THE ENCYCLOPEDIA OF
HIGH-TECH CRIME
AND CRIME-FIGHTING

Michael Newton

Checkmark Books®

An imprint of Facts On File, Inc.

The Encyclopedia of High-Tech Crime and Crime-Fighting

Copyright © 2004 by Michael Newton

Checkmark Books
An imprint of Facts On File, Inc.
132 West 31st Street
New York NY 10001

Library of Congress Cataloging-in-Publication Data

Newton, Michael, 1951—
The encyclopedia of high-tech crime and crime-fighting / by Michael Newton
p. cm.
Includes bibliographical references and index
ISBN 0-8160-4978-5 (HC) — ISBN 0-8160-4979-3 (PB)
1. Computer crimes—Encyclopedias. 2. Computer viruses—Encyclopedias. 3. Computer hackers—Biography. I. Title
HV6773.N48 2004
364.16'8—dc21
2002192847

Checkmark Books are available at special discounts when purchased in bulk quantities for businesses, associations, institutions, or sales promotions. Please call our Special Sales Department in New York at (212) 967-8800 or (800) 322-8755.

You can find Facts On File on the World Wide Web at http://www.factsonfile.com

Cover and text design by Cathy Rincon

Photographs on pages 13, 14, 15, and 116 are courtesy of Kathleen O. Arries, Forensic Anthropologist; Associate Professor of Biology, EEC Buffalo; Scientific Staff, Erie County Sheriff's Department, Buffalo, N.Y.

Printed in the United States of America

VB FOF 10 9 8 7 6 5 4 3 2 1

This book is printed on acid-free paper.

Inventor, n. A person who makes an ingenious arrangement of wheels, levers and springs, and believes it civilization.
—Ambrose Bierce
The Devil's Dictionary

If the human race wants to go to hell in a basket, technology can help it get there by jet. It won't change the desire or the direction, but it can greatly speed the passage.
—Charles M. Allen
"Unity in a University,"
speech at Wake Forest
University, 25 April 1967

Contents

Foreword

A LITTLE BIT OF HISTORY

As long as one man has and another wants, there will always be crime. The second story of the Bible is that of people breaking established rules. It is followed by an account of the first murder. And not much has changed since then. Murder, robbery, theft, and rape are part of humankind's history.

To maintain order, most societies establish laws, rules of behavior that people are expected to obey. Those who do not are punished as an example and a warning to the rest. Laws that are unenforced soon cease to be effective. So when a crime is committed, it is vital to society to quickly identify the law-breaker. Only by the swift detection, capture, and punishment of the criminal can order be maintained.

That is society's interest. Those who break the law have another interest, mainly to cover up their crimes and elude detection for as long as possible, preferably forever.

For a long time, the advantage was with the criminal. If the criminal could commit a crime and leave its scene undetected, he or she stood a good chance of escaping justice. Those charged with law enforcement had to rely on luck, witnesses, and any obvious clues that the criminal might have left behind. Luck was often with the careful criminal, who made sure not to leave behind any incriminating evidence.

A larger danger in those times was that the wrong person could be arrested and convicted for a crime. Identifications by victims and witnesses are not 100 percent reliable. Suspects developed by police through witnesses, analysis of past behavior of known felons, and the interpretation of whatever evidence was found on crime scenes had little chance of proving their innocence once accused of a crime. The real criminal was not likely to confess, nor was law enforcement likely to admit the possibility of mistakes. Justice was swift, punishment brutal, and mistakes were made.

It was not until the latter part of the 19th century that matters began to improve. Advances in science aided both law enforcement officials and those who stood falsely accused of crimes.

One concern of the justice system was the identification of repeat offenders. Until the late 1800s police relied upon their memories to identify those who had been previously arrested. In 1878 the development of the dry-plate photographic process made it possible to record images of people taken into custody. Police, however, were slow to make use of this new technology.

In 1879, while working for the French Prefect of Police, Alphonse Bertillon proposed that a series of 14 different measurements taken of a prisoner would positively identify him. In November 1882 his system was adopted on a trial basis, and in February 1883 a prisoner calling himself "Dupont" was identified as one who had been previously arrested under the name "Martin." By the end of 1884 Bertillon's method had led to the identification of more than 300 repeat offenders. By then Bertillon had embraced the new technology of photography, establishing a rogues' gallery of felons, their images preserved in what are now the traditional full face and profile "mugshots."

The Bertillonage system was universally accepted until the turn of the century when two cases, one in England and the other in the United States, pointed out its deficiencies. In England in 1901 one of a pair of identical twins, Albert and Ebenezer Fox, stood accused of theft. But which one? Their Bertillon measurements identical, they could only be identified through fingerprints. Once their identities were established, Ebenezer went to jail and Albert was set free.

Two years later, in the United States, a prisoner named Will West arrived in Fort Leavenworth Prison. However, based on his Bertillon measurements, "Will West" was already incarcerated there. As it turned out there were two men, one William West, the other, Will—with the same features and the same Bertillon measurements. Only through fingerprints could the men be properly identified.

At the same time, the use of fingerprints to solve crime was growing. The earliest known case was in 1879 in Tokyo, where Scottish doctor and missionary Henry Faulds used a sooty handprint left at the scene of a theft to exonerate the man police had arrested for the crime. A second man arrested a few days later confessed, his hand print matching that found on the scene.

In 1892 Juan Vucetich of the Argentine police solved the double murder of two children using a bloody print found on a doorpost to show that their mother had committed the deed. Scotland Yard had its first arrest and conviction using fingerprints in 1902. This was for a burglary. The Yard's first murder conviction from prints came in 1905.

Other methods of identification were also being developed. The year 1902 saw the first attempts to employ ABO blood typing to solve crimes. In 1916 Dr. Leone Lattes of the University of Turin's Institute of Forensic Medicine used ABO grouping to exonerate a suspect in an assault.

Some years later, the growing science of forensic ballistics was beginning to allow investigators to match bullets and expended cartridge cases to the weapons that had fired them. In 1915 a man named Charlie Stielow was arrested for a murder committed with a .22 pistol in Orleans County, New York. Stielow was tried, convicted, and sentenced to be executed in Sing Sing. Those convinced of his innocence persevered, and finally his life was spared and he was set free when it was demonstrated that the pistol recovered from him could not have fired the fatal shot. Further developments in the 1920s and 1930s by such experts as Calvin Goddard of the U.S. Army's Ordnance Reserve and Sir Sydney Smith, Medico-Legal Adviser for the British government in Egypt, led to the methods of firearms identification that are being used to the present day.

Of course, just as law enforcement used technology to combat crime, the criminal class was not slow to employ it for their own ends. To cite one example, fingerprints have long been a bane to the criminal, especially those who don't wear gloves while committing crimes. Efforts to disguise or alter prints have been made throughout the years, most of them unsuccessful. The only known case of a man succeeding in fully and permanently blanking out his prints was that of Robert Phillips, aka Roscoe Pitts. In 1941 Dr. Leopold Brandenburg grafted skin from Phillips's abdomen onto his fingertips, successfully obscuring his fingerprints. Unfortunately for Phillips, when he was next arrested, police used his palmprints to identify him.

THESE DAYS

In 1977 I began my career with the Baltimore Police Department's (BPD) Crime Laboratory. As a crime laboratory technician and later as a supervisor, my job was (and still is) to document crime scenes and the evidence found on them. My job was also to search for and find that evidence with the goal of identifying those involved in the crime. In doing so, I found myself using techniques similar to those described above. Fingerprinting on the scene was still being done with brushes and powders. Once a latent print was found, it could be identified only if there was a suspect, or else after a long and tedious search through arrest records and open case files. Likewise, while spent cartridge cases and fired bullets could be matched to recovered weapons, linking them to other crimes in which the weapon had been used required the long process of manually sifting through evidence from past cases.

Blood found on the scene was matched to suspects and victims through ABO grouping and similar genetic markers. Semen and other bodily fluids were useless unless the person from whom they came secreted these markers. And all too often, more than one of the people involved in the crime had identical marker profiles, making a positive identification impossible.

Gradually, though, technology caught up to our needs. By the early 1980s the BPD Crime Lab began using cyanoacrylate (Super Glue) fumes to develop prints on surfaces that were previously considered unsuitable for processing. Lasers gave us another tool with which to find still more latent prints. And then our evidence-gathering capability again increased with the use of deoxyribonucleic acid (DNA) analysis. Not only could we better compare blood and semen from victims and scenes to those suspected of committing the crimes, but such items as the mouths of soda bottles, the handles of weapons, and the triggers of handguns now bore invisible traces, which if properly recovered could positively identify a suspect.

If I were asked to pick the one recent scientific advance that changed law enforcement most radically, I would have to choose the computer. Its effect on crime and crime fighting, and the satisfaction one gets from doing the job, has been amazing. Computers are used in the analysis of crime patterns. Reports, crime scene diagrams, and facial composites—back in 1977 all of these were prepared by hand, and not always done as accurately or presented as neatly as we would have liked. Computers now allow us to do these jobs more thoroughly and professionally.

This, however, is administrative office stuff that, while important, is secondary to the main goal—putting the bad guys in jail. And it is in this area that the computer best serves law enforcement.

Police departments on the local, state, and federal levels have established massive databases that hold digital records of inked prints of those arrested, latent prints recovered from crime scenes, lands and grooves from fired bullets, firing pin impressions from spent cartridge cases, and DNA patterns from body fluids recovered on crime scenes and taken from sex offenders.

The use of these computer databases gives law enforcement a powerful weapon. No longer do police need to develop a suspect to have a recovered print matched to a suspect. Entering the print into an AFIS (Automated Fingerprint Identification System), a fingerprint examiner can sometimes make a match in a case without witnesses or suspects within 24 hours of the crime being committed. Similar databases exist to match recovered bullets and cartridge cases from one scene to those on another and to the gun that fired them. Still another does the same for the DNA patterns from recovered evidence and known offenders. Thanks to these tools, law enforcement no longer needs to rely on luck, witnesses, and obvious clues to identify participants in crimes.

These databases also turn back time. Investigations of crimes that occurred five, 10, even 20 years ago are given new life as more and more information is gathered and criminals who walked free for far too long are identified and arrested for their past misdeeds.

More important, with the ability to make faster and more accurate identifications comes the opportunity to free those falsely accused of or unjustly imprisoned for crimes they did not commit. Just as the beginnings of fingerprint, firearms, and ABO

comparisons lead to the exoneration of the innocent, so too is DNA comparison freeing or clearing those wrongly suspected or convicted.

Just how much modern science and technology has affected the world of crime and crime fighting is explored in the following work. Just as the author did in his previous volumes on kidnappings and serial killers, Michael Newton ably uses the encyclopedia format to closely examine this subject, concentrating mainly on the advances in DNA and computers, but also exploring other technologies such as personal protection, fingerprint recovery, and how such sciences as anthropology, podiatry, and dentistry play their part in the solving of crimes.

The reader should be warned. Mr. Newton's work may challenge some dearly held ideas and concepts. Who can read about the number of people exonerated by DNA and other evidence and not question the validity of past convictions and executions? Who can feel absolutely secure sitting at their computer terminals with the presence of so many worms, viruses, and cyber-scams out there? Who can continue to enjoy certain cop shows knowing how things are done in the real world?

On the other hand, knowledge that this technology exists also may provide its own sense of security. No longer will predators be anonymous. The means to track them by the traces they leave behind are there. Unjust convictions may become fewer and fewer as the means to identify the true criminals improve. And the awareness of the schemes used by computer thieves and outlaws to separate us from our money and disrupt our lives is one of the first tools needed in protecting ourselves from them.

In this regard, Michael Newton's *Encyclopedia of High-tech Crime and Crime-fighting* serves us well, discussing the dangers and benefits of today's technology and how it is used and misused by both sides of the law.

—John L. French,
Supervisor,
Baltimore City Police Crime Laboratory

Bibliography: Patricia Barnes-Svarney, et al. *The New York Public Library Science Desk Reference.* New York: Stonesong Press/Macmillan, 1995; Larry Ragle, *Crime Scene.* New York: Avon Books, 2002; Gus Russo, *The Outfit.* New York: Bloomsbury, 2001; Jay Siegel, Pekka J. Saukko, and Geoffrey C. Knuper, eds. *The Encyclopedia of Forensic Sciences.* London: Academic Press, 2000; Sydney Smith,

Mostly Murder. New York: Dorset Press, 1988; Frank Smyth, *Cause of Death, The Story of Forensic Science.* New York: Van Nostrand Reinhold, 1980; Jurgen Thorwald, *Crime and Science.* New York: Harcourt, Brace and World, 1967; "What Every Law Enforcement Officer Should Know About DNA Evidence." CD-ROM. National Commission on the Future of DNA Evidence, National Institute of Justice; "The History of Fingerprints." Latent Print Examination. Available online. URL: http://onin.com/fp/fphistory.html. Updated February 17, 2003. Accessed March 25, 2003.

Author's Note

Entries in *The Encyclopedia of High-Tech Crime and Crime-Fighting* are alphabetically arranged. SMALL CAPITALS within the text denote a subject with its own discrete entry elsewhere in the book. "Blind" entries provide further cross-referencing for certain topics, as where one or more individuals are treated collectively—e.g., SCHNEIDER, Bjorn. See FASTLANE. While thousands of computer viruses exist today, a representative sampling was arbitrarily chosen for this volume to include (a) notorious examples and (b) lesser-known viruses discussed as examples of various types.

Introduction

"May you live in interesting times."

Robert F. Kennedy, visiting South Africa in July 1966, invoked that phrase in a globally publicized speech, describing it as an ancient Chinese curse. Linguists and historians in the past four decades have found nothing to support Kennedy's claim, which appears to be pure invention, but his instincts were true. Interesting times are those marked by conflict and courage, peril and progress, fear and fascination.

For good or ill, we live in interesting times.

Children of the post–World War II "baby boom," now middle-aged, were ill prepared for the 21st century. Their generation was raised on novels, films, and Saturday morning cartoons that predicted an era of intergalactic travel and adventure, hover cars and ray guns, global peace and harmony. Reality is rather different, with nonstop wars and terrorism, the AIDS pandemic, deforestation and global warming, and fossil fuel crises. Space exploration has languished, for the most part, with manned flight halted at the moon and our neighbor Mars inviolate outside of sci-fi fantasies. At the same time, however, even as humanity gave up on colonizing outer space, technicians labored to invent a new dimension: cyberspace.

It is the new frontier, a virtual realm where reality itself is fluid, and rules—if they exist at all—seem made to be broken. And like every other frontier in the long parade of human history, the new domain has outlaws.

It seems to be a law of nature that criminals always outpace law enforcement in adopting and adapting new technology. From six-guns to automatic weapons, Model-T Fords to Lear jets, adding machines to the Internet, lawbreakers always get there first, while law-abiding servants of the people lag behind.

The reasons for this law-and-order gap are twofold. First, law enforcement and the related private security industry are by nature both reactive and conservative. Both *respond* to threats of criminal activity as they arise. "Pro-active" law enforcement is, in fact, no more than an aggressive drive against crimes recognized from past experience. Investigators and technicians in the field do not anticipate new problems on a daily basis, much less when the crimes defy pedestrian imagination.

Second, the police are forced to work within a framework of established laws, which always lag behind criminal trends, mending fences after the fact. Offenses must be legally defined, parameters and penalties debated, guidelines for investigation clarified, budgets approved. The process may take months or years, and even when it is accelerated—as in the congressional response to terrorist attacks of September 11, 2001—implementation of new legislation still takes time.

The "9/11" crisis, in fact, provides a perfect case in point for how criminals run circles around sedentary law enforcement agencies. Slipping through loopholes in the extant security and immigration statutes, terrorist leader Osama bin Laden used American flight schools to train his suicide pilots for airline hijackings that would level the World Trade Center and gravely damage the Pentagon. Rather than risk his men by sending them aboard those planes with firearms, he armed them with simple knives permitted under short-sighted airline security regulations. In the wake of September 11, new regulations were enacted pertaining to screening of luggage—which played no part whatever in the 9/11 attacks—and even when those statutes were passed in record time, airline and airport spokesmen reported that installation of the newly mandated security devices might take three years or more to complete.

Criminals, for their part, are bound by none of the restrictions that hamper law enforcement. The most notorious of them are innovators, always thinking of new ways to victimize the public. As the Reno gang "invented" train robbery in 1866, and Jesse James pioneered daylight bank robbery a few years later, so modern felons labor nonstop to take full advantage of new technology, seeking more efficient ways to beat the system and avoid detection in the process. "High-tech" crimes are defined by their era. When bank robber Henry Starr abandoned horses and made his first getaway by automobile, in 1914, he was on the cutting edge of outlaw technology, and it served him well for the next seven years. Today a computerized thief in Moscow can steal millions from a New York bank without leaving his apartment—and he stands a better chance than Starr ever did of escaping with the loot, unrecognized.

A thread of inevitability runs throughout recorded human history. The discovery of electricity paved the way, albeit unpredictably, for the invention of modern computers. Before the invention of transistors, glass vacuum tubes regulated the flow of electricity inside computers—the largest and most powerful of its day being the Electronic Numerical Integrator and Computer (ENIAC) built at the University of Pennsylvania in 1946. ENIAC weighed almost 60,000 pounds, filled a 30-by-50-foot room, and cost more than $3.2 million to build. Transistors were invented in 1958, and the first case of American computer crime was recorded the same year. By 1976, U.S. authorities had logged 374 cases of "computer abuse"—including four cases of frustrated owners who shot their own computers in fits of rage.

The rest is history.

Some high-tech crimes are simply variations on familiar themes, their ancient motives—greed, desire, revenge, religious and political fanaticism—coupled with new technology to become at once more profitable and more threatening to organized society. Such crimes as theft, fraud, stalking and harassment, espionage, sabotage, and terrorism are as old as *homo sapiens,* but new advances in communications, data storage and retrieval elevate common felons to new levels of achievement.

At the same time, certain modern crimes are truly that: without computers and associated hard- or software they would not exist. "Phreaking"—the art of defrauding long-distance telephone carriers with computers or other devices—has existed only since the final quarter of the 20th century. Computer "hacking," likewise, is a product of the 1960s, turned to crime (for sport or profit) even as aging pioneers in the field volubly defend an illusory "hacker ethic." Child pornography may be as old as the first camera, but its present global proliferation—complete with "morphing" of victims' bodies and faces to confound investigators—is a product of our interesting times. Drug dealers and addicts have existed throughout history, but only in the past three decades have synthetic "designer drugs" been manufactured with an eye toward societal demographics. Embezzlers have always plagued financial institutions, but before the cyberage they were unable to grow rich by "data diddling" and "salami slicing." (See the CYBERCRIME entry for definitions.)

Progress always has a price. No advance in technology comes without corresponding changes in society, both good and bad. It is the challenge of a free society to use modern technology for the greatest benefit, while restraining those who would corrupt new inventions and use them for personal gain, to the detriment of their neighbors and in violation of the law. It remains for future historians to judge how well that task has been achieved, or whether cyberspace shall prove to be an ungovernable Wild Frontier.

Entries A–Z

ABENE, Mark: hacker "Phiber Optik"

Hailed in some quarters as "the digital age's first full-fledged outlaw hero," condemned by prosecutors as a nefarious Internet marauder, New York native Mark Abene—a.k.a. "Phiber Optik"— seemed an unlikely HACKER at first glance. A high school dropout, Abene first encountered computers while killing time in the electronics department of a Queens department store where his mother worked. Beginning with an inexpensive Radio Shack TRS-80 computer, dubbed the "Trash-80" by hackers, Abene learned rapidly by trial and error, networking with like-minded youth in cyberspace. In the late 1980s, he was a founding member of an informal hackers' syndicate dubbed the MASTERS OF DECEPTION.

Abene's specialty was penetrating corporate computers and cheating telephone networks of money on long-distance calls. To that end, he practiced at home on an old telephone receiver, researching its codes so exhaustively that the phone eventually fell apart. Convicted on state charges of computer trespass in 1991, Abene received probation and continued his hacking career without letup. He was arrested a second time in 1993, as part of a federal crackdown on the Masters of Deception, was indicted on multiple charges and held for trial in New York. Abene ultimately pleaded guilty on two counts—one each of computer intrusion and conspiracy—and was sentenced to one year in prison on November 3, 1993. Judge Louis Stanton, intent on "sending a message" to prospective hackers, proclaimed from the bench

that "hacking crimes constitute a real threat to the expanding information highway."

Abene's friends and supporters, including coworkers at the New York–based ECHO bulletin-board system, were dismayed by Phiber Optik's prison sentence. An outpouring of e-mail support for Abene ranged from incoherent obscenities to advice on survival in prison: "Try not to get killed," one fan suggested, while another urged Abene to "skip the country." Phiber Optik surrendered in January 1994 to serve his time in a minimum-security facility in Pennsylvania, and emerged from prison physically unscathed. Upon release, he was treated to a welcome-home party by hundreds of supporters, at a posh Manhattan nightclub. *New York* magazine subsequently dubbed him one of the city's 100 smartest people.

ACME Rent-a-Car: illegal use of satellite technology

James Turner, a resident of New Haven, Connecticut, got more than he bargained for when he rented a van from the local branch of Acme Rent-a-Car in the fall of 2000. Turner knew the vehicle came equipped with GPS (global positioning satellite) technology, but he assumed the equipment was installed as a convenience for renters. "I was not aware of what GPS could do," he later told reporters. "I thought it was an onboard navigation system, to use when you got lost."

With that in mind, Turner was "very, very surprised" to learn, upon returning the van, that Acme had fined him $450 for driving at excessive speeds while the vehicle was in his possession. Since Turner had charged the rental fee to his bank debit card, the fines were in fact extracted from his account before he returned the van. Nor was Turner's case the only one of its kind, as revealed by subsequent investigation. One unlucky renter's bank account had been completely drained by fines, without his knowledge, based on fine print in the rental contract which allowed Acme to dun its customers for violating traffic laws.

James Turner took Acme to small claims court, asserting that the company had no right to invade his privacy or to usurp police authority by charging renters $150 each time they exceeded an arbitrary speed limit. Connecticut's Department of Consumer Protection entered the fray in July 2001, filing criminal charges against Acme's New Haven office. According to the complaint, not only were Acme's speeding fines illegal, but the company "did not notify consumers when [it] withdrew money out of credit card and ATM accounts to pay these illegal fees." Acme's lawyers responded that the practice of fining lead-footed drivers "saves by discouraging speeding." As for the state's complaint, attorney Max Brunswick declared, "If they say it's not fair practice, we will give [Turner] his money back. We are not out to make money on this."

Civil libertarians were less concerned about individual monetary losses than about the implications of satellite tracking applied to individuals at random, throughout society. David Sobel, general counsel for the Washington-based Electronic Privacy Information Center, remarked on Acme's case that "the challenge right now is to ensure, before these services and capabilities are widely deployed, that rules are in place." Robert Smith, of the Privacy Foundation, expressed concern for "a long-term problem that's not going away. Most people are innocent [but] they still get tracked."

Ironically, GPS tracking systems—developed for military combat applications—were initially installed in rental cars as a crime-fighting measure, enabling companies to pinpoint missing vehicles if they were not returned on time by would-be auto thieves. A benefit to renters was the peace of mind obtained from knowing they could not get lost while driving in an unfamiliar area. It was a short step from that point, however, to surveillance of consumers via hardware that permitted rental companies to track a driver's speed or other "dangerous" behavior. As Max Brunswick, the attorney, told the media, "You

have a problem in rental cars, that people don't treat them like their own cars. The main reason to put in the GPS receivers is not to track the people but to track the vehicles. With this device you can track within a city block anywhere in the world."

And that, critics say, is part of the problem. Privacy advocates note that rental car records might be obtained by angry spouses in divorce litigation or by employers seeking to spy on their traveling workers. Rental companies using the GPS hardware universally deny any intent to violate consumer privacy or profit from their high-tech "safety" equipment, but critics remain skeptical. Connecticut authorities advise consumers nationwide to read the fine print in their rental contracts and to question personnel in charge of renting cars about the firm's resort to GPS technology. If any aspect of the contract is unclear, or if the company announces its intent to act in a policeman's role, consumers are advised to take their business elsewhere.

ADAMS, Kenneth See FORD HEIGHTS FOUR

ADOPTION Fraud: Internet con games

As civilized societies have long attempted to regulate the process of child adoption, so have outlaw profiteers sought means of circumventing legislation meant to safeguard children, birth parents, and adoptive parents alike. In the 19th century—and later, in some parts of Canada and the United States—"baby farmers" contrived to arrange illegal adoptions, selling infants to the highest bidders (or, in some extreme cases, killing the children while billing their mothers for ongoing care). Modern technology offers new avenues of profit for unscrupulous adoption "facilitators," no longer restricted to word of mouth or discreet newspaper advertisements.

The Internet has been a goldmine for swindlers who offer infants for adoption, then collect a handsome finder's fee with no intention of delivering the human "merchandise." In some cases, the children offered for adoption may exist, although descriptions of their race, gender, and physical condition may be false; in other cases, there are no babies at all, no pregnant mothers waiting to deliver. There are only websites and mail drops for payments that vanish without a trace.

Since the mid-1990s, Internet adoption fraud has ranked among the fastest-growing types of cybercrime. As Bill Pierce, founder of the National Council for Adoption, told an interviewer in August 2000, would-be adoptive parents "are getting burned on the Internet at a rate that is inconceivable." Richard Pearlman, executive director of the Chicago-based Family Resource Center, told the *Los Angeles Times* in January 2001: "The Internet makes it possible to trade in human lives. There is so much potential to make money in the adoption field that no one is above bad practice." Robert Tuke, president of the American Academy of Adoption Attorneys in 2001, agreed. "Whereas before the con artist would ply their trade by mail or in person," Tuke informed the *Times,* "on the Internet they can reach a wider audience easier and disguise easier who they are." Prospective parents are "especially vulnerable" in Tuke's view, often caught by swindlers "in a highly emotional state."

The most prolific Internet adoption swindler on record is Sonya Furlow, a resident of Philadelphia who victimized at least 44 couples in the late 1990s, stealing at least $200,000 from victims spanning the United States. One pair of victims, Steve and Kelly Motl of Wisconsin, shelled out $10,000 to Furlow's operation—ironically dubbed Tender Hearts Family Services—beginning in the spring of 1998. In addition to Furlow's "finder's fee," the payments were allegedly intended to support a pregnant young woman named Laurel through her confinement and delivery of her child. In fact, as the Motls learned to their ultimate sorrow, there was no child—and no "Laurel." Furlow had simply lied and kept the money for herself.

Another couple, Ken and Kelly Mostrom, refinanced their home and paid Furlow $3,500 before the "facilitator" sent them a terse e-mail, explaining that the nonexistent birth mother had changed her mind and decided to keep her baby. There was, of course, no refund on the "finder's fee." Roy and Kelly Kaiser, of Philadelphia, researched adoption thoroughly, intending to "be smart" about their choices, but they still fell into Sonya Furlow's web. Once again, Furlow promised a child in return for $3,500, but a last-minute phone call reported that mother "Elise" had reneged on the deal. John and Terry Nakai, from Colorado, paid Furlow $4,500 on behalf of an alleged birth mother named "Dakota," then balked at making further payments as they noted gaps in Furlow's story, including a claim that "Dakota" was suddenly stricken with cancer. Finally, came Furlow's angry telephone message: "I don't think I want to deal with people like you. If you

don't even care when cancer's involved, I'm going to tell Dakota to pick another couple."

The end came for Furlow after Charles Elliott, a Philadelphia accountant and fraud investigator, received a complaint against Tender Hearts from one of his regular clients. After contacting several victimized couples, Elliott handed his information to the FBI, and Furlow was indicted on multiple counts of mail fraud. She pleaded guilty in August 2000, receiving a sentence of three years and 10 months in prison from a judge who denounced her for preying on the "fundamental human need to have a family."

Furlow was not alone in practicing adoption swindles on the Internet, by any means. Jill and Steven Hopster, from Redmond, Washington, broke the mold for adoptive parents in 2000 by specifically requesting a biracial infant. After conclusion of a contract with the birth mother of one such child, the Hopsters were dismayed to find the woman offering "their" child to other couples on the Internet. Investigation demonstrated that the mother had, in fact, deceived them in regard to both the baby's race and legal status. Another couple, left anonymous in media reports, spent 10 weeks in Tijuana, Mexico, waiting for delivery of their new child before a "facilitator" told them the mother had changed her mind—and again, no refunds were forthcoming. (The facilitator in that case, Adrienne Lewis, faced legal complaints from 18 couples in May 2001.)

The most notorious case of international adoption fraud to date involves the so-called "Internet twins," exposed by a British tabloid newspaper on January 16, 2001. A couple from northern Wales, Alan and Judith Kilshaw, revealed on that date that they had paid a U.S. adoption broker £8,200 ($12,000) to facilitate adoption of six-month-old twin girls from Arkansas. The Kilshaws had already named the girls Belinda and Kimberly, when they discovered that broker Tina Johnson had sold the twins to a California couple, Richard and Vickie Allen, for £4,000 ($6,000) in October 2000. To rectify the "error," Johnson then persuaded the Allens to return the girls to their birth mother, one Tranda Wecker, in order to complete the more lucrative transaction.

While the Allens vowed to sue for custody, and the Kilshaws filed adoption papers in Arkansas, British prime minister Tony Blair vowed strict enforcement of an international Adoptions Act (ignored since its passage in 1999), and FBI agents began investigating the swindle in America. On January 18, British police served the Kilshaws with an emergency protection order and placed the twins in foster care, pending resolution of the case in court. Six days later, a court in Missouri awarded custody to Aaron Wecker, the twins' biological father, but the babies remained in British foster care. The Allens and the Kilshaws met on February 1, airing their dispute on Oprah Winfrey's television show, and Tranda Wecker hired attorneys to fight for custody of the twins on February 8. Richard Allen was arrested on March 1, 2001, charged with child abuse on accusations from two teenage baby-sitters, and the Allens withdrew their bid for custody of the twins despite his not-guilty plea. Five days later, on March 6, Arkansas judge Mackie Pierce denied custody to both the Allens and Kilshaws, remanding settlement of the case to a court in Missouri, where the twins were born. FBI agents raided Tina Johnson's Caring Heart Adoption service on March 14, in El Cajon, California, seeking evidence for possible indictments. Finally, on April 9, 2001, Britain's highest court ordered the twins returned to Missouri, for settlement of custody between their biological parents.

As hazards for would-be adoptive parents multiply in cyberspace, the National Adoption Center (NAC) offers safety tips for those who surf the Web in search of children. NAC spokesperson Gloria Hochman offers the following advice to prospective parents:

1. Be certain the advertised adoption agency is duly licensed in the state where it operates.
2. Request the agency's annual reports and verify its record of successful adoptions.
3. Shun Internet websites that do not provide an agency's physical address and telephone number. Verify the address and telephone number before proceeding further.
4. Avoid websites that promise quick adoptions. Baby-shopping on the Internet does not absolve the parties from obeying state and federal statutes governing adoptions.
5. Determine who funds the website. Legitimate adoption agencies are normally funded by some government agency or by a reputable charity.
6. Make no payments without itemized bills, detailing all expenses. If the worst comes to pass, that documentation facilitates lawsuits and/or criminal prosecution for fraud.

The story of Internet adoptions is not universally bleak, however. Even couples victimized by swindlers on the Web are sometimes favored with a happy end-

ing. Such was the case for two of Sonya Furlow's victims, Steve and Kelly Motl. Late in 2000, still relying on the Internet, the Motls successfully adopted a new daughter, Grace, and report themselves completely satisfied.

AHNEN, Steven: hacker "Code3"

A resident of Sarasota, Florida, born April 13, 1958, Steven Ahnen was a member of a HACKERS syndicate known to its members as "PIRATES WITH ATTITUDE." The reference to piracy was no idle boast, since members of the group engaged in wholesale theft of software on the Internet, stealing more than 5,000 copyrighted programs in the late 1990s, operating through a hidden website based on the campus of a Quebec university. On May 4, 2000, a federal grand jury in Chicago indicted 12 hackers and five accomplices employed by Intel Corporation on charges of conspiracy to infringe copyrights. Steven Ahnen, known to fellow hackers as "Code3," was among 13 defendants who pleaded guilty in an effort to reduce penalties.

"AIDS" Virus Warnings: Internet hoax

While several real-life computer VIRUSES have employed the name of AIDS or the HIV virus in their titles, this notorious Internet warning, broadcast via e-mail, refers to a virus that does not exist. The apparent deliberate effort to spark Internet panic is recognizable as a hoax because it is unsigned, and because no computer virus has the power to attack and disable hardware as described. The usual warning method reads as follows, with grammatical errors intact:

THEREE IS A VIRUS GOING AROUND CALLED THE A.I.D.S VIRUS. IT WILL ATTACH ITSELF INSIDE YOUR COMPUTER AND EAT AWAY AT YOUR MEMOR THIS MEMORY IS IRREPLACEABLE. THEN WHEN IT'S FINISHED WITH MEMORY IT INFECTS YOUR MOUSE OR POINTING DEVICE. THEN IT GOES TO YOUR KEY BOARD AND THE LETTERS YOU TYPE WILL NOT REGISTER ON SCREEN. BEFORE IT SELF TERMINATES IT EATS 5MB OF HARD DRIVE SPACE AND WILL DELETE ALL PROGRAMS ON IT AND IT CAN SHUT DOWN ANY 8 BIT TO 16 SOUND CARDS RENDERING YOUR SPEAKERS USELESS. IT WILL COME IN E-MAIL CALLED "OPEN:VERY COOL! :) DELETE IT RIGHT AWAY.

THIS VIRUS WILL BASICLY RENDER YOUR COMPUTER USELESS. YOU MUST PASS THIS ON QUICKLY AND TO AS MANY PEOPLE AS POSSLE!!!!! YOU MUST!

AIRPORT Security

In the wake of airborne terrorist attacks that claimed some 3,000 American lives on September 11, 2001, airport and airline security is a matter of paramount importance both to government officials and to the millions of travelers who fly each day around the world. It remains to be seen whether new security devices and techniques, coupled with stricter legislation passed since "9/11," will in fact make air travel safer, or simply cause increased delays and aggravation for commercial passengers.

The world's first airline hijackings (or "skyjackings") occurred in Peru, with two planes commandeered by political dissidents on February 21 and 23, 1931. Sporadic incidents were recorded over the next 30 years, mostly involving defectors from communist nations, but the United States did not experience its first skyjacking until May 1, 1961, when a Korean War veteran of Puerto Rican extraction diverted a National Airlines flight to Havana. Skyjackings proliferated through the 1960s and became a standard terrorist tactic in the early 1970s, compelling airports worldwide to install metal detectors (for passengers) and X-ray devices (for carry-on luggage). The U.S., Israel, and a few other nations also stationed armed "sky marshals" on selected flights, particularly those scheduled for high-risk areas. Although sky marshals frustrated a handful of skyjackings and killed or wounded several terrorists, their numbers were never sufficient to end the threat. Rather, skyjacking seemed to run its course and taper off as U.S. relations with Cuba, and Middle East peace initiatives, sapped support from major radical groups. Still, occasional skyjackings and bombings of commercial aircraft continued into the 21st century, capped by the tragic events of September 2001.

Modern guidelines for U.S. airport security are established by Civil Aviations Security (CAS), a division of the Federal Aviation Administration (FAA). FAA/CAS agents are found in every American airport, prepared for immediate threat-response, and most major U.S. airports have their own police forces (or officers assigned from the local metropolitan police department). Since September 11, uniformed troops of the National Guard are also found in airports nationwide, generally stationed near security checkpoints barring access from the airport concourse to departure and arrival gates. CAS guidelines have three main goals in terms of security: (1) to prevent attacks on airports or aircraft; (2) to prevent accidents or injuries due to transport of dangerous materials; and (3) to ensure the safety of passengers.

Step one in the airport security chain is identity confirmation on both passengers and airport employees. Upon check-in, all passengers are required to present a photo ID (and a passport, if traveling internationally). The ID must be presented a second time, with the passenger's ticket and boarding pass, before he or she boards an aircraft at the departure gate. Travelers are also briefly questioned on check-in, specifically asked whether they personally packed their luggage, if the bags have been in their possession at all times, and whether any third party has asked them to carry objects aboard the plane. Those questions are designed to prevent terrorists from slipping explosive devices onto a flight without risk to themselves (as happened in at least one incident during the 1980s, when a young woman unwittingly carried a disguised bomb in her luggage as a favor for a new "boyfriend").

Airport and airline employees, from janitors to pilots and flight attendants, are also required to carry photo ID clearly stating the subject's name, position, and access privileges. Ten-year background checks were supposedly required for airport/airline personnel even before September 2001, but the system remains deeply flawed. On December 14, 2001—three months after the worst terrorist attacks in U.S. history—officials at San Francisco International Airport revealed that 29 employees with full access to aircraft and runways were convicted felons (including sex offenders, kidnappers, and individuals convicted of firearms violations). The ex-convicts were discovered after airport officials belatedly screened fingerprints for 3,000 of their 13,000 employees. (The other 10,000 background checks were still in progress.) Apparently relieved that "only" 1 percent of their employees thus far had turned out to be felons, airport officials declared that those ex-convicts discovered on staff had "lost their access to secure areas"—but they would not be fired.

Access to airport departure and arrival gates has been restricted since September 2001 to passengers with valid tickets. Prior to reaching the terminal gates, all passengers are required to pass through metal detectors, while their carry-on baggage is xrayed. Federal legislation passed since 9/11 mandates installation of new equipment to x-ray check-through baggage as well, but airports around the country have predicted that they will miss the mandatory installation deadline by several years, due to shortages of equipment and funding. In addition to weapons— now including knives of any size, formerly those with blades of four inches and longer— airline passengers and personnel are forbidden from transporting the following items without specific authorization:

Explosives including fireworks, ammunition, sparklers, matches, gunpowder, or signal flares

Pressurized containers including hair spray, oxygen tanks, propane tanks, spray paint, or aerosol insect repellent

Poisons including arsenic, cyanide, or any pesticides and insecticides

Corrosives including acids, lye, drain cleaner, mercury, and automobile batteries

Household items including any solvents, bleach, pool chemicals, flammable liquids, or flammable perfume in bottles of 16 ounces or larger

Failure to declare weapons or any of the items listed above when boarding an aircraft may result in criminal prosecution, with penalties including prison time and stiff fines. It is furthermore illegal even to joke about weapons, explosives, hijacking, or other such threats in an airport or on board an airplane, pranksters being liable to arrest and criminal prosecution even when they are unarmed and have no criminal intent.

The majority of airport metal detectors operate on the pulse induction (PI) principle. PI systems typically employ a coil of wire on one side of an

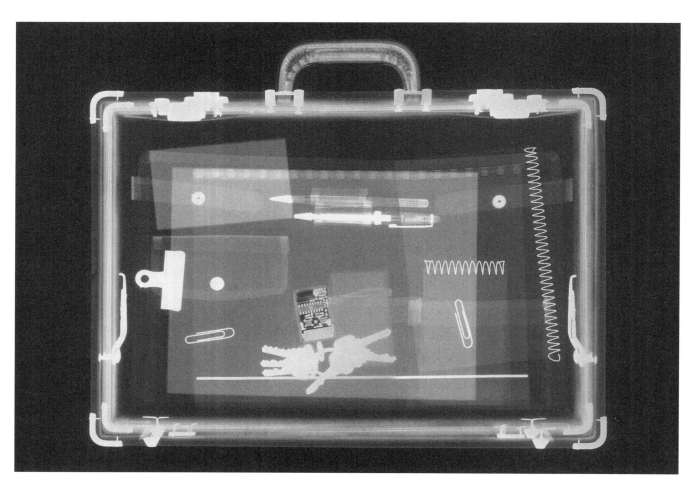

An X ray of a briefcase. X-ray technology plays a key role in airport security. (Lester Lefkowitz/CORBIS)

arch as a transmitter and receiver. Short, powerful pulses of electric current pass through that coil, each generating a momentary magnetic field. As each pulse ends, the magnetic field reverses polarity and collapses, thereby sending another burst of current (called the "reflected pulse") through the coiled wire. Common PI metal detectors send out anywhere from 25 to 1,000 pulses per second, depending on the model, with each reflected pulse lasting some 30 microseconds (millionths of a second). When a metal object passes through the arch, the electric pulse creates an opposite magnetic field around the object, thereby triggering a longer-than-normal reflected pulse, detected by a built-in "sampling circuit," which notes discrepancies in the length of any reflected pulse and sounds an audible alarm. Many newer metal detectors are "multizone" models, equipped with multiple transmit-receive coils at different heights, to increase their sensitivity.

Prior to September 2001, passengers who triggered alarms from airport metal detectors after emptying their pockets (and sometimes removing jewelry and other items) might be double-checked with hand-held metal detectors, frisked for hidden weapons, or asked to disrobe in private examination rooms. Since 9/11, random frisks and double-scans of passengers have become routine, including requests that some travelers remove their shoes for inspection prior to boarding. One security firm, Adams Electronics, offers special "HF-1 Detector Gloves" with built-in, battery-powered metal detectors, thereby leaving both of an inspector's hands free in the event hand-to-hand self-defense is required. The HF-1 gloves are made from Kevlar and Nomex, protecting the wearer's hands from being cut, punctured, or burned (in the event that an incendiary device is uncovered).

While passengers are individually screened, their carry-on luggage passes through an X-ray system that typically divides objects scanned into three categories: organic, inorganic, and metal. Most airport units operate on a dual-energy X-ray system, generating X rays in the range of 140 to 160 kilovolt peaks (KVP)—a reference to the X ray's penetrating power. (Higher KVP means greater penetration.) In dual-energy systems, X rays pass through the object being examined, then strike a detector that passes the X rays to a filter, which in turn blocks out lower-energy rays. The remaining high-energy X rays then strike a second detector, whereupon computer technology compares the images from both detectors to present the clearest possible picture. Items are usually displayed in color on the viewing monitor, with organic materials always depicted in orange, while the colors for inorganic material and metal varies depending on the unit's manufacturer. Most explosives are organic, and would thus be among the objects highlighted in orange. Airport security personnel are (theoretically) trained to identify weapons, ranging from obvious handguns and knives to improvised explosive devices (IEDs), but once again, human negligence and faulty equipment make the system far from perfect. One example: on December 30, 2001 (11 weeks after 9/11, with strict new procedures in place), passenger Barry Brunstein was arrested in Memphis, Tennessee, for attempting to carry a loaded pistol on board an airliner. Prior to arrival in Memphis that day, he had carried the gun aboard two other flights, departing Tampa and Atlanta, without being stopped.

X-ray scanning systems are admittedly imperfect, even with the best technicians in charge. Electronic devices, such as laptop computers, contain so many intricate components that an intelligent bomber could easily hide explosive devices within. Requiring travelers to remove their computers from cases and turn the computers on still fails to guarantee that a small explosive charge is not concealed inside. To that end, chemical "sniffers" are employed—essentially "an automated chemistry lab in a box." Security personnel rub a cloth over the suspect device or article of baggage, then "read" the cloth with the sniffer, detecting any trace residue of chemicals commonly used to build bombs.

Examination of checked luggage, in airports where it presently occurs at all, is carried out by one of three different methods. *Medium* X-ray systems are fixed devices that scan whole pallets of cargo or luggage for contraband items. *Mobile* X-ray units are contained within large trucks, capable of scanning loaded luggage carts or vans as they drive slowly past a stationary target. *Fixed-site* X-ray systems are whole buildings constructed as massive scanners, examining tractor-trailers of luggage parked inside. Legislation passed since September 2001 mandates X-ray screening of all checked luggage in every American airport, but purchase and installation of large units at ticket check-in counters remains problematic. (When all else fails, bomb-sniffing dogs are sometimes used to check luggage before it is loaded aboard an aircraft.)

An alternative method to standard X-ray inspection is found in computer tomography (CT) scanner systems. The CT scanner is a hollow tube that surrounds luggage, slowly revolving while bombarding it with X rays, recording the data and creating a highly detailed "slice" (tomogram) of the bag. From there, the CT scanner calculates mass and density of objects inside the bag, reporting on any items that fall within the normal range of dangerous materials. Most European airports run all checked baggage through CT scanners, and while many American airports possess the technology, it has not been used consistently because its slow rate of operation plays havoc with tight airline schedules. Before 9/11 only overtly suspect bags were subjected to CT scans. Even today, the devices are not universally available or consistently employed in the United States.

How effective are the latest airport security regulations in America? On September 28, 2001, President George W. Bush called for installation of two reinforced cockpit doors on commercial airliners, each door with a separate key. He further suggested increasing the number of armed sky marshals to cover "most" domestic flights and increased federal control of airport security measures, though he stopped short of requiring that screeners be made federal employees. Bush announced his plan to work with Congress and pass new security regulations "in an expeditious way," but some accused the president of paying mere lip service to heightened security. On December 30, 2001, Bush's Department of Transportation discarded new rules that would have required airport screeners to be high school graduates—a regulation that would have dismissed one-fourth of the nation's 28,000 airport security agents.

Bush's strange reversal brought heated criticism from experts in the field of airline security. James Hall, former chairman of the National Transportation Safety Board, told reporters, "We're dealing with very sophisticated and trained individuals who are trying to blow up our commercial aircraft. These screeners are going to be an important line of defense, and it seems to me we should have higher educational standards for them." Meanwhile, a federal investigator sneaked three knives past airport screeners in Miami, while similar experiments defeated X-ray devices in Fort Lauderdale and Philadelphia. Billie Vincent, former FAA security director, angrily dismissed Bush's improvements as "more of the half-assed measures that got us into the September 11 hijackings and will produce the same half-assed results."

"AIRSNORT": wireless password decryption program

Introduced in August 2001, AirSnort is a wireless local area network (WLAN) surveillance tool that passively monitors transmissions, computing encryption keys upon collection of sufficient data. After collecting 100MB to 1GB of data, AirSnort is reportedly able to produce the target password in less than one second.

Local area networks are theoretically protected by a built-in security, the Wired Equivalent Privacy (WEP) system—also labeled the "802.11b standard"—which automatically encrypts data as it is transmitted. But system analysts agree that WEP leaves much to be desired in terms of real security. In fact, AirSnort designers Blake Hegerle and Jeremy Bruestle insist they went public with their creation in hopes of spurring WLAN technicians to install better security systems. As Bruestle told *Wired News,* "We felt that the only proper thing to do was to release the project. It is not obvious to the layman or the average administrator how vulnerable 802.11b is to attack. It's too easy to trust WEP. . . . It's easy to be complacent. AirSnort is all about opening people's eyes."

Or opening their networks to pernicious HACKERS, as the case may be. The AirSnort website maintained by Hegerle and Bruestle includes detailed instructions on downloading their program and the hardware required to use it effectively. Mark Denon, a freelance technology writer, found it "very easy" to access networks using AirSnort. "I've been able to connect to networks when standing outside of businesses, hospitals, or Internet cafés that offer the service," he told *Wired News.* "You can jump in and use the network to send e-mail or surf the Net, and often it's quite possible to access whatever information is moving across the network."

One benefit for hackers using AirSnort is the program's virtual untraceability. As inventor Hegerle explains, AirSnort does not communicate in any way with other computers on the target network. As a passive eavesdropper, it simply listens to the network's flow of traffic, capturing sufficient data to decode a busy network's password in three or four hours. Low-traffic networks take longer to crack, but Bruestle notes that data collection need not be continuous. AirSnort can revisit a network over several days of intermittent snooping, until sufficient data is collected to decrypt the password.

ALEJANDRO, Gilbert: exonerated by DNA evidence

On the night of April 27, 1990, a woman in Uvalde County, Texas, was attacked in her home by a stranger who forced a pillowcase over her head, then raped her. Unable to describe her assailant's face, the victim recalled his general build and his clothing, including a cap, gray T-shirt and dark shorts. Police canvassed the neighborhood and questioned three men, one of whom wore clothes matching the rapist's description. None were detained for a lineup, but the victim later identified suspect Gilbert Alejandro via mug shots from a previous arrest.

At trial, Alejandro's only defense was an alibi provided by his mother, testifying under oath that he was at home when the rape occurred. Against that testimony, prosecutors offered the victim's shaky identification, buttressed by testimony from FRED ZAIN, chief medical examiner of nearby Bexar County. Zain told the court that a DNA test of semen found on the victim's clothing matched Alejandro's DNA "and could only have originated from him." Jurors convicted Alejandro, and he was sentenced to a 30-year prison term.

On appeal it was discovered that Fred Zain had grossly misrepresented results of the Bexar County DNA tests in Alejandro's case. The first test performed, in July 1990, had produced inconclusive results, while a second test performed three months later actually excluded the defendant as a source of the semen on file. Alejandro's lawyers filed a writ of habeas corpus and he was released to his parents' custody, his movements tracked by an electronic monitor. A Uvalde County judge reviewed Alejandro's case on July 26, 1994, receiving testimony that the 1990 DNA test had excluded Alejandro as a suspect. Two members of the original trial jury also testified that their guilty verdicts were based solely on Fred Zain's false testimony. As a result of that hearing, Alejandro's conviction was overturned, and Uvalde County prosecutors dismissed all charges on September 21, 1994. Alejandro later sued Uvalde County for false imprisonment and was awarded $250,000 in damages for his four-year incarceration.

Fred Zain, meanwhile, was fired by Bexar County in 1993, and later charged with aggravated perjury, evidence tampering, and fabrication for his part in Alejandro's wrongful conviction. Jurors acquitted him at trial, in 1998, but 100 more convictions based upon his testimony are under review across

Texas. Despite his cash award, Gilbert Alejandro remains understandably bitter toward Zain. "He should be put away for a long time," Alejandro told reporters, "like I was put away in prison doing hard labor."

ALEXANDER, Richard: exonerated by DNA evidence

In 1996 a sexual predator known only as the River Park Rapist terrorized female residents of South Bend, Indiana. Police arrested 30-year-old Richard Alexander that August, charging him with four of the attacks on the basis of eyewitness statements from victims. DNA testing excluded him as a suspect in one of those rapes, and some investigators were skeptical of the other three cases, Detective Sergeant Cindy Eastman telling reporters, "We had a gut feeling that Alexander was not the guy." Supporting that belief, at least three more similar rapes were reported after Alexander's arrest. Still, task force officers and prosecutors forged ahead with their case. Alexander's first trial ended with a hung jury in June 1997. At his second trial, in March 1998, jurors acquitted him of one rape but convicted him of two others. Alexander received a 70-year prison term for those crimes.

He caught a break five years later, when alleged burglar and child-molester Michael Murphy confessed to one of the rapes for which Alexander stood convicted. New DNA tests were ordered, and their findings conclusively exonerated Alexander of an attack committed on August 7, 1996. Four days later, on December 12, 2001, he was released from custody by order of the St. Joseph County Superior Court. Authorities now say two rapists are suspected in the River Park attacks, and that five of those crimes remain under active investigation.

ALIBRIS/INTERLOC: Internet vendor charged with fraud

An Internet bookseller and provider of communications services headquartered in Emeryville, California, Alibris was charged with illegally intercepting customer communications and possessing unauthorized password files in November 1999. According to the specific federal charges, filed on November 22, Alibris and its corporate predecessor Interloc, Inc. (formerly operating in the Greenfield, Massachusetts, area) intercepted thousands of e-mail messages sent by on-line bookseller Amazon.com to Alibris clients using Interloc e-mail addresses. Those interceptions, conducted between January and June 1998, were allegedly designed to give Alibris/Interloc an unfair competitive advantage over Amazon.com and other vendors.

As U.S. Attorney Donald Stern explained: "In this case, an Internet service provider intercepted mail passing through its network to gain a business advantage. The continued growth of e-commerce depends on the security of electronic transactions. We are committed to prosecuting the electronic theft of valuable intangible business property with the same vigor we have applied to the theft of valuable physical property in the past."

Martin Manley, president and chief executive of Alibris, told reporters that none of the e-mails intercepted and stored on his company's computers had ever been opened, but the company chose not to defend itself in court. A plea agreement, dated November 25, 1999, recorded Alibris's agreement to pay $250,000 in settlement of the federal claim. It was a bargain, even so, since conviction at trial carried a potential fine of $250,000 on each separate count of e-mail interception.

"ALICIA": computer virus

First reported in July 1998, "Alicia" is described as a "dangerous memory-resident, polymorphic, parasitic virus which attaches to the end of .com and .exe files." Once that infestation is accomplished, the virus infects files located while searching disk directories, using DOS functions FindFirst/Next. Alicia also attacks computer archives, adding to them its "infected dropper"—a dummy program bearing one of the following file names: hdbk.com, hdnk.com, hddk.com, hdok.com, hdpk.com, kdhd.com.

The Alicia virus seeks out archive files by using filename extensions. The list of extensions includes .zip, .arj, .rar, .ace, .ha, .arc, .pak, .lzh, .lha, and .zoo. When attacking archives, the virus dissects their internal formats, creates a new record, and writes its own infected dropper. The eight archive formats affected by Alicia are .zip, .arj, .rar, .ace, .ha, .pak/arc, .lzh/lha, and .zoo.

The virus delivers its payload on May 24, or upon executing an infected dropper. In either case, it displays the string "Alicia X Version Gamma 0.1 X by Star0 IKX In honor of B0z0ikx." Despite potential havoc caused before the virus is identified, expert technicians report that the infected strings are easily extracted after diagnosis.

"A Little Girl Is Dying": Internet hoax

Built-in denials aside, this widely circulated Internet hoax is a chain letter and it accomplishes precisely nothing. Anyone familiar with the American Cancer Society knows that while that organization accepts donations for research, it does not distribute any funds to cancer patients. The original hoax e-mail reads:

You guys. . . . this isn't a chain letter, but a choice for all of us to save a little girl that's going to die of a serious and fatal form of cancer. Please sent this to everyone you know . . . or don't know at that. This little girl has 6 months left to life her life, and as her last wish, she wanted to send a chain letter telling everyone to live their life to fullest, since she never will. She'll never make it to prom, graduate from high school, or get married and have a family of her own. By you sending this to as many people as possible, you can give her and her family a little hope, because with every name that this is sent to, the American Cancer Society will donate 3 cents per name to her treatment and recovery plan. One guy sent this to 500 people!!!! So, I know that we can sent it to at least 5 or 6. Come on you guys. . . . and if you're too selfish to waste 10-15 minutes and scrolling this and forwarding it to EVERYONE, just think it could be you one day. . . . and it's not even your $money$, just your time. Please help this little girl out guys, I know you can do it!! I love you guys!

A variation on the theme, perhaps intended as a form of personal harassment, invokes the name of a real-life physician who in fact has nothing to do with the chain letter's circulation. With his surname and address deleted in the interest of privacy, that version reads:

PLEASE FORWARD THIS TO HELP THIS LITTLE GIRL ALL FORWARDED E-MAILS ARE TRACKED TO OBTAIN THE TOTAL COUNT.

Dear All:

PLEASE pass this mail on to everybody you know. It is the request of a special little girl who will soon leave this world as she has cancer. Thank you for your effort, this isn't a chain letter, but a choice for all of us to save a little girl that's dying of a serious and fatal form of cancer.

Please send this to everyone you know . . . or don't know. This little girl has 6 months left to live, and as her dying wish, she wanted to send a letter telling everyone to live their life to the fullest, since she never will. Shel'll [sic] never make it to prom, graduate from high school, or get married and have a family of her own.

By you sending this to as many people as possible, you can give her and her family a little hope, because with every name that this is sent to, The American Cancer Society will donate 3 cents per name to her treatment and recovery plan. One guy sent this to 500 people!!!! So I know that we can send it to at least 5 or 6. Just think it could be you one day. It's not even your money, just your time!!!

"PLEASE PASS ON AS A LAST REQUEST"

Dr. Dennis ——, Professor
Department of Developmental and Molecular Biology
[Institution deleted]

ANDERSON, Marvin Lamont: wrongly convicted; cleared by DNA

A Virginia resident, convicted of rape in 1982 on the basis of a victim's eyewitness testimony, Marvin Anderson received a 210-year prison sentence at his trial. He was paroled in 1997, after serving 15 years, but the stigma of his rape conviction followed Anderson as he attempted to rebuild his life. New legislation signed by Governor Jim Gilmore in May 2001 allowed Anderson's lawyers to petition for DNA

Marvin Anderson clutches his absolute pardon from Virginia governor Mark Warner as he and his sister walk out of the capitol in Richmond on Wednesday, August 21, 2002. Anderson received his pardon after being exonerated of rape charges by DNA evidence. (AP)

testing of semen recovered from the original crime scene. "I knew once they did the testing it would exonerate me," Anderson told reporters. "I knew because I didn't do this."

His longstanding assertion of innocence was vindicated in December 2001, when results of DNA testing excluded Anderson as a possible suspect in the rape. The test results partially matched DNA from two convicted sex offenders in Virginia's data bank, but the evidence samples were too degraded for a positive match to be made on either suspect. Anderson, for his part, was the 99th convicted felon cleared by DNA testing in the United States since the procedure was discovered. "I'm not bitter," he told interviewers. "There's no anger. What happened to me was a mistake by many people, not just any one individual."

Prior requests for DNA testing in Anderson's case had been stalled when authorities reported semen evidence missing from their files. The crucial evidence was rediscovered in 2001, in time for Virginia's new statute to waive the existing deadline on submission of exculpatory scientific evidence. Anderson has announced his intent to seek a pardon from Governor Gilmore. A spokesperson for Gilmore's office denied any knowledge of the case on December 7, 2001, but told reporters, "We would look forward to reading his clemency petition."

"ANDROID": computer worm

Initially reported in May 2000, "Android" is a worm virus spread via Internet channels by e-mail attachments that, when opened, target ultra.exe Windows executable files. One week after infecting a computer, the worm delivers its payload, erasing files with the following extensions on both local and remote drives: .ico, .doc, .txt, .htm, .jpg, .gif, .zip, .rar. The damaged files, once erased, are not recoverable. On the fifth of any month thereafter, the worm drops its android.bmp file with the "ANDROID" text in it, and registers it in the computer's system as wallpaper.

ANGELL, Brian: Internet swindler

A resident of Warwick, Rhode Island, 30-year-old Brian Angell was one of 17 persons arrested for fraud following a two-year federal sting operation dubbed Operation OPERATION SMARTCARD.NET. The defendants were accused of buying and reselling hundreds of counterfeit "smart cards" that provided users with illegal free access to DirecTV, a satellite television service. Spokesmen for the Justice Department and U.S. Customs estimated that use of counterfeit access cards resulted in a $6.2 million yearly loss to the legitimate satellite television industry. Angell and three other Smartcard defendants pleaded guilty in August 2001. Two months later, in Providence, U.S. District Judge Mary Lisi sentenced him to one year's probation and a $5,000 fine.

ANTARAMIAN, Michael Harry: alleged software pirate

On June 1, 2000, FBI agents arrested 52-year-old Michael Antaramian and 47-year-old Fred Hariri on federal charges of conspiracy and criminal copyright infringement. The California residents—Antaramian of Sacramento, Hariri from Glendale—were accused of illegally copying software and high-security computer chips used in the arcade-style video games "NFL Blitz 2000" and "Golden Tee Golf 99." Both games use sophisticated technology to prevent unauthorized reproduction of their software, but Antaramian allegedly developed a method of circumventing the security systems. After copying the chips and software, federal prosecutors say, he then supplied the software to Hariri, who in turn sold it to others.

Following a brief courtroom appearance in Sacramento on June 2, Antaramian was released on his own recognizance and ordered to appear in Los Angeles federal court six days later. Hariri, meanwhile, was arraigned in Los Angeles on the day of his arrest and posted $25,000 bond to secure his release. If convicted on all charges, both defendants face a maximum of 15 years in federal prison and fines of $750,000 each. Antaramian was also named in an additional forfeiture count, which would compel him (if convicted) to surrender all materials related to the copyright infringement scheme. Both defendants are considered innocent of any crime until their cases are resolved by trial or plea bargains.

ANTHROPOLOGY, Forensic: identifying skeletal remains

Anthropology—literally the study of human beings—is broadly divided into three subfields: cultural anthropology (the study of cultures, societies, lifestyles, beliefs, etc.); archaeology (the study of past cultures, via dwellings and relics left behind); and physical (or biological) anthropology (involving all physical and/or biological aspects of the primate order from prehistoric times to the present). A broad

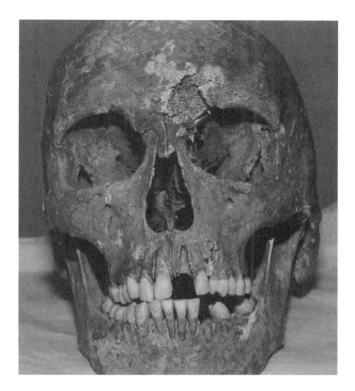

The skull of an 1812 soldier is cleaned and ready for the anthropologist to make a facial approximation. The skull is covered in latex and gauze to make a mold. (Kathleen O. Arries)

field in its own right, physical anthropology is further subdivided into various specialties, including osteology (study of bones). Within the field of osteology we find another sub-specialty: forensic anthropology—the study of skeletal remains as they are relevant to legal cases.

In essence, forensic anthropologists examine skeletal remains (a) to identify the subject, where feasible; and (b) to determine cause of death, where evidence exists. Incomplete or badly damaged remains make the task more difficult—sometimes impossible—but some facts are discernible even from incomplete skeletons. A skull may reveal the subject's race (though interracial marriages confuse the issue) and sex (with a 25 percent margin of error when the skull alone is found). In adult subjects the pelvis identifies gender (with a 10 percent margin of error), but no difference is seen in prepubescent males or females. Long bones of the arms and legs give a fair indication of height and may help suggest age. Bones may also be dated with fair accuracy, to determine if a skeleton is "new" (and thus of concern to police) or a relic from earlier

times (as when aboriginal graves are disturbed). Old injuries or abnormalities become definitive in cases where detailed X rays of missing persons are available. While evidence of soft-tissue injury is wiped out by decomposition, skeletal remains may still reveal cause of death if they display unhealed fractures, knife or bullet wounds, a broken hyoid bone (from strangulation), and so forth.

The most dramatic task performed by forensic anthropologists is facial reconstruction from skulls or their fragments. Work in this field dates from the early 1940s. Pioneers included FBI technician William Krogman and I. A. Gerasimov, in Russia. Once sex and race are determined, science yields to art as modeling clay is applied to the skull, reconstructing the subject's face in part from careful measurements and partly from the sculptor's imagination. Race helps determine the shape of eyes, nose, and lips, but much of the rest remains guesswork. Without photographs or eyewitness descriptions, forensic anthropologists cannot determine whether a subject was fat or thin in real life, scarred or tattooed, bearded or balding. Hair styles, created with wigs,

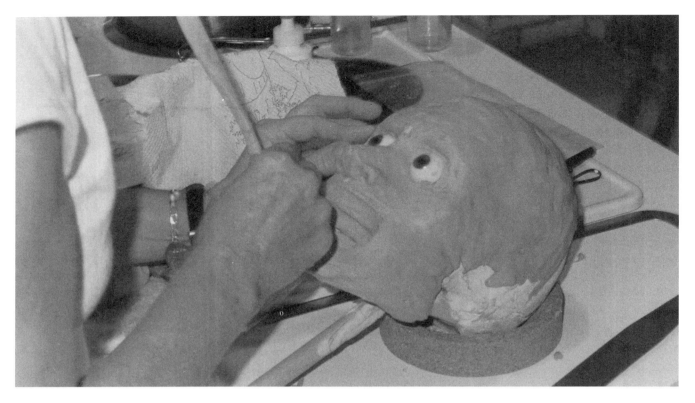

Strips of clay are placed on the mold and smoothed out to the desired tissue depths. Applying the nose, lips, and ears takes an artist's touch. The finished approximation of the soldier as he might have looked before his death. (Kathleen O. Arries)

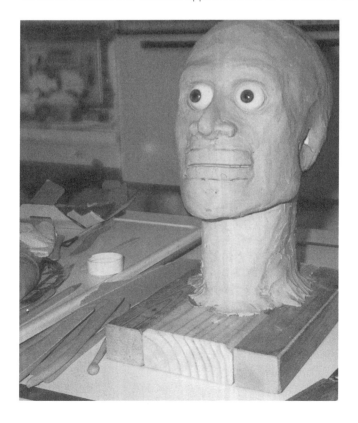

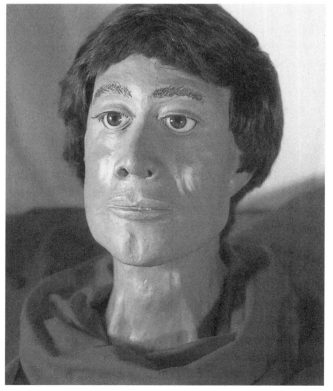

A police officer kneels at the edge of a shallow grave where the dirt has been removed to reveal the image of a woman. Her polyester clothes are still intact after nine years in the ground. (Kathleen O. Arries)

generally spring from pure speculation. Still, in some cases the models may jog memories, leading authorities to witnesses who may have known the anonymous subject in life.

The same technique may be used to "age" images of missing persons, whether they be runaways, kidnap victims, or fugitives from justice. Modern computer technology makes aging of photographs simple, and such photos are often seen on posters of missing children or fugitive felons, including members of the FBI's "Ten Most Wanted" list. While photos dominate the "aging" field, clay models are also sometimes used. One such model, sculpted in Philadelphia by Frank Bender, led directly to the arrest of longtime fugitive John Emil List. In New Jersey, List had shot and killed five members of his family on November 9, 1971, then disappeared, starting a new life as "Robert Peter Clark." He was still at large on May 21, 1989, when Bender's "aged" bust of List appeared on the TV show *America's Most Wanted*. Recognition by neighbors led the FBI to List's Virginia workplace 10 days later; he was

convicted on five murder counts in April 1990 and sentenced to life imprisonment.

Various professional organizations exist to promote understanding and proper application of forensic anthropology. The Canadian Association of Physical Anthropology was founded at Banff in 1972, so that practitioners from Canada "should not have to travel to Kansas in order to meet each other professionally." Five years later, the American Board of Forensic Anthropology was created "to provide, in the interest of the public and the advancement of the science, a program of certification in forensic anthropology." The board's website lists numerous certified members who are available for consultation with law enforcement agencies, attorneys, and the like. The 300-member Midwest Bioarchaeology and Forensic Anthropology Association was created in 1994, "in an effort to support communication on both formal and informal levels." Members of these organizations (and others abroad) regularly share information on major cases, including investigation of mass graves discovered around the world, from Central America to Bosnia-Herzegovina and the Far East.

ANTIABORTION Groups On-line

The 1973 U.S. Supreme Court decision in *Roe v. Wade,* legalizing abortion on demand, ranks as one of the most controversial judicial decisions in American history. In terms of conflict generated, it equals the 1857 Dred Scott decision (proclaiming that blacks had no civil rights), the 1896 decision in *Plessy v. Ferguson* (legitimizing "separate but equal" segregation of the races) and the 1954 ruling in *Brown v. Topeka Board of Education* (banning segregation in public schools). Pro-choice advocates hailed *Roe v. Wade* as a landmark victory for U.S. women, while antiabortion forces, chiefly fundamentalist Christians, denounced the ruling as a step toward genocide and eventual divine punishment.

Despite the heated rhetoric and scattered protests outside women's clinics, the first act of "pro-life" terrorism was not recorded until February 18, 1978, when a clinic was firebombed in Cleveland, Ohio. The next act of violence came a full year later, on February 19, 1979, with an arson attempt at a clinic in Hempstead, New York. Following Ronald Reagan's 1980 election as president, with public support from the religious far right and repeated attacks on *Roe v. Wade* from Reagan himself, the tenor of "pro-life" dissent changed radically. Almost overnight, the terrorist "Army of God" launched a guerrilla campaign against women's clinics nationwide, while individual fanatics cast themselves in vigilante roles, staging repeated attacks on abortion facilities and their personnel. A conservative tabulation of U.S. "pro-life" violence between 1980 and 2000 includes three kidnappings, seven murders; 17 attempted murders; 40 clinic bombings; 163 arson incidents; 80 attempted bombings or arson attacks; 115 cases of assault and battery; 60 burglaries; 882 incidents of vandalism; 420 cases of stalking; 526 bomb threats; 8,246 harassing phone calls; and 33,800 arrests in riotous demonstrations. In 2001, dozens of American clinics received envelopes in the mail alleged to contain anthrax, while murders of abortion providers continued in New York, Canada, and Australia.

From the start of their campaign against *Roe v. Wade,* "Christian soldiers" have formed strange alliances across the far right of the political spectrum. Militant white supremacist groups including the Aryan Nations, White Aryan Resistance, and several factions of the Ku Klux Klan joined the "pro-life" crusade, proclaiming abortion to be part of a "Jewish conspiracy" designed to reduce white numbers in America while minorities proliferate. One of the antiabortion movement's most popular tactics—publication of Wanted posters with the photographs, home addresses, and telephone numbers of clinic physicians and nurses—was pioneered in 1985 by the Carolina Knights of the Ku Klux Klan (later the White American Party, its leader convicted of conspiracy to share loot from bank robberies by neo-Nazis).

In recent years, as scrutiny from law enforcement and the media has restricted their activities, extremists of the "pro-life" movement have relied heavily on the Internet to communicate and plan their functions, while offering praise and support to convicted terrorists, encouraging others to follow their "Christian" example. The mock Wanted (or "*Un*wanted") posters have been featured on various websites for years, providing stalkers with the basic information they require to locate, harass—and sometimes murder—abortion providers. (Those who flaunt the posters, meanwhile, insist that they are merely intended to direct group prayers or allow peaceful Christians to voice their displeasure over ongoing abortions.) The same websites feature gory photographs of alleged "murdered children"—i.e., aborted fetuses—and Biblical invocations of God's wrath against perceived sinners.

Support for convicted clinic bombers and assassins is virtually universal on "pro-life" Internet websites.

The official "Army of God" website includes the predictable "Wanted Posters of Enemies," along with posthumous attacks on murdered physicians and praise for their killers. It also supports the "White Rose Banquet," a yearly fund-raising event held in honor of imprisoned clinic terrorists, which features prominent guest speakers from the Christian right. Proceeds from the banquet are allegedly contributed to families of those imprisoned, but as with most religious ventures, no public accounting is made of the cash collected. The sixth annual White Rose Banquet, held on January 21, 2002, was sponsored by convicted clinic bomber Michael Bray and his Reformation Lutheran Church of Bowie, Maryland. In addition to hawking Bray's self-published book, *A Time to Kill,* the church's Internet website had this to say about the banquet (errors uncorrected):

With the exception of January Y2K, the White Rose Banquet has been held each year since 1996 to recognize the sacrifices the saints of Christ have made to protect the unborn. It is a time when we gather together and read letters from prisoners and be updated on their unjust incarceration. In addition, there will be an auction of Prisoners of Christ artifacts, memorabilia, and handicrafts. Each year one or two prisoner's families receive receive the entire proceeds of the banquet and auction to help while their love one in imprisoned.

Items donated by prisoners in the past have included: handicrafts, pencil sketches, including calligraphy of the Ten Commandments, by [Florida death row inmate] Paul Hill, artwork by Shelley Shannon [jailed for attempted murder in Kansas], the black leather jacket worn by James Mitchell as he burned a baby killing center in Northern Virginia, denim jacket [clinic arsonist] Joshua Graff wore while performing his acts of kindness towards the unborn, and the watch used by Dennis Malvasi to time his incendiary device to blow up Planned Parenthood in NYC.

Again, The Annual White Rose Banquet is held to honor and to recognized the action our brothers and sisters have taken to protect the unborn from the bloody abortionist.

The Almighty says that He honors those who honor Him. We would do likewise. We will give honor where honor is due!

Join us again in celebration of those who have suffered years in prison for honoring God by sacrificing their lives and freedom for the sake of the innocent ones. . . .

Like unto previous years, we will read letters from saints in bonds. And shall we not auction some of their personal wares again as relics? In this time of national darkness, it is good to rejoice in the sacrifices offered by our brothers and sisters. . . .

We also reserve the right to discriminate between the wicked and the righteous and shall refuse tickets to known abortion proponents who come only to gaze and spy upon our celebration. On the other hand, we may choose to let certain members of that low class participate according to our good pleasure.

Some "pro-life" groups are even more blatant in their on-line support of terrorist activities. The American Coalition of Life Activists (ACLA), another sponsor of the White Rose Banquet, maintains close relations with "Reverend" Bray's Maryland church, and describes its own activities on a separate website thus (errors intact):

The ACLA published "reward" posters offering local activists and groups cash rewards for their anti-abortion activities[.] In preparation for the day when they hope abortion rights will be outlawed, ACLA has launched its so-called "Nuremberg Files Project." "The goal of our project," according to David Crane, the group's national director, "will be to gather all available information on abortionists and their accomplices for the day when they may be formally charged and tried at Nuremberg-type trials for their crimes. The information in these files will be specifically the kind of evidence admissible in a court of law." He added, "The Project will set up several secret archives which will be safe from seizure by those who would allow criminal child-killers to go free."

"We don't want to make the mistakes that allowed so many Nazis to escape justice after World War II," said Paul deParrie, one of the assistants involved in the project. "We intend to have extensive files on each of them which will permit prosecutors to easily identify the criminal perpetrators and bring the appropriate judgment against them.". . . .

Last year the ACLA published a poster called "the deadly dozen." According to Crane, "It exposed 12 abortionists nationwide. The media and the federal government called it a 'hit list.' Some of the abortionists were even tracked down on their vacations and told they were put on a hit list. So, what we could probably never accomplish with our exposure campaign, the government did for us very effectively! We do praise God for that. Like in the Scripture where 'the wicked flee and no man pursueth, but the righteous are as bold as lions,' we've seen fear in the hearts of the wicked."

The ACLA's "reward" offer for antiabortion commandos was described on-line as an effort to "Reward the diligence and success of activist groups working within the ACLA guidelines by offering rewards of $500 for persuading an abortionist to stop murdering the unborn. And offering rewards of $1,000 to end the killing by closing any abortion facility. This gives them some cash to work on the next abortionist, or abortion facility." While no "ACLA guidelines" were provided, the group's public support for convicted arsonists, bombers, and murderers speaks for itself. As for the "Nuremberg Files," it is noteworthy that the name of New York physician Barnett Slepian was crossed out on the ACLA's website the same day a sniper murdered him, on October 23, 1998.

Such rhetoric—and cash offers—have not gone unchallenged by pro-choice activists. In 1999 Planned Parenthood and four physicians, targeted by antiabortion websites as criminals and "baby butchers," sued a dozen "pro-life" leaders under federal racketeering statutes and a 1994 law making it illegal to incite violence against abortion providers. A jury in Portland, Oregon, ruled for the plaintiffs and ordered the antiabortion defendants to pay $109 million in damages, but that verdict was overturned by a federal appellate court on March 28, 2001. The appellate court ruled that website messages and Wanted posters were protected by the First Amendment to the U.S. Constitution unless the defendants "threatened to commit violent acts, by working alone or with others." Conversely, they could not be punished if they "merely encouraged unrelated terrorists" to attack clinics and doctors.

"Pro-life" rhetoric reached a new low after September 11, 2001, when antiabortion activists blamed *Roe v. Wade* for Palestinian terrorist attacks on New York City and the Pentagon. One website posted the following message from Troy Newman, self-described director of "Operation Rescue West" (errors preserved):

Today the LORD has visited our land in judgment. An invading force has pierced the shores of our country to wreck havoc on us, on our cities and our people.

Because the immutable character of God never changes, let us consider for what cause the Lord has smitten us.

Could it be that the blood of over 44,000,000 pre-born children has brought this destruction to our shores?

I have heard the networks and the President say, "We must punish the perpetrators!" While we must

17

seek justice, it is America who is guilty of a far greater crime—the murder of our own innocent children.

So prior to sending aircraft carriers and heavy bombers to destroy the terrorist compounds let us look inwardly, to ourselves, for certainly we are covered head to toe with innocent blood and we value human life no more than the terrorists flying the jetliners.

Today is a day of mourning and weeping in repentance. Cry to our God and beg for His forgiveness! America deserves, yes warrants the judgment of God. . . .

America is in the clutches of remedial judgment! God has tried to wake us up with shark attacks, great forest fires, earthquakes, huge storms and long droughts, school shootings, financial upheaval and power outages. Now look to the LORD with sorrow and be saved or pound your fists in the sand and we will tread ever forward to final destruction!

Understand America . . . Because we have not hated bloodshed (abortion), bloodshed (World Trade Towers, Pentagon) will pursue America. . . .

America, God is not blessing you so stop asking for it. Instead fall on your knees and beg the LORD to save America. Mr. President appoint for a day of fasting and mourning. Pastors and Elders call for weeping and sackcloth. Americans repent for the innocent blood shed upon our land.

"ANTIWIN": computer virus family

Identified for the first time in July 1997, the "Antiwin" group of computer viruses are classified as dangerous memory-resident, parasitic, encrypted viruses. The several viruses write themselves to the end of executed .exe files, but are also "smart" enough to check file names and avoid infection of various utilities and anti-virus applications that would otherwise expose their presence in a system.

The Antiwin viruses use on-the-fly encryption/decryption, so that their code is encrypted in a computer's memory, as well as in the damaged files. Furthermore, the viruses carry their own bugs, which may freeze computers when the target files are attacked.

In some cases the Antiwin viruses display a message reading "Use registered copies of MS Windows" when an infected computer freezes. Others contain the text "Greetings from MrStrange, Kiev T. G. Shevchenko University >Antiwin<, (c) by MrStrange." The master copy of the Antiwin virus also contains the text: "MrStrange hails you from Kiev! My first virus."

AOL V4.0 Cookie Chain Letter: Internet hoax

Broadcast on the Internet as a purported attempt to expose corporate malfeasance at America Online (AOL), this malicious hoax distributed by e-mail has no basis in reality. Its source remains unknown, with disgruntled employees or dissatisfied subscribers making up the list of "usual suspects." The message reads as follows:

From a former AOL employee:

I'll try and cut through the crap, and try to get to the point of this letter.

I used to work for America Online, and would like to remain anonymous for that reason. I was laid off in early September, but I know exactly why I was laid off, which I will now explain:

Since last December, I had been one of the many people assigned to design AOL 4.0 for Windows (AOL 4.0 beta, codenamed Casablanca). In the beginning, I was very proud of this task, until I found out the true cost of it. Things were going fine until about mid-February, when me and 2 of my colleagues started to suspect a problem, an unexplainable 'Privacy Invasion', with the new version. One of them, who is a master programmer, copied the finished portion of the new version (Then 'Build 52'), and took it home, and we spent nearly 2 weeks of sleepless nights examining and debugging the program, flipping it inside-out, and here is what we found.

Unlike all previous versions of America Online, version 4.0 puts something in your hard drive called a 'cookie'. (AOL members click here for a definition). However, the cookie we found on Version 4.0 was far more treacherous than the simple Internet cookie. How would you like somebody looking at your entire hard drive, snooping through any (yes, any) piece of information on your hard drive. It could also read your password and log in information and store it deep in the program ode. Well, all previous versions, whether you like it or not, have done this to a certain extent, but only with files you downloaded. As me and my colleagues discovered, with the new version, anytime you are signed on to AOL, any top AOL executive, any AOL worker, who has been sworn to secrecy regarding this feature, can go in to your hard drive and retrieve any piece of information that they so desire. Billing, download records, e-mail, directories, personal documents, programs, financial information, scanned images, etc. Better start keeping all those pictures on a floppy disk!

This is a totally disgusting violation of our rights, and your right to know as well. Since this is undoubtedly

'Top Secret' information that I am revealing, my life at AOL is pretty much over. After discovering this inform attain, we started to inform a few other workers at America Online, so that we could get a large enough crew to stop this from happening to the millions of unfortunate and unsuspecting America Online members. This was in early August. One month later, all three of us were unemployed. We got together and figured there was something we had to do to let the public know.

Unemployed, with one of us going through a divorce (me) and another who is about to undergo treatment for Cancer, our combined financial situation is not currently enough to release any sort or article. We attempted to create a web page on three different servers containing in-depth information on AOL 4.0, but all three were taken down within 2 days. We were running very low on time (4.0 is released early this winter), so we figured our last hope to reveal this madness before it effects the people was starting something similar to a chain letter, this letter you are reading. Please do the following, to help us expose AOL for who they really are, and to help us and yourself receive personal gratification for taking a stand for our freedom:

1. Forward this letter to as many people as you can (not just friends and family, as many as you can)!
2. Tell people who aren't on America Online in person, especially important people (Private Investigators, Government workers, City Council)
3. If the information about the new version isn't exposed by the time AOL is released early this winter, for your own protection, DON'T DOWNLOAD AOL 4.0 UNDER ANY CONDITION!!!

Thank you for reading and examining this information. Me and my colleagues hope that you will help us do the right thing in this situation. Enjoy America Online (just kidding!).

Regards, A former AOL employee

AOL Database Scam: Internet fraud technique

Beginning in June 1999, a message circulated on the Internet directing America Online subscribers to "verify" their registration by visiting a website unconnected to that company. Those who heeded the warning and followed the steps laid out for them at the bogus website were, in fact, providing unknown persons with their AOL passwords and user names. The original message read:

Subject: AOL Database Corruption, Please View!
MIME-Version: 1.0
Content-Type: text/plain; charset="us-ascii"
Content-Transfer-Encoding: 7bit
X-mailer: AOL 2.5 for Windows
To: undisclosed-recipients:;

Dear Member:

Hello. I am your AOL Technical Representative. Section 56 of our data base has lost all Linux functions. When your account logged onto our system, we were temporarily able to verify it as a registered user. Approximately 90 seconds ago, your verification was made void by loss of data in Section 56. Now, due to AOL verification protocol, it is mandatory for us to reverify you.
    Please visit http://216.33.20.4/biz3/AOLTech142/index.html for more information.

Regards,
Michelle
Community Action Team
America Online, Inc.

*Have you heard about AOL's newest and easiest to use software: Version 4.0? You can upgrade for free at keyword: Update. With AOL 4.0, you can send multiple files, change screen names without signing off, customize your toolbar, and much, much more. Upgrade today!!

Presumably, the addition of an advertisement made the scam message seem more legitimate. It is unknown how many AOL subscribers may have fallen for the hoax and given up their passwords. A similar fraud, posing as an AOL giveaway program, made the Internet rounds beginning in September 1999. Like the original, it directed victims to a website resembling AOL's, but which existed solely to collect personal information about those who logged on. That message read (with errors intact):

Subject: AOL Giveaways!!!

For out AOL members. Thank you for enjoying the best internet service on the net. Because we value our customers during our current update members must please submittheir information to be eligible for our FREE drawing of cash and prizes on November 12, 1999. Winners will be randomly selected and notified through email. Best of luck to our Members! Aol Staff "http://216.33.20.4/az2/tryfree/index.html"> CLICK HERE

AOL4FREE Scams: Internet swindles and hoaxes

As exposed by HOAXBUSTERS, THE "AOL4Free" charade evolved through three phases, beginning in 1996 with an AOL4Free Macintosh program, written by a former Yale computer science student and distributed to hundreds of users, providing illegal free access to America Online that cost the company between $40,000 and $70,000 in service charges. The March 1997 issue of *CSI Computer Security Alert* noted that the (anonymous) author of the program was arrested and pleaded guilty to defrauding AOL. Any attempt to replicate or use the AOL4Free program subjects all users to criminal prosecution on the same charge.

Part two of the AOL4Free story involves a fake virus warning broadcast on the Internet as a hoax. The e-mail message reads:

VIRUS ALERT!!!
DON'T OPEN E-MAIL NOTING "AOL4FREE"
Anyone who receives this must send it to as many people as you can. It is essential that this problem be reconciled as soon as possible. A few hours ago, I opened an E-mail that had the subject heading of "AOL4FREE.COM". Within seconds of opening it, a window appeared and began to display my files that were being deleted. I immediately shut down my computer, but it was too late. This virus wiped me out. It ate the Anti-Virus Software that comes with the Windows '95 Program along with F-Prot AVS. Neither was able to detect it. Please be careful and sent this to as many people as possible, so maybe this new virus can be eliminated.

Ironically, while that warning is a complete hoax, there is an aol4free.com Trojan horse file at large "in the wild" that creates fraudulent AOL accounts while deleting all files on the C drive of an infected computer. Unlike the nonexistent virus from the "warning" hoax, however, this real-life version is a DOS program that leaves Macintosh computers unscathed while attacking Windows software. It runs the DOS deltree command on the C drive of an infected machine, thereby deleting all files in a given directory, including the directory itself and any subdirectories. In that manner, the C hard drive is soon wiped clean.

On balance, it seems safe to say that any and all messages bearing the AOL4Free title should be deleted on arrival without being opened, since none of the three versions offers anything more than time-wasting annoyance, while the more serious forms may involve loss of critical data or criminal prosecution for weak-willed users.

"AOL Riot": threatening Internet hoax

The following hoax message represents an effort to coerce participation in an Internet chain letter attacking America Online. The VIRUSES and computer technology it describes do not exist, nor have any of the HACKERS' screen names provided been linked to real-life individuals. The message read (with original errors):

AOL RIOT JUNE 1, 1998
WARNING:

You must forward this letter to 10 people or your account will be terminated on June 1, 1998. All recipients of this e-mail are being tracked. When you received this, when you forwarded it, who you forwarded it to, is all on record. We are AOL's most elite hacker group, known as LcW. We have hacked AOL's (easily infiltrated) systems on numerous occaisions. We have shut down AOL keywords, we can kick any AOL Staff member off for 24 hours, we have gained access to Steve Case's account, we have created AOL's most famous hacking programs (Fate X, HaVoK, HeLL RaIsEr, MaGeNtA) and we can certainly get your credit card info. However, if you sent this to 10 people, like you are told, you will escape unharmed. We won't terminate your account and you will be able to continue using AOL. So if you know whats best for you, you will send this to 10 people as soon as possible. If you think we are bluffing. . . . just wait till June 1, and see if you can sign or not.

CAUTION: THERE WILL BE A VIRUS UPLOADED ON AOL'S MAIN SERVER ON JUNE 1, 1998. ANY USERS WHO HAVEN'T FORWARDED THIS MESSAGE WILL AUTOMATICALLY HAVE THE VIRUS DOWNLOADED INTO THEIR SYSTEM. WE SUGGEST YOU FORWARD THIS MESSAGE OR YOUR COMPUTER WILL BE FRIED.
* * * * *
Because of the outrage of AOL's increasing prices, LcW has decided to create a riot on May 1, that will cause havoc on AOL. We will be sending viruses our to thousands of AOL users. We will be terminating accounts. We will be hacking into Guide chat rooms and kicking guides offline. There will be no AOL

Staff—just complete pandemonium. If you want to join this riot, we urge you to! You won't have to worry about being TOSed or Reported because there will be no Guides online! So do whatever you want—punt, scroll, tos, just turn AOL into a war zone!

* * * * *

LIST OF LcW HACKERS ON AOL

We represent LcW
The following Hackers will be co-ordinating the Riot and hacking AOL's mainframe computer, and uploading viruses into the system.

WaReZxHaCk
MaGuS
ReDxKiNG
HaVoK
SkiD
SeMeN
NoStRa
PhoneTap
InetXWeb
Psy Acid
PoiSon iV
PaUsE
CooLant
InFeRnO
Xstatic
Chronic Burn
Zone Degreez
WaTcHeR

AOL RIOT ON JUNE 1, 1998—You have been warned LcW is taking over America Online. This is not no fucking joke either. You have been warned.

The warning offered no explanation for the confusion of dates, with the "riot" variously scheduled for May 1 and June 1, 1998, but since no disturbance was noted on either date, it hardly mattered.

AOL Upgrade Warning: Internet hoax

Yet another hoax targeting America Online, this bogus warning cautions Internet users against the perils of a nonexistent upgrade supposedly offered by e-mail with an infected attachment. It reads (with grammatical errors intact):

Attention Friends

Another scam on the lurch on the AOL net. . . . BEWARE!!!!!! If you receive an e-mail that is titled "Fwd: America Online 4.0 Upgrade" or that has an attached file called "Setup40.exe" Do not download the program it is NOT Aol 4,0 it is a program that will e-mail your SCREEN NAME and your PASSWORD to two or more people during two blackouts of your computer screen. DO NOT DOWNLOAD DELETE IT!!! Please E-Mail this letter to as many people as possible to avoid damage. . . . thanks!!!

Spokesmen for America Online reply, for the record, that "AOL does not circulate ANYTHING to customers by way of e-mail with attached files. All AOL software is distributed through keyworded download areas on the service."

"APOKALIPSA": computer virus

First identified in October 2000, the "Apokalipsa" computer virus was rated nondangerous by expert analysts and may in fact have ceased to exist "in the wild." The virus wrote itself to the end of executed .exe files and apparently decrypted only in the year 2000, displaying the following messages:

Wellcome to 21st century.
Author (Martin Zdila—MATOSoft) wish you no viruses in your computer (except me—APOKALIPSA).
I (virus) was born in SLOVAKIA in 1997/98. Don't panic, I am harmless virus what is waiting for APOKALIPSA. Press any key to continue.
Oh my God . . . APOKALIPSA is here !!!
ALL DATA ON YOUR DISK ARE DESTROYED, FOREVER! . . . ha ha ha. I got you! Great joke, isn't it ?!

In fact, no disks were erased and the virus's built-in trigger for the year 2000 seems to have rendered it inoperative thereafter.

AREA Code 809 Scam: Internet hoax based on actual fraud

This curious message, circulated for the first time in February 2000, refers to an actual telephone scam but garbles the details and incorporates various factual errors that make the warning useless. The 809 telephone area code is assigned to the Dominican Republic, charged as an overseas call despite the fact that it can be dialed in the same manner as a domestic long-distance call. Some numbers in that country are pay-per-call numbers, similar to "900" numbers in the United States, but unlike the U.S., Dominican statutes provide for no recorded warnings before those numbers are dialed. The 809 area code therefore has been used to bilk callers of cash, but the Internet warning is erroneous in several respects, including the pretense that it emanates from the (legitimate) ScamBusters website. The hoax message reads (with errors preserved):

SPECIAL ALERT—DON'T EVER DIAL AREA CODE 809
This is pretty scary—especially given how they try to get you to call. Be sure you read this and pass it on to all your friends & family so they don't get scammed!

SCAM: Don't Respond To Emails, Phone Calls, Or Web Pages which tell you to Call An "809" Phone Number. This is a very important issue of Internet ScamBusters! Because it alerts you to a scam that is spreading *extremely* quickly—can easily cost you $100 or more, and—is difficult to avoid unless you are aware of it. We'd like to thank Paul Breummer and Brian Stains for bringing this scam to our attention. This scam has also been identified by the National Fraud Information Center and is costing victims a lot of money. There are lots of different permutations of this scam, but HERE'S HOW IT WORKS:

Permutation #1: Internet Based Phone Scam Via Email You receive an email, typically with a subject line of "*ALERT*" or "Unpaid account." The message, which is being spammed across the net, says: I am writing to give you a final 24hrs to settle your outstanding account . . . If I have not received the settlement in full, I will commence legal proceedings without further delay. If you would like to discuss this matter to avoid court action, call Mike Murray at Global Communications on at 1-809-496-2700.

Permutation #2: Phone Or Pager Scam You receive a message on your answering machine or your pager which asks you to call a number beginning with area code 809. The reason you're asked to call varies: it can be to receive information about a family member who has been ill, to tell you someone has been arrested, died, to let you know you have won a wonderful prize, etc. In each case, you're told to call the 809 number right away. Since there are so many new area codes these days, people unknowingly return these calls. If you call from the US, you will apparently be charged $25 per-minute! Sometimes the person who answers the phone will speak broken English and pretend not to understand you. Other times, you'll just get a long recorded message. The point is, they will try to keep you on that phone as long as possible to increase the charges. Unfortunately, when you get your phone bill, you'll often be charged more than $100.00.

HERE'S WHY IT WORKS: The 809 area code is located in the British Virgin Islands (the Bahamas). The 809 area code can be used as a "pay-per-call" number, similar to 900 numbers in the US. Since 809 is not in the US, it is not covered by US regulations of 900 numbers, which require that you be notified and warned of charges and rates involved when you call a "pay-per-call" number. There is also no requirement that the company provide a time period during which you may terminate the call without being charged. Further, whereas many US phones have 900 number blocking to avoid these kinds of charges, 900 number blocking will not prevent calls to the 809 area code. We recommend that no matter how you get the message, if you are asked to call a number with an 809 area code that you don't recognize, investigate further and/or disregard the message. Be *very* wary of email or calls asking you to call an 809 area code number. it's important to prevent becoming a victim of this scam, since trying to fight the charges afterward can become a real nightmare. That's because you did actually make the call. If you complain, both our local phone company and your long distance carrier will not want to get involved and will most likely tell you that they are simply providing the billing for the foreign company. You'll end up dealing with a foreign company that argues they have done nothing wrong. Please forward this entire issue of Internet ScamBusters! To your friends, family and colleagues to help them become aware of this scam so they don't get ripped off.

The actual ScamBusters website disavows any link to this e-mail, although a form of the warning (minus errors) may be found on that site. Among the errors noted by ScamBusters are the following:

1. ScamBusters has never warned anyone to avoid dialing 809 numbers under any and all circumstances.
2. Likewise, the website asks no one to forward its articles to friends or broadcast them across the Internet at large.
3. Contrary to the hoax e-mail's implication, the 809 area code is not new, but has been in use for years.
4. More significantly, the 809 area code is not "located in the British Virgin Islands (the Bahamas)." In fact, the British Virgin Islands and

Bahamas are not the same country, nor does either share the 809 area code with the Dominican Republic. The Bahamian area code is 242, while that of the British Virgin Islands is 284.

ARMORED Vehicles

Armored or "bulletproof" vehicles have long been a staple of crime and crime-fighting, as well as military action. Prohibition-era gangsters like Chicago's Al Capone protected themselves from bootleg rivals with armored limousines, and the 1930s Barker-Karpis gang used similar vehicles (some equipped with smokescreen generators) to escape from police after their daylight bank holdups. Private security firms, in turn, initiated use of armored vehicles for shipping cash and other valuable merchandise, a practice that continues to the present day. Increasingly, as the threat of terrorism or ransom kidnapping spreads throughout the world at large, high-ranking government and business figures seek advanced security in transit for themselves, their families, and their associates.

Civilian armored vehicles typically rely on steel plating, shatter-resistant glass, and special "run-flat" bulletproof tires to protect their drivers and passengers. Weapons and gun ports are also frequently included, to give the targets of attack a fighting chance at self-defense. Drawbacks of heavily armored vehicles include reduced speed and increased fuel consumption, all of which comes with a greatly inflated price tag. Manufacturers are typically close-mouthed about specifics of their armor plating, but multiple layers of tempered steel and occasional lighter materials such as Kevlar are standard for civilian vehicles. Military and police vehicles often employ more expensive, bulkier armor, including the following types:

Composite armor, true to its name, incorporates layers of different substances, each with different protective properties against specific kinds of attack. One system employs steel armor inlaid and reinforced with a network of titanium rods; another sandwiches heat-absorbing chemical layers between steel plates; yet another provides layers of rubber between armor plates to absorb the shock waves of explosive rounds on impact.

Explosive reactive armor (ERA) actually employs a layer of explosive material between thick steel plates, attached like shingles to the existing armor of a military vehicle, but spaced somewhat away from it. On impact of an armor-piercing round, the explosive layer detonates, flinging the steel plates apart and absorbing most of the incoming round's destructive force before it reaches the primary target.

It is presently illegal for American civilians to purchase or possess armor-piercing ammunition, either in the form of small arms "cop-killer" rounds or larger military ordnance, but black-market sources make most forms of weaponry available to terrorists, revolutionaries, and well-financed criminal gangs. Three common anti-armor rounds designed specifically for military use are:

1. Armor-piercing, fin-stabilized, discarding sabot (APFSDS) rounds. The projectile in one of these shells is a long, small-diameter dart with tail fins, made of some extremely hard and dense material such as tungsten carbide or depleted uranium. Because it is much smaller than the bore of the weapon that fires it, the dart is encased in a light alloy sleeve (the "sabot") which disintegrates and falls away upon firing. The dart—or "penetrator"—itself is designed to pierce armor and shatter inside the vehicle, spraying any occupants with white-hot shrapnel and fragments of the vehicle's own ruptured plating.

2. High explosive anti-tank (HEAT) ammunition. These shells penetrate armor by using the "Monroe effect" of detonating explosives at a critical distance from the target. HEAT projectiles are cylindrical full-bore shells containing several pounds of high explosives. The front of each round is a hollow cone lined with copper or some other dense material, its extended nose bearing a piezoelectric crystal at the tip. The crystal is crushed on impact, generating an electric pulse that passes to a detonator at the base of the round's explosive payload. When the charge explodes, a detonation wave passes around the cone and collapses it in a "focusing" action, converting it to a fast-moving (16,000 mph) jet of molten material and high-explosive gas. Heat and velocity combine to penetrate the armor, incinerating the vehicle's occupants on contact and detonating any live ammunition in the round's path.

3. High-explosive squash-head (HESH) ammunition. These rounds premiered in World War II

23

and have been constantly refined over the past half-century. Each HESH round is a blunt-nosed projectile filed with plastic explosive that "squashes" against its target on impact, then detonates from a fuse in the base of the charge. Rather than piercing the armor, the HESH round's massive shock wave dislodges a large steel "scab" from the vehicle's interior plating, which then ricochets around inside the vehicle with killing force.

Use of such destructive ammunition would be excessive and counterproductive for bandits intent on robbing an armored truck of cash—and it would hardly be necessary. When neo-Nazi members of The Order robbed a Brink's truck at Ukiah, California, of $3.8 million on July 19, 1984, three shots from a .308-caliber semiautomatic rifle pierced the armored truck's windows and persuaded the guards to surrender. The bandits scarcely needed the harmless cardboard tube, which they had painted to resemble a bazooka rocket-launcher.

ARSON Investigation

According to a 1998 report from the Federal Emergency Management Administration (FEMA), arson is the leading cause of fire-related property damage in the United States, also resulting in an average of 500 deaths per year, nationwide. The FBI's *Crime Classification Manual* (1992) lists seven motives for deliberate fire-setting. They include:

VANDALISM

Subcategories of this motive include willful and malicious mischief (wherein motive may be determined by choice of targets) and peer-group pressure (most commonly seen in juvenile offenders).

EXCITEMENT

Variants of this motive include fire-setting by thrill-seekers, by arsonists craving attention, by those seeking recognition as "heroes" (firefighters sometimes fall into this category), or sexual deviants who achieve satisfaction from the act of setting fires.

REVENGE

A more "rational" form of fire-setting, this form may target individuals, specific groups or institutions, or society in general. It may also include acts of intimidation, as in the case of fires set to discourage particular activities (e.g., the testimony of a witness, purchase of specific property, etc.).

CRIME CONCEALMENT

Fire destroys evidence, and various arsonists have used it to conceal acts of murder, suicide, burglary, theft, or embezzlement, and to destroy crucial records pertaining to disputed property or activities.

PROFIT

These fires are normally set to obtain an insurance payoff, to liquidate property, to dissolve a failing business, to eliminate unwanted inventory, or to eradicate competition.

EXTREMISM

Fires in this category include acts of TERRORISM and discrimination (if indeed there is any discernible difference between the two acts), and arson incidents committed during riots. Religious fanaticism may be a factor, in addition to political or racial concerns. (In 1999 a self-styled Satanist confessed to burning more than 30 Christian churches across the Midwest.)

SERIAL ARSON

Defined as compulsive, repetitive fire-setting. Indeed, repetition alone seems to distinguish this category from the "excitement" motive listed above. FBI taxonomists confuse the issue by creating a subcategory for *spree* arsonists (who set multiple fires without an emotional "cooling-off" period between incidents), and by adding a *mass* arson category for offenders who set multiple simultaneous fires at one location. (The latter, clearly, has nothing to do with "serial" arson, which by definition involves successive and separate incidents.)

Arson investigators begin their task by studying the complex chemical process that is fire. Each fire consists of three basic elements: fuel, oxygen, and heat. The physical state and shape of the fuel, available oxygen, and the transmission of heat all play critical roles in development of a specific fire. Investigators must also understand the basics of building construction, including materials used and the nature of any fire-protection systems in place, which determine the course of a fire's development and progress.

The first step in any fire investigation is determining a blaze's point of origin. Only when the point of origin has been determined can authorities discover how and why a blaze began. This "backwards" investigation must be fully documented via field notes, diagrams and sketches, photographs, and collection of fire scene evidence. If investigators can eliminate accidental causes—faulty equipment, careless smoking, flammable liquids, lightning, electrical failures, and spontaneous combustion—they are ready to proceed in search of a deliberate incendiary cause for the fire. That evidence may include traces of accelerants) gasoline, kerosene, etc.) or the remnants of an incendiary/explosive device recovered from the fire scene. Various mechanical sensors and specially trained dogs assist investigators in the discovery of accelerants and other clues at a fire scene. That evidence, in turn, may prove vital in tracing the arsonist (or, in the alternative, for use in attempts at PSYCHOLOGICAL PROFILING of an unknown fire-setter).

Collection of evidence at any crime scene must conform to rigorous forensic standards if that evidence is to withstand legal challenges in court. Photographs and fire-scene sketches document the points where evidentiary items were initially discovered, and each fire department or law enforcement agency follows established procedures to document the chain of custody between discovery and trial. Modern computer software, such as the FireFiles system, provides arson investigators with case-management tools to organize various details of the case, track evidence from collection through analysis, and to help in preparation of technical reports.

ASPARTAME Hoax: Internet smear campaign

The artificial sweetener aspartame, marketed under various brand names, has come under fire on the Internet since a 1996 scientific study reported an increase in brain tumors among laboratory animals ingesting the chemical, although no direct causal link was asserted and medical opinion later varied on the subject, as the incidence of tumors leveled off while use of aspartame continued to increase nationwide. In December 1999 a letter began circulating on the Internet, allegedly written by one Betty Martini, described as a lecturer at the World Environmental Conference. Its contents were entirely false, misleading, and defamatory to various popular products and their manufacturers, with no basis whatever in fact. That message read (complete with errors):

WORLD ENVIRONMENTAL CONFERENCE and the MULTIPLE SCLEROSIS FOUNDATION & FDA IS SUING FOR COLLUSION WITH MONSANTO.

Article written by Betty Martini

I have spent several days lecturing at the WORLD ENVIRONMENTAL CONFERENCE on ASPARTAME: Marketed as 'NutraSweet,' 'Equal,' and 'Spoonful.' In the keynote address by the EPA, they announced that there was an epidemic of multiple sclerosis and systemic lupus, and they did not understand what toxin was causing this to be rampant across the United States.

I explained I was there to lecture on exactly that subject. When the temperature of Aspartame exceeds 86 degrees F, the wood alcohol in ASPARTAME converts to formaldehyde and then to formic acid, which in turn causes metabolic acidosis. (Formic acid is the poison found in the sting of fire ants.) The methanol toxicity mimics multiple sclerosis; thus, people were being diagnosed with having multiple sclerosis in error. The multiple sclerosis is not a death sentence, where methanol toxicity is. In the case of systemic lupus, we are finding it has become almost as rampant as multiple sclerosis, especially Diet Coke and Diet Pepsi drinkers. Also, with methanol toxicity, the victims usually drink three to four 12 oz. Cans of them per day, some even more. In the case of systemic lupus, which is triggered by ASPARTAME, the victim usually does not know that aspartame is the culprit. The victim continues its use aggravating the lupus to such a degree, that sometimes it becomes life threatening.

When we get people off the aspartame, those with systemic lupus usually become asymptomatic. Unfortunately, we cannot reverse the disease. On the other hand, in the case of those diagnosed with Multiple Sclerosis, (when in reality, the disease is methanol toxicity), most of the symptoms disappear. We have seen cases where their vision has returned and even their hearing has returned. This also applies to cases of tinnitus.

During the lecture I said "If you are using ASPARTAME [NutraSweet, Equal, Spoonful, etc.] and you suffer from fibromyalgia symptoms, spasms, shooting pains, numbness in your legs, cramps, vertigo, dizziness, headaches, tinnitus, joint pain, depression, anxiety attacks, slurred speech, blurred vision, or memory loss, you probably have ASPARTAME DISEASE!"

People were jumping up during the lecture saying, "I've got this. Is it reversible?" It is rampant. Some of the speakers at my lecture were even suffering from these symptoms. In one lecture attended by the Ambassador of Uganda, he told us that their sugar industry is adding aspartame! He continued by saying that one of the industry leader's son could no longer walk due in part to product usage! We have a very serious problem.

Even a stranger came up to Dr. Episto (one of my speakers) and myself and said, "Could you tell me why so many people seem to be coming down with MS?" During a visit to a hospice, a nurse said that six of her friends, who were heavy Diet Coke drinkers, had all been diagnosed with MS. This is beyond coincidence. Here is the problem. There were Congressional Hearings when Aspartame was originally included as a sweetener in 100 different products. Since this initial hearing, there have been two subsequent hearings, but to no avail.

Nothing has been done. The drug and chemical lobbies have very deep pockets. Now there are over 5,000 products containing this chemical and the PATENT HAS EXPIRED!!!!

At the time of this first hearing, people were going blind. The methanol in the Aspartame converts to formaldehyde in the retina of the eye. Formaldehyde is grouped in the same class of drugs as cyanide and arsenic—DEADLY POISONS!!! Unfortunately, it just takes longer to quietly kill, but it is killing people and causing all kinds of neurological problems. Aspartame changes the brain's chemistry. It is the reason for severe seizures. This drug also causes birth defects. There is absolutely no reason to take this product. It is NOT A DIET PRODUCT! The Congressional record said, "It makes you crave Carbohydrates and will make you FAT." Dr. Roberts stated that when he got patients off aspartame, their average weight loss was 19 pounds per person.

The formaldehyde stores in the fat cells, particularly in the hips and thighs. Aspartame is especially deadly for diabetics. All physicians know what wood alcohol will do to a diabetic. We find that physicians believe that they have patients with retinopathy, when in fact, it is caused by aspartame. The aspartame keeps the blood sugar level out of control, causing many patients to go into a coma. Unfortunately, many have died. People were telling us at the conference of the American College of Physicians, that they had relatives that switched from saccharin to an aspartame product and how that relative had eventually gone into a coma. Their physicians could not get the blood sugar levels under control. Thus, the patients suffered acute memory loss and eventually coma and death. Memory loss is due to the fact that aspartic acid and phenylalanine are neurotoxic without the other acids found in protein. Thus it goes past the blood brain barrier and deteriorates the neurons of the brain.

Dr. Russell Blaylock, neurosurgeon, said, "The ingredients stimulates the neurons of the brain to death, causing brain damage of varying degrees. Dr. Blaylock

has written a book entitled "EXCITOXINS: THE TASTE THAT KILLS" Health Press 1-800-643-3665). Dr. H.J. Roberts, diabetic specialist and world expert on aspartame poisoning, has also written a book entitled "DEFENSE AGAINST ALZHEIMER'S DISEASE" (1-800-814-9800). Dr. Roberts tells how aspartame poisoning is escalating Alzheimer's Disease, and indeed it is. As the hospice nurse told me, women are being admitted at 30 years of age with Alzheimer's Disease. Dr. Blaylock and Dr. Roberts will be writing a position paper wit some case histories and will post it on the Internet.

According to the Conference of the American College of Physicians, "We are talking about a plague of neurological diseases caused by this deadly poison." Dr. Roberts realized what was happening when aspartame was first marketed. He said, "His diabetic patients presented memory loss, confusion, and severe vision loss." At the Conference of the American College of Physicians, doctors admitted that they did not know. They had wondered why seizures were rampant (the phenylalanine in aspartame breaks down the seizure threshold and depletes serotonin, which causes manic depression, panic attacks, rage and violence).

Just before the Conference, I received a fax from Norway, asking for a possible antidote for this poison because they are experiencing so many problems in their country. This "poison" is now available in 90 PLUS countries worldwide. Fortunately, we had speakers and ambassadors at the Conference from different nations who have pledged their help. We ask that you help too. Print this article out and warn everyone you know. Take anything that contains aspartame back to the store. Take the "NO ASPARTAME "TEST" and send us your case history. I assure you that MONSANTO, the creator of Aspartame, knows how deadly it is. They fund the American Association, American Dietetic Association Congress, and the Conference of the American College of Physicians. The New York Times, November 15, 1996, ran an article on how the American Dietetic Association takes money from the food industry to endorse their products. Therefore, they cannot criticize any additives or tell about their link to MONSANTO.

How bad is this? We told a mother who had a child on NutraSweet to get off the product. The child was having grand mal seizures every day. The mother called her physician, who called the ADA, who told the doctor not to take the child off NutraSweet. We are still trying to convince the mother that the Aspartame is causing the seizures. Every time we get someone off of aspartame, the seizures stop. If the baby dies, you *know whose fault it is, and what we are up against. There are 92 documented symptoms of aspartame, from coma to death. the majority of them are all-neurological, because the aspartame destroys the nervous system.*

Aspartame Disease is partially the cause of what is behind the mystery of the Desert Storm healthy problems. The burning tongue and other problems discussed in over 60 cases can be directly related to the consumption of Aspartame product. Several thousand pallets of diet drinks were shipped to the Desert Storm troops., (Remember heat can liberate the methanol from the aspartame at 86 degrees F.) Diet drinks sat in the 120 degree F Arabian sun for weeks at a time on pallets. The servicemen and women drank them all day long. All of their symptoms are identical to aspartame poisoning. Dr. Roberts says consuming Aspartame at the time of conception can cause birth defects."

According to Dr. Louis Elsas, Pediatrician and Professor of Genetics at Emory University, In his testimony before Congress. The phenylalanine concentrates in the placenta, causing mental retardation. In the original lab tests, animals developed brain tumors, phenylalanine breaks down into DXP, a brain tumor agent.) when Dr. Episto was lecturing on aspartame, one physician in the audience, a neurosurgeon, said, "When they remove brain tumors, they have found high levels of aspartame in them." Stevia, a sweet food, NOT AN ADDITIVE, which helps in the metabolism of sugar, would be ideal for diabetics, has now been approved as a dietary supplement by the FDA for years, the FDA has outlawed this sweet food because of their loyalty to MONSANTO.

If it says "SUGAR FREE" on the label—DO NOT EVEN THINK ABOUT IT. Senator Howard Hetzenbaum wrote a bill that would have warned all infants, pregnant mothers and children of the dangers of aspartame. The bill would have also instituted independent studies on the problems existing in the population (seizures, changes in brain chemistry, changes in neurological and behavioral symptoms). It was killed by the powerful drug and chemical lobbies, letting loose the hounds of disease and death on an unsuspecting public. Since the Conference of the American College of Physicians, we hope to have help of several world leaders.

Again, please help us, too. There are a lot of people out there who must be warned, please let them know this information. The author, Betty Martini, can be reached at 770-242-2599.

A later version of this warning letter is identical in all respects except that the author's name has been changed to "Nancy Markle." Title and contents notwithstanding, the Multiple Sclerosis Foundation has publicly disavowed any knowledge of a link between the disease or its symptoms and any artificial sweeteners. The American Diabetes Association has likewise denounced the hoax and refuted its claims with respect to diabetes, while the Food and Drug Administration has attested to aspartame's safety for human consumption. Finally, none of the organizations named have filed or anticipate filing litigation of any sort against Monsanto Corporation or any other manufacturer of artificial sweeteners.

"ASSIGNATION": computer virus family

Identified for the first time in June 1996, the "Assignation" family includes no dangerous, memory-resident parasitic viruses. The several viruses write themselves to the end of executed .exe files, simultaneously installing the "Assignation.653" virus into the infected computer's memory and setting the system's date to February 5. No other viruses manifest themselves, but the Assignation virus displays the following text strings:

> *"Assignation.426,436": 386*
> *Virus—by Qark/VLAD—1996*
> *"Assignation.653":*
> *kraD evoL*
> *Hello. . . . This is Assignation Virus V1.00 . . . ^_^*
> *Today You will have a Date for Someone :-)*
> *May Be with you friend, Brother, or Dark Lover :-)*
> *Copy Allright By Dark Lover ^_^ 04/22/1996*
> *in Kaohsiung, Taiwan, R.O.C.*

ATKINS, Herman: exonerated by DNA evidence

On April 8, 1986, a female shoe-store clerk was confronted by an unmasked gunman who stole $130 from the store's cash register, then raped her twice and forced her to fellate him, all the while threatening to "blow [her] brains out." While giving her statement at the Riverside County, California, sheriff's office, the victim saw a wanted poster on fugitive Herman Atkins, sought for assaulting two Los Angeles policemen, and she identified him as her attacker. Atkins was arrested in Phoenix seven months later, held over for trial on charges of rape and armed robbery. At trial in 1988, his wife testified that Atkins was at home (in Los Angeles) with no car on the day of the rape. Jurors convicted him on all counts, and he received a 45-year prison term; a second trial in Los Angeles County added two years and eight months for the assault on the patrolmen.

In 1993, encouraged by reports of other inmates freed from custody when DNA testing exonerated them of rape and other crimes, Atkins contacted the New York-based CARDOZO INNOCENCE PROJECT. California authorities resisted petitions for a new DNA test in Atkins's case, but an appellate court ordered the test in August 2000. A report filed on January 15, 2001 excluded Atkins as a suspect in the rape, and he was freed in February 2001, the 64th inmate cleared by DNA evidence since American courts first admitted its use for appeals in 1993. Greeting reporters with a smile, Atkins proclaimed, "Now God, me and the people of California and the United States know I am an innocent man."

AUGUSTINE, Tyrone: software copyright pirate

A resident of Cambridge, Massachusetts, born May 13, 1971, Augustine was employed by Intel Corporation in December 1998, when he entered into a criminal conspiracy with four coworkers and a HACKERS' syndicate christened "PIRATES WITH ATTITUDE." The plotters collaborated to collect and bootleg more than 5,000 computer software programs stockpiled on a covert website based on the campus of a Quebec university. The Intel gang agreed to trade their company's software for free access to programs maintained on the Canadian website, and Augustine went further, arranging to ship critical pieces of Intel hardware to Canada at the company's expense, but without the knowledge of his employers. A federal grand jury in Chicago indicted 17 of the pirates on May 4, 2000, charging each with one count of conspiracy to violate U.S. copyright laws. Those charged included Augustine, his four coworkers, and 12 of the hackers from Pirates with Attitude. Tyrone Augustine was among 13 defendants in the case who pleaded guilty as charged. As of December 2001, no date had yet been fixed for sentencing.

AUSTRALIAN Society of Forensic Dentistry

As its name suggests, the Australian Society of Forensic Dentistry (ASFD) is a professional organization devoted to the promotion of forensic ODONTOLOGY in the nation of Australia, to facilitate identification of murder, accident, and disaster victims. The ASFD's 48 identified members in 2001 reportedly included all practicing dentists in Australia, but membership is open (at a price of $45 per year) to "any professional who has an interest in the application of dental techniques for forensic purposes." The sole member listed from outside Australia for 2001 was Dr. Hirofumi Aboshi, a professor of dentistry at Nikon University in Tokyo. The ASFD's website includes links to similar organizations around the world and provides contact information for members available to consult on a contract or emergency basis.

"AZATOTH": computer virus

Reported initially in October 1999, "Azatoth" is another "benign" virus—as opposed to the dangerous, memory-resident, encrypted parasitic viruses that may paralyze or destroy entire systems. It writes itself to the end of .exe files that have been opened or executed, thereafter deleting the file anti-vir.dat and disabling resident driver tbdrvxxx. Azatoth displays the following text strings:

mandragore/DDT
[azatoth]
windblows must die! enjoy linux!

B

"BABYLONIA": computer virus

Reported for the first time in December 1999, "Babylonia" is a memory-resident, parasitic Windows virus with worm and backdoor capabilities. It utilizes codes that are found on Windows 9x computers only, therefore limiting its impact, but it attacks several types of files within the vulnerable systems: Windows executable files; Windows help files; and the Winsock library (thus transmitting its replicants to the Internet at large).

Babylonia installs itself into Windows memory when an infected .exe file is executed, scanning the Windows kernel for required function addresses and implanting itself as a memory-resident system driver (VxD). Once installed, the virus commandeers a block of Windows VxD memory and copies itself there, afterward creating an additional file on the C drive, labeled c:\babylonia.exe. That file is a virus component afterward run as a stand-alone application, releasing additional virus features. During self-installation, Babylonia also scans the system drivers for AVP9 and SPID antivirus monitors, altering them to prevent virus scans.

Once installed, the Babylonia virus interrupts three kinds of Windows file access functions: file opening; renaming; and reading/modifying file attributes. Whenever an executable file is accessed thereafter, the virus attaches itself to the file's end, thereby increasing its size. To gain control of files, Babylonia employs "entry point obscuring" technology, scanning the file entry code and overwriting it at some point to achieve penetration.

Windows Help files (.HLP) also fall prey to the Babylonia virus, infected by means of a program that modifies the internal file structure, adding Babylonia's script to the "system" area, and thereafter forcing the Help system to execute a specially prepared binary Windows32 program, itself a "start-up" polymorphic routine that replicates the main virus code and executes it as a Windows32 application.

When attacking a vulnerable computer's wsock32.dll library, Babylonia patches in a program to activate the memory-resident virus copy and send the virus to the Internet at large, via infected e-mail attachments. The attached virus file is identifiable by the label "x.exe." Alternative file names built into the virus, but never displayed due to bugs in the system, include i-watch-u; babylonia; surprise!; jesus; buhh; and chocolate. When the infected attachment is opened, Babylonia installs itself into the new computer's system and displays two fake messages:

Loader Error
 API not found!

Loader Error
 Windows 95 [or NT] required!
 This program will be terminated.

While installing itself in a computer system, the Babylonia virus also creates a stand-alone backdoor program unconnected to the virus code itself, which registers itself as a "service process" invisible to a scan of the computer's task list. That file is copied to the Windows system directory with the kernel32.exe name and is registered to the auto-run section of the system registry as HKLM\Software\Microsoft\Windows\CurrentVersion\Run. That done, the backdoor program automatically connects to a hackers' website in Japan and downloads additional files, after which the backdoor program exits.

Files downloaded from the Japanese website are "virus plugins," permitting the author of the virus to utilize infected computers at will—upgrading the virus, installing new backdoors and "Trojan" programs, corrupting data, and so forth. Four plugins are identified to date. The first, named dropper.dat, creates, executes, and then deletes a file labeled c:\instalar.exe, which reinstalls Babylonia if it has already been detected and removed by the computer's legitimate user. The second file—named greetz.dat—lurks until January 15, then writes and executes commands displaying the following message:

W95/Babylonia by Vecna (c) 1999
Greetz to RoadKil and VirusBuster
Big thankz to sok4ever webmaster
Abracos pra galera brazuca!!!
Eu boto fogo na Babilonia!

A third plugin file, named ircworm.dat, installs a worm virus variously labeled 2kBug-MircFix.exe and 2kbugfix.ini, but laboratory tests suggest the program contains "bugs" of its own that prevent the worm from spreading as intended. The final plugin program—poll.dat—provides the virus's author with information about the infected computer and sends a message reading "Quando o mestre chegara?" to the e-mail address babylonia_counter@hotmail.com.

"BADASS": computer worm

Identified in October 1999, "BadAss" is a computer worm virus spread on the Internet via MicroSoft Outlook. The worm is a Windows.exe file virus which appears to be based on the "MELISSA" virus, bearing very similar functions and sequence of instructions in its code. BadAss is transferred by means of e-mail messages with infected attachments bearing the name badass.exe, but the file can be manually renamed and will afterward spread with the new name, presumably unrecognized by recipi-

ents who might otherwise identify and delete it unopened.

When the infected attachment is opened, thereby executing the worm's .exe file, BadAss delivers its payload in the form of serial message boxes, then opens the MS Outlook database, retrieves e-mail addresses from the built-in address book, and sends infected messages to all addresses listed therein. The subject line of infected messages includes the text "Moguh," while the message reads: "Dit is wel grappig! :-)". Its series of preliminary message boxes are distinctively insulting. The first reads as follows:

Kernel 32
An error has occured probably because your cunt smells bad. Is this really so?
    [Yes]   [No]

A move of the mouse cursor to the [No] button is automatically overridden, shifting it repeatedly to [Yes] until the [Yes] button is finally clicked. Thereupon, a second message is displayed while the infection routine proceeds.

WIN32
Contact your local supermarket for toilet paper and soap to solve this problem.
    [OK]

BadAss will not send messages twice from the same infected computer. Instead, it automatically suspends activity after infected messages have been sent to all addresses retrieved from the computer's address book.

"BADTRANS": computer worm

A prolific worm virus spread via Windows Win32 systems, "Badtrans" was discovered in November 2001. It consists of two primary components, a worm and a "Trojan" program that operate independently of one another. The worm segment of Badtrans sends e-mail messages with infected attachments to addresses found in the infected computer's address book, while the Trojan program transmits selected information on the infected computer—including passwords, keyboard log, and other user's information—to a specified e-mail address, for later use by the virus's writer.

Corruption occurs when recipients of infected messages open the e-mail attachments, thereby activating Badtrans, whereupon the worm installs itself in the system registry. At the same time, Badtrans drops an additional win32.dll file—a "keyboard hooker"—which spies on all text entered through the computer's keyboard. In some instances, the worm deletes its original infected file once installation on the target system is complete.

Badtrans spreads via e-mail in one of two ways, either extracting new addresses from the victim's address book or retrieving them from the incoming e-mail box. Once the addresses are secured, the worm begins transmitting bogus e-mail messages without the victim's knowledge, each bearing its own infected attachment. Outgoing messages may include the victim's legitimate e-mail return address or some fake address, randomly chosen from the following list:

"Admin" <admin@gte.net>
"Administrator" <administrator@border.net>
"Andy" <andy@hweb-media.com>
"Anna" <aizzo@home.com>
"Anna" <lindaizzo@home.com>
"JESSICA BENAVIDES" <jessica@aol.com>
"Joanna" <joanna@mail.utexas.edu>
"JUDY" <JUJUB@AOL.COM>
"JUDY" <JUJUB271@AOL.COM>
"Kelly Andersen" <Gravity49@aol.com>
"Linda" <lgonzal@hotmail.com>
"Mary L. Adams" <mary@c-com.net>
"Mon S" <spiderroll@hotmail.com>
"Monika Prado" <monika@telia.com>
"Rita Tulliani" <powerpuff@videotron.ca>
"Support" <support@cyberramp.net>
"Tina" <tina08@yahoo.com>
"Tina" <tina0828@yahoo.com>

The subject line of Badtrans-infected e-mails is sometimes blank, but frequently contains "Re:" followed by the actual subject of a previous e-mail, lifted from the victim's address book. The message text is generally blank. Attachments bearing the worm's code typically carry one of the following filenames:

Card (or CARD)
docs (or DOCS)
fun (or FUN)
HAMSTER
Humor (or HUMOR)
Pics (or PICS)
images (or IMAGES)
info

Me_nude (or ME_NUDE)
README
New_Napster_Site
news_doc (or NEWS_DOC)
S3MSONG
SEARCHURL
SETUP
Sorry_about_yesterday
stuff
YOU_are_FAT! (or YOU_ARE_FAT!)

Badtrans does not send infected messages twice to the same e-mail address, instead storing all e-mails utilized in a Windows system directory file and checking the file's contents before a new message is dispatched. The worm's spying Trojan program stores information to a log file and later sends it on to randomly selected e-mail addresses drawn from the 22 listed below (with their servers):

bgnd2@canada.com
cxkawog@krovatka.net
DTCELACB@yahoo.com
eccles@ballsy.net
fjshd@rambler.ru
I1MCH2TH@yahoo.com
JGQZCD@excite.com
muwripa@fairesuivre.com
OZUNYLRL@excite.com
rmxqpey@latemodels.com
S_Mentis@mail-x-change.com
smr@eurosport.com
ssdn@myrealbox.com
suck_my_prick@ijustgotfired.com
suck_my_prick4@ukr.net
thisisno_fucking_good@usa.com
tsnlqd@excite.com
udtzqccc@yahoo.com
WPADJQ12@yahoo.com
XHZJ3@excite.com
YJPFJTGZ@excite.com
ZVDOHYIK@yahoo.com
mail.canada.com
imap.front.ru
mx2.mail.yahoo.com
inbound.ballsy.net.criticalpath.net
mail5.rambler.ru
mx2.mail.yahoo.com
mta.excite.com
fs.cpio.com
mta.excite.com

inbound.latemodels.com.criticalpath.net
mail-fwd.rapidsite.net
mail.ifrance.com
smt.myrealbox.com
mail.monkeybrains.net
mail.ukr.net
usa-com.mr.outblaze.com
mta.excite.com
mx2.mail.yahoo.com
mx2.mail.yahoo.com
mta.excite.com
mta.excite.com
mx2.mail.yahoo.com

BAILEY, Roosevelt Tobias Jr.: software pirate

A resident of Indianapolis, Roosevelt Bailey Jr. operated with accomplice Terry Lorenzo Barber (of Radcliff, Kentucky) to procure and sell bootleg computer software between December 1997 and May 1998. Using a variety of corporate fronts— Atlanta Micro Systems, Indiana Micro Systems, World Technologies Group, and so forth—the partners hawked their illicit products by telephone and at weekend computer shows across the Midwest. Their hottest item, a CD of bootleg Adobe software valued at $4,768 on the legitimate retail market, was sold by Bailey and Barber for $75 per copy. In their six months of operation, the pirates cleared $25,053 while cheating copyright holders out of $1,434,589.

Arrested in June 1998, Barber pleaded guilty to federal charges of trafficking in counterfeit computer software. On May 10, 2001 he was sentenced to four months' community confinement and three years' probation, and also ordered to pay restitution in the amount of $25,053. Bailey struck a separate bargain with federal prosecutors, pleading guilty to trafficking in counterfeit computer software, and tax evasion for the years 1996 and 1997. On June 1, 2001, a federal judge sentenced him to 18 months' imprisonment plus three years' supervised probation following release from custody.

BAKER, Jake: alleged cyberstalker (case dismissed)

A resident of Ann Arbor, Michigan, Jake Baker was accused by U.S. federal authorities of collaborating with the Canadian Arthur Gonda (present whereabouts unknown) to harass and threaten a female classmate of Baker's at the University of Michigan.

As specified in the indictment, Baker and Gonda allegedly exchanged a series of e-mails between November 29, 1994, and January 25, 1995, in which they aired desires to kidnap, rape, and murder the woman in question. The e-mails were private, but Baker afterward prepared a kind of synopsis which he posted to the Internet newsgroup "alt.sex.stories." A criminal complaint was filed, and Baker was arrested on February 9, 1995, and detained overnight. On February 10 a U.S. magistrate extended his detention, deeming Baker a threat to the community at large. A psychological examination refuted that finding, and Baker was allowed to post bond on March 10, 1995. He thereafter filed a motion with a U.S. district court in Michigan to quash a five-count superseding indictment filed on February 14, 1995.

Prosecutors responded to Baker's motion by noting that federal law prescribes a fine and five-year prison term for any defendant who "transmits in interstate or foreign commerce any communication containing any threat to kidnap any person or any threat to injure the person of another." They further maintained that Baker's exchange of e-mails with Gonda revealed "the evolution of their activity from shared fantasies to a firm plan of action." The court disagreed, ruling that the "shared fantasies" of Baker and Gonda never rose to the standard of a "true threat" required for prosecution under federal law. Description of the intended target(s) as "female college students who lived in Defendant Jake Baker's dormitory at the University of Michigan in Ann Arbor, Michigan" was deemed too vague to constitute a threat against any specific individual, though one acquaintance of Baker's was named as the "type" of victim desired. Likewise, the court found no intent to carry out a crime expressed in any of the messages. The indictment was accordingly dismissed on June 21, 1995.

BALTUTAT, Brian: software pirate

A resident of Wyandotte, Michigan, 21-year-old Brian Baltutat maintained a website called "Hacker Hurricane," where 142 pirated computer software programs were offered free of charge to all comers. According to the federal charges filed against him, an estimated 65,000 persons took advantage of the site to download various programs, thereby swindling the legitimate vendors out of untold revenue. Baltutat pleaded guilty to a federal charge of copyright infringement on October 12, 2000, before Judge

Julian Cook. On January 30, 2001, Baltutat was sentenced to three years' probation, including 180 days of home confinement, 40 hours of community service, and financial restitution to various software manufacturers. In addition to those terms, Baltutat was barred from engaging in any Internet activity without specific permission from the U.S. Probation Department. He was further ordered to inform any persons whose computers he may use about his conviction and sentence.

BANK Giveaway: Internet hoax

A preposterous fraud on its face, this Internet chain letter has nonetheless duped thousands into circulating it with promises of untold wealth from a bizarre pyramid scheme. The original message (with clumsy errors intact) reads as follows:

Need some extra cash for the summer? It is really very simple. Attached to this message is a tracking program. For every person you to, you earn $10.00. For every person they send it to, you get $5.00, and so on. Basically, the more people you send this to, the more cash you earn. This is funded by national banks everywhere, who believe that summers should be more fun, and want to help children and young adults learn to manage money. As you can see, all you need to to as many people as you can. From a week to a month later, you will receive a check in the mail for however much money you earned by sending this, and how many people they sent it to. Good luck, and await the check!

Hello, my name is Betsy. This really works, please don't delete it! If you choose not to read it, at least send it to people so that they can have a chance. I got this e*mail and tried it. Exactly a week later, I received a check for $180.00! It was perfect timing, I?m going to Florida soon and really need the extra cash. Thanks sooo much for sending this to me, I hope someone else out there turns out as happy as I did!

BARBER, Terry Lorenzo   See BAILEY, ROOSEVELT

BATH & Body Works Giveaway: Internet hoax

Circulated for the first time in November 1999, this Internet chain letter claims that the firm of Bath & Body Works will send a $50 gift certificate to anyone who forwards the message to 13 people. Needless to say, the offer is a fraud. It reads (with errors preserved):

Hi. I am, Michele Cordova, the founder of Bath & Body Works and I want your business. We are trying a new advertising campaign through the power of YOU, the consumer. In order for this to work, you need to send this e-mail to 13 people and I know that is not a lucky number but that is the number we need in order for this to work. Our computer tracking system will keep count of how many people you send it to so don't feel like you have to send to to thirteen people all at once. You may not send it to the same person more than once unless you internet pals accidentally delete the message, we wouldn't want them to miss out on this great offer. To compensate you for your hard work, we are going to send you a $50 dollar gift certificate redeemable in any store nationwide. This is not a joke, it will be your loss if you don't send this to 13 PEOPLE. Thanks again!

Michele Cordova
Founder of Bath & Body Works

Since the e-mail itself contains no advertisement for the firm in question, it is difficult to see how sending it around the Internet could lure new customers. That careless oversight is typical of cyber-hoaxers, whose wit and imagination often seem distinctly limited.

BAUER, Linda: Internet swindler

A resident of Hastings, Minnesota, Linda Bauer was one of 11 defendants charged in connection with the federal sting operation known as OPERATION SMART-CARD.NET. All were accused of trafficking in counterfeit "smart cards" that provided users with illegal free access to DirecTV, a satellite television service. Those sales, conducted primarily via the Internet, cost the legitimate satellite TV industry an estimated $6.2 million per year before the ring was shut down in July 1999, with the defendants pocketing an estimated $516,000. Bauer was one of five accused in the case who pleaded guilty as charged. No sentence had been imposed at the time of this writing (December 2001).

"BEANHIVE": computer virus

Only the second known Java system virus (after "StrangeBrew"), "BeanHive" was found in the wild during February 1999. The virus consists of two parts, the "starter" and "main" components, infecting computers by an unusual method. When attacking a target, BeanHive replicates by means of its starter system only, while the main virus code remains on a remote Web server maintained by a hackers' group known as Codebreakers. Running an infected Java program causes the BeanHive starter to read its virus code from the remote server and execute it, searching for Java files in various directories and infecting them with the virus starter only. No trace of the main virus code remains when BeanHive releases control of the infected system.

BeanHive's unique operating system has advantages and built-in limitations. Its mode of infection permits the virus to hide its code within corrupted files, increasing their length only slightly and thereby escaping detection in a cursory search. Retention of the main virus code on a remote Web server also permits the writer to upgrade BeanHive periodically, without using Trojan or backdoor components to invade widely scattered computers. A major weakness of the virus is its inability to replicate outside of very limited conditions, since systems run as Java applets or any of the more popular Web browsers are immune to its effects.

BeanHive's starter is a Java program containing only 40 lines of code. Upon seizing control of a target computer, it connects to the remote Web server, downloads the main virus code, and runs it as a subroutine. The main BeanHive virus code, divided into five parts, includes the following components:

a98b34fr.class: file access functions
be93a29f.class: preparing file for infection (Pt. 1)
c8f67b45.class: preparing file for infection (Pt. 2)
dc98e742.class: inserting virus starter into victim file
e89a763c.class: file format parsing

BELL, Corethian: exonerated by DNA evidence

A resident of Cook County, Illinois, 23-year-old Corethian Bell telephoned police one night in July 2000, reporting that he had found his mother shot to death in her Calumet City apartment. In fact, she had been stabbed and sexually assaulted, the struggle leaving bloodstains from a second party on the walls, while semen traces were recovered from the victim's clothing. Authorities suspected Bell, and he obliged them with a videotaped confession to the crime, thus insuring his indictment on capital

murder charges. A second woman was raped and stabbed in December 2000, five blocks from the first crime scene, but police were confident they had their man in custody and drew no link between the attacks.

A suspect was later booked for the second crime, while Bell sat in jail awaiting trial, and DNA tests were ordered to confirm the new suspect's guilt in that case when he refused to confess. Police were startled when the second suspect's DNA also matched blood and semen samples lifted from the apartment where Bell's mother was slain in July 2000. Bell's case was one of several profiled by the *Chicago Tribune* in 2001, detailing incidents of negligence and worse on the part of Cook County authorities, including multiple wrongful convictions and several apparent cases of deliberate "frame-ups" over the past decade. From his cell, Bell confirmed that he had confessed only after 50 hours of near-constant interrogation, allegedly including physical abuse by relays of detectives. On January 4, 2002, Bell was released from custody, all charges dismissed by the state at a hearing before Circuit Court Judge Daniel Darcy. Even with conclusive evidence of another suspect's guilt, some local police remained stubbornly fixated on Bell. "He gave us a statement," Sergeant Stan Salura told reporters. "I believe that is factual." As for Bell, he dismissed the incident as a "crazy thing" and sought to get on with his life. "I feel so good," he told the press upon release. "Let's go. I'm hungry."

BILL Gates Giveaway: Internet hoax

It was perhaps inevitable that one of the world's richest software developers should himself become the subject of an Internet giveaway hoax. Several variants of this fraudulent message have circulated since November 1997. The original, repudiated by Microsoft spokesmen, reads (with errors intact):

FROM: GatesBeta@microsoft.com
ATTACH: Tracklog@microsoft.com/Track883432/-
TraceActive/On.html

Hello Everyone,

And thank you for signing up for my Beta Email Tracking Application or (BETA) for short. My name is Bill Gates. Here at Microsoft we have just compiled an e-mail tracking program that tracks everyone to whom this message is forwarded to. It does this through an

Bill Gates (Microsoft Corporation)

unique IP (Internet Protocol) address log book database. We are experimenting with this and need your help. Forward this to everyone you know and if it reaches 1000 people everyone on the list you will receive $1000 and a copy of Windows98 at my expense. Enjoy.

Note: Duplicate entries will not be counted. You will be notified by email with further instructions once this email has reached 1000 people. Windows98 will not be shipped until it has been released to the general public.

Your friend,
Bill Gates & The Microsoft Development Team.

BIOMETRICS: high-tech security techniques

Biometrics is, broadly, the use of automated technology to identify individual persons via specific physiological or behavioral characteristics. *Physiological* biometrics employs various devices to define identity from data gathered by direct measurement of the human body. Examples include fingerprint scanning, hand geometry, iris or retina scanning, and facial geometry. *Behavioral* biometrics tracks a subject's specific actions—speech patterns, handwriting, or even something as seemingly neutral as typing on a computer keyboard.

In addition to those broad categories, biometrics is further defined as passive or active techniques. *Passive* biometrics, including voice and facial scans, may be employed without the subject's knowledge or cooperation. (In the case of vocal scans, recordings obviate even the need for a subject's physical presence.) *Active* biometrics, by contrast, demands personal cooperation for scanning of hands, eyes, or signatures with various computerized devices. Manufacturers of those devices describe their respective systems as "fail-safe," while Hollywood depicts a steady stream of super-villains defeating biometric scanners with false eyes, counterfeit fingerprints— even amputated body parts removed from legitimate users. A more likely approach to defeating biometric scanners would involve computer HACKERS or physical interference with the hardware.

Biometrics has a number of diverse applications for modern law enforcement, government, and private security. The most obvious, *identification*, employs a "one-to-many" search to discover an individual's identity. As a case in point, security cameras at an airport or other facilities may photograph suspect individuals and use a biometric system to compare the suspect's likeness with a large database of known lawbreakers, foreign agents, and so forth. The related process of identity *verification* executes a "one-to-one" search, comparing the claimant of a particular identity with recorded characteristics of the known individual. Thus, a thief using a stolen credit card to withdraw funds from an automatic teller machine (ATM) might be photographed, examined, and denied the cash—or stalled with automated delaying tactics while police are summoned to the scene.

Physiological biometric verification devices, particularly those employing fingerprint scans or hand geometry, may be employed for many purposes, incorporated in a wide variety of everyday objects. Some companies use biometrics to monitor employee time and attendance, thereby eliminating time cards and improving payroll accuracy by eradication of "buddy-punching" scams. Access control in secure areas is critical to many governmental, law enforcement, correctional, and corporate operations. Devices currently designed with built-in biometric scanners include vaults and safes, custom vehicles, home security systems, personal computers and various weapons—

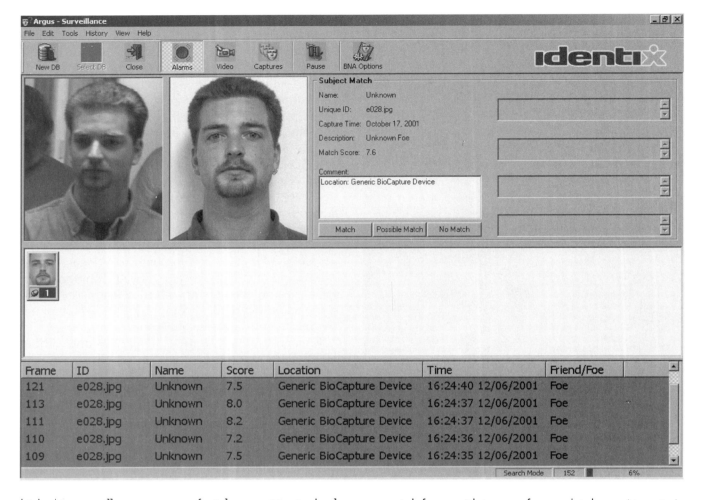

Linked to surveillance cameras, facial recognition technology can match faces with images from a database. (Identix Inc.)

including "SMART GUNS" designed to fire only if held in particular registered hands.

Interest in biometric security devices increased dramatically after the terrorist attacks of September 11, 2001. Manufacturers were naturally pleased with the rash of new orders, but they noted certain problems with the existing technology. Among them:

1. The performance of biometric devices in daily real-world situations does not match test results obtained in vendor-controlled laboratories. Advertising claims aside, no system provides 100 percent security and some can be defeated more easily than others. Even the best scanners sometimes reject authorized users or fail to catch imposters, and a small percentage of the population (for reasons unexplained) cannot be reliably

registered in current biometric systems. In short, while installation of biometrics at airports and other "hot spots" would clearly improve security standards, breaches would still be recorded.

2. Employee-facing systems are significantly cheaper and easier to operate than passenger-facing systems designed to scan large numbers of unknown subjects around the clock. Employees may be subject to background checks and punitive action (including dismissal and/or prosecution) for attempting to defeat security systems. The general public—airline customers, for example—may scheme to frustrate the scanners in a variety of ways, ranging from simple disguises to plastic surgery. Passengers who travel rarely may undergo natural changes with time, from aging, injury, or disease. Finally, the sheer number of

subjects—millions of travelers, versus hundreds or thousands of employees—vastly increases the scope and expense of security systems.

3. Biometric systems are limited by the integrity of the initial enrollment process. Individuals who create a false identity before enrolling in a biometric system—as by presenting a counterfeit passport or driver's license— will normally be deemed legitimate unless they duplicate another name enrolled in the system. Biometrics cannot prevent individuals from assuming false identities, only from impersonating subjects previously catalogued.

4. Biometric *identification* and *verification* address separate issues, with the latter generally much simpler and less expensive. Subjects seeking verification, as noted above, are compared to a known exemplar and accepted or rejected on that basis. In broader identification scans, the subject may claim no particular identity at all, requiring comparison of his or her facial scan with known subjects numbering in the tens of thousands. The further a search extends, including external data-

bases like the FBI's, the more expensive and time-consuming it becomes.

5. Biometric scanners use templates, rather than raw images, to perform their comparisons. Each template is a small computer file based on distinctive individual characteristics—and like any other computer file, it is vulnerable to damage or tampering. Even without interference, each personal interaction with the scanner varies slightly—even microscopically. No two fingerprints are applied in precisely the same manner, for instance, thus insuring that air-tight 100-percent accuracy is unattainable by any mechanical system.

As of early 2002, biometric scanning devices employed at most major American airports—including Chicago's O'Hare Airport, San Francisco International, Charlotte/Douglas (in North Carolina) and Reagan National (in Washington, D.C.)—were restricted to access screening of employees. Eight U.S. and Canadian airports have experimented with use of biometric scanners to let citizens circumvent immigration lines, but enrollment of the population

 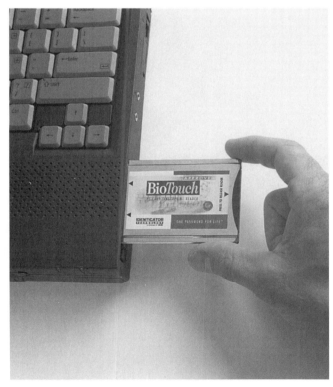

The BioTouch™ PC Card features an optical fingerprint reader, allowing secure access for laptop users. (Identix Inc.)

at large is a daunting prospect, if not impossible. Iceland's Keflavik International Airport uses facial scans to check passengers against a surveillance "hot list," facilitated by the airport's relatively low volume of traffic. While "9/11" increased demands for facial-scan technology as a cure-all for future terrorist attacks, various problems remain. They include:

1. Variance between enrollment and surveillance devices. Enrollment in facial-scan systems normally involves use of a clear photograph, including passport photos, drivers' licenses, or mug shots. Surveillance is maintained by video cameras, with significantly lower resolution than the original images, making it possible for subjects to slip through the net unrecognized.
2. Environmental changes at the surveillance point. Anything from altered lighting to a change in angle of the surveillance camera's wall mount may result in poor resolution and the failure of a system to identify enrolled subjects.

Fingerprint scanners provide physical access to secure areas. (Identix Inc.)

3. Changes in a subject's appearance. Alterations sufficient to confuse surveillance systems may include a gain or loss of weight, a change of hairstyle, aging, application of cosmetics or prosthetics, even the wearing or removal of eyeglasses.

Despite its present limitations, biometric scanning will clearly expand in the future, finding new applications in both law enforcement and private industry. Hand and fingerprint scans have traditionally been used for access control to secure areas, but iris and retinal scans offer a new level of security, while making deception more difficult. Airline passengers may in future be required to provide some biometric data prior to traveling, in the interest of greater security. Similar enrollment may be required upon issuance of passports for international travel. Integration of existing FBI and other criminal databases would potentially apprehend hundreds of fugitives each year. Finally, surveillance systems will certainly expand, presumably becoming more effective and reliable.

At the same time, wide-scale implementation of biometric surveillance raises legal and ethical questions yet unanswered. Is it physically and/or economically feasible to make biometric enrollment mandatory for all travelers (much less all residents) of America or any other nation? What safeguards can be imposed to guarantee that biometric systems do not violate individual rights to privacy? How will human agencies respond to the inevitable errors every technological system produces from time to time? Will use of biometrics alone create a dangerous sense of false security? Until those questions are satisfactorily answered, full-scale biometric surveillance remains poised on the line between established fact and science fiction.

BJORLIN, Kaj: fugitive software pirate

Identified by U.S. federal prosecutors as a member of the software rip-off consortium dubbed "PIRATES WITH ATTITUDE," Swedish native Kaj Bjorlin was among 17 defendants indicted on May 4, 2000, for conspiring to infringe copyrights on more than 5,000 computer software programs. Defendants in the case included 12 members of Pirates with Attitude and five employees of Intel Corporation, the latter charged with illegally furnishing computer hardware and software to a covert website in Quebec. By May 2001, 14 of the defendants had either pleaded guilty as charged or had been convicted at trial. Only Bjor-lin—known on-line as "Darklord"—and another defendant from Belgium remain at large, outside the present reach of U.S. authorities.

"BLACKSUN": computer virus

Noted for the first time in June 1998, "BlackSun" is classified as a dangerous, memory-resident, encrypted boot virus. It attaches itself to the master boot record of an infected computer's hard drive and thereafter replicates to the boot sectors of any floppy disks accessed by the system. Error messages reading "GetDiskParameters" are returned when the victim attempts to access infected disks. Furthermore, if the digits for a month and day are the same (e.g., August 8: "8/8") and the infected computer's clock strikes zero seconds, the BlackSun virus erases all CMOS memory (Complementary Metal Oxide Semiconductor, the battery-backed RAM used on modern computers to store hardware configuration data) and thereby disables the system entirely.

BLOODSTAIN Evidence

Every bloodstain tells a story. Aside from DNA testing, which may identify the donor of a particular stain—and thus distinguish between offenders and victims—the shape, number, and placement of bloodstains may chart the course of a crime for experts trained to interpret such evidence. The very presence of blood (or its lack) at a crime scene tells investigators whether a murder victim was killed on the spot, or perhaps slain elsewhere and transported to a separate dump site. If the latter, authorities may later seek warrants for the search of prospective murder scenes, in hopes of discovering where the crime actually occurred.

A murder scene with body and bloodstains intact is more useful to detectives and technicians in their search for answers to an unsolved crime. Scientific analysis of bloodstain patterns is a relatively new phenomenon, dating approximately from the 1950s. In 1955, during trial of Ohio's controversial Sam Sheppard case, Dr. Paul Kirk testified that blood-spatter evidence enabled him "to establish the relative position of the attacker and victim at the time of the . . . beating. He was able to determine that the attacker administered blows with a left hand, which was significant in that Dr. Sheppard was right-

handed." (Sheppard was initially convicted, nonetheless.) By 1983 an International Association of Bloodstain Pattern Analysts was organized, its studies documenting the fact that bloodstain evidence at crime scenes may reveal:

- The source of particular stains
- The relative position of persons and objects at the time of impact
- The number of separate impacts
- Whether impact was inflicted with a blunt or sharp object
- The distance blood traveled, and its velocity
- The elapsed time between impact and examination by authorities
- The movement of persons and objects after impact (including blood smears, drag marks, footprints, etc.)

A blood-spatter pattern is determined by multiple factors, including the distance a drop of blood falls, the force with which it falls (arterial spray versus dripping from a vein, oozing from wounds or flung from an upraised bludgeon, etc.), whether it falls vertically or diagonally, and the type of surface it strikes. In addition to charting the course of an attack, bloodstains may also preserve contact marks from other objects: footprints, fingerprints, tool marks, fabric patterns, tire marks, and so forth. In the case of the Army doctor Jeffrey MacDonald—a case as controversial in its time as that of Dr. Sheppard 30 years earlier—crime lab technicians used blood-spatter evidence to demonstrate that the defendant bludgeoned his wife and young daughters to death, then stabbed himself in the chest to simulate an assault by third parties. (As in the Sheppard case before it, substantial evidence today suggests that MacDonald may, in fact, be innocent.) Similar evidence may be gleaned from shootings, stabbings, explosions, or hit-and-run accidents.

Some bloodstains are invisible to authorities by the time they begin to process a crime scene. Perpetrators may exert great energy to clean up a scene, but blood evidence is very difficult to eradicate. Even when stains are expunged beyond visibility to the naked eye, traces may be found by using luminol, a chemical spray that causes covert bloodstains to fluoresce. In such instances, blood evidence may be found beneath carpets and floorboards, concealed in the pattern of fabric or wallpaper, or hidden in sink traps and plumbing. Wherever it lies, bloodstain evidence may prove guilt by placing an absent victim at the scene (through DNA), thus challenging a suspect's alibi. In these days when science allows identification of one individual to the exclusion of all others on earth (except an identical twin), blood evidence is more important than ever to prosecutors and police.

BLOODSWORTH, Kirk: exonerated by DNA evidence

On July 25, 1984, a nine-year-old girl was found dead in a wooded area of Baltimore County, Maryland. She had been raped, strangled, and beaten with a rock found at the murder scene. Five witnesses claimed to have seen the child walking with a man on the day she was killed, and they collaborated with police to produce a sketch of the unknown suspect. Soon, an anonymous telephone call directed authorities to Baltimore resident Kirk Bloodsworth. The five alleged eyewitnesses identified him as the man last seen with the victim, while a neighbor of Bloodsworth's recalled his confession of doing "a terrible thing" on the day of the crime. On March 8, 1985, Bloodsworth was convicted of rape, sexual assault, and first-degree premeditated murder, drawing a sentence of death.

Bloodsworth's attorney appealed the conviction, contending that police illegally withheld evidence pointing to another suspect and that the "terrible thing" Bloodsworth confessed to his neighbor was a failure to buy his wife a taco salad as promised. The Maryland Court of Appeals overturned his conviction in July 1986 and remanded the case for a new trial. Convicted a second time, Bloodsworth was spared but received two consecutive life sentences. An appeal of the second conviction was denied, but Bloodsworth had been busy in the meantime, studying the British case of serial killer COLIN PITCHFORK, convicted on the basis of DNA evidence. Bloodsworth's attorney petitioned for release of the state's evidence for more sophisticated testing and the prosecution finally agreed, delivering the victim's clothing in April 1992. Semen from the underpants was compared with Bloodsworth's DNA, excluding him as a possible suspect in June 1993. The FBI Crime Laboratory repeated the test on June 25, 1993, with identical results.

Although Maryland statutes forbid presentation of new evidence more than one year after a defendant's final appeal, Baltimore County prosecutors joined Bloodsworth's attorney in petitioning for a pardon. Bloodsworth was released from prison on June 28, 1993, and the governor granted his pardon six months later. No other suspects have yet been charged in the case.

"BLUE Box": device used in telephone fraud

Invented sometime in the late 1960s, the "blue box" is a tone-generating device that signals telephone company equipment that a call has been terminated, while in fact the conversation continues without being billed for additional time. Refinements on the original device include a "black box" that emits an electronic signal that a call did not go through (when in fact it did), and a "red box" that simulates the sound of coins being loaded into a pay telephone. Such devices are employed by HACKERS—commonly dubbed "phreakers"—to cheat phone companies throughout the world, with yearly losses estimated in the millions of dollars. Employment of any device to suppress billing information is a federal crime in the United States, placing the "phreaker" at risk of prosecution for interstate wire fraud.

BLUE Mountain Cards: target of slanderous
Internet hoax

Since March 1999 Blue Mountain Cards, an Internet greeting card company, has been plagued by false rumors and warnings that the simple act of opening a greeting card on the firm's website might cause a reader's computer system to crash. In fact, no such problem exists, the malicious rumor surviving as a cyberspace equivalent to the false claim that Procter & Gamble's "moon and stars" logo meant that company was run by worshipers of Satan. Jared Schutz, executive director of Blue Mountain, has offered the following response to the anonymous e-mail campaign.

It is very frustrating and difficult for us to dispel these rumors, but please help us in doing so by passing this email along to your friends and spreading the word that there is no way that bluemountain.com can spread a virus. Our electronic greeting cards are simply web pages that you view with your browser. Our email notifications are only text messages without any attached files. When someone sends or receives cards from our site, they do not actually download to their computer any file that might contain a virus. We are worried that these rumors are hurting our free card efforts, and hope that you can help us set the record straight.

BODY Armor

Written history does not record the first use of protective body armor by fighting men (or women), but shields, helmets, and injury-resistant clothing certainly date from the earliest days of armed human conflict. Leather and wood were used extensively before technology allowed the manipulation of various metals, and steel remained the epitome of armor for generations thereafter. Bandits and G-men fought their epic battles of the 1930s wearing crude steel plates in fabric vests that slipped over their heads like sandwich signs, and such cumbersome gear remained the norm until bullet-resistant fabrics like DuPont's Kevlar, Honeywell's GoldFlex and Zylon, or the European firm Akzo's Twaron were developed in the 1960s and 1970s.

The National Institute of Justice (NIJ) rates body armor on a scale of ballistic protection levels. The armor is tested not only for resistance to actual penetration, but also for minimization of blunt force trauma (either from projectile impact or direct blows from a hand-to-hand assailant). Blunt trauma is measured by the dent inflicted on a soft clay pad behind the armor, with a maximum depth of 1.7 inches permitted for physical safety. The NIJ's armor rankings are:

This body armor is specially designed for tactical operations where total protection is necessary.
(Courtesy of Point Blank Body Armor, Inc.)

I—Blocks .38 Special round-nose lead projectiles traveling at 850 feet per second (fps) and .22-caliber Long Rifle ammunition at 1,050 fps. This armor, also protects the wearer against birdshot charges from a shotgun, but is not recommended for use against any higher-velocity ammunition.

IIA—Consisting of 16 to 18 layers of Kevlar, this armor is designed to cope with most threats encountered in urban shooting situations. It will stop various rounds including 9-mm full metal jacket (FMJ) projectiles traveling at 1,090 fps and .357 Magnum jacketed, hollow-point (JHP) projectiles traveling at 1,250 fps.

II—With 22 to 24 layers of Kevlar, this thickness should stop bullets including 9-mm FMJ rounds traveling at 1,175 fps and .357 Magnum jacketed, soft-point (JSP) projectiles traveling at 1,395 fps. Most shotgun pellets are also deflected.

IIIA—Offering 30 to 32 layers of Kevlar, IIIA level armor stops numerous rounds including 9-mm FMJ projectiles traveling at 1,400 fps (the usual muzzle velocity for most 9-mm submachine guns) and .44 Magnum rounds at the same velocity. Its blunt-trauma protection rating is the highest offered by soft armor, thus allowing for more effective return fire in a gunfight.

III—To repel most rifle bullets, this armor abandons soft fabrics to employ 1/4-inch specially treated steel, 1/2-inch ceramic armor plates, or 1-inch polyethylene plates. Blunt trauma should be minimized, but the armor is heavier and is not concealable.

IV—Finally, to protect against armor-piercing rifle bullets, this armor is crafted from 3/4-inch ceramic plates.

Special circumstances require special armor, beyond those listed above. Bomb-disposal personnel require full-body coverage in the event of an explosion, typically combining both ballistic-resistant and fire-retardant fabrics, some of which protect the wearer from projectiles traveling up to 2,250 fps. A typical bomb-disposal suit would include an armored coat (sleeves included), removable collar and groin protector, armored trousers (often open at the rear for comfort, providing front-coverage only), a helmet with fragment-resistant face shield, an armored chest plate, with special boots and gloves (available for cases where an explosive device must be disarmed, rather than simply transported). "Bomb blankets" are also available to screen personnel or to shroud small devices and contain shrapnel in the event of a blast.

Manufacturers are quick to stress that no body armor is ever 100 percent bulletproof. Likewise, special stab-resistant fabrics or fabric combinations may be needed to deflect blades, in the event of an assault with knife or sword. Armor-piercing ammunition has been banned from civilian sales in the U.S. for many years, but sufficient quantities of "cop-killer" bullets are still available to render many forms of concealable armor superfluous. Factors to consider in selecting body armor include:

Threat assessment The type of protection required obviously varies from person to person. A motorcycle racer needs less (or different) protective clothing than a bomb-disposal technician. If an assailant's weapons are known, armor may be adjusted accordingly.

Comfort Uncomfortable armor is more likely to be removed and abandoned, thus making it useless when a crisis finally arrives. A compromise between comfort and coverage must be attained in order for the gear to be effective.

Concealability If an assailant knows his target is wearing a protective vest, he may fire at the head or lower body and inflict fatal wounds without regard to the armor. Various situations, such as diplomatic functions or corporate gatherings, may also require discretion on the part of those wearing protective gear.

Cost The better the armor, the higher its price. Urban patrolmen forced to purchase their own Kevlar vests have more limited options (and consequent greater exposure) than wealthy corporate CEOs or military personnel whose equipment is funded by taxpayers.

Coverage Some vests offer only front-and-back protection, while others wrap around the wearer's torso to include side coverage. Various other garments, including entire business suits, may be crafted from thin layers of bullet-resistant fabric, albeit with some sacrifice of fashion points. Tactical vests, worn outside the clothing by officers on SWAT teams and other assault

units, offer 50 percent more protection on average than vests designed to be worn under shirts or jackets.

Mobility Armor becomes a handicap if it retards the wearer's movement, making him or her a proverbial "sitting duck." Whether fleeing an attack or fighting back, a certain amount of mobility is required for survival.

Temperature A primary concern for wearers of protective clothing, heat buildup may prove uncomfortable in some situations, or debilitating (even lethal) in others. Whenever possible, armor intended for long-term use should be tailored to the environment where it will be worn. Some modern (more expensive) vests include built-in cooling systems for extra comfort.

Weight Heavy armor induces fatigue with prolonged wear, and it also reduces mobility. In most cases, this issue arises most often with Class III or IV armor, and in bomb-disposal suits. Ceramic and polyethylene plates weigh less than steel, and may be preferred if they provide equivalent protection from rifle bullets.

In addition to "bulletproof" clothing, various tactical shields are also available. Special canine "vests" are sold for police dogs in firefight situations, and projectile-resistant fabric may be crafted into a variety of other shapes. Some of the more common forms include use as upholstery (for office furniture or car seats), and in backpacks or briefcases (which may be used to shield an otherwise unprotected person).

"BOOM": computer virus

This encrypted virus, discovered in January 1997, contains macro viruses that attack basic components of Windows and Excel systems. Opening a compromised file infects the system and permits the virus thereafter to alter documents saved by the "File-SaveAs" function. On starting Microsoft Word, the virus sets an infected computer's System macro to be triggered at 13:13:13—that is, 1:13 P.M. and 13 seconds—whereupon the menus are renamed as follows: Datei; Bearbeiten; Ansicht; Einfügen; Format; Extras; Tabelle; and Fenster. The virus then prints out the following message:

Mr. Boombastic and Sir WIXALOT are watching you!!
Mr. Boombastic and Sir WIXALOT: Don't Panik, all
things are removeable!!! Thanks VIRUSEX!!!

Next, the virus creates a new template and produces the following message:

Greetings from Mr. Boombastic and Sir WIXALOT!!!
Oskar L., wir kriegen dich!!!
Dies ist eine Initiative des Institutes zur Vereidung und Verbreitung von Peinlichkeiten, durch in der Öffentlichkeit stedhende Personen, unter der Schirmherrschaft von Rudi S.!

"BOSTON Strangler": renewed scientific investigation

Ten years before the term "serial killer" entered popular usage, Boston was terrorized by an elusive predator who raped and strangled women in their homes, slaying 11 between June 1962 and July 1964. According to conventional wisdom, the case broke in November 1964, when 33-year-old Albert DeSalvo was jailed on rape charges, subsequently confessing to the "Boston Strangler" crimes and adding two more victims police had failed to count on their official list. A plea bargain engineered by lawyer F. Lee Bailey sent DeSalvo to prison for life on unrelated charges. He was murdered there in November 1973, and while DeSalvo never stood trial for the Boston murders, the case was officially "solved."

Or was it?

The case against DeSalvo has been widely criticized for over 30 years. Deviations in *modus operandi* led some critics to suggest multiple stranglers at large in Boston, while Mafia hit man Vincent Barbosa confided to a journalist that DeSalvo had been paid to "take a fall" for the actual (still unidentified) killer. An alternative suspect, convicted two-time killer George Nassar, was accused in one theory of feeding DeSalvo vital details on the murders while they shared a ward at Bridgewater State Hospital.

Finally, more than a quarter-century after DeSalvo was murdered in prison, forensic scientists revisited the Boston Strangler case in an effort to determine whether or not DeSalvo committed the murders to which he confessed. His body was exhumed in October 2001, for extraction of DNA material unknown to pathologists at the time of the original murders. The material was slated for comparison with evidence collected in the case of 19-year-old Mary Sullivan, the strangler's last victim, found dead on January 4, 1964.

Announcements of "new evidence" in the Boston case were made on December 6, 2001, with James Starrs—a professor of law and forensic science at George Washington University—promising "blockbuster results." Another GWU spokesman, Paul Fucito, said of the DNA findings: "Whether they announce one way or another whether [DeSalvo] did it or not, I think that will be a fairly conclusive announcement." He added that the DNA report would "be revealing enough that it will give the Boston authorities the incentive to look at their evidence and their findings and maybe compare notes and maybe bring the investigation forward."

In fact, by December 2001, neither DeSalvo's family nor Mary Sullivan's believed DeSalvo was the Boston Strangler. That opinion was apparently supported on December 6 by reports that Prof. Starrs's "All-Star Forensic Science Team" had discovered foreign DNA from *two* individuals on Sullivan's body and clothing, neither of the samples linked to DeSalvo. As Professor Starrs told the press, "It's indicative, strongly indicative, of the fact that Albert DeSalvo was not the rape-murderer of Mary Sullivan. If I was a juror, I would acquit him with no questions asked." Sullivan's nephew, Casey Sherman, had an even more emphatic statement for the press.

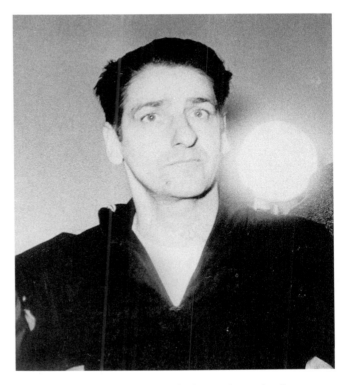

Recent DNA tests have cast doubt on the guilt of confessed serial murderer Albert DeSalvo. (Author's collection)

43

"If he didn't kill Mary Sullivan, yet he confessed to it in glaring detail, he didn't kill any of these women."

Retired Massachusetts prosecutor Julian Soshnick disagreed, retorting, "It doesn't prove anything except that they found another person's DNA on a part of Miss Sullivan's body." Seeming to ignore that neither donor was DeSalvo, Soshnick stood firm: "I believe that Albert was the Boston Strangler." Another retired investigator, former Boston homicide detective Jack Barry, cited DeSalvo's detailed confessions. "He just knew so much," Barry said, "things that were never in the paper. He could describe the wallpaper in their rooms." Dr. Ames Robey, Bridgewater's supervisor in the 1960s and the chief psychiatrist who evaluated DeSalvo, found the confessions less persuasive. "He was a boaster," Dr. Robey told reporters. "I never believed it for a minute."

In any case, the DNA discovery still stopped short of solving Boston's most famous murder case. Professor Starrs believes at least one of the DNA samples recovered from Sullivan's body belongs to her killer, but as he admitted in December 2001, "We cannot tell you the $64,000 question as to whose it is."

BOYANOVSKY, Brian: computer software pirate

A resident of Beaverton, Oregon, born June 26, 1975, Brian Boyanovsky was one of five Intel Corporation employees charged on May 4, 2000, with conspiracy to violate federal copyright laws. Acting in concert with members of a HACKERS' gang calling itself "PIRATES WITH ATTITUDE," the Intel employees illegally provided company hardware and computer software to establish a covert "Sentinel" website, operating from a college campus in Quebec. Before the syndicate was broken up, more than 5,000 stolen software programs were disseminated through the site, with a retail value in excess of $1 million. Within a year of their arrest, Boyanovsky, his four coworkers and eight of the self-styled pirates had filed guilty pleas in federal court. Sentencing was deferred until the remaining cases were resolved.

BRAVO, Mark Diaz: exonerated by DNA evidence

On February 20, 1990, a female patient of a Los Angeles psychiatric hospital complained to staff members that she had been sexually assaulted. During successive police interviews, she named several different assailants, one of them Mark Bravo, a hospital orderly. Bravo was ultimately charged with rape after the victim told police she was "sure" of his guilt. Semen recovered from a blanket at the alleged crime scene matched Bravo's blood type, found in only 3 percent of the American population. Jurors later convicted Bravo of rape, and he was sentenced to an eight-year prison term.

Bravo's appeal of the conviction was denied in 1992. A year later, he filed a post-conviction motion for DNA testing on the blanket, a semen-stained sheet, and the victim's underpants. The motion was granted, and a subsequent report, dated December 24, 1993, revealed that none of the semen stains matched Bravo's DNA. His lawyer filed a writ of habeas corpus on January 4, 1994, and Bravo was released from prison three days later. By that time, the victim had also recanted her testimony accusing Bravo of rape.

BREDING, Ryan   See FASTLANE

BRISON, Dale: exonerated by DNA evidence

On the night of July 14, 1990, while walking home from a neighborhood convenience store, a female resident of Chester County, Pennsylvania, was grabbed from behind by a man who seized her throat and pressed a knife into her back, commanding that she walk in front of him. Stabbed moments later, she lost consciousness briefly, waking as the attacker dragged her into some bushes near an apartment complex. There, she was raped repeatedly before the man fled. The victim subsequently identified Dale Brison as her attacker, and he was arrested. At trial, the prosecution introduced a hair "consistent" with Brison's, found by police at the crime scene. Brison requested a DNA test, but the court denied his motion. Brison's mother corroborated his alibi—that he had been sleeping at home when the rape occurred—but jurors disbelieved the testimony, convicting him of rape, kidnapping, aggravated assault, carrying a prohibited offensive weapon, and three counts of involuntary deviate sexual intercourse. He received an aggregate sentence of 18 to 42 years in state prison on the various charges.

On appeal, in 1992, the Pennsylvania Superior Court ordered DNA testing performed on the semen stains from the victim's clothing, and Brison was excluded absolutely as a suspect in the case. County prosecutors next insisted on performing their own tests and produced identical results. Dale Brison was released from custody in January 1994, after serving three and a half years of his undeserved sentence.

BROWN, Albert: exonerated by DNA evidence

At age 19, in 1981, Oklahoma resident Albert Brown was convicted of murdering a retired Tulsa firefighter, Earl Taylor, found gagged and drowned in Lake Fort Gibson. Conviction hinged on testimony regarding human hairs—specifically, that hairs found on the gag in Taylor's mouth matched Brown's, and that hairs from Taylor's head were found in the trunk of Brown's car. Brown was sentenced to life and served 20 years before DNA testing revealed that hairs lifted from the gag were not, in fact, his.

A hearing on Brown's case was held in Tulsa on October 2, 2001, whereupon the court scheduled his release for October 16. Prosecutors initially agreed, saying a retrial was "possible but not likely." When Brown's release date arrived, however, authorities "discovered" his history of 44 prison disciplinary infractions, including allegations that Brown had conspired with others in the stabbing of a fellow prisoner. Prosecutor Dianne Barker Harold found, not surprisingly, that after being falsely imprisoned for two decades Brown had "some anger issues and authoritative issues." She also reversed the prior decision of her office, requesting six months to decide if enough evidence existed for a retrial on the Taylor homicide. Freedom remains elusive for Arnold Brown, as the state seeks ways to keep him imprisoned despite the scientific evidence that apparently exonerates him.

BROWN, Melissa S.: computer saboteur

A disgruntled employee of Christian & Timbers, an executive recruitment firm in Beachwood, Ohio, 30-year-old Melissa Brown used her computer skills to sabotage the company for spite. Working from home in the predawn hours of April 14, 2001, Brown used a coworker's ID and password to invade the firm's system, changing the chief information officer's password while he was absent on vacation. The resultant internal investigation cost Christian & Timbers more than $15,000, resulting in Brown's identification as the hacker.

A federal grand jury indicted Brown for computer fraud on July 6, 2001. She faced five years' imprisonment and/or a $250,000 fine if convicted at trial, but she chose to strike a plea bargain with prosecutors on September 14, 2001. Following her guilty plea, on November 26, 2001, Brown was sentenced to three years' probation by Judge Dan Polster in Akron, Ohio. Special conditions of her probation included seven months of home confinement with electronic monitoring and full restitution to Christian & Timbers, in the amount of $15,346.71.

"BUBBLEBOY": computer e-mail worm

The first known e-mail virus capable of infecting computers without attached data, "BubbleBoy"— discovered in November 1999—uses various tricks to activate its code directly from the body of messages sent via MicroSoft Outlook or Outlook Express. When a corrupted message is opened, the worm code takes control, gains access to the target computer's disk files and system registry, raiding the Outlook address book and sending infected messages to all addresses listed there.

Two separate tricks are utilized to spread virus copies from the newly infected computer. The first is a built-in feature of MS Outlook that permits creation of e-mail messages in HTML format—which in turn contain scripts that automatically execute (open) when the message is displayed. BubbleBoy may also bypass Internet Explorer security systems on an infected computer via a breach that allows HTML scripts to create disk files. Known as "Scriptlet.Typelib," this feature allows creation of new files in the Windows Startup folder, thus activating the worm and creating new copies the next time Windows is booted, while no Internet Explorer security messages are displayed. The initial file created on a newly infected computer is labeled "update.hta," found in the "c:\windows\start menu\programs\startup" directory. If for any reason Windows is not installed in the c:\windows directory, BubbleBoy cannot create its file and therefore fails to replicate.

Execution of the update.hta file runs the computer's Outlook application in a hidden window and creates a new (infected) message, which is then sent on to all recipients found in the victim's Outlook address book, in a manner similar to the pernicious "MELISSA" virus. The message subject line reads "BubbleBoy is back!" and the message text reads:

The BubbleBoy incident, pictures and sounds
http://www.towns.com/dorms/tom/bblboy.htm

The worm also changes Windows registration data, listing the program's registered owner as "BubbleBoy" and the registered organization as "Vandelay Industries." That done, it leaves a window open on the monitor's screen, reading: "System error, delete 'UPDATE.HTA' from the startup folder to solve this problem."

Avoiding use of HTML applications is not a guarantee of safety against BubbleBoy or similar worms, since HTA files remain installed on the computer and are therefore vulnerable. Infestation can be prevented as follows:

1. Double click on the "My Computer" desktop icon.
2. Select "View -> Folder options" from the menu.
3. Select the "File Types" tab.
4. Locate and highlight "HTML Application."
5. Click "Remove" and confirm the action.
6. Close the dialog box.

For users who wish to retain their HTML applications without risk of infection, Microsoft provides a system update to eliminate the security breach. It may be downloaded and installed from http://support/microsoft.com/supprt/kb/articles/Q240/3/08.ASP.

"BUDDYLST.SIP" Computer Virus: Internet hoax

Appearing for the first time in October 1999, this spurious warning against a nonexistent computer VIRUS has also been translated into French and circulated abroad. The original English version reads:

Objet: Fw: Danger—Virus—Danger

This is not a joke

This information came from Microsoft. Please pass it on to anyone you know who has access to the Internet.

You may receive an apparently harmless Budweiser screen saver entitled BUDDYLST.SIP.

If you do—DO NOT OPEN IT UNDER ANY CIRCUMSTANCES, but delete it immediately.

Once opened, you will lose EVERYTHING on your PC. Your hard disc will be completely destroyed and the person who sent you the message will have access to your name and password via the Internet.

As far as we know, the virus was circulated yesterday morning. It's a new virus, and extremely dangerous.

Please copy this information and e-mail it to everyone in your address book. We need to do all we can to block this virus.

AOL has confirmed how dangerous it is, and there is no anti-virus program yet, which is capable of destroying it.

Please take all the necessary precautions and pass this information on to your friends, acquaintances and work colleagues.

BUD Frog Screen-Saver Warning: Internet hoax

In January 1997 e-mail warnings circulated on the Internet alerted readers to an alleged VIRUS code hidden in copies of the popular "Bud Frog" screen-saver program created as an advertising device for Budweiser beer. While the warning itself is an evident hoax, the U.S. Department of Energy's HOAXBUSTERS website adds a proviso that third-party copies of the screen-saver program "may have been infected with a virus between when it was released and when you get it." The virus in question was apparently a Trojan horse program of undisclosed size and power. The hoax warning reads as follows:

DANGER!!! VIRUS ALERT!!!

THIS IS A NEW TWIST. SOME CREEPOID SCAM-ARTIST IS SENDING OUT A VERY DESIRABLE SCREEN-SAVER (THE BUD FROGS). BUT IF YOU DOWN-LOAD IT, YOU'LL LOSE EVERYTHING!!!!! YOUR HARD DRIVE WILL CRASH!!

DON'T DOWNLOAD THIS UNDER ANY CIRCUMSTANCES!!!

IT JUST WENT INTO CIRCULATION YESTERDAY, AS FAR AS WE KNOW. . . . BE CAREFUL.

PLEASE DISTRIBUTE TO AS MANY PEOPLE AS POSSIBLE . . . THANX

File: BUDSAVER.EXE (24643 bytes)
DL Time (28800 bps): <1 minute

BUG'S Life Screen-Saver Virus: Internet hoax

As with the popular BUD FROGS screen saver, this program, taken from the popular animated film *A Bug's Life* (1998), has also been the target of Internet rumors alleging that some copies contain a Trojan horse virus. In fact, no such infected copies have been found to date, though computer experts recommend downloading the screen saver only from its original website, as opposed to accepting it from unreliable third parties. The hoax warning circulated since May 1999 reads as follows:

Subject: FW: Another Virus!!!!!!

Someone is sending out a very desirable screen-saver, a Bug's Life—"BUGGLST.ZIP". If you download it, you will lose everything!!! Your hard drive will crash and someone from the Internet will get your screen name and password! DO NOT DOWNLOAD THIS UNDER ANY CIRCUMSTANCES!!! IT JUST WENT INTO circulation yesterday, as far as we know. Please distribute/inform this message. This is a new, very malicious virus and not many people know about it. This information was announced yesterday morning by Microsoft. Please share it with everyone that might access the Internet. Once again, pass this along to EVERYONE in your address book so that this may be stopped.

BULLOCK, Ronnie: exonerated by DNA evidence

On March 18, 1983, in Chicago, a nine-year-old girl on her way to school was accosted by a man wearing a police uniform, who forced her into his car and drove to a nearby alley, where he raped her. A second case was reported on April 18, 1983, the rapist flashing a badge at a 12-year-old before he abducted and raped her. The victims described their attacker to police, and a sketch was prepared, later used to identify suspect Ronnie Bullock. Both victims selected Bullock from a lineup and later identified him in court. Convicted at trial in May 1984, Bullock received a 60-year sentence for deviate sexual assault and a concurrent 15-year sentence for aggravated kidnapping.

An appellate court upheld Bullock's conviction in March 1987, but his motion to have the rape evidence impounded for future study was granted. Prosecutors agreed to his motion for DNA testing in June 1993, presumably confident that the results would confirm Bullock's verdict. Following a delay, in which the victim's underpants "disappeared" and were then rediscovered, testing proceeded in October 1994. The lab's report excluded Bullock as a suspect in the case, and he was released from prison on October 14, 1994, confined to his parents' home while prosecution experts duplicated the DNA tests. The secondary tests again excluded Bullock, and the charges were dismissed, liberating Bullock after he

had served 10 and one-half years of his sentence. The actual rapist has not been apprehended.

BURNS, Eric: hacker "Zyklon"

Described by federal prosecutors as the coleader of a loose-knit HACKERS' syndicate called "GLOBAL HELL" —a.k.a "total-ka0s"—Eric Burns was 18 years old in 1998, when he designed the "Web Bandit" computer program to identify vulnerable Internet targets. Operating from his home in Shoreline, Washington, Burns singled out Electric Press, a Virginia-based server that hosted web pages for NATO, the U.S. Information Agency (USIA), and Vice President Al Gore. Between August 1998 and January 1999 Burns hacked the Electric Press server four times, the invasions affecting dozens of U.S. embassies and consulates dependent on USIA for information, one attack disabling the USIA website for eight days. Burns also hacked the web pages of 80 businesses hosted by LASER.NET in Fairfax, Virginia; the web pages of two Issue Dynamics clients in Virginia and Washington, D.C.; the University of Washington's web page; web servers of the Virginia Higher Education Council; and an Internet service provider in London, England.

In most cases, Burns replaced the target web pages with his own simple messages, including his "Zyklon" screen name and professions of love for a woman named Crystal. A similar message, accompanied by crude insults, was left on May 2, 1999, after hackers invaded the White House website. Burns initially took credit for that attack in a series of e-mail correspondence, but later denied personal involvement, blaming the White House hack on fellow members of Global Hell. FBI agents arrested Burns on May 8, 1999, charging him with multiple felony counts of computer intrusion, causing damage in excess of $40,000. He pleaded guilty to one count on September 7, 1999. On November 19, 1999, Burns was sentenced to 15 months' imprisonment, three years' supervised probation, and a restitution order in the amount of $36,240.

BUTLER, Joel L.: satellite TV pirate

A resident of Millersburg, Ohio, 40-year-old Joel Butler was indicted by a federal grand jury on August 7, 2001, charged with selling and distributing 50 fraudulently altered DirecTV satellite access cards, which permitted buyers to illegally receive and decrypt pay-per-view programs and premium channels such as HBO, Showtime, and Cinemax. The illicit sales, occurring between June 1, 1997, and February 26, 2001, cost DirecTV an estimated $100,000 in legitimate income. Butler pleaded guilty to one count of the indictment on October 1, 2001.

BUTLER, Sabrina: exonerated by medical evidence

Mississippi resident Sabrina Butler, an 18-year-old unwed mother, was charged with murder in 1990 after her nine-month-old son was pronounced dead at a community hospital. Butler told physicians and police that she had found the boy unconscious in his crib, attempting to revive him with CPR techniques before rushing to the hospital. Police noted contradictions in her statement, discounting grief and Butler's diagnosis as borderline mentally retarded when they filed the murder charge. At trial, prosecutors sought the death penalty on grounds that Walter Butler had been killed during commission of another felony—specifically, child abuse. Butler's defense attorneys presented the CPR story but offered no supporting evidence. (One of the lawyers was later described by a local newspaper as an "incompetent drunk.") Butler was convicted of first-degree murder and sentenced to die.

Mississippi's Supreme Court overturned the conviction in 1992, on grounds that Butler's prosecutor had improperly urged jurors to infer guilt from the fact that Butler did not testify in her own defense. Retried in 1995, Butler had the advantage of a skilled defense attorney and belated testimony from a neighbor who confirmed her original account of attempted CPR. New medical evidence also revealed that Walter Butler suffered from cystic kidney disease and may have died from Sudden Infant Death Syndrome. His abdominal injuries were diagnosed as posthumous results of a failed attempt to revive him. Butler was acquitted after brief deliberation and released from custody.

BYNUM, Roger West: video pirate

A prolific dealer in bootleg videocassettes of motion pictures and compact discs of musical recordings, 52-year-old Roger Bynum was arrested following a raid by Prince Georges County police on July 29, 1999. The raiders seized 23,892 videocassettes and 58,975 CDs, charging Bynum with conspiracy to sell and distribute the illicit copies. He was indicted on August 23, 1999, and pleaded guilty to conspiracy on March 1, 2000. Eleven months later, on January 26, 2001, Bynum received a two-year prison sentence from U.S. District Judge Deborah Chasanow. In addition to jail time, Bynum was ordered to pay restitution of $172,500 to the Motion Picture Association of America and $290,000 to the Recording Industry Association of America. Bynum's prosecutor told the press, "Criminals who traffic in counterfeit merchandise harm the copyright holders who are deprived of control over their work and also damage consumers who wind up with inferior merchandise."

BYRD, Kevin: exonerated by DNA evidence

In 1985 a Houston woman was attacked and raped in her home by an unknown intruder. In statements to police, she repeatedly described her rapist as a white man, adding that "he had an unusual color of skin . . . a honey-brown color, but he was not black." Four months later, while shopping in a neighborhood grocery store, she glimpsed Kevin Byrd—a dark-skinned African American—and reported him to the authorities as her attacker. At trial, prosecutors convinced a jury that the victim's repeated descriptions of her assailant as "white" were in fact a "mistake" by one of the detectives assigned to her case. Byrd was convicted in August 1985 and sentenced to life in prison.

Twelve years later, in early 1997, DNA testing of semen collected in the case proved beyond doubt that Byrd was innocent. The Texas Board of Pardons and Paroles recommended to Governor George W. Bush that Byrd be pardoned immediately on grounds of actual innocence, but Bush refused until October 1997, finally compelled by adverse publicity to grant the belated pardon. Critics accused Bush of racism, noting that Byrd was the first black recipient of clemency among 15 inmates pardoned by Bush, but the reaction of Harris County authorities was even more troubling. In the wake of Byrd's pardon, the county clerk ordered "rape kit" evidence destroyed in 50 other cases, thereby making DNA tests impossible—and presumably sparing county prosecutors from further embarrassment.

"CALIFORNIA Wobbler" Computer Virus:
Internet hoax

In May 1999, Internet warnings began to circulate about a so-called Wobbler VIRUS allegedly transmitted in a file titled California. In fact, neither the file nor its encoded virus exist. As with the mythical "BUDDYLST. SIP" virus, warnings were also broadcast in French. The English original read (with errors preserved):

Subject: FW: New Virus Warning

Dear ALL

Thought you might be interested in this message. If you receive an email with a file called "California" do not open the file. The file contains the "WOBBLER" virus.

This information was announced yesterday morning by IBM. The report says . . . "this is a very dangerous virus, much worse than 'melissa' and there is NO remedy for it at this time. Some very sick individual has succeeded in using the reformat function from Norton Utilities causing it to completely erase all documents on the hard drive. It has been designed to work with Netscape Navigator and Microsoft Internet Explorer. destroys Macintosh and IBM compatible computers. This is a new, very malicious virus and not many people know about it at this time. Please pass this warning to everyone in your address book and share it all your online friends asap so that the destruction it can cause may be minimized."

All the best
Dan

Whoever "Dan" may be, no such report was ever issued by IBM and no virus resembling the "Wobbler" has yet been discovered on-line.

CALLACE, Leonard: exonerated by DNA evidence

In January 1985, a teenage resident of White Plains, New York, was accosted by two strangers as she approached her car in a mall parking lot. The men brandished knives and forced her into the backseat of a nearby sedan, where one sexually assaulted her while his companion watched. Police arrested Leonard Callace on the basis of a suspect sketch; the victim later picked his likeness from a photo lineup and identified him in court as her rapist. (The second man was never found.) Adamant in his protestation of innocence, Callace rejected a plea bargain offered by the state, which would have freed him after four months in jail. At trial, prosecutors demonstrated that Callace's blood type matched semen collected from the victim, and his alibi was uncorroborated. Jurors deliberated less than an hour before convicting Callace on four counts of sodomy, three counts of sexual abuse, one count of wrongful imprisonment, and criminal possession of a weapon. On March 24, 1987, Callace received a prison term of 25 to 50 years.

The verdict was affirmed on appeal, and Callace was denied leave to pursue further action before the state court of appeals. While serving his time, Callace learned the basic details of DNA testing from the case of another New York defendant, CHARLES DABBS. On June 27, 1991, a Suffolk County judge approved DNA testing of semen stains from the victim's clothing, which eliminated Leonard Callace as a source. He was released from prison on October 5, 1992, after serving nearly six years of his sentence. Prosecutors dismissed all charges and declined to pursue a new trial based on the victim's testimony alone.

CANDLE Memorial Chain Letter: Internet hoax

This fraudulent e-mail chain letter appeared on-line soon after the terrorist attacks of September 11, 2001, in New York and Washington, D.C. Evolving through successive incarnations, it pleads for patriots to mount a candlelight demonstration in honor of victims slain in the attacks, but careful readers will note that no date is specified for the mass turnout. Likewise, no data is available on how many candles would be required to present a light show visible from outer space. The first version of the message read:

Friday night at 7:00 p.m. EST step out your door, stop your car, or step out of your establishment and light a candle. We will show the world that Americans are strong and united together against terrorism. Please pass this to everyone on your e-mail list. We need to reach everyone across the United States quickly.

Close behind the first plea, and apparently assuming that Americans had answered the call, came this second Internet message, crediting unnamed U.S. officials for the call to action:

Pretty impressive and another statement to be made if everyone participates . . . 10:30 EASTERN TIME . . . 9:30 Central, 8:30 Mountain, 7:30 Pacific.
The U.S. has asked that everyone step out on their lawns tonight and light a candle. They will be taking a satellite picture of the U.S. and posting it on the news tomorrow morning.
Please pass this on to as many people as possible.

A third and final version of the hoax pretends that the National Aeronautics and Space Administration planned to take the satellite picture of candles burning across America.

Subject: Candle Memorial Tonight

A formal request from NASA:

10:30 EASTERN TIME . . . 9:30 Central, 8:30 Mountain, 7:30 Pacific
NASA has asked that everyone step out on their lawns tonight at 10:30 and light a candle. They will be taking a satellite picture of the US and posting it on the news tomorrow morning.
Please pass this on to as many people as possible. Thank you.

There was, of course, no candlelight memorial and no high-flying camera in attendance. If anyone was deceived by the hoax, they have managed to conceal the embarrassing fact.

"CANDYMAN": computer virus family

Logged for the first time in April 1999, the macro viruses of the "Candyman" family attack the global macros area of a target computer upon execution of an infected document and spread to other documents as they close. On the 25th of any month, Candyman deletes all files in the c:\windows and c:\dos folders, then displays a message reading:

No se olviden de CABEZAS - Pierri y Duahlde PUTOS-Cabezas Virus by CANDYMAN Bs. As. Argentina

CANTRELL, Calvin: convicted hacker

A 30-year-old resident of Grand Prairie, Texas, Calvin Cantrell was identified by federal prosecutors as a member and ringleader of an 11-member HACKERS' syndicate known as "Phone Masters." The group reportedly invaded computers of three telephone networks, in a vain attempt "to own the telecommunications infrastructure from coast to coast." When not hacking telephone company systems, the self-styled Phone Masters invaded the computers of various credit-reporting agencies, utility providers, and government computers including that of the Justice Department's National Crime Information Center. FBI data-taps secured evidence against Cantrell and two other defendants, all of whom pleaded guilty to criminal fraud and related charges in spring 1999. On September 16, 1999, Cantrell received a two-year prison sentence and was ordered to pay the victim companies $10,000.

CARDOZO Innocence Project: defenders of falsely accused
Operating from the Benjamin N. Cardozo School of
Law in New York City, the Innocence Project was
founded in 1992 by lawyers Barry Scheck (best
known for his role in the defense of O. J. SIMPSON) and
Peter Neufeld. A clinical law program for students,
supervised by law professors and university administrators, the project offers pro bono (free) legal assistance to prison inmates challenging their convictions
on the basis of DNA evidence. (The inmates are
required, however, to obtain private funding for the
actual tests, which may cost as much as $10,000.)
Limited funding and personnel currently force the
Innocence Project to decline any cases where DNA is
not the primary issue. In addition to legal defense for
imprisoned clients, the project also lobbies state legis-
latures for passage of laws authorizing compensation
of wrongly convicted and incarcerated persons. To
date, those efforts have enjoyed limited success (only
Illinois and New York have passed such laws to date),
but defense of wrongly convicted prisoners has
achieved more dramatic results. As of January 2002,
100 American inmates had been exonerated and freed
on the basis of DNA testing, 38 of those thanks to
members of the Innocence Project. Those represented
directly by the Cardozo Innocence Project include
HERMAN ATKINS, TERRY CHALMERS, EDWARD HONAKER,
and CALVIN JOHNSON JR.

CARPENTER, Claude R., II: computer saboteur
A 19-year-old resident of Lusby, Maryland, Claude
Carpenter II was hired on March 13, 2000, as a systems administrator for Network Resources, a sub-
contractor for the Internal Revenue Service. At the
time, Network Resources was performing work on
the Integrated Network Operations Management
System (INOMS) database, which contained an
inventory of all computer hardware and software
owned by the IRS. Carpenter's specific duties
included monitoring three computer servers maintained by the IRS computer center at the New Car-
rollton Federal Building in Lanham, Maryland.

Carpenter's poor work habits soon led to repeated
reprimands for misbehavior, including late arrivals
and early departures from work, unavailability to
deal with system responses and customers' requests,
and insubordinate comments to his supervisor. Three
disciplinary meetings in April 2000 resulted in Carpenter being warned that further infractions would
lead to dismissal. Still his tardiness continued, and on
May 4, 2000, his root access (the level of complete
control utilized by system administrators over a system) was restricted to a single server. On May 18,
following a dispute between Carpenter and a
coworker, Carpenter's supervisor initiated paperwork for his dismissal.

Carpenter's last day on the job, he worked a shift
from 2:00 P.M. on May 18 to 12:30 A.M. on May 19,
2000. Logging onto all three servers, including two
from which he was barred, Carpenter modified his
supervisor's computer profile and inserted a destructive code that would erase all data found on the
servers. He then tried to cover his tracks by turning
off system logs, removing history files and seeking to
have the virus code overwritten after it was executed.
Fired from his job on May 19, Carpenter tipped his
hand over the next two weeks by telephoning repeatedly, asking if everything was OK, or if anything was
wrong with the servers. His suspicious behavior
prompted project managers to shut the Lanham
servers down and remove the destructive code.

Charges of intentionally causing damage to a protected computer were still pending when Carpenter's
employers discovered more offenses. In addition to
his sabotage, Carpenter had lied under oath concerning his work history, criminal record, and illegal drug
use when he applied for the IRS job. Carpenter
pleaded guilty to one felony count on July 24, 2001,
facing a maximum sentence of 10 years in prison and
a $250,000 fine. While he might serve as little as six
months in jail, prosecutors announced their intent to
request an 18-month exemplary sentence and cash
restitution in an amount as yet undetermined.

"CAT Colonic" Computer Virus: Internet hoax
In a realm known for peculiar titles, the "Cat
Colonic" computer VIRUS stands out as one of the
more bizarre. Thankfully, based on descriptions of its
allegedly lethal behavior, it never existed in fact.
Fraudulent warnings about the virus first appeared
on the Internet in May 1999. The original bogus
alert read as follows:

*If you receive an e-mail entitled, "How to Give a Cat a
Colonic," DO NOT open it. It will erase everything on
your hard drive. Forward this letter out to as many people as you can. This is a new, very malicious virus and
not many people know about it. This information was
announced yesterday morning from IBM. Please share
it with everyone that might access the Internet. Once*

again, pass this along to EVERYONE in your address book so that this may be stopped. AOL has said that this is a very dangerous virus and that there is NO remedy for it at this time.

CELL Phone Cloning: wireless fraud technique

Every cell phone is designed to have a unique factory-set electronic serial number (ESN) and mobile identification number (MIN). "Cloned" cell phones are those reprogrammed to transmit the ESN and MIN of another (legitimate) telephone when calls are made. Swindlers obtain those numbers by monitoring radio wave transmissions and intercepting calls in progress. After "cloning," the legitimate phone shares its ESN/MIN combination with one or more additional phones—but all charges are billed to the registered owner. In a variation of the theme, called "tumbling," some bootleg cell phones are programmed to use a different stolen ESN/MIN combination for each call, running through a list of multiple numbers. This technique prevents a single legitimate user from noting a sudden rash of bogus calls on his or her monthly bill and thus delays exposure of the fraud in progress.

Profits from a cloning operation are limited only by the swindler's nerve and imagination. Small-timers simply use the phones themselves or share with friends until the fraud is discovered and the ESN/MIN combination is deactivated. Others sell cloned telephones, individually or in bulk lots. Finally, in larger cities, it is not unusual to find "customers" lined up on sidewalks or in shopping malls, waiting their turns to make long-distance calls on a "vendor's" cloned telephone for a fraction of the normal cost. Nationwide, by 2000, cell phone cloning cost the industry an estimated $650 million. Cloned cell phones are also extremely popular with drug dealers and other felons who have a vested interest in keeping their telephone records untraced.

Experiments with new forms of cell phone security are constantly ongoing, but wily thieves seem to crack each new system within months of its development. Meanwhile, the U.S. government took action in April 1998, with the Cellular Telephone Protection Act, making it a federal crime to possess, use, or traffic in any hardware or software configured to alter or modify a cell phone without proper authorization. Enforcement of the act fell to the U.S. Secret Service, which reports a doubling in the number of arrests for wireless telecommunications fraud each year since 1991.

"Cloned" cell phones are used to run up millions of dollars in fraudulent calls each year.

While the industry strives to outwit high-tech swindlers on the drawing board, legitimate cell phone users can still take certain basic steps to protect themselves from fraud. Experts recommend the following precautions:

1. Whenever possible, disable any "roaming" functions built into a cell phone. Roaming permits use of a telephone via analog systems when the caller is outside a server's normal digital range, but it also frequently defeats the purpose of secure personal identification numbers (PINs). Cloners love roaming phones for that reason and often target areas surrounding airports or interstate highways, to capture signals (and ESN/MIN combinations) from callers in transit.

2. Turn off telephones when they are not in use. Cell phones left on poll the cellular base station with the strongest signal every few seconds, thus allowing the system to route calls through the appropriate base station. At the same time, however, polling leaves a phone vulnerable to interception and cloning, even when a call is not in progress.

3. Review all bills in detail and report any fraudulent calls to the service provider. A cursory glance may not reveal the occasional bogus call generated by "tumbling," but many cloning victims are billed for dozens—or thousands—of illegitimate calls in a single month.

CENTURION Ministries: defenders of the wrongfully accused America's first Innocence Project, Centurion Ministries was organized in 1983 by James McCloskey, a corporate executive-turned-minister who earned his master of divinity degree from Princeton University. Operating from Princeton since its foundation, Centurion Ministries describes its singular mission as a campaign "to liberate from prison and vindicate individuals who are completely innocent of crimes for which they have been convicted and imprisoned." More than a dozen inmates have been freed to date through the efforts of McCloskey and his staff, including EDWARD HONAKER and CLARENCE MOORE, cleared on the basis of DNA evidence.

In a 1989 article, "Convicting the Innocent," McCloskey maintained that wrongful convictions occur primarily from one or more of seven causes: (1) a widespread "presumption of guilt" against those charged with crimes; (2) perjury by police officers; (3) false testimony by prosecution witnesses; (4) illegal manipulation or suppression of evidence by prosecutors; (5) shoddy police work (as opposed to deliberate frame-ups); (6) incompetent defense counsel; and (7) misconceptions by jurors concerning evidence and testimony.

Because of its small staff and meager resources, Centurion Ministries holds potential clients to a stringent standard. As described on the group's website, cases are accepted only if: the inmate has been sentenced to death or life imprisonment, with no

Jim McCloskey poses near a board listing cases being worked on by his organization, Centurion Ministries. (AP)

parole for at least 15 years; the inmate is "100% innocent," with no involvement in the crime (thereby excluding cases of accidental death or self-defense); the inmate must be indigent and have exhausted all standard legal appeals; and the case does not involve child molestation, since such cases "require a special expertise that CM does not possess." Inmates who meet those strict criteria are invited to contact Centurion Ministries for a review of their cases.

"CHAINSAW": computer worm

Named after the 1974 cult classic horror film *Texas Chainsaw Massacre*, "Chainsaw" is a network worm capable of spreading on the Internet. The worm installs itself on a targeted computer by copying its code to the Windows system directory (filename winmine.exe) and to the root directory of the disk drive currently in use (filename chainsaw.exe). Chainsaw next registers itself in the system registry, then exits and triggers its infection procedure during the next Windows startup.

Once installed and activated, Chainsaw sends a message to the "alt.horror" online news group, incorporating a tag line from the movie's original poster and reading as follows:

From: "Leatherface" <hacked.up.for@bbq.net>
Subject: CHAINSAWED
Newsgroups: alt.horror
Message body:
WHO WILL SURVIVE
AND WHAT WILL BE LEFT OF THEM?

Chainsaw also attempts to send copies of itself from the newly infected computer, seeking targets vulnerable through a "backdoor" Trojan program, firing off corrupted messages to randomly selected addresses in an endless loop. Those transmissions include a "denial-of-service" code that causes Windows 9x computers to crash on receipt of the infected files. At the same time, Chainsaw disables the "ZoneAlarm" Internet protection utility to facilitate its attack. Newly infected remote computers may display the following message, lifted from the opening moments of *The Texas Chainsaw Massacre*:

THE FILM WHICH YOU ARE ABOUT TO SEE IS AN ACCOUNT OF THE TRAGEDY WHICH BEFELL A GROUP OF FIVE YOUTHS. IN PARTICULAR SALLY HARDESTY AND HER INVALID

BROTHER FRANKLIN. IT IS ALL THE MORE TRAGIC IN THAT THEY WERE YOUNG. BUT, HAD THEY LIVED VERY, VERY LONG LIVES, THEY COULD NOT HAVE EXPECTED NOR WOULD THEY HAVE WISHED TO SEE AS MUCH OF THE MAD AND MACABRE AS THEY WERE TO SEE THAT DAY. FOR THEM AN IDYLLIC SUMMER AFTERNOON DRIVE BECAME A NIGHTMARE. THE EVENTS OF THAT DAY WERE TO LEAD TO THE DISCOVERY OF ONE OF THE MOST BIZARRE CRIMES IN THE ANNALS OF AMERICAN HISTORY, THE TEXAS CHAINSAW MASSACRE . . .

CHALMERS, Terry Leon: exonerated by DNA evidence

Defendant Terry Chalmers was arrested following the rape and robbery of a young woman in White Plains, New York, on August 18, 1986. The victim first identified his photo from an array of police mug shots, then twice selected him as her attacker from police lineups. At trial, Chalmers's alibi remained uncorroborated, and the victim identified him again. On June 9, 1987, he was convicted of rape, sodomy, robbery, and two counts of grand larceny, drawing a prison term of 12 to 24 years.

Chalmers first appealed his conviction on grounds that the police lineups were improperly conducted. On July 18, 1990, the New York Supreme Court's appellate division rejected that argument, finding that police conduct was proper in the case, and that the victim's courtroom identification of Chalmers made the lineups superfluous. Chalmers next applied to the CARDOZO INNOCENCE PROJECT for aid, and its lawyers obtained physical evidence from the case for DNA testing. On July 26, 1994 those tests eliminated Chalmers as a possible donor for the semen traces recovered by authorities in August 1986. Chalmers's conviction was vacated, with the rape and sodomy charges dismissed on January 31, 1995. Authorities stalled for three months before dropping the larceny charges. Terry Chalmers was released after serving eight years of his undeserved sentence.

CHANAL, Pierre: serial murder suspect indicted by DNA

Between 1980 and 1987, eight young men either vanished or were found brutally murdered in the Marne region of France, northeast of Paris. Several of the victims were soldiers, based at one or another of three army camps located in what soon became known as the "Triangle of Death." Pierre Chanal, himself a senior warrant sergeant with the crack 4th Dragoons commando regiment, fell under suspicion in 1988, after he kidnapped and raped a Hungarian hitchhiker in the same region. Convicted and sentenced for that crime, Chanal was free again by August 2001, when French authorities announced their intent to charge him with multiple murders.

DNA testing, unavailable to French authorities in 1988, had recently been applied to several human hairs discovered in Chanal's van—the same vehicle in which he was earlier caught red-handed, his male victim trussed up in a parachute harness, while Chanal videotaped his rape and torture. Results of those DNA tests indicated a "very strong probability" that Chanal murdered three of the previous victims, including 19-year-old Trevor O'Keefe, an Irish tourist found strangled and buried in a shallow grave during August 1987. Five counts of murder were dismissed on August 14, 2001, since the victims have never been found, but Chanal was ordered to stand trial for the deaths of O'Keefe and two others. At this writing, no trial date has been set. Unlike America's legal system, the French Napoleonic Code presumes a suspect's guilt until innocence is proved in court.

CHEMICAL & Biological Weapons (CBW)

Between September 18 and October 9, 2001, an unknown person or persons mailed several letters from New Jersey, addressed to the U.S. Senate office building in Washington, D.C., and to media outlets in New York and Florida. The envelopes contained anthrax spores, which infected some two dozen victims, six fatally. White House spokesmen linked the mailings to the TERRORISM attacks of September 11, 2001, but no proof of that charge was forthcoming. FBI agents mounted a massive coast-to-coast search for the killer(s), but at this writing (in mid-October 2002) the G-men have not taken legal action against any or released any trial-worthy evidence.

On the one-year anniversary of the anthrax murders, President George W. Bush called for war with Iraq, alleging that Iraqi dictator Saddam Hussein had illegally stockpiled "weapons of mass destruction" while scheming to launch new attacks against the United States. Bush's own CIA chief disagreed, reporting that Hussein was more likely to retaliate for an invasion than to launch a unilateral assault, but the real irony of the war-hawk position was

revealed on October 9, 2002, when the Associated Press published documents proving that U.S. military forces had conducted secret testing of chemical and biological weapons (CBW) on some 3,000 soldiers in the 1960s. While belatedly couched in terms of "an effort to develop defenses against such weapons," the illegal tests prompted critics to ask whether U.S. leaders were any more responsible or trustworthy than Iraq's Hussein.

As suggested by its name, CBW involves two distinct and separate groups of elements. *Chemical* agents are manmade, including a wide variety of drugs and poisons, hallucinogens, defoliants, toxic metals, and nerve agents (often called "nerve gases," though they may not be in gaseous form). Some applications of chemical warfare verge on slapstick comedy, as when the Central Intelligence Agency planned to spike Fidel Castro's cigars with LSD (to cause him to make erratic, nonsensical speeches) or to dust his clothes with a depilatory (thereby causing fallout from his famous beard). At the other end of the scale are deadly serious applications, such as the September 1957 assassination of Soviet defector Nikolai Khokhlov in Frankfurt. The assassin sprinkled Kokhlov's food with thallium, a rare toxic metal. The result is described by author John Barron in *KGB* (1974).

Hideous brown stripes, dark splotches, and black-and-blue swellings disfigured his face and body. A sticky secretion oozed from his eyelids, and blood seeped through his pores; his skin felt dry, shrunken, and aflame. At the mere touch of his hand, great tufts of hair fell out. . . . Tests on September 22 showed that Kokhlov's white corpuscles were being swiftly and fatally destroyed, his bones decaying, his blood turned to plasma, and his saliva glands atrophying.

Biological agents, by contrast, are destructive organisms found in nature—bacteria, viruses, spores, parasites—though some may be genetically altered in labs to enhance their offensive application. Unlike chemical weapons, biological warfare has been used at least since the Middle Ages, when rotting livestock carcasses were catapulted over castle walls to spread death and disease under siege. Some modern scholars also believe the "Black Death," which claimed one-third of the known world's population between 1347 and 1351, may have begun as a primitive form of "germ warfare." A century later, European diseases began decimating aboriginal people in the Western

Hemisphere, and not always by accident. Cruel settlers in the U.S. and Mexico sometimes resolved their local "Indian problem" by offering Native Americans treacherous gifts of poisoned food or smallpox-infected blankets.

Modern chemical warfare left its mark on Europe during World War I, with the use of toxic gas by both sides producing results so horrific that it was banned by the subsequent Geneva Convention. Suspicion of CBW research by Japan and Nazi Germany prompted the U.S. military to begin its own production of chemical and biological weapons in 1942 and to continue for nearly three decades beyond V-J Day (victory over Japan, 1945). American diplomats leveled charges of CBW violations against North Korea in the early 1950s and later made similar accusations against the Soviet Union and the People's Republic of China. In the United States, meanwhile, military researchers conducted a series of covert tests that are only now coming to light, in the first decade of the 21st century. The tests revealed in October 2002 included:

"Devil Hole I"—Designed to test dispersal patterns of the nerve agent sarin after release from rockets and artillery shells in aspen and spruce forests similar to those in the USSR, this experiment was carried out in the summer of 1965 at the Gerstle River test site near Fort Greeley, Alaska.

"Devil Hole II"—Another test at the Gerstle River site, this time involving the nerve agent VX, deployed against mannequins dressed in military uniforms, seated in U.S. Army trucks.

"Big Tom"—A 1965 test that involved spraying bacteria over the Hawaiian island of Oahu to simulate a biological attack on an island compound. Researchers used *Bacillus globigii*, a bacterium believed harmless at the time (later found to cause serious infections in persons with weakened immune systems).

Those acknowledged tests do not include the deliberate exposure of some 3,000 U.S. soldiers to CBW agents in the name of national defense, and rumors persist of other tests still concealed from the public at large. Author Ed Regis reports, in *The Biology of Doom* (1999), that the U.S. program employed 4,036 persons at its peak and tested various agents on 2,000 human volunteers before "its abrupt cancellation in 1969." After decades of gov-

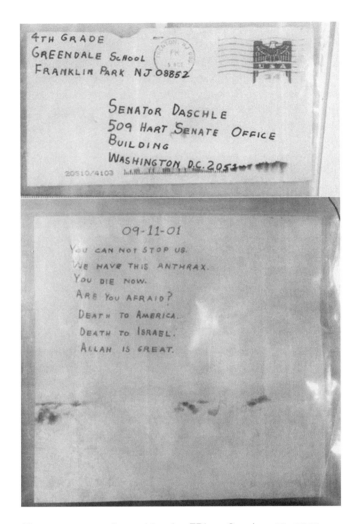

These images released by the FBI on October 23, 2001, show the envelope and letter sent to the office of former Senate Majority Leader Tom Daschle containing anthrax. (AFP/CORBIS)

ernment lies and evasions, however—beginning with the Vietnam "credibility gap" and proceeding through Watergate, the Church Committee hearings on intelligence abuses (1975–76), and the Reagan era's Iran-Contra scandal—some critics contend that the testing never really stopped at all. Indeed, a report published in the *New York Times* one week before the terrorist attacks of September 11, 2001, revealed that the Pentagon had conducted recent CBW experiments and that its scientists had "further plans to genetically engineer a more virulent form of the bacterium that causes anthrax, a deadly disease ideal for germ warfare." When the anthrax mailings began two weeks later, FBI agents initially blamed Muslim extremists, but later suggested the infected letters may have been sent by someone employed at a covert U.S. laboratory. Critics took no solace from claims issued by the Bush White House, that all American CBW experiments were "completely consistent" with international treaties.

Another nation with an unsavory record of CBW experimentation was South Africa under the fallen apartheid regime. According to reports aired in 1998, that country's white-supremacist government employed a renowned cardiologist, 50-year-old Dr. Wouter Basson, to develop and deploy CBW agents against opponents of the repressive apartheid regime. Dubbed "Dr. Death" by his critics, Basson allegedly sought to produce bacteria that would kill only blacks, along with "vaccines" to sterilize black women. Testimony before the nation's Truth and Reconciliation Commission also suggested that Dr. Basson, operating after 1983 from South Africa's Roodeplaat Research Laboratories, cultivated strains of anthrax, cholera, and botulinum, while studying the use of illegal drugs like Ecstasy, THC, and LSD for "crowd control." Basson's team, dubbed "Project Coast," reportedly developed covert assassination tools (including a syringe disguised as a screwdriver), concocted plans to distribute T-shirts poisoned with hallucinogenic drugs in black townships, and schemed to poison imprisoned black leader Nelson Mandela with thallium (the same toxic metal used by the Soviets to kill Nikolai Khokhlov in 1957). Project Coast additionally is said to have produced poisoned beer, chocolate, cigarettes, and envelope glue. Mandela disbanded the unit upon becoming president in 1993.

The only known criminal use of CBW agents to date occurred in Japan, in the case of the cult known as Aum Shinrikyo ("Supreme Truth"). The sect's "venerable master," Shoko Asahara, prophesied an imminent apocalypse, predicting that 90 percent of the earth's population would die in poison gas attacks by 1997, but he was finally unable to wait for his own deadline. Seven residents of Matsumoto were killed in June 1994, with another 200 injured, after cultists released sarin nerve gas in a residential neighborhood. Nine months later, on March 20, 1995, the incident was repeated on a Tokyo subway train, leaving 12 persons dead and 5,500 in treatment for nonfatal injuries. Several cultists were in custody, captured with $7 million in cash and enough sarin to kill 4 million people, when other sect members released phosgene gas at Yokohama's main railroad terminal on April 19, 1995, injuring 300 persons. Two days later, another 25 persons were hospitalized after a gas attack on a Yokohama shopping mall. Cyanide canisters were retrieved from a Tokyo train station on July 4, 1995, disarmed before they could release their deadly contents. By that time, Shoko Asahara and more than a dozen of his disciples were in custody, awaiting trial on multiple murder charges. Several were convicted at trial, and the cult was officially disbanded by court order on October 30, 1995.

CHEMICAL Castration: medical control of sex offenders

In an age when sexual assault—and particularly sexual abuse of minors—has become a high-profile crime and a "hot button" issue in political debates, new methods of prevention are constantly under debate. Convicted offenders are subject to increasingly severe prison sentences, ranging literally into thousands of years for some multi-victim child molesters, and experimental statutes in several American jurisdictions now permit detention of inmates judged "sexually dangerous" to society beyond completion of their statutory terms. While those laws—and corresponding statutes mandating public broadcast of a paroled sex offender's home address—remain under heated attack by defense attorneys and civil libertarians, all concerned agree that prison time and subsequent registration of known sex offenders with police do little or nothing to prevent recidivism.

Sex criminals repeat their crimes—against adult or minor victims, male or female—because of deepseated urges and desires. Sterilization of repeat offenders, believed to be a "cure" as late as the 1930s in Germany, in fact does nothing but eliminate the criminal's ability to procreate. Surgical castration, likewise, has proved ineffective in those cases where the sexual assaults stem from rage, sadism, or any other cause unrelated to production of testosterone. In recent years, a less invasive but equally controversial method has been mandated in several states, involving "chemical castration" by means of medication that lowers the testosterone level, thereby reducing a subject's sex drive.

The drugs of choice for chemical castration are Depo-Provera and Depo-Lupron (medroxyprogesterone acetate), which operate by lowering the blood serum testosterone levels in males who receive the injections. Sexual drive is reduced by influencing the hypothalamus portion of the brain that stimulates the pituitary gland to release hormones that in turn control sperm production. The drugs are alleged to reduce recidivism among serial sex offenders from 87 percent to a mere 2 percent, but medical researchers question those statistics, noting that men subjected to the drugs can still obtain an erection, engage in sexual intercourse, and ejaculate.

California was the first state to impose chemical castration as a legal penalty (or remedy) through a statute passed by the state legislature on August 28, 1996, and signed by Governor Pete Wilson on September 18. The law provides that any person convicted of specified sex offenses against a victim under 13 years of age may be required to undergo medroxyprogesterone acetate treatment during parole for a first offense, and all repeat offenders must receive the treatment during their parole. Those treatments would in fact begin prior to an inmate's release from prison and would continue through the term of that parole unless the state department of corrections demonstrates to the board of prison terms that the treatments are no longer necessary.

Immediate objections were raised by the American Civil Liberties Union and its California affiliate. ACLU spokesperson Valerie Navarro told reporters, "There are problems regarding the right to privacy, the right to procreate, the right to exercise control over one's body." The ACLU termed chemical castration "barbaric, unconstitutional and ultimately ineffective in protecting our children," predicting that the new law would be challenged in court. "Society has an overwhelmingly important interest in keeping children safe," Navarro said. "But this is a simplistic and ultimately ineffective response to the problem of child abuse. As medical and psychiatric experts have testified, the complex reasons that impel people to assault children cannot be eliminated by giving people shots. This measure is nothing more than an election year bill that won't do anything to make it safer for our children."

Dr. Michael Meek and the California Psychiatric Association raised concerns of greater import to most Californians than the civil rights of convicted child molesters. "It's a bad law as written," Dr. Meek told the press. "The classic example would be someone who molests children because voices tell him to molest children. Well, they're doing it from a psychotic point of view because voices tell them. Progesterone is not going to help them at all." Dr. Fred Berlin of Johns Hopkins Hospital also derided the notion that progesterone is a cure-all for sex crimes. "The notion we can give someone a shot once a week, and walk away from them and feel comfortable," Berlin said, "I think is a very naïve point of view."

Naïve or not, the notion of a quick fix instantly appealed to lawmakers in other states. Over the next three years, similar statutes were enacted in Georgia, Iowa, Louisiana, Montana, Oregon, and Wisconsin. Alabama governor Don Siegelman sponsored legislation offering a choice of chemical or surgical castration to any male defendant who sought probation on a first-time conviction for rape, sodomy, sexual torture, or first-degree sexual abuse of a victim under 13 years of age. (Female offenders, as in all other states so far, would be exempt and unaffected by the law.) As of March 2000, the costs for progesterone treatment of paroled sex offenders averaged $2,400 per subject, per year.

Aside from potential failure, medical experts point out that use of progesterone-related drugs poses a potentially lethal health risk for subjects who suffer from obesity, diabetes, pulmonary disease, or high blood pressure—issues ignored in the statutes passed to date. Known side effects of the treatment in males include breast enlargement, tumors, and edema. Women who have used the medication to correct menstrual irregularity for two months or more, meanwhile, report a history of malignant breast tumors, venous thromboses, and an increased tendency toward hemorrhage. Prevailing medical (as opposed to public and political) opinion suggests that use of progesterone should be evaluated on an individual basis, rather than on mandatory terms as specified by existing state legislation. A 1991 research report that recommended Depo-Provera chiefly for use with serial rapists and homosexual pedophiles also added the following cautionary notes:

1. Antitestosterone agents should be employed only if there is
   a. substantial risk of repeated offenses in the period during which behavior therapy has been initiated but has not yet been effective or
   b. a risk that any single offense will produce substantial harm to a victim as, for example, an act of child molestation as opposed to an act of exhibitionism.
2. Such agents should be employed for as short a time as possible. Their use should be tapered once

evidence is gained that behavior therapy is becoming effective.

3. Such agents should be given at the lowest dose necessary to produce the required reduction in sexual drive.

4. Such agents should be employed in cases in which continued monitoring of plethysmograph recordings and plasma testosterone levels can occur.

5. Such agents should not be employed as the sole therapeutic approach.

6. Such agents should only be employed in cases in which competent consent can be obtained or in which a guardian can approve their administration.

The latter point is of particular concern with regard to juvenile offenders, as new research continues to report disturbing side effects of chemical castration. In addition to those already noted, recent studies now report extreme weight gain (up to 50 percent of body weight) in some subjects; hyperinsulinemic response to glucose load; compromise of gastrointestinal or gall bladder functions; chills; phlebitis; nausea and vomiting; headaches; hypoglycemia; leg cramps; and sleep disturbances (including bizarre nightmares).

A report on chemical castration in the *New England Journal of Medicine* (February 12, 1998) added support to arguments of those who believe the treatment benefits society via control of sexual offenders. Citing a study of 30 male subjects' recurring deviant sexual behavior, including 25 convicted pedophiles, the article found treatment with a new drug—triptorelin—more effective than Depo-Provera in curbing recidivism (and less risky in terms of medical side effects) when used in combination with traditional psychotherapy. Used primarily in Europe at the present time, triptorelin has yet to gain widespread acceptance in the United States, but the news encouraged proponents of chemical castration in their long-running effort to defeat skeptical challenges. Medical effectiveness, however, still does not address the constitutional issues raised by civil libertarians, and the controversy will doubtless continue until finally settled before the U.S. Supreme Court at some future date.

CHILD Pornography and Solicitation On-line

Pornography is big business on the World Wide Web. According to one Nielsen NetRatings report, 17.5 million Americans visited Internet porn sites from their homes in January 2001 alone, a 40 percent increase over the next most recent survey, from September 2000. The Web's premier porn site—PornCity.net—scored more hits than ESPN.com or the Internet book vendor barnesandnoble.com. Since most porn sites charge visitors for any view beyond a brief "free sample," the profit potential is enormous—$970 million in 1998, according to the research firm Datamonitor. A report from Forrester Research estimates that cyber porn sales (including videos and other merchandise purchased on-line for home delivery) matched overall Internet book sales in 1999 ($1.3 million) and far exceeded the $800 million spent on airline tickets. By a very conservative estimate, 40,000 sex-oriented websites existed in March 2001, and the number was steadily rising.

Those figures, however, refer only to "legitimate" porn sites, wherein the models (and presumably the visiting "surfers") are certified adults. Despite poorly documented complaints from church groups that some 200,000 Americans suffer from Internet porn addiction, legislative efforts to impose "decency" standards on the Web have thus far been defeated in the courts. Only in the area of child pornography has legislation been approved to punish vendors and recipients.

It was not always so. While child molestation is a crime in every American state (with the age of consent varying from one jurisdiction to another), no federal ban on child pornography existed until 1977, when the Sexual Exploitation of Children Act banned the production, interstate shipment, and advertisement of such items. Seven years later, settling a point of persistent uncertainty, the Child Protection Act of 1984 defined as "children" any person below the age of 18 years. The Child Sexual Abuse and Pornography Act of 1986 tightened bans on production and advertisement of child porn, without regard to interstate operations. The Child Protection and Obscenity Act of 1988 made it illegal to use computers for transmission or advertisement of child pornography; it also criminalized the buying, selling, or otherwise obtaining custody of children for the purpose of producing porn. Interstate or foreign shipment of three or more child porn images by any means (including computers) became a federal crime in November 1990. The Telecommunications Act of 1996 bans use of any interstate or international communications medium to solicit sexual acts from minors. Finally and most controversially, the Child

The logo for "Crimes Against Children," a unit of the FBI that incorporates "Operation Candyman," an operation that broke up a computer-based pornography ring that targeted children. (AP Photo/Kenneth Lambert)

Pornography Prevention Act of 1996 amends definition of the term to include any simulated depiction of children having sex—even if the models are themselves legal adults or the images include only nonexistent "virtual" children. (Artists and civil libertarians continue to battle the latter provision in court.)

Despite the seeming glut of legislation and increasing international cooperation between law enforcement agencies (at least in North America and western Europe), the lucrative trade in "kiddy" porn still thrives. Frustration over inability to capture foreign dealers and producers has prompted certain U.S. agencies—notably the FBI and Customs Service—to initiate covert domestic "sting" operations that sometimes smack of entrapment. In such cases, the agency generates its own advertisements for child pornography, then arrests all those who attempt to purchase the items (generally material confiscated in previous raids). Since some of those arrested have no prior police records, the agencies involved have been accused of "creating crime" to inflate their own lagging arrest and conviction statistics. At the very least, it can be argued that their time and money would be

better spent pursuing producers and vendors of child pornography, rather than soliciting private individuals to break the law by purchasing a magazine or videotape.

And to be sure, there are enough legitimate targets at large to keep any agency busy, without attempting to seduce others. A sampling of recent cases includes:

August 2001 Three members of a Houston, Texas, team that searches for missing children were indicted on federal child pornography charges following an FBI investigation. Defendants Henry Gerdes, Jason Krieg, and Thomas McBarron were all members of the South Texas Advanced Tactical Search and Rescue unit, a missing-person recovery unit for which Krieg served as the official spokesman. Police in Dickinson, Texas, received a tip in July 2001 that the suspects intended to create a child porn Internet site. FBI agents joined the investigation and raided the suspects' homes on August 28, seizing computers, disks, tapes, and two vehicles. All three defendants were charged with sexual exploitation of a child and conspiracy to produce child pornography; Krieg faced an additional charge of sexually assaulting a juvenile. Authorities say the trio taped two teenage boys having sex and that Krieg taped himself having sex with an underage girl. At that, police seemed satisfied that "We got them early on in this project."

November 2001 Ronald C. Kline, a 61-year-old judge of the Orange County (California) Superior Court, surrendered to federal agents at the courthouse on November 9 and was charged with possessing child pornography, his bail set at $50,000. Authorities targeted Judge Kline after receiving tips from a private group that surfs the Internet seeking child-pornography traders. Apparently, an unnamed member of the group hacked into Kline's computer and reported his findings to police. According to Kline's attorney, "The photos were discovered when a HACKER in a remote location infected [Kline's] computer with a VIRUS and made an unauthorized copy of the entire contents of his hard drive." Those contents included child porn images and a private diary in which Kline allegedly confessed his preoccupation with adolescent boys. Trial on the charge was still pending in March 2002, when Judge Kline stood unopposed for reelection in Orange County. Meanwhile, an alleged victim has contacted police, claiming that Kline molested him between 1976 and 1978, when the witness was a child and Kline was a lawyer in private practice.

December 2001 Authorities in Winnipeg, Manitoba, vowed to "leave no stone unturned" in their investigation of what they called the province's "largest and most sadistic Internet child-abuse case" to date. Bryan William Larsen, a 41-year-old computer programmer and member of Manitoba's Crocus Grove Nudist Resort was arrested on December 13, following investigation of what police spokesmen termed a "pedophile ring." The owners of Crocus Grove called the arrest "very disturbing" and "a total shock." Raiders seized 100,000 computer images from the suspect's home, allegedly posted to eight different websites that the defendant operated from his apartment. Also seized were a camera, binoculars, 40 pairs of young girls' panties, and assorted other evidence. The alleged pedophile ring was uncovered through an international law enforcement effort dubbed "Project Snowball," intended to crack down on Internet pornography worldwide. Participants included local Canadian officers, as well as members of the Royal Canadian Mounted Police. Aside from Larsen, Canadian authorities report that Project Snowball has thus far identified 406 suspects in British Columbia, 946 in Ontario, 436 in Quebec, 232 in Alberta, 82 in Manitoba, 61 in Nova Scotia, 52 in Saskatchewan, 35 in New Brunswick, 20 in the Northwest Territories, eight in Newfoundland, six on Prince Edward Island, and four in the sparsely settled Yukon.

January 2002 Responding to an "epidemic" of child pornography—which they dubbed "our hidden crime, our hidden shame"—police in Toronto, Ontario, announced the arrest of three suspects, with 200 more still at large. Suspect Blair Evans, a 51-year-old physicist formerly involved in national defense work, was arrested on January 18, charged with making, possessing, and distributing child pornography. Police raiders confiscated some 200,000 "horrendous" computer images at his home, said to depict the sexual abuse of "tens of thousands of

innocent children, some as young as six months old." At the time of his arrest, Evans was on probation for a 1999 child-porn conviction, involving 6,000 illicit photographs. The arrest in that case, dating from 1996, had cost Evans his government job and prompted his wife to divorce him before he was sentenced to eight months in jail. Toronto authorities declared their city a major hub in the global child-porn trade, noting that the number of cases with international links had nearly doubled—to 500—between 2000 and 2001. "It's not an expansion," said Corporal François Dore of the Ottawa Provincial Police, "it's an explosion."

January 2002 In Vancouver, British Columbia, 67-year-old retired city planner John Robin Sharpe faced trial on two counts of possessing child pornography and two more of possession with intent to distribute. Initially charged in May 1996, when police and customs officials raided his home to seize books and computer disks, Sharpe had challenged Canada's child pornography possession statute before the British Columbia Supreme Court, arguing that the law was too broad and therefore violated free-speech provisions of the Canadian constitution. He won that case in January 1999, with the decision upheld by the B.C. Court of Appeal, but the Supreme Court of Canada reversed that finding and affirmed the statute's constitutionality in January 2001, thus allowing Sharpe's trial to proceed.

March 2002 Patrick Quigley, a 47-year-old former social worker in Charlottesville, Virginia, pleaded guilty to distributing child pornography he downloaded from the Internet. At the time of his arrest, Quigley was an investigator for Child Protective Services.

Supporters of a tough crackdown on child-porn purveyors and their customers note that children injured by the traffic are not only those compelled to perform for the cameras. Increasingly, it appears that some predatory pedophiles draw inspiration from Internet porn, then go on to abuse children themselves, either for personal pleasure or as part of some perverse commercial enterprise. Some cases in point:

June 2001 Rev. William Cabell, a graduate of Yale Divinity School and Princeton Theological Seminary—serving since 1990 as pastor of

Faith United Church of Christ in State College, Pennsylvania—was jailed for crossing state lines to have sex with a minor. The arrest followed a protracted Internet chat-room correspondence with a 14-year-old boy in New Jersey. After eight months of on-line flirtation, Cabell drove to meet his adolescent paramour at a restaurant in Piscataway, New Jersey, and found himself confronted with an undercover FBI agent. Cabell was released on $100,000 bond pending trial, confined to house arrest, and barred from using a computer. Critics of such sting operations denounce law enforcement for translating "harmless" fantasies into criminal action, which might otherwise never occur.

August 2001 Authorities in Nassau County, New York, arrested three suspects—identified as James Warren, Beth Loschin, and Michael Montez—on charges of kidnapping and sexually abusing a 15-year-old girl from Wrentham, Massachusetts. The child disappeared from her home on August 3, allegedly abducted after she struck up a friendship with defendant Warren on the Internet. Warren and Loschin then allegedly held the girl for a week as their sex slave, on Long Island, and "loaned" her to Montez for two days of abuse. They were jailed after the child escaped and telephoned police, directing officers to her kidnappers. Warren faced one count of kidnapping, 10 counts of sodomy, six counts of rape and one count of sexual abuse; Loschin was charged with eight counts of sodomy, six counts of rape and one count of sexual abuse; Montez faced three counts of kidnapping, plus five counts each of rape, sodomy and endangering the welfare of a child. The two male defendants were held without bond, while Loschin was unable to raise her $80,000 bail. Queens prosecutor Richard Brown ranked the crime "among the most despicable cases of sexual assault on a minor that I have seen in my ten years as district attorney. In addition to the utter depravity of this crime and the lasting damage such an ordeal inflicts on a child, the fact that the victim and the Nassau defendants met in an online chat room is terrifying to us all, especially those of us who are parents." Resolution of the case was postponed indefinitely on August 15, 2001, when defendants Warren and Loschin waived their constitutional right to a speedy trial.

August 2001 While the Long Island case was still making national headlines, 43-year-old Darrell Crawford was arrested in Charlestown, Rhode Island, charged with transporting a 16-year-old Rhode Island girl across state lines for purposes of prostitution. FBI agents who captured Crawford say the case may also involve at least three other juvenile victims. According to charges filed against him, Crawford met the victim in July 2001, on a telephone chat-line, and persuaded her to work for him as a prostitute. Running away from home, the girl allegedly met Crawford and a still-unidentified female accomplice, joining them on a trip to Boston, where she serviced an average of five men per night until July 15, earning $100 for intercourse and $50 for oral sex, giving all the money to Crawford. After briefly returning home on July 16, the girl allegedly returned to Boston with Crawford 10 days later, continuing work for the pimp until her mother tracked her down and took the girl to police on August 13, 2001.

How common are such cases? According to a media report published the same month as the Boston and Long Island arrests, 19 percent of underage Internet users surveyed had received unwanted sexual solicitations within the past year; 5 percent received solicitations that frightened or upset them; 3 percent received "aggressive" solicitations involving off-line contact or attempts to stage a personal meeting; 70 percent of those solicited were using home computers at the time; and 49 percent of those solicited kept the fact a secret. In an era when thousands of children run away from home every year, and suspect JOHN ROBINSON, a.k.a. "Slavemaster," faces trial as the first Internet serial killer, on-line predators seem to qualify as a serious and growing threat.

"CHOLERA": computer worm

Identified in September 1999, the "Cholera" computer worm spreads by means of infected e-mail attachments transmitted via the Internet and local networks. It arrives as a file named setup.exe, attached to e-mails with the subject "OK" and a message body containing only a "smiley" face. It derives its name from an encrypted text string in its code reading: CHOLERA—Bacterium BioCoded by GryYo/29A.

Upon initial execution when the infected attachment is opened, Cholera installs itself to the Windows directory, with the filename rpcsrv.exe, writing instructions that force Windows to run the file on its next startup. In the case of a computer with multiple Windows installations, a copy of the virus may be found in each. Cholera conceals its activity by displaying a fake warning dialog box that reads:

Cannot open file: it does not appear to be a valid archive. If you downloaded this file, try downloading the file again.
[OK]

Transmission of the virus to remote computers is accomplished on the next Windows startup, when Cholera takes control, registers itself in Windows memory as a hidden application, and then runs two additional routines. The first spreads Cholera throughout the local network, identifying network drives, scanning them for Windows directories, and repeating the installation routine. The second sends infected e-mails far and wide, employing addresses gleaned from disk files in the victim's Windows directory and subdirectories. Cholera sends 10 messages during each subsequent round of activity.

CHRISTOPHER Mineo Jr. Disappearance:
Internet hoax

Designed as an appeal for help in locating a missing child, this fraudulent e-mail has been in circulation on the Internet since early 2001. Investigation by the U.S. Department of Energy's HOAXBUSTERS website and others indicate that no such person has been reported either missing or abducted from Brooklyn or anywhere else in the United States. The original plea read:

I am asking you all, begging you to please, forward this email on to anyone and everyone you know, PLEASE. I have a 5 year old son named Christopher John Mineo Jr, nickname C.J. I am from Brooklyn N.Y. He has been missing since November of 98. If anyone anywhere knows anything, seen anything, please contact the original screen name that sent this. Which is CMINE00295 @aol.com I am including a picture of him.

All prayers are appreciated!! It only takes 2 seconds to forward this on, if it was your child, you would want all the help you could get.

Please
Christopher John Mineo Sr.

The attached photograph depicts a young boy of Hispanic appearance, true identity unknown. Aside from the total lack of evidence supporting any such incident, further proof of a hoax is found in the fact that the disappearance date was altered to May 11, 2001, in later versions of the e-mail.

COAKLEY, Marion: exonerated by forensic evidence

A native of Beaufort, South Carolina, who later moved to New York City, Marion Coakley was an African-American day laborer with a tested IQ of 70. On the night of October 13, 1983, while Coakley attended a church prayer meeting, one of his neighbors was raped and robbed in her home. The victim subsequently accused Coakley and he was arrested, lab tests allegedly demonstrating that his blood-type matched the rapist's. At trial, jurors ignored Coakley's alibi witnesses and convicted him of rape and robbery, whereupon he received a 15-year prison term.

Two years later, Coakley convinced attorneys Barry Scheck and Peter Neufeld of his innocence, prompting them to launch a renewed investigation of the case. Students from the Cardozo criminal law clinic joined in the project, attempting to arrange for DNA tests, but the court blocked testing on grounds that the "DNA fingerprint" results were still (in 1986) an unproven form of personal identification. Instead, the defense team retested semen samples from the crime scene and proved that Coakley's blood-type did not, after all, match the rapist's. Coakley was released from prison, and the rape remains officially unsolved. Their experience in this case prompted Scheck and Neufeld to found the CARDOZO INNOCENCE PROJECT, which now serves as the last line of defense for wrongfully convicted prisoners in cases where scientific evidence is decisive.

COCA-COLA Giveaway: Internet hoax

Launched on the Internet in February 2000, this fake "sales promotion" is yet another time-wasting hoax, unsanctioned by the company whose name it bears. Computer-savvy readers will recognize the physical impossibility of the process described. The pitch reads:

Coca-Cola is offering four free cases of diet coke or regular coke to every person you send this to. When you have finished sending this e-mail to as many people as you wish, a screen will come up. It will then ask where you want your free coke products sent. This is a sales promotion to get our name out to young people around the world.

We believe this project can be a success, but only with your help. So please start e-mailing and help us build our database. Thank you for your support!

Always Coca-Cola,
Mike Hill
Director of Marketing Coca-Cola Corporation
Atlanta, Georgia
www.cocacola.com

It is unknown how many recipients may have been duped by this fraudulent offer, but any participants in the mythical scheme wait in vain for their free Coca-Cola.

"COCAINE": computer virus

A polymorphic parasitic virus, discovered in July 1999, "Cocaine" has three components. The first attacks Windows executable files; the second infects MicroSoft Word Normal templates; and the third sends out e-mails with infected message attachments. Four months after infection, Cocaine delivers its payload by displaying message boxes with the header "W32/Wm.Cocaine" and text randomly selected from the following seven variants:

Chop your breakfast on a mirror . . .
I will occupy, I will help you die . . .
I will run through you, now I rule you . . .
Master of Puppets, I'm pulling your strings . . .
Taste me you will see, more is all you need . . .
Veins that pump with fear, sucking darkest clear . . .
Your life burns faster, obey your master . . .

Cocaine's first infection routine attacks Microsoft Word, if that program is installed on the host computer. Word's virus warning protection is disabled as Cocaine modifies the system, replacing the original normal.dot template with an infected replicant, importing the main virus code from the c:\cocaine.sys file it installed. From the infected Word template, Cocaine jumps next to Windows. When scanning for Windows executable files to attack, Cocaine avoids antivirus programs and "bait" warning files by

ignoring any file names that contain the letter "V" or any numerals. That accomplished, the virus proceeds to "hook" and infect e-mail access files, in preparation for expanding to the Internet at large.

When sending out e-mails, Cocaine first searches archived messages for attachments to corrupt. If none are found, the virus appends its own infected normal.dot or Windows executable files to the messages and thus perpetuates itself via the Internet. The subject fields for Cocaine-infected e-mails are randomly selected from the following list:

Improvement to your page
Kewl page!
Secret stuff!
You must see this . . .
Your page r0x0r!

Analysts note that Cocaine was the first computer virus to process Windows 2000 addresses, in addition to the more common Windows 95/98 and Windows NT addresses, while searching for access to the kernel32.dll image.

"CODE Red": computer virus

The Code Red (or CodeRed) virus, alternately known as "Bady," was initially unleashed in June 2001, officially described for the first time in a Microsoft security bulletin dated June 18. Named for a caffeinated soft drink favored by some computer programmers, the virus is an Internet worm that replicates between Windows 2000 servers running Microsoft's Internet Information Services (IIS) and the Microsoft Index Server 2.0 or the Windows 2000 Indexing Service. Using a specially crafted code string, the virus overwrites various modules and thus forces systems to access an incorrect address, which reproduces 100 copies of the worm on each infected machine. Ironically, a defect in the virus code produces thousands of copies, rather than the 100 originally intended, thereby wasting huge amounts of memory and slowing server operations to a crawl.

English-language websites attacked by the Code Red virus are defaced by a message reading: "Welcome to http://www.worm.com! Hacked by Chinese!" That message sparked fears of deliberate international sabotage, with the People's Republic of China initially (but wrongly) suspected in a cyberspace version of 19th-century paranoia concerning the so-called Yellow Peril. In order to disprove the allegation, Chinese authorities closed 8,000 cyber-cafés in July 2001, while President Jiang Zemin called for stronger legislation governing use and abuse of the Internet by Chinese citizens. China's crackdown on Internet use by an estimated 26.5 million citizens predictably spawned charges of censorship, as new legislation imposed stricter licensing policies, banned cybercafés in the vicinity of public schools, and mandated installation of software enabling local authorities to monitor websites downloaded on public computers. As for Code Red itself, a spokesman for China's Office of Network Coordination and Information told Reuters on July 30, 2001, that the virus was too sophisticated for the average Chinese HACKER. "I've never heard of anything so powerful in China," the officer declared. "This is not something that an ordinary person has the skill to create." No Code Red cases at all were reported from China, but neighboring South Korea was less fortunate, reporting 13,000 computers infected during late July.

Predictions of a massive Code Red attack on U.S. government computers timed for July 31, 2001, failed to come true, as the day passed without incident. Ronald Dick, director of the U.S. National Infrastructure Protection Center (NIPC) told reporters on that Tuesday afternoon that 4,000 sensors around the globe had failed to detect any upsurge in Code Red activity. The collective sigh of relief was premature, however, as a new form of the virus—labeled Code Red II— was identified "in the wild" on August 4, 2001, spreading much faster than the original worm. Unlike its predecessor, Code Red II attempts to "backdoor" infected systems, creating a hidden path for outsiders to enter and sabotage websites. South Korea, once again hard hit, reported infection of computers at Hyundai Motors, the Ssangyong Group, and other major industrial systems.

Systems vulnerable to the Code Red virus or Code Red II may be "cured" by downloading a Microsoft patch from http://www.microsoft.com/technet/security/bulletin/MS01-033.asp. That site also includes detailed instructions for deleting virus codes from the memory of an infected computer. At this writing, the author(s) of the Code Red virus and its Code Red II successor remain unidentified.

COHEN, Earl: convicted by DNA evidence

A repeat sex offender in Kentucky, born in 1964, Earl Cohen logged his first rape conviction in the late 1980s. Blood samples were secured from Cohen for the state's DNA database. That evidence sent him back to prison for another rape in 2001.

Cohen's second known victim was attacked in Louisville, in April 2001. Forensic evidence from the backseat of the victim's car was compared against samples on file. Cohen was duly arrested and convicted by a jury on October 21, 2001.

"COLOMBIA": computer virus

Classified by analysts as a dangerous "stealth" macro virus, Colombia was discovered in the wild during April 1999. It infects the global macros of a targeted computer when an infected document is opened, then spreads to other documents when they are created, opened, or closed by the host's user. Colombia turns off the Word virus protection system and also disables the Tools/Macros and View/Toolbars menus.

"Stealth" notwithstanding, the virus reveals itself on arrival by trying to format any floppy disk in the computer's A drive and printing out "Linea <counter number> Esquema a" to the status bar. If the counter exceeds 99, Colombia automatically deletes all data on the C drive by executing the command format.com in a hidden DOS window. As each newly infected document is closed, the following message is displayed:

Publicidad para Colombia!!
COLOMBIA
Salvado por Colombia
Se salv el Diskette

COLUMBIA House Giveaway: Internet hoax

Launched on the Internet in November 1999, this chain letter pretends to issue from the music distributor Columbia House. A giveaway to the e-mail's bogus nature is the inclusion of a website other than that of the actual company itself—and perhaps the name of its alleged author. The original reads:

Hi. My name is Richard Douche. I am the president of Cyber Productions for Columbia House. We are in a fierce competition with companies such as Amazon.com and Music Blvd, among many others. Because of this, I have been authorized to offer 10+ free cd's of your choice to any person who participates in our promotion. We at Columbia House understand that your time is very important to you, and that you don't want to have to fill out a form and mail it in to us. With this in mind, we have developed a simplistic way for anyone who receives this email to participate. All you have to do is send this message to your friends! Yes, it is that simple. Now you are wondering how many CDs you get, and how to get them. It all depends on how many people you send this message to. You are required to send this email to the address below to receive your first 10 CDs. Cyberpromotions@n2music.com In addition, you get another CD for every person you forward this to. For example, if you send this to Cyber Promotions, along with 10 of your friends, you would receive a total of 20 CDs. Remember to sent this to Cyber Promotions or you WON'T RECEIVE YOUR CDS!! We will email you back promptly asking for your CD selections. Again, thank you for your participation!!

Richard Douche
President, Cyber Promotions

"COOL Video" Promotion: Internet hoax

As with most Internet hoaxes, this e-mail, posted for the first time in May 1999, offers a reward of sorts for dispersing copies of the original message. In this case, it is fair to say that the laugh is on those duped into playing the game. The message reads (with errors uncorrected):

OK here's the deal, this works. I don't know how . . . but it works, you have to send it (this) to no less than 11 people. Some how, from the return path generated, you'll receive . . . something, and it is funny!!!!

This is the coolest thing I've ever gotten! All you have to do is send it to 11 people and this little video comes up on your screen and shows the funniest clip. i can't tell you what it is but i was laughing so hard! So spend a few seconds to send this and you'll be glad you did! thanks!

"COOL Worm": computer worm virus

Initially reported in February 2002, the "Cool Worm"—also known as "Menger" and "JS Exploit-Messenger"—is a computer worm virus spread via the MSN Messenger instant messaging (IM) service. While not judged particularly dangerous in itself, it was viewed by analysts as a possible precursor to more destructive worms designed to attack and spread through IM systems on the Internet. As in the case of many other worms and viruses, "Cool Worm" replicates and sends itself to targets found on an infected system's address list, but it appears to have no other function and no destructive payload.

"Cool Worm" exploits a vulnerability in MSN Messenger that was recognized in December 2001, for which Microsoft created a patch in early February 2002. "Cool Worm," meanwhile, had been able to capitalize on the weakness, prompting widespread criticism of the delay between problem recognition and remediation. Analysts warn that any Internet messenger service is a natural target for HACKERS and virus writers, facilitating rapid spread of new viruses across the country and around the world.

COTTON, Ronald: exonerated by DNA evidence

In July 1984, two female residents of Burlington, North Carolina, were attacked in separate incidents by a serial rapist who invaded their apartments, cut telephone lines, and afterward looted their homes of cash and other valuables. Suspect Ronald Cotton was arrested on August 1, 1984, after one victim identified his photograph, then picked him from a police lineup. Charged with one of the rapes, Cotton was tried in January 1985. Prosecutors noted that a flashlight found in his home "resembled" one carried by the rapist, and that rubber from his tennis shoes was "consistent" with evidence found at the crime scene. Jurors convicted him on one count each of rape and burglary.

North Carolina's Supreme Court overturned that conviction on appeal, because the trial judge had excluded testimony that the rapist's second victim had selected a different suspect from a police lineup. Prior to Cotton's second trial, the alternative suspect—already imprisoned for similar crimes—admitted to a cellmate that he was guilty of the Burlington attacks. Cotton's new trial judge refused to admit the convict's statement into evidence, and Cotton was convicted again—of both rapes, this time—in November 1987. Cotton received a sentence of life for the rapes, plus 54 years on two counts of burglary. The verdict was affirmed on appeal in 1988.

New lawyers took over Cotton's case six years later, filing a motion for DNA testing that was granted in October 1994. Semen samples from one victim had deteriorated beyond the point of testing, but samples from the second excluded Ronald Cotton as a suspect in May 1995, while matching samples from the imprisoned alternative suspect found in the State

Bureau of Investigation's DNA database. Cotton was released from prison on June 30, 1995, and pardoned by the governor in July. The pardon made him eligible for $5,000 in state compensation, based on a 1948 statute granting $500 for each year of wrongful incarceration up to a maximum of 10 years. His attorneys thus far have been unsuccessful in their efforts to secure passage of new legislation granting increased compensation.

CRACKER Barrel Giveaway: Internet hoax

Reported for the first time in November 2000, this on-line hoax pretends to be a sales promotion for the Cracker Barrel chain stores, but in fact has no connection to that company. Such items have become so abundant on the Internet that the U.S. Department of Energy's HOAXBUSTERS website was moved to speculate "if these are actually hoaxes or are the latest advertising gimmick." In either case, no such giveaway program has been acknowledged or sanctioned by Cracker Barrel. The hoax message reads:

My name is Junior Johnson, founder of Cracker Barrel. In an attempt to get out name out to more people in the rural communities where we are not currently located, we are offering a $50 gift certificate to anyone who forwards this email to 9 of their friends. Just send this email to them and you will receive an email back with a confirmation number to claim your gift certificate.

Sincerely,
Junior Johnson
Founder of Cracker Barrel

Hey guys,
DON'T DELETE THIS EMAIL
It really works, I tried it and got my Gift certificate confirmation number in 3 minutes.

The anonymous postscript notwithstanding, no such gift certificates are offered for this scheme. As with similar hoaxes, the mechanism by which Cracker Barrel might confirm the dispersal of e-mails remains unexplained.

CREDIT Card Fraud

In the "old days"—that is, prior to the late 1980s and the advent of Internet "e-commerce"—credit card swindlers were required to steal cards them-

selves, or else buy stolen cards from a motley collection of pickpockets, muggers, purse-snatchers, and burglars. Next, in order to use a stolen card, the swindler or an accomplice was required to physically present the card for purchase of merchandise, risking arrest if its theft had been reported to police or credit agencies. Today, technology has minimized those risks and made the process simpler for prospective thieves. Indeed, cyberbandits no longer need to see a credit card, much less steal it, before they launch illicit spending sprees.

Credit (and debit) card fraud is huge business in modern America. Visa Corporation reported a $490 million loss from such crimes in 1997, while reporting that the rate of fraud had dropped from previous years. Gregory Regan, special agent in charge of the U.S. Secret Service's financial crimes division, calls credit card fraud "the bank robbery of the future." Unlike Jesse James and John Dillinger, however, modern credit card thieves utilize high technology to execute their crimes from a safe distance—sometimes the far side of the world.

A wide range of devices presently in use permits cyberthieves—dubbed "carders"—to steal numbers from credit cards and users they have never seen. HACKERS penetrate Internet databases to download credit card information on customers by the thousands, while others spy on Internet orders and lift the numbers in transit from nonsecure websites. Electronic devices attached to telephone lines can record and translate credit card numbers transmitted via tones from touch-tone phones. At the relatively crude end of the scale, "skimmers" planted in various commercial enterprises (restaurants, department stores, gas stations, etc.) use electronic scanners to record coded data from the magnetic strips of credit cards used for legitimate purchases. Once the credit card number and expiration date are recorded, the data may be sold, traded, or simply used by individual thieves to order merchandise on-line, without ever presenting the card itself for examination. If all else fails, software available on-line permits carders to use algorithms employed by various credit companies to manufacture counterfeit cards in the name of fictitious customers.

Computer technology also facilitates mass transactions involving thousands of credit card numbers in a single deal. Where old-fashioned thieves would have required a suitcase to carry 100,000 stolen credit cards, the same number of stolen or counterfeit numbers may be swiftly transmitted via e-mail, or stored for future use on compact disks. "Virgin" numbers—i.e., those not previously used in fraudulent transactions, may demand a higher price. CARLOS FELIPE SALGADO JR., a carder arrested in May 1997, pleaded guilty to multiple felony counts after attempting to sell a CD-ROM with 100,000 stolen credit card numbers to an undercover FBI agent. At that, he might have escaped law enforcement's attention—as many others do—if he had resisted the urge to boast of his ongoing scam in various Internet chat rooms, confessing to strangers that he had sold hundreds of credit card numbers for five dollars apiece.

Federal law in the United States limits consumer liability to $50 in the case of fraudulent credit card transactions, but the rules are different for *debit* cards, which allow direct withdrawals from a customer's personal checking account. The $50 stop-loss rule applies to debit cards only if customers report a card's loss within two business days of realizing it is gone. After that, the customer's liability increases to $500 for the next 60 days. Any customer failing to report bogus debits beyond 60 days from the date a card was lost or stolen faces potential bankruptcy, as he or she may lose the full contents of the checking account, plus any overdraft line of credit in place to prevent checks from bouncing. By the time a careless customer notices the illicit withdrawals—particularly if they come in small, irregular amounts—it may already be too late. Thus far, only California has passed legislation imposing a statutory $50 cap on consumer liability for debit card fraud.

Telephone calling card numbers are stolen in the same manner as credit and debit card numbers, by means ranging from high technology to time-honored "shoulder surfing" (peering over a caller's

The Internet has made credit card fraud much simpler for prospective thieves, allowing them to commit their crimes from a safe distance.

shoulder as he or she dials in the number). Unlike "phreaks" who use BLUE BOXES and other devices to cheat telephone companies, card thieves bill their calls to real-life customers—again, with the risk that brief calls to "normal" numbers (as opposed to hours-long chats with a friend in Moscow or Sri Lanka) may go unnoticed for months on end.

The best form of security against credit or debit card fraud is personal attention to bank statements and monthly billings. Some credit card companies routinely alert their customers if charges are made from an unusual location or using a long-dormant card, but most accept charges as genuine unless a customer complains.

CRINER, Roy Wayne: exonerated by DNA evidence

On September 27, 1986, 16-year-old Deanna Ogg was raped, then beaten and stabbed to death in Montgomery County, Texas. Police initially described the missing murder weapon as a tire tool, but the implement was never found. An informer's statement led detectives to Roy Criner, a 21-year-old logger from New Caney. Murder charges were filed, then dismissed in the absence of a weapon, leaving Criner to face a lesser charge of aggravated sexual assault.

At trial in 1990, three witnesses claimed Criner had boasted of raping a hitchhiker whom he threatened with a screwdriver. Police now changed their description of the murder weapon, deeming Ogg's wounds "consistent with" a screwdriver—but no blood was found on a screwdriver confiscated from Criner's pickup truck in 1986. Tire tracks from the crime scene failed to match Criner's vehicle, and a pubic hair found on Ogg's body matched neither the victim nor Criner. Still, jurors were convinced by testimony that Criner's blood type matched semen samples lifted from Ogg's corpse. Upon conviction, Criner received a 99-year prison sentence.

DNA testing, performed by a private laboratory in 1997, determined that Criner was not the source of semen found on Ogg's body in 1986. Montgomery County prosecutors requested a second test by the Texas Department of Public Safety's crime lab and obtained the same result. District Judge Michael Mayes sent Criner's case to the Texas Court of Criminal Appeals with recommendations for a new trial, but appellate judge Sharon Keller rejected the motion in May 1998, ruling that "overwhelming direct evidence" proved Criner's guilt. Keller cited no such evidence to support her judgment, but suggested that

Roy Criner, left, embraces his father after his release from the Montgomery County jail in Conroe, Texas. After he had spent a decade behind bars, his conviction was debunked by DNA evidence. He was released in advance of an expected pardon by then-governor George W. Bush. (AP)

the semen evidence was meaningless, since Criner might have worn a condom and Ogg was "known to be promiscuous," presumably engaging in sex with several partners each day.

That strange decision touched off a firestorm of media criticism, spearheaded by the *Houston Press*. Another DNA test was performed in 2001, on saliva recovered from a cigarette butt at the crime scene. (Criner was a nonsmoker.) DNA from the saliva matched the semen found on Ogg's corpse, thereby eliminating any theory of consensual sex at some earlier time. Montgomery County District Attorney Mike McDougal recommended clemency to the Texas Board of Pardons and Paroles on July 28, 2001. The 18-member board voted unanimously to approve the petition, and Governor George Bush announced his intent to pardon Criner on August 14, 2001. As for Ogg's murderer, her brother James suggested to reporters, "They ought to pull in everybody [who knew Deanna] and say, 'DNA test on everyone.' They will find the person." To date, no such effort has been undertaken in Montgomery County and the case remains unsolved.

CRUZ, Rolando: exonerated by DNA evidence

Sometime after 1:00 P.M. on February 25, 1983, 10-year-old Jeanine Nicario was kidnapped from her home in Naperville, Illinois. Authorities found her two days later, raped and bludgeoned to death in a wooded area of DuPage County, four miles from her home. On May 8, 1983, 19-year-old Rolando Cruz approached homicide detectives to report alleged "dream visions" of the murder, thereby presenting himself as a suspect. Cruz later claimed his statements— which incriminated two acquaintances— were motivated by a $10,000 reward offered for information on the case. The plan backfired on March 8, 1984, when he was arrested along with 21-year-old Stephen Buckley and 20-year-old Alejandro Hernandez. Held in lieu of $3 million bond, each of the trio faced 12 charges, including multiple counts of murder, rape, deviate sexual assault, aggravated liberties with a child, aggravated kidnapping, home invasion, and residential burglary.

Detective John Sam resigned from the DuPage County Sheriff's Department in December 1984, voicing doubts about the three defendants' guilt, but his superiors remained confident. Prosecutors illegally withheld Cruz's "dream vision" statement from defense attorneys, but introduced it as evidence at trial, in January 1985. Several witnesses were called to testify that Cruz and Hernandez had admitted intimate knowledge of the crime, while defense attorneys failed to pursue their alibis. Jurors convicted Cruz and Hernandez on February 22, 1985, but failed to reach a verdict on Buckley. On March 15, 1985, Judge Edward Koval sentenced Cruz and Hernandez to die.

Authorities were surprised on November 8, 1985 when confessed serial killer Brian Dugan, already charged in two other Illinois murders, admitted killing Jeanine Nicario himself, without accomplices. Eleven days later, Dugan received two consecutive life sentences for the slayings of a seven-year-old girl and a 27-year-old nurse. On March 28, 1986, the *Chicago Lawyer* published an article claiming that DuPage County authorities believed Dugan guilty of Nicario's murder, but the state attorney's office denied the report, calling Dugan's confession a hoax. Judge Robert Nolan, presiding over Stephen Buckley's retrial, officially ruled

Dugan's story fictitious and inadmissible on September 5, 1986—but prosecutors dismissed all charges against Buckley six months later, releasing him on March 5, 1987.

On January 19, 1988, the Illinois Supreme Court overturned the convictions of Cruz and Hernandez, ordering new and separate trials for the pair. On September 2, 1989, over prosecution objections, Judge Edward Koval ruled the Dugan confessions admissible at retrials of Cruz and Hernandez, but it made no difference. Cruz was convicted a second time, on February 1, 1990, and again sentenced to death. Jurors failed to reach a verdict on Hernandez in May 1990, but his third trial resulted in conviction on May 11, 1991. Instead of death, this time Judge John Nelligan sentenced Hernandez to 80 years for murder, 20 years for kidnapping and 12 years for residential burglary, making the terms concurrent.

The Illinois Supreme Court upheld Cruz's second conviction on December 4, 1992, then reversed itself and ordered a new trial on July 14, 1994, finding that the second trial court made errors in the admission and exclusion of evidence. An appellate court granted Hernandez a new trial on January 30, 1995, citing jury misconduct and Judge Nelligan's failure to disclose the problem. New evidence was revealed on September 24, 1995, when results from a DNA test excluded Rolando Cruz as Jeanine Nicario's rapist. The same test found that Brian Dugan "shared DNA traits" with semen samples from the prosecution's rape kit. Cruz was acquitted on November 3, 1995, after police lieutenant James Montesano recanted his prior testimony and admitted lying under oath about Cruz's "dream vision" statement. Charges against Hernandez were dropped on November 17, 1995, while a special prosecutor was appointed to investigate official misconduct in the case.

DuPage County Sheriff Richard Doria announced in June 1996 that an internal investigation revealed no evidence of perjury by any of his officers, Lt. Montesano's sworn admission notwithstanding. A grand jury was convened to study the case, and in December 1996 it returned a 47-count indictment against Montesano and three other detectives, along with three former prosecutors. The so-called "DuPage Seven" were acquitted on all counts in 1999, prompting critics to describe the verdict as a "whitewash." The Nicario murder remains officially unsolved today.

CULT of the Dead Cow: hacker syndicate

Reportedly organized in 1984 and based at Lubbock, Texas, the HACKER syndicate known as the Cult of the Dead Cow (cDc) describes itself as "a leading developer of Internet privacy and security tools" whose goal is "to create and promote technologies that provide ordinary computer users with comprehensive online privacy solutions." Furthermore, its stated mission "is to eliminate the abuse of Internet privacy that is rampant in the United States and throughout the world." Critics argue that such noble-sounding aims are simply a cover for old-fashioned hacking, and they support their claim by noting the cDc's 1998 release of a program dubbed "BackOrifice," which seemed to place invasive "Trojan" technology within the grasp of relatively unskilled Internet users, permitting stealthy invasion of systems running Windows 95 or Windows 98 technology.

The "cult," meanwhile, pleads innocence of any sinister design. In November 2000, responding to exposure of the FBI's Web-surfing Carnivore software, the cDc offered "a helping hand in America's time of need," announcing "an ongoing effort to create and deploy best-of-breed electronic surveillance software." Hacker "Oxblood Ruffin," self-described "foreign minister" of the cDc, declared in an Internet posting: "This will be better than other available tools. We wish to provide infrastructure as part of a successful, multi-layered pyramidal cybercrime strategy. Our system will provide information to help federal prosecutors determine their legal strategy before anyone is tried or even indicted."

Satire or simple foolishness? A partial answer may lie in yet another cDc communiqué, wherein the group "declared war" on the Church of Scientology. That broadside read in part:

We believe that El Ron Hubbard is actually none other than Heinrich Himmler of the SS, who fled to Argentina and is now responsible for the stealing of babies from hospitals and raising them as "super-soldiers" for the purpose of overthrowing the U.S. Fed. Govt. in a bloody revolution. We fear plans for a "Fourth Reich" to be established on our home soil under the vise-like grip of oppression known as Scientology!

Such antics aside, no identified members of the cDc have been prosecuted to date. Associates of the group, while never publicly named, appear on its website with such screen names as "Suicidal Amoeba," "Drunkfux," "The Nightstalker," "Deth Vegetable," "DilDog," and "Myles Long."

CYBERANGELS: volunteer opponents of Internet harassment

Organized by Curtis Sliwa's Guardian Angels in 1995, as a private remedy to the modern epidemic of CYBERSTALKING and Internet harassment, Cyberangels is a nonprofit group staffed entirely by volunteers, including some 9,000 members in 74 nations. The organization's website receives an average of 500 to 600 daily complaints involving on-line threats, malicious rumors, and other forms of harassment. About 20 percent of those incidents involve students, ranging from elementary school to the university level, with complaints including reference to racial slurs, individual death threats, and "hit lists" mimicking the Columbine High School massacre of April 1999.

In its first three years of operation, Cyberangels received excellence awards from various on-line organizations including The Widow's Web, the Family Friendly Site, the Crete (Illinois) Police Department, Cops Online, Skylight Productions (Award for Peace, 1997), Saving Our Children-United Mothers, the Oregon State Police, and WHOA! (Women Halting Online Abuse). At the same time, however, the group was criticized by *Wired* magazine for its "gung-ho moralism" and alleged use of illegal search-and-seizure methods, including banned downloading and trading in CHILD PORNOGRAPHY to entrap suspected pedophiles.

That picture changed in late 1998, when New Jersey attorney Parry Aftab took over as the volunteer executive director for Cyberangels, giving the outfit a major face-lift. Aftab described the change for *Wired News* in March 2000: "Even their logo was dark and undercover, these eyes staring out at you and funny-looking wings. Now we're all angels and hugs. Of course, meanwhile, we're doing undercover work with Customs to catch child pornographers." FBI spokesmen describe Aftab's revamped Cyberangels as "an invaluable resource to law enforcement," instrumental in the arrest and conviction of "at least three child predators" by early 2000.

Cyberangels volunteers do not confine their efforts to on-line pedophiles, however. Most of the complaints received involve cyberstalking in the form of threats or rumors posted by minors and targeting classmates. Cyberangels specialized in stripping Internet stalkers of their treasured anonymity, exposing their real-world identities to victims, school administrators—and to law enforcement agencies in areas where Internet harassment is a criminal offense. Director Aftab describes cyberstalking as "really a stupid thing to do." For the record, Aftab notes, "People who do this all think they're anonymous and they're wrong. Everybody is traceable online."

Threats of schoolyard violence in America are taken seriously, Aftab notes: "You have to treat every threat as real and pass it on to law enforcement." In an age when even joking about weapons may produce suspension or expulsion from public schools, Internet "jokers" of dubious taste are advised to think twice before testing their right to free speech in cyberspace. A collateral Cyberangels program, dubbed Teen Angels, enlists local teenage volunteers to counsel their peers on the dangers of posting threats and rumors on-line.

On March 29, 2000, Cyberangels joined the United Nations Educational, Scientific, and Cultural Organization (UNESCO) in hosting a Kids International Summit at the New York City Police Museum. The all-day event launched "Wired Kids," the official website of UNESCO's North American "Innocence in Danger" program, educating children and their parents to some of the dangers found lurking on-line. Cyberangels may be accessed for further information or to file complaints at http://www.cyberangels.org/stalking/.

CYBERCRIME: computer-related crime and punishment

Rapid advances in computers since the 1980s, coupled with the advent of the Internet, have created new frontiers for lawbreakers and law enforcement alike. Computer-related or -assisted crimes vary widely, from personal intimidation and petty vandalism to multimillion-dollar thefts affecting giant corporations and espionage on a global scale. Even murder, the ultimate crime, may be facilitated by the World Wide Web—as demonstrated in 2001 by the case of JOHN EDWARD ROBINSON, a.k.a. "Slavemaster," billed in media reports as the first Internet serial killer.

Computer crime is not a new phenomenon, by any means. The first record of a computer-related crime dates from 1958, and 374 cases of "computer abuse" were logged by 1976 (including four instances of frustrated owners shooting their own computers, two "fatally"). The first federal prosecution of a computer crime occurred in 1966. Today, law enforcement agencies and civilian watchdog groups in the U.S. alone receive yearly complaints numbering in the tens of thousands. Cybercrimes evolve as rapidly as new technology, spurred on by the dark side of the human imagination, but a representative sampling would include the following offenses:

Hacking Whether performed by bored, precocious teenage "nerds" or sophisticated gangs akin to organized crime, the illicit penetration of corporate or government computer systems by unauthorized outsiders today is viewed as a significant threat to national and global communications infrastructures. "Idealistic" hackers deny any interest in monetary gain and insist their penetrations are designed to preserve "freedom of information," but purely mercenary hackers—sometimes dubbed *crackers* to emphasize their criminal motives—dedicate themselves to large-scale theft of cash, confidential information, and the like. Another problem area, described by computer aficionados as "darkside hacking," involves deliberate cybervandalism by such perpetrators as the "LEGION OF DOOM" and its rivals from the "MASTERS OF DECEPTION."

Theft of cash In 1994 a Russian hacker named VLADIMIR LEVIN stole more than $10 million from Citibank Corporation without ever setting foot in the United States. Internet transfers of cash and securities between banks and other financial institutions are routine today, subject to interference and diversion by cyberbandits who invade corporate systems, steal passwords and bank account numbers, and divert huge sums to accounts under their own control. Techniques such as "lapping" (employee diversion of incoming cash to a bogus account) and "kiting" (use of normal delays in processing financial transactions to create the appearance of assets where none exist) victimize financial institutions from within. Another form of internal theft, nicknamed "salami slicing," occurs when employees shave small sums from numerous sources (as in the case of a computer operator for a New York garment-making firm, who stole two cents from the federal income tax withheld on each coworker's weekly paycheck). Automatic teller machines (ATMs), meanwhile, lose an estimated $200 million per year to various frauds. At the same time, Internet CREDIT CARD FRAUD, involving theft or counterfeiting of credit and debit card numbers by the hundreds of thousands, levies a staggering toll against various financial institutions. The problem's gravity may be judged by Visa Corporation's report for 1997, listing losses of $490 million as an improvement over previous years.

"Phreaking" Akin to hackers, both in spirit and technique, "phreakers" are those who employ various devices (such as the classic "BLUE BOX") to cheat telephone companies on long-distance calls. Once again, some "purists" profess to regard their efforts as a blow for freedom of communication, while others unapologetically turn a profit on sale of charge-evasion devices and stolen calling numbers. Precise figures for losses from telephone fraud are unavailable, but industry spokespersons suggest that long-distance fraud costs the industry between $4 billion and $8 billion yearly; all forms of telecommunications fraud combined may top $15 billion per year, with wireless fraud alone exceeding $1 billion.

"Data diddling" Employed in a variety of settings, this technique involves manipulation or falsification of computer data for personal profit or other illegal motives. One case, reported in 1997, involved crackers who penetrated the computers of maritime insurance companies, inserting registration data for non-existent ships and purchasing large insurance policies on the mythical vessels, then "sinking" them to collect the payoffs.

Extortion and/or blackmail As before the invention of computers and the Internet, these crimes involve coercion of tribute payments to prevent some threatened action by the extortionist or blackmailer. As early 20th-century racketeers sold "protection" (from themselves) to frightened neighborhood merchants, so cyberthugs victimize individuals or corporations via e-mail and the World Wide Web. On June 2, 1996, the *Times* (London) reported that various banks and investment firms in the U.S. and Britain had "secretly paid ransom to prevent costly computer meltdown and a collapse in confidence among the customers." None of the threats—said to emanate from cyberterrorists in America and Russia—or the payoffs (up to £13 million per incident) had been reported to

authorities. Florida resident MICHAEL PITELIS was arrested in August 2000 for attempting to extort $1 million from a Massachusetts corporation, threatening to expose software secrets. The same month, Kazakhstan native OLEG ZEZOV was charged with blackmailing the Bloomberg financial news company for $200,000. In May 2001 Russian operator Alexei Ivanov (see VASILY GORSHKOV) faced charges of victimizing firms across the U.S. with similar threats.

Bootlegging and piracy Lumped together by U.S. prosecutors as "intellectual property theft," these offenses include any unauthorized duplication and/or distribution of copyrighted material. The items most often bootlegged include computer software, motion pictures, and music, but any material covered by U.S. or international copyrights and patents is likewise subject to misappropriation. Profit motives were once considered essential for prosecution of such cases, but enactment of the No Electronic Theft (NET) Act on December 16, 1997, criminalized software piracy and other forms of bootlegging whether the items were sold or given away as a "public service."

Malicious programming Since the 1980s, thousands of computer VIRUSES and worms have been unleashed upon the Internet by programmers around the world. Some are benign, with no more impact on their host computers than a brief, amusing video display, while others—like "MELISSA" and the "CODE RED" virus—cause global damage to corporate and personal computers estimated in the billions of dollars. Certain nations seem to spawn a disproportionate number of virus writers—160 separate viruses were traced to Bulgaria alone between 1989 and 1993—but no part of the world is presently immune. Almost as numerous are hoaxes, circulated on the Web by pranksters with too much free time on their hands. While most malicious programs are broadcast at random, often in the form of infected e-mail attachments, some are written with more specific targets in mind. Corporate victims fall prey most often to disgruntled past or present employees, while government computer systems may be targeted by foreign agents or domestic activists. "Logic bombs"—destructive codes that lie dormant within a computer until triggered by a specific signal—have been found within the systems of several U.S. agencies. (At that, federal spokesmen estimate that they detect no more than 10 percent of all attempted intrusions per year.)

Espionage Whether corporate or political, spying has been facilitated by the Internet. In 1986, a systems administrator at the Lawrence Berkeley Laboratory in California discovered that crackers from "Chaos," a West German group, had hijacked the computer account of a former employee and used it to steal U.S. military data for sale to the Soviet KGB intelligence agency. Three members of "Chaos" were indicted on espionage charges, while a fourth died mysteriously. The survivors were convicted at trial in 1990, receiving prison terms of 20 months to five years, with fines totaling $9,000. Eight years later, a group calling itself the "Masters of Downloading/2016216" claimed to have cracked the Pentagon's communications system, stealing software for a military satellite system and threatening its sale to terrorists, but the threat was never realized. Worldwide, various corporations are constantly on guard against attempts to penetrate computer systems and steal financial records, lists of customers, proprietary software, or other valuable secrets.

Cyberstalking Most of the crimes discussed so far are financially or politically motivated, targeting government or commercial institutions, but cyberstalking is uniquely personal. As malicious individuals in daily life stalk celebrities, family members, ex-lovers, and former friends, harassing their targets with phone calls and letters or worse, so their counterparts in cyberspace spew venom on-line. E-MAIL BOMBING is one common harassment technique, the target inundated with hundreds or thousands of unwanted messages, sometimes including personal threats. Other forms of cyberstalking may include posting of personal data or photos at large on the Web (as in the Wanted posters utilized by some ANTIABORTION GROUPS to intimidate physicians) or hacking of personal computers with malicious intent. CYBERANGELS, a civilian volunteer group committed to opposing on-line stalkers, reports an average of 650 complaints per day on its website year-round.

Child pornography and solicitation While child molestation is a crime in every U.S. jurisdiction, no federal law banned production or sale of child pornography prior to 1977, with "children" legally defined in 1984 as any person below the age of 18 years. Further U.S. legislation has since been enacted to ban advertisement of child pornography (1986); use of computers to transmit, sell, or receive child pornography (1988); possession of three or more images depicting sex with children (1990); inducement of minors to participate in child pornography (1996); and possession of any image that *appears* to depict sex with children, even when the models are adults "morphed" with computer graphics to resemble children or where "virtual children" are depicted without use of live models (1996). The latter provision is especially controversial facing determined legal attacks from artists and civil libertarians who maintain that nonexistent children have no rights and cannot suffer harm. To date, despite prosecution of some notorious defendants—including teachers, ministers, judges, and other public officials—legislation seems largely ineffective at curbing child pornography, particularly that which is produced outside the United States.

"Mousetrapping" Designed to create a literal captive audience for otherwise unwelcome advertising, "mousetrapping" involves the creation of alluring websites with built-in snares that prevent on-line visitors from escaping once they log on to the site. While any type of advertisement may be used in mousetrapping, the more objectionable forms—especially on sites that lure minors with promised images of rock stars or other celebrities—are those for gambling, lotteries, pornography and psychics. The undisputed king of American mousetrapping, Pennsylvania operator JOHN ZUCCARINI, has reportedly earned millions from his many websites, while logging more than 60 lawsuits from the Federal Trade Commission. Visitors to Zuccarini's websites (and their many copycats) are unable to escape by any normal combination of keystrokes, bombarded meanwhile by a rapid-fire barrage of advertisements displayed as individual "windows."

Identity theft This offense differs from simple credit card theft in both its scope and potential damage to the victim. Felons who obtain sufficient personal data about an intended target, whether from on-line sources or primitive "dumpster diving," are often able to create their own persona with someone else's name, Social Security number, and other vital information. While certain bizarre cases of celebrity impersonators rank among the most notorious incidents of identity theft—a West Indian immigrant spent years posing as the son of comedian Bill Cosby—middle-class victims suffer the greatest damage. In one egregious case, the ex-convict impostor ran up more than $100,000 in credit card debts, obtained a federal home loan, and purchased high-ticket items ranging from guns and motorcycles to houses before filing bankruptcy, all in his victim's name. The offender also tormented his victim with mocking telephone calls, immune from federal prosecution since no statute then penalized identity theft. The victim and his wife spent more than $15,000 to restore their credit and good names, while the thief escaped with a brief jail term (for giving a false name when purchasing a firearm) and paid no restitution. The case, and others like it, inspired Congress to pass new legislation on identity theft in 1998.

Internet fraud These crimes occur so frequently and evolve so rapidly that no detailed accounting is feasible, but certain broad categories are worthy of note. *On-line auctions* generate more fraud complaints than any other Internet activity, most commonly when buyers bid on some valuable piece of merchandise and receive a counterfeit item or nothing at all. (Losing bidders are also sometimes approached to buy "surplus" items that never arrive.) Shills are also frequently employed to create a false impression of interest in some item and artificially inflate its price. *Retail fraud* involves the same basic scams, including nondelivery or bait-and-switch techniques. *Business opportunity fraud* advertises spurious "work at home" schemes, generating millions of "spam" e-mail messages daily, bilking thousands of gullible respondents for wasted "processing fees." *Money laundering,* while not a fraud upon the average consumer, uses financial institutions (and sometimes charities) to "wash" vast sums including profits from organized crime and forbidden political contributions. *Investment fraud* includes manipulation of securities via the "pump-and-dump" technique (inflating the

prices of worthless stocks before they are sold) and "cybersmear" campaigns that deflate stock prices by attacking a company's reputation. In extreme cases, such activities not only defraud traders and damage individual companies, but may also affect the stock market as a whole. Cyberfraud allegations are heard by the Internet Fraud Complaint Center, a joint operation of the FBI and the Justice Department's National White Collar Crime Center (NW3C).

Because all law enforcement is reactive, the U.S. federal response to cybercrime has naturally lagged behind illicit innovations in the field. Today, most cases are handled by the Justice Department's Computer Crime and Intellectual Property Section (CCIPS), consisting of some two dozen U.S. attorneys who concentrate solely on cybercrime issues. Founded in 1991 as the Computer Crime Unit, elevated to "section" status five years later, CCIPS employs prosecutors with expertise in such diverse subjects areas as encryption, electronic privacy laws, copyrights, e-commerce and hacking. Addressing the U.S. Senate on February 16, 2000, Attorney General Janet Reno called CCIPS "the cornerstone of our prosecutor cybercrime program. Current CCIPS responsibilities include:

Litigating cases This involves not only prosecuting felons charged with violation of relevant federal statutes, but also filing lawsuits against corporations and organizations deemed liable to civil penalties under prevailing federal law. Those penalties may include fines, reimbursement of parties damaged by some illegal action, and injunctions barring further proscribed activities.

Training CCIPS spearheads efforts to train local, state, and federal agents or prosecutors in the legal aspects of combating cybercrime. It does not provide technical training in use of computers or other high-tech devices, however, although such courses are offered to agents in training at the FBI Academy.

International liaison Confronted with the global Internet, CCIPS cannot afford a parochial approach to crime-fighting. Its leaders chair the G-8 Subgroup on High-tech Crime, which maintains a round-the-clock contact point for mutual assistance of investigators fighting cybercrime in 15 collaborating nations. CCIPS also plays a leading role in the Council of Europe Experts' Committee on Cybercrime and participates in a similar unit for the Organization of American States in Latin America. On November 23, 2001, in Budapest, the U.S. and 29 other nations signed the Council of Europe Cybercrime Convention, drafted over a four-year period to facilitate international cooperation among diverse law enforcement agencies.

Policy and legislation　While it does not have the final word, CCIPS is tasked with proposing federal policy and legislation in the field of cybercrime, accommodating needs of the private sector where possible, and closing loopholes in extant legislation, to prevent today's felons from avoiding prosecution tomorrow.

One area of heated debate on cybercrime policy involves the handling of juvenile cases. Proliferation of personal computers gives millions of children free access to the Internet, supervised only by parents or guardians who are sometimes overworked, preoccupied, or simply negligent. The result may include minors being exposed to sexually explicit material and gambling websites, or it may go further, spawning criminal activity on the part of precocious young felons. Stripped of face-to-face interaction with merchants and other business persons, juveniles find themselves on a level playing field where Internet fraud is concerned. Armed with stolen or counterfeit credit card numbers, available today at bargain rates, minors can run up huge bills for merchandise. Telephone fraud also appeals to young "phreakers," and many notorious hackers have launched their careers during adolescence. Federal investigators note that "juveniles appear to have an ethical 'deficit' when it comes to computer crimes," citing studies that reveal 34 percent of university undergraduates freely admitting to software piracy, while 16 percent admit illegal hacking of computer systems to gain desired information.

Prosecution in such cases is frequently hampered by statutes limiting the liability and punishment of minors for their crimes. While each state maintains its own juvenile code, federal regulations are embodied in the Juvenile Justice and Delinquency Prevention Act. Justice spokesmen note that "As a threshold matter, it is important to note that a juvenile proceeding is not the same as a criminal prosecution. Rather it is a proceeding in which the issue to be determined is whether the minor is a 'juvenile delinquent' as a matter of status, not whether he or she is guilty of committing a crime." A finding of "delinquency" is therefore not a criminal conviction, although it may result in confinement, mandatory counseling, and other remedial action. Banning access to computers for a fixed amount of time is common punishment for underage cybercriminals.

As cybercrime has spawned new regulatory agencies, so it has also produced a new breed of defenders for those accused. The on-line HACKER'S DEFENSE FOUNDATION solicits contributions for those accused of computer penetrations, and at least a handful of attorneys now profess to specialize in defending indicted cyberoutlaws. Oscar Figueroa, a San Francisco lawyer, promotes himself on-line as "a semantic warrior committed to the liberation of information," specifically inviting clients who are "charged with committing a computer-related criminal offense, such as hacking, cracking, phreaking, identity theft, copyright infringement or trade of theft secrets [*sic*]." Given the government's increasing preoccupation with computer-related crimes, it seems unlikely that Figueroa and other champions of the accused will suffer from a shortage of clients in the foreseeable future.

CYBERSTALKING: on-line harassment

In August 1999, U.S. Attorney General Janet Reno addressed one of America's newer criminal problems in a report to Vice President Al Gore. In reference to its subject, that document noted—

Although there is no universally accepted definition of cyberstalking, the term is used in this report to refer to the use of the Internet, e-mail, or other electronic communications devices to stalk another person. Stalking generally involves harassing or threatening behavior that an individual engages in repeatedly, such as following a person, appearing at a person's home or place of business, making harassing phone calls, leaving written messages or objects, or vandalizing a person's property. Most stalking laws require that the perpetrator make a credible threat of violence against the victim; others include threats against the victim's immediate family; still others require only that the alleged stalker's course of conduct constitute an implied threat. While some conduct involving annoying or menacing behavior might fall short of illegal stalking, such behavior may be a prelude to stalking and violence and should be treated seriously.

After reviewing the report, Vice President Gore told reporters, "Make no mistake: this kind of harassment can be as frightening and as real as being followed and watched in your neighborhood or in your home."

Psychologists maintain that most stalkers, whether on-line or off, are motivated by a desire to control their victims. As in cases of domestic violence, most identified offenders are male, the majority of complaining victims female. In many cases the parties had a prior relationship, and harassment begins when the victim seeks to break the link. Lack of physical contact in cyberstalking cases sometimes makes on-line harassment seem more benign than traditional stalking, but such is not always the case. Cyberstalkers may have greater access to a victim's personal data—with more opportunities to disrupt personal and professional lives—than a prowler dependent on lurking in shadows. At the same time, geographical distance is no longer a barrier to harassment, with swift global access assured by the Web. Internet anonymity encourages rash behavior from certain personality types, and as in more traditional cases, cyberstalking may be a prelude to physical confrontation.

Modern technology opens a world of new possibilities for stalkers as they torment their chosen victims. Instead of buying stamps and stationery to send a dozen threatening letters, the cyberstalker can resort to E-MAIL BOMBING, sending thousands of messages for free, in a fraction of the time required to scrawl one note on paper. More sophisticated offenders use custom programs to send messages at regular or random intervals, without being physically present at a computer terminal. Third parties can be enlisted to join the harassment via Internet chat rooms or bulletin boards, as where a stalker posts controversial or alluring messages in the victim's name, complete with home address, e-mail address, and/or telephone number. Cases cited in Attorney General Reno's report include the following:

California A 50-year-old ex-security guard in Los Angeles sought revenge on a 28-year-old woman who rejected his romantic overtures. Posing as his victim, the man posted numerous on-line messages with the woman's phone number and home address, in which "she" detailed fantasies of being raped. On six separate occasions, men inspired by the messages came to the woman's home at night, knocking on her door

and announcing their desire to rape her. The offender was finally arrested, pleading guilty in April 1999 to one count of stalking and three counts of soliciting a sexual assault, the combined charges making him eligible for six years' imprisonment.

Massachusetts Prosecutors indicted a man who used anonymous Internet remailers to harass and blackmail a female coworker. The messages threatened to reveal the victim's past sexual activities to her new husband unless she granted sexual favors to the stalker. Instead of landing a hot date, he wound up in jail.

California An honors graduate from the University of San Diego, convinced that five female students had belittled him and caused others to join in the ridicule, spent 12 months bombarding his targets with threatening e-mails, sometimes four or five messages per victim, each day. After the stalker's arrest and prior to his guilty plea on cyberstalking charges, police determined that none of the women had ever met their unbalanced tormentor.

Texas A 55-year-old Longview resident was arrested for criminal solicitation in June 2001, after a Yahoo representative told police that someone using the suspect's computer had posted chat-room pleas for assistance in having his wife "kidnapped, gang-raped, tortured and humiliated." In custody, the suspect confessed to that offense, citing "long-term marital problems," and also admitted to storing CHILD PORNOGRAPHY on his computer. He was held in lieu of $200,000 bond, pending trial.

Such incidents, unfortunately, are on the rise in America and around the world. No comprehensive records of cyberstalking exist today, but some Internet service providers (ISPs) and law enforcement agencies record complaints received. Nationwide, according to the U.S. Justice Department's records, 8.2 million women (one in every 12) and 2 million men (one in every 45) have been stalked at some time in their lives; 1 percent of all American women and .4 percent of American men reported stalking incidents in 1999. That same year in the U.S., more than 80 million adults and 10 million children had access to the Internet. Roughly applying the statistics of "normal" stalking to cyberspace, we may extrapolate nearly 1 million cyberstalking victims in a given year. Indeed, the number may be considerably higher, since 19 percent of juvenile Internet users surveyed in 2001 had received at least one unwelcome sexual solicitation within the past year. The Los Angeles District Attorney's Office reports that e-mail or other electronic communications were a factor in 20 percent of some 600 cases handled by its Stalking and Threat Assessment Unit in 1998; an identical percentage of cases handled by the Manhattan D.A.'s Sex Crimes Unit also involved cyberstalking. Finally, a study on sexual victimization of female college students, conducted at the University of Cincinnati in 1996 and 1997, found that 13 percent of 4,446 women surveyed had experienced stalking incidents, with 25 percent of those offenses ranked as some variety of cyberstalking.

Efforts are under way to curb the problem at various levels. Police need time and funding to acquire expertise in all areas of CYBERCRIME, and many smaller departments are still deficient in computer equipment and expertise. The Justice Department's 1999 survey revealed that a majority of cyberstalking victims do not report the harassment to authorities, often assuming that law enforcement will not take them seriously. And indeed, that has been the case in some jurisdictions, where victims were advised to simply "turn off the computer" or to return and file a report if the on-line harassment graduated to physical confrontation. One couple, harassed by Internet postings that offered their nine-year-old daughter for sex, including the family's telephone number, filed repeated futile complaints with their local police department before FBI agents finally stepped in and arrested the stalker. G-men quickly determined that the local police had no computer expert on staff and that the detective assigned to the case had never logged onto the Internet.

As with any other crime that transcends state or national boundaries, cyberstalking creates jurisdictional problems for law enforcement. Far-flung departments rarely communicate well with each other, and others are divided by bitter rivalry—the Los Angeles County Sheriff's Department and LAPD being prime examples. Federal intervention is likewise resented by many state or local law enforcement agencies, who carry grudges over prior instances of high-handed intrusion. If a victim in Manhattan is harassed by a stalker in Connecticut—much less London or Moscow—investigation and solution of the case becomes a burden local officers are generally unequipped to bear.

Inadequate legislation is another problem in dealing with cyberstalkers. At last count, 16 American states had stalking statutes that explicitly cover electronic communications, and the laws in several other states are broad enough that cyberstalking may be covered, depending largely on a prosecutor's whim. In other states, however, some kind of physical confrontation may be required for harassment to qualify as "stalking" under legal definitions. In those areas, it may be possible to prosecute cyberstalkers under other statutes—including a variety of state and federal laws that forbid using mail or telephone lines to transmit threats. One unexpected stumbling block for investigators is the federal Cable Communications Policy Act of 1984, which prohibits disclosure of cable subscriber records to law enforcement without a court order *and* advance notice to the subscriber. As more individuals utilize cable companies as their ISPs, authorities find it difficult (or impossible) to secretly investigate certain offenders.

Internet anonymity poses another complication for investigators, available to potential cyberstalkers in two forms. One allows individuals to create a free electronic mailbox through a website, and while most servers demand identifying information from users, it is rarely (if ever) authenticated. Where payment for a mailbox is required, untraceable money orders are gladly accepted, the signature's validity irrelevant. Cyberstalkers also use anonymous remailers, special mail servers that strip identifying information and transport headers from e-mail before it is sent. Near-perfect anonymity can be achieved by forwarding a message serially through several such remailers, until it is effectively untraceable.

While adult victims of cyberstalking still get short shrift from some police departments, children are more aggressively protected on all levels. Federal authorities eagerly prosecute on-line sexual predators, as do most state and local agencies. The FBI's Maryland-based initiative dubbed "Innocent Images," launched in December 1998, secured 232 felony convictions during the following year. The U.S. Customs Service's CyberSmuggling Center, housed at Sterling, Virginia, also has a special unit devoted to cases of Internet child exploitation. In March 1998 the National Center for Missing and Exploited Children unveiled a new CyberTipline for leads on child abuse. If all else fails, the volunteer organization CYBERANGELS logs an average 650 complaints of cyberstalking per day on its website, giving top priority to threats against children.

Even when ill-equipped to deal with cyberstalking, most police departments strive to do their best—and sometimes they accomplish it with irony. In April 2001 a cyberstalker known on-line as "Giblet Gravy" began harassing the Rowlett, Texas, police department with numerous e-mails. Officers ignored the early messages, until they became increasingly vulgar and insulting. Over time they identified the sender as 38-year-old John Germer, and turned the tables on their nemesis in December 2001, with an e-mail informing Germer that a warrant had been issued for his arrest on misdemeanor harassment charges. Within hours, Germer's attorney contacted police to arrange his client's surrender.

DABBS, Charles: exonerated by DNA evidence

In the predawn hours of August 12, 1982, a female resident of Westchester County, New York, was attacked while walking near her home. A man grabbed her from behind, dragged her into a nearby alley, and shoved her down a flight of stairs. Upon regaining consciousness, the victim found herself confronted by three men, two of whom held her down while the third raped her. She identified the rapist as Charles Dabbs, a distant cousin. The other two assailants were never apprehended.

At trial, prosecutors relied on the victim's identification of Dabbs, including references to his "distinctive laugh," and noted that the blood type of semen stains found on the victim's clothing matched Dabbs's Type O blood. Jurors convicted him of first-degree rape on April 10, 1984, and Dabbs received a prison term of 12 to 20 years. His conviction was upheld on appeal, but the Westchester County Supreme Court granted Dabbs's request for DNA testing of the evidence on November 21, 1990. A private laboratory concluded that Dabbs was not the source of semen found on the victim's clothing, and the court acknowledged his innocence on July 31, 1991. The charges were officially dismissed three weeks later, on August 22, 1991. Dabbs was released after serving seven years of his sentence.

DAVE Matthews Chain Letter: Internet hoax

Circulated for the first time in September 1999, this Internet chain letter capitalizes on the fame of pop musician Dave Matthews to promote another sympathy hoax. Veterans of Internet scams will note language very similar to the "A LITTLE GIRL IS DYING" hoax and others. As usual, the mechanics of the payoff process are left unexplained, defying the limits of modern computer technology. The message reads (with errors uncorrected):

Hi! This is Dave Matthews from The Dave Matthews Band. I got America Online just a little while ago and my screenname will be sent to you if you pass this on. I get a list of the people who send this to at least another 5 people online and my secretary will send all of you my screenname. I go online at least once a week. The reason I am doing this is because this little girl needs our help and I thought that I could use my fame to help out this sick little girl. Ok Listen I Just Spent 13 hours Getting Screen Names Just So that I Could Help a Little Girl So Read The bottom This isn't a chain letter.

Ok you guys. . . . This isn't a chain letter, but a choice for all of us to save a little girl that's dying of a serious and fatal form of cancer. Please send this to everyone you know . . . or don't know at that. This little girl has 6 months left to live, and as her dying wish, she wanted to send a chain letter telling everyone to live their life to the fullest, since she never will. She'll never make it to prom, graduate from high school, or get married and have a family of her own. But by you sending this to as many people as possible, you can give her and her family a little hope, because with every name

Dave Matthews, Internet hoax victim. (Matthew Mendelsohn/CORBIS)

that this is sent to, the American cancer society will donate 3 cents per name to her treatment and recovery plan. One guy sent this to 500 people!!!! So, I know that we can sent it to at least 5 or 6. Come on you guys. . . . And if you're too damn selfish to waste 10-15 minutes scrolling this and forwarding it to EVERYONE, (more than one person): you're one sick puppy, and two: just think it could be you one day . . . and it's not even your $money$, just your time. I know that ya'll will impress me!!!! I love y'all!!!!!

Another that I am putting money towards is: Tamara Martin and she has severe lung cancer due to second hand smoke. This chain was a final attempt to get her healthy again. Every letter sent gets 6 cents from me. Please send this to 10 people. (by the way for those who take 2 minutes to send this, what comes around goes around.)

I am putting a lot of money towards this and thanks to all my fans -

> *I*
> *love*
> *y'all!!*
> *Love,*
> *Dave Matthews*

As expected, Matthews and his band have disavowed any link to this hoax and no donations to specific cancer victims are made in any case by the American Cancer Society. Ironically, the authors of these copycat hoaxes never seem to note the built-in contradiction between their claims that "this isn't a chain letter" and the "dying wish" of some mythical child to send a *chain letter* around the world.

"DAVINIA": computer worm

An Internet worm virus spread through e-mail messages using Microsoft Outlook and Microsoft Word 2000, Davinia was reported for the first time in February 2001. It arrives as an e-mail in HTML format, with an empty subject line and body, but a script embedded in the message executes automatically when the e-mail is displayed, opening a browser window and downloading a page from the worm's Internet site. That page contains another script in turn, which opens a Microsoft Word document on the same website, disabling Microsoft Word 2000 antivirus protection without the user's knowledge. Next, Davinia gains access to the target computer's Microsoft Outlook address book and sends infected e-mails to all addresses listed there. The final payload is delivered after all addresses are exhausted, when the worm creates a file named littledavinia.vbs in the Windows system directory and proceeds to overwrite all hard disk files and installs an HTML page. When activated, the destructive page displays this message:

VBScript: Onel2 - Melilla
Hola, tu nombre es <name>.
Tu email es <email address>.
Yo soy Onel2, y vivo en Melilla
una ciudad del norte de Africa.
Estoy enamorado de una chica llamada Davinia.
Ella es la mas guapa del mundo.
Es como una diosa.
Igual que yo me contagie de amor
de Davinia, tus archivos se van a
contagiar de amor de esta pagina

Davinia(chica) y Davinia(virus) rompen
    corazones y archivos.
littledavinia version 1.1 esta en camino . . .

DAVIS, Chad: hacker "Mindphasr"

A 19-year-old resident of Green Bay, Wisconsin, Chad Davis, known on-line as Mindphasr, was described by federal prosecutors as a founder of the HACKER syndicate known as GLOBAL HELL. He was arrested by FBI agents on August 30, 1999, charged with hacking into a U.S. Army computer system at the Pentagon in June 1999 and maliciously interfering with military communications, modifying the contents of an army Web page. U.S. Attorney Thomas Schneider told reporters, "Even though the intrusion involved an unclassified Army computer network, the intruder prevented use of the system by Army personnel. Interference with government computer systems are not just electronic vandalism, they run the risk of compromising critical information infrastructure systems."

At the time of the Pentagon hack, Davis was already a suspect in other computer intrusions. FBI agents had executed a search warrant on his Wisconsin home on June 2, 1999, seeking evidence of his connection to the Global Hell gang. He pleaded guilty to the Pentagon intrusion on January 4, 2000, and received a six-month jail sentence on March 1, 2000. Davis also received three years' probation for his offense and was ordered to pay restitution in the amount of $8,054.

DAVIS, Gerald Wayne: exonerated by DNA evidence

Police in Kanawha County, West Virginia, received a rape complaint on February 18, 1986. The alleged victim claimed she had taken some laundry to be washed at the home of Gerald Davis, a family friend, who attacked and raped her when she returned for the items hours later. According to her statement, Davis's father—Dewey Davis—was also present in the house but made no effort to assist her during the attack. Searching the Davis home, authorities found a shoe and jacket belonging to the victim. While both Davis and his father claimed innocence of any wrongdoing, they were jailed on charges of kidnapping and sexual assault.

At trial, in May 1986, state police chemist FRED ZAIN testified that DNA tests could not exclude Gerald Davis as a possible source of semen found on the vic-

tim's underwear. Both defendants maintained that they had done nothing while the victim washed her clothing, but jurors disbelieved their story. Gerald Davis was convicted of kidnapping and two counts of sexual assault, while his father was found guilty of abduction, first-degree sexual abuse and second-degree sexual assault. Both defendants received prison terms of 14 to 35 years, reduced to a flat 10 years on appeal.

The defendants gained new hope in 1993, following revelations that Zain, the police chemist, had committed perjury and falsified test results in numerous criminal cases. West Virginia's Superior Court granted a petition to repeat DNA tests on semen recovered from the victim, and those tests excluded Gerald Davis as a semen donor. Prosecutors demanded a second test, this time on Davis's sheets and underpants, contending that Davis could have raped the victim without ejaculating. The new tests revealed no trace of the alleged victim's DNA, and Gerald Davis was released to home confinement on March 16, 1994, pending retrial. Jurors acquitted him on December 4, 1995, and charges against his father were subsequently dismissed.

DAYE, Frederick Rene: exonerated by DNA evidence

On the evening of January 10, 1984, a young woman was attacked by two men while leaving a San Diego, California, drugstore. One assailant forced the victim into her own car from the driver's side, then opened the back door for his accomplice. Inside the car, the men rifled her purse and stole six dollars, then removed several articles of jewelry before they ripped off the victim's clothes and raped her. Afterward the two men dumped their victim on a nearby residential street and fled in her car. A witness to the crime identified the men as Frederick Daye and David Pringle, both soon arrested on charges of kidnapping, robbery, rape, and auto theft. The victim identified Daye's mug shot as a likeness of her rapist and picked him out of a lineup at police headquarters.

The defendants were tried separately, with Pringle pleading the Fifth Amendment from the witness stand at Daye's trial. Blood typing on a semen stain from the victim's clothing matched Daye's Type B blood, and prosecutors noted that he had given police a false name at the time of his arrest. Jurors convicted him on August 14, 1984, after deliberating for nearly eight hours. Daye was sentenced to life imprisonment with possible parole on the kidnapping charge, plus 14 years and eight months on various other counts. David Pringle was convicted in a later trial and likewise sentenced to prison. An appellate court affirmed Daye's conviction on February 29, 1986, and California's Supreme Court declined to review the case.

David Pringle surprised authorities with a confession to the rape and kidnapping on February 1, 1990, his statement exonerating Daye and naming another man as his accomplice. The San Diego County Superior Court appointed an attorney to investigate the claim, and while a writ of habeas corpus was denied on August 11, 1992, the court ruled that Daye was entitled to new representation. Destruction of the original trial evidence was scheduled for October 1992, but last-minute motions preserved it for DNA testing, with a $2,000 grant to complete the procedure. Those tests, completed on April 21, 1994, excluded Daye as a source of semen collected from the victim's clothing following the rape. Daye's conviction was overturned on September 27, 1994, after he had served 10 years of his sentence.

"DEADMAN": computer viruses

The computer virus known as Deadman presently appears in two variant forms, identified respectively in February and June 1999. The original virus is today known as Deadman.576, described by analysts as a "non-dangerous nonmemory resident parasitic virus." It searches for executable files and writes itself to the end of any such files discovered. If an asterisk (*) appears in the file's command line, Deadman.576 freezes the infected computer and displays a message reading:

It seems to be all right.
*.exe
[FALSE]
Copyright © 1998–99 by Deadman

The second variant, known as Deadman.943, is described by analysts as a dangerous nonmemory-resident encrypted parasitic virus. It searches out and attaches itself to both command and executable files, scanning all subdirectories of the infected computer's hard drive. It may also erase random sectors from the target computer's C drive and typically displays the following message:

Program too big to fit in memory
[Napoleon]
Copyright © 1998–99 by Deadman [SOS]

DEAL, Steve   See FASTLANE

"DEATH Ray" Computer Virus: Internet hoax

With the plethora of computer VIRUSES identified over the past decade, there would seem to be no need for fabricating more out of thin air, but hoaxers still persist, spreading alarm across the Internet with their efforts. The so-called Death Ray virus was initially reported by the *Weekly World News*, a tabloid known for its "creative" journalism (including photos of President Bill Clinton welcoming extraterrestrial creatures to the White House). Since the original "exposure" of this nonexistent virus, thousands of Internet users have been confronted with the following warning, which has no basis whatsoever in reality.

A deadly new computer virus that actually causes home computers to explode in a hellish blast of glass fragments and flame has injured at least 47 people since August 15, horrifying authorities who say millions of people are risking injury, blindness or death every time they sit down to work at their PC!

"Computer viruses of the past could disable your computer, but this virus goes a step further—and can kill you," declared Martin Heriden, a computer expert who specializes in identifying computer viruses. "This virus doesn't carry the usual 'markers' that enable it to be detected. It slips through the cracks, so to speak.

"It is an extremely complicated process. But suffice it to say that the virus affects the computer's hardware, creating conditions that lead to dangerous short circuits and power surges. The end result? Explosions—powerful explosions. And millions of Internet users are at risk."

The virus, nicknamed Death Ray by experts like Heriden, surfaced in England on August 1. A 24-year-old college student was permanently blinded when his 15-inch color monitor exploded in his face.

"So how do you protect yourself? I wish I knew," said Heriden. "You either stop using the Internet or you take your chances until we can get a handle on this thing and get rid of it for good."

Efforts to locate "Martin Heriden" are unavailing. Although someone of that name may well exist, somewhere on earth, no such computer expert has been found to date in the United States or Europe. He, like the Death Ray virus itself, is presumably a figment of some practical joker's fertile imagination.

DENNIS, Scott D.: computer saboteur

A resident of Anchorage, Alaska, Scott Dennis was employed in 1999 as a computer system administrator for the U.S. District Court. During December of that year, Dennis became disgruntled at a plan to let more users access "Judsys," a private mail list server normally restricted to computer system administrators of the U.S. courts. Rather than voice his displeasure through channels, Dennis decided to launch a series of "mail bomb" attacks against Judsys and its host computer, operated by the U.S. District Court for the Eastern District of New York. During December 1999 and January 2000, Dennis flooded Judsys with e-mail "spam" on at least five occasions, forcing the host computer to be taken off-line and reconfigured.

Despite his efforts to remain anonymous, Dennis was traced by federal technicians who identified the Internet Protocol (IP) addresses for computers used in the attacks. On April 18, 2000, Dennis was indicted for interfering with a government computer. He pleaded guilty on January 19, 2001, and received a three-month jail sentence, to be followed by three months' home confinement and one year of supervised release. Dennis was also ordered to perform hours of community service and agreed to let federal authorities monitor his computer activity. In addition to his jail time and probation, Dennis paid $5,300 in restitution to the New York federal court and ISP Internet Alaska.

DESIGNER Drugs

Also widely known as "club" drugs for their prevalence at trendy nightclubs and teenage "rave" parties, designer drugs are synthetic substances created by changing the molecular structure of existing drugs—normally amphetamines or methamphetamines, PCP, and fentanyl—to create new drugs with similar or enhanced pharmacological effects. Designer drugs initially came into vogue as an attempt to circumvent the Controlled Substance Act of 1970, which strictly regulated various psychoactive drugs (including LSD, amphetamines, and methamphetamines). A 1986 amendment to that law banned all existing designer drugs *and* all possible variations of any controlled substance, whether or not those variations had yet been imagined or manufactured.

As with other outlawed drugs, of course, a legislative ban has done no more than whet the public appetite while raising prices on the street. The effects of designer drugs vary widely, depending on potency and the latest recipe employed by their illicit manufacturers. Club drugs derived from methylenedioxymethamphetamine (MDMA), frequently sold as "Ecstasy," produce feelings of euphoria, but increased dosages may also generate paranoia, depression, irrational violence, and hallucinations similar to those produced by LSD. Gamma hydroxybutyrate (GHB), once sold in health food stores as a performance-enhancer for body builders, is a central nervous system (CNS) depressant abused for its intoxicating effects. When taken in large doses or combined with other CNS depressants such as alcohol or sedatives, GHB can produce fatal respiratory depression. Undesirable side effects common to many club drug users include hypertension, increased heart rate, blurred vision, tremors and seizures, impaired speech, dehydration, and progressive brain damage. Psychological symptoms of designer drug abuse include confusion, irritability, amnesia, insomnia, and severe anxiety. The confusion was evident among four thieves at Noblesville, Indiana, on August 24, 2001. Intent on stealing the heroin-mimic OxyContin from a local pharmacy, the raiders instead escaped with oxytocin, a drug used to induce labor in pregnant women. "I don't know if they used any," Detective Todd Uhrick told reporters. "They were all pretty dumb."

As with any other deviant subculture, designer drug users apply various street names to their chemicals of choice. Among them are the following:

MDMA   Adam, B-bombs, Bean, Blue kisses, Blue lips, Crystal, Clarity, Cloud nine, Dead road, Debs, Decadence, Dex, Diamonds, Disco biscuits, Doctor, Dolls, Driver, Ecstasy, Essence, Eve, Exiticity, Gaggler, Go, Greenies, Gum opium, Happy drug, Herbal bliss, Kleenex, Love drug, Mini beans, Morning shot, Nineteen, Rave energy, Ritual spirit, Scooby snacks, Speed for lovers, Strawberry shortcake, Sweeties, Ultimate Xphoria, Wafers, West Coast turnarounds, Wheels, Whiffledust

Fentanyl   Apache, China girl, China town, Dance fever, Friend, Goodfellas, Great bear, He-man,

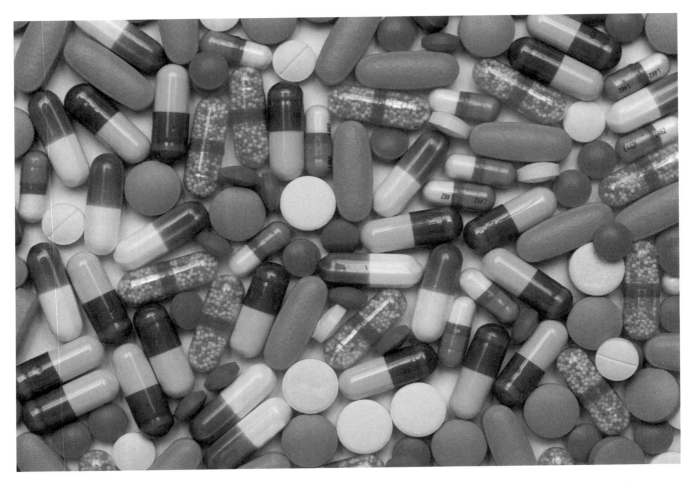

Designer drugs are synthetic substances created by changing the molecular structure of existing drugs—normally amphetamines or methamphetamines, PCP and fentanyl—to create new drugs with similar or enhanced pharmacological effects.

Jackpot, King ivory, Murder 8, Poison, Tango & Cash, TNT

Dimethyltryptamine AMT, Businessman's LSD, Businessman's special, Businessman's trip, DET, DMT, Fantasia, 45-minute psychosis

Alpha-ethyltryptamine Alpha-ET, ET, Love pearls, Love pills, Trip

Methcathinone Bathtub speed, Cadillac express, Cat, Gaggers, Go-fast, Goob, Qat, Slick super-speed, Somali tea, Star, Stat, The C, Tweeker, Wild cat, Wonder star

Ketamine Cat valium, Honey oil, Jet, Ket, Kit kat, Purple, Special "K," Super acid, Super C, Vitamin K

GHB Georgia home boy, Grievous bodily harm, Liquid ecstasy, Scoop

Nexus (4-bromo-2, 5-dimethoxyphenethylamine) Bromo, MFT, Spectrum, Toonies, Venus

Rohypnol Forget me drug, La rocha, Lunch money drug, Mexican Valium, Pingus, R-2, Reynolds, Roaches, Roachies, Roofies, Rope, Row-shay, Ruffies, Ruffles, Wolfies

DESKTOP Sales, Inc.: computer trademark pirates

A computer hardware firm based in the Chicago suburb of Gurnee, Illinois, Desktop Sales pleaded guilty on November 19, 1998, to violating federal trademark laws by distributing computer memory boards in counterfeit International Business Machine Corp. (IBM) boxes. As outlined in the federal complaint and plea agreement, Desktop purchased inexpensive computer memory chips and modules used to upgrade the memory capacity of personal computers, then packaged them in fake IBM boxes for resale at premium prices. Between January 1991 and May 1993, Desktop sold approximately 30,000 of the mislabeled units, earning $11.1 million—a net profit of $1.1 million over and above the price obtainable without counterfeit packaging.

Following acceptance of the guilty plea, U.S. District Judge Robert Gettleman imposed the maximum fine on Desktop Sales—a total of $3.3 million, or triple the firm's illegitimate profit from sales of the counterfeit products. U.S. Attorney Scott Lassar afterward told reporters, "The resolution of this case ensures that IBM will be made whole for the violation of its trademark and that the defendant will pay the maximum fine for illegally infringing that trademark." IBM vice president and assistant general counsel D. J. Rosenberg added his vote of confidence for the prosecution, declaring that "IBM greatly appreciates the outstanding job done by the Department of Justice in this case. This type of action by the Department is extremely valuable in protecting IBM's trademarks which represent the high quality and reliability our customers have come to expect." By the time its guilty plea was filed in federal court, Desktop Sales had been reborn as VisionTek.

"DEEYENDA" Computer Virus: Internet hoax

Yet another mythical virus described in hyperbolic e-mail warnings is "Deeyenda," said (falsely) to obliterate all files on the hard drive of any infected computer. The hoax warning's language is similar to equally spurious alerts broadcast in relation to the nonexistent "GOOD TIMES" virus, suggesting the work of a determined joker or a rather unimaginative copycat. Knowledgeable Internet users will be aware that the Federal Communications Commission (FCC) does not broadcast computer virus warnings and has no responsibility to do so. The usual Deeyenda warning reads as follows (misspellings in the original):

***********VIRUS ALERT***********

VERY IMPORTANT INFORMATION, PLEASE READ!

There is a computer virus that is being sent around the Internet. If you receive an email message with the sub-

ject line "Deeyenda," DO NOT read the message, DELETE it immediately!

Some miscreant is sending email under the title "Deeyenda" nationwide, if you get anything like this DON'T DOWNLOAD THE FILE! It has a virus that rewrites your hard drive, obliterates anything on it. Please be careful and forward this e-mail to anyone you care about.

Please read the message below.

Alex

----FCC WARNING!!!!!----
DEEYENDA PLAGUES INTERNET

The Internet community has again been plagued by another computer virus. This message is being spread throughout the Internet, including USENET posting, EMAIL, and other Internet activities. The reason for all the attention is because of the nature of this virus and the potential security risk it makes. Instead of a destructive Trojan virus (like most viruses!), this virus referred to as Deeyenda Maddick, performs a comprehensive search on your computer, looking for valuable information, such as email and login passwords, credit cards, personal inf., etc.

The Deeyenda virus also has the capability to stay memory resident while running a host of applications and operation systems, such as Windows 3.11 and Windows 95. What this means to Internet users is that when a login and password are send to the server, this virus can copy this information and SEND IT TO UN UNKNOWN ADDRESS (varies).

The reason for this warning is because the Deeyenda virus is virtually undetectable. Once attacked your computer will be unsecure. Although it can attack any O/S this virus is most likely to attach those users viewing Java enhanced Web Pages (Netscape 2.0+ and Microsoft Internet Explorer 3.0+ which are running under Windows 95). Researchers at Princeton University have found this virus on a number of World Wide Web pages and fear its spread.

Please pass this on, for we must alert the general public at the security risks.

DIEKMAN, Jason Allen: hacker "Shadow Knight"

A resident of Mission Viejo, California, 18-year-old Jason Diekman launched a series of illegal computer intrusions from his home in 1998. His targets included NASA's Jet Propulsion Laboratory (JPL) in nearby Pasadena, another NASA computer at Stanford University, and "hundreds, maybe thousands" of computers on university campuses across the United States. At the same time, Diekman used the Internet to capture an estimated 500 credit card numbers, which he used to purchase more than $6,000 worth of computer equipment, stereo speakers and clothing.

The operation that blew Diekman's cover was a relatively amateurish tap on a local cable television provider. Orange County authorities traced Diekman and charged him with grand theft in that case, but the charges were expanded when he failed to appear for a July 2000 court hearing. Federal authorities had traced him in the meantime, and he was indicted for his HACKER exploits on July 26, 2000. Local police nabbed him again August 20, 2000, and Diekman pleaded guilty on charges of theft and failure to appear, accepting a 75-day jail sentence. He was transferred to federal custody on September 21, 2000, facing felony charges that carried a maximum sentence of 26 years in prison and a $750,000 fine.

On November 6, 2000, Diekman pleaded guilty on two hacking charges and one count of using unauthorized access devices (the stolen credit card numbers) to make illegal purchases. As part of that guilty plea, he admitted causing $17,000 worth of damages to various NASA computers. The charges carried a maximum sentence of 16 years in federal prison. While free on $100,000 bond in that case and awaiting sentencing, Diekman involved himself in another Internet fraud, inducing three accomplices to make wire transfers of cash to Diekman via Western Union, charging the amounts to stolen credit card numbers. FBI agents arrested Diekman on April 18, 2001, slapping him with multiple charges of hacking and wire fraud. On August 1, 2001, he pleaded guilty to one count of wire fraud and one count of obtaining information from a protected computer. Diekman was held without bond pending sentencing in federal court. He was scheduled for sentencing on October 15, 2001, but his court appearance was indefinitely postponed in the wake of September 2001 terrorist attacks in New York City and Washington, D.C.

"DIESEL": computer virus

Discovered in April 2000, "Diesel" is a nonmemory-resident parasitic virus rated "non-dangerous" by expert analysts. Upon infecting a computer, it searches system directories and subdirectories for Linux executable files, then writes itself into the middle of each file located, thus increasing the file's size. That done, it restores control to the host. Diesel contains the following text string:

/home root sbin bin opt
[Diesel: Oil, Heavy Petroleum Fraction Used In Diesel Engines]

"DION": computer virus

Rated "non-dangerous" by analysts, this memory-resident, encrypted, parasitic virus was initially discovered in June 2001. It infects Windows systems, lurking in memory as a hidden service process, and waits to infect various applications as they are run. As files are infected, Dion creates a .DLL "dropper" file in the Windows system directory, identified by a name with eight random digits (e.g., 23895741.DLL, 09563512.DLL, and so forth). On the 20th day of each month thereafter, at 8:10 P.M., Dion presents itself with video effects. The first display, at center-screen, appears as

..::[MUSIC IS LIFE]::..

Moments later, a brightly colored "DION" text appears on the desktop, moving from left to right, border to border, until that text fills the monitor's screen.

DIONNE, Diane: software pirate

A resident of West Palm Beach, Florida, born April 11, 1961, Diane Dionne was one of 17 defendants indicted by U.S. authorities for software piracy on May 4, 2000. Prosecutors identified her as a member of the HACKERS' syndicate known as PIRATES WITH ATTITUDE, responsible for stealing and illegally distributing more than 5,000 computer software programs via a covert Internet website based on a Canadian university campus. Those indicted for conspiracy to infringe U.S. copyrights included 12 members of Pirates with Attitude and five employees of Intel Corporation, the latter charged with supplying computer hardware and software valued in excess of $1 million. Dionne was among 13 defendants who pleaded guilty as charged in 2001.

DISNEY Giveaway Offer: Internet hoax

In August 1998 an e-mail variant of the BILL GATES GIVEAWAY fraud began to make the Internet rounds, this one invoking the name of the Walt Disney Company. As in other, similar cases, Disney bears no responsibility for the offer and has publicly repudiated it, noting that the firm has no interest whatsoever in alleged e-mail tracking devices. The message reads:

Hello Disney fans,
And thank you for signing up for Bill Gates' Beta Email Tracking. My name is Walt Disney Jr. Here at Disney we are working with Microsoft which has just compiled an e-mail tracing program that tracks everyone to whom this message is forwarded to. It does this through an unique IP (Internet Protocol) address log book database.

We are experimenting with this and need your help. Forward this to everyone you know and if it reaches 13,000 people, 1,300 of the people on the list will receive $5,000, and the rest will receive a free trip for two to Disney World for one week during the summer of 1999 at our expense. Enjoy.

Note: Duplicate entries will not be counted. You will be notified by email with further instructions once this email has reached 13,000 people.

Your friends,
Walt Disney Jr., Disney, Bill Gates &
The Microsoft Development Team.

DNA Evidence

Often described as the basic building block of life on earth, deoxyribonucleic acid (DNA) is the substance that transmits genetic traits. Discovered by scientists James Watson and Francis Crick, DNA was admitted as legal evidence for the first time in 1985 and sent a criminal suspect—British serial killer COLIN PITCHFORK—to prison for the first time in January 1988. Since then, the science of DNA analysis and comparison—sometimes dubbed "DNA fingerprinting"—has assumed strategic importance in many criminal trials where conviction or acquittal hinges on traces of blood, semen, hair, or other evidence containing genetic material.

To the best of modern scientific knowledge, only identical twins display precisely the same DNA, but all human DNA has certain traits in common and a relatively small percentage of it is used to determine identity. In fact, while human beings have 23 million pairs of chromosomes containing DNA, only 3 million pairs—13 percent of a subject's entire genome—varies from person to person. (Half of each pair is drawn from the subject's father and half from the mother.) The key to analyzing DNA evidence lies in comparison of genetic material found at a crime scene with a suspect's DNA in those segments that differ.

Two different kinds of "polymorphic regions"—areas with great diversity in DNA—are found within each genome, respectively dubbed sequence polymorphisms and length polymorphisms. *Sequence polymorphisms,* or simple substitutions of bases within genes, are generally of little value in criminal cases. *Length polymorphisms,* by contrast, are variations in the physical length of a DNA molecule. Forensic DNA evidence uses length polymorphism found in "non-coding" DNA (the portions which do not transmit genetic codes) by examining unique variations in repeat sequences of DNA. Because a specific sequence may be repeated from one to 30 times in a row, those regions are dubbed "variable number tandem repeats" (VNTRs). The number of VNTRs determines a DNA fragment's length, and the number found at specific places in the DNA chain (loci) is unique to a specific individual (again, excluding identical twins).

The scientific procedure used to isolate a subject's DNA profile is called *restriction fragment length polymorphism* (RFLP) analysis, developed in the 1980s by Britain's Dr. Alec Jeffries. In essence, it simply means that analysts count the number of VNTR repeats at various distinctive loci to determine a subject's statistically unique DNA "fingerprint." Microscopic comparison of a known subject's DNA profile with the same information from an anonymous evidence sample should reveal if the genetic material lifted from a crime scene was produced by the suspect in custody. Comparison proceeds through several steps, including:

1. *Isolation of the DNA.* Genetic material found at crime scenes is frequently contaminated by contact with soil or other extraneous materials, commingling of bodily fluids from two or more subjects, and so forth. Thus, before analysis can proceed, the DNA must be cleaned and isolated for study. Failure to perform this step correctly leaves the evidence open to serious challenge by a suspect's defense team.

2. *Reduction of the large genome to manageable fragments.* This step is accomplished by application of "restriction enzymes"—bacterial enzymes that recognize specific four-to-six-base sequences and cut the DNA at predictable base pairs. Human DNA is thus broken down into millions of fragments ranging from 100 base pairs to longer segments in the tens of thousands. Distinctive VNTR loci may then be more conveniently examined.

3. *Arrangement of the DNA fragments by size via gel electrophoresis.* In this step, DNA is placed into a slab of agarose (a gel derived from seaweed, used to solidify various culture media) and exposed to an electric field. Since DNA is negatively charged, it will be drawn toward the field's positive electrode, with smaller fragments moving through the agarose more quickly than larger ones. The relative size of each fragment is determined by how far it moves through the agarose within a specific time frame.

4. *Isolation of specific DNA strands.* DNA fragments separated by gel electrophoresis begin to disintegrate within a day or two. Permanent preservation is achieved via the "Southern Blot" technique, which isolates single strands for more detailed examination. To accomplish this end, DNA is first denatured from its original double helix into a single strand, thus freeing nucleotides to base-pair with DNA probes in the final step (described below). A positively charged nylon membrane is used to lift negatively charged DNA from the agarose gel (the "blot"). Since DNA remains invisible at this stage, one more step is required to permit visual comparison.

5. *Imprinting of the DNA on film.* Specific VNTR sequences on a DNA strand are located by means of a "DNA probe," created from a sequence complementary to that of a known VNTR locus, which binds to matching sequences on the nylon membrane. The probe includes a radioactive compound which allows it to be located and to produce a picture of the DNA strand via direct

Model of DNA double helix structure. (PhotoDisc)

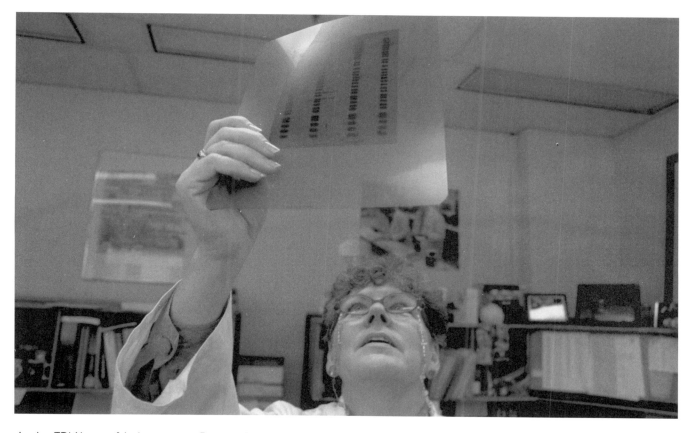

At the FBI National Laboratory in Boston, DNA analysis is carried out to find evidence in certain criminal cases. (Amy Toensing/CORBIS SYGMA)

contact with special X-ray film. The final DNA photograph displays dark bands at each point where the DNA probe has bound itself to the suspect sample.

Mathematics finally determines identity when DNA strands are compared. A match on one VNTR locus is no more significant than a single digit lifted from a suspect's street address, where millions of addresses may contain, for example, the number "3." Comparison of many loci found on different chromosomes, however, tell a very different story. Each VNTR locus has about 30 length variants (alleles), each of which occurs at a known frequency within the human population. When these are multiplied, using four loci, the odds of replicating a particular allele combination are approximately one in 5 million. The FBI typically tests 13 loci, with 26 different DNA bands, pegging the odds of two unrelated individuals matching the same profile at more than one in 100 *billion*. Since the entire population of Earth is less than 7 billion (in 2002), DNA "fingerprint" identification may fairly be labeled conclusive.

As a new form of evidence in the 1980s and early 1990s, DNA faced challenges from courts and attorneys who questioned the value of the testing as positive evidence. Most jurors still have only a vague understanding of DNA analysis and require a crash course in the testing procedure at trial, before they can reach an informed verdict. Even then, prosecutors and defense attorneys have no recourse against jurors who misunderstand the evidence or simply refuse to consider it. A prime example was the case of Orenthal James (O. J.) SIMPSON, acquitted of double murder in 1995 despite damning DNA evidence from the crime scene. In the wake of Simpson's acquittal, one juror told reporters: "I didn't understand the DNA stuff at all. To me it was just a waste of time. It was way out there and carried absolutely no weight with me."

Various improvements in DNA analysis have made the identification of subjects more streamlined and more precise since testing was initiated. RFLP analysis requires large amounts of relatively high-quality DNA, so that small or contaminated samples often yield inconclusive results. In 1983, California scientist Kary Mullins developed an alternative, the *polymerase chain reaction* (PRC) system, which permits amplification of very small DNA samples. (The procedure earned a Nobel Prize in chemistry for Mullins in 1993.) With the PCR system, a tiny amount of specific DNA can be replicated exponentially within hours, thus making the test sample virtually unlimited.

Aside from capability of testing smaller samples, science has also devised new ways of extracting DNA from sources formerly too difficult or too contaminated for use as evidence. Several nations, including Britain and the United States, have built extensive DNA databases, collecting unique profiles by the hundreds of thousands from military personnel, convicted felons, government employees, and voluntary submissions from the general public at large. Crime labs have improved training of technicians and have established formal protocols for handling DNA evidence, thus reducing contamination of samples. The most common forensic uses of DNA evidence today are proving guilt, exonerating innocent suspects, establishing paternity, and identifying anonymous human remains.

Conviction of criminals who leave genetic material at a crime scene is vastly simpler today than 20 years ago, when blood type and hairs were merely deemed "consistent" between a suspect and recovered crime scene evidence. A suspect with a common blood type might be convicted of rape or some other serious crime, when the only other evidence against him is a mistaken eyewitness identification—and indeed, many U.S. prison inmates convicted on precisely such evidence had been exonerated since the advent of DNA testing. Comparison of suspect samples with a database of known offenders often surprises investigators. British police, for example, report that their database of 360,000 DNA profiles from repeat offenders scores more than 500 positive matches in outstanding cases per week. The U.S. lags behind that impressive total, with Virginia authorities reporting 10 cases solved per week by DNA, while detectives in Washington state cleared five "cold" cases with the new technology in July 2001 (includ-ing three old rape cases solved in one day). A disturbing case in point from the U.S. is that of DENNIS FRITZ, where belated DNA testing identified the perpetrator of an Oklahoma rape-murder as one of the chief prosecution witnesses used to convict an innocent defendant at trial.

Even DNA from pets may be useful in solving a criminal case. The men who murdered Elizabeth Ballard in 1998, planting her corpse in the New Mexico desert, were captured after police recovered a single dog hair from the victim's body, and later matched it via DNA testing to a pit bull owned by one of the killers. Blood from a Seattle dog helped convict the gang members who murdered its owners. Traces of dog feces on another suspect's shoe sent him to prison for an Indiana triple murder. Dog urine sprayed on a truck tire in Iowa identified the pickup's driver as a prime suspect in the dog owner's death. Beth Davis, speaking for a veterinary genetics lab in Davis, California, told the press in 2001: "A lot of the technology is a fallout from the human genome project. We just applied that to animals."

Encouraged by such cases, police have eagerly applied DNA technology to their backlog of unsolved crimes. Texas became the first state to indict an unknown rapist solely on the basis of DNA evidence, in August 2001. The offender remains unknown today, but his "John Doe" indictment prevents a five-year statute of limitations from protecting him in the event that he is ultimately captured. New Hampshire police used DNA to convict 40-year-old Joseph Whittey of murder in 2001, 20 years after he killed and sexually assaulted an elderly widow, and they now hope DNA may help them solve 26 more slayings from the 1990s.

DNA evidence is especially helpful in linking serial offenses, when rapists or killers often travel widely to avoid detection, counting on a lack of communication between police departments to cover their tracks. In Fort Collins, Colorado, analysis of DNA samples from an unknown subject who raped five women between May and September 2001 linked the offender to six more rapes and a murder committed in Pennsylvania between July 1997 and August 1999. Without DNA profiles, police departments separated by some 1,750 miles would have no clue that they were seeking the same predator. August 2001 saw authorities in Michigan use DNA to link crimes committed between 1986 and 1990, though the killer still remains at large. Washington state detectives believed one serial killer was responsible for 11 murders of women on the Yakima Indian reservation, until DNA evidence linked imprisoned convict John Bill Fletcher Jr. with two of the slayings, while clearing him of nine others. In Vancouver, British Columbia, where 50 prostitutes are missing and presumed murdered since the 1980s, detectives scoured a farm for evidence in February 2002 and used DNA samples from kin of the victims to indict suspect Robert William Pickton on two counts of first-degree murder.

Exoneration of those falsely accused or imprisoned is perhaps the greatest public service performed by DNA analysts, since it remedies injustice *and* informs authorities (if they were not already conscious of the fact) that unknown criminals remain at large. DNA cleared its first innocent suspect, a British citizen accused of two rape-murders, in 1985. Since the late 1980s, more than 100 U.S. prison inmates have been liberated after DNA analysis proved they were innocent of murder, rape, or other heinous crimes. Ten have been freed from death row, condemned for the crimes of others, and those cases—including several deliberate frame-ups by corrupt authorities—have sparked new debates over capital punishment in America. Illinois governor George Ryan declared a moratorium on executions in January 2000, after learning that 13 inmates had been wrongfully sentenced to death. Nationwide, FBI analysts report, DNA analysis of crime scene evidence exonerates primary suspects in 30 percent of all cases examined. That statistic alone offers cause for concern, with its implication that nearly one-third of all inmates convicted on less precise evidence—blood type alone, "consistent" hairs, etc.—may indeed be innocent.

Exoneration of the innocent—or confirmation of guilt, in some cases—is not inexpensive. In July 2000 San Diego, California authorities began a review of 560 convictions obtained prior to 1992, when DNA testing became routine. The tab: $5,000 per case. Prosecutors in other jurisdictions refuse to perform the tests themselves, leaving defendants to raise the money by any means available. Organizations like the CARDOZO INNOCENCE PROJECT do their part, but they are perpetually short of funds, fighting time and official intransigence on behalf of penniless defendants.

State opposition to DNA review is particularly strident in cases where inmates have already been executed, while maintaining their innocence to the bitter end. A case in point, now under review, is that of Ellis Wayne Felker, in Georgia. Felker was condemned for the 1981 rape slaying of 19-year-old Evelyn Ludlam. His case made national headlines when the U.S. Supreme Court agreed to review it on an expedited basis, examining his challenge of a new statute curtailing federal appeals. The court refused to delay Felker's execution on grounds that new evidence of his innocence had not been discovered, and he was electrocuted on November 15, 1996. Today, though private attorneys pursue posthumous DNA testing in Felker's case, his prosecutors scorn the effort as "a total waste of time."

The new vogue in DNA testing has created a vast backlog of cases awaiting disposition. By July 2000, evidence from 180,000 American rape cases was stored in various labs around the country, each item waiting its turn while trials are placed on hold, justice delayed for victims and defendants alike. Aside from cases still awaiting trial, more than 1 million American convicts have petitioned for DNA tests in their various cases. If only 5 percent are truly innocent—versus the FBI's prevailing 30 percent—it means some 50,000 innocent persons are caged in the United States for crimes they did not commit.

Thousands of persons—some sources say *hundreds* of thousands—disappear without a trace each year in the United States. At the same time, authorities discover the remains of *hundreds* who may never be identified. Decomposition may obscure not only a corpse's identity, but also cause of death, leaving the question of natural death versus accident or homicide forever unanswered. Nationwide, thousands of families seek closure, mourning the unexplained loss of their children, siblings, parents, or spouses.

Prior to the advent of DNA testing, "John Doe" or "Jane Doe" remains were sometimes identified via dental records, skeletal abnormalities, or (if flesh remained) by means of scars, tattoos, and birthmarks. Today, bone fragments or a single strand of hair may be sufficient for identification, provided that DNA is found within the sample. Where known DNA from a missing person is available—as from blood or tissue samples—a positive match can normally be made. If no samples exist from the subject himself, technicians can still use the methods applied in paternity testing to see if the deceased was related to members of a particular family, thereby resolving the issue in most cases.

In September 2001, after several nationally publicized cases of babies switched at birth in hospital maternity wards, a Wisconsin company called Innovative Control Systems announced development of a new "Surelink" DNA kit, designed to prevent such mistakes. The kit screens DNA from blood found in the infant's umbilical cord and a sample from the mother, both collected in the delivery room. The samples are placed in a tamper-proof pouch and filed in a secure location, where the DNA material allegedly remains intact and testable for at least a decade. If questions of maternity arise within that time, the genetic evidence is available to resolve all doubts.

More common by far than switched infants is the threat of child abduction in America. Authorities disagree on the frequency of such incidents, but recent FBI estimates claim an average of 300 "stranger abductions" per year, for an average of one kidnapping every 29 hours. Some of those victims are recovered without injury; others are molested or murdered; some are never seen again. In a few bizarre cases, pedophiles or other mentally unstable individuals have held children captive for years on end, imposing new identities that override a child's initial memories of home and family. When children are found dead, as in the notorious Lindbergh case from 1932, decomposition may retard identification or obscure cause of death.

Authorities in various states hope DNA testing may remedy some of those problems. Science cannot protect children from predators, but at least it can attempt to verify identity when they are found at last, alive or dead. In August 2001, Indiana State Police officers began distributing kits that allow parents to collect and store DNA samples from their children, with 1,000 kits passed out in Evansville alone by January 2002. Presumably the kits would replace more traditional fingerprint cards, especially for children under seven years of age, whose fingerprints are often indistinct and difficult to read. The kits require no blood samples, instead relying on swabs taken from a child's mouth. Commercial kits typically cost between $25 and $75, but authorities note that parents can achieve the same result by keeping a child's used toothbrush, along with hair samples (roots included), and storing the items in a freezer against future need.

DNA testing is sometimes useful in famous criminal cases, as well as the obscure. Following the East Coast terrorist attacks of September 11, 2001, many victims killed in the explosion and collapse of New York's World Trade Center were too badly damaged for simple identification by visual means. DNA testing was employed in the worst cases, using samples obtained from toothbrushes, hairbrushes, and other known belongings of those trapped in the rubble. By October 24, 2001, eight victims had been identified using DNA evidence exclusively. As Marion DeBlase told reporters, following identification of her husband, James, "You have to come to some kind of closure somehow, as each day goes by, but it's very difficult to come to terms with it when you have nothing to hold on to." With initial estimates of 4,339 missing (later reduced to under 3,000), police had collected some 2,600 DNA samples from family members by late October.

On the very day of the New York terrorist attacks, media reports noted the emergence of DNA evidence in another famous case. In 1975, ex-convict James Riddle Hoffa was fighting to regain control of the Teamsters Union, lost when he was imprisoned for bribery and jury-tampering in the 1960s. Although granted clemency by President Richard Nixon in 1972, Hoffa was barred for a decade from participating in union affairs—a ruling he bitterly contested, described by some reporters as part of a corrupt bargain between Nixon and reigning Teamster president Frank Fitzsimmons. Hoffa disappeared on July 30, 1975, when he left home to keep a lunch date with union and underworld acquaintances at a Michigan restaurant. The presumed victim of a gangland murder "contract," Hoffa remains missing today, while theories abound as to where and how his remains were concealed.

On September 11, 2001, FBI spokesmen announced that DNA tests had identified samples of Hoffa's hair recovered from a car driven by Charles ("Chuckie") O'Brien on the day of Hoffa's disappearance. O'Brien, 66 years old in 2001 and retired to Florida, was raised in Hoffa's home but never formally adopted by the family. For more than a quarter-century he denied Hoffa's presence in the vehicle the day he disappeared, but federal agents now refute that claim. No charges have been filed to date, and Hoffa's daughter, St. Louis municipal judge Barbara Crancer, remains skeptical that the murder will ever be solved. "Unless they can break Chuckie down," she told *USA Today*, "I don't see it moving forward." Crancer's brother, James P. Hoffa, is the current Teamsters Union president and has urged investigators to pursue the case aggressively. The "new" evidence was revealed only after the *Detroit Free Press* filed a lawsuit under the Freedom of Information Act, forcing the FBI to open its files on the Hoffa case. Assistant U.S. Attorney Keith Corbett told reporters the obvious: "This is a 26-year-old case. There are a lot of hurdles to get over in bringing a case after this long."

With the advance of DNA testing, new legislation has evolved to control its application in criminal cases. The U.S. House of Representatives, on October 2, 2000, passed a law to provide individual states with federal grants to expedite testing of evidence collected from crime scenes and from convicted offenders. The money was expected to benefit states like Michigan, where 15,000 blood samples from known sex offenders had been collected since 1991, with barely 500 samples analyzed and catalogued during the next nine years. The bill was introduced by Rep. Bart Stupak, who told reporters, "Right now, state and local police departments cannot deal with the number of DNA samples from convicted offenders and unsolved crimes. States simply do not have enough time, money or resources to test and record these samples."

At the same time, juvenile offenders in Kentucky were exempted from providing DNA samples for a newly established database on sexual offenders. That decision was announced on August 21, 2001, by the Kentucky Court of Appeals. Acting in the case of a juvenile sex offender identified only as "J.D.K.," convicted of molesting and sodomizing his nine-year-old sister and an eight-year-old friend, the court unanimously ruled that juveniles could not be required to contribute DNA samples for state police files, where DNA profiles of 3,200 adult sex offenders already reside. Critics of the decision noted that many repeat offenders (including serial killers) commit their first sexual assaults in adolescence, thus granting opportunity for swift identification in later cases if samples are preserved, but the Kentucky judges felt themselves constrained by state law. As Judge Sara Combs declared from the bench, "By employing the words 'convicted' and 'felony'—words which the legislature itself has expressly defined and to which it has given technical meaning—it is plainly intended that juveniles adjudicated in district court not be included in the DNA database." (In Kentucky and most other jurisdictions, felonies are those offenses punishable by confinement for one year or more in state prison.)

States have adopted various methods in their efforts to compile useful DNA databases. Some states make sample contribution mandatory for convicted criminals, with jailers in Maine and New York empowered to place reluctant donors in solitary confinement, there extracting the samples by force if necessary. California's legislature adopted a different approach, assigning misdemeanor penalties to inmates who withhold DNA samples, but requiring prison officials to obtain separate court orders for each sample forcibly obtained. About 40 percent of California's prison inmates are presently "required" to donate DNA samples, but the misdemeanor statute carries no weight with those serving long terms—particularly inmates jailed for life or condemned to death row. Compared to the risk of indictment for additional sex crimes or murders, the threat of misdemeanor punishment—a maximum of one year's confinement in county jail—is no threat at all. To date, California has collected DNA profiles on 200,000 inmates convicted of qualifying felonies, but hundreds more resist and fight costly delaying actions in the courts. Inmate Fred Clark, serving 20 years at Vacaville's state medical facility, spoke for many other California inmates when he challenged authorities, saying, "If I don't submit, what are you going to do? Put me in jail? I tell you what. When I die, you can have all the DNA you want."

The reaction of local prosecutors to DNA testing varies from one location to the next. All are happy to use the new technology in pursuing convictions, but many resist application of testing to cases already resolved. San Diego provides a welcome change from official obstructionism, prosecutors volunteering in July 2000 to offer free DNA testing for any inmates claiming the results would set them free. Texas, by contrast, leads all other states in executions and in fighting to the last ditch against reviews of evidence in old cases. A state law enacted in April 2001 permits Texas inmates to seek post-conviction DNA analysis, but prosecutors in some jurisdictions seek to undermine the law by disposing of evidence before it can be tested. In December 2001, eight months after the statute took effect, the *Houston Press* reported that Harris County prosecutors were busily destroying rape kits, bloody clothing, semen swabs and other items of biological evidence from sexual assault cases. A prior statute permits county clerks to destroy trial evidence two years after conviction in noncapital felonies where a defendant is sentenced to more than five years, thus rendering DNA tests impossible in many cases. A spokesperson for the Harris County district attorney reported that 2,740 pounds of evidence had been destroyed in October and December 2001.

Under President Bill Clinton, the U.S. Justice Department set aside $750,000 for DNA testing of convicted felons, to resolve doubt in dubious cases, but Republican attorney general John Ashcroft scuttled the program in December 2001, announcing that the money would be used instead for identification of World Trade Center victims killed in the September 11 terrorist attacks. Justice spokesman Charles Miller assured reporters that "there's nothing sinister here," but some defense attorneys claimed to see a pattern in the new administration's disregard for civil rights (and President George W. Bush's record of excusing slipshod prosecution tactics during his stint as governor of Texas). John Pray, a professor at the University of Wisconsin Law School in Madison, opined, "It's safe to say that if you take away $750,000 that was earmarked, there's going to be some people who would have taken the test that would have proved them innocent." Virginia defense attorney Jerry Lyell was more direct, telling the press in response to Ashcroft's announcement, "It sounds a little fishy. To hear them cutting back, especially such a small amount comparatively . . . might suggest that their hearts weren't in the right place in the first place."

DONATIONS for Cartridges Offer: Internet scam
A strange and apparently pointless Internet scam was launched in October 2001, with circulation of a message promising charitable donations in return for used inkjet printer cartridges. The message reads as follows:

Subject: Don't throw out your empty inkjet cartridges. Now you can help. . . .

Help us raise $1 million for the Families of Freedom Scholarship fund by sending us your trash!

Every day, over one million empty inkjet cartridges are thrown out, ending up in our landfills. Now, if you send us your empty inkjet cartridges instead of throwing them away, we will donate money to a great charity that is trying to raise $100 million dollars to aid families affected by the terrorist attack of September 11, 2001.

Several weeks ago, President Bill Clinton and Bob Dole announced their involvement in a project called the Families of Freedom fund. The goal of the fund is to raise $100 million in order to establish scholarship money for the children of those tragically killed in the terrorist attacks.

IQ Inkjets is trying to help.

For every empty inkjet cartridge you send to us, we donate $1 to the fund. With your help, we will collect one million empty cartridges in the next six months and donate $1 million to the fund. We are proud to be a part of this great charity drive and thank you for your efforts in helping us.

Please CLICK HERE to go to our collection website and send us your empty inkjet cartridges. Or, you can send your empties to:

IQ Inkjet Products
Suite 1009
2944 Prosperity Avenue
Fairfax, VA 22031

Thanks for your support. We look forward to receiving your empty cartridges soon.

Intrigued by this message, a member of the U.S. Department of Energy's HOAXBUSTERS team launched an investigation of IQ Inkjet Products. Whereas the Families of Freedom Scholarship Fund is a recognized charity, the Web page linked to the IQ appeal proved to emanate from a website in Taiwan, whose contents were hidden. From there, the link led to another site in San Diego, California—and then to the Philippines, where IQ Inkjet has its headquarters. That firm's legitimate website, in turn, carried no information concerning any appeal for old cartridges or charitable donations deriving therefrom. Finally, Hoaxbusters turned to the mailing address in Fairfax, Virginia, which houses a truck rental and storage yard, with no connection to IQ Inkjet. At this writing, the cartridge donation appeal seems to be an elaborate and fruitless practical joke.

DOTSON, Gary: exonerated by DNA evidence
On the night of July 9, 1977, a Chicago woman told police she had been kidnapped and raped by two men while walking near her home. The attackers allegedly forced her into a car and assaulted her there, one man afterward trying to scratch words on her stomach with a broken beer bottle. Composite sketches of the

two men were prepared, and the woman later identified suspect Gary Dotson from a police mug book, then picked him out of a lineup. Semen stains from the woman's underpants matched Dotson's blood type, and a pubic hair recovered from her clothing was deemed "similar" to Dotson's. Convicted of rape and aggravated kidnapping in July 1979, Gary Dotson received a prison term of 25 to 50 years.

The case began to unravel in March 1985, when the alleged victim recanted her testimony, reporting that she had lied to conceal a consensual act of sex with her boyfriend. Dotson's judge refused to order a new trial, insisting that the "victim's" original testimony was more believable than her new statement, eight years after the fact. The governor of Illinois likewise refused to accept the woman's revised statement and denied Dotson's petition for a pardon, but on March 12, 1985, he did commute Dotson's sentence to time served, pending good behavior. That parole was revoked in 1987, after Dotson's wife accused him of domestic violence, and the Appellate Court of Illinois affirmed Dotson's rape conviction on November 12, 1987. The governor granted Dotson a "last chance parole" on December 24, 1987, but an arrest for barroom brawling two days later sent Dotson back to prison once more.

In 1988 Dotson's new lawyer submitted the original trial evidence for DNA testing, unknown at the time of conviction nine years earlier. Those tests excluded Dotson as a donor of semen samples from the victim's clothing, and a new trial was ordered by the Cook County Criminal Court. In light of the DNA evidence and their "victim's" shaky credibility, prosecutors declined to retry the case. Dotson's conviction was overturned on August 14, 1989, after he had served a total of eight years in prison.

"DRAGONBALL": computer worm

Identified for the first time in February 2001, this Internet worm virus is written in Visual Basic Script (VBS) and spreads via e-mails using Microsoft Outlook and IRC. Ironically, internal errors prevent DragonBall from operating correctly, but it still has the potential to infect computers. When the script runs initially, it replicates itself in the following system directories:

```
C:\windows\winsock.vbs
C:\windows\sysdir.vbs
C:\windows\system\millioner.vbs
```

```
C:\windows\system\dragonball.vbs
C:\windows\system\dragonball.cab
```

In the next phase of its attack, DragonBall changes keys in the system registry and the win.ini file, creating two new keys and altering others. Next, the worm opens Microsoft Outlook's address book and creates and sends an infected message to each address found, reading:

Subject: Hello ;]

Body: Hi, check out this game that I sent you (funny game from the net ;]).

Attach: dragonball.vbs

Once again, the worm's built-in bugs prevent it from spreading via e-mail, but the following dialogue box is displayed:

Dragon Ball Z by YuP
Thank you, and bye bye DragonWorld!!!
   [OK]

When the user closes that dialogue box, DragonBall seizes control of the computer's keyboard and mouse, running MediaPlayer with a file downloaded from the Internet, displaying the following text:

@ECHO ON
ECHO DraGon Ball [Z] by YuP
ECHO Thank you and bye bye dragon world!!

DRAPER, John T.: hacker "Cap'n Crunch"

New Jersey native John Draper was one of the premier American "phreakers"—hackers who experiment with different means of swindling telephone companies on long-distance charges. He is generally acknowledged as the inventor of the "BLUE BOX," though Draper credits the original technique to others in his published memoirs. In either case, he ranks among the first hackers involved in phone line manipulation and as one of the first imprisoned for wire fraud in the cyberage.

Draper's first "experiments" with telephone fraud date back to his teenage years, when—as described by one anonymous admirer—he tried "to convince pay phones to return his coin *and* put through his calls." In 1969, a year after his honorable discharge from the U.S. Air Force with service in Vietnam, Draper met a blind teenage "phreaker" and aspiring radio disc jockey. According to Draper, his new acquaintance and another friend pioneered the trick of using high-frequency tones to complete long-distance calls without payment. Musical instruments were initially used, and Draper derived his "Cap'n Crunch" nickname by using the plastic whistle from a cereal box to produce 2600-herz tones in pursuit of free phone calls. Among other tricks, he discovered a "secret" number in Vancouver, British Columbia that, when accessed, permitted free conference calls for an unlimited number of callers.

Draper and company were satisfied to keep a low profile, enjoying their own "experiments" in private, but others soon caught on to the blue box technique and its derivatives. In early 1971 the *San Jose Mercury* broke a story concerning the use of blue boxes by members of organized crime, provoking a swift reaction from federal authorities. The heat increased in October 1971, after *Esquire* magazine published an article titled "The Secret of the Little Blue Box," including a sampler of "phreaking" techniques. Against his better judgment, Draper had consented to an interview for the piece, and he was arrested in early 1972.

Convicted of wire fraud and sentenced to a minimum-security prison five months after his arrest, Draper quickly purchased a radio and modified it to pick up the frequency of walkie-talkies carried by his guards. He also modified a prison pay phone to make "collect" calls without any charge to the recipient. In his spare time, Draper instructed fellow inmates in the fine points of "phreaking" and constructing their own blue boxes. In return for those tutorials, he was protected by more physical inmates from the rigors of extortion, sexual assault, and other perils of incarceration. Draper recalls that it was "quite a challenge" teaching prisoners—including many virtual illiterates—to invade the telephone system and construct "cheese boxes" for free receipt of incoming toll calls.

Released on five years' probation, Draper was arrested once more in April 1974, after letting a friend use his computer to "modify" commercial telephone service. Draper later claimed the plan was "practically shoved down [his] throat," but federal prosecutors took a different view and he was sent back to jail for violating his probation. Prior to his second arrest, Draper and another hacker comrade also pulled "the White House toilet paper prank,"

wherein they allegedly used CIA codes to access President Richard Nixon directly, warning him that "Los Angeles is out of toilet paper!"

Back in the free world for good, Draper continued his computer experiments in a legitimate vein, creating the EasyWriter word processing program for the Apple II computer. In a nod to the old free-spirit days, Draper named the program after the 1969 film *Easy Rider,* starring Peter Fonda and Dennis Hopper.

"DRILLER": computer virus

Discovered in October 2000, "Driller" is a memory-resident, parasitic, polymorphic virus that infects Windows executable files with .exe, .scr and .cpl filename extensions. Driller also lingers in the system memory as a component of the infected Windows program, accessing and corrupting 15 different kernel functions as it spreads. When a file is infected, Driller encrypts its code and writes it to the end of the file, concealing it within an 8K segment of the target file. Internal bugs sometimes disrupt the infection process and present a Windows "error" message when the application is run. Thereafter, on Fridays, Driller replaces the startup page of Microsoft Internet Explorer and Netscape Navigator with a link to the website found at http://www.thehungersite.com and displays the following copyright text:

> [Virus TUAREG by The Mental Driller\29A]
> -This virus has been designed for carrying the TUAREG engine-

DUNKIN Donuts Boycott: Internet smear campaign

Soon after the terrorist attacks of September 11, 2001, some anonymous Internet hoaxer launched a malicious smear campaign against the Dunkin Donuts snack shop chain, attempting to incite a national boycott over the false claim that the company had sympathy with Arab terrorists. The message reads:

> *Attention all Americans:*
> *Boycott Dunkin Donuts!!*
>
> *In Cedar Grove, NJ, a customer saw the owner of a Dunkin Donuts store burn the U.S. flag. In another Dunkin Donuts store in Little Falls, a customer saw a U.S. flag on the floor with Arabic writing all over it.*

We are starting a nationwide boycott of all Dunkin Donuts. Please make sure this gets passed on to all fellow Americans during this time of tragedy. We Americans need to stick together and make these horrible people understand what country they are living in and how good they used to have it when we supported them. Numerous fastfood companies are at Ground Zero, giving away free food to volunteers. Where is Dunkin Donuts in all of this?

Boycott Dunkin Donuts!!!!!! Pass it on. . . .

No evidence exists that either of the incidents described above ever took place, nor has the Dunkin Donuts chain felt any impact from the anonymous call to arms. Apparently, recipients of the hoax e-mail were more intelligent than its author.

DURHAM, Timothy Edward: exonerated by DNA evidence
An Oklahoma college student, Timothy Durham was accused of molesting an 11-year-old Tulsa County girl in 1991. At trial in 1993, 11 alibi witnesses testified that Durham was 300 miles away from Tulsa when the crime occurred, but jurors convicted him regardless, and the court imposed a stunning sentence of 3,120 years in prison. DNA tests performed in 1997 proved Durham innocent, and he was subsequently released from prison. The crime remains unsolved today.

EASTMAN, Richard Mark: indicted on DNA evidence
Police in Peel, Ontario, were baffled by the murder of 63-year-old Muriel Holland, raped and strangled to death at a local senior's home on August 27, 1991. Eleven years and four months elapsed before they finally broke the case, as a result of Canadian legislation requiring all defendants convicted of serious offenses to provide blood samples for a national DNA data bank. Richard Eastman was serving time for an unrelated felony when lab technicians matched his DNA to semen samples lifted from the Holland crime scene in 1991. Authorities charged him with first-degree murder in January 2002, evoking public expressions of gratitude from Holland's family. Eastman denies involvement in the murder, and his trial has not been held thus far. He is presumed innocent until convicted by a jury of his peers.

"ECLIPSE": computer virus
Discovered in February 1990, the "Eclipse" computer virus is a nonmemory-resident companion virus which targets Windows executable files, renames them with a .bin extension, and copies itself to the infected file. On August 11 the virus displays this message:

[Eclipse] virus
11 August 1999: a day I will never forget!
by Black Jack/LineZer0/Metaphase

ELF Bowling/Frogapult: Internet virus hoaxes
Since December 1999 the Internet game distributor Nstorm (http://www.nstorm.com) has been victimized by malicious e-mail chain letters falsely claiming that two of its games are infected with an unidentified virus. The games singled out for attack are "Elf Bowling" and "Frogapult." To date, no infected copies of the game have been documented, and no fault has been found with Nstorm's website, though future discovery of games infected by some third party naturally cannot be ruled out. Nick Schoeneberger, developer of the games for Nvision Design Inc., has issued the following statement in regard to Nstorm's products.

Our company has produced a number of freely emailed and downloadable computer games which have been the subject of a hoax virus warning. We have contacted Symantec (makers of Norton Anti-Virus) and they have certified all of our games virus-free on this web page: http://www.symantec.com/avcenter/venc/data/y2kgame. hoax.html

ELFASSY, Raphael: accused of telemarketing fraud
A 21-year-old resident of Pierrefonds, Quebec, Raphael Elfassy was one of three defendants arrested on July 24, 2001, charged with conspiracy, fraud in excess of $5,000, and theft of communications via CELL PHONE CLONING. The arrests resulted from a joint international investigation dubbed "PROJECT

COLT," including collaboration of the Royal Canadian Mounted Police, Sûreté du Québec, the Montreal Urban Community Police Department, the FBI, U.S. Customs Service and U.S. Postal Service.

Prosecutors said Elfassy and his two alleged accomplices, 24-year-old Ross Taylor and 28-year-old Atiba Thomas, had run a telemarketing boiler room for six months prior to their arrest, placing free calls to the United States on cloned cell phones and swindling gullible victims with offers of a bogus tax scheme. The three allegedly posed as attorneys, announcing to prospective victims that they (the targets) had won $50,000. In order to receive their mythical prize, each victim was required to pay a 10 percent "tax" out of pocket. Worthless checks in the amount of $10,000 were mailed to victims as a show of "good faith," found to be fraudulent only after the American dupes had written checks of their own, ranging from $2,000 to $5,000. Investigators identified 16 victims who were swindled of an average of $5,000 each over six months. Trial of the defendants is pending.

E-MAIL "Bombing": Internet harassment technique

E-mail bombing (or "flooding") is defined as the malicious sending of numerous, often identical messages to a particular recipient with the intent of causing aggravation or, in extreme cases, disabling the target's mail server. Depending on the target—protected government and corporate computer systems, for example—the harassment may be criminal, leaving the "bomber" liable to fines or prison time. E-mail bombing is generally distinguished from the annoyance of "mass mailer" computer VIRUSES by the fact that (a) one target is singled out for flooding; (b) target selection is not typically random or haphazard; and (c) mail bombing generally does not infect or damage targeted computers aside from consuming memory or bandwidth.

Because e-mail harassment and other forms of CYBERSTALKING are now prosecuted with increasing frequency, e-mail bombers seek refuge in anonymity. One method of concealing their identity is through the use of anonymous remailers, widely available on the Internet. Another and more popular method is for the bomber to visit an Internet mailing service—such as Lyris or Shagmail—and subscribe to dozens (or hundreds) of e-mail "newsletters" via the target's address. Shagmail provides a prime example of the

system in action. As of January 2002 it offers 76 daily or bi-weekly newsletters, replete with "spam" advertising, to which unwitting targets may be subscribed by an enemy, with no attempt to verify the subscriber's address or identity. Once the flood of "spam" begins, victims are forced to "unsubscribe" from each list individually—a process often hampered by apparent glitches in the system, wherein victims are informed erroneously that they "are not subscribed" to the list in question, even as the messages keep pouring in. Shagmail administrators, meanwhile, stolidly ignore complaints and insist that their advertising-driven enterprise is "just for fun."

One unexpected venue of e-mail bombing during recent years has been the corporate battleground, where firms have secured their computer systems against outside attack but often overlook the threat from disgruntled employees within. A 1997 survey conducted by the FBI and the Computer Security Institute disclosed that 80 percent of 562 organizations polled saw employees as more likely sources of computer attack and sabotage than outside HACKERS. Of the firms surveyed, 43 percent reported one to five internal computer attacks in the previous year. Even governments are vulnerable to disgruntled keyboard saboteurs, as demonstrated by the cases of CLAUDE CARPENTER II and SCOTT DENNIS.

Most e-mail servers now provide some sort of screening software or a "killfile" capability for weeding out unwanted correspondents, but the weakness lies in their technology. Even the best can only weed out "spam" with certain words or codes displayed in the subject line—naming an advertisement or a product, for example—and the mechanism is simply avoided by altering titles or subjects. Furthermore, since many victims of e-mail bombing are listed as willing subscribers to the newsletters that flood their systems, the mass mailings do not qualify as spam. One provider with an answer to the problem is PrimeMail, whose "PrimeShield" system allows subscribers to set a daily e-mail limit, beyond which all incoming messages are discarded before reaching the customer's in-box. One obvious drawback to the system is the impossibility of predicting how many legitimate messages may be received on a given day. Even with PrimeShield, an e-mail bomber striking early in the day could jam the target's mailbox and prompt the system to discard all later messages, regardless of their source.

E-MAIL Tax Plan: Internet hoax

Since May 1999 a message circulated on the Internet has warned subscribers of an impending tax on e-mail. This warning described a nonexistent congressional bill, allegedly proposed for the benefit of the U.S. Postal Service. No such legislation has in fact been submitted to Congress, and the Postal Service publicly denies any attempt to recoup its losses from e-mail traffic via taxation. The original message reads (with errors intact):

* * * * * * * *

Dear Internet Subscriber: Please read the following carefully if you intend to stay online and continue using e-mail: The last few months have revealed an alarming trend in the Government of the United States attempting to quietly push through legislation that will affect your use of the Internet. Under proposed legislation (Bill 602P) the U.S. Postal service will be attempting to bilk email users out of "alternative postage fees". Bill 602P will permit the Federal Govt. to charge 5 cents surcharge on every email delivered, by billing Internet Service Providers at source. The consumer would then be billed inturn by the ISP. Washington D.C. lawyer Richard Stepp is working without pay to prevent this legislation from becoming law. The U.S. Postal Service is claiming that lost revenue due to the proliferation of email is costing nearly $230,000,000 in revenue per year. You may have noticed the recent ad campaign "There is nothing like a letter". Since the average citizen received about 10 pieces of email per day in 1998, the cost to the typical individual would be an additional 50 cents per day, or over $180 per year, above and beyond their regular Internet costs. Note that this would be money paid directly to the U.S. Postal Service for a service they do not even provide. The whole point of the Internet is democracy and non- interference. If the Federal Govt. is permitted to tamper with our liberties by adding a surcharge to e-mail, who knows where it will end. You are already paying an exorbitant price for snail mail because of bureaucratic inefficiency. It currently takes up to 6 days for a letter to be delivered from New York to Buffalo. If the U.S. Postal Service is allowed to tinker with email, it will mark the end of the 'free' Internet in the United States. One congressman, Tony Schnell (R) has even suggested a "twenty to forty dollar per month surcharge on all Internet service" above and beyond the government's proposed email charges. Note that most of the major newspapers have ignored the story, the only exception being the Washingtonian which called the idea of email surcharge "a useful concept whose time has come"

(March 6th 1999 Editorial) Don't sit by and watch your freedoms erode away! Send this email to all Americans on your list and tell your friends and relatives to write their congressman and say "No!" to Bill 602P Kate Turner assistant to Richard Stepp Berger, Stepp and Gorman Attorneys at Law 21 Concorde Street, Vienna, VA.

* * * * * * * *

"EMPEROR": computer virus

First identified in May 1999, this memory-resident, polymorphic, multipartite virus is rated "extremely dangerous" by computer analysts. It infects DOS .com and .exe files by writing its code to the end of the infected files. "Emperor" also overwrites the hard drive's Master Boot Record (MBR) and the boot sector of infected floppy disks with its own loading routing, thereby installing the virus into system memory on rebooting. Emperor also contains numerous debugging routines and is adept at bypassing antivirus protection on the computers it attacks. At the same time, internal bugs sometimes cause the target system to freeze when infected programs are executed. While infecting the MBR or floppy disk boot sector, Emperor erases substantial blocks of memory. A more destructive routine involves erasure of data on the target computer's hard drive, coupled with display of the following message:

EMPEROR

I will grind my hatred upon the loved ones. Despair will be brought upon the hoping childs of happiness. Wherever there is joy the hordes of the eclipse will pollute sadness and hate under the reign of fear. In the name of the almighty Emperor. . . .

This routine is executed any time the infected system is rebooted between 5:00 A.M. and 10:00 A.M., accompanied by display of a further text string reading:

the EMPEROR virus
written by Lucrezia Borgia
In Colombia, 1999

"EPSILON": computer viruses

Initially discovered in September 1996, the Epsilon computer virus exists in two forms, both rated as dangerous memory-resident companion viruses.

"Epsilon.513" contains bugs that disrupt its function and often freeze the infected system, while displaying the text string: Epsilon 1.0 © 15.3.1995 B.T.Pir8. The "Epsilon.1498" variant overwrites various hard disk sectors with the following text:

*Epsilon 1.9 © 27.4.1995 B.T.Pir8 * This virus was written in the city of Brno, Czechoslovakia (4Ever!), Europe (No such bloody America!). Drink only Tuzemsky Rum and fuck only Slovak girls! * A word to AEC, especially BBS Sysop and Mrnutstik & comp.: You are bloody fucked idiots! I'll destroy your dirty sickening BBS. Get ready, stupid idiotic lunatics! Get ready for WAR!!! * Message to Grisoft: Your AVG 3.3 is nice but not very successful on Epsilon, I'm afraid.*

ERDMANN, Ralph: pathologist who falsified medical evidence

In Texas, where he plied his trade as a circuit-riding medical examiner, Dr. Ralph Erdmann was nicknamed "Dr. Death." He won the moniker from prison inmates and defense attorneys, based on the consistency with which Erdmann provided testimony in felony cases, sending dozens of accused murderers to death row. Apparently a tireless civil servant, Dr. Erdmann operated in 40 of the Lone Star State's 47 counties, once charging prosecutors $171,000 for 400 autopsies in a single year. His medical verdicts invariably supported police theories in the cases he examined—so dependably, in fact, that one investigator later told reporters, "If the prosecution theory was that death was caused by a Martian death ray, then that was what Dr. Erdmann reported."

And therein lay the problem.

Erdmann's reputation began to unravel in 1992, when relatives of one deceased man obtained a copy of Erdmann's autopsy report, noting the weight of a spleen surgically removed years earlier. The body was exhumed, revealing that no autopsy had been performed. Lubbock attorney Tommy Turner was appointed as a special prosecutor to review Erdmann's work. In the process, he examined 100 autopsies and found "good reason to believe at least 30 were false." In fact, as one judge noted, police sometimes refrained from sending bodies to Erdmann because "he wouldn't do the work. He would ask what was the police theory and recite results to coincide with their theories."

When Erdmann did operate, he made bizarre and disturbing mistakes which prosecutors managed to conceal from jurors. In one case, Odessa prosecutors were forced to dismiss murder charges after Erdmann lost the victim's head, including with it the fatal bullet wound. In another he claimed to have examined a victim's brain, but exhumation revealed no cranial incisions. Yet another case found Erdmann mixing organs from two bodies in the same container and offering false testimony on the cause of death. Turner's investigation disclosed that Erdmann sometimes allowed his 13-year-old son to probe wounds during autopsies, and on several occasions his wife sold bones removed from murder victims.

It should not be supposed that Erdmann always ruled defendants guilty, though: if police believed a death was accidental, he could skew the evidence in that direction just as well. One such case involved 14-month-old Anthony Culifer, smothered with a pillow by his mother's live-in boyfriend. Erdmann blamed the child's death on pneumonia, his finding reversed by a second autopsy nine years later. In a similar case, a woman found by Erdmann to have choked on her own vomit was in fact murdered by a violent ex-boyfriend. The killer was eventually sentenced to life imprisonment, while Erdmann was ordered to pay the victim's family $250,000. It was Erdmann's testimony in capital cases that made him most dangerous, though, with at least four defendants executed on his word alone. At least 20 more condemned inmates in Texas have appealed their verdicts since Erdmann's misconduct was revealed.

In 1992 Dr. Erdmann appeared before a judge in Randall County, pleading guilty to seven felony counts of perjury and falsifying autopsy results. It was merely the tip of the iceberg, as civil suits began to multiply across Texas, but authorities seemed satisfied. As part of the plea bargain, Erdmann was stripped of his medical license, sentenced to 10 years' probation with 200 hours of community service, and ordered to repay $17,000 in autopsy fees. He moved to Seattle, Washington, where police found him with a cache of weapons in June 1995, thereby violating terms of his probation. Texas hauled Erdmann back to serve his time, and while he was eligible for parole after serving 30 months, public protests scuttled his first parole bid in March 1997.

(See also: GILCHRIST, JOYCE; ZAIN, FRED).

ERICSSON/NOKIA Telephone Giveaway: Internet hoax

In late 1999 a fraudulent e-mail began to circulate on the Internet, offering free Nokia telephones to any participants in a familiar chain letter scheme. Curiously, that hoax prompted another, as the competing Ericsson company was targeted by a similar hoax in April 2000. Neither firm is responsible for the e-mails sent out in its name, and no free phones will be forthcoming to those duped by the scheme. The Ericsson message reads:

Dear customer

Our main competitor, Nokia, is giving free mobile phones away on the Internet. Here at Ericsson we want to counter this offer. So we are giving our newest WAP-phones away as well. They are specially developed for Internet happy customers who value cutting edge technology. By giving free phones away, we get valuable customer feedback and a great Word-of-Mouth effect. All you have to do, is to forward this message to 8 friends. After two weeks delivery time, you will receive

a Ericsson T18. If you forward it to 20 friends, you will receive the brand new Ericsson R320 WAP-phone. Just remember to send a copy to Anna.Swelund@ericsson. com—that is the only way we can see, that you forwarded the message.

Best of luck
Anna Swelund
Executive Promotion Manager for Ericsson Marketing

Any rights not expressly granted herein are reserved. Reproduction, transfer, distribution or storage of part or all of the contents in any form without the prior written permission of Ericsson is prohibited except in accordance with the following terms. Ericsson consents to you browsing Ericsson World Wide Web pages on your computer or WAP-phone and printing copies of these pages for private use only.

This doubtless ranks as the first time recipients of a chain letter were both encouraged to send it on *and* legally forbidden to do so, but the warning had no effect in any case, as Ericsson repudiated the message in its entirety.

"ESMERALDA": computer virus

Initially catalogued in January 2000, "Esmeralda" is a memory-resident, parasitic virus that targets Windows 95 systems. Upon the opening of .exe files, Esmeralda writes itself to the end of the infected file, thereafter randomly erasing sectors on the infected computer's C drive. While active, it displays the following text:

> *ESMERALDA*
> *para Esmeralda Vera Vera*
> *Bucaramanga, Colombia, 1999*

"ETHAN": computer virus

Discovered in 1998, the "Ethan" computer virus draws its name from Edith Wharton's classic novel *Ethan Frome* (1911). It is a Word macro virus that replicates within Word 97 programs, corrupting Word's normal.dot documents and template. On first contact, Ethan replicates by creating a file named "c:\ethan.__" and thereafter strikes randomly, changing the properties of various Word documents as they are opened. Typical changes include alteration of a document's title to "Ethan Frome," change of

A fraudulent e-mail circulated in 1999 offered free Nokia phones in a familiar chain-letter scheme. A similar hoax followed offering free Ericsson phones. (Nokia)

author's name to "EW/LN/CB," and change of a company's name to "Foo Bar Industries, Inc." ("Foo Bar" is a variant spelling of the slang term "fubar"—an acronym for "*f*ucked *u*p *b*eyond *a*ll *r*ecognition.") In addition to tampering with documents, Ethan was also designed to deliver another payload on the first workday of each month between April and December 1999. On the relevant dates it displayed the following messages (presented with errors as shown in the original):

On April 1—

Y2K! Spread the word

This is not an April fools joke. I wish it were! The year 2000 is fast approaching, and the word still needs to be spread about the implications and dangers of the millennium bug commonly referred to as the Y2K bug. The virus that has infected this word document was written to help spread the word about the Y2K bug, and educate you so you can prepare yourself and your family for Saturday January 1, 2000. Today until January 1, 2000, on the first business day of each month, I will give you a lesson in Y2K preparation. Spread the word. Knowledge is power!

On May 3—

Hello again!

Lets start our first lesson to help prepare you for the millennium bug. Although I don't personally believe there will be food shortages, power shortages, gas shortages as a result of the computer bug, there will be food, power and gas shortages by hoarding nitwits that fear the millennium bug. As a result, I highly recommend that you begin to stockpile bottled water (1-month supply), canned food (1-month supply), and as much gas as you can store (keep your vehicle gas tank always topped up starting December 1st). That's it for this month. See you next month!

On June 1—

How's the weather?

Right now it's pretty warm out, so you are probably not thinking much about the winter. But remember the millennium bug is expected to hit in the middle of winter. If you're in a northern climate, like the Great White North (Canada), I suggest you consider purchasing a good airtight wood stove, and at least a face cord of wood. Even if there are no disruptions in natural gas,

or oil, or electricity, the wood stove is a great way of reducing your heating bills. And if there is a problem, you will be comfortable in your own heated home, unlike your unprepared neighbors (remember the Canadian ice storm last year!) That's it for this month. See you next month!*

On July 2—

Did you get the stove?

Last month I recommend purchasing a gas stove to help heart your home in the event that your supply of electricity, gas, or oil was interrupted. This month I would like to suggest that you purchase a portable generator and enough gas cans to store gas to power the generator. The generator can be used to power lighting and small electrical appliances should the power be disrupted. That's it for this month. See you next month!

On August 2—

Getting back to basics

In this installment, I would like to suggest that you consider purchasing candles, matches, flashlights, and batteries. These items will be invaluable during those cold, dark nights should the power companies fail in their Y2K conversion. Don't plan on relying on the banks or credit/debit cards. Start each month, and stash away enough money to last you at least 2 months. This money should include enough money to pay the rent/mortgage, utilities, FOOD, etc. Remember cold hard cash is accept EVERYWHERE. That's it for this month. See you next month!

On September 1—

A Limerick

The millennium's not far away Get onto your coding today Fix it or fudge it The boss won't begrudge it If everything works on the day! That's it for this month. See you next month!

On October 1—

Three months to go

Getting nervous? If you've followed my advice over the past months, there should be nothing for you to worry about. We will survive the Y2K bug, but preparation will insure that if there is any Y2K crisis, it will only be small bump in the road, not a major pothole for you. That's it for this month. See you next month!

On November 1—

Two months to go
    Personally, I don't believe that there will be a major, global Y2K crisis. I trust the banks with my money. I trust MOST of the industrial sector, and I trust the power and water agencies to provide me with power and water over the infamous weekend. I even trust the Russians and there nuclear arms! BUT you can never be too careful. Take care. Be prepared. Use common sense. That's it for this month. See you next month!

On December 1—

Good Luck (30 days to go)
    Well, this will be the final installment in the Y2K preparation lessons. If you have followed my advice over the past few months, you will be in excellent shape to bring in the New Year. May the New Year bring you health and happiness. Best wishes. Bye!

EUROPEAN Institute for Computer Anti-Virus Research

An unofficial organization devoted to combating computer VIRUSES in Europe and beyond, the European Institute for Computer Anti-Virus Research (EICAR) recruits members from leading universities, industry, government, the military and law enforcement, while cooperating with the media and privacy advocates "to unite efforts against writing and proliferation of malicious code like computer viruses or Trojan Horses, and, against computer crime, fraud and the misuse of computers or networks, inclusive [of] malicious exploitation of privacy data."

With that broad mission in mind, members of EICAR are pledged to uphold a particular code of conduct that includes the following strictures:

1. "Total abstinence" from any publications or other activity that could promote panic at large— "i.e., no 'trading on people's fears'."
2. "Abstaining from the loud and vociferous superlatives and factually untenable statements in advertising, e.g., 'all known and unknown viruses will be recognised'."
3. Withholding any information suited to development of viruses from unauthorized third parties. Exchange of data between serious researchers and/or research institutions is permitted when all have passed inspection and accept the EICAR code of conduct.

In action, EICAR seeks to operate as a "Cyber Defense Alliance" (CDA), defined by organization spokesmen as "a framework of support that endeavours to create a 'User Friendly Information Society.'" Reaching beyond the bounds of Europe, the CDA is envisioned as "a global initiative that includes legal frameworks, research, technical measures, and organisational co-operations in support of the objective." More specifically, that objective includes:

- Global cooperation with other security and antivirus organizations
- Support for the European Commission's Convention on Cyber Crime
- Support for the EC's Research Technology Development Information Security Technology Program
- Warning, verification, and reporting of new computer viruses
- Compilation of a central database on malicious codes
- Establishment of a unified convention for naming new viruses
- Certification and licensing of antivirus researchers with standard recognized requirements
- Support for antivirus research and enhancement of defense mechanisms
- Improved public education and awareness of the problem

By 2001, various EICAR task forces were involved in debate on the issues listed here, developing policy statements while actively continuing research on computer viruses at a more practical level. Constant networking is maintained with similar groups, such as the Asian Anti-Virus Research Association.

"EVERYTHING You Never Wanted to Know"
Survey: Internet scam
The following Internet message poses as a means for subscribers to make new friends, but in fact it gives the anonymous author access to personal information on anyone foolish enough to respond. A relatively "innocent" use of that information might be its sale to some Internet advertising consortium. On the other hand, it could as easily be used in CYBERSTALKING for malicious purposes. The message reads:

Everything you never wanted to know and were afraid to ask

Here's what you're supposed to do. Copy this entire e-mail and change all the answers so they apply to you. Then send it to everyone you know, INCLUDING me. So you should get back a lot of get-to-know-you e-mails. You'll learn a lot about your friends that you maybe didn't know. Please take 5 minutes of your day to do this.

FULL NAME:
NICKNAME(s):
HOMETOWN:
BORN:
CURRENT RESIDENCE:
CROUTONS OR BACON BITS:
FAVORITE SALAD DRESSING:
DO YOU DRINK:
SHAMPOO & CONDITIONER OR
   JUST CONDITIONER:
HAVE YOU EVER GONE SKINNY DIPPING:
DO YOU MAKE FUN OF PEOPLE:
FAVORITE COLORS:
HAVE YOU EVER BEEN CONVICTED OF
   A CRIME:
BEST ON-LINE FRIENDS:
ONE PILLOW OR TWO:
PETS:
FAVORITE TYPES OF MUSIC:
DREAM CAR:
TYPE OF CAR YOU DRIVE NOW:
WHAT TYPE OF CAR WAS YOUR FIRST CAR:
TOOTHPASTE:
FAVORITE FOOD:
DO YOU GET ALONG WITH YOUR PARENTS:
FAVORITE ICE CREAM:
FAVORITE SOFT DRINK:
FAVORITE TYPE OF FAMILY GAME TO PLAY:
WHAT IS YOUR BAD TIME OF DAY:
FAVORITE TIME OF YEAR:
ADIDAS, NIKE, OR REEBOK:
FAVORITE PERFUME OR COLOGNE:
FAVORITE WEBSITE:
FAVORITE SUBJECT IN SCHOOL:
FAVORITE MOVIE YOU HAVE SEEN RECENTLY
   OR FAVORITE TYPE OF MOVIE:
LEAST FAVORITE SUBJECT:
FAVORITE ALCOHOLIC DRINK:
FAVORITE SPORT TO WATCH:
MOST HUMILIATING MOMENT:
CRAZIEST OR SILLIEST PERSON YOU KNOW:
WHAT DO YOU LOOK FOR IN
   THE OPPOSITE SEX:

SAY ONE NICE THING ABOUT THE PERSON WHO SENT THIS TO YOU:
PERSON YOU SENT THIS TO, WHO IS LEAST LIKELY TO RESPOND:

"EXEHEADER": computer viruses

First noted in July 1996, this family of parasitic computer viruses includes at least 13 variants. All write themselves into the free space (or "cave") found in .exe headers, thereby concealing themselves since the file size does not increase. "ExeHeader" viruses contain the following text strings:

"Bane.256": [Bane]
"Bosco.a": BOSCO
"Bosco.b,d:" BOSCO D'SOUZA
"Bosco.c": ROYDEN D'SOUZA
"Dina.271": Dina v4.4r
"Dina.283": Dina v4.2r
"Dragon.400": DRAGON-2 Anti
"HeaderBug.324":C:\DOS\SMARTDRV.EXE=Header-Bug=
"Hobbit.416": HOBBIT
"Mike.252": (c) MIKE.
"Morality": MORALITY
"Mz1": Mz1 Copyright (c) 1992 by Ç ñ á
"Renegade.416": Renegade
"Retro": [Dying_Oath] by Retro
"Vlad.337": [Serrelinda], Rhince/VLAD
"XAM.278": XAM

Variations of the ExeHeader virus perform in different ways upon invading a target computer. They include:

ExeHeader.396 A dangerous virus that infects files as they are executed, converting .exe files to the .com format. After successfully corrupting 256 files, the virus begins to erase large disk sectors.

ExeHeader.440 Another dangerous virus, infecting both .exe and .com files. In some cases the virus then manifests itself with a video display.

ExeHeader.AntiArj Designed to corrupt only sectors that contain the header of ARJ archives (a protected archive system named for its creator, Robert Jones).

ExeHeader.Clust An encrypted cluster virus that contains the following test strings:

"Clust.a": [Clust2] JT/Trident
"Clust.b": [Clust2B]
"Clust.c": [Clust2C]

ExeHeader Bosco A virus that searches out and deletes .chk files ("chunks" of data collected for future repair and saved to a computer's root directory when Windows 95/98 runs its Scandisk program, following any malfunction).

ExeHeader.Dragon.400 A stealth virus that installs itself as a device driver, thereafter intercepting the "write" and "read" commands to legitimate device drivers. If the accessed data contain .exe headers, the virus inserts itself automatically.

ExeHeader.Joan A stealth virus that installs itself into an infected computer's High Memory Area. It contains the text string:

>Joan v1.2 by KiKo NoMo of T.N.T. Taipei/Taiwan
1995/08

ExeHeader.Ming While corrupting files, this virus sometimes (but not always) displays the message:

Written By Crazy Lord (Ming)
Made in Hong Kong

ExeHeader.Olya A dangerous stealth virus that overwrites disk sectors with the text "Olya Kibina" on the 26th day of April.

ExeHeader.Pure Similar in operation to ExeHeader.Joan, this variant is another stealth virus that attaches itself to a computer's High Memory Area.

ExeHeader.SkidRow Triggered whenever the month and date share the same numerical value—1 January, 2 February, and so forth—this virus displays the following messages:

"ExeHeader.SkidRow.415,427":
This is Skid-Row Virus
Written by Dark Slayer
* in Keelung. Taiwan *
"ExeHeader.SkidRow.432":
This is Skid-Row Virus
Written by Dark Slayer
% in Keelung. Taiwan %

ExeHeader.XMA.278 After installing itself, this variant attaches to each tap on the infected computer's keyboard, checking system buffers for .exe file headers and copying itself into any such headers located.

EXPLODING Gel Candles Warning: Internet hoax

Beginning in June 2001 the Internet was flooded with alerts announcing an alleged recall of gel candles, peculiar (and futile) in that it names no specific brand, recalling firm or other agency. The U.S. Department of Energy's HOAXBUSTERS team investigated the gel candle safety issue and was able to document one recall, in June 1998, of Glade brand candles that were found to burn a bit too intensely. No further recalls have been ordered on any brand of candles since that time, and no explosions have ever been recorded. The hoax message reads:

Subject: IMPORTANT INFORMATION—Gel candles

Thought you all should read this for your own safety

Hi all, My former secretary had a terrible thing happen to her and her family last week, and I wanted to share it with all of you so that you could be warned and warn your friends and family as well. She had a gel candle burning in her bathroom . . . it exploded and caught her house on fire . . . the house burned down and they have lost everything. The fire marshal told her that this is not the first incident where a gel candle has exploded and caused a fire. He said that the gel builds up a gas, and often times it explodes and sets fire to the room it is in, which is what happened to her. The fire was so hot it melted the smoke alarm, and they didn't discover the fire until there was an explosion, which was her toilet blowing up, and then it was too late . . . the entire upstairs was engulfed in flames. Smoke damage and water damage have destroyed what wasn't destroyed by fire. I know that there are roomies and friends that I don't have on this list because I can't remember how to spell their screen names . . . please pass this along to anyone I missed. I wouldn't want this to happen to anyone else. Her family is devastated. All their mementos and everything of value and meaning are gone. I'm not trying to scare anyone . . . just a friendly warning to all of you about the use of gel candles left unattended. Thanks and take care.

NOTE: Marty and I know a lady who loved the gel candles. She had one burning on her mantle and it caught fire just like in the message above. She was at home at the time and saw it happen and grabbed the candle to keep it from setting her home on fire and it came apart in her hand. She suffered third degree burns to her hand and 3 fingers! Please, if you or anyone you know have these candles, don't light them, they are dangerous. Please, pass this on.

FAIN, Charles: exonerated by DNA evidence

Nine-year-old Daralyn Johnson was kidnapped on February 24, 1982, while walking to school in Nampa, Idaho. School administrators assumed she was absent due to illness, and Daralyn's parents knew nothing of her disappearance until she failed to return home that afternoon. Police soon learned that she had never reached the school. Her corpse was found three days later, in a ditch near the Snake River. Autopsy results showed that Daralyn had been raped, then drowned. Pubic hairs from an unknown subject were retrieved from her underpants and one stocking.

Seven months after the murder, an informant directed police to sanitation worker Charles Fain. Detectives noted that his light-brown hair appeared to match the hairs recovered from Daralyn's body. Fain also resided one block from Daralyn's home in September 1982, but at the time of the murder he had lived 360 miles away, in Redmond, Oregon. At his second interrogation, in October 1982, Fain agreed to a polygraph examination and passed it, the examiner reporting that Fain told the truth when he denied participation in Daralyn's rape and murder.

Still, local prosecutors charged him with the crime and held Fain for trial in 1983. The polygraph results were inadmissible in court, and while an Oregon librarian testified on Fain's behalf, describing him as a regular customer around the time of the Idaho murder, jurors chose to believe an FBI technician who described the crime scene hairs as "similar" and "con-

sistent" to Fain's. Convicted of first-degree murder, kidnapping and rape, Fain was sentenced to death in February 1984. Still maintaining his innocence, he converted to Christianity in prison and joined fellow inmates in a legal contest for the right to hold religious services on death row (victorious in 1989).

DNA analysis was unknown at the time of Fain's conviction and death sentence, but science caught up with his case in 2001, after he had served more than 17 years in prison. "Overall," he told reporters, "I believed I was going to get out because I was innocent. When this DNA stuff started coming on the news, something just told me it was going to be part of this case." Indeed, testing proved beyond doubt that the pubic hairs found on Daralyn Johnson's body in 1984 were not Fain's, a result confirmed by independent prosecution testing on June 28, 2001. One week later, Idaho attorney general Al Lance joined defense attorneys in petitioning a federal court to grant Fain a writ of habeas corpus. U.S. District Judge B. Lynn Winmill voided Fain's conviction on July 6, 2001, and remanded his case to the original trial court for further action.

Attorney General Lance, while cooperative to a point, still declared, "It is important to the interests of justice that there be no misunderstanding as to the meaning of this announcement. DNA testing was not available at the time of Fain's trial and conviction. It is available today and, appropriately, has been used in this case. While this new evidence does show the need for further review, it would be wrong to say that it proves Fain's innocence. The DNA testing proves only one thing. It proves that the pubic hairs found on the victim's clothing did not belong to Charles Fain. That fact in itself does not mean that Fain did not commit these crimes. This evidence does not exonerate Mr. Fain."

And yet, despite such face-saving pronouncements, it did precisely that. Fain was released from custody on August 24, 2001, after prosecutors declined to retry the case against him. formally dismissing the charges. Fain expressed no bitterness at the system that had falsely imprisoned him, telling journalists, "I gave that up a long time ago. That is the one thing I know I can do: forgive." To date, the murder of Daralyn Johnson remains unsolved.

"FAMILY Pictures" Computer Virus: Internet hoax

Beginning in March 2001, bogus warnings of yet another nonexistent computer virus began to circulate on the Internet. A spokesman for the U.S. Department of Energy's HOAXBUSTERS website suggests, with wry humor, that this fraud may have been perpetrated by someone fed up with browsing through photo albums. The original warning reads (with original errors):

Subject: Virus to look out for

DO NOT OPEN "NEW PICTURES OF FAMILY" It is a virus that will erase your whole "C" drive. It will come to you in the form of an E-mail from a familiar person. I repeat a friend sent it to me, but called & warned me before I opened it. He was not so lucky and now he can't even start his computer! Forward this to everyone in your address book. I would rather receive this 25 times than not at all.

Also: Intel announced that a new and very destructive virus was discovered recently. If you receive an e-mail called "FAMILY PICTURES," do not open it. Delete it right away! This virus removes all dynamic link from your computer. Your computer will not be able to boot up.

"FANTASMA": computer virus

Identified for the first time in October 1996, "Fantasma" is a dangerous, memory-resident, parasitic virus that attaches itself to the end of .com and .exe files when they are opened or executed. Begin-

ning in the year 2000, the virus delivers a payload on March 5 of each successive year, overwriting boot sectors of the infected computer's hard drive with a Trojan program that displays the following text:

Internal Error
Virus FANTASMA. Mexico 1996

"FASTLANE": alleged software pirate gang

On February 15, 2001, the U.S. Justice Department indicted nine defendants, alleged members of a gang known to its members as Fastlane, for stealing more than $1 million in copyrighted computer software, games, and movies via nonpublic Internet sites. Those charged in the nine-count indictment included 36-year-old Steve Deal (a.k.a. "Doobie"), of Charlotte, North Carolina, and Trenton, New Jersey; 31-year-old Tony Walker (a.k.a. "SyS"), of San Diego, California; 26-year-old Ryan Breding (a.k.a. "river"), from Oklahoma City; 25-year-old Glendon Martin (a.k.a. "TeRRiFiC"), of Garland, Texas; 22-year-old Shane McIntyre (a.k.a. "Crypto"), from Boynton Beach, Florida; 20-year-old Bjorn Schneider (a.k.a. "airwalker"), of Falmouth, Massachusetts; 19-year-old James Milne (a.k.a. "lordchaos"), from Shawnee, Kansas; 19-year-old Tae Yuan Wang (a.k.a. "Prometh"), of Bellevue, Washington; and 19-year-old Kevin Vaughn (a.k.a. "DaBoo"), from Raleigh, North Carolina.

According to government spokesmen, the gang was broken when an FBI undercover agent infiltrated its ranks and was asked to provide a computer for one of Fastlane's Internet websites, for illicit distribution of stolen software. The agent agreed and thereafter monitored the gang's operations via that computer, spying from within. Prosecutors tracked illegal downloads and distribution of copyrighted software between January and September 2000, when Steve Deal was arrested and released on $10,000 bond. Eight of the defendants were charged with multiple counts of copyright infringement and conspiracy, while Vaughn was indicted for conspiracy alone.

As detailed in the charges, Fastlane was founded in November 1999, with members inside the U.S. and abroad. Defendants Deal, McIntyre, Schneider, and Wang were the managing brains behind Fastlane. Martin, Milne, and Vaughn allegedly operated the gang's computers and websites, where stolen software—dubbed "warez" by the pirates—was stored. Breding and Walker allegedly provided hardware in return for free access to the stolen software, games, and movies. Fastlane websites included the "Super Dimensional Fortress Macros" (SDFM) site operated by an FBI undercover agent between January 7, 2000, and September 20, 2000. Defendants Deal, Schneider, McIntyre, and Wang also reportedly participated in management of the SDFM site, downloading thousands of copyrighted programs that included operating systems, utilities, word processing software, data analysis and spreadsheet applications, communications programs, graphics, desktop publishing, and games. During nine months of operation, the SDFM site alone downloaded more than 1,900 gigabytes and distributed more than 697 gigabytes of software, including Microsoft Office 2000, Microsoft Windows Millennium, Adobe Framemaker v6.0, Corel Custom Photo SE, Symantec PCAny-where, and McAfee VirusScan—collectively valued in excess of $1 million.

Other sites affiliated with Fastlane included Sacred Halls (SH), maintained by defendant Milne at a university in Kansas and remotely accessed from his Shawnee home; The Good News, maintained by defendant Martin in Ohio and remotely accessed from Texas; and 4:20, maintained by defendant Vaughn at a university in North Carolina. FBI agents were assisted in their investigation by agents of the Interactive Digital Software Association, the Business Software Alliance, the Software and Information Industry Association, and the Motion Picture Association of America.

No trial has yet been scheduled for the Fastlane defendants as of January 2002. Justice Department spokesmen remind the public that indictments contain only charges and are not proof of guilt. If convicted, defendants charged with conspiracy to infringe copyright face a maximum sentence of five years in prison and a $250,000 fine on each count. Copyright infringement carries a maximum sentence of three years in prison and a $250,000 fine on each count. Financial restitution is mandatory in the event of conviction.

FBI Computer Crimes Unit

Although the Federal Bureau of Investigation (FBI) has used computers for decades, for all manner of tasks including data storage and FINGERPRINT identi-

fication, no concerted effort toward tracking criminals in cyberspace was made in Washington before the late 1990s. The first such unit was apparently based in the Cleveland field office, spawned by an executive order from President Bill Clinton that created a new Infrastructure Protection Task Force. By year's end, similar units were operating from FBI field offices in New York City, San Francisco, and Washington, D.C. On February 25, 1997, the bureau announced that a similar unit would soon be operational in its Los Angeles field office, coordinating efforts across the country. Supervisory special agent John McClurg told reporters, "A number of other cities are actually on the verge of reaching that point in which they have the expertise [in tracking cybercriminals] that is certifiable. Los Angeles is very close. Teams are being formed across the U.S. in the field offices."

As described in FBI press releases, the computer crime unit was designed to bridge a gap between domestic criminal investigations and the bureau's national security function, operating internationally if evidence led investigators beyond the continental United States. Still, it was July 1999 before the FBI formally announced its "war" on computer criminals, in a press release from the Seattle field office. There, 10 agents were assigned to cybercrime full-time, assisted by two assistant U.S. attorneys. Cases specifically earmarked for handling by the unit included CHILD PORNOGRAPHY, drug dealing, or financial crime, and intrusion into computer networks by disgruntled employees or recreational "HACKERS." In April 2000, Washington spokesmen felt confident enough to announce creation of a new InfraGuard program, described as "just one portion of a larger plan to tackle computer crimes as networks become more valuable to international commerce and carry more important information." By that time, FBI computer squads were collaborating full time with other agencies, via the Justice Department's National Infrastructure Protection Center and its Internet Fraud Complaint Center.

Ted Jackson, special agent in charge of the Atlanta field office, told reporters that the FBI considers computer crime "the new form of terrorism. Someone involved in attacking your system can cause more problems than bombs." The bureau was determined to root out cybercriminals, Jackson insisted. "When you're at your computer and do something illegal, and you affect commerce or government, we're going to do everything in our power to bring you before the bars of justice."

FBI investigators recognize two basic kinds of computer crime: (1) crimes facilitated by computers, as money laundering, transmission of pornography, or different kinds of fraud; and (2) crimes where a computer itself is the target of intrusion, data theft, or sabotage. Federal investigators derive their authority from computer crimes legislation passed by Congress, including some statutes—wire fraud, interstate transmission of threats or ransom demands, and so forth—enacted long before the first computer was invented. In theory, the FBI investigates a case only when federal statutes have been violated, and the U.S. attorney's office supports investigation with an agreement to prosecute if federal violations are substantiated. Under prevailing law, unless a subject voluntarily discloses information, FBI agents may only gather evidence pursuant to a search warrant, court order, or a federal grand jury subpoena.

Those are the rules, but civil libertarians remind us of the FBI's history, including numerous illegal break-ins, wiretaps, and all manner of criminal harassment against minority groups spanning the better part of a century, from the bureau's creation in 1908 through (at least) the early 1990s. Voices of concern were raised with the unveiling of the FBI's Carnivore program, a software tool designed to scan the Internet at large (some say illegally, at random) for evidence of crime in cyberspace, and bureau explanations of the software's "surgical" precision did little to pacify outspoken critics. Likewise, the passage of sweeping new search-and-surveillance legislation in the wake of September 2001's terrorist attacks on New York City and the Pentagon suggested broad potential for abuse. It remains to be seen how federal agents and prosecutors will use their new powers, or whether they will once more exceed their authority in the name of "national security."

FCC Religion Broadcasting Ban: Internet hoax

Since February 2000 a series of fraudulent e-mails have circulated on the Internet, claiming that the Federal Communications Commission (FCC) is plotting to eradicate religious programming in America. Despite FCC repudiation of the lie—and the fact that religious broadcasts seem to increase in number with each passing month—the hoax lives on in cyberspace and still apparently wins the odd gullible convert

from time to time. The original (with errors uncorrected) reads:

Please chare this with everyone! We don't need to sit back and be passive on this one. This is really scary and once you read it you'll realize that CBS would even be forced to discontinue "Touched By An Angel" because they use the word "God" in every program. Madeline Murray O'Hare, an atheist, successfully eliminated the use of Bible reading and prayer from schools fifteen years ago. Her organization has now been granted a Federal Hearing on the same subject by the Federal Communications Commission (FCC) in Washington, DC. Their petition, No. 2493, would ultimately pave the way to stop the reading of the Gospel of our Lord and Savior Jesus Christ, on the airwaves of America. They took this petition with 287,000 signatures to back their stand. If this attempt is successful, all Sunday Worship services being broadcast either by radio or television will stop. This group is also campaigning to remove all Christmas Programs, Christmas songs and Christmas carols from public schools. You can help! We need one million signed letters. This would defeat their effort and show that there are many Christians alive, well and concerned in our country. Please print this letter then cut off and sign the form below. PLEASE DO NOT SIGN JOINTLY, such as "Mr. & Mrs." Each person should sign one letter separately, and mail it in separate envelopes. Be sure to put "Petition 2495" ON THE ENVELOPE when you mail the letter. This has to go out regular mail. It's important that you do it right away. Please e-mail this letter to all your friends and relatives and to anyone else you feel led to. Or photo copy it and mail it. Christians must unite on this. Please do not take this lightly. You don't have to be a "Bible Thumper" to realize the significance of the disappearance of another good influence in our lives, and of particular concern, that of the next generation's lives. We did once and lost prayer in schools and in offices across the nation. We cannot let this attempt succeed. Below is a sample letter that you can copy and send, or draft your own personal message to voice your concern.

Send letter to:

Date: January ___, 2000

*Federal Communications Commission
Washington, DC 20054*

Re: Petition 2493

Dear Sirs;

I am an American and am very thankful for my American Heritage. Our forefathers founded this country under the premise of a strong belief and faith in God and His principles. I am also very much aware of the role that our Christian faith has played in the freedom that we Americans now enjoy. Therefore, I protest any effort to remove from radio or television, programs designed to nurture faith in God, or to remove Christmas programs, Christmas songs and Christmas carols from public airwaves, schools, office buildings, etc.

> *Sincerely.*
> *Name:*
> *Address:*
> *City:*
> *State & Zip Code:*

FCC spokespersons insist that there is no Petition 2493 (or 2495, for that matter) and that if such a petition were submitted the commission would ignore it. Likewise, the FCC has no jurisdiction over what is done, said, or broadcast in "schools, office buildings, etc." Finally, while televangelists frequently harp on the theme, the late activist Madalyn Murray O'Hair left no "organization" behind at the time of her death to continue working for the strict separation of church and state. The alleged conspiracy against religious broadcasting simply does not exist—except in the imaginations of certain doomsday preachers who find it useful as a fund-raising ploy.

"FIASKO": computer virus

Described by analysts as a harmless, nonmemory-resident, parasitic, polymorphic virus, "Fiasko" was first reported in January 2000. It attacks Windows systems exclusively, searching out executable files and infecting the first two found in each directory, writing itself to the end of each file. Its innocuous payload is delivered in the following display:

mort's virus
FIASKO '99—10x 4 nothing . . .

"FILTH": computer virus

Discovered in February 2000, "Filth" is classified as a dangerous, memory-resident, parasitic, stealth virus that attacks Windows systems, writing itself to the

end of executable files. Each time an infected file is executed, the virus takes control, switches to Windows kernel mode, and replicates itself in memory as a driver. In the process of infection, Filth corrupts various file access functions, including the "Find File" and "Read File" commands. In some cases, a bug in the virus damages Windows to the extent that it cannot be restarted. Filth presents the following text:

Cradle of Filth
krad

FINGERPRINTS

Fingerprints have been used as a form of identification for at least 4,000 years, the first known record dating from ancient Babylonia, where several captured army deserters were forced to leave marks of their fingers and thumbs as a permanent record. Two thousand years ago, the Chinese used thumbprints as seals for official documents, and the next millennium saw Chinese river pirates compelled to provide ink prints of their thumbs. Fingerprints made their first appearance in a criminal trial in pre-Christian Rome, after a senator was murdered and his killer left bloody handprints on the wall. Shape and size, rather than ridge detail, acquitted the prime suspect in that case and later convicted the senator's wife.

"Modern" fingerprint identification dates from 1788, when German analyst J. C. A. Mayer declared for the first time that each fingerprint is unique. Mark Twain and Sir Arthur Conan Doyle made fictional references to fingerprint identification in the 19th century, but practical identification waited for the near-simultaneous work (in 1892) of William Herschel in India, Henry Faulds in Japan, and Francis Galton in England. It was Galton who first proposed a practical system of fingerprint classification and filing, improved and expanded by Sir Edward Henry in 1899–1900. Meanwhile, in Argentina during 1891, a competing classification system was developed by Juan Vucetich, still used in most Spanish-speaking countries. Official fingerprinting made its way to the United States in 1902, when New York state adopted the technique to eliminate fraud on civil service tests. By 1908 the U.S. armed forces had adopted universal fingerprinting of all personnel, and America witnessed its first criminal conviction based on fingerprints three years later. J. Edgar Hoover often boasted of the FBI's vast fingerprint collection, including not only convicted criminals and military personnel, but also persons printed for a wide variety

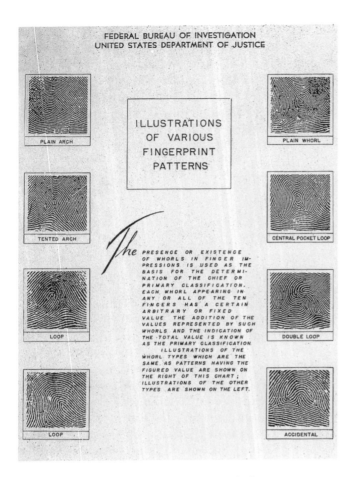

FEDERAL BUREAU OF INVESTIGATION
UNITED STATES DEPARTMENT OF JUSTICE

ILLUSTRATIONS
OF VARIOUS
FINGERPRINT
PATTERNS

PLAIN ARCH

TENTED ARCH

LOOP

LOOP

PLAIN WHORL

CENTRAL POCKET LOOP

DOUBLE LOOP

ACCIDENTAL

The PRESENCE OR EXISTENCE OF WHORLS IN FINGER IMPRESSIONS IS USED AS THE BASIS FOR THE DETERMINATION OF THE CHIEF OR PRIMARY CLASSIFICATION. EACH WHORL APPEARING IN ANY OR ALL OF THE TEN FINGERS HAS A CERTAIN ARBITRARY OR FIXED VALUE. THE ADDITION OF THE VALUES REPRESENTED BY SUCH WHORLS AND THE INDICATION OF THE TOTAL VALUE IS KNOWN AS THE PRIMARY CLASSIFICATION. ILLUSTRATIONS OF THE WHORL TYPES WHICH ARE THE SAME AS PATTERNS HAVING THE FIGURED VALUE ARE SHOWN ON THE RIGHT OF THIS CHART; ILLUSTRATIONS OF THE OTHER TYPES ARE SHOWN ON THE LEFT.

Fingerprints are classified based on eight basic patterns. (Kathleen O. Arries)

of government positions, driver's licenses and so forth. (Even casual tourists visiting FBI Headquarters were invited to donate fingerprints, purportedly to help identify victims of future natural disasters.)

With billions of fingerprints from millions of persons on file, each subject with his or her separate fingerprint card, identifying anonymous prints from a specific crime scene might require weeks of eye-straining effort. Even reducing the field to a smaller subset—e.g., convicted burglars or kidnappers—still left technicians with thousands of cards to examine, each bearing 10 fingerprints. Today, the process is greatly streamlined by an Automated Fingerprint Identification System (AFIS), capable of scanning and rejecting hundreds of prints per hour. Recent improvements in software also "clean up" smudged prints and facilitate identification of partials.

Ironically, just when fingerprint scanning became nearly effortless, the very use of fingerprints themselves was called into question at a murder trial in Philadelphia. Defendants Carlos Llera-Plaza, Wilfredo Acosta, and Victor Rodriguez faced possible execution if convicted of running a Pennsylvania narcotics syndicate that committed at least four murders between 1996 and 1998. Defense attorneys for the trio challenged the scientific validity of fingerprint evidence, winning a decision from U.S. District Judge Louis Pollak on January 7, 2002, that barred fingerprint experts from linking crime scene prints to specific defendants. Acting in response to a 1993 U.S. Supreme Court decision requiring federal judges to take a more active role in weighing the admissibility of scientific evidence, Pollak ruled that experts may testify about similarities between "latent" crime scene prints and "rolled" fingerprints on file, but they may not claim specific latent prints positively match a criminal suspect. Judge Pollak found that, unlike DNA evidence, the error rate of fingerprint data has never been calculated, that the evidence itself has never been scientifically tested, and that no universal standards exist for a "match."

Prosecutors filed an immediate appeal of Judge Pollak's decision, noting that his ruling "would deprive the government of vital evidence in this case, in which latent fingerprints directly link defendants to heinous murders. If carried to its logical conclusion, the court's reasoning would virtually eliminate any expert opinion on the myriad subjects on which subjective expert opinion has always been welcomed in the federal courts."

At a February hearing on Judge Pollak's decision, FBI fingerprint analyst Stephen Meagher cited the bureau's proficiency test as sufficient grounds for Pollak to trust expert testimony. British fingerprint expert Allan Bayle, appearing for the defense, noted that FBI tests used the same sample prints for three years in a row and branded the bureau's six-week training program "a joke." Of the final proficiency test, Bayle said, "They're not testing their ability, and they're not testing their expertise. If I gave my experts this test they would fall about laughing." Furthermore, Bayle noted, there were no international standards for fingerprint comparison and identification: British courts required 16 specific "Galton points" of identity, Australian authorities demanded 12, and FBI experts often made do with 10 matching points. Meagher, recalled to the stand by Judge Pollack, reluctantly acknowledged that "there certainly have been erroneous [fingerprint] identifications testified to in the United States," but denied that the FBI had ever made such a mistake. Coming hard on the heels of sweeping scandals in the FBI's crime laboratory and reports that G-men had framed various innocent persons on murder charges across the United States, leaving three to sit in prison for 25 to 30 years each, Meagher's blanket endorsement of FBI methods was less than compelling.

FLESH-EATING Bananas: Internet panic attack

First circulated on-line in February 2000, this fraudulent warning purports to emanate from the Centers for Disease Control (CDC). It has been publicly repudiated by both the CDC and the Food and Drug Administration but still continues to surface periodically. The original message reads (with errors preserved):

Subject: URGENT warning

Dear Friend,

Please forward to everyone you love!! This is VALIDATED FROM THE CDC. (center for disease control in atlanta georgia)

Warning:

Several shipments of bananas from Costa Rica have been infected with necrotizing fasciitis, otherwise known as flesh eating bacteria. Recently this disease has decimated the monkey population in Costa Rica. We are now just learning that the disease has been able to graft itself to the skin of fruits in the region, most notably the Banana which is Costa Rica's largest export.

Until this finding scientist were not sure how the infection was being transmitted. It is advised not to purchase Bananas for the next three weeks as this is the period of time for which bananas that have been shipped to the US with the possibility of carrying this disease. If you have eaten a banana in the last 2-3 days and come down with a fever followed by a skin infection seek "Medical Attention"!!!

The skin infection from necrotizing fasciitis is very painful and eats two to three centimeters of flesh per hour. Amputation is likely, death is possible.

If you are more than an hour from a medical center burning the flesh ahead of the infected area is advised to help slow the spread of the infection.

The FDA has been reluctant to issue a country wide warning because of fear nationwide panic. They have secretly admitted that they feel upwards of 15,000 Americans will be affected by this but that these are acceptable numbers.

Please forward this to as many people you care about as possible as we do not feel 15,000 people is an acceptable number.

Manheim Research Institute
Center for Disease Control
Atlanta Georgia

It should go without saying that no responsible physician or medical researcher advises patients to burn themselves as an antidote to any known disease or infection. The CDC's official response to this false rumor reads:

The Centers for Disease Control and Prevention, National Center for Infectious Diseases states that the current email rumor circulating about Costa Rican bananas causing the disease 'necrotizing fasciitis' is false.

We have not heard any reports of cases of necrotizing fasciitis associated with bananas. There is no evidence that necrotizing fasciitis is transmitted by food. The bacteria which most commonly cause necrotizing fasciitis live in the human body. The usual route of transmission for these bacteria is from person to person.

FLETCHER, John Bill Jr.: indicted by DNA evidence

Convicted of multiple felony charges in 1987, 45-year-old John Bill Fletcher Jr. was serving a 43-year sentence at the Washington State Penitentiary in Walla Walla when he received some bad news in December 2001. While DNA test results were being used to free wrongfully convicted inmates all over the country, more than 100 at last count, the same tests had a dramatically different impact on Fletcher's case. Far from liberating Fletcher, DNA profiling had linked him to an unsolved murder that would keep him in prison for the rest of his life.

Fletcher was on parole from Texas, after serving seven years of a 20-year aggravated rape conviction, when he moved to Washington's Yakima County in October 1986. Old habits die hard for a sociopath, and Fletcher was jailed in August 1987, after his latest rape victim identified him. Fletcher had kidnapped the woman, raped her and stabbed her 16 times before she escaped, after disarming Fletcher and stabbing him in the leg with his own knife. A second victim came forward after Fletcher's arrest, leading to his ultimate conviction on two counts of first-degree rape, plus one count each of robbery and assault. At the time, he was also suspected in the rape-slayings of Theresa Branscomb (stabbed to death in February 1987) and Bertha Cantu (killed the same way, five months later), but scientific evidence was inconclusive.

"It was extremely frustrating at the time," investigator Jim Hall told the press. "It was one of those things where you knew what was going on but couldn't prove it. Technology has finally caught up with him." Bloodstains from Fletcher's station wagon matched Branscomb's DNA, and Fletcher confessed to both slayings after he received assurances that prosecutors would not seek the death penalty. He was formally charged with two counts of first-degree murder on December 10, 2001.

FLICK, Kevin: satellite TV pirate

A 43-year-old resident of Petersburgh, Ohio, Kevin Flick was arrested by federal agents on August 18, 2000, charged with selling and distributing electronic devices primarily used for unauthorized decryption of direct-to-home satellite television transmissions. According to details of the indictment, between January 1, 1998, and June 30, 1999, Flick sold and installed television satellite dish systems for at least 125 clients in northern Ohio and western Pennsylvania. At the same time, he provided those customers with access cards illegally altered to permit free reception and decryption of "premium" channels such as HBO, Showtime, and Cinemax, normally offered for a monthly fee by DirecTV. Prosecutors estimated that his illegal operation cost DirecTV a total of $250,000, for an average of $2,000 per hacked access card. Flick pleaded guilty to one felony count on September 5, 2000, as part of a bargain with federal prosecutors. On November 16, 2000, U.S. District Judge Patricia Gaughan sentenced Flick to six months in jail and three years' supervised probation, plus $250,000 restitution to DirecTV and a $100 levy for a federal Crime Victims' Fund.

"FOG": computer worm

Catalogued for the first time in June 2001, Fog is an e-mail worm with two significant variants. Both forms send themselves throughout the Internet as e-mails with file attachments; upon infecting a new host, they report back to an IRC (Internet Relay Chat) channel with information about the infected computer. A backdoor system is then activated, granting remote access to the computer and permitting a distant saboteur to inflict further damage.

The first Fog variant—Fog.a, also known as Apbot—displays the following message box when an infected file is opened:

> Explorer
> > i reb00t
> > > [OK]

When the "OK" button is pressed, Fog automatically copies itself into the Windows system directory and the Windows fonts directory, using the names "AntiVirus.exe" and "Times New Roman.exe," respectively. Fog also checks the infected computer's in-box for any e-mails with file attachments and replies to each with an infected message reading:

> Subject: I think you sent me a virus . . . heres a cleaner
> Message: I took my computer to the shop and they ran this, and told me to sent it to you.. hope this helps.
> Attachment: AntiVirus.exe

At the same time, Fog searches out and attempts to erase the following processes, including antivirus applications:

ANTI-TROJAN.EXE
ANTS.EXE
APLICA32.EXE
AVCONSOL.EXE
AVP.EXE
AVPCC.EXE
AVPM.EXE
AVP32.EXE
BLACKD.EXE
BLACKICE.EXE
CFIADMIN.EXE
CFAUDIT.EXE
CFINET.EXE
CFINET32.EXE
CLEANER3.EXE
IAMAPP.EXE
IAMSERV.EXE
ICLOAD95.EXE
ICLAODNT.EXE

ICMON.EXE
ICSUP95.EXE
ICSUPNT.EXE
IFACE.EXE
LOCKDOWN2000.EXE
MINILOG.EXE
MOONLIVE.EXE
NAVAP32.EXE
PCWallIcom.EXE
SAFEWEB.EXE
SPHINX.EXE
TCA.EXE
TDS2-98.EXE
TDS2-NT.EXE
VSECOMP.EXE
VSHWIN32.EXE
WEBSCANX.EXE
WRADMIN.EXE
WRCTRL.EXE
ZONEALARM.EXE

Fog.a also includes the following copyright text:

[Fist of God]
[Remote DDoS]
[v2.7b]

"Fog.b" confuses the issue, inasmuch as it is also sometimes known as Apbot. Like Fog.a, it deletes files and terminates applications including those listed above, while sending itself to new host machines via infected e-mail attachments. The message dispatched by Fog.b reads as follows:

Subject: Virus Alert!
Message: Businesses of all kinds have suffered today as a virus has been unleashed, please find the attached cleaner and run it. You cannot tell if you have this virus until you run the cleaner.
Attachment: regsrv32.exe

"FORD Heights Four": inmates exonerated by DNA evidence
Described in a *Chicago Tribune* report as "almost certainly the largest single, proven miscarriage of justice in Illinois history," the case of the "Ford Heights Four" began at 2:15 A.M. on May 11, 1978, when 28-year-old Larry Lionberg and his fiancée, 23-year-old Carol Schmal, were kidnapped from a Homewood gas station. Police later discovered them in an abandoned Ford Heights townhouse: Schmal had been raped and both victims were killed with close-range gunshots to the head.

Authorities had no leads in the case until an anonymous telephone call sent them looking for five young blacks on May 17. Those arrested were Kenneth Adams, Paula Gray, Verneal Jimerson, William Rainge, and Dennis Williams. On the day of his arrest, Williams recalls, a white officer warned him, "Nigger, you're gonna fry." While investigators juggled evidence—and buried testimony pointing to four other suspects—the sole female defendant was offered a bargain she could not refuse. In exchange for testimony against her supposed accomplices, Paula Gray would receive immunity from prosecution. Fearing for her life, Gray readily agreed.

In light of local sentiment and official malfeasance, the result was predictable. Adams, Jimerson, Rainge, and Williams were convicted on all charges: Jimerson and Williams were sentenced to die for the murders; Rainge was sentenced to life imprisonment; Adams received a 75-year prison term. The four maintained their innocence, and their convictions were overturned on appeal in 1983, but all four were convicted again in a 1985 retrial, with Williams once again sentenced to die. There the matter rested until May 1995, when condemned killer Girvies Davis—hours away from his own execution—urged a friend, journalism professor David Protess, to investigate the Ford Heights case. Preliminary research showed gaping holes in the prosecution's case, and Protess assigned some of his students from Northwestern University to find the truth. What they uncovered was a frame-up fueled in equal parts by racism and the desire to clear a shocking case at any cost.

Paula Gray, the state's "star" witness with a tested IQ of 55, freely admitted lying under oath to save herself from prison. Worse yet, the students discovered that another informant had named four other suspects on May 17, 1978—suspects ignored by the police in their single-minded zeal to convict the "Ford Heights Four" already charged. One of those suspects, Ira Johnson, was serving 74 years for a separate murder when Protess found him in prison. Johnson signed an affidavit naming his deceased brother Dennis as Carol Schmal's killer, further admitting that he and two other gunmen—Arthur Robinson and Juan Rodriguez—killed Larry Lionberg.

Police and prosecutors dismissed the new evidence as fraudulent, but the Illinois Supreme Court felt otherwise, overturning Verneal Jimerson's conviction and death sentence on grounds that Paula

Gray had lied under oath at his trial. Freed on bond pending retrial, Jimerson worked with the journalistic team to free his friends. That freedom came in June 1996, when DNA test results positively excluded all four defendants as participants in Carol Schmal's rape. Ira Johnson, Arthur Robinson, and Juan Rodriguez were indicted on July 3, 1996, subsequently convicted and sentenced for the Ford Heights double slaying.

No police officers were charged with any crime in the Ford Heights frame-up, but state authorities offered to pay the four exonerated inmates $35,000 each for their 18 years in prison. Understandably reluctant to accept that low-ball offer, the Ford Heights Four sued Cook County, its sheriff's department and various individual officers for false imprisonment. In March 1999 the case was settled out of court, for a reported $36 million. A gag order was imposed to suppress details of the settlement. Dennis Williams, still embittered and distrustful, reportedly still telephones a friend or relative each time he leaves his home, to have an iron-clad alibi prepared in case authorities come after him again with more false charges.

"FREEZER": computer virus

A dangerous, memory-resident, parasitic virus, first identified in September 1996, "Freezer" is known in two variants, labeled "Freezer.830" and "Freezer. 980." The latter is encrypted, but both perform in identical fashion, writing themselves to the end of .com and .exe files as the files are opened. Thereafter, both versions erase the infected computer's CMOS (*c*omplementary *m*etal *o*xide *s*emiconductor) memory sectors, which hold the time, date and system setup parameters. Both viruses contain the text string "I am Freezer," with the 980 variant adding "V2.0" to the message.

FRITZ, Dennis and Williamson, Ronald:
exonerated by DNA

Authorities in Ada, Oklahoma, labored for five years to solve the 1982 rape-murder of 21-year-old Debra Sue Carter. In May 1987 they arrested two suspects: 34-year-old Ronald Williamson and 37-year-old Dennis Fritz, a respected junior high school teacher and neighbor of the victim. Both men denied involvement in the crime, but they were charged and held for trial on the basis of forensic

evidence including hairs and semen, deemed "consistent" with their own by methods common prior to the advent of DNA testing. At trial, in April 1988, the prosecution also relied heavily on testimony from jailhouse "snitches," including one Glen Gore, who claimed the defendants had confessed the crime in private conversations. Upon conviction, Williamson was sentenced to die, while Fritz received a life prison term. Williamson successfully appealed his conviction and won a new trial, but he was convicted again and once more sentenced to die. At one point in his death row odyssey, Williamson came within nine days of execution, summoned to the warden's office to discuss disposal of his corpse.

A stay of execution saved his life on that occasion, and Williamson remained persistent, winning another appeal in 1998. This time, before convening a third trial, prosecutors agreed to DNA testing of evidence found at the Carter crime scene. Fritz's lawyers, including Barry Scheck from the CARDOZO INNOCENCE PROJECT, joined that effort and the tests exonerated both men of involvement in the crime. They were released from prison on April 15, 1999. Prosecution witness Glen Gore, meanwhile, was implicated by DNA testing as Carter's actual slayer, a disclosure that prompted him to stage a jailbreak from the Lexington Correctional Center one day before Fritz and Williamson were liberated. Gore surrendered to police on April 20, 1999.

On June 12, 2000, Dennis Fritz appeared before the U.S. Senate Judiciary Committee in Washington, D.C., to describe his ordeal. Appearing in support of proposed legislation to mandate DNA testing in relevant cases, Fritz told his audience:

At the time of my conviction in 1988, DNA testing had just been accepted by the scientific community. For years while in prison, I repeatedly petitioned the courts to allow me to get my DNA tested. I was flat out denied by one court after another. By the time I got in touch with Barry Scheck and Peter Neufeld, I had lost seven court decisions, and I had just about lost hope. . . .

The refusal of the state of Oklahoma to compare my DNA with the crime scene evidence was only one of the reasons why I lost all those years of my life. The other reason was my trial attorney's ineffectiveness. First, he had no real incentive to defend me since he had only received $500 for representing me in a capital murder case. And besides that, he had never handled a murder *case in his life. In fact, he had never handled any type of criminal case whatsoever, due to the fact that he was a civil liabilities lawyer. . . .*

It is more than past time to put an end to these unmerciful travesties of injustice that occur when the truth is hidden or disregarded. I appeal to you, the members of this committee, to enact the necessary laws to fully assure that no human being will ever have to suffer unjustly for something of which they are totally innocent.

FROST, Ray: alleged Internet swindler

A resident of Syracuse, Indiana, Ray Frost was one of 11 defendants arrested by federal investigators during a sting operation dubbed OPERATION SMART-CARD.NET. The targets were purveyors and purchasers of counterfeit "smart cards" used to steal pay-per-view programming from DirecTV, a satellite television company. The investigation began in September 1998 and continued for 22 months, with U.S. Customs agents selling counterfeit access cards through a website established specifically for the sting. Five of the 11 Smartcard defendants have pleaded guilty to date (as of January 2002), while felony charges are pending against Frost and five others. Prosecutors stress that indictments are merely accusations and are not proof of guilt.

"FUXX": computer virus

This "flooder" virus, initially recognized in September 2000, is designed to attack mobile telephones rather than personal computers. It accomplishes that function by dispatching a blizzard of SMS (short *message service*) text messages, similar to those received by a pager. SMS gateways typically employed for such attacks include:

sms.link.btn.de
www.free-sms.com
www.lycos.de
www.mobidig.net
www.nm-info.de
www.pcteam.de

G

"GALICIA": computer viruses

Described by analysts as a nondangerous, nonmemory-resident, parasitic virus, "Galicia" was initially discovered in November 1996, with a variant form identified in August 1997. The original form is now designated "Galicia.a" or "Galicia.800," while the newer variant is dubbed "Galicia.b" or "Galicia.840." Both forms write themselves to the beginning of .com files on an infected computer. In the "odd" months—January, March, May, July, September and November—both viruses write themselves to the MBR (*m*aster *b*oot *r*ecord) of the infected computer's hard drive. Galicia.a contains the text string "Galicia contra telefonica!" while its variant presents the text "Antitelefónica Galicia!"

"GALLERY": computer virus

First identified in September 1997, "Gallery" is defined by expert analysts as a harmless, memory-resident, parasitic virus, which writes itself to the end of .com files as they are executed by an infected computer. There is no payload or outward manifestation of the virus. It contains the text string "Art Gallery++."

GAP Giveaway Offers: Internet hoaxes

In May 1999 the following giveaway offer made its first appearance on the Internet, claiming to emanate from the popular GAP clothing chain. In fact, it seems to be a variation on the fraudulent BILL GATES GIVEAWAY scam and has no validity whatsoever. The original message (complete with errors) read:

Subject: FW: FREE clothes from GAP

Everyone loves free stuff!

Abercrombie & Fitch have recently merged to form the largest hottie outfitter company in the world! In an effort to remain at pace with this giant, the GAP has introduced a new email tracking system to determine who has the most loyal followers. This email is a beta test of the new clothing line and GAP has generously offered to compensate those who participate in testing process. For each person you send this e-mail to, you will be given a pair of cargo pants. For every person they give it to, you will be given an additional Hawaiian print T-shirt, for every person they send it to, you will receive a fishermans hat!

GAP will tally all the emails produced under your name over a two week period and then email you with more instructions. This beta test is only for Microsoft Windows users because the email tracking device that contacts GAP is embedded into the code of Windows 95 and 98. Is you wish to speed up the "clothes receiving process" then you can email the GAP's P.R. rep for a free list of email addresses to try, at. . . . gollygap@yahoo.com

(this was forwarded to me, it's not me saying this . . .) I

know you guys hate forwards, but I started this a month ago.

A week ago, I got an email from the GAP asking me for my address I gave it to them yesterday and got a load of merchandise in the mail from the GAP!!!!! It really works! I wanted you to get a piece of the action, you won't regret it

Six months later, in November 1999, a new version of the GAP giveaway hoax began to circulate on-line, this one purportedly signed by the company's founder. Again, it is presented with various errors intact.

Subject: FREE Gap gift certificates

Hi! My name is Janelle McCann, Founder of the Gap. You have probably heard about the e-mail from Abercrombie and Fitch offering twenty five-dollar gift certificates to every five people you sent that letter to.

My question is: DID IT WORK? Most of you who tried it will probably say NO. But this letter is NOT a prank like others you have experienced. I am offering thirty-five dollar gift certificates to every seven people you send this to. When you have finished sending this letter to as many people as you wish, a screen will come up.

It will tell you how much you have earned in Gap gift certificates. Print that screen out and bring it to your local Gap store. The sales clerk will give you your certificates and you can SHOP BABY! This is a sales promotion to get our name out to young people around the world.

We believe this project can be a success, but only with your help. Thank you for your support!

Sincerely,
Janelle McCann
Founder of the Gap

GEISSBERGER, John: software pirate

A resident of Columbia, South Carolina, born May 15, 1962, John Geissberger was one of 17 defendants indicted for software piracy by federal authorities on May 4, 2000. Twelve of the 17 charged were identified as members of a HACKER syndicate known to its members as "PIRATES WITH ATTITUDE" (PWA). Geissberger and four others were employees of Intel Corporation, charged with illegally furnishing computer hardware used by the gang to maintain a covert web-

site in Quebec. The Intel employees were compensated for their role in the conspiracy with free access to software programs stolen by members of the larger gang.

As described by prosecutors, Geissberger and his coworkers made their arrangement with the hacker gang in December 1998, shipping sophisticated hardware to Canada at Intel's expense, but without the firm's knowledge or approval. Geissberger's specific role in the plot involved clearance of the illegal shipment through Canadian Customs. Within a year of their arrest, Geissberger and his four Intel cohorts all pleaded guilty to the charges filed against them. Eight PWA members also struck plea bargains, while a ninth was convicted at trial. At this writing (in January 2002), two members of the gang remain fugitives in Europe.

GHOST.EXE Trojan Virus: Internet hoax

The "Ghost.exe" computer program was initially distributed as a free screen saver, including advertisements for the Access Softek software firm. It displays a Halloween background with ghosts flying around the monitor screen, but the flight pattern changes on any Friday the 13th to let ghosts emerge from the screen saver's window and pursue a wider flight path. Whether the deviation frightened some nervous user or not is unknown, but messages circulated on the Internet soon began to warn that Ghost.exe contained a Trojan program damaging to host computers. That tale grew in the telling, until panicky e-mails alleged the screen saver's nonexistent virus could erase computer hard drives. The program's developers were then deluged with angry calls and nervous queries, having included their names and telephone numbers in the program's "About" box. Individual reassurance seems to have no effect on the tide of rumor, however, and Internet warnings about Ghost.exe are now probably more numerous than computers displaying the screen saver itself.

GILCHRIST, Joyce: forensic chemist linked to frauds

An African-American native of Oklahoma City, Joyce Gilchrist was drawn to the mysteries of police work while still a student at the University of Central Oklahoma. By 1980, when she obtained her degree in forensic chemistry, Gilchrist was already employed in the Oklahoma City Police Department's crime lab, working on some 3,000 cases between 1980 and

1993. In 1985 she was named the Oklahoma City Police Department's "civilian employee of the year." Gilchrist made a compelling witness at trial, invariably supporting prosecution theories with the kind of scientific evidence guaranteed to make a jury sit up and take notice. Legendary Oklahoma City district attorney Bob Macy was especially enamored of Gilchrist's technique, and police dubbed her "Black Magic" for her startling conviction rate. "It was in reference to a homicide case," Gilchrist later told *60 Minutes II,* "where the defense attorney referred to me in his closing argument as a sorcerer . . . and stated that I seemed to be able to do things with evidence that nobody else was able to do."

And that, in fact, was the problem.

In 1987 another forensic chemist, John T. Wilson of Kansas City, wrote an angry letter to the Southwestern Association of Forensic Scientists (SAFS), asserting that Gilchrist offered "scientific opinions from the witness stand which in effect positively identify the defendant based on the slightest bit of circumstantial evidence." Wilson took the unusual step of criticizing a colleague after several Oklahoma defense attorneys asked him to review Gilchrist's testimony from preliminary hearings. Convinced that Gilchrist had presented false evidence in court, Wilson ultimately testified against her in three separate murder cases. Although he "got major heat" for siding with the defense in those cases, Wilson told interviewers that he "felt I had an ethical obligation" to do so. "When I read the transcripts and saw what she was saying, I was really shocked. She was positively identifying hair, and there's no way in the world you can do that without DNA."

As a result of Wilson's letter, the SAFS conducted its own investigation and determined that Gilchrist had violated the group's code of ethics, resulting in a formal censure. In 1988 the Oklahoma Criminal Court of Appeals overturned Curtis Edward McCarty's murder conviction, based on the fact that Joyce Gilchrist gave the court "personal opinions beyond the scope of scientific capabilities." (A new trial was ordered, resulting in a second conviction and death sentence for McCarty, but the evidence from his case remained under scientific review in 2001.) In 1989 the same appellate court overturned another murder conviction, finding that Gilchrist had improperly used hair analysis to testify that James Lucas Abels had been "in very close and possibly even violent contact" with the victim.

Such disclosures notwithstanding, Gilchrist was promoted to supervisor of the Oklahoma City crime lab in 1994 and continued to testify in criminal cases through the remainder of the decade. It was only in August 1999, after her rebuke by federal judge Ralph Thompson, that her career began to implode. At issue was the rape-murder conviction of Alfred Brian Mitchell, sentenced to death largely on the strength of Gilchrist's scientific testimony. Specifically, Gilchrist had testified that tests performed on semen samples in the case were "inconclusive," when she knew defendant Mitchell should have been excluded as a suspect by the test results. Judge Thompson bluntly labeled her testimony "untrue" and overturned Mitchell's rape conviction. (The murder conviction was allowed to stand, but Mitchell's death sentence was later overturned by the 10th Circuit Court of Appeals.)

As a result of Judge Thompson's ruling and criticism arising from similar cases, police removed Gilchrist from the crime lab in March 2000 and assigned her to an administrative post. Seven months later, the Association for Crime Scene Reconstruction expelled Gilchrist for offering sworn testimony that misrepresented evidence. On April 25, 2001, Oklahoma Attorney General Drew Edmondson announced that his office would review several death penalty cases that hinged on Gilchrist's testimony, further requesting that the Oklahoma State Bureau of Investigation review Gilchrist's work in search of possible criminal violations. An FBI report, published on the same date, alleged that Gilchrist misidentified hairs and fibers or gave testimony "beyond the limits of forensic science" in at least eight felony cases. Most ominous was the reported fact that Gilchrist's testimony had sent 23 defendants to death row, with 11 of those inmates subsequently executed.

Defense attorney David Autry, counsel for several defendants convicted with help from Gilchrist, told reporters, "It was common knowledge within the defense bar and should have been to the DA's office that she was incompetent and malicious. She survived because she made close cases for the prosecutors and secured convictions in particularly heinous crimes." One of those she convicted, alleged rapist Jeffrey Todd Pierce, was released from prison on May 7, 2001, after serving 15 years, when DNA tests proved him innocent of the crime. Following that reversal, Governor Frank Keating ordered a sweeping review of some 1,200 cases involving Gilchrist. On September 25, 2001, Gilchrist was formally dismissed from her job, Police Chief M.T. Berry citing "laboratory mismanagement, criticism from court challenges and flawed casework analysis." Gilchrist's attorney tried to put a bold face on the situation, claiming that his client was "totally and completely a scapegoat" for other, unnamed wrongdoers.

In October 2001 a federal grand jury subpoenaed all evidence from 10 of Gilchrist's murder cases, including nine wherein defendants had been executed and one in which the accused was serving life without parole. By November 2001, Oklahoma investigators had isolated 165 Gilchrist cases which they deemed deserving of further study in depth, reporting that another year or more would be required to complete that review. The Oklahoma Indigent Defense System (OIDS), spearheading renewed DNA testing in various Gilchrist cases, issued a statement that, "whether it was intentional or just negligence, the fact is that her testimony was used to secure death sentences in cases where these people might have been sentenced to life. If just one of these people would have been sentenced to life without her testimony, the entire criminal justice system has been undermined."

Despite the insistence of Oklahoma attorney general Edmondson that "I am personally satisfied that no innocent person was executed," grave doubts remain. An example of the danger posed by Gilchrist's malfeasance is demonstrated in the case of Malcolm Rent Johnson, executed in January 2000 for the 1981 rape-murder of a woman in Oklahoma City. Johnson proclaimed his innocence to the end, despite Gilchrist's testimony that semen found on the victim's bed was "consistent" with Johnson's blood type. Police and prosecutors blocked all attempts at DNA testing while Johnson was alive, but a July 2001 memo obtained by the media seems to indicate that Gilchrist lied under oath at Johnson's trial: specifically, the document states that no sperm was found in semen samples from the crime scene, while Gilchrist testified to the opposite result. In his summation at the 1981 proceedings, D.A. Bob Macy called Gilchrist's testimony "damning, it's condemning, it's conclusive." Today, the state has done a curious turnabout, claiming that Johnson would have been convicted and condemned on the basis of eyewitness testimony alone, without Gilchrist's contribution to the case.

One version or the other must be false.

To date, no charges have been filed against Joyce Gilchrist for perjury or any other criminal offense. A review of her various cases continues, with all sides pledged to the pursuit of truth (although authorities in Oklahoma doggedly resist new DNA testing in any case where inmates have been executed on the basis of Gilchrist's "scientific" testimony). Regardless of whether she faces prosecution at some future date, cases like that of Joyce Gilchrist, RALPH ERDMANN, and FRED ZAIN have shaken the faith of many Americans in the modern system of capital punishment.

"GINGER": computer virus

Ranked as a "harmless," memory-resident, stealth multipartite virus, initially discovered in October 1996, "Ginger" now exists in at least three variants, dubbed "Ginger.2774," "Ginger.2782," and "Ginger.Orsam.2624." All infect the master boot record (MBR) sector of a target computer's hard drive, slightly altering the address of the Active Boot Sector from which DOS is loaded. Subsequently, while loading from an infected sector, the viruses also write themselves to the end of any .com and .exe files accessed. Ginger.2774 and Ginger.2782 contain the following text strings:

You can't catch the Gingerbread Man!!
Bad Seed—Made in Oz
COMSPEC=\COMMAND.COM
CHKDSK MEM
10/23/92

Ginger.Orsam.2624 contains the text strings:

Orsam—Made in Oz
You can't catch the Gingerbread Man!!
COMMAND

"GLITTER": computer viruses

First noted in September 1996, the "Glitter" family of nonmemory-resident, encrypted, parasitic computer viruses are ranked "not dangerous" by expert analysts. Two variants are known thus far, identified as "Glitter.1207" and "Glitter.1462." Both search out .com and .sys files on an infected computer, then write themselves to the ends of any such files located. Glitter.1207 includes the following text:

Glitter ver 1.0, Coded by Siddharth
SID IS IN YOUR RAM CHIPS
Greetings from Siddharth Bombay-92

Glitter 14.62 includes the text:

Glitter ver 1.03, Coded by DDISARTHH,
Hi Avi Guess Who?
Greetings from Siddharth, Mumbai 400 092

On May 8, July 4, September 3 and November 5 the Glitter.1462 variant also displays the following message:

Wish you a Happy Birthday
Love Guess Who?

"GLOBAL Hell": hackers' syndicate

Described by federal prosecutors as "a real gang, just like the Crips and Bloods," the hackers' organization known as Global Hell (gH) surfaced on May 2 1999, with an attack of cybervandalism on the White House website, based in Washington, D.C. Six days later, FBI agents arrested gH member ERIC BURNS for that incident and other attacks on U.S. government websites spanning the period from August 1998 through January 1999. One day after Burns was arrested, hackers defaced the White House website a second time, launching additional attacks against sites maintained by the FBI, various Cabinet departments, and the U.S. Information Agency. The FBI and White House websites were shut down for 24 hours, while the damage was repaired and new security firewalls were installed. A subsequent copycat attack on the U.S. Senate website claimed credit for another group, calling itself the "Masters of Downloading," and included insults describing members of Global Hell as "a group of special-ed students."

The FBI struck back on May 26, 1999, with raids targeting eight homes in California, Washington, and Texas. During one Houston raid, G-men seized a computer from the home of teenage suspect PATRICK GREGORY, who told reporters afterward that his parents were "really mad. . . . The computer had all their financial information and stuff on it." None of the suspects were arrested in those raids, but federal analysts used information from the confiscated computers to build a series of indictments.

Global Hell retaliated for the raids on Thursday, May 27, with new attacks on the FBI and Interior Department websites. Their message of defiance read: "FBI declared war by raiding lots of gH members. Now, it's our turn to hit them where it hurts . . . by going after every computer on the Net with a .gov prefix [sic]. We'll keep hitting them until they get down on their knees and beg." In response to that attack, G-men announced that federal arrest warrants had been issued for 16 hackers, climaxing a yearlong investigation of illegal on-line activity. One of those named was Wisconsin teenager CHAD DAVIS, identified in court documents as a founder of Global Hell.

Threats notwithstanding, the gang remained aggressively defiant. Three weeks after the FBI search of his home, on the night of June 26–27, Davis hacked into a computer at the Pentagon and replaced the U.S. Army's standard Web page with a message reading: "Global Hell is alive. Global Hell will not die." G-men arrested Davis for that hack on August 30, 1999, and he pleaded guilty on January 4, 2000, receiving a six-month jail term and three years' probation. Eric Burns pleaded guilty to his charges on September 7, 1999, sentenced to 15 months in prison and three years' probation, plus an order to pay $36,240 in restitution to his victims.

Despite their high-level hacks, federal spokesmen denigrated gH members as mediocre operators. "It is not that these are super whiz kids," one anonymous FBI agent told reporters. "It is the technology that gives them the ability to cover their tracks enough that you can have a hard time making a criminal case against them." As for motives, computer analyst Drew Williams told the *Washington Post,* "They are into bragging rights. They are vandals who are into it for the sense of chaos." David Remnitz, chief executive of a New York-based computer security firm, told the *Post,* "The Global Hell types may have shown a skill for self-promotion, but not the kind of sophistication that you see in truly dangerous computer criminals of the sort who penetrate systems to steal proprietary information." That disclaimer aside, U.S. Attorney Thomas Schneider said of the gang, "Interference with government computer systems [is] not just electronic vandalism. They run the risk of compromising critical information infrastructure systems."

Patrick Gregory was the third gH member to face retribution in court, named as a leader of the gang and charged with one count of conspiracy for hacking and telecommunications fraud. Described by FBI agents as "a known street gang member in the Houston area," Gregory reportedly had turned to computers as "his way out" of trouble but found only more of the same. On April 12, 2000, he pleaded guilty as charged; on September 6, 2000, Gregory received a 26-month prison term, plus three years' probation and an order to pay more than $154,000 in restitution to parties he had damaged.

Even on his way to prison, Gregory failed to grasp the significance of Global Hell's actions. "I don't understand why they look at us as such bad people," he told an interviewer from the television program "20/20." Assistant U.S. Attorney Matthew Yarbrough had an answer to that question ready and waiting. "If you deface a website of a company that is making $18 million a day, you are committing a pretty serious crime," he told reporters. "We can't treat this problem as if it's just kids. Everyone has to start taking this very seriously."

The latest gH member to face charges is 17-year-old Rhode Island resident DENNIS MORAN, known on-line as "Coolio." Moran's computer was seized in a February 2000 raid by FBI agents, seeking evidence to link him with the May 1999 government website attacks. Investigators also sought to blame "Coolio" for more recent incidents, including "denial of service" attacks on some of the Internet's largest commercial websites: Yahoo, eBay, E-Trade, and Amazon.com. Other targets allegedly included an anti-drug organization (D.A.R.E.), an Internet security firm (RSA Security), and the U.S. government's Chemical Weapons Convention website. "Coolio" reportedly left the image of Walt Disney cartoon characters on websites he attacked, according to investigators on the case. Moran pleaded guilty to three misdemeanor counts on January 2, 2001, agreeing to accept a jail term of nine months to one year, plus payment of $15,000 restitution to his victims.

GODSCHALK, Bruce: exonerated by DNA evidence

In July and September 1986, two women were raped at the Kingswood Apartments in King of Prussia, Pennsylvania. One victim was unable to describe her attacker, but the other glimpsed his face reflected in a bedroom mirror and gave police a vague description, including a reference to his distinctive shirt and sneakers. Bruce Godschalk, a 26-year-old unemployed landscaper from Radnor, was later arrested for the crimes. Police found no clothing similar to the rapist's in Godschalk's apartment, but one victim identified him as her attacker and a fellow inmate claimed Godschalk had talked about the rapes in jail. More to the point, Godschalk himself confessed in custody, but soon recanted, claiming that his state-

ments were coerced by police. Convicted of rape in 1987, he received a 10- to 20-year prison sentence.

In 1993 Godschalk filed a motion for DNA testing of forensic evidence in the case, but two state courts rejected the bid. Seven years later, supported by attorneys from the CARDOZO INNOCENCE PROJECT, Godschalk filed a federal lawsuit to compel DNA testing on March 22, 2000. Montgomery County prosecutors again resisted the effort, but on March 27, 2001 a federal judge overruled state objections, finding that Godschalk was not constitutionally barred from seeking new tests of the evidence. Those tests, financed by money from his late mother's estate, excluded Godschalk as a source of the semen recovered from the crime scenes. He was released on February 14, 2002, after serving 15 years of his sentence.

Montgomery County District Attorney Bruce Castor Jr. still appeared to have his doubts about the case as Godschalk was released, although he agreed to dismiss all charges in the case. "This is one of those situations where I can't tell you what the truth is," Castor told reporters. "As a prosecutor, I have to be sure. And we're not sure. It's frustrating because I think the evidence is compelling that he's guilty, and the evidence is compelling that he's innocent. I don't like uncertainty. We can't prove it beyond a reasonable doubt, so we let him go. I am not convinced that Bruce Godschalk was innocent. What I am convinced of is that he cannot be proven innocent [sic] beyond a reasonable doubt. And in this business, a tie goes to the defendant."

Godschalk's reaction to that strange declaration was terse and direct: "He's insane."

"GOLDFISH": computer virus

An encrypted virus reported for the first time in September 1996, "GoldFish" contains two macros: AutoOpen and AutoClose. It infects files on opening or closing, and depending on the nature of the system infected it may display the following dialogue box:

GoldFish
I am the GoldFish,
I am hungry, feed me.

The virus then waits for its unwilling host to select one of the choices offered: "fishfood," "worms," "worm pryme," or "core." No specific damage to infected systems is reported, marking GoldFish as a minor annoyance, rather than a danger.

GONDA, Arthur See BAKER, JAKE

"GONER": computer worm

On December 3, 2001, analysts employed by the McAfee computer security firm reported thousands of their clients had received copies of a new computer worm virus, dubbed Goner. The worm is transmitted by e-mail with a subject line reading "Hi" and text asking the recipient to view an attached screensaver program. Infection occurs when the attachment is opened, whereupon Goner sends copies of itself to all e-mail addresses listed in the victim's Microsoft Outlook address book, or through the ICQ instant messaging system. At the same time, Goner attempts to delete any security or antivirus programs installed on the newly infected computer.

McAfee spokesmen placed Goner on "outbreak" status, a high-alert warning last employed when the "LOVELETTER" virus caused global damage measured in billions of dollars. The first samples of Goner were identified in Europe, principally France and Germany. By December 4, 2001, security firms including McAfee and Symantec had released updates of their antivirus software to detect and defeat Goner infections.

One week after Goner surfaced, its creators were arrested in Jerusalem. Meir Zohar, chief of the Israeli police computer crimes squad, identified the culprits as four teenage HACKERS, placed under house arrest after confessing their role in creating and sending the worm. Israeli adults convicted of generating a computer virus face prospective five-year prison terms, while the maximum sentence for juveniles is 30 months. Still, it appeared that mere confessions might not be enough to make the case against Goner's creators. "After five days," Zohar told reporters, "they will be released unless we find something."

"GOOD Times" Computer Virus: Internet hoax

Since November 1994 a variety of Internet warnings have been circulated, warning recipients of a computer virus called "Good Times" which does not exist in fact. The U.S. Department of Energy's HOAX-BUSTERS website has exposed the fraud repeatedly, but still it lives on, outpacing denials and alarming recipients with predictions of dire consequences should they encounter the mythical virus. The initial warning, circulated in November and December 1994, read:

Here is some important information. Beware of a file called Goodtimes. Happy Chanukah everyone, and be careful out there. There is a virus on America Online being sent by E-mail. If you get anything called "Good Times," DON'T read it or download it. It is a virus that will erase your hard drive. Forward this to all your friends. It may help them a lot.

While experts were busily debunking the original hoax, a second Good Times warning began to make its rounds on the Internet. This one included claims that the Federal Communications Commission (FCC) had issued an alert against the virus—when, in fact, that organization has no part in detecting computer viruses or Trojans and has never issued any such warning. The second bogus message reads as follows:

The FCC released a warning last Wednesday concerning a matter of major importance to any regular user of the InterNet. Apparently, a new computer virus has been engineered by a user of America Online that is unparalleled in its destructive capability. Other, more well-known viruses such as Stoned, Airwolf and Michaelangelo pale in comparison to the prospects of this newest creation by a warped mentality.

What makes this virus so terrifying, said the FCC, is the fact that no program needs to be exchanged for a new computer to be infected. It can be spread through the existing e-mail systems of the InterNet. Once a computer is infected, one of several things can happen.

If the computer contains a hard drive, that most likely will be destroyed. If the program is not stopped, the computer's processor will be placed in an nth-complexity infinite binary loop—which can severely damage the processor if left running that way too long. Unfortunately, most novice computer users will not realize what is happening until it is far too late.

Two years after the original Good Times hoax was circulated, a humorous spoof of the hoax itself appeared on the Internet, proving that even hoaxers may not have the last laugh.

December 1996
READ THIS:

Goodtimes will re-write your hard drive. Not only that, but it will scramble any disks that are even close to your computer. It will recalibrate your refrigerator's coolness setting so all your ice cream goes melty. It will demagnetize the strips on all your credit cards, screw up the tracking on your television and use subspace field harmonics to scratch any CD's you try to play.

It will give your ex-girlfriend your new phone number. It will mix Kool-aid into your fishtank. It will drink all your beer and leave its socks out on the coffee table when there's company coming over. It will put a dead kitten in the back pocket of your good suit pants and hide your car keys when you are late for work.

Goodtimes will make you fall in love with a penguin. It will give you nightmares about circus midgets. It will pour sugar in your gas tank and shave off both your eyebrows while daring your girlfriend behind your back and billing the dinner and hotel room to your Discover card.

It will seduce your grandmother. It does not matter if she is dead, such is the power of Goodtimes, it reaches out beyond the grave to sully those things we hold most dear.

It moves your car randomly around parking lots so you can't find it. It will kick your dog. It will leave libidinous messages on your boss's voice mail in your voice! It is insidious and subtle. It is dangerous and terrifying to behold. It is also a rather interesting shade of mauve.

Goodtimes will give you Dutch Elm disease. It will leave the toilet seat up. It will make a batch of Methanphedime [sic] in your bathtub and then leave bacon cooking on the stove while it goes out to chase gradeschoolers with your new snowblower.

Listen to me. Goodtimes does not exist.

It cannot do anything to you. But I can. I am send-ing this message to everyone in the world. Tell your friends, tell your family. If anyone else sends me another E-mail about this fake Goodtimes Virus, I will turn hunting them into a religion. I will do things to them that would make a horsehead in your bed look like Easter Sunday brunch.

GORSHKOV, Vasily, and Ivanov, Alexei:
indicted hackers

In a world largely deprived of boundaries by the Internet, law enforcement officers and private security agents employed to solve CYBERCRIME must concern themselves not only with thieves and vandals in their own vicinity, but also with conspirators around the world. One particular source of vexation for American authorities in the 21st century has been Russia, where hackers dwelling (theoretically, at least) beyond the FBI's long reach have plagued commercial institutions. In January 2000 a Russian operator known only as "Max" stole 300,000 credit card numbers from CD Universe, in an extortion bid. Nine months later, a penetration of Microsoft's high-security network was traced to a still unidentified hacker in St. Petersburg. VLADIMIR LEVIN, a Russian living in America, was convicted and imprisoned in 1999 for using his computer to steal $12 million from Citibank.

Even those operations, however, paled beside the efforts of 25-year-old Vasily Gorshkov and 20-year-old Alexei Ivanov, two Chelyabinsk natives who settled in Washington state and there launched a computer hacking and extortion scheme so massive that FBI spokesmen took the unprecedented step of warning the public before their investigation was completed. That press release, issued in March 2001, warned American consumers that organized hackers based in Russia and Ukraine had stolen more than 1 million credit card numbers nationwide, while attacking the computer networks of more than 40 businesses scattered across 20 states. Eight months later, on November 10, 2001, the G-men had two alleged prime movers of the global plot in custody.

According to a federal indictment issued in Seattle, Gorshkov and Ivanov spent two years victimizing various corporations, banks, and school districts, spawning 20 counts of computer-related theft, extortion, and fraud. The charges allege that Gorshkov and Ivanov stole credit card numbers by the tens of thousands, along with other sensitive information downloaded from targets that included PayPal (the world's largest on-line payment company) and the Central National Bank of Waco, Texas. In a high-tech variation on the age-old "protection" racket, the defendants purportedly downloaded sensitive files from an intended target's computer, then demanded employment as "security consultants" to keep the stolen data secret, at fees ranging from $15,000 to $100,000. In one case, federal investigators claim, Gorshkov and Ivanov published the secret information even after they were "hired" to maintain its security.

Lacking jurisdiction to arrest the suspects in Russia, FBI agents mounted an elaborate sting operation to lure them stateside. In June 2000 the bureau established a bogus security firm dubbed "Invita," leasing office space in Seattle, and then contacted Ivanov with an offer of employment as a hacker. To demonstrate his skill, Ivanov hacked into Invita's computer system, whereupon FBI agents invited him and his partner Gorshkov to visit Seattle in person. On arrival for their November 10, 2001, "job interview," the Russians were asked for further demonstrations of their hacking prowess. While establishing a link to their home server in Chelyabinsk (on an FBI computer equipped with a "sniffer" program that recorded every keystroke), the suspects allegedly boasted of their prior activities and promised the assembled undercover agents that "the FBI could not get them in Russia."

Seattle was another story, though, and the pair soon found themselves in custody, confronted with charges that could keep them out of circulation and off the Internet for years to come. With the assistance of their sniffer program, federal agents downloaded 1.5 gigabytes of incriminating material from the remote server in Chelyabinsk—so much data, in fact, that Seattle court recorders estimate it could require 1 million pages to print out a hard copy of the evidence. Ken Kanev, a Seattle attorney retained to defend Vasily Gorshkov, has challenged the admissibility of that evidence, but the issue remains unresolved at this writing (in February 2002). As for the defendants, they retain a presumption of innocence until their case is tried—and they seem to have achieved martyr status in Russia, where the website for *Khaker Magazine* includes a message board filled with recriminations for U.S. authorities. One anonymous poster warned: "Watch out Russian hackers! You see what kind of low-life tactics the Americans are capable of, so work more carefully!"

"GOTCHA": computer viruses

Reported in four variants since November 1996, the "Gotcha" memory-resident-parasitic viruses are rated "harmless" by analysts who have evaluated them. "Gotcha.605" and "Gotcha.607" write themselves to the ends of .com files only, while the variants "Gotcha.666" and "Gotcha.1781" may infect either .com or .exe files. All forms contain the following text strings:

EXECOM
E=mc2 GOTCHA!

Gotcha.666 includes the text: "E=mc^2 MULATTOED YA THROUGH THE WHITE GOYIM SHIKSES!" Gotcha.1781 displays the message "LEGALIZE CANNABIS" with a picture of a green marijuana leaf, while presenting the following text:

Do you think Cannabis should be legalized? (Y/N)
I'm glad you agree with me!
And what about Alcohol, should that be illegal too?
 (Y/N)
Hmm, I don't agree, but I respect your opinion.
You are a HYPOCRITE!!!

"GRAVEYARD": computer virus

Initially reported in August 1997, "Graveyard" is a dangerous, memory-resident, encrypted, parasitic virus that writes itself to the end of .com files as they are executed by an infected computer. Debugging any program thereafter results in crashing the system with potential loss of valued data. This virus includes the text string "Graveyard!"

GRAY, Anthony: exonerated by DNA evidence

Maryland native Anthony Gray was arrested in 1991, accused of raping and murdering a woman at Chesapeake Beach. Although innocent of the crime, he was intimidated by police into confessing. Gray pleaded guilty in October 1991, convinced that he would be convicted and executed if he went to trial before a jury. As part of the plea bargain, Gray received a double life sentence and subsequent appeals based on his limited intellect were rejected. DNA tests finally identified the true killer, but despite that suspect's guilty plea in 1997, Gray remained in prison. More testing proved that Gray had not been present at the crime scene, resulting in his belated release on February 9, 1999.

GRAY, Joseph: satellite TV pirate

A 71-year-old resident of Rantoul, Illinois, Joseph Gray was one of 17 American defendants indicted during 2001 as a result of the federal sting operation dubbed OPERATION SMARTCARD.NET. Those arrested were accused of purchasing or selling counterfeit access cards, which allowed unauthorized reception and decryption of satellite television services offered by the firm DirecTV. FBI agents estimated that DirecTV lost $6.2 million in revenue from the fraud between 1998 and 2000, when the sting operation began producing arrests. Gray purchased 30 counterfeit satellite access cards from FBI undercover agents and traded his own merchandise for another 60 of the bogus "Euro" cards, which he then re-sold to other individuals. Gray pleaded guilty as charged on June 14, 2001. He faced a maximum sentence of five years' imprisonment and a $500,000 fine.

GREEHEY, Kevin: alleged satellite TV pirate

Another defendant snared by OPERATION SMART-CARD.NET, Kevin Greehey was a resident of Sarasota, Florida, when federal agents arrested him in August 2000. With nine others, Greehey faced felony charges of buying and selling counterfeit access cards, which permitted their users to illegally receive and decrypt satellite television transmissions without paying TV providers their normal monthly fees. One provider, DirecTV, lost an estimated $6.2 million before federal agents intervened, duping would-be dealers and pirates with counterfeit "Euro" cards. Four of those indicted with Greehey pleaded guilty as charged, but Greehey and four more defendants were still awaiting trial at last report (in January 2002). All are presumed innocent unless they are convicted at trial. In that event, each felony count filed against them carries a maximum penalty of five years in prison and a $500,000 fine.

GREEN, Edward: exonerated by DNA evidence

In July and August 1987, a serial rapist terrorized women in Washington, D.C. The predator claimed his first victim on July 3, near a local high school; a second woman, attacked at the same place on August 5, fought her way clear without being raped. Based on physical descriptions offered by the two victims, Washington police later arrested suspect Edward Green in the vicinity of the attacks. The first victim picked his photograph from among several others displayed by police; both women also selected Green from lineups at police headquarters and identified him as their assailant at trial. Forensic experts testified that Green's blood type was "consistent" with the rapist's, based on semen samples recovered from the first victim. Jurors deliberated three hours before convicting Green of rape but acquitting him of assault on the second victim.

Prior to sentencing, Green's lawyer filed a motion for postponement pending completion of a DNA test on the state's forensic evidence. Prosecutors opposed several delays, but time was granted by the judge. A final report, issued in February 1990, excluded Edward Green as a source of the semen found on the first victim's clothing. Green's attorney used that finding as the basis for a motion for a new trial, granted at a special hearing on March 19, 1990. The U.S. attorney's office agreed to dismissal of the rape charge, while Green remained incarcerated for an unrelated drug violation.

GREEN, Kevin Lee: exonerated by DNA evidence

A Marine Corps corporal stationed in southern California, Kevin Green went out for a late-night cheeseburger on September 30, 1979, and returned to find that his 20-year-old pregnant wife had been assaulted in their home, raped, and severely beaten. Dianna Green survived the beating but her unborn child, already two weeks overdue, did not. Emerging from a coma in October, with brain damage and memory loss, Dianna named her husband as her attacker and he was arrested on March 25, 1980, later convicted of sexual assault, attempted murder (of his wife), and second degree murder (of their child). He received a prison term of 15 years to life.

DNA testing was unknown at the time Green went to prison, and by the time he learned about it in the early 1990s he could not afford the $10,000 required for tests on the prosecution's evidence from his case. As luck would have it, in 1996 a DNA test performed on serial killer Gerald Parker linked him to the rape of Dianna Green, and Parker later confessed to the crime. Kevin Green by then had survived inmate attacks and suicide attempts in prison and gone on to earn a college degree in social sciences. Upon his release after DNA testing exonerated him, state legislators discovered that California had no legal mechanism for compensating wrongfully convicted persons. A special bill, passed in 1999, awarded Green $100 for each day he was incarcerated. Today he lives in Missouri and travels widely as a public speaker.

"GREEN River Killer": cold case solved via DNA

Beginning in January 1982, an unknown predator killed at least 40 women around Seattle and Tacoma, Washington; nine more listed as missing are also presumed to be dead. Many of the victims were prostitutes, working along the infamous "Sea-Tac Strip." A few were runaways or hitchhikers. While skeletal remains were found as late as 1988, authorities have not confirmed another slaying in the series since October 1984. The killer's favorite dumping ground led journalists to christen him the Green River Killer.

While theories and suspects abounded in the haunting case, police were unable to solve it. Public interest waned and funds ran out. Nearly two decades after the last confirmed murder, it seemed the case would remain an eternal mystery—like the identity of London's Jack the Ripper or the elusive New Orleans Ax Man—but modern science intervened to shed new light on the murky affair.

DNA evidence lay beyond the reach of American police in 1984. Its first use in a murder trial, against British serial slayer COLIN PITCHFORK, would not make headlines until 1986. The trail in Washington was cold by then, but DNA has an advantage over witnesses and other transitory evidence: if undisturbed by man or nature, it remains to tell its story years, decades, even centuries after the fact.

So it was in the Green River case. One of the original manhunters, King County sheriff Dave Reichert, announced formation of a new task force in June 2001, to test skin cells recovered from materials used to strangle some of the murderer's victims. Most, predictably, would belong to the victims—but Reichert hoped some might be traced to the killer himself. As detective Tom Jensen told reporters, "It's too bad we didn't have this technology back when it was going on, because the case would have been better handled, probably solved."

The best hope for working with 19-year-old evidence lay in the polymerase chain reaction (PCR)

process, described by Dr. Beverly Himick of the Washington State Patrol Crime Lab as "a chemical photocopier." In essence, PCR processing takes a microscopic DNA sample and generates multiple copies at high speed, thereby providing forensic scientists with sufficient material to complete their varied tests. Semen recovered from three of the Green River victims was tested, the DNA compared with evidence collected over time from various suspects and known sex offenders in Washington state. In early October 2001, Detective Jensen presented Sheriff Reichert with three DNA printouts: two samples were obtained from victims Marcia Chapman and Opal Mills, murdered in 1982; the third—a saliva sample—had been taken from a suspect by police in 1987.

All three matched.

On November 30, 2001, King County detectives arrested 52-year-old truck painter Gary Lee Ridgway at his place of business, charging him with first-

DNA evidence directly linked Gary Ridgway to numerous murders in the Green River killings that haunted Washington State in the 1980s. (Reuters NewMedia Inc./CORBIS)

degree murder in four of the 49 Green River cases. According to prosecution press releases, DNA samples obtained from the corpse of 21-year-old Carol Christensen (killed in May 1983) matched Ridgway's DNA so precisely that "it can be estimated that not more than one individual (excluding identical twins) in the world's population would exhibit this DNA profile." Semen retrieved from 31-year-old Marcia Chapman's body was degraded, displaying only nine of 13 possible DNA markers, but all nine matched Ridgway's. Experts placed the odds of another white male matching all nine markers at one in 645 million—more than double the entire U.S. population. Sperm from at least two men was found with the body of 16-year-old Opal Mills, and while DNA results were inconclusive, tests did not exclude Ridgway as a possible donor. No foreign DNA was found on 17-year-old Cynthia Hinds, but Ridgway was charged in her case because Hinds was discovered with Chapman and Mills on August 15, 1982. Both she and Chapman were pinned underwater with heavy rocks, and small stones were inserted by the killer into their vaginas.

With Ridgway in custody, police revealed that they had considered him a suspect in the Green River murders since February 1983, when a Seattle prostitute accused him of violent behavior. Two months later, a pimp watched hooker Marie Malvar climb into a pickup truck with her "trick." When she failed to turn up the next day, her pimp traced the pickup to Ridgway's house and alerted police, but Ridgway denied any knowledge of the incident. Questioned again in April 1984, Ridgway admitted frequent contact with prostitutes—a fact confirmed by sporadic surveillance—but again denied any other wrongdoing. In November 1984 a prostitute informed detectives that Ridgway had tried to strangle her during sex, before she broke free and escaped. Ridgway acknowledged that attack but claimed the woman bit him first, and no charges were filed. In 1985, Ridgway allegedly told detectives that he was obsessed with prostitutes and that they "affect him as strongly as alcohol does an alcoholic." A saliva sample was obtained from Ridgway in 1987, then routinely filed away for 14 years, until Sheriff Reichert launched a fresh investigation of the case.

Authorities seemed confident of Ridgway's guilt. "DNA is sort of the physical last link," one investigator told reporters on December 5, 2001, "but it does nothing more than verify what our circumstantial evidence has said before. It's nowhere close to the

sole evidence in this case." Indeed, for some that raised a question as to why Ridgway was not arrested earlier. Harold Coleman, chief executive officer for a Seattle-based DNA testing firm, told journalists that PCR testing "has been widely available since 1996," performed by his own lab under contract for the Indiana State Police and other law enforcement agencies. The Washington State Patrol's crime lab remained "woefully underfunded," unable to perform PCR tests before mid-1999, and Green River fell through the cracks, with new cases assigned top priority. As Coleman suggests, "The DNA was just sitting there in the evidence locker. I think they just didn't think to send it out for somebody else to do it."

Delays notwithstanding, King County authorities maintain that the Green River case is now closed. It remains to be seen if a jury will agree, or if new murder charges will be added to those already filed against defendant Gary Ridgway.

GREGORY, Patrick W.: hacker "MostHateD"

A 19-year-old resident of Houston, Texas, Patrick Gregory was a member of the "Total-Kaos" HACKER syndicate from 1997 through May 1999; he also joined CHAD DAVIS (a.k.a. "Mindphasr") to create a second gang in February 1998, dubbed "GLOBAL HELL." While active in both groups, Gregory used stolen access devices—including telephone numbers, Personal Identification Numbers (PINs), and credit card numbers—to access teleconference facilities provided by AT&T, MCI, Sprint, Latitude Communications, and various other telephone companies. Members of "total-kaOs" and "Global Hell" staged daily conference calls lasting six hours or longer, to discuss and plan their invasions of protected computer networks across America and around the world.

In addition to illegally obtaining free telephone service worth thousands of dollars, Gregory admitted using various access devices to eavesdrop on third-party conference calls and to disrupt operations of the several companies he victimized. In June 1998 he billed $4,200 to an innocent third party for teleconferences conducted with his fellow conspirators. Four months later, Gregory disrupted teleconference classes at Dallas (Texas) Community College, resulting in charges of $18,500 to the school. He further admitted to sharing stolen computer passwords and credit card numbers with other members of "total-kaOs" and "Global Hell," while joining his cronies in criminal penetration of numerous computer systems around the globe. Typically, the gangs replaced corporate Web pages with cybergraffiti advertising their own syndicates; on other occasions, whole systems were crashed as a prank. In April 1999, with other "Global Hell" hackers, Gregory invaded computer systems operated by the White House, the U.S. Army, Ameritech, U.S. Cellular and several other companies, causing damage estimated between $1.5 million and $2.5 million.

Investigation by the FBI ultimately terminated Gregory's Internet crime spree, resulting in federal charges of computer hacking and conspiracy to commit telecommunications fraud. On April 12, 2000, Gregory pleaded guilty before U.S. District Judge Jorge Solis. Five months later, on September 6, 2000, Gregory was sentenced to 26 months' imprisonment followed by three years' supervised probation, and was ordered to pay his victims $154,529.86 in restitution. U.S. Attorney Paul Coggins afterward told reporters, "I'm proud of the sophisticated investigative work done by the newly established North Texas Regional Computer Forensic Lab and the collaborative efforts of local, state and federal agencies working together to aggressively crack down on the explosion of CYBER-CRIMES and cybercrooks."

HACKERS and Hacking

Wherever the subject of CYBERCRIME is raised, hacking immediately comes to mind and lingers as the foremost example of lawlessness linked to computers. It was not always so, however, and some purists—including the original hackers, now in their 50s and 60s—complain that the term has been grossly abused, its original meaning long since forgotten.

The original self-described "hackers" were a group of 1960s students at the Massachusetts Institute of Technology, obsessed with computers and programming in the days before desktop or laptop computers existed, vying for precious time on MIT's bulky mainframes. A small, insular clique, they wore the hacker label proudly and lived to explore the expanding realm of cyberspace. Believing that all knowledge and computer software should be freely shared, the in-crowd bitterly resented patents, copyrights, and other roadblocks to what they described as "freedom of communication." Still, the pioneers insist, their small society had "strict unwritten rules" against malicious mischief or using their skills for personal profit.

Such rules, whether unwritten or inscribed in statute books, never succeed in curbing lawlessness for very long. With passing time, as access to computers grew more common, so hackers multiplied exponentially—and their self-definition changed radically in the process. As now used in the media—and, frankly, among many hackers themselves—the term now applies to anyone, regardless of motive, who executes unauthorized penetration of other (usually protected) computer systems. Whether the goal is simple snooping for the thrill of it, political dissent in cyberspace, bank robbery, or global espionage, all hackers stand together in the media spotlight—and in court, if they are captured, since federal statutes passed in the 1990s make any such penetration a criminal act.

Old-school hackers resent the blanket condemnation, insisting that cybercriminals be dubbed "crackers" or "darkside hackers" to distinguish their greed and malice from the pure motives of the alleged majority. Apologists such as hacker-turned-on-line-columnist Douglas Thomas maintain that the original "elegant" hacker ethic still survives. "Most hackers," Thomas wrote in 1998, "consider two things taboo: destroying information and making money off a hack. Those two things are enough to get you shunned in most hacker circles, or at least give you a very bad reputation." At the same time, countless pro-hacker websites and newsletters praise "phreakers" who defraud long-distance carriers of millions of dollars every year, and defend hackers who vandalize corporate or government websites in the name of "freedom."

As for police and prosecutors, they refuse to let their hunt for cybercriminals bog down in a swamp of semantics. Their attitude: Whether a burglar breaks into a gallery to steal paintings or simply to admire them, he is still a burglar and should pay the penalty prescribed by law.

Vowing to prosecute is one thing, but arresting disembodied criminals in cyberspace is something else entirely. Many police departments lack the expertise to identify anonymous hackers, crackers, thieves, and cyberstalkers. When offenders are identified, some of the cases present investigators with a jurisdictional labyrinth: thieves in Hong Kong or Moscow using computers based in London or Singapore to rob banks in New York or Los Angeles. The pursuit requires training, equipment, and funding that some law enforcement agencies do not possess. Successful prosecution demands collaboration in a field where rivalry between agencies is sometimes more bitter than the animosity between police and criminals.

FBI Director Louis Freeh, testifying before the U.S. Senate in February 2000, frankly admitted that G-men were no match for savvy cybercriminals. "Even though we have markedly improved our capabilities to fight cyberintrusions," he said, "the problem is growing even faster and we are falling further behind." Among the countless incidents that trouble law enforcement:

June 1991   KEVIN POULSEN's arrest by FBI agents capped an eight-year hacking spree that compromised government laboratories and military computers, while invading the privacy of various civilians (including Hollywood celebrities). In custody, Poulsen claimed the "hacker ethic" had "dictated his every act"—including manipulation of radio giveaway contests that graced him with $22,000 in cash, two free trips to Hawaii, and two $50,000 sports cars.

July 1994   Russian hacker VLADIMIR LEVIN organized a plot to steal more than $10 million from Citibank, transferring the money to foreign accounts.

February 1995   FBI agents arrested hacker KEVIN MITNICK, climaxing a series of corporate and government computer intrusions dating from the 1970s, when Mitnick was 13 years old. His sixth (and so far last) conviction, in March 1999, earned Mitnick a 46-month prison term plus a court-ordered ban on any use of computers for another four years after his release.

March 1997   A teenage hacker known on-line as Jester penetrated the NYNEX phone system (now Bell Atlantic) in Worcester, Massachusetts. His "innocent" meddling disabled the network, knocking out the town's telephone service and disrupting radio transmissions at a nearby airport.

January 2000   A Russian hacker known only as Maxus stole more than 300,000 credit card numbers from CD Universe in an attempted extortion scheme. The plot failed, but the offender remains unidentified.

February 2000   Computer vandals attacked Yahoo, the world's most popular website, shutting it down for three hours in what authorities called the most serious incident of organized Internet sabotage to date. The "denial of service" (DOS) attack flooded Yahoo's data centers with mock requests for information, clogging the system's routers and forcing a shutdown. Other attacks the same month disabled the eBay on-line auction service and Amazon.com's book dealership.

October 2000   A sustained penetration of Microsoft's high-security networks was traced to a Russian internet service provider (ISP), but the culprit was not apprehended.

February 2001   Hackers incensed by school dress codes in Salem, Oregon, invaded the school district's computer system and vandalized its website.

March 2001   An FBI press release blamed organized hacker syndicates in eastern Europe—primarily Russia and Ukraine—for stealing more than 1 million credit card numbers and invading the computer networks of more than 40 businesses in 20 U.S. states.

September 2001   In the wake of massive terrorist attacks on the World Trade Center and the Pentagon, American hackers debated launching a cyber-vigilante campaign against computer systems in Afghanistan and other nations perceived as terrorist havens. Calling themselves the Dispatchers, composed of 60-odd self-styled "computer security enthusiasts," the group chose as its spokesman a hacker known only as the Rev. The announced declaration of war was instantly denounced by a German hackers' syndicate, the Chaos Computer Club, while the FBI's National Infrastructure Protection Center issued an advisory to warn global corporations of possible accelerated hacking in the name of "patriotism." No evidence exists that the proposed attacks ever occurred.

January 2002   A man who discovered a security breach in a website maintained by the *Poteau* (Oklahoma) *Daily News & Sun* and reported it to the newspaper's publisher received a sentence of three years' probation and a $1,000 fine after confessing that he also downloaded protected files from the site.

January 2002   Hackers invaded and defaced the website of the Texas state lottery. No data or financial losses were reported by authorities. The offenders remain unidentified.

While law enforcement struggles to keep up with cybercriminals, producers and vendors of security-related software welcome the Internet crime wave. American corporations spent $4.2 billion on security software in 1999 alone, and the February 2000 DOS attacks described above sparked another spending spree, with an additional $200 million shelled out for updates and new systems, with security spending expected to top $7.4 billion in 2002. Security analysts blame haphazard network construction for most of the breaches, careless cyber architects making things easy for hackers and crackers. In the wake of the Yahoo shutdown, Network Associates advertised "the first and only service that can detect and remove the denial-of-service attack agent!" Sales by Seattle-based WatchGuard Technologies rose more than 60 percent in one week following the February 2000 attacks, while SonicWALL of Silicon Valley posted a 513 percent revenue hike in the subsequent quarter. High on the list of hot new devices were "zombie" scanners, built to identify remote computers used as hack-attack conduits. Still, for all their good intentions, new systems themselves are typically cracked within days or weeks of release to the public sector.

Though none will admit it, several computer security firms are widely suspected of hiring "darkside" hackers—also known as "black hats"—to advise them on little-known tricks of the trade. Such allegations raise concerns about which side the black hats really serve, and the various security firms take pains to insist that any "former" darkside hackers on their payroll are reformed, confirmed "white hats" who have abandoned—some say returned to—the "hacker ethic." The only certainty in cyberspace is that intrusions will continue, with prosecutions lagging behind security firms racing one another to cash in on America's latest crime wave.

HACKER'S Defense Foundation

Organized as the Hacker's Defense Fund in 1994, this organization—if such it may be called—adopted its present name in December 1997. According to the "mission statement" published on its website, the Hacker's Defense Foundation (HDF), led by president Michael Roadancer, "does not condone, support, or defend blatant criminal acts." Rather, the official line proclaims:

> *The Hacker's Defense Foundation is a Not-for-Profit foundation dedicated and committed to the advancement of the hacking community, through education, of the social, political, and legal implications of the uses of technology, and seeks to enlighten the public and law enforcement about hacking community [sic], through education, that hackers are not the lawless goons that law enforcement, the news media, and Hollywood portray them as.*

The HDF's "educational" function is apparently fulfilled via brief website editorials. No advice is offered on how to join the HDF, no donations are solicited, and no evidence presently exists that the group has actually defended any indicted hackers. As to what the HDF has done since 1997, President Roadancer reports: "To be blunt: not a whole hell of a lot on the outside. We have had some meetings, drawn up a lot of paperwork, and I spoke at con[vention]s very sporadically. Hackerz.org's webserver got hacked and trashed by a member of the community and we lost about a years [sic] hard work."

Apparently, "the community" has yet to be properly educated concerning respect for its own, much less the prevailing laws of the land.

"HAIKU": computer worm

Identified in February 2000, "Haiku" is a worm virus spread on the Internet, in the form of a Windows executable file. It is recognizable by its e-mail attachments, labeled haiku.exe. When such a message is received and the attachment opened, Haiku installs itself in the system and lies in wait for the host computer to restart, at which time it sends out copies of itself attached to e-mails, targeting addresses from the host's address book. Upon installing itself, Haiku displays a dialogue box like the following:

Haiku Generator

> *Reflected light*
> *Wind garden flurry silence*
> *Flashing rainbow silence*
>   *[OK]*

The "poem" offered here is one of countless variations generated from a random mass of 198 nouns, verbs, adjectives and adverbs available to the worm. The verse produced is not a haiku poem, incidentally, since the randomly generated lines ignore the classic structure: five syllables in the first and third lines, with seven in the second.

To spread itself abroad, Haiku scans the infected host's Explorer personal folder, extracting e-mail addresses from any .doc, .htm, .html, .rtf or .txt files located. Next, the worm connects to the Internet using SMTP (simple *m*ail *t*ransfer *p*rotocol) technology and sends a copy of itself to each address retrieved. That task accomplished, Haiku removes itself from Windows memory on the original infected host. Its message appears as follows:

Subject: Fw: Compose your own haikus!
Message: :))

————Original Message————

> *"Old pond . . .*
> *a frog leaps in*
> *water's sound."*
> *—Matsuo Basho.*

DO YOU WANT TO COMPOSE YOUR OWN HAIKUS?

Haiku is a small poetry with oriental metric that appeared in the XVI century and is being very popular, mainly in Japan and the USA.

It's done to transcend the limitation imposed by the usual language and the linear/scientific thinking that treat the nature and the human being as a machine.

It usually has 3 lines and 17 syllables distributed in 5, 7 and 5. It must register or indicate a moment, sensation, impression or drama of a specific fact of nature. It's almost like a photo of some specific moment of nature.

More than inspiration, what you need in order to compose a real haiku is meditation, effort and perception.

DO YOU WANT TO COMPOSE YOUR OWN HAIKUS?

Now you can! it is very easy to get started in this old poetry art. Attached to this e-mail you will find a copy of a simple haiku generator. It will help you in order to understand the basics of the metric, rhyme and subjects which should be used when composing a real haiku . . . just check it out! it's freeware and you can use and spread it as long as you want!

Subsequently, in one case of every 16 infections, the Haiku worm automatically connects to a remote Internet server and retrieves a "/haiku_wav/Haiku .wav" file which displays the following message:

[I-Worm.Haiku, by Mister Sandman]

> *Did you know*
> *The smallest box may hold*
> *The biggest treasure?*

HAMMOND, Ricky: exonerated by DNA evidence

In the early evening of November 20, 1987, a female resident of Hartford, Connecticut, was snatched from a city sidewalk, forced into a waiting car by a stranger who drove her to a rural area outside of town and there sexually assaulted her. After the attack, the kidnapper drove his victim to an unfamiliar neighborhood and left her with a warning that she would be killed if she reported the incident. She told police nonetheless, but arrest of a suspect was delayed since the victim had no clue to her rapist's identity.

Ricky Hammond was subsequently charged with the attack, after the victim identified his photograph and accurately described certain details of his car, including the make and model, scratches in the paint, a torn child's seat, and a wristwatch hanging from the gearshift. Forensic tests on hair retrieved from Hammond's car found it consistent with the victim's hair. Prosecutors hit an apparent snag when tests performed on semen from the victim's clothes excluded Hammond, as to both blood type and DNA, but a court accepted the district attorney's argument that the evidence must have been "contaminated," since the victim's testimony was so detailed and persuasive. Jurors bought the same story, convicting Hammond of kidnapping and sexual assault in March 1990, whereupon he received a 25-year prison sentence. Hammond's motions for a new trial and more detailed forensic testing on available evidence were routinely denied.

Hammond appealed his conviction on three grounds: (1) that the trial court erred in denying his motion for a new trial based on exculpatory blood and DNA analysis; (2) that the court also erred in rejecting his motion for further DNA testing; and (3) that the prosecution made improper statements to the jury, thus infringing on his right to a fair trial. On February 25, 1992, Connecticut's Supreme Court overturned his conviction and remanded the case for further proceedings, noting that the trial judge had ignored or misunderstood "the logical inconsistencies in the prosecution's case, the evidence suggesting that the chemical alteration of the assailant's DNA was physically impossible, or the absence of any evidence that the defendant's scientific tests were unreliable." After serving two years of his sentence, Hammond was acquitted at his second trial and released from custody.

"HAPPYTIME": computer worm

Initially discovered in May 2001, the "HappyTime" worm virus is written in VBS (*Virtual Basic Script*) language and spreads via e-mails using Microsoft Outlook Express or the MSMAPI (*Myrinet Synchronized Multichannel Application Programming Interface*) system. HappyTime first appears as an e-mail message, either presented in HTML format or with an HTML-formatted attachment. If the e-mail itself is in HTML format, the virus code within its body executes automatically upon the message being opened; otherwise, the HTML attachment must be opened with a double click to achieve the same effect.

On activation, HappyTime first replaces the target computer's desktop wallpaper with a new HTML file containing the worm's viral code. In most cases, this change is not visible to the host's user, as any background picture displayed on-screen will remain unaltered. Infection of the desktop wallpaper allows HappyTime to seize control each time the desktop is displayed, whether on startup or when other applications are closed down. Once basic infection is achieved, HappyTime invades all HTM files found in the Windows WEB subfolder, thereby insuring that the worm code is activated each time an infected file or folder is opened. Those activations, in turn, free the worm to locate and infect all other files with extensions .htm, .html, .asp, or .vbs.

While the infection of various files is in progress, HappyTime also modifies the registry values of Microsoft Outlook Express, forcing the program to create messages in HTML format with its stationery tool. Each of those messages in turn contains the HappyTime viral code. When the worm's program has been executed 366 times by the infected host computer, HappyTime launches one of two variant spreading routines. The first raids MS Outlook's address book and sends infected messages to every address found there, while the second sends infected "replies" to any messages found in the system's inbox. The infected messages have no text, but carry an attached file labeled "Untitled.htm."

A final twist is delivered by HappyTime when the sum of the month and date equal 13—as on March 10, August 5, and so forth. On those dates, the worm seeks out and erases all .exe and .dll files found on the infected host computer's hard drive.

HARIRI, Fred See ANTARAMIAN, MICHAEL

HARRIS, William: exonerated by DNA evidence

A state champion athlete from Rand, West Virginia, 17-year-old William Harris was looking forward to college with scholarships in hand when a neighbor was raped near her home in December 1984. Jailed on the basis of a shaky eyewitness identification, Harris was later convicted after state serologist FRED ZAIN testified that his blood type matched that of the rapist. Harris received a 10- to 20-year prison sentence and was still incarcerated a decade later, when West Virginia authorities discovered that Zain had presented false evidence in various felony cases. DNA tests were performed on the semen smears recovered by police in Rand, and Harris was cleared of all charges. The exoneration came too late to salvage his athletic and scholastic careers, however. It was small consolation when Zain, disgraced, was charged with perjury in West Virginia and Texas.

HARRY Potter Warning: Internet hoax

Lifted more or less intact from *The Onion*, a satirical magazine, this hoax "warning" began to circulate on the Internet in September 2000. Ironically, although its author(s) apparently had nothing more than fun in mind, the views expressed precisely echo the actual complaints of various right-wing Christian groups across America, which have condemned the popular series of novels (and in several cases demanded its removal from libraries) on specious grounds that the books "promote witchcraft" or even "teach Satanism." The original hoax warning reads (with errors preserved):

This is the most evil thing I have laid my eyes on in 10 years . . . and no one seems to understand its threat. The Harry Potter books are THE NUMBER ONE selling children's books in our nation today. Just look at any Barns & Noble or Waldenbooks storefront. Go to Amazon.com and read the reviews. Hear the touting by educators and even Christian teachers about how "It's great to see the youth so eagerly embracing the reading experience!" Harry Potter is the creation of a former UK English teacher who promotes witchcraft and Satanism. Harry is a 13 year old 'wizard.' Her creation openly blasphemes Jesus and God and promotes sorcery, seeking revenge upon anyone who upsets them by giving you examples (even the sources with authors and titles) of spells, rituals, and demonic powers. I think the problem is that parents have not reviewed the material. The name seems harmless enough . . . Harry Potter. But that is where it all ends. Let me give you a few quotes from some of the influenced readers themselves: "The Harry Potter books are cool, 'cause they teach you all about magic and how you can use it to control people and get revenge on you enemies," said Hartland, WI, 10-year-old Craig Nowell, a recent convert to the New Satanic Order of the Black Circle. "I want to learn the Cruciatus Curse, to make my muggle science teacher suffer for giving me a D." [A 'muggle' is an unbeliever of magic.]

Or how about the REALLY young and innocent impressionable mind of a 6 year old when asked about her favorite character: "Hermione is my favorite, because she's smart and has a kitty," said 6-year-old Jessica Lehman of Easley, S.C. "Jesus died because He was weak and stupid."

And here is dear Ashley, a 9 year old, the typical average reader of Harry Potter: "I used to believe what they taught us at Sunday School," said Ashley, conjuring up an ancient spell to summon Cerebus, the three-headed hound of hell. "But the Harry Potter books showed me that magic is real, something I can learn and use right now, and that the Bible is nothing but Boring lies."

DOES THIS GET YOUR ATTENTION!! If not, how about a quote from a High Priest of Satanism: "Harry is an absolute godsend for our cause," said High Priest Egan of the First Church of Satan in Salem,

MA. "An organization like ours thrives on new blood—no pun intended—and we've had more applicants than we can handle lately. And, of course, practically all of them are virgins, which is gravy." [Since 1995, open applicants to Satan worship have increased from around 100,000 to now . . . 14 MILLION children and young adults!]

It makes me physically ill, people! But, I think I can offer you an explanation of why this is happening. Children have been bombarded with action, adventure, thrills and scares to the point Hollywood can produce nothing new to give them the next 'high.' Parents have neglected to see what their children are reading and doing, and simply seem satisfied that 'Little Johnny is interested in reading.' AND . . . educators and the NEA are PUSHING this with NO WARNING as to the effects or the contents. Still not convinced? I will leave you with something to let you make up your own mind.

And finally, a quote from the author herself, J.K. Rowling, describing the objections of Christian reviewers to her writings: "I think it is absolute rubbish to protest children's books on the grounds that they are luring children to Satan," Rowling told a London Times reporter in a July 17 interview. "People should be praising them for that! These books guide children to an understanding that the weak, idiotic Son of God is a living hoax who will be humiliated when the rain of fire comes, . . . while we, his faithful servants, laugh and cavort in victory."

My hope is that you will see fit to become involved in getting the word out about this garbage. Please FWD to every pastor, teacher, and parent you know. This author has now published FOUR BOOKS in less than 2 years of this 'encyclopedia of Satanism' and is surely going to write more. I also ask all Christians to please pray for this lost woman's soul. Pray also for the Holy Spirit to work in the young minds of those who are reading this garbage that they may be delivered from its harm.

A later variant of the Potter hoax claimed (falsely) to originate with the American Family Foundation, whose spokespersons have publicly repudiated the fraud.

HATE Groups On-line

American and European racist groups discovered cyberspace in the 1980s, communicating internationally on bulletin board services (BBSs) such as the Aryan Nations Net and the Chicago Liberty Net. The Aryan Nations Net was created by "Pastor" Richard Butler (of the Aryan Nations cult based at Hayden Lake, Idaho) and Louis Beam, a rootless

Above, Racist groups like the Ku Klux Klan maintain numerous Internet websites. (Southern Poverty Law Center)
Below, Neo-Nazi activists Louis Beam (in white suit) and Richard Butler (with bullhorn) were among the pioneers of Internet racist propaganda. (Southern Poverty Law Center)

member of the Ku Klux Klan who also briefly graced the FBI's "Ten Most Wanted" list, pursued on charges of sedition. (He was acquitted, with other defendants in that case, in April 1988.)

While never specifically threatening criminal action, the Butler-Beam BBS participated in the same tough talk traditionally beloved by Klansmen and Nazis, including thinly veiled threats toward specific enemies. Referring to the leader of the Southern Poverty Law Center (SPLC), whose civil lawsuits bankrupted various racist groups (and finally the Aryan Nations itself), Beam wrote: "According to the word of our God, Morris Dees has earned two (2) death sentences. . . . Thy will be done on earth as it is in heaven." When such rhetoric was combined with instructions on bomb making and an unstable readership, acts of criminal violence were sure to follow, as when Klansmen set fire to the SPLC's Montgomery, Alabama, office on July 28, 1983.

The first Internet website devoted to white supremacist dogma was launched in March 1995 by Don Black, a former Alabama Klansman lately paroled from a three-year term in federal prison. Resettled in Florida, Black recognized the magic of the Web. "There's a potential here to reach millions," he told reporters. "I think it's a major breakthrough."

Black's latest tiny group would not prosper, but others swiftly followed his example. In 1998 the SPLC counted 163 "hate" sites on the Internet, increasing to 254 in 1999, 305 in 2000, and 366 in 2001. Most were operated by various KKK factions, neo-Nazi groups, racist skinhead gangs, and "Christian Identity" cultists (members of a sect believing that Jews and nonwhite "mud people" were spawned in the Garden of Eden, after Eve had sex with Satan in reptile form). Those groups and websites listed by SPLC as "other" still had obvious racist or neo-Nazi roots. They included Louis Beam himself, with organizations calling themselves the National Association for the Advancement of White People; Jew Watch; Nigger Watch; White Power Central; and Jew Grinder 88 (the numerals a veiled reference to the eighth letter of the alphabet—i.e., "HH"—as an abbreviation of "Heil Hitler!").

The advent of extremist "patriot militias" in America after 1995 added new firepower to the far right, and many (if not most) of those groups maintained close ties to older, more traditional racist movements like the Klan and Aryan Nations. By 1998, SPLC counted 248 "patriot" sites on the Internet, increased

to 263 in 2000, but the next year saw that movement on the wane, membership in various pseudo-militias plummeting along with the number of Web links. By the end of 2001, the number of Internet sites maintained by militiamen and their allies had dwindled to 155 and was steadily declining.

By the start of the 21st century, "white power rock"—a brand of violent music imported from Britain in the mid-1980s—had become one of the racist right's most powerful recruiting tools, speaking to the anger and frustration felt by most skinheads. The lyrics, typified by those of lead singer George Burdia from the band "Rahowa!" (short for Racial Holy War) illustrate why neo-Nazi skinheads have surpassed all other factions in arrests for hate crimes in America and Western Europe.

You kill all the niggers and you gas all the Jews
Kill a gypsy and a commie too.
You just killed a kike, don't it feel right?
Goodness gracious, Third Reich!

HAWAIIAN Good Luck Totem: Internet hoax

A common example of an Internet chain letter, the Hawaiian totem message disavows any intent to profit from gullible readers, yet preys on their superstition for the purpose of an apparent practical joke. It is replicated on the World Wide Web—with or without artwork—in thousands of variations, contributing to the junk mail (or "spam") that drives many Internet subscribers to distraction.

Hawaiian GOOD LUCK TOTEM

This totem has been sent to you for good luck. It has been sent around the world ten times so far. You will

receive good luck within four days of relaying this totem. Send copies to people you think need good luck. Don't send money as fate has no price. Do not keep this message. The totem must leave your hands in 96 hours.

Send ten copies and see what happens in four days. You will get a surprise. This is true, even if you are not superstitious.

Good luck, but please remember: 10 copies of this message must leave your hands in 96 hours . . .

HAWKINS, Frank C. Jr.: satellite TV pirate

A 53-year-old police lieutenant in Canton, Ohio, Frank Hawkins Jr. was indicted by a federal grand jury on October 18, 2000, charged with selling and distributing mechanical devices for unauthorized decryption of satellite cable television programming and direct-to-home satellite services. As charged in the indictment, Hawkins accepted $750 between April 12 and April 17, 2000, for the illegal alteration of five DirecTV access cards. Suspended without pay following his indictment, Hawkins retired from the Canton Police Department in January 2001. A month later, on February 23, 2001, he pleaded guilty before U.S. District Judge James Gwin and received a sentence of one year's probation, plus a $2,000 fine payable within 30 days.

HAYES, Robert: exonerated by DNA evidence

A 35-year-old resident of Broward County, Florida, Robert Hayes was employed as a groom at the Pompano Harness Track when a female coworker, Pamela Albertson, was raped and strangled to death in 1990. Albertson was found clutching several hairs in her hand, believed to come from her assailant, and prosecutors claimed that DNA tests performed on the hairs proved they belonged to Hayes. Convicted of murder in 1991, he was sentenced to a term of life imprisonment.

On appeal, Hayes's lawyers demonstrated that while Hayes is an African American, the hairs retrieved from Albertson's hand in 1990 belonged to a white man. They also provided expert testimony that DNA extracted from the suspect hairs had been contaminated during testing and did not in fact link Hayes to the crime. Florida's Supreme Court overturned the conviction in 1995 and remanded the case to Broward County for retrial, where Hayes was acquitted of all charges in July 1997. Leaving prison penniless, Hayes returned to his native Canton,

Mississippi, and was hired to drive a city dump truck, caring for horses at a local amusement park in his spare time. The rape-murder of Pamela Albertson remains unsolved today.

HEART Attack Survival Technique: Internet hoax

Circulated sporadically on the Internet since July 1999, this hoax appears innocuous but may have tragic results for a gullible reader in isolated cases. Specifically, the solo heart-attack remedy recommended in the e-mail message does not work. Spokesmen for the American Red Cross and the American Heart Association agree that heart attack victims typically lose consciousness within a matter of seconds, and those who do not are in no need of cardio-pulmonary resuscitation (CPR). The bottom line: Anyone who feels him/herself in the early stages of a heart attack should dial 911 for medical assistance, rather than experimenting with futile home remedies. The bogus warning reads:

Subject: Heart Attack Information

For your information. This will also be posted on the Health & Wellness portion of the intra-net.

HOW TO SURVIVE A HEART ATTACK WHEN ALONE

A person, of any age, can have a heart attack. Without help the person whose heart stops beating properly and who begins to feel faint, has only about 10 seconds left before losing consciousness. However, these victims can help themselves by coughing repeatedly and very vigorously. A deep breath should be taken before each cough, and the cough must be deep and prolonged, as when producing sputum from deep inside the chest. A breath and a cough must be repeated about every two seconds without let up until help arrives, or until the heart is felt to be beating normally again.

Deep breaths get oxygen into the lungs and coughing movements squeeze the heart and keep the blood circulating. The squeezing pressure on the heart also helps it regain normal rhythm. In this way, heart attack victims can get to a phone and, between breaths, call for help.

Tell as many other people as possible about this, it could save their lives!

—from Health Cares, Rochester General Hospital via Chapter 240's newsletter AND THE BEAT GOES

ON . . . (reprint from The Mended Hearts, Inc. publication, Heart Response)

HELSINGIUS, Johan: Internet privacy advocate

A native of Helsinki, Finland, Johan Helsingius—known on-line as "Julf"—operated the Internet's most popular anonymous remailer (penet.fi) until 1996, when he was driven out of business by a flurry of unfounded allegations suggesting involvement in criminal activity. None of the charges were substantiated, but the aggravation proved too much and Helsingius retired from the trade, leaving other anonymous remailers to provide bashful Internet subscribers with the illusion of complete security from prying eyes.

Helsingius hit his first snag with the law in 1995, when the Church of Scientology claimed some unknown penet.fi subscriber was posting cult secrets on the Internet. Police raided Helsingius's office in

Finnish private computer consultant Johan Helsingius operated a re-mailer of electronic messages until he was forced to shut down his server because of claims he was relaying child pornography on the Internet. (AP)

response to the complaint, and a Finnish court ultimately ruled that Helsingius must reveal the subscriber's true e-mail address. Rather than violate the confidentiality of his customers, Helsingius scrapped the service and retired on August 30, 1996. As he told reporters when announcing his decision, "I will close down the remailer for the time being because the legal issues governing the whole Internet in Finland are yet undefined. The legal protection of the users needs to be clarified. At the moment the privacy of Internet messages is judicially unclear."

Worse lay in store for Helsingius after *The Observer*, a British Sunday tabloid newspaper, claimed that penet.fi had been used to transmit CHILD PORNOGRAPHY around the world. Finnish police investigated that claim, as well, and pronounced it false. Sergeant Kaj Malmberg of the Helsinki Police Crime Squad told reporters that Helsingius had limited his service in early 1995, so that the remailer could not transmit photographs. "The true amount of child pornography in [the] Internet is difficult to assess," Malmberg said, "but one thing is clear: We have not found any cases where child porn pictures were transmitted from Finland."

Helsingius, meanwhile, seemed unwilling to give up entirely on the Internet privacy issue. As he told an interviewer in September 1996, "I will try to set up a task force which will include Internet experts together with representatives of civic organizations and authorities. The task force could take a stand on issues such as the network's practical operation methods and the misuse of the network. I hope that the results of this task force will support the development of the network."

As for the importance of Internet privacy, Helsingius said, "It's important to be able to express certain views without everyone knowing who you are. One of the best examples was the great debate about Caller ID on phones. People were really upset that the person at the receiving end would know who was calling. On things like telephones, people take for granted the fact that they can be anonymous if they want to and they get really upset if people take that away. I think the same thing applies for e-mail."

As for specific examples, Helsingius noted, "It's clear that for things like the Usenet groups on sexual abuse, people need to be able to discuss their own experience without everyone knowing who they are. Where you're dealing with minorities—racial, political, sexual, whatever—you always find cases in which people belonging to a minority would like to discuss things that are important to them without having to identify who they are."

To date, no task force as imagined by Helsingius has been organized and the issue of anonymous e-mails remains controversial, but advances in computer technology enable law enforcement agencies to trace most messages without undue difficulty.

HERNANDEZ, Alejandro See CRUZ, ROLANDO

HERR, Adrian Frederick: software pirate

A 30-year-old resident of Laguna Hills, California, Adrian Herr was a prolific software pirate who operated from his home, advertising on the Internet and in computer magazines. According to the federal investigators who arrested him in 2000, Herr made between $20,000 and $30,000 selling bootleg copies of Microsoft software, including the popular Windows 98, Windows 2000, Office 2000 and Publisher 2000 programs. He produced counterfeit CDs himself and used false Microsoft labels to make them appear legitimate.

Authorities reached a tentative agreement with Herr in April 2000, whereby he promised to quit the bootleg software business in return for waiver of prosecution on pending felony charges, but within a few weeks Herr resumed posting ads on the Internet and hawking his wares through *Recycler* magazine. He was then arrested and slapped with two felony charges of copyright infringement. Herr pleaded guilty on February 26, 2001, before U.S. District Judge Alicemarie Stoler. He faced a maximum sentence of 10 years in prison and a $500,000 fine for reneging on his initial bargain with the feds.

HICKS, Anthony: exonerated by DNA evidence

In November 1990 a female resident of Madison, Wisconsin, told police she had been raped by an unknown black man who knocked on her apartment door, then forced his way inside, twice assaulting her before he fled the scene. The 26-year-old victim saw her attacker's face briefly, when he barged into the flat, but was not permitted to see him again for the duration of her ordeal. Anthony Hicks was subsequently jailed for a traffic offense in Madison, whereupon a police dispatcher examined a composite sketch of the rape suspect and told detectives, "That looks like that black guy we just brought in."

Hicks was placed in a lineup, whereupon the victim identified him as her assailant. Hicks passed two polygraph tests, suggesting he was innocent, but the test results were inadmissible in court.

At trial, prosecutors introduced certain pubic hairs found at the crime scene, identified as "consistent" with samples taken from Hicks. The Wisconsin state crime lab had no DNA testing facility at the time, and while defense attorney Willie Nunnery employed a private analyst to test the hairs, the samples proved too small for conclusive testing under the restricted fragment length polymorphism (RFLP) analysis system most commonly used. Nunnery learned that a more efficient method of DNA testing—the polymerase chain reaction (PCR) method—was available from a lab in California, but he elected to skip those tests and used a Chicago expert to contest the prosecution's findings of "consistency" between the hairs. Jurors convicted Hicks in December 1991 and he received a 19-year prison term.

More advanced DNA testing, under the PCR system, was performed on the evidence in 1993, whereupon Hicks was excluded as a suspect in the rape. Wisconsin's Court of Appeals reversed Hicks's conviction and ordered a new trial, that decision affirmed by the state supreme court "in the interest of justice" when prosecutors appealed. Hicks was released in 1996, after spending four and a half years in prison. (His alleged victim, meanwhile, stands by her identification to the present day, insisting she picked the right man.)

Upon his release, Hicks sued attorney Nunnery for malpractice in failing to pursue the PCR tests in 1991. Jurors in that civil case believed the test would almost certainly have resulted in acquittal for Hicks. They found Nunnery negligent and ordered him to pay Hicks $2.6 million for the time that he was wrongfully imprisoned. Nunnery, outraged, told reporters, "I think it was totally unfair and unprecedented. I was doing all I could to provide aid and assistance to my client. I think I will be vindicated. This, too, shall pass."

"HIDER": computer viruses

Classified as dangerous, nonmemory-resident, encrypted parasitic viruses, the "Hider" variants were first catalogued in May 1998. Three forms are presently recognized, all of which infect .exe and .com files (except command.com) by writing themselves to the ends of the respective files. The viruses deliver their payloads on the 13th of each month. "Hider.1782" displays the following message:

Anston Rant is back for more!
Whoa, looks like you be missin some files there, Bud!

The variants identified as "Hider.2143" and "Hider.2169," meanwhile, display this message:

Anston Rant Returns! Miss me, folks?
I'd trash some data, but my medication kicked in!

"HIV": computer virus

Identified for the first time in October 2000, "HIV" is ranked by analysts as a dangerous, memory-resident virus targeting Windows executable files and MSI (*Medium Scale Integration*) archives. The virus further utilizes "entry point obscuring" methods to conceal itself within infected files, a process assisted by its small size (about 6KB in length). HIV is also armed with anti-debugging techniques, freezing the infected host system if debugging programs are encountered. In Windows 98 systems, HIV disables file protection safeguards by overwriting the default.sfc file with empty data. A similar technique employed against sfcfiles.dll on Windows 2000 is defeated as Windows blocks access or automatically restores deleted files from its backup.

When infecting MSI archives, the HIV strain searches for executable files and overwrites their program entry routines with a code that displays the following message when the program is run:

[Win32.HIV] by Benny/29A
This cell has been infected by HIV virus.

Another angle of attack for HIV involves replacement of HTML files in the current directory with XML files, achieved by writing an xml suffix to the existing filename. That done, HIV contrives to hide the modified files by setting a Windows registry key to conceal extensions for XML files. Finally, HIV opens the Windows Address Book (WAB) database, retrieves any e-mail addresses found there, and dispatches infected messages to each. Those messages read:

From: press@microsoft.com
Sent: 2010/06/06 22:00
Subject: XML presentation

Message: Please check out this XML presentation and send us your opinion. If you have any questions about XML presentation, write us.
Thank you.
The XML development team, Microsoft Corp.
Attached file: press.txt

The attachment, of course, contains HIV's viral code and proceeds to infect the new host when the press.txt file is opened, thus perpetuating the routine.

HOAXBUSTERS: Internet debunking site

Maintained by the U.S. Department of Energy's Computer Incident Advisory Capability (CIAC), the Hoaxbusters website is dedicated to exposing Internet hoaxes and thereby minimizing their potential damage, ranging from simple aggravation to swindles and loss of commerce precipitated by fraudulent "warnings" about mythical defects in various legitimate products or services. Such hoaxes circulate about the Internet with other junk e-mail ("spam"), but are often couched in terms that make them resemble public service announcements or other worthwhile communications. Some deliver attachments infected with computer VIRUSES and thereby deliver a payload more damaging than simple anxiety.

The Hoaxbusters website divides hoaxes into 11 broad categories. They include:

1. *Malicious code warnings* related to viruses, Trojan programs, and other Internet menaces allegedly found "in the wild," which do not in fact exist.
2. *Urban myths,* including reports and warnings of dire events which never took place in reality, sometimes calculated to produce fearful reactions in their target audience.
3. *Bogus giveaways,* typically claiming that cash or some other valuable prize has been offered by a major corporation, inviting readers to participate in mythical contests or similar time-wasting activities.
4. *Inconsequential warnings* that propagate anxiety concerning real-life matters that are either obsolete (in that the problem has long since been solved) or that were virtually harmless in the first place.
5. *Sympathy letters and requests for help* on behalf of some allegedly needy person, often the victim of an accident or illness. In hoax cases, the person

allegedly requesting aid either does not exist or else has no such problem and has not broadcast appeals for help. Such pleas may constitute a form of CYBERSTALKING when they generate volumes of unwanted e-mail or other contact with the allegedly needy person.

6. *Traditional chain letters,* typically threatening bad luck if the recipient does not forward duplicates or—in cases of Internet fraud—send money to a list of persons named in the message.
7. *Threatening chain letters,* including malicious threats of harm against the recipient, his property, or some third party if the chain is not perpetuated.
8. *Scam chain letters,* presented as communications from a legitimate firm, which in fact are designed to swindle the recipients in some way.
9. *Scare chain letters* that warn random recipients of impending danger to others, frequently naming women as the endangered parties.
10. *Jokes* couched in terms of fanciful warnings referring to improbable events or disasters, such as the end of the world or some regional catastrophe.
11. *"True legends,"* defined by the Hoaxbusters website as "real stories and messages that are not hoaxes but are still making the rounds of the Internet." No criminal or malicious intent generally lies behind such messages, but they still add to the recipient's daily load of time-wasting spam.

Hoaxbusters advises recipients of any hoax messages to ignore them and/or to employ any available e-mail filter programs that may screen such items out upon delivery. In no case should chain letters be perpetuated, nor should cash or any other item be sent to strangers in response to e-mail requests. Attachments to unwanted e-mails and those sent by strangers are best left unopened, as they may contain damaging virus codes. Any threats received should be reported to law enforcement agencies or to some private organization such as CYBERANGELS, which is equipped to trace the offending messages. E-mails that solicit cash or other valuables may also be reported to the U.S. Justice Department's Internet Fraud Complaint Center, at <http://www.fbi.gov/interagency/ifcc/ifccoverview.htm>.

"HOBO": computer virus
Initially discovered in January 1998, "Hobo" is rated as a harmless, memory-resident, partly encrypted parasitic virus which copies itself to the infected host's Interrupt Vectors Table. It also searches out .com files in the current directory and writes itself to the end of each one located. No payload is delivered and no manifestations present themselves thereafter. Hobo contains the following text:

*.com
'Hobo' Created by Sozer

HOLDREN, Larry: exonerated by DNA evidence
In December 1982 a female resident of Charleston, West Virginia, was attacked while jogging, dragged into a highway culvert, and there repeatedly raped. Charleston resident Larry Holdren was identified by both the victim and an off-duty FBI agent, who testified under oath that he observed Holdren walking near the crime scene on the day of the attack. Convicted at trial on six counts of sexual assault, Holdren received a sentence of 30 to 60 years in state prison. He served 15 years of that term before DNA testing—unavailable at the time of his trial—conclusively excluded him as the source of semen recovered from the victim and the crime scene.

HONAKER, Edward: exonerated by DNA evidence
In the predawn hours of June 23, 1984, Samuel Dempsey and his girlfriend, Angela Nichols, were sleeping in their car, parked beside a rural Virginia highway, when a stranger woke them, brandishing a pistol and identifying himself as a police officer. The man ordered Dempsey out of his car and into the nearby woods. He then dragged Nichols to a nearby pickup truck and drove her to a more secluded area, where she was raped and sodomized repeatedly. Authorities prepared a sketch of the suspect from descriptions offered by Dempsey and Nichols, including his military-style camouflage fatigues.

Authorities still had no leads in the case when a second woman was raped, 100 miles from the scene of the original crime. That victim said her rapist resembled a neighbor, 40-year-old Edward Honaker, but Honaker had an airtight alibi and was never charged with the crime. He was photographed by detectives, however, and that photo made its way to Nelson County, where Dempsey and Nichols identified Honaker as their assailant of June 23. Honaker owned a pickup resembling the kidnapper's vehicle, and a search of his home turned up camouflage clothing similar to the rapist's.

There were problems with the prosecution's case from the beginning. First, Honaker once again had an alibi corroborated by four witnesses. Nichols described her rapist as left-handed, whereas Honaker was not. The rapist's semen contained motile sperm, while Honaker had undergone a vasectomy eight years earlier. Although the rapist had disrobed and forced Nichols to perform oral sex, she did not recall a large surgical scar across Honaker's stomach. Finally, while the kidnapper had ranted at length about his Vietnam war experience, Honaker had no such military record.

Nelson County prosecutors forged ahead despite those stumbling blocks. At trial, they dismissed the corroboration of Honaker's alibi as "a put-up job" concocted by friends and relatives to deceive the court. Honaker's vasectomy was dismissed with a claim that sperm found on vaginal swabs came from Sam Dempsey. Dempsey and Nichols testified against Honaker, identifying him under oath as their assailant. Finally, a state forensic expert told jurors that hair found on Nichols's clothing after the rape "was unlikely to match anyone" other than Honaker. Convicted on seven counts of rape, sodomy and sexual assault, Honaker received three life terms in prison plus 34 years.

In the wake of that crushing verdict, Honaker contacted CENTURION MINISTRIES for help in appealing his conviction. Investigators soon discovered that Nichols's first description of the rapist was inconsistent with Honaker and that some of Dempsey's testimony was induced via hypnosis. Centurion Ministries then joined forces with the CARDOZO INNOCENCE PROJECT to pursue DNA testing of evidence collected by police. Prosecutors reluctantly furnished the evidence, and a lab report of January 13, 1994, identified two different seminal deposits in the samples preserved, mismatched between the vaginal swab and a stain found on Nichols's shorts. DNA results positively excluded Edward Honaker as a source of either sample. A second report, dated March 15, 1994, concluded that while Samuel Dempsey could not be excluded as a source of the clothing stain, he likewise had not produced the semen swabbed from Nichols's vagina. In June 1994 Nichols admitted an affair with a third party unknown to Dempsey, but the secret lover was also excluded by DNA tests as a source for the vaginal samples. The June 1984 rapist remains unidentified.

Virginia statutes forbid introduction of new evidence more than 21 days after trial, regardless of the circumstances, so Honaker was forced to seek a pardon from Governor George Allen. Lawyers filed a clemency petition on June 29, 1994, and Allen officially pardoned Honaker on October 21, 1994, freeing him after he had served 10 years in prison. "It's mind-boggling what our system can do," Honaker told reporters at the prison gates. "What happened to me can happen to any man alive. DNA was my salvation." Governor Allen refused financial compensation on grounds that all officials involved in the case "acted in complete accordance with the law."

HONDA Giveaway: Internet fraud

Another Internet giveaway hoax, this one targeting Honda Motors with fraudulent claims of free vehicles offered in return for circulating chain letters online, was first reported in September 1999. As with the BILL GATES hoax, the GAP giveaway fraud, and others, this offer has no validity and has been publicly repudiated by Honda. The original message reads (with errors uncorrected):

Subject: FW: New Wheels! Please forward this . . . (fwd)

First off, I just want everyone to know this is the real thing. I forwarded this message to everyone I know about 6 months ago and last week a Honda employee showed up at my house with my brand new 1999 Civic EX!!! It is so funny because I never believed these things worked and actually sent this one as a joke to all my friends. But they forwarded the message too and now I have received a new car!!!

My best friend actually hasn't gotten his car yet but he checked the balance of his Honda Account and it has reached nearly $11,000!!! If you like Honda's or you just want a new car, please forward this message it is the real thing.

Bob Stanley, Denver Colorado

Friends,

Look I know this sounds too good to be true, and that's what I thought too. But I called Honda's headquarters in Japan and spoke to an American representative myself and it really is true! They assured me that this the real thing! I still wasn't convinced but I called three weeks later and my Honda account balance has reached *the unbelievable sum of $12,500!!! So even if you don't believe this, forward it anyway so my account will continue to grow until I get my brand new Prelude!!!*

Steve Kelly, Minneapolis Minnessota

Dear valued customers:

Here at Honda we have been well known for over 20 years for providing the best in reliabillity, comfort, and style. Over the years we have risen to be one of the top auto industries here in Japan. But that isn't enough. We want to be number one in the US. Now our twentieth anniversary for making cars is here!!! This is the perfect opportunity for you and us here at Honda to celebrate our 20 years of excellent service. We have been trying to think of ideas to get more people to know about our cars. And with technology and e-mail being the wave of the future, we want to jump on this opportunity. So we have set up a rewards system to repay those who help us spread the word about Honda. Our marketing staff has designed a special program that traces this message as it travels across the US. Anyone who forwards this e-mail, will immediately have an account at their local Honda dealer opened in their name. This account will initially be opened with a credit of $1,000 toward any new or used vehicle at their participating dealership. For each person you forward this e-mail to, the amount of $200 will be added to your account. If the recipients of this e-mail forward it you will be rewarded an additional $100 for each person it reaches and if they forward it your account continues to grow in $100 increments. You can log onto our website at http://www.Honda.com to check the balance of your account. If things go well and everyone participates you should see your account grow quite quickly. Follow the on screen instructions to order the specific make and model of Honda you want to buy with your account. We hope that this is a rewarding experience for you and us. Our goal is to reach over 1 million computers by the year 2000.

I thank you for your time and business.

Sincerely,
Kageyama Hironobu
Senior Honda Marketing Advisor

HOWLAND, Gregory: software pirate

A Massachusetts Institute of Technology graduate and resident of Bethesda, Maryland, Gregory Hol-land was 39 years old in 1998, when he began selling bootlegged computer software on the Internet. Doing business as Howland Enterprises Inc. and Middlemarch Networks, Howland advertised copies of Apple software on various Internet newsgroups, including Mac OSX server, WebObjects 4, OpenStep 4.2 User, and OpenStep 4.2 Developer. The least expensive versions of these programs, in the aggregate, still retailed for more than $6,000, while Howland offered his copies for a fraction of that price.

In September 1998 Howland sold copies of OpenStep 4.2 User and OpenStep 4.2 Developer for $170 to a Denver company, Black Hole Inc. After receiving the software, a Black Hole representative advised Howland that he was selling bootlegged programs and advised him to "stop this practice immediately before you wind up busted by the man." Howland agreed and refunded Black Hole's money, but the business was too lucrative for him to simply walk away. A short time later Apple representatives learned of the Black Hole transaction and a Boston member of the firm contacted Howland via e-mail in February 1999, using the name "Alex Lamb" as he sought to purchase bootleg programs. Howland readily agreed to sell "Lamb" copies of the OpenStep programs for $100 plus $15 shipping. He mailed the package from his home address on February 22, 1999.

FBI agents entered the case at that point, maintaining the "Alex Lamb" façade while they negotiated further illegal transactions. Between April and June 1999, Howland sold the feds 39 CDs containing illegal bootleg copies of various Apple programs, charging $2,060 for software valued in excess of $60,000 at legitimate retail prices. The FBI never paid Howland for those disks, arresting him instead, but he admitted selling 25 to 50 copies to other Internet customers at $50 each, for an alleged total profit of $1,250 to $2,500. The price charged to Black Hole Inc. in September 1998 suggests Howland may have understated his profits in the case by $3,000 to $6,000, assuming he was truthful concerning the number of CDs sold.

Howland pleaded guilty to one count of willful copyright infringement on June 13, 2001, facing a maximum sentence of five years in prison and a $250,000 fine. Stephen Schenning, U.S. attorney for the district of Maryland, told reporters, "This office and law enforcement agencies recognize the significance of intellectual property to our nation's economy and will aggressively prosecute people committing these crimes." Schenning described Howland's prosecution as part of the U.S. Justice Department's nationwide Intellectual Property Initiative, launched in July 1999 under provisions of the federal No Electronic Theft (NET) Act.

HSU, Eugene You Tsai: accused cyber-spy

A naturalized U.S. citizen residing in Blue Springs, Missouri, Eugene Hsu was arrested by Customs Service officers on August 30, 2001, charged with conspiring to sell advanced military encryption devices to the People's Republic of China. Arrested at the same time was David Tzu Wvi Yang, a Taiwan native and permanent resident alien living in Temple, California.

According to spokesmen for the U.S. Customs Service, the arrests climaxed a four-month investigation centered in Baltimore. Hsu and Yang reportedly contracted with an undercover Customs officer to sell and transport KIV-7HS encryption devices, deemed so advanced and sensitive that special approval from the National Security Agency is required before the equipment can be exported. In fact, according to Allan Doody, Customs special agent in charge for Baltimore, the KIV-7HS device is listed among "the most sensitive items on the U.S. munitions list." According to its developer, Rainbow Technologies, the device provides "high-speed cryptographic functions in Time Division Multiple Access architectures to provide secure high-bandwidth, wide-area, networked data exchange via satellite over a broad range of data rates."

Customs agents pursued their investigation with help from Mykotronx, a Rainbow Technologies subsidiary and supplier of the KIV-7HS. The agents posed as middlemen who could facilitate export of the devices to a third party, one Charlson Ho, affiliated with a Singapore company called Wei Soon Long. According to the charges filed, Eugene Hsu pursued the transaction even after Customs agents informed him that no export license would be approved for export of the KIV-7HS devices to China and that such export would violate the federal Arms Control Export Act. Hsu's alleged partner in the scheme, David Yang, reportedly told agents on August 24 that the units were ready for transport from Los Angeles to Singapore via Taipei, and from Singapore on to China. No KIV-7HS units actually changed hands before the suspects were arrested.

Customs was alerted to the pending transaction in May 2001, when Hsu contacted Mykotronx in Columbia, Maryland, to ask the retail price of KIV-7HS units. A Mykotronx security officer thereafter informed federal agents of the overture, since the KIV-7HS is restricted to U.S. government use. Customs asked Mykotronx to tell Hsu that all future discussions would be conducted through an intermediary import/export firm in Maryland—in fact, a Customs front staffed by the agency's undercover officers. Between May 2, 2001, and August 18, 2001, a Customs agent recorded various telephone conversations with Hsu, David Yang, and Charlson Ho in Singapore (who planned to buy the units for resale in China). Those conversations, and Hsu's alleged willingness to violate federal law, formed the basis of charges filed against Hsu and Yang.

Spokesmen for the U.S. Justice Department stress that indictments are simply accusations of criminal activity and are not in themselves proof of guilt. All criminal defendants are presumed innocent until they are convicted by a jury or agree to a plea bargain with their prosecutors. Hsu's attorney has informed reporters that his client had no part in "a deeper Chinese government conspiracy and had no idea what he was getting into." If convicted on the charges filed, Eugene Hsu and David Yang face a maximum penalty of 10 years in federal prison and a $1 million fine.

HU, Jinsong: accused cyberstalker (exonerated)

A 26-year-old doctoral candidate at California State Polytechnic University in Pomona, Jinsong Hu was considered a promising student until early 1995, when a former girlfriend accused him of sexually harassing her via e-mail. Initially charged under California's stalking law, Hu spent six months in the Orange County jail before jurors acquitted him in June 1995. Although Jiajun Wen also accused Hu of verbal and written harassment, the bulk of prosecution evidence against him consisted of e-mails which Hu denied writing, blaming the barrage of messages on a still-unidentified impostor. A university computer expert testified that she had traced the offending e-mails back to Hu's account. Hu countered that Wen knew his password and numerous others had access to his e-mail server. Jurors accepted his claim that most of the harassing e-mails were fraudulent, and that some he did send had been altered by persons unknown, but the Caltech administration was unmoved by Hu's acquittal, expelling him in October 1995.

Hu's expulsion polarized the Caltech faculty and student body, while reports of e-mail harassment and CYBERSTALKING increased dramatically on campuses across the nation. Investigators conceded that e-mails were easily altered (or "spoofed"), and at least one message sent to Jiajun Wen was later traced to an acquaintance of her new boyfriend, living in Salt Lake City, but the expulsion order remained in force. Caltech geology professor Yuk Yung told the *Los Angeles Times,* "E-mail is the bread and butter of an institution like this. But it is very hard to prove that the person whose name is on it indeed sent it, and that it has not been tampered with—especially here, where these kids all have extraordinary computing ability." Jinsong Hu was one year from completion of his studies when he was expelled, described by his faculty adviser as a brilliant scholar who scored first among nearly 1 million students taking the Chinese equivalent of the Graduate Record Exam (GRE) prior to entering Caltech.

Hu's case hinged on four specific e-mail messages, the first allegedly sent to Wen when they broke up in August 1994, three others sent to Wen's new boyfriend in January 1995. The latter messages included references to sexual encounters between Hu and Wen and a warning: "If you are beginning to suffer now, tell Jiajun about it. She knows what it means." Hu maintains that he knew nothing of the messages until a later date in January 1995, when he found his e-mail account disabled by a Caltech computer administrator. His expulsion was ordered by a three-member panel, apparently ignoring the trial court's finding in Hu's criminal case. While conceding that Hu had an alibi for the time when two e-mails were sent, the panel decided that he could have written a program to make his computer send messages while he was not at the terminal.

"HYDRA": computer worm

An Internet worm written in Visual Basic and spread via e-mails with an attached .exe file, "Hydra" was noted for the first time in June 2001. When a recipient clicks on the attachment, Hydra copies itself to the Windows directory under the name msserv.exe and logs that file in the Windows registry auto-run keys as follow:

HKEY_CURRENT_USER\Software\Microsoft\Windows\CurrentVersion\Run

HKEY_CURRENT_USER\Software\Microsoft\Windows\CurrentVersion\RunServices

HKEY_LOCAL_MACHINE\Software\Microsoft\Windows\CurrentVersion\Run

HKEY_LOCAL_MACHINE\Software\Microsoft\Windows\CurrentVersion\RunServics

Hydra lingers in Windows memory as a hidden application and spreads itself further on the Internet by connecting to Microsoft Outlook, where it registers itself as Outlook's "NewMail" and "ItemSend" events handler. Under "NewMail," when a message is received, Hydra scans the e-mail for its own infection (and deletes it if a virus code is found), then opens clean messages and scans them for .exe attachments (deleting those, as well). For "ItemSend," Hydra searches outgoing e-mails for any attached files and replaces those found with its own infected .exe attachment. If outgoing messages have no attachments, Hydra creates one to further spread the infection. E-mails sent between 1:00 and 2:00 P.M. on any Friday the 13th are further modified with the following text added to the beginning of each message:

[I-Worm.Hydra] . . . by gl_st0rm of [mions]

Hydra conceals itself in several ways, first deleting the msconfig.exe file from the Windows system directory, then searching out and terminating the following antivirus applications as found:

Amon
AntiVir
AVG
  AVP Monitor
  Dr. Web
  File Monitor
  F-Secure
  F-STOPW
  InoculateIT
  Iomon98
  Kaspersky Anti-Virus
  navpw32
  NOD32
  Norman Virus Control
  Norton AntiVirus
  Registry Editor
  Registry Monitor

Task Master
Trend PC-cillin
vettray
Vshwin

Curiously, Hydra also installs and activates SETI (*Search* for *Extra*terrestrial *Intelligence*) software on infected host computers, downloaded to the Windows directory as MSSETI.EXE from one of the following websites:

ftp://ftp.cdrom.com/pub/setiathome/setiathome-3.03.i386-winnt-cmdline.exe

ftp://ftp.let.uu.nl/pub/software/winnt/setiathome-3.03.i386-winnt-cmdline.exe

ftp://ftp.cdrom.com/.2/setiathome/setiathome-3.03.i386-winnt-cmdline.exe

ftp://alien.ssl.berkeley.edu/pub/setiathome-3.03.i386-winnt-cmdline.exe

ftp://setidata.ssl.berkeley.edu/pub/setiathome-3.03.i386-winnt-cmdline.exe

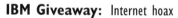

IBM Giveaway: Internet hoax

In June 1999 another variant of the BILL GATES GIVE-AWAY began circulating on the Internet, this one promising free computer hardware to participants in a mythical e-mail promotion. As with the other give-away schemes that surface periodically, this one is a fraud and has been publicly repudiated by IBM spokespersons. The original message read (with errors intact):

Subject: Free Computer Equipment!!!
Date: Monday, June 28, 1999 6:35 PM

Hey, I just wanted to let you guys know about this great new PC I just got from IBM!

Hewlett-Packard and Gateway have just merged to form the biggest computer supplier in the world! Bigger than Dell, bigger than IBM, bigger than them all! In response to this amazing merger, IBM has set aside 250,000 free computers to reward and keep it's most loyal and trusted customers! I've already got mine, read on to see how you can get yours!!!

This email has a special encoding which will let IBM know every time you send it to one of your friends or relatives. The first 250,000 people who send this to at least 15 of their friends will receive a brand new IBM computer! After you sent this to your friends, and qualify, IBM will contact you via email, and get your shipping address. Send them your address, and in a couple of days, a brand new computer, complete with printer,

and 19" monitor is sitting on your doorstep! You must hurry, because the offer ends July 31 of this year.

Here's the catch, though. Each of your friends must send this to at least 5 people or you won't be eligible, so choose your friends wisely! Remember, a true friend will send this along for you! That's all it takes, no strings attached! No purchase necessary!!! You don't even have to have previously purchased a computer from IBM! They want to earn or keep your future business, and they're willing to pay for it!!!

"ICECUBES": computer worm

Reported for the first time in November 2000, "Ice-cubes" is an Internet worm VIRUS in the form of a Windows executable file, spread via infected e-mail attachments. When the attachment is opened, Ice-cubes automatically installs itself into the new host system and delivers its payload with a giggle, pre-senting a humorous dialogue box that appears to "configure" a Windows Icecubes program. That box includes "manufacturer's default settings (not to be edited)" which instruct the computer to—

- "Crash every 2 days"
- "Crash after 5000 bytes of un-saved changes"
- "Create incredibly large files"
- "Fail AutoRecovery at 17 percent"
- "Decrease boot speed by 70 percent"
- "Annoy me with that sodding paperclip when I least expect it"

During installation, Icecubes copies itself to the Windows system directory under the filename wsock2.dll (not to be confused with legitimate files wsock32.dll or wsock2.vxd). Thereafter, the worm moves on to infect the original wsock32.dll Windows library, normally locked against writing, by using a "rename" command that replaces the original wsock32.dll file with an infected one upon the system's next restart. Once having infected WSOCK32.DLL, Icecubes monitors all outgoing data. When a message is sent, the worm automatically prepares a duplicate with its own infected attachment and text reading:

Subject: Windows Icecubes!
Text: I almost forgot. Look at what I found on the web. This tool scans your system for hidden Windows settings, better known as -Windows Icecubes-. These settings were built in by the Windows programmers. I think you might want to change them a little, just take a look! :)

On July 1 Icecubes displays the following message on all infected computers:

W9x.Icecubes / f0re [1z0]
Windows detected icecubes on your harddrive.
This may cause the system to stop responding.
Do you want Windows to remove all icecubes?

IDENTITY Theft

Identity theft is the blanket term for any type of crime wherein the offender uses another individual's legitimate personal information to commit acts of fraud or deception, typically (though not exclusively) for illicit financial gain. The criminal activity extends beyond mere CREDIT CARD FRAUD, for example, since offenders literally assume the victim's identity, often using the assumed name to purchase cars and houses, rent apartments, take out loans, book travel reservations. The assumed identity may also be employed for outright criminal activity and furnished to authorities when the offender is arrested, posts bond, and so forth. If unchecked, the impact on a victim may be devastating, both emotionally and financially.

Unlike DNA or FINGERPRINTS, personal data in modern society consists mainly of numbers—particularly Social Security, credit card, bank account, and telephone calling card numbers. Any or all of those numbers may be obtained by thieves in a variety of ways, ranging from purse-snatching, "dumpster diving," and "shoulder surfing" at pay phones or automatic teller machines to purchase through illegal channels. And in today's world, the vendors of stolen personal data operate primarily on the Internet. Experts on identify theft warn consumers against responding to "spam" e-mail that requests personal information in return for some illusory prize or reward. Likewise, circumspection must be used when making on-line credit card purchases or when relaying personal data on the telephone. Cellular phones are more risky than traditional land lines, since conversations can be intercepted—literally plucked from the air—without resort to clumsy (and illegal) wire tapping equipment.

Identity theft became a federal crime in 1998, with passage of the Identity Theft and Assumption Deterrence Act, imposing a maximum sentence of 15 years' imprisonment, plus a fine and forfeiture of any personal property used to commit the offense. Separate federal statutes impose additional penalties for various collateral offenses, including identification fraud, credit card fraud, computer fraud, mail fraud, wire fraud, or financial institution fraud. Each of these federal offenses are felonies that carry substantial penalties, in some cases as high as 30 years' imprisonment, fines, and criminal forfeiture of property. The U.S. Justice Department accepts on-line complaints via its Internet Fraud Complaint Center, at http://www1.ifc-cfbi.gov/index.asp.

Examples of identity theft range from the trivial to the fantastic. A nursing home employee in Elkhart, Indiana, was arrested on March 9, 2002, for stealing an 87-year-old Alzheimer's patient's Social Security number. The object: to restore the offender's telephone service after she fell behind on her monthly payments. In Oregon, meanwhile, police raiders seized 85 computer disks from a fraud suspect's home, revealing personal data collected on every holder of a state driver's license. The disk labeled "B" contained names, home addresses, birth dates, and driver's license numbers for 269,889 individuals. Also recovered in the raid were credit cards, death certificates, Social Security cards, and applications for medical residency at Oregon Health and Science University Hospital. The suspect was initially held on $1,000 bond, then released a day later due to overcrowding at the local jail.

Prosecutors and financial institutions offer the following tips for self-defense in the new age of rampant identity theft:

1. *Keep personal information on a strict "need to know" basis.* Banks and credit card companies already have your information on file. They do not telephone to request or "verify" such data. When unknown callers offer prizes, "major credit cards," and so forth in return for personal information, demand a written application form—or better still, hang up. Keep your Social Security card in a safe place; do not carry it with you or have the number printed on checks. Defeat "dumpster divers" by shredding or burning crucial documents before they are discarded. Abstain from posting personal information on the Internet—to genealogical or class reunion sites, chat rooms, or questionable vendors. When traveling, have mail held at your local post office until you return, thus preventing theft of credit card statements and other critical documents from your mailbox. When using public telephones or ATMs, be wary of eavesdroppers and "shoulder surfers." Give out no vital information on a cell phone anywhere, at any time.

2. *Check financial information regularly and thoroughly.* Bank and credit card accounts issue monthly statements. If yours do not arrive on time, call the institution(s) and inquire. If statements have been mailed to an unauthorized address, report the fraud immediately and demand copies of all missing statements. Examine monthly statements in detail, confirming all charges and/or debits as legitimate. Report immediately any unauthorized activity on the accounts.

3. *Periodically request copies of credit reports.* These should list all bank and financial accounts under a subject's name, including loans and mortgages. Report any unauthorized activity to the proper authorities.

4. *Maintain detailed records of banking and financial accounts for at least one year.* Financial institutions are required by law to maintain copies of checks, debits and other transactions for five years, but customers without records of their own may have no way to dispute unauthorized charges or signatures.

If, despite these precautions, you still become a victim of identity theft, swift action is required to minimize financial loss and to preserve your reputation. The following contacts can provide assistance:

1. *The Federal Trade Commission.* Report violations by telephone (toll-free) at 1-877-ID THEFT (877-438-4338) or by mail to Consumer Response Center, FTC, 600 Pennsylvania Avenue, N.W., Washington, DC 20580.

2. *The Postal Inspection Service.* For cases of suspected mail fraud or illicit misdirection of mail, contact the nearest post office for telephone numbers and complaint forms.

3. *The Social Security Administration.* Report misuse of Social Security numbers by telephone to 1-800-269-0271.

4. *The Internal Revenue Service.* Report theft of information from tax records or misuse of personal data to commit tax violations by telephone to 1-800-829-0433.

5. *The three principal credit reporting agencies.* Their fraud units may be contacted at the following numbers and addresses:
   a *Equifax*: call 1-800-525-6285 or write to P.O. Box 740250, Atlanta, GA 30374-0250.
   b *Experian* (formerly TRW): call 1-888-397-3742 or write to P.O. Box 1017, Allen, TX 75013.
   c *Trans Union*: call 1-800-680-7289 or write to P.O. Box 6790, Fullerton, CA 92634.

6. *All creditors with whom your name or personal data has been fraudulently used.* This may include long-distance telephone companies, as well as banks, credit card companies, automobile dealerships, etc.

7. *All financial institutions where you have accounts.* Whether an identity thief has tampered with the accounts or not, the institutions must be warned of a fraud in progress to prevent further losses and assist in apprehending the offenders.

8. *Major check verification companies.* These contacts are useful if checks have been stolen or bogus checking accounts established in a victim's name. If any merchant has received bad checks in your name, contact the merchant's verification company. The major firms and their phone numbers are:

CheckRite: (800) 766-2748
ChexSystems: (800) 428-9623 [for closed accounts]
CrossCheck: (800) 552-1900
Equifax: (800) 437-5120

National Processing Co.: (800) 526-5380
SCAN: (800) 262-7771
TeleCheck: (800) 710-9898

For sheer audacity—or comic relief—23-year-old identity thief Thomas Seitz takes the prize. A New Jersey computer buff, Seitz blamed the U.S. Security and Exchange Commission (SEC) for seducing him into a life of cybercrime. After all, he told authorities, if the SEC did not post thousands of names and Social Security numbers on its public website, Seitz would not have taken out car loans in 14 of the listed names—and he would not stand convicted of bank fraud today. It was simply too tempting, Seitz maintained. Granted, his first 12 on-line loan applications under various pseudonyms were rejected, but he received $15,000 on his 13th attempt. Next, using the stolen identity of a 57-year-old electronics executive in Salt Lake City, Seitz obtained a $44,000 auto loan, an on-line insurance quote and two credit cards to pay for the policy. When it came to obtaining fake ID in his victim's name, Seitz found that he had 300 websites to choose from. "I knew I did something illegal," Seitz admitted, "but I always came out of a situation pretty much better than I anticipated." That is, until a car dealer tried to register his newly purchased vehicle and Seitz was arrested for using a counterfeit driver's license. At that point, he admitted, "I had no defense."

"IDIOT": computer viruses

Initially reported in May 1997, the "Idiot" computer virus now exists in two variants, known as "Idiot.2032" and "Idiot.2592." Both are ranked by analysts as dangerous, memory-resident, parasitic viruses, containing the text string: =\/\= IDIOT VULTURE =/\/=. Idiot.2032 is encrypted, while its later variant is not.

Both versions of the Idiot virus operate in the same manner, seizing control when an infected file is executed, whereupon they infect the following files: c:\dos\fdisk.exe, c:\dos\undelete.exe, c:\dos\mem.exe, and c:\dos\expand.exe. Idiot then infects any files that are executed, opened, or accessed with the Get/Set File Attribute, using a complex technique to insert themselves into the middle of each target file. The virus thus appears to have no entry point and so becomes more difficult to locate. "Bugs" in the virus may deliver an additional destructive payload, corrupting the files that are infected and thereby rendering them useless.

IFFIH, Ikenna: convicted Internet hacker

A 28-year-old resident of Boston, Massachusetts, Ikenna Iffih was indicted by federal prosecutors on February 23, 2000, for hacking into various government and corporate computer systems, interfering with their operations for malicious personal amusement. According to the charges filed, Iffih obtained unauthorized access to a corporate Internet account in April 1999, using that account to illegally penetrate a computer operated by the U.S. Defense Logistics Agency. Next, he used a "telnet proxy" service to disguise his actual computer address, making it appear that his address was that of the government's computer. He then invaded the website of Zebra Marketing Online Services (ZMOS), an Internet service provider that hosts corporate Web pages and provides other Internet services for corporate clients. Iffih's attack on the ZMOS website damaged the firm's main computer, in Washington state, and caused the company a significant loss of revenue.

Still not satisfied, between May and August 1999 Iffih devoted himself to invading a Maryland computer research project Web server maintained by the National Aeronautics and Space Administration (NASA). At one point he seized control of the NASA system, allowing Iffih to read, modify, or delete any files found therein. At the same time, he installed a "sniffer" program to intercept and record passwords of legitimate users transmitted over the NASA network, archiving the data for later personal use. Next, using the captive NASA computer as a launching pad, Iffih defaced the U.S. Interior Department's Web page with cyber graffiti and invaded various computers operated by Northeastern University in Boston, illegally copying files that contained personal information on many students, alumni, administrators, and faculty members. FBI agents, collaborating with members of the U.S. Immigration and Naturalization Service, arrested Iffih before he could put that private data to personal use.

Iffih's indictment included three charges: (1) intentionally intercepting and endeavoring to intercept login names and passwords transmitted to and through a NASA computer; (2) intentionally and illegally accessing the ZMOS website used for interstate and foreign commerce, causing significant damage; and (3) willfully and maliciously interfering with a U.S. government communication system, thereby hindering and delaying transmission of communications. If convicted on all counts at trial, Iffih faced a maximum 10-year prison sentence and a $250,000 fine. To avoid that punishment, he pleaded guilty on June 29, 2000, and was sentenced to two years' probation, plus forfeiture of all personal computer equipment and payment of $5,000 restitution to Zebra Marketing Online Services.

"ILLUSION": computer virus family

Now recognized in several variants, the first "Illusion" virus was reported in July 1998. Researchers classify the whole family as "very dangerous," memory-resident, parasitic viruses, which write themselves to the ends of executed .com files. Bugs within the several viruses produce erratic behavior, ranging from sporadic self-replication to crashing an infected system. Idiot viruses consistently delete the following antivirus files from infected hosts:

```
anti-vir.dat
avp.crc
chklist.ms
chklist.tav
ivb.ntz
smartchk.cps
```

On July 4 and any Friday falling on the second of a month, Illusion erases selected hard drive sectors and displays the following message on-screen:

—*IlluSioN viRus coded by ThE_WiZArD in Spain (1997)*—

When you know your time is close at hand
Maybe then you will begin to understand
Life down there is just a strange Illusion . . .

"INDONGA": computer viruses

Found on the Internet today in four variants, the "Indonga" computer virus was initially logged in June 1997. Its current forms are variously known as "Indonga.2062," "Indonga.2125," "Indonga.3652" and "Indonga.4010." All four are classified by expert analysts as "very dangerous," memory-resident, encrypted parasitic viruses that write themselves to the ends of .com and .exe files. Damage inflicted on host computers is determined by the virus variant involved and by the host system's date.

Indonga.2062 and 2125 infect executed .com files (with the exception of command.com), erasing disk sectors on September 22 and 24, while displaying the following messages on-screen:

Indonga.2062—

PINDONGA Virus V1.4 (Hecho en ARGENTINA)
Programado por: OTTO (16/9/77)
Saludos a: MAQ-MARIANO-SERGIO-ERNESTRO-
*   COSTRA*
PD: Alguien mate a Bill Gates (EL WINDOWS SE
*   CUELGA)*

Indonga.2125—

PINDONGA Virus. (Hecho en ARGENTINA)
Programado por: Otto (16/9/77)
Saludos a: MAQ-MARIANO-SERGIO-ERNESTRO-
*   COSTRA*
PD: Alguien mate a Bill Gates (El WINDOWS SE
*   CUELGA)*

Indonga.3652 and 4010 infect all accessed .com and .exe files (including command.com), with Indonga.3652 erasing disk sectors on February 25, March 21, August 27 and September 16, while displaying the following message:

PINDONGA Virus V5.6 (Hecho en ARGENTINA)
Programado por Otto (16977)
Saludos a MAQ-MARIANO-SERGIO-ERNESTRO-
*   COSTRA-PABLIN*
PD: Alguien mate a Bill Gates (EL WINDOWS SE
*   CUELGA)*
PINDONGA Virus (Programado por OTTO en
*   ARGENTINA) 16977.*

"INFINITE": computer virus

Logged initially in August 2000, "Infinite" is a non-memory-resident, encrypted parasitic virus which searches for Windows executable files in the Windows system and current directory, infecting and corrupting all it finds. Infection occurs when the virus finds a "cave"—unused code or data—in the body of a file and implants itself there. "Infinite" contains a text string reading: "Win32.Infinite (c) 2000 Billy Belcebu/iKX".

INSTANT Message Discontinuation: Internet hoax

In June 1999 a warning circulated on the Internet, advising recipients that America Online's Instant Message service would be discontinued the following month. Subscribers were urged to petition for continuation of the service—which, in fact, was not endangered in the first place. The message was yet another hoax, one of many aimed at AOL during the 1990s. The original warning read (with errors uncorrected):

Dear America Online and Instant Message users,

Our America Online staff is planning to take away our Instant messages by July 14, 1999. If you want to keep your Instant Messages free of charge, sent this mail to everyone you know. It will be used as a petition. Each person you send this to, counts as one "signature." If this petition gets 100,000 "signatures," our Instant Messages will still be available at no extra charge. If America Online does not receive 100,000 "signatures," Instant Messages will still be available, but only to those who bay an extra 15.00 dollars a month. If you do not care about getting any further Instant Messages, please send this for the sake of those who want to keep their Instant Messages free of charge. Thank you for your time and consideration.

Robert McDoggan
America Online
Assistance Director

"INTEGRATOR": computer virus

Ranked by analysts as a dangerous, nonmemory-resident, encrypted parasitic virus, Integrator was reported for the first time in July 1998. Upon invading a new host computer it searches for .com files and writes itself to the end of each one located. On November 20 it freezes the infected system. This virus contains the text string: "Black Crow Integrator v1.00."

INTEL/AOL Merger: Internet hoax

This hoax, circulated on the Internet in December 1999, appears to combine elements of a classic hoax and E-MAIL BOMBING. The message itself describes a nonexistent merger of two cyberspace giants, unaccountably resulting in a mythical cash giveaway. The punch line is delivered with inclusion of an e-mail address for the author's "brother's girlfriend"—who presumably was flooded with inquiries at the time. The original message read (errors intact):

Subject: Real money

I'm an attorney, and I know the law. This thing is for real. Rest assured AOL and Intel will follow through

with their promises for fear of facing an multimillion dollar class action suit similar to the one filed by Pepsico against General Electric not too long ago. I'll be damned if we're all going to help them out with their e-mail beta test without getting a little something for our time.

My brother's girlfriend got in on this a few months ago. When I went to visit him for the Baylor/UT game she showed me her check. It was for the sum of $4,324.44 and was stamped "Paid In Full".

Like I said before, I know the law, and this is for real. If you don't believe me you can e-mail her at jpiltman@baylor.edu. She's eager to answer any questions you guys might have.

This is not a joke. I am forwarding this because the person who sent it to me is a good friend and does not send me junk. Intel and AOL are now discussing a merger which would make them the largest Internet company and in an effort make sure that AOL remains the most widely used program, Intel and AOL are running an e-mail beta test. When you forward this e-mail to friends, Intel can and will track it (if you are a Microsoft Windows user) for a two week time period. For every person that you forward this e-mail to, Microsoft will pay you $203.15, for every person that you sent it to that forwards it on, Microsoft will pay you $156.29 and for every third person that receives it, you will be paid $17.65. Within two weeks, Intel will contact you for your address and then send you a check. I thought this was a scam myself, but a friend of my good friend's Aunt Patricia, who works at Intel actually got a check for $4543.23 by forwarding this e-mail.

Try it, what have you got to lose????

INTERNET Access Charges: cyberhoax

Beginning on November 6, 1998, a scare message circulated on the Internet warned users of an impending financial charge for on-line access. Early versions of the warning blamed the Federal Communications Commission (FCC) for the mythical tax, while later variants simply fingered "the government" or "Congress." In any case, the warning was a fraud, as revealed by a formal FCC statement that the commission "has no intention of assessing perminute charges on Internet traffic or of making any changes in the way consumers obtain and pay for access to the Internet." The most common version of the warning read (errors preserved):

Date: Wednesday, January 06, 1999 10:03 PM

Looks Like Congress has found another way to tax us.

There is a new bill in US Congress that will be affecting all Internet users. You might want to read this and pass it on. CNN stated that the government would in two weeks time decide to allow or not allow a charge to your (OUR) phone bill each time you access the internet.

Please visit the following URL and fill out the necessary form!

The address is http://www.house.gov/writerep/

If EACH one of us, forward this message on to others in a hurry, we may be able to prevent this from happening! (Maybe we CAN fight the phone company!)

Various hoax indicators include the facts that (a) "Congress" does not vote as a single unit on any bill; (b) without a particular bill number protests have no impact; and (c) this particular "alert" was circulated while the 105th Congress was adjourned.

INTERNET Cleanup Day: Internet hoax

This e-mail warning, circulated in various forms on the Internet, is another hoax concocted by some practical joker. There is, needless to say, no such thing as "Internet Cleanup Day," and the process described would dismantle the Internet, not "clean" it. The original hoax message reads (with errors intact):

Subj: Internet Cleanup Day

THIS MESSAGE WILL AGAIN BE REPEATED IN MID FEBRUARY.

Attention

It's that time again!

As many of you know, each year the Internet must be shut down for 24 hours in order to allow us to clean it. The cleaning process, which eliminates dead email and inactive ftp, www and gopher sites, allows for a better working and faster Internet.

This year, the cleaning process will take place from 12:01 a.m.. GMT on February 27 until 12:01 a.m. GMT on February 28 (the time least likely to interfere with ongoing work). During that 24-hour period, five powerful Internet search engines situated around the world will search the Internet and delete any data they can find.

In order to protect your valuable data from deletion we ask that you do the following:

1. Disconnect all terminals and local area networks from their Internet connections.
2. Shut down all Internet servers, or disconnect them from the Internet.
3. Disconnect all disks and hard drives from any connections to the Internet.
4. Refrain from connecting any computer to the Internet in any way.

We understand the inconvenience that this may cause some Internet users, and we apologize. However, we are certain that any inconvenience will be more than made up for by the increased speed and efficiency of the Internet, once it has been cleared of electronic flotsam and jetsam.

We thank you for your cooperation.

"IRINA" Computer Virus: Internet hoax

The "Irina" virus hoax began as a publicity stunt, launched by Guy Gadney, (former) head of electronic publishing for Penguin Books in London. The hoax was designed to generate advance publicity for an interactive book titled *Irina*, but created a global Internet panic instead. Condemned by antivirus experts as "extremely irresponsible and dangerous," the stunt brought a formal apology from Penguin. The original message, including reference to a nonexistent college and professor, read (with errors preserved):

FYI

There is a computer virus that is being sent across the Internet. If you receive an e-mail message with the subject line "Irina", DONOT read the message. DELETE it immediately. Some miscreant is sending people files under the title "Irina". If you receive this mail or file, do not download it. It has a virus that rewrites your hard drive, obliterating anything on it. Please be careful and forward this mail to anyone you care about.

(Information received from the Professor Edward Prideaux, College of Slavonic Studies, London).

IVANOV, Alexei See GORSHKOV, VASILY

"JACKAL": computer viruses

The "Jackal" title is presently worn by two distinct and separate computer viruses. The first, initially detected in May 1996, is described by analysts as a dangerous, memory-resident, multipartite virus. It attacks the master boot record (MBR) of an infected host and changes the address of the active boot sector, writing itself to the new address. Upon booting the host system, "Jackal" is then executed in lieu of the original boot sector. Thereafter, the virus writes itself to the end of .com and .exe files that are accessed by the host. "Jackal" also sporadically reformats sectors of the infected host's hard drive.

The second Jackal variant, identified in March 1998, is a macro virus which replicates itself as various files on the host computer are opened or saved with new names. At the same time, it erases the following popular antivirus applications as they are located.

```
C:\eSafe\Protect\*.dll
C:\f-macro\f-macro.exe
C:\PC-Cillin 95\Lpt$vpn.*
C:\PC-Cillin 95\Scan32.dll
C:\PC-Cillin 97\Lpt$vpn.*
C:\PC-Cillin 97\Scan32.dll
C:\Program Files\AntiViral Toolkit Pro\Avp32.exe
C:\Program Files\AntiViral Toolkit Pro\*.avc
C:\Program Files\Command Software\F-PROT95\
    *.dll
```

```
C:\Program Files\Command Software\F-PROT95\
    *.exe
C:\Program Files\McAfee\VirusScan95\Scan.dat
C:\Program Files\McAfee\VirusScan\Scan.dat
C:\Program Files\Norton AntiVirus\Viruscan.dat
C:\Program Files\Symantec\Symevnt.386
C:\Program Files\FindVirus\Findviru.drv
C:\Program Files\Cheyenne\AntiVirus\*.dll
C:\Program Files\Cheyenne\Common\Cshell.dll
C:\TBAVW95\Tbscan.sig
C:\Tbavw95\Tb*.*
C:\VS95\*.dll
```

On the first day of any month, Jackal inserts its own name as a password in various documents. On the 27th of each month it inserts the password "ULTRAS." Throughout May and on the fifth, ninth, 17th and 25th of other months it displays the following message:

Microsoft Office 97
Error, is necessary will update files

Jackal then attaches the following disk format commands to the infected host's c:\autoexec.bat file:

@ECHO OFF
CLS
ECHO Microsoft Corp. 1983–1997 All rights reserved
ECHO Goes preparation to renovation of your system files
ECHO Please wait this can occupy several minutes

```
FORMAT C: /U /C /S /AUTOTEST > NUL
ECHO.
ECHO.
ECHO.
ECHO Error at renovations of files
```

On the 15th and 30th of each month Jackal deletes the following files:

```
c:\*.*
c:\windows\*.*
c:\windows\system\*.*
```

"JACKWILD": computer virus

A macro virus of Polish origin rated "dangerous" by computer analysts, "JackWild" was initially reported from Poznan, Poland, in April 1998. Its 11 encrypted macros include AutoClose, AutoExec, AutoNew, AutoOpen, FileExit, FileNew, FileSave, FileSaveAs, FileTemplates, ToolsMacro, and Utils. The most immediate and obvious symptom of a JackWild infection is an alteration of colors seen in many Windows elements, coupled with a display reading: "Colors 95 modified by Jack Wild."

JAMES, Jonathan: first incarcerated juvenile hacker

A Miami, Florida, HACKER whose name was initially withheld from the media due to his age, 15-year-old Jonathan James—a.k.a. "c0mrade"—made a series of computer intrusions between August 23, 1999, and October 27, 1999, penetrating a military computer network used by the Defense Threat Reduction Agency (DTRA). The DTRA, as its name suggests, is a Defense Department agency charged with reducing the threat of various attacks on the United States, including any assault with nuclear, biological, or chemical weapons. As he later confessed to authorities, James gained unauthorized access to a computer server in Dulles, Virginia, and installed a "backdoor" program that intercepted more than 3,300 messages sent to and from members of the DTRA staff. The program also captured 19 user names and passwords of DTRA employees' computer accounts, including 10 on military computers.

A previous intrusion, later linked to James, had targeted 13 computers of the National Aeronautics and Space Administration (NASA), housed at the Marshall Space Flight Center in Huntsville, Alabama. Using two different Internet service providers, James mounted that offensive on June 29–30, 1999, downloading NASA proprietary International Space Station software valued at some $1.7 million. As a result of that intrusion and theft, NASA computers were shut down for three weeks in July 1999, costing the agency $41,000 in labor and hardware replacement expenses.

No previous juvenile hacker had ever served time in America, but the Justice and Defense Departments were determined to make an example of James. On September 21, 2000, after pleading guilty on two counts of juvenile delinquency, he was sentenced to six months' confinement and ordered to write letters of apology to NASA and the Defense Department. As U.S. Attorney Guy Lewis told reporters in Miami, "This case should send a clear message to our community that, given the appropriate case, we will aggressively prosecute to the full extent of the law."

J. Crew Giveaway: Internet hoax

In November 1999 a new chain letter appeared on the Internet, claiming (falsely) that the J. Crew clothing retail chain was offering gift certificates to all participants in an e-mail advertising scheme. The hoax is reminiscent of others and refers specifically to similar false messages targeting GAP stores. The message read (with grammatical errors intact):

Hello readers!

My name is Robert Crensman. I am sure you are all well aware of the free offerings made from Gap and the free gift certificates offered from Abercrombie and Fitch. I am the Senior President of J. Crew, and I am offering a great deal in compliance to these other great offers.

For every ten people you forward this two, your AOL screen name will receive an online J. Crew gift certificate worth fifty dollars. There is no limit on how many people you can sent this to. This is simply an online promotion to increase the usage of our internet website. We appreciate your help in passing on this letter. Thank you for your support!

Feel free to visit our online store at http://www.jcrew.com

Sincerely,
Robert Crensman
Senior President of J. Crew

JENKINS, Vincent H.: exonerated by DNA evidence

An African-American resident of Buffalo, New York, born in 1939, Vincent Jenkins had a long record of arrests and convictions. By age 43, he had already spent a total of 28 years behind bars for various offenses. He was, in short, one of the "usual suspects" questioned often by Buffalo police when they had crimes to solve, his photo displayed in mug books for victims who did not recognize their assailants.

One such incident occurred in 1982, when a woman strolling through the Tiffts Farm nature preserve was assaulted and raped. Before fleeing, her attacker said, "The liquor made me do it." Vaginal and cervical swabs, taken at a local hospital, revealed semen traces from two different donors. The victim told police that she had performed consensual sex with her husband several hours before the rape. She scanned mug books in vain, unable to identify her assailant, but provided police with a vague description.

Four weeks after the attack, Vincent Jenkins was arrested and exhibited to the victim. Despite watching him for 25 minutes, she refused to name Jenkins as the rapist. Police next ordered Jenkins to speak, but the victim also failed to identify his voice. She changed her mind only after detectives and agents of the prosecutor's office convinced her that Jenkins "must be" the rapist, because of his criminal record. Jenkins was convicted at trial and received a life sentence.

Attorney Barry Scheck and the CARDOZO INNOCENCE PROJECT finally rescued Jenkins from prison, after he had served more than 16 years on his latest conviction. DNA tests performed in 1999 conclusively excluded Jenkins as the source of either semen sample recovered from the alleged rape victim in 1982. Oddly, the woman's husband was also excluded as a donor of both samples, which placed the prosecution in a precarious position. Barry Scheck described what happened next, in a televised interview.

When the testing was completed, [the victim] had indicated at the time of the sexual assault that her husband had had prior consensual sex with her 24 hours earlier. The DNA testing showed, very interestingly— it was done blindly—that Jenkins did not match either of the two DNA patterns, either the predominant pattern that was found on the vaginal swab and on the cervical swab, and a trace amount of male DNA that was found on the cervical swab, which is exactly . . . what you would expect from prior consensual sex.

That would be the trace presumably of her husband. She is still married to that gentleman. And when the knowns were tested, it turned out that the trace amount of DNA did not come back and match her husband. At that point, despite . . . requests to the prosecutor that they really didn't want to do it to these people, because going back and saying to her, well, you know, of course she was insisting the tests were wrong, but . . . I think that is highly unlikely, because it was cross validated with victim samples and everything else. We have prosecutors coming into court and saying, well, what really happened in this case is that there were three rapists, you know, there was this defendant, who didn't ejaculate, and she didn't notice that two other people raped her in the park that afternoon.

With results of the DNA tests in hand, Buffalo prosecutors agreed not to oppose a motion in state court to vacate Jenkins's conviction, but they fought Scheck's efforts to have a federal court declare Jenkins innocent. Vincent Jenkins, a prison convert to Islam now known as Warith Habib Abdal, was finally released from custody on September 11, 1999.

"JESSICA": computer virus

Currently recognized in two variants, called "Jessica.1234" and "Jessica.1345," the original strain of this virus was initially logged in June 1997. It is a memory-resident, parasitic virus deemed "not dangerous" by analysts who have studied its effects. Both variants write themselves to the ends of executed .com and .exe files on an infected host computer, thereafter erasing the antivirus programs chklist.cps and chklist.ms if either is found in the system. On August 10 each variant displays an on-screen message:

Jessica.1234—

Dear Jessica:
I love you!!!
Wanderer V1.2

Jessica.1345—

Dear Jessica: This is to commemorate our pure and deep friendship which began in R405,PUDY,1992. My wanderlust comes from the love of freedom . . .
Wanderer V1.1 NT

JIMERSON, Verneal See FORD HEIGHTS FOUR

"JINDRA": computer viruses

Two variants of the "Jindra" virus are presently known, both identified for the first time in February 1998. Expert analysts rank both as "very dangerous," although they operate in different ways. The original virus, now labeled "Jindra.2049," is classed as a "very dangerous," nonmemory-resident, parasitic polymorphic virus which searches infected hosts for .com files (excluding command.com) and writes itself to the end of each one located. It also erases the following antivirus programs if found within the host system:

```
C:\AGUARD.DAT
C:\AVG*.GRS
C:\DOS\VSAFE.COM
CHKLIST.MS
```

On the 21st and 22nd of any month, Jindra.2049 erases the system's CMOS (complimentary metal oxide semiconductor) disk sectors and displays the following message on-screen: "Jindra&Pastika je zde!!!" Depending on the system's time, Jindra.2049 may also insert its variant, known as "JindraBoot." This is a memory-resident boot virus that writes itself to boot sectors of floppy disks and the infected host's C drive. Upon infecting its 101st file, JindraBoot erases the host's CMOS and other disk sectors, thereby compounding the damage begun by Jindra.2049.

JOHNSON, Calvin Crawford, Jr.: exonerated by DNA evidence

One night in early 1983, a female resident of Clayton County, Georgia, woke to find a prowler straddling her back as she lay face down in bed. The man choked her unconscious with a belt, then waited for her to revive before he wrapped a towel around her head, raping and sodomizing her before he fled the scene. The victim, a white woman, had briefly glimpsed her African-American attacker's face and subsequently viewed police mug books. She identified Calvin Johnson Jr., a 25-year-old mail carrier with a 1981 burglary conviction, as her assailant and Johnson was arrested, charged with both the rape in question and another sexual assault committed two days earlier.

At trial, in November 1983, jurors acquitted him of the first assault but convicted him of rape and

Calvin Johnson Jr., right, and his attorney Peter Neufeld leave the courtroom after a judge freed him from prison. Johnson, who spent 16 years behind bars for a brutal rape, was cleared after DNA evidence proved another man was responsible for the crime. (AP)

burglary in the later case. On the day he was sentenced to life imprisonment, Johnson told the court, "With God as my witness, I have been falsely accused of these crimes. I'm an innocent man, and I pray in the name of Jesus Christ that the truth will eventually be brought out."

Legal appeals proved fruitless, but Johnson finally received assistance from the CARDOZO INNOCENCE PROJECT, committed to reexamining cases where DNA evidence may cast new light on dubious convictions. Semen samples preserved from the original case were tested in November 1998 and proved conclusively that Johnson was innocent of the crime for which he stood convicted. After various administrative delays, Judge Matthew Simmons ordered a new trial for Johnson and he was released from custody in June 1999, after District Attorney Bob Keller formally dropped the charges. Keller, who had prosecuted Johnson 16 years earlier, told reporters, "I didn't feel he should spend one more day in prison." Still, despite shaking Johnson's hand for the news cameras, Keller insisted, "I don't think this was a miscarriage or a failure of the system. It points out the tremendous advantages of new testing that we didn't have in 1983. It is a tragedy when a person spends so much time in prison, and I'm sorry for that."

Johnson, for his part, told the press, "I had faith that in some way, some day, the truth would come out, and I kept the faith." Johnson's 70-year-old father, meanwhile, saw no cause for celebration in his son's belated release. "I don't celebrate tragedies," he declared. "It's something that should've happened 16 years ago, so I'm not going to celebrate now. It's as simple as that."

"JOIN the Crew" Computer Virus: Internet hoax

One of the more pervasive Internet hoaxes is a warning of a VIRUS transmitted by e-mail messages titled "Join the Crew." At the time this hoax first appeared and was exposed as fraudulent, no virus had yet been created which could infect a target computer simply by opening an e-mail message. Today such viruses *do* exist—BUBBLEBOY was the first identified—but various experts (including the otherwise reliable HOAX-BUSTERS website maintained by the U.S. Department of Energy) still maintain that viruses can only be transmitted via extraction and execution of infected e-mail attachments. The original hoax message read:

IMPORTANT—VIRUS Alert!!!

Take note!

Someone got an email, titled as JOIN THE CREW.
It has erased his hard drive.
Do not open up any mail that has this title.
It will erase your whole hard drive.
This is a new email virus and not a lot of people know about it, just let everyone know, so they won't be a victim.

Please e-mail this to everyone you know!!!
Remember the title: JOIN THE CREW

JONES, Joe C.: exonerated by DNA evidence

In the early morning hours of August 24, 1985, three women left a Topeka, Kansas, nightclub and walked to their cars in the parking lot. Instead of leaving at once, they sat talking between the two vehicles for several minutes and were thus engaged when a man armed with a pistol suddenly appeared, moving between the cars and ordering one woman to step out. He dragged the woman to another vehicle nearby, forced her inside, and drove to a different part of town where she was raped.

Joe Jones, a homosexual, was present at the nightclub on the date of the attack. The two eyewitnesses identified him as the kidnapper, and while his alleged victim initially picked another assailant from police mug shots, she later changed her story and likewise fingered Jones. When police searched Jones's home, they found a pair of pants resembling those the rapist wore. At trial, a Topeka shopkeeper testified that Jones was in his store at the time of the assault, dressed in different clothing, but jurors disregarded the statement. Evidence of Jones's homosexuality was deemed inadmissible by the court. On February 13, 1986, he was convicted of rape, aggravated kidnapping, and aggravated assault, sentenced to life imprisonment on the kidnapping charge with shorter concurrent prison terms on the other two counts.

On February 2, 1987 Jones filed a motion of remand with the Kansas Supreme Court, seeking a new trial on the basis of ineffective legal counsel and newly discovered evidence. Since his conviction, Jones had learned of another defendant's conviction for sexual assaults with an identical modus operandi, and psychologists were called to testify that Jones was a victim of "unconscious transference," the victim and witnesses recalling his face after previously glimpsing him at the nightclub. The motion for remand was granted on February 13, 1987, but only for the purpose of examining the other suspect. A hearing was convened, at which the other inmate naturally denied committing any additional assaults, and prosecutors noted that the second suspect's photograph had been examined by the witnesses before they identified Jones. The motion for a new trial was denied.

Next, Jones's attorney filed another appeal to the state supreme court, on grounds that Jones's sexual orientation should have been allowed as evidence at trial, and that the trial court wrongfully excluded evidence pointing to another suspect. That motion was denied on March 3, 1989.

In 1991, as news of DNA testing reached the defense team, Jones's lawyers were granted permission to test forensic evidence recovered in the case. After some difficulty and the transfer of the evidence to a second laboratory, test results determined on October 25, 1991, that Jones could not have produced semen samples recovered from the victim in 1985. Jones's attorneys moved for a new trial on December 18, 1991, but the prosecution stalled, demanding repetition of the DNA tests. A second round of testing produced identical results on April 13, 1992, and the DNA evidence was ruled admissible on June 17, 1992. Jones's conviction was vacated, with an order for a new trial, but the prosecution declined to refile charges and Jones was released from prison the same day, after serving six and one-half years of his undeserved sentence.

JONES, Ronald: exonerated by DNA evidence

An African-American native of Chicago, born July 6, 1950, Ronald Jones provides another example of the grave injustice that has prompted many Illinois residents to demand an overview of the state's justice system and application of capital punishment statutes. His wrongful conviction and death sentence is scarcely more alarming than the malicious attitude of prosecutors who blocked his release from prison for nearly two years after Jones was proved innocent of any crime.

On March 10, 1985, a 28-year-old mother of three was raped and murdered at an abandoned motel on Chicago's South Side. Seven months elapsed before police detectives extracted a confession from Jones, a 34-year-old alcoholic who lived in the same neighborhood. Authorities insisted the confession was voluntary, but Jones claimed he had signed it only after he was beaten by Detectives Steven Hood and John Markham. According to Jones's sworn testimony, Hood struck him several times across the head with a blackjack, before Markham said, "Don't hit him like this because he will bruise," and then proceeded to punch Jones repeatedly in the stomach.

Voluntary or otherwise, the confession was dubious. Jones described the murder victim as a prostitute, when in fact she had no record of prostitution. Still, Judge John Morrissey admitted the confession as evidence and disregarded Jones's testimony of police brutality. At trial in 1989, prosecutors argued that semen recovered from the victim belonged to Jones, even though the samples were too small for a conclusive blood test using then-current technology. Jones was convicted by a jury and Judge Morrissey sentenced him to die.

Five years later, in 1994, attorney Richard Cunningham asked Judge Morrissey to permit DNA testing on the forensic evidence, but Morrissey twice refused. Reminded that prosecutors had claimed the semen was Jones's, Morrissey sneered from the bench, "Save arguments like that for the press. They love it. I don't." On appeal of those decisions, the Illinois Supreme Court overruled Morrissey and ordered the DNA tests to proceed in 1997. The results conclusively excluded Ronald Jones as a source of the semen, but prosecutors still refused to acknowledge his innocence. More tests were ordered by the state, with the same result. Finally, after 22 months of "reinvestigating the case," state's attorneys dropped all charges when confronted with an order for a retrial. He was released from custody, belatedly, on May 17, 1999. The murder case remains unsolved today.

"JORGITO": computer viruses

First identified in June 1996, the "Jorgito" computer virus now exists in two variants, dubbed "Jorgito.636" and "Jorgito.730." Both are memory-resident, parasitic viruses, rated nondangerous by computer analysts. Both write themselves to the ends of executed .exe files on the infected host computer, thereafter delivering slightly different payloads. On March 14 of any year after 1998, both display a message reading "Jorgit_ Was Here." The newer version, Jorgito.730, also adds text reading:

Córdoba
Argentina

JOYANES, Francisco Javier Arjona: software pirate

A 23-year-old Spanish citizen residing in Los Angeles, California, Francisco Joyanes teamed with a fellow Spaniard, 31-year-old Maria Yolanda Sola Lirola, to operate an Internet website known as Software-Inc.com in March 1998. The operation began in Spain, but moved to the United States in November 1998. According to incorporation papers for the enterprise, Software-Inc.com had its main office in the Bahamas, with a branch office in Spain, but it operated primarily from a storefront on Wilshire Boulevard in Los Angeles. Between March 1998 and October 2000, Joyanes and Lirola manufactured bootleg copies of various commercial software programs and offered them for sale on their website without permission from the original vendors, thereby amassing an estimated $900,000 in illicit revenue.

U.S. Customs Service agents were alerted to the bootleg operation by private investigators from Adobe Systems Inc., Autodesk Inc. and Macromedia, three California software companies victimized by the scam artists. A year-long federal investigation was launched, climaxed with the filing of criminal charges on October 16, 2000. Joyanes and Lirola were each charged with one count of copyright infringement, one count of conspiracy to commit wire fraud, and one count of criminal forfeiture. The maximum penalty at law for each count is five years' imprisonment, plus three years' supervised release and a $250,000 fine. Both defendants pleaded guilty as charged on January 5, 2001, their pleas including an agreement to forfeit ownership of the Software-Inc.com domain name, $900,000 in cash, a 2000 Chevrolet Corvette convertible, and a large quantity of computer and electronic equipment. On August 7, 2001, both defendants received 21-month prison terms, followed by three years' supervised parole and an order to pay $900,000 in restitution to their corporate victims.

"JUICE": computer virus

Rated "harmless" by computer analysts who have studied its effects, "Juice" is a nonmemory-resident, parasitic virus initially logged in June 1996. Upon invading a new host, it searches out .com files and writes itself to the end of each one found. No outward manifestation of the virus has been noted. It contains the following text strings:

Found cunt juice in C:\WINDOWS\MSD.EXE
Clean, Drink, Abort
*.COM

"KALIOSTRO": computer virus

Noted for the first time in September 1997, "Kaliostro" is rated by computer analysts as a "non-dangerous," memory-resident, partly encrypted virus which writes itself to the end of opened or executed .exe files. Three .exe files thus far immune to its effects are ading.exe, dos4gw.exe and drweb.exe. In some cases, Kaliostro also interferes with modem function, transmitting a message in Russian that translates as "password ok." Kaliostro contains the following text string:

òá òá òá. . . . I am Kaliostro 3.0 (c) Dred

KASHPUREFF, Eugene E.: convicted hacker

In 1993 the National Science Foundation designated the cyber-firm Network Solutions (a.k.a. InterNIC) as the exclusive registrar of all Internet domain names containing the generic abbreviations ".com" (for commercial entities), ".edu" (for educational institutions), ".gov" (for government entities), ".net" (for computer networks and Internet service providers) and ".org" (for nonprofit organizations). By the end of the decade, InterNIC administered more than 1.2 million domain names and its Internet website logged an average 1 million visits per day. InterNIC also administers the popular "WHOIS" directory that identifies names and addresses used on the Internet. Registration via InterNIC was free until 1995, when the firm began to charge $100 for each new domain name, thereby evoking angry protests throughout cyberspace.

Eugene Kashpureff, a resident of Belfair, Washington, born in 1965, offered another avenue of registration via his AlterNIC system, but since InterNIC enjoyed a monopoly on ".com" domains he was forced to rely on alternatives such as ".ltd" and ".sex." Tired of playing second fiddle by 1996, Kashpureff used his computer expertise to launch "Operation DNS Storm," conceived as a stealth attack on InterNIC's on-line monopoly. After a year of effort, Kashpureff was ready. For nine days in July 1997—between July 10 and 14, and again between July 21 and 24—thousands of Internet users logging on to InterNIC were involuntarily rerouted to AlterNIC's website, thus impeding registration of their domain names. He might have escaped detection, but ego won out over caution and Kashpureff boasted of his campaign to the media, claiming that he could hijack e-mail sent to any website in the world—or any nation, for that matter.

A criminal complaint and arrest warrant were issued against Kashpureff on September 12, 1997, by which time he had absconded to Canada. Extradition procedures were initiated, and Kashpureff was jailed for nearly two months in Toronto, pending resolution of his case. Finally, on December 24, 1997, he waived extradition and Canadian authorities delivered him to the FBI for arraignment in Brooklyn, New York. On March 19, 1998 Kashpureff pleaded guilty to one count of computer fraud before

U.S. District Judge Allyne Ross. He faced a maximum sentence of five years in prison and a $250,000 fine, but was sentenced in August 1998 to a mere two years' probation and a token $100 fine.

"KEEPER": computer viruses

Logged for the first time in January 1995, the "Keeper" virus now appears on the Internet in at least nine variant forms, all classified by analysts as memory-resident, parasitic viruses. The variants include "Keeper.Acid.694," "Keeper.China.777," "Keeper.Eleet.726," "Keeper.Enemy.644," "Keeper.Fly.1036," "Keeper.Joker.1080," "Keeper.Lurker.546," "Keeper.Massacre.742," and "Keeper.Massacre.775." All write themselves to the ends of target files, after which their actions vary. All contain a text string crediting their authorship to an otherwise anonymous "Crypt Keeper," hence the family's generic name.

Keeper.Acid.694, Keeper.Eleet.726 and Keeper.Enemy.644 write themselves to the ends of .exe files and infect the files as they are executed, whereupon Keeper.Acid displays the following message:

Your PC is on an [Acid Trip] . . . Try again later. . . .

The two Keeper.Massacre variants attach themselves to both .com and .exe files, then delete the files rather than simply infecting them, when they are executed. Keeper.China.777, ranked as a dangerous, nonmemory-resident virus, searches for .com files (excluding only command.com) and writes itself to the beginning of each file located, erasing the pertinent disk sectors next time the host computer's clock strikes 1:00 P.M. It also contains the following text strings:

*.COM

COMMAND.COM

The China Syndrome Version 1.00a Written by: Crypt Keeper

Well, I guess you found the sectors . . . You got a warning . . . This program was written in the city of Cincinnati. Non-destructive version -!- 182 d00d.

Keeper.Fly.1036 and Keeper.Joker.1080 are ranked as dangerous, memory-resident, parasitic viruses which copy themselves to the top of an infected host's system memory but do not correct the computer's memory control block (MCB), making the system vulnerable to a crash. Keeper.Fly searches out and overwrites the following antivirus files:

clean.exe
cpav.exe
flushot3.com
f-prot.exe
nav.exe
scan.exe
tbscan.exe

If any of those files is executed it displays the message:

Not enough memory.
[The Fly] Version 1.00 by Crypt Keeper
Be afraid . . . Be very afraid . . .

Keeper.Joker, true to its name, displays one of the following messages each time an infected file is executed on the host system:

You have the Joker]I[virus by Crypt Keeper [Joker 3]
Please insert tractor-feed toilet paper into printer
Impotence error causing erection at port address 3E2
IRQ 5 This program requires Microsoft Windows.

Computer hungry: Insert 5-1/4 inch HAMBURGER in drive A:

Missing Light Magenta/Olive ribbon in printer.

Not enough memory.

Packed file corrupt.

Bad command or file name

Bad or missing command interpreter.

KELSEY Brook Jones Alert: Internet hoax

Circulated for the first time in October 1999, this plea for help in recovering a missing child refers to an actual case, but the girl in question was found safe at a neighbor's house within hours of being lost. She was not abducted or harmed, she is not still missing, and the Internet message did not originate with her parents. The point of the ongoing hoax is anyone's guess, but recipients are urged to break the chain and simply delete it. The message reads (with errors preserved):

Subject: PLEASE KEEP THIS GOING

I am asking you all, begging you to please forward this email on to anyone and everyone. As most all of you know, I have a 5 years old daughter named Kelsey Brooke Jones. We are from Southern Minnesota. She has been missing since 4pm Oct. 11, 1999. The police were notified shortly after. If anyone anywhere knows anything, sees anything, please contact me if you have my number. The police don't recommend I put my number online, but you can contact the Police, a missing person report has been filed. I am including a picture of her. All prayers are appreciated!! I hope I have covered enough East Coast, Midwest, and West Coast people to spread out the search for this little girl. It only takes 2 seconds to "forward" this on, if it was your child, you would want all the help you can get.

KENADEK, Richard D.: software pirate

A 46-year-old resident of Millbury, Massachusetts, Richard Kenadek operated a computer bulletin board service (BBS) known as Davey Jones's Locker, with subscribers in 36 U.S. states and 11 foreign countries. For a yearly fee of $99 (or $49 for three months) those subscribers were permitted to download bootleg copies of commercial software programs without paying the normal retail charges. FBI agents armed with a criminal search warrant raided Kenadek's home on June 10, 1992, seizing several computers, six modems, and a list of Kenadek's subscribers. Kenadek was not arrested at the time, but his bulletin board was eradicated. Spokesmen for the Software Publishers Association (SPA) claimed that Davey Jones's Locker had illegally distributed more than $675,000 worth of bootleg software before it was closed.

Ilene Rosenthal, the SPA's director of litigation, told reporters, "This is one of the first instances that we are aware of where the FBI has shut down a private bulletin board for distributing copyrighted software. It clearly demonstrates a trend that the government is recognizing the seriousness of software copyright violation." Still, it was August 31, 1994 before federal agents got around to arresting Kenadek, charging him with software piracy and

conspiracy to commit wire fraud. If convicted on all counts, he faced a maximum of six years in prison and $270,000 in fines. A March 1995 plea bargain spared him from that punishment, resulting in a sentence of six months' home confinement and two years of supervised probation.

KENNEDY, Thomas: satellite TV pirate

A 46-year-old resident of Cranston, Rhode Island, Thomas Kennedy was one of 17 defendants arrested during a U.S. Customs Service sting known as OPERATION SMARTCARD.NET. According to the federal charges filed against him, Kennedy purchased 166 counterfeit satellite access cards from undercover Customs agents between November 1998 and June 1999, afterward reselling them to third parties who thereby avoided paying monthly fees to legitimate service providers. Kennedy pleaded guilty in November 2000 to one count of illegally selling an electronic device. Noting his record of prior convictions for similar offenses, U.S. District Judge Mary Lisi sentenced him to 14 months in federal prison on February 15, 2001.

"KERPLUNK": computer virus

Recognized initially in July 1998, "Kerplunk" is described as a dangerous, memory-resident, oligomorphic and stealth parasitic virus, which intercepts 23 separate DOS functions of file accessing, searching, memory allocation, and other procedures. Kerplunk writes itself to the end of .com and .exe files as they are accessed on the host computer system. In an effort to conceal itself, the virus temporarily deactivates its stealth routines when any of the following antivirus or other programs are executed: ARJ, BACKUP, CHKDSK, DEFRAG, HIT, MSBACKUP, PKZIP, SPEEDISK, TELIX, and UC.

If Kerplunk locates a Novell internetwork packet exchange (IXP) driver on the host system, it automatically accesses the Novell Network and produces network faults that hamper operation. If the user's name is Supervisor, Kerplunk contacts Novell Netware to execute the following functions at different times:

1. From the first through the fourth day of any month, it disables all Supervisor privileges.
2. On any Sunday it cancels the host computer's login procedure.

3. On any Monday it sets Supervisor privileges to allow for Guest logins.
4. If the time is prior to 9:00 A.M. Kerplunk reboots the host's server.
5. If the time is between 9:00 A.M. and 2:00 P.M., it randomly cancels network connections.

If, on the other hand, the user's name is *not* Supervisor, Kerplunk clears the screen on Novell's server and presents the following message: "Permanent system error. Please hit the computer NOW!"

"KEYPRESS": computer viruses

At least 12 variants of the "Keypress" virus, first noted in July 1996, are now reported at large on the Internet. All but one are classed by analysts as dangerous, memory-resident, parasitic viruses that write themselves to the ends of .com and .exe files as they are opened or executed. In the case of .com files, the viruses then overwrite the first 16 bytes of data with their own routines. "Keypress.935" and "Keypress.1000" both erase the disk sectors they infect, while "Keypress.1199" causes the host computer to reboot erratically, at unexpected times. "Keypress.BBS.1258" intercepts the Open File function, and if the name of that file should be user.bbs, it overwrites the file with data providing login information and maximum privileges for a new, unknown user. The remaining dangerous versions of Keypress signal their activity with monitor displays as follows:

Keypress.1216.b and Keypress.1216ß—SAMSOFT

Keypress.1216.d—
FREDDY_SOFT_FREDDY_SOFT_FREDDY_SOFT

Keypress.1236—SADDAM, the inferiority of the chaos

Keypress.1250 and Keypress.1479—Mubark is caw

Keypress.1600—HELLO SHSHTAYY
GOODBYE AMIN
OO ZAGAZIG UNIVER

The sole nondangerous variant of Keypress is known as "Keypress.Ufo," a memory-resident, multipartite virus that writes itself at the ends of .com and .exe files as they are accessed. Its harmless payload is delivered via video effects that display the following message:

The U F O Club
UFO-4 By Faisal-Andre-Akhmad Kip Gading Jakarta Utara

"KHIZHNJAK": computer viruses

First reported from "the wild" in June 1996, the tongue-twisting "Khizhnjak" computer virus now exists in at least eight variant forms. All are classified as nonmemory-resident, parasitic viruses that search for .com files on the host computer's current directory and write themselves to the end of any such files located. Some variants of Khizhnjak search both the A and C drives in their quest for files to infect. Some of the Khizhnjak versions are considered harmless, while others erase infected files and disk sectors. Different variants display the following messages on-screen:

Khizhnjak.834: Mason Hardkiller (c) 1995, (XAPïA-HOB-âÇä) . . .

Khizhnjak.Areg: (c) 1993 AREG Soft

Khizhnjak.ASV: Alexander S. Virus! "SUKA ver 1.0

Khizhnjak.DeathLord.752: Death Lord. So I dub thee unforgiven

Khizhnjak.DeathLord.933: Created by Death Lord

Khizhnjak.Genesis: !!!GENESIS THE BEST BAND IN THE WORLD!!!

Khizhnjak.Hallo: Hallo! I have got a virus for you!

Khizhnjak.Happy: "Don't worry, be happy!"

KIDNEY Harvest Warnings: Internet hoax

A classic hoax that has passed into the realm of urban legend, the kidney harvest warning—sometimes with other organs featured on the menu—has found its way into novels and Hollywood films. The concept may date from 1978 and the fright film *Coma*, but fear of covert organ "harvesters" reached a point in the 1990s where Anglo-European tourists in Latin America were physically attacked by mobs who suspected they were seeking children to kidnap for their body parts. To date, no such case has been documented in police annals or the legitimate news media. A common example of the hoax warning reads (errors intact):

"It's Not a Joke"

Dear Friends,

I wish to warn you about a new crime ring that is targeting business travelers. This ring is well organized, well funded, has very skilled personnel, and is currently in most major cities and recently very active in New Orleans.

The crime begins when a business traveler goes to a lounge for a drink at the end of the work day. A person in the bar walks up as they sit alone and offers to buy them a drink. The lat think the traveler remembers until they wake up in a hotel room bath tub, their body submerged to their neck in ice, is sipping that drink. There is a note taped to the wall instructing them not to move and to call 911. A phone is on a small table next to the bathtub for them to call. The business traveler calls 911 who have become quite familiar with this crime. The business traveler is instructed by the 911 operator to very slowly and carefully reach behind them and feel if there is a tube protruding from their lower back. The business traveler finds the tube and answers, "Yes." The 911 operator tells them to remain still, having already sent paramedics to help. The operator knows that both of the business traveler's kidneys have been harvested.

This is not a scam or out of a science fiction novel, it is real. It is documented and confirmable. If you travel or someone close to you travels, please be careful.

Another e-mail report:

Yes, this does happen. My sister-in-law works with a lady that this happened to her son's neighbor who lives in Houston. The only "good" thing to this whole story is that the people doing this horrible crime are very in tune to what complications can happen afterwards because of the details precautions they take the time to set up before leaving the room. The word from my sister-in-law is that the hospital in Las Vegas (yes, Vegas) prior to transferring him back to Houston stated that these people know exactly what they are doing. The incision, etc. was exact and clean. They use sterile equipment etc. and the hospital stated that other than the fact that the victim looses a kidney there has not been any reports of other complications due to non-sterile, etc. tactics that were used. Please be careful.

Another e-mail report:

Sadly, this is very true. My husband is a Houston Firefighter/EMT and they have received alerts regarding this crime ring. It is to be taken very seriously. The daughter of a friend of a fellow firefighter had this happen to her. Skilled doctor's are performing these crimes (which, by the way have been highly noted in the Las Vegas area)! Additionally, the military has received alerts about this.

If more information on the above subject is received it will be verified and passed on to keep you updated on this material.

KISLYANSKY, Leonid and Michael: software pirates

A father-son team of software bootleggers, Leonid and Michael Kislyansky operated with several accomplices in Cleveland, Ohio, doing business as Alpha Com, Inc. (a.k.a Cyber Mag, Inc.). Between December 25, 1998, and October 25, 1999, they sold more than 28,000 copies of counterfeit Microsoft software programs—valued in excess of $15,518,000—for $577,289. After the operation was exposed in October 1999, the Kislyanskys also allegedly tried to subvert prosecution by offering bribes to two witnesses. The federal indictment filed against them included two counts of criminal copyright infringement and two counts of corrupting or attempting to corrupt potential witnesses, thereby preventing them from talking to the FBI.

Both defendants pleaded guilty in 2001 to the copyright infringement charges, while the bribery counts were dismissed as part of the bargain. U.S. District Judge Lesley Wells sentenced the pair on April 2, 2001, consigning Leonid Kislyansky to prison for 18 months, while his son got 12 months and one day. Both defendants were further sentenced to three years' supervised release after serving their time and were ordered to pay Microsoft compensation in the amount of $577,289. Leonid Kislyansky was also charged a "special assessment" of $100 for court costs.

"KLINGERMAN" Virus Alert: Internet hoax

Circulated for the first time in May 2000, this spurious message warns readers of an epidemic with a twist: the deliberate dissemination of a deadly virus by mail 17 months before terrorists shocked the nation by mailing anthrax spores to various high-profile targets. In the case of Klingerman, there was no threat beyond unreasoned panic, since the virus does not exist, and no such sinister envelopes have been mailed or received anywhere on earth. The original warning reads (with errors uncorrected):

Subject: Very Serious Information!!!

This is an alert about a virus in the original sense of the word . . . one that affects your body, not your hard drive.

There have been 23 confirmed cases of people attacked by the Klingerman Virus, a virus that arrives in your real mail box, not your e-mail in-box.

Someone has been mailing large blue envelopes, seemingly at random, to people inside the US. On the front of the envelope in bold black letters is printed, "A gift for you from the Klingerman Foundation." When the envelopes are opened, there is a small sponge sealed in plastic. This sponge carries what has come to be known as the Klingerman Virus, as public health officials state this is a strain they have not previously encountered.

When asked for comment, Florida police Sergeant Stetson said, "We are working with the CDC and the USPS, but have so far been unable to track down the origins of these letters. The return addresses have all been different, and we are certain a remailing service is being used, making our jobs that much more difficult.

Those who have come in contact with the Klingerman Virus have been hospitalized with severe dysentery. So far seven of the twentythree victims have died. There is no legitimate Klingerman Foundation mailing unsolicited gifts. If you receive an oversized blue envelope in the mail marked, "A gift from the Klingerman foundation," DO NOT open it. Place the envelope in a strong plastic bag or container, and call the police immediately.

The "gift" inside is one you definitely do not want.

PLEASE PASS THIS ON TO EVERYONE YOU CARE ABOUT.

KOTLER, Kerry: exonerated and convicted by DNA evidence
A resident of Suffolk County, New York, Kerry Kotler was accused in 1981 of raping a female neighbor on two occasions, the first allegedly occurring in 1978 and the second in 1981. In the first instance, the victim said she arrived home to find a ski-masked stranger at her home who raped her at knifepoint and robbed her of some jewelry. Unable to identify

her assailant, the victim reported a simple burglary and told police nothing of the rape. Three years later, she said, a masked man waylaid her outside her back door and again raped her while holding a knife to her throat, then stole $343 in cash. Before fleeing that time, the rapist warned that he might "come back for another visit" in the near future.

After the second rape, the victim scanned police mug books and reportedly selected Kerry Kotler from among 500 other photographs; she later picked him from a police lineup as well, claiming to recognize both his face and his voice. The Suffolk County crime lab analyzed semen stains from the victim's underpants and reported that three non-DNA genetic markers matched suspect Kotler's blood. At trial in 1983, jurors deliberated for two days before convicting Kotler on two counts of first-degree rape, two counts of first-degree burglary, two counts of second-degree burglary, and one count of first-degree robbery. Kotler received a prison term of 25 to 50 years.

Kotler's initial appeal, seeking reversal of the verdict prior to sentencing, alleged prosecutorial misconduct and deficiencies in the court's charge to the jury. It was denied on December 2, 1983. His next effort, before the state Appellate Division, sought reversal based on erroneous admission of testimony, insufficient evidence to convict and excessive sentencing, but his conviction was affirmed on March 3, 1986. A year later, on March 10, 1987, Kotler brought another motion to set aside his conviction, this one based on false testimony by a police officer, concealment of evidence and improper cross-examination of Kotler regarding his prior criminal record. That motion was also denied, on July 7, 1988, but the appellate court ordered a hearing on whether certain documents had been improperly concealed from the defense before trial. Subsequent to that hearing, on January 8, 1990, Kotler's motion was again denied.

Meanwhile, Kotler had begun to educate himself on the science of DNA testing. He contacted the Legal Aid Society for help in September 1988 and obtained the necessary funds from relatives. Forensic evidence from the case was submitted for testing on February 15, 1989, but the laboratory found an insufficient amount of DNA present for reliable analysis. Kotler's legal aid attorney then suggested a second lab and the tests were repeated in February 1990. Those tests excluded Kotler as a source of semen found on the victim's clothing, but prosecutors rejected the findings. Since DNA from Kotler *and* the suspect stains revealed a "similar" allele (gene), the state hypothesized that part of the semen had come from a consensual sex partner, and another part from Kotler.

To resolve the argument, a third battery of tests was scheduled at yet another laboratory, with the same results. Blood samples were also obtained from the victim's husband (and only reported consensual sex partner), with test results excluding both Kotler and the husband as sources of the suspect semen. Technicians from two laboratories signed a joint statement attesting to that fact on November 24, 1992. The Suffolk County court vacated Kotler's conviction on December 1, 1992, and released him on his own recognizance, after serving 11 years of his sentence. Prosecutors dismissed all charges against him on December 14, 1992.

There is an ironic post script to Kotler's story of exoneration. On April 8, 1996, one month after winning a $1.5 million legal judgment for wrongful imprisonment, Kotler was arrested for another rape, this one committed on August 12, 1995. DNA tests performed on semen from the latest victim's clothing matched Kotler's samples, already on file from his previous case. The victim reported that Kotler carried a water bottle and tried to wash away evidence after the rape, but new collection methods frustrated the attempt. Convicted of first-degree rape and second-degree kidnapping, Kotler was sentenced to a prison term of seven to 21 years.

"KUSUMAH": computer virus

First logged in July 1997, the "Kusumah" virus now exists in two variants, labeled "Kusumah.2588" and "Kusumah.3968." Both are memory-resident, parasitic viruses, rated nondangerous by computer analysts. Both write themselves to the ends of any .com and .exe files accessed on the host computer, then search out and infect the command.com file. At some indeterminate time after infection, the viruses produce the following displays:

Kusumah.2588:

```
+-< INGAT SHALAT.!! >-+
|    UNIVERSITAS      |
|  JEND. ACHMAD YANI  |
|  << E l e k t r o >> |
+ ---------------- +
|  (C) KUSUMAH SASMITA |
+ ---------------- +
```

Kusumah.3968: *Moslem Power Never End. (P)*
KuSuMaH's ElEkTr0 UnJaNi

On Fridays, the viruses create new files—selamat.com for Kusumah.2588 and gerilya.com for Kusumah.3968—and write their programs into those. Execution of those programs displays the following on-screen messages:

Kusumah.2588: *Create by: KUSUMAN SASMITA,*
UNJANI Bdg-Cmh. (C) KuSuMaH'S.

Kusumah.3968: *Gerilyawan Elektro UNJANI*
Bdg-Cmh (C) KuSuMaH'S.

KWON, Il Hyung: exonerated by DNA evidence

A student at the University of Tennessee in Knoxville, 26-year-old Il Hyung Kwon was arrested for assault and public exposure on April 10, 1997, following an attack on a female student in the school's library. He faced a six-month jail sentence and a $1,000 fine, in addition to expulsion from the university, until July 9, when a Tennessee Bureau of Investigation laboratory completed DNA testing on semen traces left from the assault and cleared him of all charges. Detective D. R. Cook, employed by the University of Tennessee Police Department, told reporters, "I'm pleased with the results, that he has been exonerated. I'm sorry for any embarrassment and inconvenience he has suffered." The school's associate general counsel, Ron Leadbetter, confirmed that no disciplinary measures would be pursued, saying, "It's a really unfortunate situation. Everybody acted in good faith. The hearing process worked. It allowed us to find out what happened; it exonerated someone who was innocent."

Il Kwon's attorney, Samuel King Lee, was less charitable in his description of the incident. His client, Lee declared, "was wrongfully accused, made a victim, and labeled the perpetrator of a heinous sexual crime. Aside from exposing Mr. Kwon to public ridicule and causing upheaval in his life and new marriage, these wrongfully brought charges put Mr. Kwon in jeopardy of criminal sanctions, including six months' incarceration and a $1,000 fine. Albeit, Mr. Kwon's most significant concern was the likelihood of permanent expulsion from the university and preclusion from employment as an engineer."

Lee noted that in cases filed by scholastic authorities, "guilt does not have to be proved beyond a reasonable doubt. In Mr. Kwon's case, since he was present in the library at the time the alleged assault occurred, and since only his wife could corroborate his alibi, but for the DNA evidence that excluded him as a suspect, it is more than probable that he would have been permanently expelled."

LaMACCHIA, David M.: accused software pirate

A 20-year-old student at the Massachusetts Institute of Technology in Cambridge, David LaMacchia was indicted by federal authorities on April 7, 1994, on charges of wire fraud. The government accused LaMacchia of establishing a computer bulletin board service (BBS) where he encouraged visitors to freely trade copyrighted software valued in excess of $1 million. U.S. Attorney Donald Stern announced the indictment, telling reporters, "In this new electronic environment it has become increasingly difficult to protect intellectual property rights. Therefore, the government views large-scale cases of software piracy, whether for profit or not, as serious crimes and will devote such resources as are necessary to protect those rights." If convicted, LaMacchia faced a maximum penalty of five years in prison and a $250,000 fine.

Prosecutors hit a snag when they brought their case, filed under a 1952 federal statute designed to prevent fraud by telephone, before U.S. District Judge Richard Stearns in Boston. Stearns dismissed the charge on December 28, 1994, finding that wire fraud per se did not apply to software piracy. Specifically, Stearns wrote in his decision, the government's "interpretation of the wire fraud statute would serve to criminalize the conduct not only of persons like LaMacchia, but also the myriad of home computer users who succumb to the temptation to copy even a single software program for private use." Judge Stearns furthermore found that statutes applying to copyright infringement, as then written, would not apply to LaMacchia's case in the absence of a profit motive. Rather than appeal the decision, authorities concentrated on revising and expanding federal statutes. LaMacchia's case may therefore be considered a proximate cause for passage of the broader No Electronic Theft (NET) Act in 1997, penalizing copyright infringement regardless of the pirate's motive.

"LAUNCH Nuclear Strike Now" Computer Virus: Internet hoax

Despite the date contained within this e-mail message, it was noted for the first time on the Internet in September 2001. The message purports to warn readers of a new computer virus with (literally) cataclysmic effects, but it is in fact a practical joke with no foundation in reality. The message reads:

Hi guys. I just got this in the mail, from Symantec, so I thought I'd forward it along. It's a new virus that we should watch out for. PLEASE FORWARD THIS TO EVERYONE YOU KNOW. THIS IS VERY IMPORTANT.

Virus Update, 1/22/00
Symantec Virus Alert Center

Hello Subscriber,

As part of our ongoing effort to keep Symantec clients up to date on virus alerts, this e-mail is being sent to all

Symantec subscribers. A new, deadly type of virus has been detected in the wild. You should not open any message entitled "LAUNCH NUCLEAR STRIKE NOW". as this message has been programmed to access NORAD computers in Colorado and launch a full-scale nuclear strike on Russia and the former Soviet states. Apparently, a disgruntled ex-Communist hacker has designed a pernicious VBScript that actually bypasses the U.S. arsenal's significant security system and takes command of missiles and bombers directly. By opening the e-mail, you may be causing Armageddon. Needless to say, Armageddon will wipe out your hard drive and damage your computer.

Again, we warn you, PLEASE, DO NOT OPEN ANY E-MAIL ENTITLED "LAUNCH NUCLEAR STRIKE NOW". YOU MAY CAUSE A FULL-SCALE NUCLEAR HOLOCAUST.

As a precaution, all U.S. nuclear missiles have been set to "Do Not Authorize Launch Via E-Mail" to prevent an accidental armageddon [sic]. However, due to a Y2K bug, the possibility still exists that you may end life as we know it on this planet by opening the aforementioned e-mail.

VIRUS NAME: ArmaGeddyLee, HappyOrMay beNot00, OopsWrongButton00
TRANSMITTAL METHOD: VBScript attached to e-mail
HAZARD: Extremely Super High
AREA OF INFECTION: Detected in wild
CHARACTERISTICS: Destroys life on earth via nuclear armageddon [sic]

Please forward this warning to everyone you can. Thank you for your attention to this matter.

Sincerely,
The Symantec Anti-Virus Team

LEE, Kent Aoki: Internet Viagra peddler

A 37-year-old resident of Honolulu, Hawaii, Kent Lee was indicted by a federal grand jury on December 9, 1999, charged with wire fraud, trademark violations and selling drugs on the Internet without a prescription.

According to the charges, Lee copied the authorized website of a nonprofit organization, the Honolulu Marathon Association, which maintains its legitimate site at <www.honolulumarathon.org>. Lee created his own page at <www.honolulumarathon.com>

and there displayed the HMA's name and "King's Runner" logo (both registered trademarks) without permission. Lee's pirated website included a section in Japanese, which falsely claimed to allow Japanese marathon contestants to register on-line. (In fact, they are required to register personally, in Japan.) For that mythical service—including false promises of transportation, a course tour, and a pre-race meal—Lee charged Japanese contestants $165, $100 more than the actual registration fee. In addition to the ongoing marathon scam, Lee also established a separate website in Honolulu, from which he advertised and sold the prescription-only sexual aid Viagra without benefit of any prescriptions.

Four months after his indictment, on April 25, 2000, Kent Lee pleaded guilty in federal court on one count of wire fraud (for the marathon swindle) and one count of dispensing a misbranded drug. Some media accounts describe Lee as the first known Internet vendor of bootleg Viagra, but with so many outlaw vendors active in the current cybermarket, that charge has proved impossible to verify.

"LEGION": computer virus

Classified by analysts as a nondangerous, nonmemory-resident, encrypted parasitic virus, "Legion" was first identified on the Internet in October 1997. It searches an infected host computer for .com files and writes itself to the end of each one found, skipping any whose names begin with two-letter combinations from the text string "COSIDETSABUV-D-UWIPU." (Thus, COMMAND.COM and other critical files are spared from corruption.) When the month and day carry an equal numerical value—January 1, February 2, and so on—Legion displays the following message on-screen:

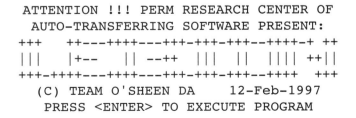

```
ATTENTION !!! PERM RESEARCH CENTER OF
  AUTO-TRANSFERRING SOFTWARE PRESENT:
+++    ++---++++---++-++-+++--++++-+ ++
|||    |+--  || --++ ||| || |||| ++||
+++-++++--++++---++-++-+++--++++  +++
   (C) TEAM O'SHEEN DA    12-Feb-1997
    PRESS <ENTER> TO EXECUTE PROGRAM
```

LEGION of Doom: 1980s hackers syndicate

Organized in the summer of 1984 and named for a gang of comic book villains, the HACKERS' collective known as the Legion of Doom apparently sprang from a computer bulletin board service (BBS) called Plovernet, run by a pair of anonymous webmasters calling themselves "Quasi-Moto" and "Lex Luthor" (arch villain of the Superman comics). According to Internet legend, Plovernet proved so popular with young computer enthusiasts and was so heavily trafficked that a major long-distance company began to block its calls. Thereafter, Lex Luthor recruited like-minded hackers to create a new bulletin board, the Legion of Doom (LoD). Original members, aside from "Luthor," included "Karl Marx," "Mark Tabas," "Agrajag the Prolonged," "King Blotto," "Blue Archer," "EBA," "The Dragyn," and "Unknown Soldier."

Dissension among the LoD's free spirits ultimately led to what some Internet historians call the "Great Hacker War" of 1990–91. The trouble apparently started when LoD leader "Erik Bloodaxe" (real name Chris Goggans) became embroiled in an on-line feud with member MARK ABENE (a.k.a. "Phiber Optik"), and Abene was expelled from the Legion. Unwilling to suffer that insult, Abene founded a rival hackers' consortium, the MASTERS OF DECEPTION, and launched a brief but hectic career of Internet chicanery that ultimately landed him in federal court. The "war" between Legion of Doom members and the Masters of Deception consisted chiefly of computer invasions and sabotage of telephone lines. The fracas was briefly interrupted in May 1990 by federal raiding parties during OPERATION SUNDEVIL, which resulted in four arrests plus seizure of 42 computers and 23,000 floppy disks, and closure of 25 electronic bulletin boards.

Internet lists of reputed LoD members include up to 58 individuals, most of them anonymous. At least 13 members were jailed at some point on charges that included hacking, wire fraud, and use of "BLUE BOXES" to cheat telephone companies on long-distance charges. A larger number listed their reasons for leaving the group as "college" or "loss of interest," suggesting that the hacker's game loses its aura of adventure as participants age. "Erik Bloodaxe" himself retired from the LoD in the early 1990s to become a corporate information security consultant, telling author Paul Taylor in 1995:

[In the early days] people were friendly, computer users were very social. Information was handed down freely, there was a true feeling of brotherhood in the underground. As the years went on people became more and more antisocial.

. . . [T]he social feeling of the underground began to vanish. People began to hoard information and turn people in for revenge. The underground today is not fun. It is very power hungry, almost feral in its actions. People are grouped off: you like me or you like him, you cannot like both. . . . The subculture I grew up with, learned in, contributed to, has decayed into something gross and twisted that I shamefully admit connection with. Everything changes and everything dies, and I am certain that within ten years there will be no such thing as a computer underground. I'm glad I saw it in its prime.

LETHAL Rodent Offal Alert: Internet hoax

In May 1998, two Internet alerts were circulated, purporting to warn readers of mortal danger resulting from contact with rat or mouse droppings and urine. To date, no such cases as those described in the e-mails have been recorded by any U.S. hospital. The Centers for Disease Control in Atlanta, Georgia, further report that such reactions are highly unlikely, and that symptoms of any such infection would not be those described in the Internet messages. The warnings are, in short, untrue. The original messages, with errors and omissions uncorrected, read:

No. 1—

A stock clerk was sent to clean up a storeroom at their Maui, Hawaii location. When he got back, he was complaining that the storeroom was really filthy, and that he had noticed dried mouse or rat droppings in some areas.

Couple of days later, he started feeling like he was coming down with stomach flu, achy joints, headache, and he started throwing up. He went to bed and never really got up. Within two days he was so ill and weak. His blood sugar count was down to 66 and his face and eyeballs were yellow. He was rushed to the emergency at Pali Momi, where they said he was suffering from massive organ failure! He died shortly before midnight. None of us would have ever made the connection between his job and his death, but the doctors specifically asked if he had been in a warehouse or exposed to dried rat or mouse droppings at any time. They said there is a virus (much like the Hanta virus) that lives in dried rat and mouse droppings. Once dried, these droppings are like dust, and can easily be ingested if a person is not careful to wash their hands and face thoroughly, or wear protective gear. An autopsy was conducted to verify the doctors' suspicions. This is why it is extremely important to

ALWAYS *carefully rinse off the tops of any canned sodas or foods, and wipe off pasta packaging, cereal boxes, etc.*

Almost everything you buy in a supermarket was stored in a warehouse at one time or another, and stores themselves often have rodents. Most of us remember to wash vegetables and fruit but never think of boxes and cans. The ugly truth is . . . even the most modern, upper-class, superstore has rats and mice. And their Warehouse most assuredly does. Whenever you buy any canned soft drink, please make sure that you wash the top with running water and soap, or if not available, drink with a straw. A family friend's friend died after drinking a can of soda!

A brief investigation by the Center for Disease Control in Atlanta discovered the cause. The top was encrusted with dried rat's urine which is toxic and obviously lethal!!!! Canned drinks and other food stuffs are stored in warehouses and containers that are usually infested with rodents and then get transported to the retail outlets without being properly cleaned.

Please forward this message to the people you care about.

No. 2—

HEALTH ALERT. . . . Whenever you buy a can of coke or any other canned soft drink, please make sure that you wash the top with running water and soap or, if not available, drink with a straw.

A family friend's friend died after drinking a can of soda! Apparently she didn't clean the top before drinking from the can.

The top was encrusted with dried rat's urine which is toxic and obviously lethal!!!!

Canned drinks and other foodstuffs are stored in warehouses and containers that are usually infested outlets without being properly cleaned.

Please forward this message to the people you care about . . . Thanks.

LEVIN, Vladimir: first Internet bank robber

A 26-year-old mathematics graduate of St. Petersburg's Tekhnologichesky University, employed at the Russian computer firm AO Saturn, Vladimir Levin led a group of Russian HACKERS in the first reported Internet bank robbery. The looting began in 1994, when Levin (a.k.a. "Vova") used an obsolete 286 computer to penetrate Citibank's Cash Manager system, illegally obtaining a list of customer passwords and codes. Thereafter, he and others logged onto the system 18 times between June and August, intercepting electronic money transfers and arranging for large sums to be deposited in international accounts. A minimum of $3.7 million (one report claims $11.6 million) was eventually funneled into bank accounts his gang controlled in the United States, Finland, the Netherlands, Germany, and Israel.

Citibank customers began complaining of large losses in July 1994, and bank officials contacted the FBI. Computer tracking of the bandits required collaboration with Scotland Yard's Computer Crime Unit in London, where the Levin gang maintained one of its larger bank accounts. Levin was arrested at London's Heathrow Airport in March 1995, as he entered the country from Russia, and was held on a U.S. federal warrant charging him with bank fraud and wire fraud. He stalled extradition for 30 months with various legal arguments, first claiming that extradition was unwarranted since no U.S. computers were used to access Citibank's accounts (rejected), then opposing trial in New York on grounds that Citibank's computer was located in New Jersey (ditto). Levin's extradition fight was not assisted by the guilty plea of an accomplice, 28-year-old Russian hacker Alexei Lashmanov. Another St. Petersburg native, Lashmanov admitted transferring U.S. funds to an account he had in Israel. An attempt to withdraw $940,000 in cash from the account was foiled, leading to Lashmanov's arrest, extradition and 1995 guilty plea in New York.

As for Levin, after his arrival in New York he devoted his energy to striking a plea bargain with prosecutors. He finally pleaded guilty to one count of wire fraud, admitting the theft of $3.7 million, and was sentenced on February 24, 1998, to three years in prison, with an order to pay Citibank $240,015 in restitution. (Levin later claimed that one of the lawyers assigned to defend him was actually an undercover FBI agent sent to sabotage his case. The guilty plea was not withdrawn.)

Citibank, meanwhile, tried to put a happy face on what could have been a public relations disaster. Bank spokesmen announced that all but $400,000 of the stolen money had been recovered by federal investigators and was safely back in the original accounts. More to the point, press agents claimed, most of the illicit transfers had been accomplished with Citibank's cooperation, as part of the ongoing manhunt for Levin and company. No Citibank employees in the U.S. or abroad were found to be involved in the conspiracy. At that, the cyberlooting still damaged the public image of a major bank whose advertising boasted that "the Citi never sleeps."

LEVY, Jeffrey Gerard: first convicted U.S. software pirate

A 22-year-old senior at the University of Oregon in Eugene, Jeff Levy apparently misunderstood the point of his studies for a major in public policy management. When not occupied with class work, he was busy bootlegging computer software programs, musical recordings, computer games, and digitally recorded movies, posting the various items to an Internet website where members of the general public could illegally download them free of charge. University officials blew the whistle on Levy after they noted an unusual volume of bandwidth traffic generated from a Web page on the school's server. FBI agents and Oregon State Police then launched an investigation, confirming that thousands of pirated software programs, movies, and music recordings were featured on Levy's website. Following a search of Levy's apartment, with seizure of various hardware, Levy became the first defendant charged under the No Electronic Theft (NET) Act of 1997.

If convicted on all counts, Levy might have faced three years in prison and a $250,000 fine, but he avoided any meaningful punishment with a plea bargain on August 20, 1999. Three months later, on November 24, 1999, he was sentenced to two years' probation, with a waiver of the court's original ban on further Internet activity. Even so, spokesmen for the government and software industry tried to put a bold face on the wrist-slap. According to Mike Flynn, anti-piracy manager for the Software & Information Industry Association, "Today's sentencing represents a modest victory for all software companies large and small. Software piracy, and even online piracy by persons not intending to make a profit, can threaten the survival of a software company. . . . SIIA is confident that this conviction and sentence will spur other U.S. Attorneys to aggressively pursue cases of online piracy under the auspices of the NET Act, and send a clear message that online piracy will be vigorously prosecuted."

U.S. Attorney Kristine Olson agreed that Levy's prosecution "represents the latest step in a major initiative of federal and state law enforcement representatives working together to prosecute electronic crimes." She applauded the collaborative efforts of the FBI and state police in Oregon, predicting further operations of the same sort nationwide. From Washington, James Robertson, assistant attorney general for the criminal division, proclaimed that "Mr. Levy's case should serve as a notice that the Justice Department has made prosecution of Internet piracy one of its priorities. Those who engage in this activity, whether or not for profit, should take heed that we will bring federal resources to bear to prosecute these cases. This is theft, pure and simple."

LINSCOTT, Steven: exonerated by DNA evidence

On October 4, 1980, Chicago police found a woman murdered in her apartment. The victim was nude, lying facedown on the floor, with a nightgown wrapped around her neck. She had been beaten and stabbed repeatedly; an autopsy found evidence of sexual assault. One of the victim's neighbors, Steven Linscott, was routinely questioned as police canvassed the area. Although he claimed no knowledge of the crime at first, Linscott later contacted authorities to report memories of a dream he had on the night of the murder, which paralleled the actual event. Specifically, Linscott dreamed of a woman being beaten with a long, thin object while she lay on the ground. (Authorities confirmed the murder weapon was a tire iron.) Linscott also saw his dream-victim dying passively, without resistance, while investigators noted that the dead woman had been found with her hands forming the Hindu "ommudra" sign for placid acceptance of death.

Suspicious now, police recorded further interviews with Linscott, requesting blood, hair, and saliva samples which he willingly supplied. Testing of semen from the crime scene showed that Linscott and the killer had the same blood type. Likewise, analysis of head and pubic hairs left by the unknown suspect were tested and judged "consistent" with Linscott's samples. With that evidence in hand, police arrested Linscott for rape and murder on November 25, 1980. At trial, a Cook County jury deliberated for 10 hours before convicting him of murder and acquitting him on the rape charge. Linscott received a 40-year prison term.

Linscott appealed the conviction and it was overturned by the Appellate Court of Illinois on August 7, 1985, on grounds that the state had produced no direct evidence of Linscott's guilt and that his dream "confession" contained no admission of guilt. Prosecutors appealed that ruling to the Illinois Supreme Court, which on October 31, 1985, ordered Linscott released on bond, pending a resolution of his case. A year later, on October 17, 1986, the court found sufficient evidence for conviction and reversed the appellate court's decision, but it also noted issues of physical evidence from the trial that had not been addressed on appeal. The case was thereby remanded to the appellate court for further review.

A prosecution expert told the appellate court that only one person in 4,500 could possess "consistent" hairs when tested for 40 different characteristics, but he in fact had tested fewer than a dozen and could not recall which ones they were. On July 29, 1987, the court ruled that the expert's invalid testimony, coupled with prosecution use of it in closing arguments, effectively denied Steven Linscott a fair trial. His conviction was thus overturned once again, but prosecutors appealed to the state supreme court once more, and the appellate court was again overruled on January 31, 1991. A new trial was ordered, to begin on July 22, 1992.

In preparation for that second trial, prosecutors sought to strengthen their case by performing DNA tests that were unavailable in the early 1980s. Forensic evidence was submitted to a laboratory in Boston, which reported that semen recovered from the crime scene could not have come from Linscott. Charges were dismissed on July 15, 1992, after Linscott had served three years in prison and spent seven more under bond.

LIROLA, Maria Yolanda Sola See JOYANES, FRANCISCO

"LITHIUM": computer virus

First recorded in December 1997, "Lithium" is ranked as a nondangerous, memory-resident, multipartite, polymorphic and stealth virus, which infects .com and .exe files, along with the master boot record (MBR) of the host computer's hard drive and the boot sector of various floppy disks. Files immune to Lithium's infection include the following: ATP, AVIR, CHKD, CLEAN, CPAV, DOO, F-, FLU, ITAV, MSAV, NAV, QUA, SCAN, SKUD, TB, THS, VI-, VIR, VSAF, VSHI, VWAT, and WOLF. Video effects displayed by Lithium depend on the system date of the home computer. They may include the following:

Accecati dalla luce
byATPY
. . . 'CAUSE WE'RE ALIVE!

GENOCIDEYouthEnergy
Le note della rabbia e dell 'instabilita'
Lithium
 Lottiamo per trovare qualcosa in cui credere.
 Nauseati dai falsi e facili sorrisi
 Nerotando nel miele
 Oppressi dalla liberta!
sono il detonatore dell voglia de proseguire . . .
You'llKnowWhatNITROMeans!

LITTLE Girl Song: Internet hoax

While many Internet chain letters utilize some threat of a curse or bad luck to make recipients pass them along, others—like this example logged in August 2001—invoke the literal wrath of God to perpetuate themselves. This example, curiously, appears to draw its inspiration from a popular country-western song, "The Little Girl," recorded by John Michael Montgomery in 2000. The message reads:

Note: This is a true article that was printed in a southern newspaper less than a year ago.

TAKE A DEEP BREATH BEFORE READING THIS.

~*~*~*~*~*~*~*~*~*~*~*~*~*~*~*~

There was an atheist couple who had a child. The couple never told their daughter anything about the Lord.

One night when the little girl was 5 years old, the parents fought with each other and the dad shot the Mom, right in front of the child. Then, the dad shot himself. The little girl watched it all. She was then sent to a foster home.

The foster mother was a Christian and took the child to church. On the first day of Sunday School, the foster mother told the teacher that the girl had never heard of Jesus, and to have patience with her.

The teacher held up a picture of Jesus and said, "Does anyone know who this is?" The little girl said, "I do, that's the man who was holding me the night my parents died."

"LIZARD": computer virus

Initially identified in October 1997, "Lizard" is named for a text string found in its virus code: "Lizard by Reptile." It is described by computer analysts as a "very dangerous" Windows 95/DOS computer virus that infects (and sometimes erases) DOS .exe files on the host computer. When an infected DOS .exe file is activated, Lizard searches for the following directories:

    C:\windows\system\iosubsys\lizard.vxd
    C:\windows.000\system\iosubsys\lizard.vxd
    C:\win95\system\iosubsys\lizard.vxd

If no such directories are found, Lizard returns to the main Windows program without causing any damage to the system. However, if one or more of the sought-after files is located, the virus inserts a VxD (Microsoft virtual device) "dropper" into Windows 95. Each time Windows is loaded, it runs all installed VxD drivers automatically, whereupon Lizard takes control and installs itself, memory-resident, into the host system.

LLOYD, Timothy Allen: computer saboteur

A resident of Wilmington, Delaware, born October 16, 1967, Timothy Lloyd was employed for 11 years as chief computer network program designer for Omega Engineering Corporation, a New Jersey-based manufacturer of high-tech measurement and control devices used by the U.S. Navy and the National Aeronautics and Space Administration (NASA). On July 10, 1996, he was dismissed from that position, for reasons which Omega spokesmen have described as "performance related." According to subsequent federal indictments, Lloyd took the news badly, stealing an estimated $50,000 worth of computer equipment from Omega before he left and planting a "logic bomb" in the firm's computer system that "detonated" on July 30 to permanently delete all Omega's software. The sabotage reportedly cost Omega $12 million in lost sales or contracts and resulted directly in the layoff of 80 other employees.

Catching up with Lloyd took time, but he was indicted on January 28, 1998, by a federal grand jury in Camden, New Jersey, charged with computer sabotage and interstate transportation of stolen property. The maximum penalty for those combined charges, on conviction, included 15 years in prison and a fine of $500,000 or double actual losses caused by the crimes. Lloyd was arraigned in Newark on February 17, 1998, before Judge William Walls. His bond was set at $25,000, with trial scheduled to begin on April 20, 1998. Legal maneuvers delayed the trial for two more years, but Lloyd was convicted on one count

(computer sabotage) by a federal jury on May 9, 2000. Two months later, on July 14, Judge Walls set aside that conviction after one of Lloyd's jurors admitted that publicity surrounding the May 2000 LOVELETTER computer virus may have influenced her verdict. Prosecutors appealed that decision in April 2001, asking an appellate court to reinstate Lloyd's conviction. The conviction was reinstated on October 12, 2001, leaving Lloyd to face a maximum five years in prison and a $250,000 fine.

LOUARN, Max: international phone-card pirate

An Illinois resident, Max Louarn was identified in 1994 as a member of an international network dealing in stolen telephone calling-card numbers. According to the federal charges filed, members of the ring—including operators who used screen names such as Killer, Phone Stud, and Major Theft—stole at least 140,000 phone-card numbers between 1992 and the time of their arrest in September 1994. The numbers were offered for sale via computer bulletin boards for an average of one dollar each, after which the illicit buyers made numerous long-distance calls free of charge. Estimates of actual losses to telephone carriers including Sprint, MCI, and AT&T range from $50 million to $140 million (the larger figure based on a presumed but undocumented estimate of $1,000 in illicit calls per stolen number). Confronted with the possibility of five years in prison and a $250,000 fine, Louarn pleaded guilty in return for lighter punishment.

While Max Louarn's crimes were apparently profit-motivated from the start, some HACKERS appear to view swindling telephone companies and other large corporations as a kind of patriotic or humanitarian gesture. As independent industry analyst Martin Sellers told reporters in November 1994, "Some hackers claim they are doing this because they consider themselves guerrillas in a war aimed at keeping the information superhighway wide open and deregulated by people they consider toll-takers, like long-distance carriers and government regulators. They consider themselves electronic Robin Hoods." The U.S. Department of Justice takes a different view and continues to prosecute Internet swindlers on a regular basis.

"LOVELETTER": computer worm

Unleashed on the Internet in May 2000, the "LoveLetter" worm virus sparked a global epidemic within days, spreading via e-mail as infected messages were sent from all computers affected. Written in Virtual Basic Script (VBX), the worm functions only on computers where Windows Scripting Host (WSH) is installed (as it is by default in Windows 98 and Windows 2000). Upon infesting a new host computer, LoveLetter opens Microsoft Outlook and scans its address book, thereafter sending copies of itself to all e-mail addresses found. At the same time, the worm installs itself in the new host and destroys various files, while downloading a Trojan horse program to permit outside access. The initial message includes the following information:

Subject: ILOVEYOU
Message: kindly check the attached LOVELETTER coming from me.
Attachment: LOVE-LETTER-FOR-YOU.TXT.vbs

By immediately sending itself to all Microsoft Outlook addresses listed, with identical e-mails and infected attachments, LoveLetter was able to circumnavigate the world in a matter of hours, launched both from private and corporate computers with international connections. Since the worm installs itself into the Windows system directory, it is reactivated and repeats its mailing procedure each time Windows starts up, until it has been purged from the infected host.

To install its Trojan horse program, LoveLetter alters the URL of the computer's Internet Explorer startup page, directing the host to a new website and forcing Internet Explorer to download an .exe file named win-bugsfix.exe from that site. On its next Windows startup, the Trojan program takes control and writes itself to the Windows system directory as winfat32.exe. The Trojan program is designed to steal passwords, collecting vital information on the host computer and sending it via e-mail to a Philippines address, <mailme@super.net.ph>.

LoveLetter also spreads its infection via Internet Relay Chat (IRC) avenues, scanning a host's local drives in search of the following files: mirc.hlp, mirc.ini, mirc32.exe, mlink32.exe and scrip.ini. When any such file is found, the worm inserts a new script.ini file containing instructions that send copies of it to all users who log onto the IRC channel. In that case, the message appears as follows:

mIRC Script

Please don't edit this script . . . mIRC will corrupt, if

mIRC will corrupt . . . WINDOWS will affect and will not run correctly. thanks

Khaled Mardam-Bey
http://www.mirc.com

If a new recipient clicks on the link, a message is displayed on-screen reading:

This HTML file need ActiveX Control
To Enable to read this HTML file
—Please press 'YES' button to enable ActiveX

Should the user comply and press "YES," LoveLetter instantly gains access to the new host computer's disk files and installs itself there, inserting its code into the Windows system directory. There is no escape if the reader presses "NO," however, as the worm then intercepts mouse movement and keyboard events to reactivate itself in an endless loop of dialogue boxes, terminating only when "YES" is finally selected.

Destructive effects of the LoveLetter worm include the following, dependent on which files are found within a new host system:

- .jpg and .jpeg files are overwritten with a ".vbs" extension added to their filenames.
- Files extensions .css, .hta, .js, .jse, .sct, and .wsh are overwritten with a ".vbs" extension to the file name, after which the original files are deleted.
- MP2 and MP3 files are likewise overwritten with a ".vbs" extension to the filenames, but a new "hidden" attribute is inserted to conceal the original file.
- .vbe and .vbs files are completely overwritten by the virus code and thus destroyed.

Many variants of the LoveLetter worm now exist on the Internet, with equally destructive capabilities. Those identified to date include (errors uncorrected):

Arab Airlines—

Subject: Thank You For Flying With Arab Airlines
Message: Please check if the bill is correct, by opening the attached file.
Attachment: ArabAir.TXT.vbs

Bewerbung Kreolina—

Subject: Bewerbung Kreolina
Message: Sehr geehrte Damen und Herren!
Attachment: BEWERBUNG.TXT.vbs

Bug & Virus Fix—

Subject: Bug & Virus Fix
Message: I got this from our system admin. Run this to help prevent any recent or future bug & virus attack's. It may take a small while up update your files.
Attachment: MAJOR BUG & VIRUS FIX.vbs

Dangerous virus warning—

Subject: Dangerous Virus Warning
Message: There is a dangerous virus circulating. Please click attached picture to view it and learn to avoid it.
Attachment: virus_warning.jpg.vbs

Free sexsite passwords—

Subject: FREE SEXSITE PASSWORDS
Message: CHECK IT OUT; FREE SEX SITE PASSWORDS.
Attachment: FREE_SEXSITE_PASSWORDS. HTML.vbs

How to beat viruses—

Subject: HOW TO BEAT VIRUSES
Message: kindly check the attached VIRUS INFORMATION coming from me. This is how you can be immune to any virus. It really helps a lot!
Attachment: HOW_TO_BEAT_VIRUSES.TXT.vbs

How to protect yourself—

Subject: How to protect yourself from the ILOVEYOU bug!
Message: Here's the easy way to fix the love virus.
Attachment: Virus-Protection-Instructions.vbs

I can't believe this—

Subject: I Cant Believe This!!!
Message: I Cant Believe I Have Just Received This Hate Email. . . . Take A Look!
Attachment: KillEmAllTXT.vbs

ILOVEYOU—

Subject: ILOVEYOU
Message: kindly check the attached LOVELETTER coming from me.
Attachment: LOVE-LETTER-FOR-YOU.TXT.vbs

Important!—

Subject: Important! Read carefully!!
Message: Check the attached IMPORTANT coming from me!
Attachment: IMPORTANT.TXT.vbs

Joke—

Subject: fwd: Joke
Message: blank
Attachment: Very_Funny.vbs

Look!—

Subject: LOOK!
Message: hehe . . . check this out.
Attachment: LOOK.vbs

Mother's Day—

Subject: Mothers Day Order Confirmation
Message: We have proceeded to charge your credit card for the mothers day diamond special. We have attached a detailed invoice to this email. Please print out the attachment and keep it in a safe place. Thanks Again and Have a Happy Mothers Day! mothersday@subdi mension.com
Attachment: mothersday.vbs

New variation on lovebug—

Subject: New Variation on LOVEBUG Update Anti-Virus!!
Message: There is now a newer variant of love bug. It was released at 8:37 PM Saturday Night. Please Download the following patch. We are trying to isolate the virus. Thanks Symantec.
Attachment: antivirusupdate.vbs

New Virus—

Subject: New virus discovered!

Message: *A new virus has been discovered! It's name is @-@Alha and Omega@-@. Full list of virus abilities is included in attached file @-@info.txt@-@. For the last information go to McAfee's web page. Please forward this to everyone you care about.*
Attachment: *info.txt.vbs*

Official virus and bug fix—

Subject: *IMPORTANT: Official virus and bug fix*
Message: *This is an official virus and bug fix. I got it from our system admin. It may take a short while to update your system files after you run the attachment.*
Attachment: *Bug_and_virus_fix.vbs*

PresenteUOL—

Subject: *PresenteUOL*
Message: *O UOL tem um grande presente para voce, e eh exclusivo. Veja o arquivo em anexo. http://www.uol.com.br*
Attachment: *UOL.TXT.vbs*

Recent virus attacks—

Subject: *Recent Virus Attacks-Fix*
Message: *Attached is a copy of a script that will reverse the effect of the LOVE-LETTER-TO-YOU.TXT.vbs as well as the FW:JOKE, Mother's Day and Lituanian Siblings.*
Attachment: *BAND-AID.DOC.vbs*

Susitikim—

Subject: *Susitikim shi vakara kavos puodukui . . .*
Message: *Kindly check the attached LOVELETTER coming from me.*
Attachment: *LOVE-LETTER-FOR-YOU.TXT.vbs*

Variant test—

Subject: *Variant Test*
Message: *This is the variant to the vbs virus.*
Attachment: *IMPORTANT.TXT.vbs*

VBS Killer—

Subject: *Yeah, Yeah another time to DEATH . . .*
Message: *This is the Killer for VBS.LOVE-LETTER.WORM.*

Attachment: *Vir-Killer.vbs*

Virus warnings—

Subject: *Virus Warnings!!!*
Message: *VERY IMPORTANT PLEASE READ THIS TEXT. TEXT ATTACHMENT.*
Attachment: *very_important-txt.vbs*

You may win $1,000,000—

Subject: *You May Win $1,000,000! 1 Click Away*
Message: *kindly check the attached WIN coming from me.*
Attachment: *WIN.vbs*

You must read this—

Subject: *You must read this!*
Message: *Have you read this text? You must do it!!*
Attachment: *C:\NOTES.TXT.exe*

"LUCY": computer viruses

Discovered on the Internet in October 1997, the "Lucy" virus now exists in two recognized variants, dubbed "Lucy.5086" and "Lucy.5286." Both are classed by analysts as dangerous, memory-resident, parasitic polymorphic viruses that write themselves to the ends of .com and .exe files as they are accessed on the host computer. While installing themselves as memory-resident, the viruses also scan the host's system memory for certain antivirus programs and disable them. At the same time, other antivirus programs are immune to attack, including: avg, chkdsk, clean, drweb, findviru, f-prot, guard, hiew, ice, nod, scan, tb, -v, virstop, viverify, and vshield. The Lucy viruses also have bugs, one of which causes Lucy.5286 to occasionally display the following message on-screen:

Hi, do you know that AndreaP is actually better than LucyV? Takze ak sa cam chce, tak to meno zmente. :-).

PS. Pochadzam[e] (ja I ona) z GJH. (mozno)

"LUNCHTIME": computer virus

Noted initially in March 1998, "LunchTime" is classed as a nondangerous, memory-resident, parasitic virus. Once a host computer is infected, LunchTime activates whenever any program is executed, searching for .exe files on the C drive and writing itself to the ends of those located. LunchTime apparently originates from Poland, and Polish antivirus programs with the name MKS* are immune from infection, although antivirus data files chklist.cps and chklist.ms are deleted by the virus. True to its name, LunchTime delivers its payload every day between noon and 2:00 P.M., displaying the following message:

Po co tak ciezko pracujesz?
Zrób sobie przerwe I idz na lunch.

Twój dysk twardy zostal zakodowany do godziny 14:00. O tej godzinie zostanie odkodowany. Jesli wylaczysz komputer wczesniej, stracisz na nim dane bezpowrotnie.

Czas do donca przerwy: 1:59:00

NIE WYLACZAJ ANI NIE RESETUJ KOMPUTERA!!!

LUSTER, Dale: indicted for satellite TV piracy

A resident of Dallas, Texas, Dale Luster was one of the defendants indicted for trading in counterfeit satellite television access cards, as part of "OPERATION SMARTCARD.NET" in August 2000. The arrests and charges followed a 22-month nationwide investigation by the U.S. Customs Service, during which undercover agents sold counterfeit "smart cards" to various traders and logged their resale to third parties. Four of the original defendants pleaded guilty soon after their arrests, but Luster's case was unresolved at this writing (in February 2002). Justice Department spokesmen note that an indictment is simply an accusation of criminal wrongdoing, and is not proof of actual illicit behavior. Indicted defendants are presumed innocent until they plead otherwise or are convicted at trial.

"MAKE a Loan" Pyramid Scheme: Internet fraud

Initially reported in July 2001, this Internet get-rich-quick plan falls into the category of pyramid (or "Ponzi") schemes that are banned by law in all states—even when transmitted by computer. Interstate participation in the scheme violates federal law, as well as various state criminal statutes. The original message reads:

This offer is sent to you because you sent me mail and you might like to try this, just like I did. Sometimes the simple way works best.
 RECEIVE more than $20,000,—IN THE NEXT 8 DAYS! . . . OR WHATEVER!
 Repeat this process every 10 days and you will be earning $60,000,—month after month!! There is no High Yield Interest Program (HYIP) that will give you this kind of profit in such a short time!

  And all you risk is $8.08,—

 It takes only $8.08,—and 2 days work to receive $22,220,—within 8 days. In these 2 days . . . can you find 10 people who need money so much, that they are willing to repeat this process to get their hands on $22,220,—in just 8 days?

 To begin with, create your free e-gold account at www.e-gold.com !!!

 Next, you send
 a $2.02 loan to the e-gold account in #1 position,
 a $2.02 loan to the e-gold account in #2 position,
 a $2.02 loan to the e-gold account in #3 position and
 a $2.02 loan to the e-gold account in #4 position.

 E-gold charges a 1% fee which leaves $2 per deposit.

 As each new person sign up and send $2.02 to the #1 account, the revised letter moves your account one level higher.

 When your account number reaches the top level, you will have $22,220 in your e-gold account.

1) E-gold: 334794
2) E-gold: 330960
3) E-gold: 334861
4) E-gold: 334864

#1) 1000 × 10 = 10000 people × $2 = $20,000,—
#2) 100 × 100 = 1000 people × $2 = $2,000,—
#3) 10 × 10 = 100 people × $2 = $200,—
#4) 10 people × $2 = $20,—

After sending $2.02 to the e-gold account in the number 1 position, remove that number, move the other 3 numbers up and put your e-gold account number in the #4 position.
 Perfect performance by 10 people and a little luck brings more than $20,000 within 8 days.
 BE HONEST!! RESPECT YOUR KARMA AND YOU WILL HAVE MORE MONEY IN YOUR LIFE.!! LIVE YOUR LIFE FREE!!

"MAKE Money Fast" Pyramid Scheme:
Internet fraud

Another computerized get-rich charade, first seen on the Internet in July 2000, this plan includes false claims that pyramid schemes are somehow legal if participants sell a service, instead of merely exchanging cash. Police and prosecutors strongly disagree. Ironically, this particular swindle has itself become the target of an Internet hoax, claiming (again, falsely) that the message contains a destructive computer virus. The original message reads (with errors intact):

Hello! I've got some awesome news that I think you need to take two minutes to read if you have ever thought "How could I make some serious cash in a hurry???", or been in serious debt, ready to do almost anything to get the money needed to pay off those bill collectors. So grab a snack, a warm cup of coffee, or a glass of your favorite beverage, get comfortable and listen to this interesting, exciting find!

Let me start by saying that I FINALLY FOUND IT! That's right!. found it! And I HATE GET RICH QUICK SCHEMES!! I hate those schemes like multi-level marketing, mail-order schemes, envelope stuffing scams, 900 number scams . . . the list goes on forever. I have tried every darn get rich quick scheme out there over the past 12 years. I somehow got on mailing lists for people looking to make money (more like 'desperate stupid people who will try anything for money!').

Well, when I was a teenager, these claims to 'get me rich quick' sounded irresistible! I would shell out $14.95 here, $29.95 there, $24.95 here, and another $49.95 there. I had maxed out my new Circuit City Card AND my Visa . . . I was desperate for money!! So, I gave them all a chance but failed at every one of them! Maybe they worked for some people, but not for me. Eventually, I just tossed that JUNK MAIL in the trash when I got the mail. I recognized it right away. I can smell a money scam from a mile away these days, SO I THOUGHT. . . . I thought I could sniff out a scam easily. WAS I WRONG!!. . . . I LOVE THE INTERNET!!!

I was scanning thru a NEWSGROUP and saw an article stating to GET CASH FAST!! I thought . . . "Here on the Internet?? Well, I'll just have to see what schemes could possibly be on the internet." The article described a way to MAIL A ONE DOLLAR BILL TO ONLY FIVE PEOPLE AND MAKE $50,0000 IN CASH WITHIN 4 WEEKS! Well, the more I thought about it, the more I became very curious. Why? Because of the way it worked AND BECAUSE IT WOULD

ONLY COST ME FIVE DOLLARS (AND FIVE STAMPS), THAT'S ALL I EVER PAY. . . . EVER!!

Ok, so the $50,000 in cash was maybe an tough amount to reach, but it was possible. I knew that I could at least get a return of $1,000 or so. So I did it!! As per the instructions in the article, I mailed out ('snail mail' for you e-mail fanatics) a single dollar bill to each of the five people on the list that was contained in the article. I included a small note, with the dollar, that stated "Please Add Me To Your List." I then removed the first position name of the five names listed and moved everyone up one position, and I put my name in position five of the list. This is how the money starts rolling in! I then took this revised article now with my name on the list and REPOSTED IT ON AS MANY NEWSGROUPS AND LOCAL BULLETIN BOARD MESSAGE AREAS THAT I KNEW. I then waited to watch the money come in . . . prepared to maybe receive about $1000 to $1500 in cash or so. . . . But what a welcome surprise when those envelopes kept coming in!!! I knew what they were as soon as I saw the return addresses from people all over the world-Most from the U.S., but some from Canada, even some from Australia! I tell you, THAT WAS EXCITING!! So how much did I get in total return? $1000? $5000? Not even!!! I received a total of $23,343!!! I couldn't believe it!!

Let's review the reasons why you should do this: The only cost factors are for the five stamps, the 5 envelopes and the 5 one dollar bills that you send out to the listed names by snail mail (US Postal Service Mail). Then just simply repost the article (WITH YOUR NAME ADDED) to all the newsgroups and local BBS's you can. Then sit back and, (ironically), enjoy walking (you can run if you like! :o) down your driveway to your mailbox and scoop up your rewards!! We all have five dollars to put into such an easy effortless investment with SPECTACULAR REALISTIC RETURNS OF $15,000 to $25,000 in about 3-5 weeks! So HOLD OFF ON THOSE LOTTERY NUMBERS FOR TODAY, EAT AT HOME TONIGHT INSTEAD OF TAKEOUT FROM McDONALDS AND INVEST FIVE DOLLARS IN THIS AMAZING MONEY MAKING SYSTEM NOW!!! YOU CAN'T LOSE!!

So how do you do it exactly, you ask? I have carefully provided the most detailed, yet straightforward instructions on how to easily get this underway and get your cash on its way. SO, ARE YOU READY TO MAKE SOME CASH!!!?? HERE WE GO!!!

THE LIST OF NAMES IS AT THE END OF THIS ARTICLE.

OK, Read this carefully. Get a printout of this information, if you like, so you can easily refer to it as often as needed.

INSTRUCTIONS:

1. Take a sheet of paper and write on it the following: "Please add my name to your list". This creates a service out of this money making system and thus making it completely legal. You are not just randomly sending a dollar to someone, you are paying one dollar for a legitimate service. Make sure you include your name and address. I assure you that, again, this is completely legal! For a neat little twist, also write what slot their name was in: "You were in slot 3", Just to add a little fun! This is all about having fun and making money at the same time!

2. Now fold this sheet of paper around a dollar bill,(no checks or money orders), and put them into an envelope and send it on its way to the five people listed. The folding of the paper around the bill will insure its arrival to its recipient. THIS STEP IS IMPORTANT!!

3. Now listen carefully, here's where you get YOUR MONEY COMING TO YOUR MAILBOX. Look at the list of five people; remove the first name from position one and move everyone on the list up slot one on the 1 slot, position 3 will now become position 2, 4 will be 3, 5 will be 4. Now put your name, address, zipcode AND COUNTRY in position 5, the bottom position on the list.

4. Now upload this updated file to as many newsgroups and local bulletin boards' message areas & file section as possible. Give a catchy description of the file so it gets noticed!! Such as: "NEED FAST CASH?, HERE IT IS!" or "NEED CASH TO PAY OFF YOUR DEBTS??", etc. And the more uploads, the more money you will make, and of course, the more money the others on the list will make too. LET'S ALL TAKE CARE OF EACH OTHER BY BEING HONEST AND BY PUTTING FORTH 120 PERCENT INTO THIS PROFITABLE & AMAZING SYSTEM!!! You'll reap the benefits, believe me!!! Set a goal for the number of total uploads you'll post, such as 15-20 postings or more! Always have a goal in mind!!! If you can UUE encode the file when uploading, that will make it easier for the people to receive it and have it downloaded to their hard drive. That way they get a copy of the article right on their computer without hassles of viewing and then saving the article from the File menu. Don't alter the file type, leave it as an MS-DOS Text file. The best test is to be able to view this file using Microsoft's Notepad for Windows 3.x or WordPad for Windows '95. If the margins look right without making the screen slide left or right when at the ends of the sentences, you're in business!

5. If you need help uploading, simply ask the sysop of the BBS, or "POST" a message on a newsgroup asking how to post a file, tell them who your Internet provider is and PEOPLE WILL ALWAYS BE GLAD TO HELP. I would try to describe how to do it but there are simply too many internet software packages with slightly different yet relatively simple ways to post or upload a file. Just ask for help or look in the help section for 'posting'. I do know that for GNN, you simply select 'POST' then enter a catchy description under the subject box, choose 'ATTACH', selecting 'UUE' and NOT 'TXT', then choose 'Browse' to go look for the file. Find your text file CASH.TXT and click on it and choose 'OK'. Place a one line statement in the main body section of the message post screen. Something like "Download this to read how to get cash arriving in your mailbox with no paybacks!" or whatever. Just make sure it represents its true feasibility, NOT something like . . . "Get one million dollars flooding in your mailbox in two days!"

You'll never get ANY responses!

6. And this is the step I like. JUST SIT BACK AND ENJOY LIFE BECAUSE CASH IS ON ITS THE WAY!! Expect to see a little money start to trickle in around 2 weeks, but AT ABOUT WEEKS 3 & 4, THE MONEY STORM WILL HIT YOUR MAILBOX!! All you have to do is take it out of the mailbox and try not to scream too loud (outside anyway) when you realize YOU HIT THE BIG TIME AT LAST!!

7. So go PAY OFF YOUR BILLS AND DEBTS and then get that something special you always wanted or buy that special person in your life (or the one you want in your life) a gift they'll never forget. ENJOY LIFE!

8. Now when you get low on this money supply, simply re-activate this file again; Reposting it in the old places where you originally posted and possibly some new places you now know of. Don't ever lose this file, always keep a copy at your reach for when you ever need cash. THIS IS AN INCREDIBLE TOOL THAT YOU CAN ALWAYS RE-USE TIME AND TIME AGAIN WHEN CASH IS NEEDED!

[Name List Deleted]

*** *AGAIN, HONESTY IS THE BEST THING WE HAVE GOING FOR US ON THIS PLAN.*

"MAKE Money Fast" Virus Warning: Internet hoax

This hoax, broadcast on the Internet for the first time in August 2000, has the distinction of being the first (and so far *only*) hoax directed toward an illegal operation. It is unknown whether the authors of the original "MAKE MONEY FAST" PYRAMID SCHEME are connected in any way to this hoax, but the fraudulent warning—unlike the original scheme itself—is not a violation of existing law. The original text reads (with errors uncorrected):

******VIRUS ALERT******
******VIRUS ALERT******
******VIRUS ALERT******

There is NEW VIRUS rapidly affecting computers on the internet. This new virus is insidious, in that it transmitted as a USENET message. Usenet is the "news group" area on the internet that users can openly discuss and exchange information on a wide variety of topics.

What makes this virus DOUBLY DANGEROUS, is that it is disguised as a common chain letter. Chain letters have been passed across usenet almost since it's beginning. Lately, a common chain letter subject is MAKE MONEY FAST.

The Make Money Fast (MMF) chain is read by thousands of people daily. It is also known as: "Easy Cash", "Make Cash Fast", "Turn 5$ into $50,000" and many others. They are all basically the same scheme, in which the reader send $1 to each of the 5 people at the bottom of the list, then moves his name onto the list.

The MMF Virus, as it has been doubed, rides along on these chain letters as a "hidden binary attachment". Since most news reader programs (computer programs used to read USENET messages) will automatically decode and store binary attachments, there is NO SAFE WAY to protect yourself from infection.

The virus attackes your system the next time you run your news reader. Though the virus is transmitted during a normal usenet session, your NEXT usenet session will probably be your last for a while. As a hidden attachment, it is automatically activated with your news reader, and very quickly destroys your partition table. Generally, this is not even noticed until the next time you try to run ANY program.

The next thing the virus does is to place your micro processor into an nth-complexity infinate binary loop, *quickly destroying it. This will appear at first as a normal "lock-up" but will quickley wipe out the delicate circuitry in your system.*

The people that run usenet, at: news.admin.net-abusers are working night and day on a cure. Perhaps some day an automatic process will be able to detect the MMF Virus in usenet messages and cancel them, but that is some time off.

At this point, your ONLY hope is to NOT DOWNLOAD ANY MESSAGES that have a subject similar to above. Please, FORWARD this message to ANYONE you know that reads usenet news.

Thank you,
News.Admin.Net-Abusers

M & M Giveaway: Internet hoax

As in the case of other fraudulent Internet giveaway messages, this one promises a free gift—popular M & M chocolate candies—in return for circulating the hoax e-mail. In fact, no such gifts were offered by the manufacturer. The message appeared on the Internet for the first time in the summer of 1999, message reading as follows (errors uncorrected):

Subject: Have some fun-this is not a hoax.

Hi. My name is Jeffrey Newieb. I am a marketing analyst for M & Ms chocolate candies based in Hershey, Pennsylvania. As the year 2000 approaches, we want to be the candy of the millennium - As you may already know, the roman numeral for Y2K is M&M. We are asking you to pass on this e-mail to 5 friends. Our tracking device is calculating how many e-mails you send out. Everytime it reaches 2000 people, you will receive a free case individual (55 gram packs) of delicious M & M candies. That means the more people it reaches, the more candy you're going to get. Mmmmmm . . . yummy M & M's for the year 2000!

MARTIN, Glendon   See "FASTLANE"

"MASTERS of Deception": hacker syndicate

America's second most notorious gang of Internet HACKERS was reportedly created on a whim, in the summer of 1989. A handful of teenage computer enthusiasts in New York had kept abreast of activities claimed by an earlier group, the so-called LEGION OF

DOOM, and for various reasons they held the original group in contempt. Deciding to form a rival cyber-gang, the youths elected to call their group MOD, thereby mocking the Legion of Doom's familiar LOD initials. After choosing the acronym they debated what the cryptic letters should stand for, finally settling on "Masters of Deception" after several false starts. Founders of the MOD included Paul Stira (a.k.a. Scorpion), Eli Ladopoulos (a.k.a. Acid Phreak), and MARK ABENE (a.k.a. Phiber Optik, lately ousted from the LOD for reasons still disputed by opposing sides of the quarrel). Ladopoulos is credited with devising the new group's name, or at least its initials.

Even before the gang was organized to taunt Legion rivals, the young hackers were penetrating computer networks, "dumpster diving" for critical documents at telephone company offices, engaging in the sort of cybervandalism that attracts police attention. In the MOD's case, New York Telephone investigators Tom Kaiser and Fred Staples began to monitor the trio's system incursions since early 1989. By August, when the MOD was formed, Kaiser and Staples were in touch with cybersleuths from the New York Police Department and the U.S. Secret Service. Indictments were slow in coming, however, since "elite" hackers are adept at covering their tracks, making pursuit as difficult (if not more so) than cracking a protected system.

By early 1990 the MOD had recruited a fourth member, John Lee (a.k.a. Corrupt), lured away from a Brooklyn gang called the Decepticons. A product of the Bedford-Stuyvesant ghetto, Lee had nonetheless excelled with computers and nurtured special skill in cracking sophisticated systems. In short order, Lee became the MOD's "scout," blazing new trails for his colleagues to follow, freely sharing information downloaded from various "secure" computers. A few weeks after joining MOD, Lee found his surreptitious way onto a telephone conference line in use by members of the Texas-based LOD, and was incensed when one of the LOD's members blurted out, "Get that nigger off the line!" The ethnic slur infuriated Lee and his MOD compatriots, who launched a kind of long-distance gang war between the rival groups of hackers.

MOD scored first blood, after a fashion, by penetrating Southwestern Bell telephone networks, tracing the home numbers of LOD leaders and bombarding them with crank calls, switching their long-distance carriers without notice, and playing a host of similar pranks. LOD members retaliated by inserting racial slurs into an "official" history of the MOD posted online, further enraging Lee and company. When LOD members opened a computer security firm in May 1991, their MOD adversaries took note of the press releases and plotted a counterattack. Lee tapped the new company's telephone lines and identified its clients, subjecting them to the same telephone harassment LOD members had suffered. LOD leaders finally confirmed the taps and notified the FBI, with the investigation soon expanding beyond their wildest dreams. Over the next 12 months, federal agents linked MOD members to a January 1990 invasion of AT&T's computer system that had disrupted telephone service throughout the Northwest.

In July 1992 federal indictments were issued against Stira, Ladopoulos, Lee, Abene and a fifth MOD member. Charged with 11 counts of illegal computer intrusion, the defendants each faced a maximum penalty of 55 years in prison and $2.75 million in fines. U.S. Attorney Otto Obermaier dubbed MOD's antics "the crime of the future," noting that "this kind of conduct will not be tolerated." The accused pleaded guilty to reduced charges and were sentenced to varying prison terms, all released on parole by 1994. Meanwhile, LOD members had the last laugh. In December 1992, at a Houston hackers' convention, they sold T-shirts emblazoned with "The Hacker War" in front; on the back, a scorecard read: "LOD 1, MOD 0."

MAYES, Larry: 100th U.S. inmate exonerated by DNA evidence
Late in 1980, the female clerk at a Hammond, Indiana, filling station was kidnapped and raped by a bandit who first cleaned out the till. Police suspected 31-year-old Larry Mayes of the crime, but the victim failed to pick him out of two successive lineups. She finally selected his photo from an array of police mug shots, but only after first being hypnotized (a fact concealed by authorities for two decades). Mayes was arrested in January 1981 and the victim repeated her identification at trial the following year, whereupon Mayes was convicted of robbery, rape, and criminal deviant conduct. He received an 80-year prison sentence, and all his appeals were denied.

Members of the CARDOZO INNOCENCE PROJECT agreed to represent Mayes in 1999, seeking DNA tests of semen traces preserved in the case, but court clerks insisted that the original rape kit was lost. A two-year stalemate ensued, finally broken by Cardozo associate Fran Hardy, an Indiana University law professor, and four of her students. A clerk in Gary was finally persuaded to search the courthouse basement, and the "lost" rape kit was found. Professor Hardy filed a petition for DNA testing of the evidence on July 9, 2001, and Lake County prosecutors agreed. The test results excluded Mayes as a suspect and he was released from prison, with all charges dropped, on December 21, 2001. He was the 100th U.S. prison inmate exonerated by DNA evidence since regular testing began in the early 1990s. The 1980 rape and robbery remains unsolved today.

McCARTY, Richard: accused satellite TV pirate

A resident of Benzonia, Michigan, Richard McCarty was one of 11 defendants arrested in July 1999, as part of the federal sting dubbed "OPERATION SMART-CARD.NET." According to the charges filed against them, the defendants purchased and sold thousands of "smart cards" granting users unauthorized access to satellite television broadcasts, costing legitimate vendors an estimated $6.2 million in lost revenue per year. Officers of the U.S. Customs Service launched the sting operation in September 1998, ultimately selling more than 3,300 counterfeit access cards to black market dealers, who then resold the cards at inflated prices. Five Smartcard defendants entered guilty pleas by April 2001, but McCarty's case is one of those with charges unresolved. Spokesmen for the Department of Justice note that indictments are merely accusations of criminal activity, and all accused defendants are presumed innocent until convicted at trial.

McINTYRE, Shane See FASTLANE

McKENNA, Patrick: computer saboteur

A resident of Hampton, New Hampshire, Patrick McKenna was employed in 2000 as a help desk worker for Bricsnet, a computer application service provider for the construction and design industry based in Portsmouth, New Hampshire. Dismissed from his job on October 20, 2000, for moonlighting and other violations of company rules, McKenna used a supervisor's password to penetrate Bricsnet's computer system that night, and again on the following day. In the course of those raids he deleted 675 files (some of them irretrievable), altered billing records, modified user access levels, and sent more

than 100 Bricsnet clients e-mails falsely claiming that the firm's project center was closed. Another Bricsnet employee discovered the damage on October 21, with in-house repairs costing $13,614.

A federal grand jury indicted McKenna in November 2000, under a statute passed in 1984 forbidding unauthorized computer penetrations. If convicted on all counts, he faced five years' imprisonment and a $250,000 fine. McKenna's trial was scheduled to begin on February 16, 2001, before U.S. District Judge Joseph DiClerico in Concord, New Hampshire. Bond was waived in the case, since prosecutors did not consider McKenna a flight risk. McKenna was convicted at trial, but his punishment was relatively light. On June 18, 2001, Judge DiClerico sentenced McKenna to serve six months in federal prison, followed by two years' supervised probation. McKenna was also ordered to reimburse Bricsnet for expenses in the amount of $13,614. He thus became New Hampshire's first convicted HACKER ordered to serve prison time. FBI spokesmen explained the punitive action by noting that McKenna's "activities were meant to cause as much damage as possible. It was malicious. How do you quantify the impact when customers receive these kinds of damaging e-mails? You can't put a dollar on that."

McMILLAN, Clark: exonerated by DNA evidence

A pair of Memphis teenagers were parked on a lover's lane in Overton Park, one night in 1979, when an armed stranger approached their car, robbed the boy, and then raped his girlfriend. Although they seemed initially uncertain, both victims finally identified 23-year-old Clark McMillan as their attacker. McMillan insisted he was innocent, despite a recent conviction on federal firearms charges and police suspicion that he may have committed several similar holdup rapes around Memphis. Conviction on the federal charge earned him a two-year prison sentence, but U.S. authorities left his final disposition to the Memphis court. Convicted of aggravated rape and robbery in 1980, McMillan was sentenced to 119 years in state prison. His several appeals were rejected.

In 1997, McMillan contacted members of the CARDOZO INNOCENCE PROJECT and persuaded them to take his case. Four years of legal maneuvers ensued, before DNA tests were finally performed on semen stains recovered from the rape victim's clothing in 1979. Those tests eliminated McMillan as a possible source of the semen, and his state sentence was vacated on May 2, 2001. Prosecutor William Gibbons told reporters on that day, "The system worked. Someone who did not commit a particular crime is going to be released from our state prisons, so I think the system has worked very well." Gibbons offered no suggestions as to how McMillan should be compensated—if at all—for the 22 years he spent in custody for a crime he did not commit.

Exoneration on the rape and robbery charges was not the end of McMillan's troubles, however. Even before his release from Tennessee's state prison was confirmed, federal authorities announced that McMillan still owed them two years in jail for the ancient firearms conviction. Attorney Peter Neufeld, speaking for the Innocence Project, announced his intention to fight that decision. "If he spent 22 [years] in prison for a crime he didn't commit," Neufeld told journalists, "they should at least give him two years' credit for a case that he would have started serving in 1979."

"MELISSA": computer virus

Launched on the Internet by its author, DAVID SMITH, on March 26, 1999, the "Melissa" macro virus infects Microsoft Word documents and templates, while sending copies of itself to other victims via the Microsoft Outlook address books found on newly infected computers. Known to analysts as a "fast infector," Melissa disables Word macro-virus protection devices and changes system registries to facilitate the replication process. Messages dispatched to unsuspecting targets begin:

Subject: Important Message From [UserName]
Message: Here is that document you asked for . . .
Don't show anyone else ;-)

The message travels with an attachment bearing the virus, which not only infects the new host computer but may also permit the victim's confidential documents to be broadcast across the Internet. If the infected computer runs Microsoft Office 2000, Melissa performs an additional function disabling that program's antivirus security settings.

An additional trigger routine displayed by Melissa is activated when the current day and minute reading on the infected computer's clock are identical—e.g., May 5, at 1:05 P.M and so forth. On those occasions, the following text is inserted into any current docu-

ment in progress: "Twenty-two points, plus triple-word-score, plus fifty points for using all my letters. Game's over. I'm outta here." Melissa also presents the following comments on-screen.

WORD/Melissa written by Kwyjibo
Works in both Word 2000 and Word 97
Worm? Macro Virus? Word 97 Virus? Word 2000
*   Virus? You Decide!*
Word -> Email | Word 97 Word 2000 . . . it's a new age!

Three new variations of Melissa have surfaced since Smith's original brainchild wreaked havoc on the Web in 1999. The first variant, a computer worm dubbed "Melissa.b," masquerades as a well-intentioned warning to unwary users, including a comment in the virus code that reads: "We don't want to actually infect the PC, just warn them." That altruistic goal is mirrored in the message carrying Melissa.b:

Subject: Trust No One
Message: Be careful what you open. It could be a virus.

That warning delivered, the worm proceeds to execute its replication routine when the e-mail's infected attachment is opened. As with the original Melissa, the later version sends its own messages out to addresses lifted from the new victim's Outlook address book. Current documents are also marked with the following inserted text (errors uncorrected):

This could have had disasterous results. Be more careful next time you open an e-mail. Protect yourself! Find out how at these web sites:

http://www.eos.ncsu.edu/eos/info/computer_ethics/
*   www/abuse/wvt/worm/*
http://www.nipc.gov/nipc/w97melissa.htm
http://www.cert.org/advisories/CA-99-04-
*   Melissa-Macro-Virus.html*
http://www.microsoft.com/security/bulletins/ms99-
*   002.asp*
http://www.infoworld.com/cgi-bin/displayStory.
*   pl?990326.wcvirus.htm*

Another variant of the original virus, dubbed "Melissa.w," is also sometimes called "Melissa.AG" or "Prilissa.A." Analysts describe it as an ordinary macro virus which, like its predecessors, spreads on the Internet via infected e-mail attachments, sent to the first 50 addresses found in the new victim's Outlook address book. Those messages read:

Subject: Message From [UserName]
Message: This document is very Important and you've GOT to read this!!!

Melissa.w's payload triggers on Christmas Day, overwriting the "C:\AUTOEXEC.BAT" file with commands that try to format the C drive on its next startup. The virus then displays the following on-screen message:

C)1999—CyberNET
Vine . . . Vide . . . Vice . . . Moslem Power Never End . . .
You Dare Rise Against Me . . . The Human Era is Over,
The CyberNET Era Has Come !!!

The same payload routine also defaces any active document with 70 different geometric shapes in randomly selected colors.

The final variation of Melissa (to date, at least) is called "Melissa.bg." It is ranked by analysts as "very dangerous," possessing an unlimited mailing routing (unlike Melissa.w's built-in limitation of 50 infected e-mails). The infected message reads:

Subject: Resume—Janet Simons
To: Director of Sales/Marketing,
Message: Attached is my resume with a list of references contained within. Please feel free to call or email me if you have any further questions regarding my experience. I am looking forward to hearing from you.

Sincerely,
Janet Simons.

The bogus "résumé" contains two macros that activate whenever a document is opened or closed on the newly infected computer. Opening a document grants the virus access to the victim's Outlook address book and initiates the familiar self-replication routine. When a document is closed, Melissa.bg saves itself in the Windows startup folder, under the name explorer.doc, reactivated with each Windows startup. Its destructive payload erases all files in the root directories of drives C through Z, in addition to the following directories:

C:\My Documents*.*

C:\WINDOWS*.*
C:\WINDOWS\SYSTEM*.*
C:\WINNT*.*
C:\WINNT\SYSTEM32*.*

The following message is also presented on-screen as the virus plays out its routine.

```
 ,————————————————————————————————,
 |                                |
 |   Better You Than Me Buddy . . .   |
 |      . . . Hope You Like My vIrUs  |
 |             :)                 |
 |             :(                 |
 '————————————————————————————————'
```

"MENACE": computer worm

Reported initially in July 2001, this worm virus spreads on the Internet via America Online. "Menace" is written in Visual Basic 6.0, delivered as an e-mail attachment titled sofunny.exe. Two variant subject lines have been reported on the messages, reading either "Fwd: This is great!" or "Fwd: This is hilarious!" The message in both cases reads: "You guys have to download this! This really is funny!" When the attachment is opened, initially launching the worm, it displays the following message on-screen:

Fatal Error #6834
An unknown error has occurred.

Menace then copies itself to the new host computer's Windows directory, creating these files:

C:\WINDOWS\msdos423.exe
C:\WINDOWS\SOFUNNY.exe

Once it has infected a new host computer, Menace lies dormant until AOL is activated, then gains access to arriving e-mails and replies to each in turn with its own infected messages. Menace also steals passwords from infected computers and sends them back to its original host when AOL is active. Menace contains the following spurious copyright text: "AOL PWS for version 4, 5, & 6. Now a worm too! By Menace."

"MENDOZA": computer virus

First reported on the Internet in June 1996, "Mendoza" is ranked by analysts as a "very dangerous," memory-resident, parasitic polymorphic virus which writes itself to the ends of .com and .exe files as they are opened or executed. Upon activation, the Mendoza infects the \dos\keyb.com file and proceeds from there to deliver its payload.

In action, Mendoza searches for the pklite.exe file used to compress other files on the host computer and compromises its function so that some files cannot be compressed, while compression of others disables output to the monitor's screen. Depending on the system's date and time, Mendoza may also erase various disk sectors and/or restart the computer to display an on-screen message reading "(c) Mendoza's 1995." Files immune to Mendoza's attack include the following:

    clean.exe
    command.com
    emm.386.exe
    loadhi.com
    pcvir.exe
    power.exe
    share.exe

MICROSOFT-AOL Merger: Internet hoax

Microsoft and America Online rank high among the more popular targets for Internet hoaxes, virus warnings, fraudulent giveaway plans, and the like. This fraudulent message, circulated for the first time in October 1999, managed to involve both corporations with its announcement of a mythical merger. The original text read as follows:

Date: Thursday, October 07, 1999 10:56 AM
Subject: Broadcast: Microsoft and AOL Merger
FROM: xxxx
COMPANY: RE/MAX Commercial Services, Inc.
Subject: Microsoft and AOL Merger

I am forwarding this because the person who sent it to me is a good friend and does not send me junk. Microsoft and AOL are now the largest Internet company and in an effort make sure that Internet explorer remains the most widely used program, Microsoft and AOL are running an e-mail beta test. When you forward this e-mail to friends, Microsoft can and will track it (if you are a Microsoft Windows user) for a two week time period. For every person that you forward this e-mail to, Microsoft will pay you $245.00, for every person that you sent it to that forwards it on,

Microsoft will pay you $243.00 and for every third person that receives it, you will be paid $241.00. Within two weeks, Microsoft will contact you for your address and then send you a check. I thought this was a scam myself, but two weeks after receiving this e-mail and forwarding it on, Microsoft contacted me for my e-mail and within days, I received a check for $24800.00.

Brent Jones
FCG Inc.
Wayne PA
610 225 6787
bjones@fcg.com

MIFFLETON, Andrew: hacker "Daphtpunk"

A 24-year-old resident of Arlington, Texas, Andrew Miffleton was associated with a group of self-styled Darkside Hackers that practiced unauthorized penetration of various protected computers, often for the purpose of illegally obtaining free long-distance telephone service. Between May 1998 and February 1999, Miffleton (a.k.a. Daphtpunk) hosted a Web page for the Darkside gang on his home computer, including a list of 40 root-level passwords that granted his cronies illegal control of the computer system owned by Verio, Inc., a national Internet Service Provider (ISP). Penetration of that system reportedly cost Verio some $90,000 in losses. At the time of his arrest by FBI agents, in February 1999, Miffleton also possessed 20 electronic serial numbers and mobile identification numbers for cellular telephone service, five stolen credit card numbers and one unauthorized AT&T calling card number.

Confronted with multiple felony charges, Miffleton struck a bargain with federal prosecutors. On December 20, 1999, he appeared before U.S. District Judge Joe Kendall and pleaded guilty to one count of possessing unauthorized access devices. The maximum penalty for that charge was 10 years' imprisonment and a $250,000 fine, but Miffleton was lucky at his formal sentencing, on July 24, 2000. Judge Kendall sentenced Miffleton to 21 months in prison and a $3,000 fine, with an additional requirement that he pay restitution to Verio, Inc. in the amount of $89,480.

"MILENNIUM": computer virus

Initially logged in July 1999, its name misspelled by the original (anonymous) author, "Milennium" is a

199

parasitic polymorphic virus rated "not dangerous" by computer analysts. It utilizes functions found only in Windows 98, and is therefore unable to infect computers running Windows 95, Windows 2000 or Windows NT. Upon infecting a new host, Milennium searches the directories for executable files, infecting each in turn. After 30 files have been infected—and for each 30 thereafter—the virus displays on-screen the following message:

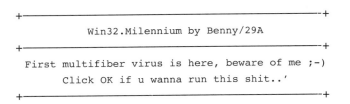

```
+———————————————————————————————+
           Win32.Milennium by Benny/29A
+———————————————————————————————+
   First multifiber virus is here, beware of me ;-)
          Click OK if u wanna run this shit..'
+———————————————————————————————+
```

In action, Milennium searches out file types *.bak, *.dat, *.exe, *.scr, and *.sfx, seizing control of each. If any file includes a debugger, Milennium subverts that security program and causes the debugger to crash. Each file discovered and stripped of protection is thereafter infected with the virus code, its size enlarged to accommodate the infestation. Computer data is not erased or otherwise lost in the process, however, thereby accounting for Milennium's "not dangerous" rating.

MILGAARD, David: exonerated by DNA evidence

Gail Miller, a nursing student in Saskatoon, Saskatchewan, left her apartment for work at 6:45 A.M. on January 31, 1969. Before reaching her usual bus stop, she was ambushed, dragged into an alley, raped, and stabbed repeatedly. A child walking to school found her body at 8:30 A.M. and police were summoned. They found a bloodstained kitchen knife at the scene and retrieved Miller's empty purse from a nearby garbage can. Detectives theoretically linked the rape-slaying with two other recent sexual assaults in the neighborhood, but they had no suspects or conclusive evidence with which to identify the stalker. A $2,000 reward for information finally led to a break in the case—or so it seemed.

David Milgaard, a 16-year-old "hippie" and drifter possessed of a long police record for theft and drug-dealing, had arrived in Saskatoon the same morning Miller was killed, traveling with friends Ron Wilson and Nichol John to visit another acquaintance, one Albert Cadrain. They reached Cadrain's home, close to the Miller crime scene, at

8:30 A.M., Cadrain noting that Milgaard's pants were torn. Milgaard and company explained that they had helped another motorist dislodge his car from a snow bank, with Milgaard ripping his pants in the process. Around 4:30 P.M., the four embarked on a trip to Alberta, then drove on to Wilson's home in Regina, arriving on February 5, 1969.

Cadrain was jailed for vagrancy in Regina a few days later and spent a week in jail. Detectives visited his cell to grill Cadrain about reports that a group of youths had gathered at his Saskatoon flat the day Gail Miller died, but he denied any knowledge of the crime. Back in Saskatoon by early March, Cadrain learned of the $2,000 reward in Miller's case and approached police with a startling new account of January 31. In his revised story, Cadrain said Milgaard had been wearing bloodstained clothes when he arrived at Cadrain's apartment, and that Milgaard seemed in a rush to leave town. While driving to Alberta, Cadrain now claimed, Milgaard had thrown a woman's cosmetics case out the car window, telling Cadrain that he had to get rid of John and Wilson because they "knew too much."

Police interrogated John and Wilson, both reporting that Milgaard had never been out of their sight long enough to commit a murder on January 31, and that his clothes were not bloodstained. As the relentless grilling continued, detectives apparently fed Wilson bits and pieces of information about the Miller crime scene, with Wilson finally deducing that he would not be released until he told police the story they wanted to hear. Nichol John, a 16-year-old drug addict, was subjected to similar pressure, once left alone in a police interrogation room with Albert Cadrain and ordered by detectives to "discuss" her statement with the Crown's star witness. By the time authorities traced Milgaard to Prince George, British Columbia, and took him into custody, John and Wilson had caved under pressure, both producing statements that incriminated Milgaard. Wilson embellished his tale to the point where Milgaard allegedly confessed that he "got the girl" in Saskatoon. John went even further, claiming she had seen Milgaard stab Gail Miller.

David Milgaard's murder trial consumed two weeks in January 1970, with Cadrain and Wilson appearing as prosecution witnesses. (Cadrain, by then, had collected his $2,000 reward. He had also been briefly confined to a psychiatric hospital, diagnosed as a paranoid schizophrenic after suffering hallucinations wherein Milgaard appeared to him in serpent form.) Nichol John faltered on the witness stand, claiming she could remember nothing of the fatal morning, whereupon Prosecutor T.D.R. Caldwell introduced her previous statement incriminating Milgaard. Two more witnesses from Regina, 18-year-old George Lapchuk and 17-year-old Craig Melnick, testified that they were watching television with Milgaard and two girls, Ute Frank and Deborah Hall, in May 1969, when a news report on the Miller slaying was broadcast. Lapchuk and Melnick (both later identified as longtime police narcotics informants) described Milgaard grabbing a pillow and demonstrating how he had murdered Miller, several times proclaiming, "I killed her!" Judge Alfred Bence criticized the Crown's witnesses, informing jurors that their testimony should be treated skeptically, but the panel convicted Milgaard on January 31, 1970. Bence sentenced Milgaard to life imprisonment and the Saskatchewan appellate court rejected his appeal in 1971. The Supreme Court of Canada subsequently declined to review his case.

Milgaard's 1979 parole bid was rejected on grounds that he still claimed to be innocent, but authorities later allowed him limited, escorted furloughs to visit his family in Winnipeg. On one such excursion, in 1980, Milgaard escaped and fled to Toronto, remaining at large for 77 days before he was cornered and shot in the back—while standing unarmed, with hands raised—by Toronto police. Milgaard survived his wound and was returned to prison, while his mother offered a $10,000 reward for information leading to Gail Miller's actual killer. Working with freelance writer Peter Carlyle-Gordge, Joyce Milgaard found Nichol John and Ron Wilson, both of whom admitted that their final statements to police (and Wilson's testimony under oath) were false. Deborah Hall refuted the testimony of George Lapchuk and Craig Melnick, asserting that Milgaard had merely fluffed up his pillow and made no admissions of guilt.

Milgaard's attorneys retained Dr. James Ferris, a forensic pathologist, to review the blood and semen evidence used against Milgaard at trial, Ferris concluding that some of the samples excluded Milgaard as a suspect, while the others were contaminated and yielded inconclusive results. While awaiting a formal review of the case in 1988, the lawyers also learned that Albert Cadrain's next-door neighbor, Larry Fisher, had been convicted and imprisoned for a series of brutal rapes in Saskatoon and Winnipeg, committed around the time of Gail Miller's slaying.

Fisher's ex-wife was located with help from CENTURION MINISTRIES, and she admitted suspecting her husband of murdering Miller. She had told police as much in 1980, after learning of the Milgaard family's $10,000 reward, but detectives ignored her statement. Interviews with Larry Fisher's victims revealed that his style of attack was similar to that used by Miller's assailant. Finally, in 1991, Justice Minister Kim Campbell asked the Supreme Court of Canada to review Milgaard's case.

The high court's ruling, issued on April 14, 1992, began with a blanket statement that Milgaard had received a "fair trial" in 1970, with no evidence of police or prosecutorial misconduct, but Ron Wilson's recantation and new evidence concerning Larry Fisher prompted a reversal of the jury's verdict, with a new trial ordered. Milgaard was released from prison three days later, after spending 23 years behind bars. Saskatchewan prosecutors declined to pursue another trial, and the province refused to compensate Milgaard for his years in prison, since he had had no opportunity to prove his innocence in court. Only in 1997, after new DNA tests provided conclusive proof of his innocence, was Milgaard finally compensated for his wrongful conviction. Larry Fisher was charged with Gail Miller's slaying in July 1997 and convicted at trial in 1999.

MILLER Beer Giveaway: Internet hoax

This fraudulent offer of free beer in return for circulating Internet chain letters was officially denounced as a hoax by the Miller Brewing Company on April 14, 1999. The note's description of a mythical e-mail tracking system echoes similar claims made in hoaxes surrounding America Online and Microsoft's Bill Gates. The message reads:

Hello:

We here at Miller Brewing Company, Inc. would like to help bring in the new millennium for everyone. We like to think of ourselves as a progressive company, keeping up with our customers. We have found the best way to do this via the Internet and email. Combining these things, we would like to make a special offer to our valued customers: If this email makes it to 2,000,000 people by 12:00 PM on New Year's Eve of 1999, we will send a coupon for one six-pack of any of our Miller Brand beverages. In the event that 2,000,000 people are reached, our tracker/counter, embedded in this message, will report to us with the list of names and email addresses. Thereafter, each email address will be sent an electronic coupon which you can print out and redeem at any Miller Brand beverage carrying store. The coupons will be sent as soon as 2,000,000 people are reached, so the sooner, the better.

Enjoy, and Cheers,
Gary D. Anderson, Chief Marketing Director
Miller Brewing Company, Inc.
http://www.millerbrewing.com

MILLER, Robert Lee, Jr.: exonerated by DNA evidence

In the mid-1980s, Oklahoma City was terrorized by the serial rape-murders of several elderly women. Police, seemingly helpless as the death toll mounted, were severely criticized for their failure to capture the unknown predator. They saw a way to clear the slate in 1987 and jumped at the chance, resulting in a classic case of justice betrayed.

Robert Miller Jr. was 29 years old, an unemployed heating and air-conditioning repairman, when he approached detectives in 1987, offering a strange solution to their frustrating dilemma. Some published accounts describe Miller as a "regular drug user," but all agree that he had no prior criminal record. Miller explained to police that he had experienced "visions" of the recent slayings and believed he had some kind of "psychic link" to the killer. As they listened to his detailed descriptions of crime scenes, questioning Miller over a span of 12 hours, detectives became convinced that *he* was to blame for the murders. Calling his videotaped ramblings a "confession," authorities charged Miller with the 1986 murders of 92-year-old Zelma Cutter and 83-year-old Anna Laura Fowler.

Apparently stunned by the accusation, Miller denied any personal role in the crimes and repeated his odd story of "seeing through the killer's eyes" in trancelike states. Police dismissed the psychic angle and enlisted forensic chemist JOYCE GILCHRIST to match Miller's hair with strands recovered from the crime scenes. Gilchrist confirmed the match, and Miller was convicted on all counts at trial, in 1988, receiving two death sentences plus a total of 725 years in prison.

Police and prosecutors evinced no concern when assaults on elderly victims continued in Oklahoma City. Another suspect, one Ronald Lott, was arrested and confessed to the assaults. When critics of the Miller prosecution pointed out the near-identical M.O. between Lott's crimes and the 1986 murders, police turned again to Joyce Gilchrist, who promptly denied any possible match between Lott and hairs recovered from the Cutter and Fowler crime scenes. Prosecutor Ray Elliott, in charge of both cases (and later an Oklahoma judge), cheerfully assured his friends, "We're going to give Robert Miller the needle. He's just blowfish."

With assistance from attorneys of the CARDOZO INNOCENCE PROJECT, evidence from Miller's case was submitted for DNA testing in 1991 and again in 1993. Results were the same in both instances, positively excluding Miller as the source of hair and semen found at either crime scene while implicating Raymond Lott. Undeterred by mere science, Ray Elliott changed his theory of the crime to claim that even if Lott *was* the rapist, Robert Miller must still have been present at both crimes in order to offer his detailed "confessions." The Oklahoma Court of Criminal Appeals disagreed in 1994, ordering a new trial for Miller on the basis of irrefutable DNA evidence. District Attorney Robert Macy, renowned for placing 60 inmates on death row, announced his intent to handle the new trial himself, but legal delays postponed the event until February 1997, when charges were finally dismissed. A contributing factor to that move was the revelation of "expert" Joyce Gilchrist's false testimony in dozens of cases throughout Oklahoma.

MILNE, James See FASTLANE

MISSING Trucks Warning: Internet hoax

Spawned by the terrorist attacks of September 11, 2001, an Internet scare message was circulated in October of that year, claiming that 30 or more trucks had been stolen from various rental companies, presumably for use by terrorists in transporting and detonating massive bombs. Despite its feasibility, in light of the 1995 Oklahoma City bombing and others, the message has been researched and denounced as fraudulent by the *Washington Post* and ABC News. No such reports of stolen trucks have been filed, alleging thefts by terrorists or otherwise. The U-Haul corporation, named as one of those losing several vehicles, also issued a formal disclaimer on October 17, 2001. The original message read:

Hey everybody,

Sorry for the mass email, but I got important news tonight. My dad works for FEMA and he's really involved with the goings on in NYC. He told me that within the last 24 hours, more than 30 Ryder, U-Haul, and Verizon trucks have been reported stolen across the country. The U-Haul and Ryder trucks were rented and then never returned, so they're considered stolen. Many of them were rented by people of Arab descent. I don't mean to make any assumptions, and I certainly don't want to scare you, but I thought you all might like to know. Be wary of these vehicles, pay attention to them, and don't walk or park near them. He said to stay out of major public places if at all possible (Crossgates, the Pepsi, downtown Albany, etc.) because recreational sites would most likely be hit on weekends. I'm sorry to cause alarm, but he told me it was ok to share this information. If you'd like to forward it to anyone you know, feel free, as there is a possibility it might save lives. I hope everyone is doing well, and give those you love an extra hug.

MITCHELL, Alfred Brian: exonerated by DNA evidence

Another Oklahoma prisoner condemned on the basis of false testimony from state forensic "expert" JOYCE GILCHRIST, Alfred Mitchell was accused of murder, rape, and sodomy in the 1991 slaying of college student Elaine Scott. Gilchrist told the trial court that "Mr. Mitchell's sperm had been found on the victim through anal and vaginal swabs," the prosecutor contending that after Mitchell "had his way with her . . . he murdered her, he beat her to death, because she was the only living witness to the crime that he had committed." Impressed by those statements, jurors convicted Mitchell on all counts and he was sentenced to die. His various appeals in Oklahoma were denied.

U.S. District Judge Ralph Thompson reversed Mitchell's rape and sodomy convictions on August 27, 1999, after discovering that Joyce Gilchrist had lied on the witness stand, while the prosecution withheld exculpatory evidence in Mitchell's case. Specifically, a review of case files had uncovered Gilchrist's handwritten notes of a conversation with FBI laboratory analysts, reporting DNA test results that excluded Mitchell as a donor of semen found at the crime scene. Branding the state's actions as "absolutely indefensible," Judge Thompson noted that:

Gilchrist's trial testimony that the DNA analysis performed by the FBI was 'inconclusive' as to petitioner was, without question, untrue. Over a year before petitioner was tried and convicted of rape and anal sodomy, [FBI] Agent Vick's DNA testing revealed that petitioner's DNA was not present on the samples tested. Petitioner's trial counsel did not receive copies of the autoradiographs developed by Agent Vick. . . . Petitioner's trial counsel did not receive copies of Gilchrist's notes, which demonstrate that she, too, was confident that only Ms. Scott's DNA was present on the vaginal swab and that only Ms. Scott and [her boyfriend's] DNA was present on the panties. Instead, the prosecution turned over only the formal FBI report discussed above which, at best, is unclear and ambiguous.

For that gross violation of judicial ethics, Thompson vacated Mitchell's rape and sodomy convictions, but allowed his death sentence for murder to stand. It remained for the 10th Circuit Court of Appeals to correct the remaining injustice in August 2001. According to that court:

Mr. Mitchell requested and received permission to conduct discovery in this habeas proceeding. As a result, he obtained hand-written notes taken by Ms. Gilchrist during telephone conversations with [FBI] Agent Vick indicating that the agent had conducted two DNA probes on the samples. These probes showed that the semen on the panties matched that of [her boyfriend] only, that no DNA was present on the rectal swab, and that the only DNA on the vaginal swab was consistent with the victim. The results thus completely undermined Ms. Gilchrist's testimony.

The district court held an evidentiary hearing, at which Agent Vick admitted there was no way to tell from his report that he had obtained no DNA results from the rectal swab, no DNA profile other than that of the victim on the vaginal swab, and no DNA profile other than that of the victim and [her boyfriend] on the panties. An expert testified at the evidentiary hearing that the DNA testing performed by Agent Vick unquestionably eliminated Mr. Mitchell as a source of the sperm. This expert reviewed Ms. Gilchrist's trial testimony implicating Mr. Mitchell through her testing . . . and stated that the testimony was based on the use of test methods Ms. Gilchrist knew were less precise than the DNA tests which eliminated Mr. Mitchell. Moreover, he pointed out that one of the tests she performed in fact excluded Mr. Mitchell. Mr. Mitchell was not provided the actual test results developed by Agent Vick or *the notes taken by Ms. Gilchrist indicating her knowledge that Mr. Mitchell had been excluded by the FBI's DNA testing.*

Ms. Gilchrist thus provided the jury with evidence implicating Mr. Mitchell in the sexual assault of the victim which she knew was rendered false and misleading by evidence withheld from the defense. Compounding this improper conduct was that of the prosecutor, whom the district court found had "labored extensively at trial to obscure the true DNA test results and to highlight Gilchrist's test results," and whose characterization of the FBI report in his closing argument was "entirely unsupported by evidence and . . . misleading." As a result, the jury convicted Mr. Mitchell of rape and forcible anal sodomy despite evidence it did not hear indicating that no such assault had taken place.

We are compelled to address the obvious by pointing out that the state's conduct in this case strikes a heavy blow to the public's "trust in the prosecutor as 'the representative . . . of a sovereignty . . . whose interest . . . in a criminal prosecution is not that it shall win a case, but that justice shall be done.'" The Supreme Court has cautioned that proper disclosure . . . is required in order "to preserve the criminal trial, as distinct from the prosecutor's private deliberations, as the chosen forum for ascertaining the truth about criminal accusations." Nonetheless, as the state takes pains to point out on appeal, our task is not to impose punishment for improper behavior but to assess whether the improperly withheld evidence raises a reasonable probability that, had it been disclosed to the jury, the result of the sentencing proceeding would have been different. . . .

Mitchell's death sentence was accordingly reversed and charges were subsequently dropped. The murder of Elaine Scott remains unsolved today.

MITNICK, Kevin David: convicted hacker

Described by admirers as "the most notorious HACKER ever captured," Kevin Mitnick boasts a series of arrests dating from his teenage years, in the 1970s. The early charges were relatively minor, including theft of Pacific Bell Telephone operators' manuals and digital alteration of connections to receive free long-distance telephone service, resulting in stern reprimands and probation. In 1983 Mitnick was convicted of hacking into a Pentagon computer system, then ordered to spend six months at the California Youth Authority's Karl Holton Training School in Stockton.

Confinement failed to curb Mitnick's reckless behavior, and he continued to commit infractions that his friends describe as "crimes of curiosity." A 1989 conviction for computer fraud earned him a one-year sentence in federal prison, followed by six months of court-ordered therapy to relieve his computer "addiction." The treatment seemed to help, as Mitnick went to work as a legitimate computer programmer, but the lure of forbidden systems proved irresistible. Arrested in 1992 for violating his 1989 federal probation, Mitnick posted bond and fled California, spending the next three years as America's first cyberspace fugitive.

The long run began to unravel on December 25, 1994, when Mitnick penetrated the computers of Tsutomu Shimomura, a computer security specialist based in San Diego, California. Shimomura's clients included the FBI, the National Security Agency, and the U.S. Air Force, insuring that any compromise of his work would produce a swift and severe official reaction. Shimomura and his colleagues were still searching for the culprit on January 27, 1995, when Berkeley software designer Bruce Koball found data stolen from Shimomura's computer stashed in one of the designer's Internet accounts on The Well, a local service provider. By February 7, further investigation had revealed that an unknown hacker was using The Well as a launching pad for raids on various corporate and university computer systems. Two days later, the phantom was traced to Netcom Online Communications Services, an Internet service provider in San Jose, California.

Shimomura flew to San Jose and persuaded Netcom administrators to cooperate in shadowing the hacker's activities. Together, they watched him copy files from Apple Computer and other "secure" systems, deprogram telephone circuits, and steal more than 20,000 credit card numbers from an on-line database. The pirate's cover was blown on February 10, 1995, when he revealed himself as Kevin Mitnick, writing to an Israeli e-mail correspondent with complaints about his photo being published in the *New York Times*. By then, Shimomura had identified Mitnick's apparent base of operations as Raleigh, North Carolina, and enlisted Sprint cellular phone engineers to help trace the hacker's address. Flying to Raleigh on February 12, Shimomura joined technicians armed with diagnostic gear to trace Mitnick's calls and pin down his location. FBI agents toured the apartment complex two days later, tracking Mitnick's telephone signals with a hand-held meter, and he was arrested on February 14, 1995, charged with 23 counts of computer and telecommunications fraud, for a maximum potential prison term of 345 years.

Mitnick pleaded guilty to one count of cellular telephone fraud in North Carolina and received an eight-month prison sentence. Thereafter, he was transferred to Los Angeles for trial on additional charges, denied bond or access to computers, and further barred from unsupervised access to telephones. Additional charges filed in California included federal probation violations plus 27 counts of illegal access, and computer and telephone fraud. Mitnick resolved both state and federal cases with another plea bargain on March 26, 1999, this time pleading guilty to five felony counts. Five months later he received a 60-month prison sentence with three years' probation and a $4,125 fine, the term to run consecutively with his sentence in North Carolina (for a total of 68 months inside). Although his plea agreement was sealed by the court, reports indicate that the court barred Mitnick from selling his story for profit and forbade any use of computers for four years after his release from prison. Mitnick served five years of his sentence and was released on January 21, 2000.

Mitnick's admirers continue to insist that he was persecuted or "framed" by authorities for displaying too much "curiosity" about modern computer technology. In the words of one sympathetic website:

> The greatest injustice in the prosecution of Kevin Mitnick is revealed when one examines the actual harm to society (or lack thereof) which resulted from Kevin's actions. To the extent that Kevin is a "hacker" he must be considered a purist. The simple truth is that Kevin never sought monetary gain from his hacking, though it could have proven extremely profitable. Nor did he hack with the malicious intent to damage or destroy other people's property. Rather, Kevin pursued his hacking as a means of satisfying his intellectual curiosity and applying Yankee ingenuity. These attributes are more frequently promoted rather than punished by society.

Mitnick's fans overlook his persistent telephone frauds and theft of credit card numbers by the thousands, as well as his personal harassment of Tsutomu Shimomura, including a series of telephone death threats between December 1994 and February 1995. "Purist" or not, such aberrant behavior strains the definition of "curiosity," and no amount of denial erases the mercenary motive evident in theft of credit card numbers and telephone service. Shimomura himself may have come closest to the truth, when he told the *Minneapolis Tribune*, "I'm curious to know what's broken in him, why he feels compelled to do this."

MOBILE Phone Virus Warning: Internet hoax

Initially circulated in May 1999, this fraudulent warning announces the discovery of a virus that targets mobile telephones by dialing selected devices and infecting them when the owner answers. No such virus exists today, and the warning is entirely spurious. The original message reads:

> Subject: GSM mobile phones Virus!
> Date: Wed, 19 May 1999 10:39:00 -0400
>
> BEWARE!!!
>
> Dear all mobile phone's owners,
>
> ATTENTION!!!
>
> NOW THERE IS A VIRUS ON MOBILE PHONE SYSTEM. All mobile phone in DIGITAL system can be infected by this virus. If you receive a phone call and your phone display "UNAVAILABLE" on the screen (for most of digital mobile phones with a function to display in-coming call telephone number), DON'T ANSWER THE CALL. END THE CALL IMMEDIATELY!!! BECAUSE IF YOU ANSWER THE CALL, YOUR PHONE WILL BE INFECTED BY THIS VIRUS.
>
> This virus will erase all IMIE and IMSI information from both your phone and your SIM card which will make your phone unable to connect with the telephone network. You will have to buy a new phone.
>
> This information has been confirmed by both Motorola and Nokia. For more information, please visit Motorola or Nokia web sites: http://www.mot.comor http://www.nokia.com There are over 3 million mobile phone being infected by this virus in USA now. You can also check this news in CNN web site: http://www.cnn.com
>
> Please forward this information to all your friends who have digital mobile phones.

"MONOPOLY": computer virus

Initially reported in August 1999, this Internet worm operates in a style similar to that of the MELISSA virus, spreading itself via e-mails sent through the Microsoft Outlook system. Whereas Melissa uses the macro language of Microsoft Office, however, "Monopoly" is written in Virtual Basic Script (VBS), its code encrypted to confound analysis. Delivery is accomplished by an e-mail attachment containing a "MONOPOLY.VBS" file, which in turn creates an image file labeled "MONOPOLY.JPG" when it is executed. At the same time, two other files are created, labeled respectively "MONOPOLY.WSH" and "MONOPOLY.VBE." When the MONOPOLY.VBE file is executed, it displays a picture of Microsoft chairman Bill Gates, his face superimposed on a Monopoly game board, with a caption reading: "Bill Gates is guilty of monopoly. Here is the proof."

The Monopoly virus spreads itself by sending out infected e-mails to all addresses listed in the current victim's Outlook address book, each with the attached file "MONOPOLY.VBS." The message reads:

Subject: Bill Gates joke
Text: Bill Gates is guilty of monopoly. Here is the proof. :-)

While the infected e-mails are being dispatched, names and addresses from the latest victim's Outlook address book, along with various personal information gleaned from the newly infected computer—registered user name, country and area code, language, Windows version, etc.—are sent to each of the following Internet addresses:

monopoly@mixmail.com
monpooly@telebot.com
mooponly@ciudad.com.ar
mloponoy@usa.net
yloponom@gnwmail.com

After those messages are sent, Monopoly changes the system registry of the infected computer to read "HKEY_LOCAL_MACHINE\Software\OUT-LOOK.Monopoly\" = "True". Once that has been accomplished, the infected computer is "immunized" against further transmission of confidential information, but the damage is already done.

MOORE, Clarence McKinley: exonerated by DNA evidence

Around 1:20 A.M. on January 14, 1986, a female resident of Somers Point, New Jersey, was wakened in her bed by a stranger who demanded money. The woman—known in court records as "M.A."—produced eight dollars from her purse, but the man

grew angry when she told him she had no more cash. He ordered M.A. to undress, then raped and sodomized her before compelling her to perform oral sex. Finally, preparing to leave, the rapist ordered her to kneel on the bed and "shake her ass" for an alleged accomplice outside her bedroom window. If she failed to comply, the rapist threatened, he would return and kill her. Four hours thus elapsed before M.A. felt safe enough to leave her bed and summon the police.

Authorities noted that M.A.'s description of her attacker was "vague": a man who "may have been black," five feet eight to five feet 11 inches tall, in his late 20s or early 30s, muscular and strong, wearing blue jeans. Initially unable to describe her rapist further, M.A. suggested to police that hypnosis "might help her remember, in more detail, his face." Hypnosis was performed by a clinical psychologist, Dr. Samuel Babcock, whereupon M.A. professed to see the rapist's face "much clearer" in her mind, with "the features . . . more detailed," and recalled that he had worn a tan suede coat with a zipper and dirt stains around one of the pockets. M.A. then collaborated with an artist to prepare a suspect sketch of her short-haired, bearded assailant. "You could tell he was black," she told police, because of his "tough street talk."

Working from M.A.'s description, Somers Point police prepared a photo lineup of possible suspects. They included a mug shot of Clarence Moore because he had a record of felony convictions spanning 18 years. The various charges included carnal abuse (1968), burglary (eight counts in 1970), marijuana trafficking (1976), robbery, and aggravated sexual assault (three counts). If that were not enough, Moore was awaiting trial for sexual assault in nearby Cape May County, suspected of two other rapes in Somers Point. Police were hardly surprised, therefore, when M.A. picked Moore's photo from the lineup she was shown on February 5, 1986.

That identification secured a search warrant for Moore's residence, where officers found several pairs of blue jeans and a suede-front jacket with sleeves, back and collar made of "sweater material." While the jacket failed to match M.A.'s description, it did have some stains on the front. Eight months after the initial photo lineup, on October 9, 1986, M.A. was shown two more sets of pictures, and selected Moore's photo from each set in turn. According to detectives, M.A. told them at that time, "I'm sure that's him. I'll never forget his face. I see it every time I close my eyes." Police collected blood and saliva samples from Moore, for comparison with crime scene evidence, but the results were not helpful. As the lab report declared: "An insufficient amount of high molecular weight human DNA [deoxyribonucleic acid] was isolated from the vaginal swabs, fitted sheet, beige blanket, yellow blanket and the light blue comforter, therefore no comparisons could be made with blood from Clarence Moore."

A pretrial hearing was convened to determine the admissibility of M.A.'s testimony induced by hypnosis, New Jersey law dictating that such testimony is allowable "if the trial court finds that the use of hypnosis in the particular case was reasonably likely to result in recall comparable in accuracy to normal human memory." In Moore's case, the trial judge found (and an appellate court agreed) that use of hypnosis "was appropriate for the victim's fear-induced traumatic neurosis" and that M.A.'s testimony therefore was admissible.

The main issue at Moore's trial, therefore, was the reliability of M.A.'s identification. Her initial statements to police noted that she had only a "very fleeting opportunity" to glimpse the rapist's face while she was "scared to death," her attacker demanding that M.A. keep her eyes closed under fear of death. Furthermore, M.A. said, she had not worn the contact lenses required to correct her myopia, and the rapist's face was "close enough to see, but not in detail." Hypnosis had apparently corrected all those shortcomings, and M.A. once again identified Moore in court. Moore's wife disputed the identification, testifying that they lived 45 minutes away from M.A.'s home, and that Moore could not have left the house for any length of time without her knowledge. She knew this, Cheryl Moore maintained, because a painful breast infection and frequent nursing of a sickly newborn infant kept her awake throughout much of each night.

The prosecutor, in his three-hour summation, told jurors that Mrs. Moore's testimony made the state's case "stronger than ever." Noting that both Moore's wife and M.A. were Caucasian, the prosecutor then sought to explain his reasoning as follows:

Here's where I ask you to really concentrate on my words because if you misunderstand what I'm saying right now, I am going to feel real bad and foolish, and you are too. So let's all understand it like adults.

Race has nothing whatsoever to do with this case, right? Right. We all know that the race of the people involved does not at all dictate whether he's guilty or anything like that. I mean, let's hope that we all feel that way, whether we are white or black or anything. Okay? So let's clear the air that the statement that I'm about to make has nothing whatsoever to do—and I hope this machine hears this—has nothing whatsoever to do with race.

This has to do with selection, okay? Here's what I mean. All of us select people in life to be with based on whatever reason, whether it's people to marry, whether it's friends, whether it's people to associate with, whether it's business people. We all make choices in life that lead us to relationships with others, and those choices may or may not be significant. . . .

Well, that can be seen, can't it, because maybe the people that you choose to date or marry or be with all appear to be blondes or it might be redheads or it might be green hair. You know, nowadays I guess green is one of the popular colors. It could be anything. You could substitute any color hair or you could substitute any particular trait. Right? . . .

You see my point? It's not a statement of race; it's a question of choice, selection of who you might want to be with, whether it is as a mate or a boyfriend or girlfriend or victim. How about that? How about that some people might choose a victim according to the way they look, whether they be blonde or blue or anything else?

So I ask you this: What did we learn when we found out that Cheryl Moore was the wife of the defendant? I suggest to you in a nonracist way that what we found out was that Clarence McKinley Moore made a choice to be with a Caucasian woman. . . .

Moore's lawyer finally objected at that point, calling for a mistrial, and while the judge denied that motion, he instructed jurors to disregard the prosecutor's comments on race as "an unfair and unreasonable inference to be drawn from the testimony and I'm convinced that it's not proper argument to the jury." Thus rebuffed on his racist appeal, the prosecutor tried another tack:

I say to you that there are two other reasons why you should find that the State's case gets stronger with the testimony of Cheryl Moore. We learned that on December 4, 1985, the defendant's wife gives birth to a child. She further tells you that from that time on up until the time he's arrested, she's disabled. I mean, she has bleeding breasts.

I ask you to consider that and infer that that would give believability to the fact that during that period of time, that is, on January 14, 1986, right in the middle of the time after the birth of the child and the disability of the wife, I ask you to infer that that is a period of time when this individual would have his greatest need for sexual release.

Again, Moore's attorney objected, noting the total absence of evidence "to even suggest that [Moore] couldn't have had sexual relations" with his wife during January 1986. The objection was sustained, and jurors were instructed once again to ignore the prosecutor's "improper inference." Undeterred, the prosecutor launched into his third and final argument, telling the jury that "if you don't believe [M.A.] and you think she's lying, then you've probably perpetrated a worse assault on her" than had her rapist. Yet again, the judge commanded jurors to ignore the inappropriate remark, but it was already too late. On March 5, 1987, Clarence Moore was convicted on three counts of aggravated sexual assault, plus one count each of second-degree burglary, second-degree robbery, and robbery with intent to commit aggravated sexual assault. Because his prior convictions classified him as a "persistent offender," Moore was sentenced to life imprisonment, with a 25-year minimum to serve before parole.

Moore appealed his conviction, and while a state appellate court found the prosecutor's "outrageous conduct violated ethical principles" and "showed a disregard of the obligation of a prosecutor to play fair and see that justice is done," still Moore's appeal was rejected on grounds that the judge's "forceful" action had "cured" any harm caused by the prosecutor's misconduct. A second appeal was rejected in 1992, and the New Jersey Supreme Court declined to review Moore's case.

By 1997, Moore had discharged his public defender and received assistance from CENTURION MINISTRIES in pursuing a federal appeal. A U.S. district judge found the prosecutor's conduct "offensive and unprofessional," but declined to overturn the state appellate court's finding that evidence produced at trial supported Moore's conviction. Finally on June 22, 2001, the Third Circuit Court of Appeals reversed Moore's conviction, declaring that the New Jersey trial "was so infected with unfairness that it was constitutionally infirm." A new trial was ordered, with Moore released from Trenton State Prison on July 25. New DNA tests were performed on semen samples gathered from the crime scene, and when these excluded Moore as a suspect in the case, the charges were dismissed.

MORCH, Peter: software thief
A citizen of Canada and Denmark, Peter Morch was employed in 2000 as an engineer with Cisco Systems,

a research and design firm in Petaluma, California. In that capacity, Morch served as a team leader for "Technical Project 1101," described by Cisco spokesmen as "pertaining to voice-over and optical networking." In September and October 2000, shortly before submitting his resignation at Cisco, Morch penetrated the company's computer system and retrieved proprietary information pertaining to various ongoing research projects, "burning" that classified data onto compact disks which Morch took with him to his new job at a competing design firm, Calix Networks in San Francisco. Upon assuming that position, Morch transferred the stolen data to a Calix laptop computer and to the company's computer network.

Cisco employees discovered the theft and reported it to federal authorities, prompting Morch's arrest for theft of trade secrets on November 20, 2000. He faced a maximum sentence of 10 years in prison and a $250,000 fine. Morch appeared in court the following day and was released on $100,000 bond pending a pretrial conference. Four months later, on March 21, 2001, the defendant pleaded guilty on one count of exceeding his authorized access to a protected computer and unlawfully obtaining proprietary information valued at more than $5,000. The plea bargain reduced his maximum sentence to five years' imprisonment and a $250,000 fine.

MORIN, Guy Paul: exonerated by DNA evidence
At 3:45 P.M. on October 3, 1984, nine-year-old Christine Jessop arrived home from school in Queensville, Ontario, a community 40 miles north of Toronto. Moments later, she left on her bicycle to meet a friend at a nearby park, stopping en route to buy gum at a neighborhood convenience store. Christine never reached the park, and in fact was never again seen alive. Three months later, on December 31, 1984, her decomposed remains were found near a rural home site, 30 miles away from Queensville. Autopsy results indicated that Christine was raped, then bludgeoned, drowned, and dismembered after death.

Evidence recovered from the crime scene appeared to confuse inexperienced detectives of the Durham Regional Police who investigated the slaying. Christine was dressed in underwear when found, the underpants stained with semen, but her parents did not recognize a sweater found near the body, and buttons recovered from the dump site failed to match those ripped from Christine's blouse. A single dark hair, recovered from the victim's necklace, may have belonged to her killer.

Authorities still had no suspect six weeks later, when Detectives John Shephard and Bernie Fitzpatrick focused on Christine's next-door neighbor, identified in Fitzpatrick's notes as "Guy Paul Morin, clarinet player, weird type guy." A 24-year-old "eccentric" who preferred beekeeping and jazz records to dating young women, Morin was marked by neighbors as "strange" for his personal habits and peculiar speech patterns. Detectives Shephard and Fitzpatrick secretly recorded an interview with Morin, and while the tape recorder unaccountably "stopped" in the midst of the interrogation, both officers later claimed Morin had made the cryptic (unrecorded) comment that "innocent little girls grow up to be corrupt." Several other suspects were identified in the Queensville vicinity, including three men with records of sexual violence toward children, but police focused on Morin (who had no criminal record) with an intensity that one critic later described as "tunnel vision."

Police obtained a sample of Morin's hair via subterfuge, and laboratory tests pronounced it "consistent" with the hair recovered from Christine Jessop's necklace. (No positive "match" between hairs is scientifically possible.) With no motive in hand, police theorized that Catherine had come home to an empty house and decided to show her musician neighbor the new recorder she had received at school. Morin, they postulated, then impulsively kidnapped and raped her, afterward killing Christine in a fit of rage or panic. An FBI profile of Christine's killer—"a night owl," "solitary," etc.—appeared to match Morin, but he denied any knowledge of the crime, expressing shock when he was charged with the murder. Police reported that carpet fibers from Morin's car were "similar" to several found on Christine's clothing, but again, no positive match could be made. Finally, detectives transferred Morin to a cell wired with microphones, shared by a policeman posing as an inmate. No confession was forthcoming, but Morin once remarked that "no one would ever know" his true relationship to Christine Jessop. Two other inmates subsequently claimed Morin had confessed the slaying in their presence, but efforts to make him repeat the alleged confession on tape were fruitless.

At trial, Morin's attorney revealed a discrepancy in the testimony of Christine Jessop's mother. Janet

Jessop initially told police she arrived home from shopping and a trip to her son Kenny's dentist around 4:10 P.M. on October 3, 1984, by which time Christine had already vanished. Morin's employer, meanwhile, confirmed that Morin left work in Toronto at 3:32 p.m., making it impossible for him to reach home and kidnap Christine before Janet and Kenny returned. Under coaxing from police, Janet Jessop later adjusted her time estimate, stating that she arrived home between 4:30 and 4:40 P.M., thus allowing Morin a few moments within which to kidnap her daughter. Even with the switch, however, the timing was highly suspect, since Morin had returned home with groceries for his family at 5:30 P.M., leaving a maximum time span of 75 minutes for Morin to rape and dismember Christine, complete a 60-mile round trip to the site where her body was dumped, remove all traces of evidence from himself and his vehicle, then finish his grocery shopping and return home. Jurors noted the discrepancy and acquitted Morin of all charges, but his prosecutors appealed that verdict to the Supreme Court of Canada, which ordered a new trial.

Legal delays postponed Morin's second trial until November 1991, by which time Christine's remains had been exhumed for a second autopsy. Amazingly, the new examination revealed gross injuries overlooked in 1985, including a bisected sternum, broken vertebrae, knife-scarred ribs, and a fractured skull (the latter directly contradicting prosecution testimony from 1985). More disturbing still was the volume of "lost" evidence: 150 slides of hair and fiber samples allegedly matched to Morin or his car, shards of plastic found on Christine's clothes, leaves and debris collected at the crime scene, a swatch of carpet and a milk carton found near the body, and so forth—all denied to Morin's defenders. One investigator "lost" his original notes on the case, then "found" a revised set more incriminating toward defendant Morin. The same detective had unaccountably stored various pieces of case evidence at his home and falsified the date on which soil samples were submitted for laboratory analysis (apparently to disguise a 12-month delay in submission of critical evidence).

Morin's attorney sought dismissal of the case on grounds of suppressed evidence, but Judge James Donnelly rejected that motion, instead praising police for their handling of the case thus far. Morin's second trial opened on November 5, 1991, and initially seemed to go well for the defense. Expert witnesses for Morin's side dismissed the hair and fiber evidence as scientifically inconclusive. Police witnesses did poorly under cross-examination, while Kenny Jessop confessed under oath that he and several other boys had repeatedly molested Christine between the ages of five and eight years, thus presenting a bevy of alternative suspects.

Surprisingly, the tide began to turn when Morin's former cellmates took the stand again, repeating their dubious claims that he had confessed the murder in jail. Strangely, where the first trial jury had dismissed these same witnesses as self-serving liars, the new panel found their testimony "very credible." Morin also took the stand in his own defense, but damaged the case with a halting, nervous performance that smacked of evasion, rather than pure innocence. Finally, in a summation heavily biased in favor

of the prosecution, Judge Donnelly urged jurors to accept the most dubious Crown evidence, while ordering the panel to ignore various points scored by the defense. Morin was thereafter convicted and sentenced to life imprisonment, ordered to serve a minimum of 25 years before parole.

Public outcry over the conviction prompted authorities to release Morin on bail, in February 1993, while he pursued his appeal. That hearing was scheduled for January 23, 1995, but it never occurred. Seeking to silence public criticism, prosecutors meanwhile ordered DNA testing on the semen stains from Christine's underwear, the results proving once and for all that Morin had no part in the crime. Charges were finally dismissed on January 22, 1995, and the case remains unsolved today.

Hacker Robert Morris Jr. created one of the earliest-recognized Internet worm viruses while a graduate student at Cornell University. He was later found guilty of violating federal computer tampering laws. (AP)

MORLEY, Christian: software pirate

A resident of Salem, Massachusetts, born April 13, 1973, Christian Morley was one of 17 defendants indicted by U.S. authorities for software piracy on May 4, 2000. Prosecutors identified Morley as a member of the HACKERS' syndicate dubbed "PIRATES WITH ATTITUDE," an affiliation shared with 11 of his fellow defendants. The other five indicted were employees of Intel Corporation, who collaborated in counterfeiting and selling bootleg software valued in excess of $1 million.

Eight of his codefendants struck plea bargains with the prosecution to reduce their punishment, but Morley preferred to take his luck at trial. Presentation of the evidence against Morley consumed a week, but jurors needed only 30 minutes to convict him of conspiracy, on May 11, 2001. Assistant U.S. Attorney James Conway chaired the prosecution, afterward telling reporters, "The trial demonstrated law enforcement's commitment to prosecute software piracy cases and the FBI's ability to successfully investigate sophisticated on-line activity."

MORRIS, Robert Tappan, Jr.: hacker "rtm"

The son of a National Security Agency scientist who once brought home an original "Enigma" decoding device and kept it as a conversation piece, Robert Morris Jr. was a 23-year-old graduate student at Cornell University in 1988, when he "accidentally" unleashed one of the earliest recognized Internet worm viruses. Launched on November 2, 1988, the "Morris worm" was reportedly designed to spread without damaging infected host computers, but bugs in the code permitted multiple infections of each computer affected, finally slowing the system down to a point where it ceased to function. Only computers using Unix were affected, but the worm still crashed some 6,000 host machines, prompting some whimsical hackers to call it the "Great Worm" (after massive dragons mentioned in the fantasy novels of J. R. R. Tolkein). Spokesmen for the U.S. General Accounting Office vaguely estimated the worm's total damage at between $10 million and $100 million, perhaps indicating that they had no real idea of its scope or final effect on the Internet. Morris was tried and convicted of violating the 1986 Computer Fraud and Abuse Act, ultimately sentenced to three years' probation, 400 hours of community service and a $10,000 fine.

MOU, Jing Jing Fan: software pirate

A 40-year-old resident of Plano, Texas, Jing Jing Mou was indicted by a federal grand jury on May 11, 2000, charged with six counts of trafficking in counterfeit Microsoft software. The indictment was filed in Los Angeles, where Mou initially pleaded innocent and was released on $50,000 bond. According to the charges filed, Mou purchased counterfeit software from a foreign manufacturer, Aventec, for shipment to an unnamed coconspirator employed by Velocity Computers in Cincinnati, Ohio. From there, the bootleg software—valued at some $18 million—was sold to retail customers. The indictment charged Mou with one count of conspiracy, two counts of trafficking in counterfeit goods, and three counts of money laundering, for a maximum prison term of 85 years if she was convicted.

Four months after her indictment, on September 25, 2000, Mou struck a bargain with prosecutors and pleaded guilty on two of the six counts filed against her (conspiracy and one count of trafficking in stolen goods valued above $600,000). The plea bargain reduced her prison time to a maximum of 25 years.

"MYSTERY": computer virus

Reported for the first time in August 2000, "Mystery" is a memory-resident, parasitic virus that replicates by infecting executable files as they are run. During infection, the virus writes itself to the "file Fixup" section, but a bug exists in the infection routine, causing some files to produce a standard Windows error message when they are attacked. At midnight, if the host computer is in use, Mystery opens and closes the CD-ROM drive and displays the following message on-screen:

Mystery by Prudentor
You are infected with Mystery! ;-)
Nothing will be killed, keep cool.

Mystery remains memory-resident by infecting the EXPLORER.EXE file on its first startup, afterward operating in the background, searching for active files, and infecting them as well.

"NADO": computer viruses

Initially reported from the Internet in June 1996 and traced to Denmark, the "Nado" family of viruses now includes at least eight variants, all but two ranked by analysts as "very dangerous," memory-resident, encrypted, parasitic viruses. All versions apparently write themselves to the ends of executed files, and some contain a bug that may corrupt files while infecting them. Nado typically creates an APRILFIRST.BAT file on the host computer's GetDisk-Space DOS registry, with a message reading: "@echo April Fool—1996—if u run this batch file your HDD will burn!" When the A drive is selected, Nado checks the system time, and if the minute count exceeds 54 it also displays the following message:

> April 1st . . . i will now kill your HardDisk

The variant forms of this virus include "Nado. Cyberbug," "Nado.Fatill," "Nado.Lover.531," "Nado.Lover.602," "Nado.Rabin," "Nado.Red-Viper.584," "Nado.RedViper.602," and "Nado. RedZar." Some of their characteristics are listed below.

Nado.Cyberbug is an encrypted virus that erases various disk sectors, determined by the host system's time display. It includes the text strings—

> *"Nado.CyberBug":*
> echo > clock[CyberBug v. 1.00]

> [made by TorNado DK]
> Cyberbug.bat

Nado.Fatill is a polymorphic encrypted virus that deletes various antivirus scanners from the host system, including F-PROT, SCAN, TBAV, and VSHIELD. It contains the text strings—

> *"Nado.Fatill":*
> [Fatal-Illusion (c) made by TorNado in Denmark '95]
> [NaE]
> echo > clock$
> Fatill10.bat

Nado.Lover.531 is rated "harmless" by computer analysts and apparently does not manifest itself in any way.

Nado.Lover.602 by contrast is a "very danger-ous" virus that infects keyboard command pro-grams, overwriting the computer's disk boot sectors with the string "[Undying Lover v1.01] [byWarB1aDE/DC '96]" and rebooting the computer each time the "Delete" key is pressed.

Nado.Rabin infects executed .com files and writes new file attributes, while also deleting the ANTI-VIR.DAT file (if found). On the third of each month, Nado.Rabin erases the Master Boot Record (MBR) from its host's hard drive, overwriting it with a text string reading—

[Yitzhak-Rabin 1.00 (c) made by TorNado in Denmark '96]

Nado.RedViper.584 and *Nado.RedViper.602* present no manifestations, but they infect executed files and frequently corrupt them in the process, thus earning their "very dangerous" rating. These variants contain the following text strings:

"*RedViper.584*": *[RedViper (c) made by TorNado in Denmark '95]*
"*RedViper.602*": *[RedViper 1.5 (c) made by Tor Nado/[DC] in Denmark '95]*

Nado.RedZar is a "harmless" encrypted virus that infects .com and .exe files as they are executed. It contains a text string reading: "*[RedZar v. 2.00 (c) made by TorNado/DC in Denmark 1996].*"

"NAKED": computer worm

Logged for the first time in March 2001, this Internet worm spreads via infected e-mail messages dispatched from the computers it invades, following a common pattern among viruses by raiding the new victim's Microsoft Outlook address book for targets. Activated when a recipient clicks on the infected message, "Naked" also deletes all .bmp, .com, .dll, .exe, .ini, and .log files from the host computer's Windows directories. As a "direct action" virus, however, Naked does not install itself as memory-resident in the computers it attacks.

When it is run, Naked displays on-screen a window labeled "Macromedia Flash Player," with a message that reads "Loading, Loading, Loading" in an endless string. Various menu buttons displayed in the bogus window are inert, except for the "Help" button. When that button is clicked, the monitor displays a window labeled "About Macromedia Flash 5 . . .," and if that in turn is clicked, the following message appears:

Flash
You're are now FUCKED! (C) 2001 by BGK
(Bill Gates Killer)
[OK]

Naked transmits itself via e-mail messages with an attached .exe file containing the worm itself. The message reads:

Attached file-name: NakedWife.exe
The Subject: Fw: Naked Wife
Message body: My wife never look like that! ;-)

Best Regards,
<UserName>

When activated by the new recipient, Naked opens MS Outlook, retrieves all addresses found in the address book, and sends duplicate messages to each (signing the new host's user name). Prurient interest does the rest, keeping this worm alive and well in cyberspace.

"NAMELESS": computer virus

Apparently launched from Russia, "Nameless" was initially reported from the Internet in July 1996. Analysts describe it as a "very dangerous," memory-resident, encrypted parasitic virus that searches for .com and .exe files, writing itself to the beginning of each such file discovered, increasing the size of each infected file to a minimum of 8,000 bytes. Depending on the host system's time and internal counters, Nameless also corrupts randomly selected sectors of the computer's hard disk. Finally, it erases various disk sectors entirely and displays a backwards-running counter of the erased sectors. Nameless contains Russian text strings, as well as the following text in English:

ABCDEFGHabcdefghCOMMAND
Nameless virus v.2.0
U my last hope . . . Please . . .
*.COM *.EXE

"NAUGHTYROBOT" Warning: Internet hoax

Circulated for the first time in 2000, "NaughtyRobot" warnings are periodically dispatched to various website administrators, with e-mail headers forged to disguise the source. Gullible recipients risk embarrassment and worse if they follow directions included in the scare message. Investigators from the HOAXBUSTERS site attribute all the mailings to a single unidentified source, but that claim is presently impossible to validate. The typical (spurious) warning message reads as follows:

Subject: security breached by NaughtyRobot

This message was sent to you by NaughtyRobot, an Internet spider that crawls into your server through a tiny hole in the World Wide Web.

NaughtyRobot exploits a security bug in HTTP and has visited your host system to collect personal, private and sensitive information.

It has captured your Email and physical addresses, a well as your phone and credit card numbers. To protect yourself against the misuse of this information, do the following:

1. *alert your server SysOp,*
2. *contact your local police,*
3. *disconnect your telephone, and*
4. *report your credit cards as lost.*

Act at once. Remember: only YOU can prevent DATA fires.

This has been a public service announcement from the makers of NaughtyRobot—CarJacking its way onto the Information SuperHighway.

"NAVIDAD": computer worm

Initially reported in January 2001, "Navidad" ("Christmas," in Spanish) is an Internet worm spread via e-mails using MAPI Outlook. It arrives as an e-mail attachment titled navidad.exe. When activated, Navidad copies itself to the Windows system directory and disables the winsvrc.vxd file, required to run various .exe files. When the victim-user tries to run those files, the monitor displays instead a message reading: "Windows cannot find WINSVRC .VXD."

Navidad also disables the host computer's regedit.exe utility, normally used to recover the registry, a problem users may overcome by renaming the infected utility regedit.com. Navidad displays a blue-eye icon in the host computer's system tray, which displays the following message if selected:

Nunca presionar este boton
Feliz Navidad
Lamentablemente cayo en la tentacion y perdio su computadora
    [OK]

NEEDLE Warnings: Internet hoaxes

There are times when the Internet seems custom-made for malicious practical jokers. In the age of AIDS and other virulent diseases, it is all too easy to incite panic via circulation of such "jokes" or urban myths. The following bogus warnings, all variations on a common theme, remain in circulation on the Web today. They read (with errors uncorrected):

Needles on Theater Seats   (May 1999)

For your information, a couple of weeks ago, in a Dallas movie theater, a person sat on something sharp in one of the seats. When she stood up to see what it was, a needle was found poking through the seat with an attached note saying, "you have been infected with HIV". The Centers for Disease Control in Atlanta reports similar events have taken place in several other cities recently. All of the needles tested HAVE been found positive for HIV. The CDC also reports that needles have been found in the coin return areas of pay phones and soda machines. Everyone is asked to use extreme caution when confronted with these types of situations. All public chairs should be thoroughly but safely inspected prior to any use. A thorough visual inspection is conssidered the bare minimum. Further more, they ask that everyone notify their family members and friends of the potential dangers, as well. Thank you. The previous information was sent from the Dallas Police Department to all of the local governments in the Washington area and was interdepartmentally dispersed. We were all asked to pass this to as many people as possible.

Needles in the ball pit   (December 1999)

Hi, My name is Lauren Archer, my son Kevin and I lived in Sugarland, TX. On October 2cd, 1994 I took my only son to McDonald's for his 3rd birthday. After he finished lunch, I allowed him to play in the ball pit. When he started whining later on, I asked him what was wrong, he pointed to the back of his pull-up and simply said "Mommy, it hurts."

But I couldn't find anything wrong with him at that time. I bathed him when we got home, and it was at that point when I found a welt on his left buttock. Upon investigating, it seemed as if there was something like a splinter under the welt. I made an appointment to have it taken out the next day, but soon he started vomiting and shaking, then his eyes rolled back into his head. From there, we went to the emergency room.

He died later that night. It turned out that the welt on his buttock was the tip of a hypodermic needle that had broken off inside.

The autopsy revealed that Kevin had died from heroine overdose. The next week, the police removed the balls from the ball pit and lo and behold. There was rotten food, several hypodermic needles: some full; some used; knives, half-eaten candy, diapers, feces, and the stench of urine. If a child is not safe in a child's play area then where?

You can find the article on Kevin Archer in the October 10, 1994 issue of the Houston Chronicle. Please forward this to all loving mothers!

Needles on Gas Pump Handles (June 2000)

*********** DANGEROUS PRANK: ***********

Please read and forward to anyone you know who drives.

My name is Captain Abraham Sands of the Jacksonville, Florida Police Department. I have been asked by state and local authorities to write this email in order to get the word out to car drivers of a very dangerous prank that is occurring in numerous states. Some person or persons have been affixing hypodermic needles to the underside of gas pump handles. These needles appear to be infected with HIV positive blood. In the Jacksonville area alone there have been 17 cases of people being stuck by these needles over the past five months. We have verified reports of at least 12 others in various states around the country. It is believed that these may be copycat incidents due to someone reading about the crimes or seeing them reported on the television. At this point no one has been arrested and catching the perpetrator(s) has become our top priority.

Shockingly, of the 17 people who where stuck, eight have tested HIV positive and because of the nature of the disease, the others could test positive in a couple years. Evidently the consumers go to fill their car with gas, and when picking up the pump handle get stuck with the infected needle.

IT IS IMPERATIVE TO CAREFULLY CHECK THE HANDLE of the gas pump each time you use one. LOOK AT EVERY SURFACE YOUR HAND MAY TOUCH, INCLUDING UNDER THE HANDLE. If you do find a needle affixed to one, immediately contact your local police department so they can collect the evidence.

***********PLEASE HELP US BY MAINTAINING A VIGILANCE AND BY FORWARDING THIS EMAIL TO ANYONE YOU KNOW WHO DRIVES. THE MORE PEOPLE WHO KNOW OF THIS THE BETTER PROTECTED WE CAN ALL BE.

Investigators note that no such incidents have been reported from any state, and that no article involving an accidental "heroine" overdose appeared in the *Houston Chronicle* of October 10, 1994 (or any other date).

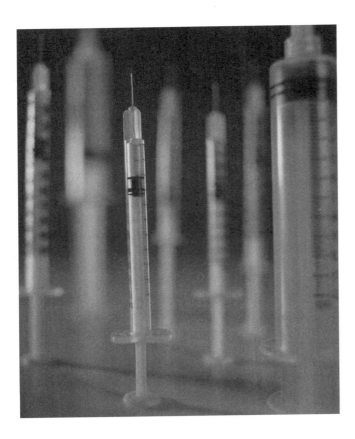

NELSON, Bruce: exonerated by DNA evidence

Another case of false accusation belatedly resolved by science comes from Allegheny County, Pennsylvania, where Bruce Nelson was accused of rape and murder in 1980. According to Terrence Moore, Nelson's alleged accomplice and sole living witness, the crime began when Moore and Nelson stole a van and drove it to a Pittsburgh parking garage, in hopes of using it to commit a robbery. In the garage, they allegedly kidnapped a woman and forced her into the van, raping her repeatedly at knifepoint before they strangled her to death with a piece of cloth. Moore was subsequently arrested and admitted his role in the slaying, but he named Bruce Nelson as the instigator and their victim's actual slayer.

Nelson was by then imprisoned on another, unrelated charge. Authorities indicted him for the rape-murder and police arranged a confrontation with Moore. At that meeting, Nelson reportedly asked Moore, "What did you tell them?" Moore allegedly replied, "I told them everything." Nelson denied any part in the crime, but prosecutors introduced his question—"What did you tell them?"—as a "confession" when he faced trial in 1982. Other evidence included Moore's fingerprints, allegedly found on the victim's purse, plus saliva "consistent" with Nelson's, found on the victim's breast, brassiere, and a cigarette butt from the crime scene. Jurors convicted Nelson of rape and murder, whereupon he received a life sentence with a concurrent 10-to-20-year prison term on the lesser charge.

Nelson's initial appeal was a *habeas corpus* petition, asserting that use of his so-called "confession" to Moore violated Nelson's Fifth Amendment right to stand silent during interrogation and his Sixth Amendment right to have counsel present during questioning. The district court rejected his petition and the Pennsylvania Supreme Court refused to review Nelson's case. On August 17, 1990, the Third Circuit Court of Appeals affirmed the state's ruling on Nelson's Sixth Amendment plea, but it overturned the Fifth Amendment ruling and remanded the case for further review by the state district court. By that time, DNA testing procedures had been discovered and recognized as evidence in court, permitting Nelson's attorney to test the saliva samples used as evidence at trial. The test excluded Nelson as a source of the saliva and his charges were dismissed on August 28, 1991.

NETSCAPE-AOL Giveaway: Internet hoax

Initially reported in May 1999, this Internet hoax provides a variation on the earlier BILL GATES chain letter fraud. Once again, a nonexistent e-mail tracking device is purportedly being tested, with money in store for those who participate in a mythical test. The original message reads:

> *Netscape and AOL have recently merged to form the largest internet company in the world. In an effort to remain at pace with this giant, Microsoft has introduced a new email tracking system as a way to keep Internet Explorer as the most popular browser on the market. This email is a beta test of the new software and Microsoft has generously offered to compensate those who participate in the testing process. For each person you send this email to, you will be given $5. For every person they give it to, you will be given an additional $3. For every person they send it to you will receive $1. Microsoft will tally all the emails produced under your name over a two week period and then*

> *email you with more instructions. This beta test is only for Microsoft Windows users because the email tracking device that contacts Microsoft is embedded into the code of Windows 95 and 98.*

> *I know you guys hate forwards. But I started this a month ago because I was very short on cash. A week ago I got an email from Microsoft asking me for my address. I gave it to them and yesterday I got a check in the mail for $800. It really works. I wanted you to get a piece of the action. You won't regret it.*

NGO, Thanh Thien: videocassette pirate

Beginning in September 1997, 41-year-old Thanh Thien Ngo ran a shop called Thuy Hang Video and Gifts in West Valley City, a suburb of Salt Lake City, Utah. As part of his stock, Ngo rented Asian-language videotapes, including various motion pictures whose labels bore the trademark of a registered distributor, Tai Seng Video Marketing. Unknown to the majority of Ngo's customers, however, the tapes were bootleg copies that he dubbed himself, then tagged with counterfeit labels to make them seem legitimate.

Representatives of Tai Seng Video Marketing discovered Ngo's operation in January 1998, and their legal department sent him a cease-and-desist letter, to no effect. Tai Seng next contacted authorities, who searched the Thuy Hang shop in March 1998, confiscating some 13,380 bootleg videotapes. Still undeterred, in April 1999 Ngo recruited two accomplices, Duc Nguyen and Phuong Kim Vo, to front a new operation in nearby Taylorsville, Utah. The terms of their transaction are murky: Nguyen and Vo reportedly purchased Ngo's remaining inventory of videotapes and equipment for themselves for $2,000, but they named their shop for him—Thien Thanh Video-Gift-Music—and Ngo helped them set up VCRs in a back room for illegal dubbing of prerecorded tapes. Ngo also reportedly "helped" with operation of the store until August 1999, when authorities staged another raid and seized 4,540 counterfeit videotapes. Of the 17,920 videocassettes seized in both raids, 8,960 bore counterfeit Tai Seng trademarks.

Nguyen and Vo each pleaded guilty to one count of misdemeanor copyright infringement in August 2000. Three months later, they received identical sentences of 36 months under supervised probation. Ngo, for his part, was indicted on multiple counts in April 2001. As U.S. Attorney Paul Warner explained the case to reporters, "The defendant piled illegality upon illegality. In other words, it isn't just like someone stitching a counterfeit Olympic logo onto a T-shirt. In this case, it is as if he were selling counterfeit Olympic shirts by stitching a counterfeit logo onto shirts that he himself had previously stolen."

Ngo cut a deal with prosecutors and pleaded guilty on May 10, 2001 to one charge of trafficking in counterfeit goods. As part of that agreement, he also admitted encouraging others to counterfeit videotapes in full knowledge that the action was illegal. Two months later, on July 17, 2001, U.S. District Judge David Sam sentenced Ngo to 10 months in prison and fined him $500. Ngo was ordered to surrender and begin serving his sentence on August 7, 2001.

In the wake of Ngo's guilty plea, U.S. Attorney Warner told the press, "Prosecuting intellectual property crime is an important part of safeguarding the foundation of the global economy in today's information age. The copyrighted motion pictures at issue in this case that were produced abroad have received vigorous protection by American law enforcement, just as American-produced motion pictures and other intellectual property deserve protection worldwide. The court's sentence accurately reflects the seriousness of the harm caused by Mr. Ngo through his repeated and undeterred counterfeiting and piracy activities. He willfully infringed on the intellectual property rights of others, despite repeated notice that the conduct was wrong and the victim objected. This case sends a clear message to others who may be tempted to engage in intellectual property theft. These federal laws will be vigorously enforced."

NONLETHAL Weapons

While the primary goal of armed combat remains the permanent incapacitation of enemies, many other situations involving military or law enforcement personnel demand weapons and tactics that do not result in loss of human life or crippling injury. Prevailing laws in the U.S. likewise restrict civilian ownership or use of deadly weapons and may dictate resort to nonlethal means of self-defense, particularly in a public setting. Whether fending off a solitary mugger on the street, defusing a volatile hostage situation, controlling prison inmates, or dispersing riotous protesters, alternative methods are needed in situations where use of deadly force is counterproductive or prohibited by law.

Nonlethal weapons, in the broadest terms, are any instruments designed for use in combat situations which do not *predictably* result in death. There are occasional exceptions to the rule, of course: asthmatics and the like may suffocate under prolonged exposure to nonlethal gas; electric stun guns may interfere with pacemakers; "flash-bang" concussion grenades might induce a heart attack or cause a subject to fall down with fatal results; rubber bullets and other "baton" rounds may kill in rare cases, if they strike a target's skull or chest with sufficient force. In general, though, nonlethal weapons are not expected to kill.

That said, there is still room for heated debate over the types, the proper design, and the use of nonlethal weapons, and that debate continues from corporate boardrooms to the Internet. Some critics stand aghast at the prospect of fielding "worse than lethal" weapons, namely those that leave their victims alive but physically or psychologically maimed (as in blinding with lasers, or scarring flesh and lungs with caustic gas). For purposes of this essay, "nonlethal" weapons are presumed to be those that neither kill nor permanently injure when used as intended, against reasonably healthy targets.

In that context, nonlethal weapons are available in many forms. Their usefulness likewise varies, arising in situations where the law forbids use of deadly force, where hostages or innocent bystanders are at equal risk with the intended targets, or when use of deadly force (though legally excused) may only make a volatile situation that much worse. With those limitations in mind, nonlethal weapons fall into several broad categories, including:

1. *Hand-held impact weapons.* The options here include a variety of clubs, flails, blackjacks, and similar weapons. Most U.S. jurisdictions limit a civilian's right to carry such instruments, and mere possession of some (brass knuckles, for example) may be criminal in itself. Law enforcement officers make extensive use of clubs and batons, but their employment is sometimes inflammatory, and they have little value against large groups of adversaries.

2. *Non-penetrating projectiles.* Typically launched from special guns, the various wooden or rubber bullets, bean-bag projectiles, and so forth deliver a painful or stunning blow at long range, thereby keeping safe distance between combatants. Some concussion grenades also discharge hard-rubber pellets as "stingers," for use in confined spaces. As with clubs, above, most U.S. jurisdictions limit ownership of these devices to police or military personnel.

3. *High-pressure liquids.* Although southern police were reviled for turning fire hoses against civil rights protesters in the 1960s, high-pressure

The Advanced M-26 model TASER gun. (AP)

hoses and "water cannons" remain a fixture of many police and military riot squads. Mounted on trucks or armored vehicles, they have seen frequent use against rowdy mobs in Europe and Asia. Serious injury may result in some cases, due to falls or violent impact with solid objects, but normal damage is limited to drenching and occasional bruises.

4. *Sprays and gases.* Great advances have been made in this field from the early days of bulky tear gas canisters (which still sometimes grow hot enough to set a house on fire). Today a wide variety of nonlethal gases and chemical sprays are available to law enforcement and military personnel. Most are designed to irritate a subject's eyes and/or respiratory system, producing disorientation, temporary blindness, and occasional nausea or unconsciousness. Most U.S.

jurisdictions permit civilian ownership of milder forms, in small amounts (Chemical Mace, and so forth). Some states require a rudimentary training course before civilians are authorized to purchase and carry such weapons.

5. *Electric stun guns.* These weapons operate by transmitting a nonlethal electric charge through the target's body, creating electronic "riffles" that disrupt synaptic pathways and result in temporary incapacitation. High on voltage but low on amperage, they are not designed to kill even with prolonged contact, but they may produce small contact burns. Physical contact with the target is required for all such weapons. Many require the stun gun itself to be pressed against an assailant's body, while others (like the Taser) fire barbed darts with slender wires attached to complete the circuit from a distance.

Stun guns are widely available in the United States by mail order and on the Internet, but purchasers should consult their local statutes to avoid placing themselves in violation of the law.

6. *Optical weapons.* As suggested by the title, these weapons interfere with vision, in order to confuse, disorient, or temporarily incapacitate the subjects. "Flash-bang" grenades produce a blinding burst of light, coupled with a concussive shock wave, to stun their targets. (Some, as noted above, also contain rubber "shrapnel" to add an element of pain without serious physical injury.) Pulsing strobe lights use the same principle to disrupt vision. Low-energy lasers may produce temporary blindness, and military technicians have reportedly studied lasers that would make the damage permanent. Obscurants, such as smoke in varied colors, can be used to disorient crowds or individuals, while masking the approach of troops or law enforcement officers.

7. *Acoustic weapons.* As with a subject's eyes, the ears may be assaulted in various ways without inflicting permanent harm. Loud music or similar sound effects are sometimes used as a means of psychological warfare, as when American troops played blaring rock-and-roll outside the besieged headquarters of Manuel Noriega, during the most recent U.S. invasion of Panama. Concussion grenades are designed to stun their targets with a thunderclap of sound. Various levels of either high- or low-pitched sound may be used to disperse crowds. Infrasound broadcasts (the nonlinear superposition of two ultrasound beams) are said to produce "intolerable sensations" including disorientation, nausea and vomiting, and involuntary defecation.

8. *Chemical weapons.* A number of tools are available here, treated separately from the sprays and gases described above. Adhesive agents include a variety of sticky, quick-drying polymer foams that can only be removed with special solvents. Chemical "barriers" consist of dense, rapidly expanding foam or bubbles that inhibit movement and obscure vision, sometimes producing foul odors and/or using dyes to mark subjects for later apprehension. Calmative agents include various sedatives, while hallucinogens confuse and disorient their targets. Lubricants, ranging from simple oil slicks to agents that turn dirt into slippery "chemical mud," impede both

attackers and subjects trying to escape. Taggants, while not technically weapons, employ chemical dyes to identify subjects (as in the explosive dye packs sometimes used to foil bank robberies).

9. *Biological weapons.* Various living organisms, including germs, bacteria, and viruses, have been used as weapons for centuries. Most of those stockpiled or custom-designed by military scientists are lethal, but countless others also exist that cause discomfort, disorientation, or temporary incapacitation without killing their victims. Rumors also persist of military experimentation with various biodeteriorative microbes—i.e., those that devour, break down, or otherwise compromise various inanimate substances, including rubber, metal, concrete, and/or petroleum products. The obvious drawback with any such agent is its relatively slow reaction time, making it a poor choice for use in short-term emergencies. The deteriorants, furthermore, would impartially attack both "friendly" and "hostile" property if carelessly dispensed.

10. *"Entanglement munitions."* Rarely used today, and having no significant value against crowds, this category involved use of nets or similar objects to snare and subdue targets. As implied by the title, the nets are fired from various specialized guns, unfurling in midair to drop over the subject. Nets may also be hand-thrown, laid as snares, or dropped from aircraft, but they would not then be described as "munitions."

Increasing emphasis on human rights throughout society and the world at large, though often honored more in the breach than by observance, will doubtless fuel new research into modes and methods of nonlethal combat. It remains to be seen whether their development and use will decrease violent conflict or cause explosive confrontations to proliferate, as fear of death or maiming injury decreases.

NORTHWESTERN University Center on Wrongful Convictions

Operating in conjunction with the CARDOZO INNOCENCE PROJECT and similar groups around the U.S., the Center on Wrongful Convictions declares itself "dedicated to identifying and rectifying wrongful convictions and other serious miscarriages of justice." Center faculty, staff and collaborating attorneys in private practice investigate cases of alleged wrongful prosecution and provide free legal representation to inmates whose cases include one or more of the following elements:

1. A claim of actual innocence—i.e., a defendant who had no involvement whatsoever in the crime(s) of which he stands convicted, as opposed to cases resting on procedural irregularities or some abusive process used to convict a suspect who is nonetheless guilty as charged.
2. DNA cases, wherein the claim of innocence is scientifically supported by testable biological evidence.
3. For cases not involving DNA, a minimum of 10 years remaining to be served on the defendant's

Scholars confirmed that prophet Nostradamus never wrote anything remotely resembling the text in an e-mail circulated during the 24 hours following the September 11 attacks. (Chris Hellier/CORBIS)

original sentence. (This requirement presumably would be moot in capital cases, where no prison term is specified.)

Prison inmates whose cases meet those criteria are invited to submit inquiries at the following address:

Center on Wrongful Convictions
Northwestern University School of Law
357 East Chicago Avenue
Chicago, Illinois 60611

"NOSTRADAMUS": computer viruses

Reported in two variations since April 1999, "Nostradamus" is a stealth macro virus written in Italian. Both versions contain three macros—AutoOpen, MacroOnFile and StrumMacro—while "Nostradamus.b" also contains a fourth: FileModelli. Nostradamus infects the Microsoft Word normal.dot file's global macros and thereafter writes itself into various saved documents. On the 31st of any month it displays the following message on-screen:

NOSTRADAMUS Virus
Barbaro impero dal terzo sarai soggiogato,
Gran parte d'individui della sua origine far perire:
Per decesso senile avverr la sua fine, il quarto colpir
Per timore che il sangue con il sangue morte ne derivi.
Centuria 3., LIX

NOSTRADAMUS Prophecy: Internet hoax

Circulated within 24 hours of the terrorist attacks on September 11, 2001, this strange offering from yet another anonymous fraud pretends to relay a Nostradamus prophecy predicting the attacks. Students of the ancient seer and his works confirm that nothing even remotely resembling this message is found anywhere in the works of Nostradamus. The fraudulent message reads (errors uncorrected):

"In the City of God there will be a great thunder, two brothers torn apart by chaos, while the fortress endures, the great leader will succumb. The third big war will begin when the big city is burning on the 11th day of the 9 month that . . . two metalbirds would crash into two tall statues in the new city and the world will end soon after"—Nostradamus 1654—

The flights that were Highjacked were from United and AA, they were numbered as follows:

11, 93, 175, and 77
11 = Today's Date
9+3 = 12 = Tomorrow
1+7+5 = 13 = Thursday
7+7 = 14 = Friday

Hopefully this is a coincidence and the terrorists can't add. but if this is correct there will either be acts of terrorism every day for the next few days or a grand event the last day. pass it around.

"NOT a Joke" Virus Warning: Internet hoax

Seen on the Internet periodically since 1999, this warning of an alleged virus is, in fact, a hoax. No such virus is known to exist at present. The original message reads (with errors intact):

****

IM SORRY GUYS>>I REALLY DONT BELIEVE IT BUT SENDING IT TO YALL JUST IN CASE!!!!!!!!!!!

This is not a joke . . . if you do not forward this e-mail to 20 other people . . . your computer will be a living hell thanks to one of our very own little ingenus viruses. I repeat this is not a joke this virus will come to you only a week after you open this piece of mail in a very undiscreet e-mail If you open this e-mail after opening others, it just might come as a letter from your "buddy" Watch out! You have one week . . . starting now. If this virus gets in it won't come back out. It will slowly delete 1 file a day from system IRQ files, startup files and win 95 kernels for registery address {1593338-489h985}

Thank you for your time. . . . #:) hahahahaha SCREW YOU!!!

****

NUCLEAR Emergency Search Team

It sounds like the plot from any one of several dozen thrillers, from Ian Fleming's *Thunderball* to James Cameron's *True Lies* and Tom Clancy's *The Sum of All Fears*. In 1974 an extortionist threatened to destroy Boston with an improvised nuclear bomb if government officials did not pay a rather modest $200,000 ransom. To encourage prompt payment, the terrorist provided diagrams that appeared to be authentic. State and federal authorities had no response plan in place for such an emergency, so they delivered the cash as ordered—but Mr. X never picked up his payoff. He remains unidentified today, and his weapon of mass destruction—if in fact it ever existed—has never been found.

That near-miss (or cruel hoax) prompted U.S. officials to create a new swift-response team to cope with future emergencies. Dubbed the Nuclear Emergency Search Team (NEST), it is comprised of more than 1,000 volunteer scientists, engineers, and technicians employed at America's nuclear laboratories and regulatory agencies, collaborating in deployment with the U.S. Army's 52nd Ordnance Group (specialized in disarming nuclear weapons). NEST regional headquarters are located at Nellis Air Force Base (outside Las Vegas, Nevada) and at Andrews Air Force Base (near Washington, D.C.).

While its existence has been publicly acknowledged since 1975, NEST operates for the most part behind a screen of secrecy. Its members are reported to have trained in emergency-response procedures with police and fire departments from New York City, Chicago, Los Angeles, San Francisco, and other large cities, but confirmation remains elusive, with details closely guarded by the Departments of Defense and Energy (controlling nuclear materials). It is known that NEST nuke-hunters employ sophisticated laptop computers (like those reported missing from the Los Alamos Nuclear Weapons Laboratory in May 2000) to detect weapons and determine their probable source via analysis of their design and materials used in construction. Other NEST tools include portable X-ray machines, sophisticated robots used to search dangerous areas, various state-of-the-art radiation detectors, and special nonmagnetic cutting tools to breach a weapon's outer shell. In their laboratories, a rotating staff of 15 to 20 NEST scientists practice constructing crude nuclear weapons with readily available technology, preparing themselves for the day when they may face such a bomb constructed by others.

In the event of a nuclear threat, NEST's reaction proceeds through seven clearly defined phases. They include:

1. *Intelligence collection.* NEST draws information from the FBI, CIA, and other agencies, collated and evaluated at the Department of Energy's (DOE) Nonproliferation Program at Lawrence

Livermore National Laboratory (LLNL) in Livermore, California. Threats are reported by outside agencies and assessed by the DOE's Office of Emergency Response.

2. *Standby alert.* Receipt of a threat activates an Operational Emergency Management Team (OEMT), essentially alerting all NEST members to prepare for action.

3. *Credibility assessment.* Any available data (such as the Boston extortionist's diagrams) is processed through LLNL's exhaustive computer database (containing "every last published word" about nuclear weapons). If the threat is deemed credible, NEST deployment proceeds to the next phase.

4. *Searching for the weapon.* NEST nuke-hunters deploy with members of the FBI's Hostage Rescue Team and/or military personnel from various elite "special mission" units. Sophisticated scanning gear is used to detect either gamma or neutron radiation. If a specific facility is threatened, the search may proceed on foot. Otherwise, roving teams may operate from land vehicles, boats, or aircraft with a variety of larger scanners. (NEST maintains its own air force and volunteer pilots, as well as specialized armored vehicles.) Within an urban setting, false alarms may be triggered by a wide variety of common objects, including medical X-ray machines and security devices, pacemakers, fresh asphalt, the dye that colors certain tiles, and even the granite used in some civic monuments. If a weapon is found, the next phase proceeds.

5. *Recovery.* Any and all necessary force may be employed to retrieve nuclear weapons before they are detonated. Killing the offenders without warning may be authorized.

6. *Ordnance disposal.* When any human threat has been neutralized, special diagnostic and assessment teams examine the suspect device. Deactivation takes priority. Proposed methods range from manual disarmament (by human hands or high-tech robots) to disabling portions of the bomb with pinpoint gunfire. Liquid nitrogen or other freezing agents may be introduced to render the mechanism inoperative. Radiation dispersal devices, consisting of a 35-foot nylon tent filled with thick, quick-drying foam may contain the threat from a ruptured canister, but they have not been tested with an actual nuclear bomb. Should these efforts fail, survivors are left to cope with the last phase of the process.

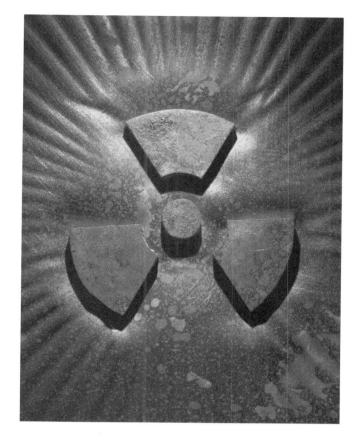

7. *Consequence management.* NEST has no direct responsibility for disaster relief, and its volunteer members have no particular expertise in this area. Given the secrecy surrounding NEST deployment, it is probable that a failed mission—i.e., detonation of a nuclear device in some populated area—would occur with little or no warning to local officials or civilians. "Consequence management" thus becomes the task of those who survive the blast and the outsiders who are eventually sent to deal with casualties and the resultant physical damage from a nuclear blast.

Federal authorities admit that NEST has evaluated "more than 110" nuclear threats since 1975, with volunteers actively mobilized to respond in "about 30" of those cases. Thus far, all threats received have been officially deemed hoaxes. Sketchy details have leaked to the media in six of those cases, although the solution in five of the cases remains "unknown"— meaning no information is available on any suspects who may have been identified or apprehended. The known cases of NEST activation include:

January 31, 1975 Los Angeles, California: A letter allegedly written by anonymous members of the radical Weather Underground organization, including a schematic drawing of a one-megaton hydrogen bomb, claimed that nuclear devices have been placed in three separate buildings. No bombs were recovered and no suspects have been publicly identified.

November 23, 1976 Spokane, Washington: Police received a ransom demand for $500,000 in small bills, threatening detonation of 10 explosive charges, each with 10 pounds of radioactive waste material. No bombs were recovered, and no suspects have been publicly identified.

January 30, 1979 Wilmington, North Carolina: The manager of a General Electric nuclear plant received an extortion letter containing a sample of uranium dioxide powder. The letter claimed that 10 gallons of enriched uranium dioxide had been stolen from the plant and would be scattered at random in an unnamed U.S. city if a $100,000 ransom payment was not forthcoming. An employee of a GE subcontractor was arrested, convicted, and sentenced to 15 years in prison for extortion. Officially, no other radioactive material was recovered.

April 9, 1979 Sacramento, California: Governor Jerry Brown received a postcard claiming that a small amount of plutonium had been released in the Capitol building to demonstrate the folly of nuclear energy development. No contaminant was found, and no suspect has been publicly identified.

November 27, 1987 Indianapolis, Indiana: An anonymous telephone caller, claiming affiliation with a Cuban political faction, warned that a homemade nuclear bomb would be detonated in a local bank overnight. No bombs were recovered, and no suspects have been publicly identified.

April 13, 1990 El Paso, Texas: Mayor Suzanne Azar received a telephone threat that a nuclear weapon built with uranium had been set to destroy a three-square-mile area of the city. No bombs were recovered, and no suspects have been publicly identified.

NEST was not involved in the Chicago arrest of Jose Padilla (a.k.a. Abdullah Al Mujahir) on May 8, 2002, allegedly for plotting with Middle Eastern terrorists to build and detonate a "dirty" nuclear bomb at some unspecified point in the United States. Attorney General John Ashcroft announced Padilla's arrest a month after the fact, on June 10, 2002, claiming the suspect was seized at O'Hare International Airport upon returning from Pakistan, where he reportedly spent time with members of Osama bin Laden's al-Qaeda terrorist network. Although a native-born citizen of the U.S., unarmed at the time of his capture, Padilla was held in military custody at a U.S. Navy brig in Charleston, South Carolina. Ashcroft, speaking to the nation on a satellite hookup from Russia, declared that warnings of Padilla's plot had been received from "multiple, independent, corroborating sources." As with previous arrests and federal warnings broadcast since the terrorist attacks of September 11, 2001, no further information was provided to support the accusation. Attorney General Ashcroft, ignoring the fact that no declared state of war exists in America, told reporters, "We have acted with legal authority both under the laws of war and clear Supreme Court precedent, which establishes that the military may detain a United States citizen who has joined the enemy and has entered our country to carry out hostile acts." A Pentagon spokesman, Lieutenant Colonel Rivers Johnson, seemed less certain, telling the press that "military officials have not decided whether to charge Mujahir or what charges to file." Regardless of charges, suspect Padilla is considered innocent under American law until proven guilty at trial.

"NUKER": computer viruses

Found today on the Internet in five recognized variants, the "Nuker" virus was initially reported in October 1996. Analysts rank the entire family as "very dangerous" memory-resident, parasitic, encrypted viruses that write themselves to the ends of .com files. The variant forms are:

Nuker.Entity infects .exe files, as well as .com files. On the first day of each month it displays the following message on-screen:

Hello user. I am a computer virus. My name is Entity. First: The keyboard is locked. Don't worry, it will be unlocked at the end of this message.

I am here because of your illegal software copying and

I am carrying a message for you from my programmer:
®Buy only ORIGINAL SOFTWARE. Today the risk of infection by a virus is very high (as you can see) and, next time, you could be visited by an harmful virus which can perform serious damage to your hard disk, floppies and backups . . . So, pay attention while getting pirated software from CDs and/or criminal BBSs. Pirating software is a federal crime.

[This warning comes from Entity virus (c) 1995 by The Nuker]

Nuker.Excess strikes on the first day of each month by slowing operations of its host computer to a crawl. When the Alt-Ctrl-Del keys are pressed to reboot the system, a message is displayed reading: "Your PC is working VERY SLOWLY today . . . What about a good PENTIUM Processor?" Random disk sectors may also be erased and the following message displayed on-screen:

```
+-|DANGER!+------------------------------------------- +
| You are infected by ExCESS Virus (c) 1995 by The Nuker  |
| ------------------------------------------------------- |
| I have destroyed your FATs but I have only ONE copy in  |
| my data area. IF YOU REBOOT NOW ALL DATA WILL BE LOST.  |
| If this isn't enough, I have altered your Master Boot   |
| Record with a formatting routine in order to low-level  |
| format the primary Hard Disk when executed. If you are  |
| so dude and you don't believe me, reboot now and look   |
| at your hard disk light spinning . . . If you don't want |
| to loose all your data then try to guess a number from  |
| 0 to 9 and pray for your answer to be correct, else . . . |
+ ------------------------------------------------------- +
```

You have 3 tries to guess the correct number!!! Enter the number:

You fucking SHIT!!! You guessed the right number!!! You are safe this time but next will come very soon and you will not be so lucky!!!

Sorry, you didn't entered the correct number! Retry, and hope you lucky!!!

Hum . . . you are lucky this time . . . Please wait while reconstructing disk structure . . .

I WAS JOKING! Your Hard Disk has been fucked up!!! Thank you for choosing another product of . . .

·T·h·e· ·N·u·k·e·r·

Nuker.Syndrome erases all files in the current directory on the first day of each month. During infection, this variant ignores files whose names begin with the following prefixes: AV, CL, -D, F-, MW, NA, SC, TB, -U and VA. Nuker.Syndrome contains the following text string:

[Syndrome virus (c) 1996 by The Nuker]
VATBF-AVSCCL-D-UMSMWNA

Nuker.Trance.1688 strikes on the first day of the month, if that date falls on a Monday, erasing various disk sectors and exchanging symbols on the monitor's screen. It contains the text string "Trance Virus (c) 1995 by The Nuker."

Nuker.Trance.1982 "shakes" the screen of its host computer by blurring images and overwrites various disk sectors with a text string reading: "This sector has been fucked up courtesy of Trancey Virus (c) 1995 by The Nuker."

"OBORA": computer virus

Initially reported from the Internet in February 1997, "Obora" is a memory-resident, parasitic virus rated "dangerous" by computer analysts. After infecting a new host computer, it waits for three files to be executed, then searches the current directory and writes itself to the end of any .exe files discovered. On Sundays it causes images on the monitor's screen to "scroll" each time the system's timer ticks off 185 seconds. On the 22nd day of any month, Obora displays the following message on-screen:

MY NAME IS TROUBLe
HELLO FROM <KETY>—

CREATED BY KEVIN

Obora contains the following text strings, which provide evidence of its author's national origin:

KETY—POLAND!!
PROSZE TU NIE GRZEBaC
96.02.12
TROUBLe—(c) by Kevin
OBORa 96 V1.0 (c) by KEVIN

OCHOA, Christopher: exonerated by DNA evidence

A native of El Paso, Texas, born in 1967, Christopher Ochoa graduated from high school with honors in 1984. Friends knew him as a quiet, soulful poet and songwriter who served as an editor for Riverside High School's literary magazine. In 1988, at age 21, he lived in Austin and worked at one of several Pizza Hut restaurants scattered around the state capital. Ochoa's roommate and close friend, Richard Danziger, worked at the same restaurant. In November 1988, the manager of another Pizza Hut in Austin, 20-year-old Nancy DePriest, was attacked in her own restaurant after hours, repeatedly raped and sodomized, then murdered execution style by close-range gunshots to the head. Coworkers reported Ochoa and Danziger to police as possible suspects in the slaying on November 10, after the pair toasted DePriest's memory at work. Detectives agreed such behavior was "odd" and picked the pair up for questioning on November 11.

Ochoa would later report that one of the arresting officers, Sgt. Hector Polanco, hurled chairs around the interview room while questioning Ochoa and threatened that "if he didn't confess they'd crush his head." Donna Angstadt, manager of the restaurant where the two suspects worked and Danziger's girlfriend at the time of his arrest, recalled her own interrogation by Polanco and Sgt. Bruce Boardman as "the most horrific, the most horrible experience I've ever been through in my life." According to Angstadt, the policemen initially accused her of supplying the murder weapon, threatening to remove Angstadt's two young children from her custody. "Your boyfriend's holding [DePriest's] head," Polanco said at one juncture, "and you're the one who pulled the trigger for your little love interest." When that approach failed, the officers told Angstadt that "if Richard gets out, he's going to hunt me down and kill me like he did Nancy DePriest."

After three days of relentless grilling, all conducted without legal counsel, Ochoa confessed to the murder in an effort to save himself from execution. The catch: in order to earn his plea bargain and confirm a life sentence, Ochoa had to help the state convict Danziger. Legal maneuvers delayed Danziger's trial until 1990, the defendant protesting his innocence at every opportunity. Ochoa, meanwhile, told relatives he, too, was innocent, but that he feared death if he recanted his statement. "They made me confess," Ochoa insisted, "and how am I going to prove my innocence now? It's my word against theirs." At trial, Ochoa described the crime in terms that judge and jury alike found "very compelling," including details of the scene only the killers (or investigating officers) should logically have known. Ochoa's testimony persuaded jurors that he and Danziger had bound and gagged DePriest, then raped and sodomized her eight different times, including two assaults after she had been shot. Danziger was convicted and sentenced to 99 years' imprisonment, with his subsequent appeals rejected.

On February 27, 1991, Danziger was attacked in prison by another inmate, Armando Gutierrez, serving 18 years for assaulting a police officer. Gutierrez knocked Danziger to the ground and kicked him repeatedly in the head with steel-toed boots, inflicting permanent brain damage. Gutierrez received an additional 25-year sentence for the assault, while Danziger was confined to Skyview psychiatric prison, thereafter sporadically unable to identify close relatives or carry on coherent conversations.

A year after Danziger's assault, in 1992, Sgt. Polanco was dismissed from the Austin Police Department for lying under oath in another murder case. An arbitrator subsequently attributed Polanco's perjury to a "memory lapse," and he was reinstated with the department. Unsatisfied with merely getting his job back, Polanco sued the department and won a $350,000 jury award for wrongful termination. Investigation of Polanco's alleged official misconduct did not extend to the DePriest murder case, but new evidence soon cast doubt on the investigation.

In early 1996, while serving a life sentence for aggravated robbery and other crimes, Texas inmate Achim Josef Marino "found Jesus" and felt himself morally obligated to clear the books on other crimes

he had committed. On February 5, 1996, Marino sent a six-page letter to the Austin *American-Statesman,* confessing that he alone was responsible for DePriest's murder. Local police began investigating Marino's confession in March 1996, but they had reached no conclusion by 1998, when Marino sent additional letters to the American Civil Liberties Union and Governor George Bush. Neither responded, and word of Marino's confession leaked to the public only in February 2000, after members of the REMINGTON CENTER INNOCENCE PROJECT took over Chris Ochoa's defense. Belated DNA test results confirmed that Marino was the sole rapist of Nancy DePriest, and Ochoa was released from prison on January 17, 2001. Danziger's release was delayed for another two months, while transfer to a managed care facility was arranged. Austin police reported that no action could be taken against the officers who secured Ochoa's false confession, since the statute of limitations had run out on their crimes.

ODONTOLOGY, Forensic: crime scene dentistry

Forensic odontology is the application of dentistry and/or dental records to police work for the purpose of identifying unknown persons, living or deceased, who may be either criminals or victims of a crime. In dealing with deceased subjects, the same techniques are also used to identify remains in accidental deaths or cases where the cause of death may be unknown.

Identification via forensic odontology proceeds in different ways, depending on whether or not the procedure involves establishment of identity or determination of guilt. In the former circumstance, technicians normally compare known dental charts and X rays with the teeth of a deceased subject whose identity is unknown. (The same methods could be used to identify living subjects, as in cases of amnesia or where a criminal suspect refuses to identify himself.) By matching the shape, size, and configuration of teeth, along with any injuries or distinctive dental work, identity may be established with a certainty equivalent to that of fingerprints or DNA testing. This technique is used hundreds of times each year in the United States, to identify mutilated victims of homicide, fires, explosions, airplane crashes, or natural disasters, and in cases where advanced decomposition rules out fingerprints or other common means of identification.

Forensic odontology may also be used to identify criminals, though in a rather different way than it is used on unknown corpses. In this application, a

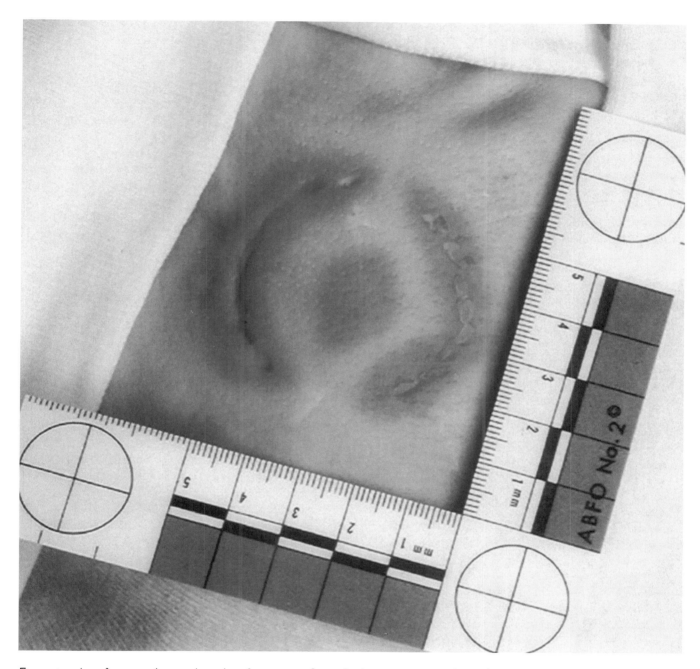

Forensic odontology can be used to identify a criminal, in which case a suspect's teeth are compared to bite marks left behind during commission of a crime. (Courtesy of C. Michael Bowers D.D.S., J.D.)

suspect's teeth are compared with bite marks left behind during commission of a crime. The bite marks may be found on human flesh (as from a fight or sexual assault) or on any other object that retains observable bite marks (as where a burglar stops to raid a victim's refrigerator and bites into a piece of cheese). In one midwestern case, a rape victim had the presence of mind to bite the rubber window molding of her attacker's car, while she was being assaulted in the front seat. The bite marks, as proof of her presence in the rapist's vehicle, supported the victim's story and sent her attacker to prison.

The most famous bite-mark case in history is that of cross-country serial killer Theodore Robert Bundy. A sexual sadist and necrophile, Bundy killed at least 30 girls and young women between January 1974 and February 1978. He claimed victims in at least four states, starting in Washington and ending his run in Florida, after a nocturnal rampage left two women dead and one gravely injured in a college sorority house. Bite marks on the buttocks of one lifeless victim were a critical piece of prosecution evidence, securing Bundy's first-degree murder conviction in July 1979. He was executed for his crimes on January 24, 1989. 11 years and nine days after inflicting the wounds that sent him to death row.

"OLD Lady with a Box" Chain Letter:
Internet hoax

This exercise in wasted time, initially circulated on the Internet in March 2001, is yet another of the countless chain letters propagated daily on the World Wide Web. Typically, those gullible enough to follow the directions contained in the message inevitably find that nothing happens. The original text reads:

Sent: Tuesday, March 06, 2001 4:14 PM
Subject: Do This! Its hysterical!!

An old lady walked into a Grocery Store. She wanted to buy the best dog food in the world for her little puppy. She went up to the cash register to buy the food. The sales-lady told her that the store did not allow old ladies to buy animal food unless they show the actual animal because a lot of old ladies like to eat the animal food themselves. So the old lady went home, got her dog and went back to the store to buy her dog food. The next day she came back to buy the best cat food around. But the Saleslady told her the same thing, so the old lady went back home and brought her cat to the Grocery Store to buy the cat food. The next day the old lady went to the Grocery Store again carrying a big container. She went up to the sales lady and said, "Put your hand inside here". The Saleslady shook her head. "NO", she said, "there is probably something in there that will bite me!". "I promise you that there is nothing in here that will bite you.", the old lady said. So the Saleslady stuck her hand inside the container and screamed.

To find out what was inside the container you must send this to at least 10 people, when it says, your mail

has been sent . . . instead of clicking OK, hit ALT-8 and the container will pop up on your screen.

OLD Navy Giveaway Offer: ### Internet hoax

Another spurious giveaway offer circulated on the Internet, starting in November 1999, this hoax pretends that free clothing will be shipped to the participants in its chain letter scheme. The offer has been disavowed by Old Navy, and circulation of the message (quoted below, with errors uncorrected), will achieve nothing beyond wasting time.

w: OLD NAVY GIFT CARD

DEAR OLD NAVY SHOPPER,

I AM LAURA THIMIS, THE FOUNDER OF OLD NAVY. AS YOU KNOW, THERE HAS BEEN SOME PRMOTION THINGS GOING ON WITH ABERCROMBIE AND FITCH AND THE GAP. NOW I WANT TO BE PART OF THE INTERNET PRMOTION "GIG".

FOR EVERY 10 PEOPLE THAT YOU SEND THIS TO, YOU GET A FREE $25.00 GIFT CARD FOR ANY OLD NAVY STORE, IN ANY PART OF THE WORLD, FROM THE U S A TO CHINA, FROM ICELAND TO PARIS!! MAKE SURE THAT YOU SEND THIS TO LOTS AND LOTS AND LOTS OF PEOPLE!!!!

AFTER YOU SEND THIS TO AT LEAST 10 PEO-PLE, YOU WILL RECIVE YOUR FREE OLD NAVY GIFT CARD IN 2–4 WEEKS!!!! WATCH THE MAIL!

"OLGA": ### computer viruses

Initially reported in November 1996, this virus now exists on the Internet in two variant forms, both rated "dangerous" by analysts. Apparently produced in Russia, the related viruses perform in different ways.

The original form, *Olga.483*, is a memory-resident, multipartite virus that writes itself to the Master Boot Record (MBR) of a host computer and into the headers of .exe files. On December 27 the virus erases all infected disk sectors. It contains the text string "SGB: 01ga++".

The later variant, *Olga.4448*, is a memory-resident, parasitic virus that writes itself to the beginning of .com files when their attributes are modified. Infected disk sectors are erased in October, while the monitor displays this message:

*You must undertake nothing, if you need the
datas stored on your default disk.*

I M A R C E N C Y
T H E   V I R U S   O L G A   W O R K I N G .
(W R I T E N   B Y   S C O R P I O N)

OLIVER, Thomas: software pirate

A resident of Aurora, Illinois, born July 14, 1965,
Thomas Oliver was an enthusiastic HACKER, known
as "Rambone" to his cronies in the syndicate of software thieves called "PIRATES WITH ATTITUDE" (PWA).
In 1999 he conspired with 11 associates and five
employees of Intel Corporation to steal and illegally
distribute more than 5,000 copyrighted software
programs, valued in excess of $1 million. Oliver was
one of 17 defendants indicted by a federal grand jury
in Chicago, on May 4, 2000, charged with stealing
the software and making it available to others via a
website based in Quebec, Canada. Kathleen McChesney, special agent in charge of the FBI's Chicago
field office, told reporters the defendants belonged to
"one of the oldest and most sophisticated networks
of software pirates anywhere in the world." By May
2001 Oliver had joined seven other PWA members in
pleading guilty on charges that carried a maximum
penalty of five years in prison and a $250,000 fine.
Financial restitution to the victims is also mandatory
under federal law.

"OLIVIA": computer viruses

Presently found on the Web in three variant forms,
"Olivia" was first identified in January 1998. All
three forms are memory-resident, encrypted parasitic
viruses, rated "dangerous" by analysts. The Olivia
variants write themselves to the ends of .com and
.exe files as they are accessed, sometimes performing
duplicate infections of the same files. They also disable various popular antivirus programs, but certain
files are immune from infection. Neither
"Olivia.2152" nor "Olivia.2374" will infect files
named command, emm386, 4dos or win; other files
immune to Olivia.2374 include chkdsk, sscan, tb,
and vt.

Olivia.2152 and Olivia.2374 deliver their identical payloads on April 10 and December 23, respectively. On those dates, they display an on-screen
message reading "Please put a love music CD into
your CD-ROM and pass [*sic*] any key to continue,"
then trigger routines to play a compact disk. The
third variant, "Olivia.3378," performs this same
function on April 10, but it does not otherwise mirror the actions of Olivia.2152. Instead, Olivia.3378
attacks Windows32 executable files, writing itself to
the end of each file infected, corrupting them with its
own bugs in the process. Its on-screen message for
the impromptu April 10 concert reads: "Put a Audio-
CD into the CD-ROM, and it [*sic*] any key . . ."

OLLINS, Calvin, et al.: exonerated by DNA evidence

On the night of October 18, 1986, medical student
Lori Roscetti was returning to her home on
Chicago's West Side, after a late study session at
Rush University, when several men forced their way
into her car. Driven to a lonely railway access road,
Roscetti was gang-raped and murdered, her body
found the next morning. Police considered several
suspects before settling on four black teenagers,
including Marcellius Bradford, cousins Calvin and
Larry Ollins, and Omar Saunders. Arrested some
three months after the crime, the latest suspects were
subjected to marathon grilling without legal counsel.
After 24 hours of threats and alleged beatings, Bradford confessed to the crime, claiming the four
ambushed Roscetti for bus fare back to Chicago's
infamous Cabrini-Green housing project. Calvin
Ollins, a 14-year-old described in court records as
"mildly retarded," also confessed to the slaying, later
claiming he was tricked by police who told him a
confession would allow him to go free.

The defendants were tried separately. Bradford
pleaded guilty to a reduced charge and received a 12-
year prison term in return for his testimony against
Larry Ollins. Three successive trials sent the other
suspects to prison for life, under highly suspect circumstances. Two key prosecution witnesses later
recanted in interviews with the *Chicago Tribune*, one
claiming he lied under oath to secure a $35,000
reward for information in the case, another telling
reporters he testified against the four defendants to
divert suspicion from himself. Police crime scene analyst Pamela Fish testified that semen stains found on
the victim's body and clothing were "consistent" with
the defendants' blood types, but subsequent findings
cast doubt on both her judgment and veracity.

The convictions and life prison terms were upheld
on appeal. (Bradford served half of his 12-year sentence and was later sent back to prison on a burglary
conviction.) Saunders and the Ollins cousins lan-

guished in prison until 2001, when a series of articles in the *Chicago Tribune* began poking holes in the prosecution's case and new attorney Kathleen Zellner submitted various pieces of crime scene evidence to an independent DNA expert, Dr. Edward Blake, for testing that was unavailable in 1987. Dr. Blake's report, submitted in November 2001, excluded any of the four accused defendants as donors of the semen recovered from Lori Roscetti's corpse and underpants. At the same time, Dr. Blake examined Roscetti's coat and jogging pants, discovering 22 more semen stains on garments which, according to Pamela Fish's sworn testimony, bore no stains at all. Those 22 stains likewise excluded the four defendants as donors, the aggregate weight of the evidence prompting Dr. Blake to brand Fish's testimony "a scientific fraud." In December 2001, Cook County prosecutors dismissed all charges against the three defendants still in prison, and they were released after serving more than 14 years.

Assistant State's Attorney Celeste Stack assured the court and the public that the original Roscetti investigation was "done in good faith, based on the best evidence we had at the time," but attorney Zellner seemed closer to the truth when she told reporters, "I cannot overstate the official misconduct, the abuse of power, the activities that went on that I believe were criminal in nature." The Illinois statute of limitations prohibits any charges being filed against investigators or witnesses who may have committed perjury in 1987, and Pamela Fish—reassigned since 1987 to an administrative post at the Forensic Science Center in Chicago—declines to comment on the case. On January 18, 2002, Zellner filed litigation seeking compensation for her clients, blaming Fish and others for submitting false evidence that resulted in imprisonment of four innocent men. Lora Roscetti, meanwhile, was further traumatized by the new revelations in her daughter's case. "It's 15 years," she said. "How are they going to find them now?" Thus far, DNA comparison with 30 additional suspects has proved fruitless, and the case remains unsolved.

"ONEMINUTE": computer virus

Initially reported from the Internet in September 1997, "OneMinute" is a nonmemory-resident, parasitic, polymorphic virus rated "not dangerous" by technical analysts. It searches out both .exe and .com files (excluding only command.com), writing itself to the end of the former and to the beginning of the latter. OneMinute also deletes the antivirus programs chklist.cps, chklist.ms, and smartchk.cps. On specific dates, it displays the following messages (with errors intact):

On 1 January—

This day in the year 1976, Chou Enlai, Premier of the State Council of China, had been left us for ever. Now, in order to express cherish the memory of this great man, let's observe one minute's silence . . . Thank you!

On 6 July—

This day in the year 1976, Chu Te, Chief of the Standing Committee of the National People's Congress of China, had been left us for ever. Now, in order to express cherish the memory of this great man, let's observe one minute's silence. Thank you!

On 9 September—

This day in the year 1976, Mao Tsetung, Chairman of the Communist Party of China, had been left us forever. Now, in order to express cherish the memory of this great man, let's observe one minute's silence. Thank you!

OPERATION Candyman: FBI Internet "sting"

In December 2000 an informant advised FBI agents that members of a Yahoo e-group (or "electronic community") were involved in posting, exchanging, and transmitting CHILD PORNOGRAPHY in violation of existing federal law. The e-group, labeled "Candyman," was advertised with a message reading: "This group is for People who love kids. You can post any type of messages you like too or any type of pics and vids you like too." Agents of the bureau's Houston field office obtained a court order permitting them to monitor and trace communications of the Candyman subscribers. Over the next 14 months, G-men identified 7,000 unique e-mail addresses for Candyman correspondents, including 4,600 inside the United States and 2,400 based in other countries.

Nationwide, FBI agents secured personal information on 1,400 Candyman subscribers, concentrating on 707 who had the highest volume of illegal photos transmitted or received. Within that group, special attention was paid to persons in positions of trust or authority, including clergymen, teachers, and law enforcement officers. At least one subject was found in each of the FBI's 56 field divisions; some districts hosted as many as 45 targets. On March 18, 2002, agents launched coordinated raids from coast to coast, searching 231 homes and places of business, arresting 86 suspects in 26 states. Of those arrested, 27 confessed to molesting children and named a total of 36 victims. As FBI Executive Assistant Director Bruce Gebhardt described the mixed bag, "They include members of the clergy, law enforcement officers, a nurse, a teacher's aide, a school bus driver, and others entrusted with protecting, nurturing and educating the American youth." U.S. Attorney General John Ashcroft told reporters, "When we pursue child pornography, the path often leads to evidence of real sexual predators who have abused real children. These individuals must be stopped. There will be no free ride on the Internet for traffickers of child pornography."

OPERATION Longarm: U.S. Customs Internet "sting"

Launched in 1992, "Operation Longarm" was the first major campaign initiated by the U.S. Customs Service (USCS) to combat CHILD PORNOGRAPHY on the Internet. Agents began the operation after they discovered that a Danish syndicate was actively soliciting and distributing illegal photographs and videos on an international scale. The "Longarm" code name was chosen accordingly, to denote cooperation between U.S. authorities and law enforcement officers abroad.

Recognition of the Danish operation came after USCS agents carried out a "controlled delivery" of foreign child pornography to an identified U.S. suspect. Upon arresting their target, the agents found unexpected quantities of child pornography stored electronically on his home computer. As USCS supervisory agent Don Huycke later told *Government Technology*, "That was the birth of Longarm. This first guy told us about a Europe-based bulletin board he had accessed to get the pictures, and when we went looking, we found this BBS in Denmark called Bamse. On it we found every type of sex act you can perceive of—animal, homosexual, urination, defecation and child porn. There were three separate child-porn rooms connected to this bulletin board."

Working from their original informant's lead, USCS agents identified three Danish websites involved in transmission of child pornography banned by federal law in the United States. Con-

sular officials delivered the downloaded evidence to police in Aulberg, Denmark, where the Bamse website was based. After initially dismissing the American concerns as "prudish," Aulberg authorities ultimately seized 16 computers and several thousand floppy disks bearing pornographic images. USCS agents reviewed the haul and identified 3,000 porn traffickers in 16 countries, including 350 within the U.S. A majority of those had visited the Danish website only once or twice, but 35 regular patrons were singled out for more intensive scrutiny.

In December 1992 Customs agents huddled with Justice Department attorneys to prepare the first-ever federal search warrant for child pornography transmitted and stored on computers. Civilian computer experts briefed the agents on proper methods of detecting and preserving evidence stored on computers. The agents were ready to strike on March 5, 1993, coordinating simultaneous raids against 35 suspects in 22 states. With thousands of illicit images in hand, all 35 defendants were convicted and sentenced to prison, their convictions upheld on appeal.

OPERATION Rip Cord: U.S. Customs Internet "sting"

This federal investigation of Internet CHILD PORNOGRAPHY allegedly began in March 1996, after the owner of an adult bookstore in upstate New York approached local police with complaints about the volume of illegal "kiddy porn" displayed on the Internet. Despite his own involvement with adult pornography, police say, the shopkeeper was sickened by the illicit images of small children sexually assaulted. So were the investigators, when they tuned in to the Web. One U.S. Customs Service (USCS) agent was apparently so shocked by what he saw that he yanked the power cord of his computer from its wall socket, and thereby coined the "Rip Cord" code name for the operation.

State and local police in New York quickly realized that they lacked the expertise and jurisdiction to cope with a national network of child pornographers. Agents of the state attorney general's office called on Customs agents for assistance, since much of the porn they were able to trace came from international vendors. Over the next 18 months, investigators cracked computer codes and traced screen names to identify more than 1,500 subjects who trafficked in child pornography and sometimes solicited sex with minors on the Internet. By September 30,

1997, 120 persons had been arrested in the U.S. and Europe, while raiders captured more than 200,000 illegal images and seized home computer equipment valued in excess of $137,000. Of those arrested before USCS agents announced their campaign, 31 defendants had been successfully prosecuted by October 1997. A sampling of those captured in New York state, identified here by their Internet screen names, includes:

"ccsnuggles"   An 18-year-old woman in Queens, New York City, arrested in 1998 for transmitting numerous illegal images. She was charged with eight counts of promoting a sexual performance by a child.

"DIAPERLUV"   The first subject arrested in Operation Rip Cord, a 27-year-old mid-level manager of a television network in New York City. He was convicted in 1997 of sending 40 child-porn images over the Internet, sentenced to five years' probation and a $2,000 fine, with mandatory forfeiture of his personal computer.

"DunEinstein"   A 44-year-old Staten Island man, arrested in 1997 for transmitting pornographic images to Rip Cord investigators. Searchers also found a substantial amount of printed matter in his home.

"ENJOLARAS97"   A 21-year-old school janitor in Buffalo, who used the principal's computer at his school (and one belonging to his ex-girlfriend) to send and receive numerous illegal images. Convicted in 1998, he was sentenced to five years' probation and 50 hours of community service.

"Gatorraid"   A 49-year-old Chautauqua County man, charged with promoting the sexual performance of a child after allegedly sending pornographic images of children and explicit e-mail messages to Rip Cord investigators. He was on-line, "chatting" with undercover agents, when the raiders arrived on his doorstep.

"Gtrfirst"   A 31-year-old public school teacher in New Paltz, charged in 1998 with promoting a sexual performance by a child after he transmitted illegal images over the Web.

"Happy51758"   A 52-year-old Albany man, convicted in 1998 of sending numerous images over the Web, some depicting children as young as age four engaged in sex with adults.

"Laughmastr"   A 28-year-old Ulster County man who sent pornographic images to Rip Cord investigators, jailed in 1997 on one count of promoting a sexual performance by a child.

"MDANO064186"   A 35-year-old used-car dealer in Ontario County, convicted in 1997 of sending illicit images to Rip Cord investigators. He was sentenced to 30 days in jail, five years' probation and a $1,000 fine.

"NYAnimal"   A 32-year-old Otsego County man, reported to Rip Cord investigators in 1997 by America Online security personnel, following complaints that he transmitted child pornography to unwilling recipients. He was charged with promoting a sexual performance by a child.

"NYRagMan"   A 40-year-old Syracuse resident, convicted in 1997 of sending 10 pornographic images of children to Rip Cord agents. He was sentenced to 100 hours of community service and five years' probation, with mandatory registration as a sexual offender.

"NateTSnake"   A 20-year-old student at State University of New York-Albany, whose career goal was to become a kindergarten teacher. Arrested for sending 10 illegal images to Rip Cord agents, he was convicted in 1997, sentenced to five years' probation and a $5,000 fine, with an order to forfeit his computer.

"Redpanda17"   A 39-year-old Westchester County man, charged in 1997 with two counts of child pornography and two counts of promoting a sexual performance by a child.

"REMY271"   A Rochester native, convicted in 1997 of sending various illegal images to Rip Cord undercover agents. He was sentenced to three years' probation and fined $1,000.

"Sanchez13"   A 27-year-old resident of Grand Island, New York, jailed after he sent 35 child-porn images to Rip Cord investigators. Convicted in 1997, he was sentenced to five years' probation with mandatory sexual counseling.

"sgzjr"   A 26-year-old resident of Queens, in New York City, arrested in 1998 after transmitting numerous illegal images. He was charged with six counts of promoting a sexual performance by a child.

"SHYDAD4U"   A 50-year-old grandfather in Albany, who sent a series of images to Rip Cord investigators, including several photos of an adult male raping a young girl. Convicted in 1997, he received a sentence of 16 months to four years in prison.

"Space.keep.touch.ch" A Swiss couple arrested in Buffalo, after they traveled to Buffalo with their two-year-old daughter, for the purpose of selling CD-ROM disks loaded with child pornography to undercover Rip Cord investigators. Both were convicted in 1997.

"TOTHEPNT" A 20-year-old Syracuse man, arrested in 1998 for sending several pages of child-porn images over the Internet, charged with promoting a sexual performance by a child.

An unnamed 17-year-old high school student in Syracuse, arrested after sending 10 pornographic images of children to Rip Cord investigators. The subject was granted youthful offender status and processed through the juvenile justice system.

In the wake of those arrests and prosecutions, with more to come, New York Attorney General Dennis Vacco told the press, "The message that the kiddy pornographers in America and across the world need to know [is] that we're going to continue to sit on the Net, and they need to pay attention, because the next chat line conversation they have might be with an investigator from my office, from the state police, from U.S. Customs. Eventually, we're going to find the producers. At the end of the day, this is not a victimless crime. The victims are those kids in the photographs."

OPERATION Smartcard.net: U.S. Customs Internet "sting"

Each year in the United States, satellite television providers lose an estimated $6.2 million to pirates who intercept signals without subscribing to the service and paying legitimate fees. That interception is accomplished primarily through use of counterfeit satellite TV access cards—called "smart cards"—which illegally give viewers free access to all satellite television programming, including high-priced pay-per-view special events. Purchase of a counterfeit card through black market channels, usually for a flat fee of several hundred dollars, saves the viewer money over time by avoiding subscription and pay-per-view fees. Distribution of such counterfeit cards is also a federal crime, bearing a maximum penalty on conviction of five years in prison and a $250,000 fine for each offense.

The federal sting campaign known as "Operation Smartcard.net" began in September 1998, after agents of the U.S. Customs Service (USCS) seized a large shipment of counterfeit "Eurocards" arriving in the country at Blaine, Washington, from a foreign supplier. USCS officers had lately noted a dramatic increase in smuggling and seizure of such cards, primarily across the U.S.-Canadian border, and Operation Smartcard.net was conceived as a means of interdicting that traffic.

In pursuance of their sting, USCS agents established a fictional Internet business called TSS, with a website offering Eurocards for sale over a warning that "unauthorized use of access cards is illegal in the U.S." Assisting in the sting were DirecTV (a legitimate satellite TV provider hard hit by pirates) and NDS Americas (a supplier of "smart card" technology that manufactured DirecTV's legitimate access cards under contract). Before the agents folded their operation and began preparing formal charges, in June 1999, they sold 3,195 illegal smart cards to bootleg dealers for resale and 382 to individuals for private use. Those sales generated $516,000 in proceeds, with the cash deposited in the U.S. Treasury. Between July 2 and 6, 1999, DirecTV and NDS used electronic countermeasures to deactivate the counterfeit access cards sold by Customs agents on their website, as well as many others previously placed in circulation prior to the sting operation. During the week of July 13–18, 1999, USCS agents armed with search warrants fanned out across the country, confiscating bootleg equipment from various suspects and interrogating 30 identified dealers in counterfeit smart cards. Federal charges were subsequently filed against 15 defendants.

Over the next 12 months, four of the Smartcard defendants pleaded guilty on reduced charges after striking bargains with the U.S. Justice Department. They included BRIAN ANGELL, in Warwick, Rhode Island; LINDA BAUER, of Hastings, Minnesota; MICHAEL POULSEN, of Mountain View, California; and MOHAMMED WALID, in Yorktown Heights, New York. A fifth defendant—THOMAS KENNEDY, of Cranston, Rhode Island—pleaded guilty in November 2000 to selling 166 phony smart cards, and the remaining suspects were eventually convicted. Sentences varied from Angell's relative wrist slap of one year's probation and a $5,000 fine to Kennedy's term of 14 months in federal prison. In the wake of Operation Smartcard.net, the U.S. Customs Commissioner told reporters that the defendants "thought they got away without paying for satellite TV. Instead, these cyber-pirates will pay in a way they hadn't expected."

OPERATION Sundevil: U.S. federal hacker roundup

Spawned by the activities of a HACKER syndicate labeled the "LEGION OF DOOM," the sweeping national campaign dubbed "Operation Sundevil" was a crackdown on individuals who had penetrated telephone company computers to obtain free long-distance service. Nationwide raids were conducted by U.S. Secret Service agents on May 7–9, 1990, resulting in seizure of 42 computers and some 23,000 floppy disks from suspects residing in Chicago, Cincinnati, Dallas, Detroit, Fort Worth, Los Angeles, Miami, Newark, New York City, Phoenix, Pittsburgh, Richmond, San Diego, San Francisco, San Jose, and Tucson. In addition to evidence of wire fraud, the captured computers and floppy disks contained a vast hoard of pirated software, plus stolen codes, passwords, and credit card numbers.

Reports issued in the wake of Operation Sundevil suggest that Secret Service agents started their sweep with a list of 300 computer bulletin boards known to offer bootlegged software or illegal access to telephone systems, but only 25 of the most egregious boards were actually affected by the May 1990 raids. Only four suspects were actually arrested in the Sundevil sweep. They included a Tucson operator known on-line as "Tony the Trashman"; "Dr. Ripco," operator of a thriving phone-fraud bulletin board in Chicago; a Pennsylvania "phreaker" known to confederates as "Electra"; and an unidentified California juvenile hacker. The paucity of arrests and prosecutions seemed to confirm a suspicion of outspoken hacker advocates—i.e., that the Sundevil raids were intended primarily to seize computers and records, rather than to incarcerate offenders. The sweep also performed a public relations function for federal law enforcement (and more specifically the Secret Service), while sending a message to hackers nationwide. Garry Jenkins, assistant director of the Secret Service, made that warning explicit on May 9, 1990, when he told the media:

> Today, the Secret Service is sending a clear message to those computer hackers who have decided to violate the laws of this nation in the mistaken belief that they can successfully avoid detection by hiding behind the relative anonymity of their computer terminals. . . .
>
> Underground groups have been formed for the purpose of exchanging information relevant to their criminal activities. These groups often communicate with each other through message systems between computers called "bulletin boards."

> Our experience shows that many computer hacker suspects are no longer misguided teenagers, mischievously playing games with their computers in their bedrooms. Some are now high-tech computer operators using computers to engage in unlawful conduct.

Given the ever-rising rates of fraud and other computer crimes in the United States, it would appear that Jenkins was wasting his breath, but federal efforts to curtail the cybercrime wave continue, albeit eternally lagging behind the curve.

OQUENDO, Jesus: convicted hacker

A 27-year-old resident of Queens, New York, Jesus Oquendo was employed in the first half of 2000 as a computer security specialist at a firm called Collegeboardwalk.com, sharing office space and a computer network with one of its investors, a Manhattan-based venture capital firm called Five Partners Asset Management LLC. In the course of his duties, Oquendo illegally altered the startup commands on the Five Partners system to automatically send him the firm's password file each time the Five Partners computers were rebooted. In July 2000, after Collegeboardwalk. com failed financially, Oquendo used the stolen passwords to remotely access the Five Partners system, secretly installing a "sniffer" program to intercept and record electronic traffic on that system, transmitting the stolen e-mails to Oquendo each morning at 4:00 A.M.

By means of the sniffer program, Oquendo also accessed a second firm connected to the Five Partners system, a Manhattan computer retail company called RCS Computer Experience. Intercepting the RCS manager's password, Oquendo was then able to invade the company's database, used to track sales and inventory. On the night of August 2–3, 2000, Oquendo used his home computer to invade the RCS system for no apparent reason, deleting the entire database and leaving a message that read: "Hello, I have just hacked your system. Have a nice day." The damage caused by Oquendo's "prank" cost RCS an estimated $60,000 in repairs.

Authorities soon traced Oquendo, a.k.a. "Sil," who also maintained a website called "AntiOffLine," described by investigators as "quirky." Arrested by FBI agents for his act of cybervandalism, Oquendo became the first HACKER tried for such crimes in the southern district of New York. He was convicted on March 7, 2001, following a week of testimony, facing a maximum sentence of five years in prison and a $250,000 fine. District Judge Loretta Preska proved merciful when she sentenced Oquendo on June 12, 2001, ordering him to serve 27 months in a minimum security federal lockup and to pay his victims $96,385 in restitution. U.S. Attorney Mary Jo White told reporters outside the courthouse, "This case demonstrates that defendants cannot maliciously damage the property of others and eavesdrop on their internal communications and expect to hide behind the anonymity of the Internet. The privacy of individuals will be protected and computer hacking will not be tolerated."

OSOWSKI, Geoffrey, and Tang, Wilson: computer stock thieves

Northern California residents Geoffrey Osowski and Wilson Tang set a standard in 2001 for federal prosecution of thieves who use computer skills to steal securities and similar items. Both were employed at Cisco Systems in 2000, 30-year-old Osowski (of Mountain View) as a financial analyst and 35-year-old Tang (from Palo Alto) as an accounting manager. Together, starting in October 2000, they devised a scheme to penetrate Cisco's computer system and transfer large amounts of company stock to their private Merrill Lynch accounts. In the course of that operation they identified control numbers used to track authorized stock option disbursals, then they forged forms purporting to authorize new disbursals, faxed the forged requests to the firm responsible for issuing Cisco shares, and directed that the shares be transferred to private brokerage accounts.

Osowski and Tang made their first raid in December 2000, transferring 97,750 Cisco shares into two Merrill Lynch accounts. Osowski received 58,250 shares on that occasion, while Tang got 39,500 shares. Osowski liquidated most of his stolen shares over the next few weeks and launched a spending spree, purchasing a Mercedes Benz 320 for $52,000, a $44,000 diamond ring, a $20,000 Rolex watch and sundry lesser items. In February 2001 the thieves went back for a second helping of Cisco stock, this time depositing 65,300 shares in Osowski's Merrill Lynch account and another 67,500 shares in an account Tang had established with Charles Schwab exceeded $7.8 million.

Cisco Systems auditors discovered the stock thefts in February 2001 and alerted FBI agents, cooperat-

ing with the investigation that identified Osowski and Tang as the thieves. Arrested on March 28, 2001, the cyberbandits were arraigned in San Jose federal court and then released on personal recognizance bonds of $100,000 each. A federal grand jury indicted both defendants on April 4, 2001, charging each with three counts of wire fraud, one count of computer fraud, and one count of conspiracy. If convicted on all counts at trial, each subject faced a maximum sentence of 25 years in prison and a $1.25 million fine, plus mandatory restitution to their victims.

Rather than take their chances with a jury, Osowski and Tang bargained with their prosecutors for reduced charges. On August 20, 2001 they both pleaded guilty to one count of computer fraud, for exceeding their authorized access to Cisco's protected system. On November 26, 2001, U.S. District Judge Ronald Whyte sentenced both defendants to 34 months in federal prison and three years' supervised parole. Additionally, they were required to forfeit assets seized at their arrest ($5,049,057 in cash, jewelry and other items, including Osowski's new Mercedes) and to pay Cisco Systems the difference between $7,868,637 and the amount federal agents recovered through sale of the confiscated items. Osowski and Tang began serving their prison terms on January 8, 2002.

OUTBACK Steakhouse Warning: Internet defamation

An anonymous writer with some unknown grudge against the Outback Steakhouse chain of restaurants launched this libelous hoax on the Internet in the mid-1990s. Aside from describing mythical events, it fabricates unheard-of symptoms for the illness in question. No such events have been recorded to date from any Outback restaurant. The original message reads:

Forward this to everyone you know!!!
BEWARE!!
FOR ALL OF YOU OUTBACK LOVERS. . . .
Outback in Spartanburg
THIS IS CERTAINLY NO JOKE!

A friend of mine went to the Outback Steak House in Spartanburg Friday night to eat. She had to send her steak back 3 times before they finally had it cooked done as was requested to start with. A few hours later she became ill, so ill in fact they took her to the hospi-

tal. The doctor after an extensive evaluation determined it was some sort of food poisoning. It just so happened she didn't eat all of her steak and had taken some home so her husband went and got it, brought it to the doctor who in turn sent it for testing to see what kind of poisoning it was to treat her effectively. By now they have had to put her into intensive care. The results came back to the doctor Saturday afternoon and showed that there was URINE from at least 3 different individuals in the meat!!!!!!!!!!!!!!!!

Needless to say they are taking action against the restaurant!!!!! She was in a room this morning and expected to be released later today. If you order at a restaurant and the order isn't right, just get your money back and leave, DO NOT SEND YOUR FOOD BACK!!!!!!!

"OVERKILL": computer viruses

Reported in three variants since July 1996, the members of this Italian "family" are rated as dangerous parasitic polymorphic viruses. "Overkill.1191" and "Overkill.1385" (the latter a memory-resident virus) search out .com files and write themselves to the beginning of each, while "Overkill.1308" writes itself to the end of .exe files. Versions 1191 and 1308 both contain a text string reading "Procedure from VCL 1.0," while 1191 includes the additional text: "Chi vuol esser lieto, sia: di doman non v'e' certezza." At various random times, Overkill halts operation of an infected host computer when the "Y" key is pressed, displaying the following messages on-screen:

Overkill.1191—

OverKill Virus—By MTZ—From Italy—Are You ready (y/n)?

Overkill.1308—

OverKill II Virus—By MTZ—From Italy—Are You ready (y/n)?

Overkill.1385—

OverKill III Virus—By MTZ—From Italy—Are You ready (y/n)?

"OVERRIDE": computer viruses

Reported in two variants since July 1996, "Override" is classified by analysts as a "non-dangerous," non-memory-resident, parasitic virus. Both search out .com files (except for command.com) and write themselves to the beginning of each file discovered. One variant, "Override.1380," reboots the infected host computer on days randomly selected from the system's counter and displays the following message on-screen:

EXTERNAL OVERRIDE

This virus is dedicated to jerk M.S.,
who almost succeeded in ruining a relation
by telling lies about my girlfriend.
If you are wondering why I have hit you,
I am still wondering why he tried to hit us . . .
The Ninth Circle.

The second virus form, "Override.1428," is more predictable, acting on Friday the thirteenth to reboot its host and display this message:

External Override.
Dedicated to the jerk who told
lies about my girlfriend and almost ruined my life.
Out of sight, not out of mind sucker!

PAGET'S Disease Warning: Internet scare campaign

Although included by HOAXBUSTERS on its website of Internet hoaxes and swindles, this message circulating throughout cyberspace since June 1999 actually describes a real-life disease. Its presentation in this message is, however, deceptive and apparently designed to frighten readers needlessly. The American Cancer Society reports that Paget's disease is associated with breast cancer and is also extremely rare, appearing in less than 1 percent of all patients suffering from that more common malady. Thus, the notion of this illness spreading rapidly throughout the population is a hoax with malicious overtones. The original message reads:

Paget's Disease

This is a rare form of breast cancer, and is on the outside of the breast, on the nipple and aureola. It appeared as a rash, which later became a lesion with a crusty outer edge. I would not have ever suspected it to be breast cancer but it was.

My nipple never seemed any different to me, but the rash bothered me, so I went to the doctor for that. Sometimes, it itched and was sore, but other than that it didn't bother me. It was just ugly and a nuisance, and could not be cleared up with all the creams prescribed by my doctor and dermatologist for the dermatitis on my eyes just prior to this outbreak. They seemed a little concerned but did not warn me it could be cancerous. Now I suspect there are not many women out there

who know a lesion or rash on the nipple or aureola can be breast cancer.

Mine started out as a single red pimple on the aureola. One of the biggest problems with Paget's disease of the nipple is that the symptoms appear to be harmless. It is frequently thought to be a skin inflammation or infection, leading to unfortunate delays in detection and care.

What are the symptoms? The symptoms include:

1. *A persistent redness, oozing, and crusting of your nipple causing it to itch and burn. (As I stated, mine did not itch or burn much, and had no oozing I was aware of, but it did have a crust along the outer edge on one side).*
2. *A sore on your nipple that will not heal. (Mine was on the aureola area with a whitish thick looking area in center of nipple).*
3. *Usually only one nipple is affected.*

How is it diagnosed?
Your doctor will do a physical exam and should suggest having a mammogram of both breasts, done immediately. Even though the redness, oozing and crusting closely resemble dermatitis (inflammation of the skin), your doctor should suspect cancer if the sore is only on one breast. Your doctor should order a biopsy of your sore to confirm what is going on.

They will take a sample of your breast tissue in that area to test for cancer.

If the cancer is only in the nipple and not in the breast, your doctor may recommend just removing the nipple and surrounding tissue or suggest radiation treatments. Had my doctor caught mine right away, instead of flaking it off as dermatitis, perhaps they could have saved my breast, and it wouldn't have gone to my lymph nodes.

This message should be taken seriously and passed on to as many of your friends as possible; it could save someone's life. My breast cancer has spread and metastasized to my bones after receiving mega doses of chemotherapy, 28 treatments of radiation and taking tamaxofin. If this had been diagnosed as breast cancer in the beginning, perhaps it would not have spread . . .

TO ALL READERS-

This is sad as women are not aware of Paget's disease. If, by passing this around on the e-mail, we can make others aware of it, and its potential danger, we are helping women everywhere. Please, if you can, take a moment to forward this message to as many people as possible, especially to your family and friends.

It only takes a moment, yet the results could save a life!

PASSWORD "Sniffers": covert rip-off software

Password "sniffers" are computer programs that monitor and record the name and password of computer users as they log on, delivering the critical information to a HACKER who has already penetrated the system and put the sniffer to work. With passwords in hand, the intruder is free to roam at will through the violated system, downloading classified information, altering or deleting files, transferring funds in the case of financial institutions, or impersonating rightful system users in a variety of other ways. As the case of KEVIN MITNICK amply illustrated, data may not only be removed, but also added and concealed without the knowledge of a system's normal user. A report in the *Wall Street Journal* suggested that hackers may have sniffed out passwords used by members of America Online, an Internet service with more than 35 million subscribers.

Another hazard for legitimate users whose passwords are stolen lies in the possibility that they may be held responsible, either inadvertently or through a deliberate "frame-up," for the unlawful actions of a hacker who has hijacked their accounts. One possible scenario might involve theft of credit card numbers, stored in a hacked account without the legitimate user's knowledge, later traced by law enforcement officers who come calling with search warrants. In similar fashion, many other forms of cyber-contraband, from stolen files to CHILD PORNOGRAPHY, may be loaded into an innocent user's computer, either for the hacker's momentary convenience or as a deliberate form of harassment.

Passwords are "sniffed" when users log onto their local area networks (LANs) and their computers are briefly vulnerable to every other computer using the same network. While the login process cannot be avoided and present PC technology sounds no alert when a password is monitored, analysts recommend frequent changes in passwords to limit the time when a stolen code may be used to the thief's advantage.

PATTERSON, James Earl: first "cold hit" on DNA evidence

A Virginia native, born January 31, 1967, James Earl Patterson was approaching his 20th birthday on January 11, 1987, when a night of "partying" on drugs and liquor turned to brutal murder. Running short of money for cocaine, Patterson decided to burglarize the home of a recent acquaintance in Prince Georges County, 56-year-old Joyce Snead Aldridge. Shortly before midnight, Patterson broke into Aldridge's home, confronting the woman with a demand for cash. Enraged when he learned that she had only a handful of coins in her purse, Patterson raped Aldridge, then stabbed her three times with one of her own kitchen knives and left her for dead. Aldridge had strength enough to call police, and she was attempting to dial her son's home number when Patterson returned, stabbing her 14 more times and leaving her dead on the floor. The crime was still unsolved a year later, when Patterson raped an 18-year-old woman he met at a party. Convicted on that charge, he was sentenced to 25 years in prison, eligible for parole in the year 2005.

Incarceration changed Patterson's life, according to later reports. He "found Jesus" in the Big House and was "born again," but repentance somehow stopped short of confessing his undisclosed crimes. A born-again reader as well as a religious convert, Patterson studied the modern advances in DNA testing, harboring fears that it might prove to be his undoing. As he later told reporters, "It always played out in the back of my mind that [the evidence] could be put together . . . that it could come back to haunt me." His own DNA had been added to Virginia's ever-growing databank in 1990, following the rape conviction, but despite his newfound religious zeal— "The crimes really tear at my heart. My prayers constantly go out to the family members of the victims."—Patterson still made no effort to wipe the slate clean. In March 1999, Prince Georges County investigators scored a first-ever "cold hit" in the Aldridge case, comparing a genetic profile of her unknown killer to samples in the state database, and they went to visit Patterson in prison. "When I saw the badges come out, it literally took my breath away," he told the press. "The day of judgment had met me."

And still he lied to authorities, denying any role in Aldridge's murder. Only when confronted with irrefutable scientific proof of guilt did Patterson change his tune and confess to the crime. In June 2000 Patterson pleaded guilty to murder, rape, forcible sodomy, and abduction with intent to defile, asking Judge James D'Alton Jr. to impose the ultimate penalty. "As I look around this courtroom, I see lives that I've wrecked," Patterson told the court. "Saying I'm sorry to these people is a hollow statement. These families were touched by me because, in some instances, they befriended me. In befriending me, it turned into their worst nightmare. . . . Your honor, I've thought about the death sentence, and I beg you to give me the death sentence. I pray today that it will be some type of closure for these families. I'm deeply sorry. . . . I just pray the Lord touches their lives and take away the pain I brought upon them." Judge D'Alton granted the request, based on the vile nature of Patterson's crime and his potential for future mayhem.

While passing his final months on death row, rejecting all appeals of his sentence, Patterson waxed philosophical on the marvels of DNA testing. "I applaud the science," he told one interviewer. "It's become a good thing. It has condemned people who needed to be condemned and released people who needed to be released." As for himself, Patterson insisted, "I feel at peace with my decision. It's either going slow or dying quickly. I'm ready to go. I could be running my head against the wall, bawling my eyes out, but it's not that way. I'm getting ready for the big transformation." That transformation came at 9:10 P.M. on March 14, 2002. Before his execution by lethal injection, Patterson told the small audience of court-appointed witnesses, "My heart goes out to the Aldridge family. God bless each and every one of you who is here tonight."

Virginia has been a persistent leader in the use of DNA science to solve criminal cases. The state's 1994 execution of serial killer TIMOTHY SPENCER was the first of a U.S. defendant convicted on the basis of genetic evidence. Statewide, a database of DNA material collected from some 180,000 convicted felons enabled Virginia police to score 300 "cold hits" in 2001, with another 92 between January 1, 2002 and the date of Patterson's execution. In the wake of that event, Virginia's state legislature passed a new law permitting collection of DNA samples from persons awaiting trial for violent crimes, rather than waiting for the outcome of their trials.

PBS/NPR Petition: Internet hoax

This fraudulent petition has circulated on the Internet since 1995, imploring readers to assist in beating back a mythical threat to the Public Broadcasting System (PBS) and National Public Radio (NPR). It apparently began with students at the University of Northern Colorado, in Greeley, who acknowledged launching the hoax and were subsequently reprimanded by university administrators. Future recipients are encouraged to delete the message without taking any action, since the threat is nonexistent. The original message reads:

Subject: PBS and NPR—petition

Please read this VERY IMPORTANT petition! I hope you will then sign it and pass it along to everyone you know. We've got to be active in saving these important institutions! Please sign! Thanks!

This is for anyone who thinks NPR/PBS is a worthwhile expenditure of $1.12/year of their taxes (as opposed to, say, Newt Gingrich's salary?), a petition follows.

If you sign, please forward on to others (not back to me).

If not, please don't kill it—send it to the email address listed here:

wein2688@blue.univnorthco.edu

PBS, NPR (National Public Radio), and the arts are facing major cutbacks in funding. In spite of the efforts of each station to reduce spending costs and streamline their services, some government officials believe that the funding currently going to these programs is too large a portion of funding for something which is seen as "unworthwhile." Currently, taxes from the general public for PBS equal $1.12 per person per year, and the National Endowment for the Arts equals $.64 a year in total.

A January 1995 CNN/USA Today/Gallup poll indicated that 76% of Americans wish to keep funding for PBS, third only to national defense and law enforcement as the most valuable programs for federal funding.

Each year, the Senate and House Appropriations committees each have 13 sub-committees with jurisdiction over many programs and agencies. Each subcommittee passes its own appropriation bill. The goal each year is to have each bill signed by the beginning of the fiscal year, which is October 1.

The only way that our representatives can be aware of the base of support for PBS and funding for these types of programs is by making our voices heard.

Please add your name to this list and forward it to friends if you believe in what we stand for. This list will be forwarded to the President of the United States, the Vice President of the United States, and Representative Newt Gingrich, who is the instigator of the action to cut funding to these worthwhile programs.

If you happen to be the 150th, 200th, 250th etc. signer of this petition, please forward a copy to:

wein2688@blue.univnorthco.edu.

If that address is inoperative, please send it to:

kubi7975@blue.univnorthco.edu.

This way we can keep track of the lists and organize them.

Forward this to everyone you know, and help us to keep these programs alive.

Thank you.

"PENPAL Greetings": Virus Warning: Internet hoax

Apparently designed to counteract an Internet chain letter, this message pursues its goal by claiming (falsely) that the chain letter itself carries a virus. Telltale signs of fraud include the fact that no program can launch itself and that no virus known to date can forward copies of itself to new recipients without regard for the host's or the recipient's e-mail system. The original message reads (with errors intact):

FYI!
Subject: Virus Alert
Importance: High

If anyone receives mail entitled: PENPAL GREETINGS! please delete it WITHOUT reading it. Below is a little explanation of the message, and what it would do to your PC if you were to read the message. If you have any questions or concerns please contact SAF-IA Info Office on 697-5059.

This is a warning for all internet users—there is a dangerous virus propogating across the internet through an e-mail message entitled "PENPAL GREETINGS!".

DO NOT DOWNLOAD ANY MESSAGE ENTITLED "PENPAL GREETINGS!" This message appears to be a friendly letter asking you if you are interested in a penpal, but by the time you read this letter, it is too late. The "trojan horse" virus will have already infected the boot sector of your hard drive, destroying all of the data present. It is a self-replicating virus, and once the message is read, it will AUTOMATICALLY forward itself to anyone who's e-mail address is present in YOUR mailbox!

This virus will DESTROY your hard drive, and holds the potential to DESTROY the hard drive of anyone whose mail is in your inbox, and who's mail is in their inbox, and so on. If this virus remains unchecked, it has the potential to do a great deal of DAMAGE to computer networks worldwide!!!!

Please, delete the message entitled "PENPAL GREETINGS!" as soon as you see it! And pass this message along to all of your friends and relatives, and the other readers of the newsgroups and mailing lists which you are on, so that they are not hurt by this dangerous virus!!!!

PERSONAL Tracking Units: individual surveillance devices

Personal tracking units (PTUs) are electronic devices used to monitor the whereabouts and movements of specific individuals, most commonly criminal defendants who have been sentenced to a term of house arrest as an alternative to prison. PTUs are worn by the surveillance subjects, typically on a locked ankle strap that emits a silent alarm if the device is removed or damaged in some way. The cheaper, more common type of PTU operates with a "tamper-proof" base set installed in the subject's home, sounding an alarm (to the police, the subject's probation officer, etc.) if the subject moves outside an established perimeter (generally his home or the adjacent property). A more advanced (and more expensive) form of PTU incorporates global positioning satellite (GPS) technology to chart the subject's actual movements with near-pinpoint accuracy. The latter devices, in various forms, may also be used for covert surveillance of individuals or specific vehicles, if they can be attached without the subject's or driver's knowledge.

PETERSON, Justin Tanner: hacker and police informer

Justin Peterson's parents divorced when he was eight years old, in 1969. By his teens, settled with his mother in Lincoln, Nebraska, Peterson displayed an avid interest in electronics. Inspired by his mother's work with computers, he bought one for himself in 1981 and left home three years later, moving to California where he worked (or posed) as a nightclub promoter and sound engineer. Living on the fringe of the Los Angeles rock-and-roll scene, calling himself "Eric Heinz"—or "Agent Steal" on-line—Peterson used his self-taught computer skills to steal a living from local radio stations. In a 1989 promotional call-in contest, he seized control of station KPWR-FM's telephones and thereby "won" a $10,000 cash prize. Overall, Peterson later admitted to *Phrack* magazine, he and a handful of accomplices collected "thousands of dollars, trips to Hawaii and a few Porsches" from similar rigged contests. As Peterson himself admitted, he was "getting pretty carried away there for a while. I invaded a lot of people's privacy. Phone taps. Credit reports. Breaking into Pacific Bell offices, etc."

Pacific Bell eventually discovered the computer intrusions and alerted police to Peterson's activities. When officers tried to arrest him, however, Peterson escaped in a high-speed chase and fled to Dallas, where he resumed his illegal activities. Authorities finally captured him in the summer of 1991, seizing computer equipment, five modems and various Pacific Bell manuals from his apartment. An FBI affidavit filed at the time expressed fear that Peterson may have eavesdropped on federal investigators. A Texas grand jury indicted Peterson on eight counts, including unauthorized computer penetration and credit card fraud, while further investigation revealed outstanding arrest warrants in California and Maryland. G-men were willing to give him a break, however. Instead of pressing their case in court, they "turned" Peterson and put him to work as an informer in the HACKER underground. "I didn't have much choice," he later told

Originally developed for the military, the SMART cellular transmitter and ankle bracelet use global positioning to track offenders in at least 20 states. (AP)

Phrack. "Most hackers would have sold out their mother." His file was sealed and transferred to California, where court records describe him as "acting in an undercover capacity" for the FBI.

Peterson's targets in L.A. and environs included notorious hackers KEVIN MITNICK and KEVIN POULSEN, both of whom interacted with the duplicitous "Agent Steal." While pursuing and informing on those targets, Peterson continued his mercenary invasions of the Pacific Bell computer system, presumably without the knowledge of his FBI contacts. The sting operation unraveled in April 1993, when Poulsen and Peterson were both arrested in Los Angeles, along with hacker cohort Ronald M. Austin, charged with rigging radio contests at three stations to fraudulently claim $22,000 in cash, two cars and two Hawaiian vacations. Peterson and Austin pleaded guilty to computer fraud on April 21, while Poulsen was indicted two days later. Peterson, facing a maximum sentence of 40 years in prison and a $1.5 million fine, was released on bail with sentencing deferred until he testified at Poulsen's trial. Federal prosecutors confronted Peterson on October 18, 1993, inquiring as to whether he had been committing more computer crimes while free on bond. Peterson denied any wrongdoing, then vanished on October 22, with a federal arrest warrant issued the same afternoon.

Peterson's *Phrack* interview, published on November 17, 1993, seemed to imply some threat from the FBI beyond a basic pursuit and arrest. "I have learned a lot about how the bureau works," Peterson said. "Probably too much." Lawyers for the defendants still remaining in L.A. accused G-men of entrapment and worse. A protest by attorney Ronald Sherman, addressed to Attorney General Janet Reno on May 19, 1994, accused Los Angeles agents of engaging "in a course of conduct which is illegal and contrary to Bureau policy." Calls for a criminal investigation of the FBI itself were rejected by the Justice Department's public integrity section, while U.S. Attorney David Schindler told reporters, "It is factually incorrect that we allowed Mr. Peterson to commit crimes." Sherman replied with the opinion that FBI agents "don't want to find this guy because then they are really in trouble. Why? Because he will tell you what he was doing for them." Kevin Mitnick had vanished, meanwhile, following Peterson's example as a fugitive.

G-men had their work cut out for them in tracking their one-time informer. Armed with multiple identities and Social Security numbers "too numerous to list" on his wanted poster, Peterson boasted to *Phrack* that "I find people for a living. I don't think it will be hard to use what I know to keep a low profile." In fact, his luck ran out nine months later, when he was captured at a Los Angeles apartment complex in the predawn hours of August 30, 1994. Charged with using his computer to steal $150,000 from a local bank two weeks before his arrest, Peterson pleaded guilty in federal court, on March 27, 1995. He faced a maximum sentence of 60 years in prison and a $2 million fine, but Judge Stephen Wilson proved lenient at his formal sentencing in November 1995, ordering Peterson to serve 41 months with three years' supervised parole, plus

$40,000 in restitution to his corporate victims. Peterson was released to a halfway house in the fall of 1998, to complete his 41-month sentence, but he soon vanished again and was declared a fugitive. Apparently tired of life on the run, however, Peterson soon surrendered and was ordered by the court to serve five more months for his latest jaunt on the lam.

PHAM, Thai H. See PLATINUM TECHNICS INTERNATIONAL

"PHANTOM": computer viruses
Between July and October 1996, Web watchers reported three different viruses employing the "Phantom" label. The two variants discovered in July 1996 are now identified as "Phantom1" and "Phantom.2201," respectively. Phantom1 is a memory-resident, parasitic, polymorphic virus, rated "not dangerous" by analysts, which writes itself to the end of open .com and .exe files. Long periods of keyboard inactivity prompt the virus to display a skull on-screen, with the caption "PHANTOM 1," followed by this message (errors uncorrected):

> *Congradulations!!! Your computer is now infected with a high performance PHANTOM virus! Coming soon: next virii based on the _C00LEST_ mutation engine all over the world: the Advanced Polymorphic Engine! Enjoy this intro! (C) 1994 by Dark Prince.*

Various bugs in Phantom1 cause it to erratically corrupt some infected files—and freeze the host system—while leaving others undamaged. Phantom's visual effects also do not function with MS-Windows or Windows 95.

Phantom.2201 is ranked as a "dangerous," memory-resident, encrypted virus that writes itself to the end of executed .com files that open from a Jump (JMP) command. After corrupting various sectors, Phantom.2201 displays the following message on-screen (errors intact):

> *HI ROOKIE! I'm a THESEASE! I live in YOUR computer—sorry. . . . Thanks to Brains in the Computer Siences!*

Phantom.2201 also adds the following text strings to the end of .arc, .dbf, and .exe files:

The PHANTOM Was HERE—Sorry . . .
Copyright (c) PHANTOM—This virus was designed in
the HUNGARIAN VIRUS DEVELOPING LABORA-
TORY. (H.V.D.L.)v1

The Phantom virus discovered in October 1996 is a stealth macro virus that infects Excel97 spreadsheets and delivers its apparently harmless payload at 4:00 P.M. (1600 hours), when the following message appears in the monitor screen's status bar:

The Phantom
Is watching you!
Beware!

PHILLIPS, Jason: convicted software pirate

A resident of Plano, Texas, born November 9, 1970, Jason Phillips was a member of the HACKERS' syndicate known to its members as "PIRATES WITH ATTITUDE" (PWA). Operating on-line as "Crov8," Phillips joined with fellow PWA members and renegade employees of Intel Corporation to steal computer hardware and software, making the stolen software available to purchasers through a website based in Quebec, Canada. Five Intel employees and 12 PWA hackers (including Phillips) were indicted by the U.S. Justice Department on May 4, 2000, charged with conspiring to infringe copyrights on more than 5,000 different software programs. Phillips was one of eight PWA members who pleaded guilty over the next 12 months, facing a maximum sentence of five years in prison and a $250,000 fine.

"PHONEMASTERS": outlaw hackers' syndicate

A gang of 11 sophisticated HACKERS "whose ultimate goal was to own the telecommunications infrastructure from coast-to-coast," the network known as "Phonemasters" was organized by ringleaders Corey Lindsly, of Portland, Oregon, and Calvin Cantrell, of Grand Prairie, Texas. All members of the group were "elite" computer enthusiasts in their 20s, skilled enough to penetrate telephone networks maintained by AT&T, Sprint, GTE, and British Telecommunications. In addition to the various telephone systems, Phonemasters also penetrated computers owned by utility providers, credit reporting agencies, air traffic control systems, and various governmental agencies (including the FBI's National Crime Information Center), using stolen teleconferencing systems to launch their attacks and cloaking their invasions with state-of-the-art encryption programs.

FBI agent Michael Morris was tipped to Calvin Cantrell's activities in August 1994, but various legal and technical stumbling blocks delayed his investigation for another four months. By December 1991, Agent Morris had obtained permission to intercept telephone impulses from Cantrell's computer modem and the data-tap interception device to accomplish his aim. Collection of evidence was still in progress during February 1995, when a member of the hacker clique alerted Cantrell that his telephone number had surfaced in FBI reports on-line. Morris in turn became aware of the leak and organized simultaneous FBI raids against the homes of Cantrell, Lindsly, and accomplice John Bosanac on February 25, 1995. Legal maneuvers stalled a resolution of the case until March 1999, when Agent Morris played data-taps for the various defendants and all three pleaded guilty to one count of theft, one count of possessing unauthorized calling card numbers, and one count of unauthorized access to protected computer systems. On September 16, 1999, Judge Jerry Buchmeyer sentenced Corey Lindsly to 41 months in federal prison and ordered him to compensate corporate victims in the amount of $10,000; Calvin Cantrell received a two-year prison term and an identical fine. John Bosanac, sentenced separately on his guilty plea, received an 18-month sentence and an order for $10,000 restitution. No other members of the Phonemasters gang have been charged so far.

PIERCE, Jeffrey Todd: exonerated by DNA evidence

At noon on May 8, 1985, a female Oklahoma City resident returned home from work to find a window of her apartment broken, the flat ransacked. While she was examining the damage, a knife-wielding stranger emerged from another room, overpowered the woman, and raped her. In her statement to police, the victim speculated that her attacker may have been the same man she briefly observed while leaving for work that morning. On that occasion, the unidentified man had been standing in some nearby shrubbery, holding what appeared to be a garden tool.

Police initially suspected that the rapist might be a groundskeeper employed by the apartment complex, one of whom was 23-year-old Jeffrey Pierce. On the day of the rape, however, a patrol officer pointed Pierce out to the victim and asked her if he was the assailant, whereupon she answered, "I don't think so." Another 10 months passed before Pierce was arrested and charged with the crime, in March 1986, after the victim changed her mind. At trial, in October 1986, the victim who initially dismissed Pierce as a suspect told the jury, "I will never forget his face." Pierce countered with two alibi witnesses who said he was eating lunch with them at the time of the rape. Jurors were finally swayed by testimony from police chemist JOYCE GILCHRIST, who declared that 28 scalp hairs and three pubic hairs recovered from the crime scene were "microscopically consistent" with Pierce's hair. Prosecutor Barry Albert told the court that the odds of Gilchrist being mistaken were "totally astronomical." Upon conviction, Pierce received a 65-year prison term.

On appeal, Pierce's attorney noted that Gilchrist had ignored a court order to provide suspect hair samples for independent testing. The Oklahoma Appeals Court agreed that her conduct was illegal but refused to order a new trial, stating that the defense had an "equal obligation" to enforce the judge's order (although what means they might have used was not explained). Gilchrist's mishandling and falsification of evidence was eventually exposed, an FBI lab report noting that she "went beyond the acceptable limits of forensic science or misidentified hair and fibers in at least six criminal cases," including that of Jeffrey Pierce.

As that scandal unfolded in May 2001, the Oklahoma State Bureau of Investigation announced the results of DNA testing on hairs from the 1985 crime scene. Those tests exonerated Pierce, and three months later identified the actual rapist as a prison inmate already serving 45 years for another sexual assault. Because the statute of limitations had expired, no further charges could be filed against the guilty party. Upon hearing the announcement, original trial juror Roy Orr told reporters, "I feel like I was part of a scam. The evidence wasn't correct, and we counted on the police department and forensic specialists to be honest and truthful, and that wasn't the case." Joyce Gilchrist, promoted to an administrative post in 1993 and placed on leave of absence when the scandal broke, told the television program *60 Minutes II*, "I've never lied in court. I've always told the truth. I've never lied to anyone about anything. If you don't want to know the truth, don't ask me because I'm not going to sugarcoat anything for you. I'm going to tell it to you. . . . I'll tell it to you just the way it is."

Legislation to financially compensate wrongfully imprisoned inmates was introduced in the Oklahoma State Senate on May 9, 2001, two days after Pierce was freed from prison. Despite initial optimism, the bill was defeated 11 days later. Rather than settle for the state's apology, Pierce's attorneys filed a $75 million federal lawsuit on April 1, 2002 against Joyce Gilchrist, former District Attorney Bob Macy and the Oklahoma City Police Department, charging the defendants with false imprisonment and violation of Pierce's civil rights. The lawsuit remains unresolved at this writing.

"PIKACHU": computer worm

Also sometimes called "Pokemon," after the Japanese television cartoon series in which the "Pikachu" character appears, this worm virus was initially reported on the Internet in September 2000. It spreads, like so many others, via infected e-mail attachments sent using Microsoft Outlook. The infected attachment bears the title "PikachuPokemon.exe," while the worm itself consists of a Win32 .exe file written in Visual Basic 6.0.

When infecting a new host computer, Pokemon overwrites the system's original c:\autoexec.bat file with instructions that delete all existing files in the Windows and Windows system directories, thereafter searching MS Outlook's address book and dispatching messages to other unsuspecting victims. Those messages read:

> Subject: Pikachu Pokemon.
> Text: Great Friend! Pikachu from Pokemon Theme have some friendly words to say.
>
> Visit Pikachu at http://www.pikachu.com
> See you.

To each e-mail message, Pikachu appends itself in the infected attachment. Upon opening, it displays the trademark logo of the yellow cartoon character, while infection of the new host computer proceeds.

"PIRATES with Attitude": international hackers' syndicate

Organized in the early 1990s, the HACKER consortium known to its members as "Pirates with Attitude" (PWA) was apparently created with the purpose of using illicit means to turn a profit in cyberspace. Members in Belgium, Canada, Sweden, and the United States communicated via private Internet Relay Chat (IRC) channels dubbed "#pwa" and "#tude" in pursuit of their illegal schemes. (The attitude was displayed in PWA's motto. Members called themselves "The Group That Gives Slightly Less Than a Fuck.") The group also maintained numerous File Transfer Protocol (FTP) sites on the Internet, configured for the transfer of pirated software stored in bulk on the various sites. One site operated by PWA members, known as "Sentinel," was among the first FTP sites on the Internet, operating from late 1995 until January 2000. Based at the University of Sherbrooke in Sherbrooke, Quebec, "Sentinel" was established specifically as a "WAREZ" site—cyberspeak for a site trafficking in stolen software—and was not accessible to the general public. Access was limited to authorized users. Those users, in turn, were selected by alleged PWA leader ROBIN ROTHBERG, a.k.a "Marlenus," a resident of North Chelmsford, Massachusetts.

Members of PWA were granted access to the Sentinel FTP site on a "merit" basis, required to upload software files from other sources in return for permission to browse and download the programs of their choice. Authorities would later charge that Rothberg also authorized access by 100 other individuals who had negotiated private terms. Between January 1998 and January 2000, more than 5,000 copyrighted software programs were illegally stored and traded via the Sentinel site, in flagrant violation of U.S. and international copyright laws. While Sentinel was active, an estimated 1,200 gigabytes of software were uploaded to the site, with more than 4,300 gigabytes downloaded by visitors. The programs included operating systems, utilities, applications such as word processing and data analysis programs, and games and MP3 music files, including, programs published by Adobe, IBM, Lotus Microsoft, Norton, Novell, and Oracle.

Within PWA, members were assigned specific roles, including "suppliers" (who funneled software programs to the group from major companies), "crackers" (who stripped away the copy protection commonly embedded in commercial software), "packagers" (who tested programs and prepared them for release), and "couriers" (who transferred software to PWA's FTP sites). One PWA supplier, employed by Microsoft, was JUSTIN ROBBINS—a.k.a. "Warlock"—of Charlotte, North Carolina, valued for his access to expensive cutting-edge programs. In addition to stealing software himself, Robbins also granted Rothberg access to Microsoft's internal network, using Robbins's identification and password.

Another phase of the PWA conspiracy, launched in December 1998, involved the enlistment of various Intel Corporation employees to furnish computer hardware that the Sentinel FTP site's storage capacity. Intel workers who joined in the plot were later identified as 27-year-old TYRONE AUGUSTINE, of Olympia, Washington; 23-year-old BRIAN BOYANOVSKY (a.k.a. "Boynger"), of Beaverton, Oregon; 36-year-old JOHN GEISSBERGER, from Columbia, South Carolina; 28-year-old BRIAN RILEY, of Olympia, Washington; and 24-year-old GENE TACY, also from Olympia. In pursuance of the conspiracy, Intel's rogue employees shipped the requisite hardware to Canada at Intel's expense but without the company's knowledge, Geissberger assisting its clearance through Canadian customs. Tacy thereafter configured Intel's servers to make software readily accessible. In return for those services, the Intel moles were granted free access to Sentinel.

In July 1999 the U.S. Department of Justice announced a law enforcement initiative aimed at combating the new epidemic of software piracy and copyright infringement, both domestically and abroad. The Sentinel FTP site was an early target of that investigation, combining efforts of the FBI and Canadian authorities. Raiders seized the Quebec computer on January 13, 2000, and PWA leader Rothberg was arrested on February 3, 2000. Indictments followed three months later, on May 4, charging 17 defendants with conspiracy to infringe copyrights on more than 5,000 computer software programs valued in excess of $1 million. Those indicted, aside from Rothberg, Justin Robbins, and the five Intel employees, included: 42-year-old STEVEN AHNEN (a.k.a. "Code3"), of Sarasota, Florida; Swedish citizen KAJ BJORLIN (a.k.a. "Darklord"); 39-year-old DIANE DIONNE (a.k.a. "Akasha"), from West Palm Beach, Florida; 27-year-old CHRISTIAN MORLEY (a.k.a. "Mercy"), of Salem, Massachusetts; 34-year-old THOMAS OLIVER (a.k.a. "Rambone"), from Aurora, Illinois; 29-year-old JASON PHILLIPS (a.k.a. "Crov8", of Plano, Texas; 30-year-old JASON SLATER (a.k.a. "Technic"), from Walnut Creek, California; 34-year-old MARK STONE (a.k.a. "Stoned"), of Cypress, California; Belgian national MARK VEERBOKEN (a.k.a. "Shiffie"); and 40-year-old TODD VEILLETTE (a.k.a. "Gizmo"), of Oakdale, Connecticut.

Federal prosecutors described the PWA as "one of the oldest and most sophisticated networks of software pirates anywhere in the world," their indictment hailed as "the most significant investigation of copyright infringement involving the use of the Internet conducted to date by the FBI." Despite the massive software thefts involved, each defendant was charged with one count of conspiracy to infringe copyrights, the maximum sentence upon conviction including five years in prison and a $250,000 fine (or twice the gross gain of any particular defendant from the scheme).

Over the 12 months following the mass indictment, PWA members Rothberg, Ahnen, Dionne, Oliver, Phillips, Robbins, Slater, Stone, and Veillette pleaded guilty as charged. Guilty pleas were also received from all five of the turncoat Intel Corporation employees. Christian Morley took his chances with a federal jury and was convicted on May 15, 2001, later sentenced to two years in prison. Eleven of those who pleaded guilty (excluding Rothberg, Ahnen and Robbins) were sentenced on April 19, 2002: Jason Slater received an eight-month prison term, followed by six months' community confinement; Thomas Oliver was sentenced to six months' community confinement with electronic monitoring and a $5,000 fine; the other nine drew terms of community or home confinement that ranged from three to six months each, plus 200 hours of community service, five years' probation and fines up to $5,000. Rothberg, as PWA's leader, was sentenced separately, on May 15, 2002, to an 18-month prison term. Sentencing on defendants Ahnen and Robbins, both described as "cooperative," was deferred to a later date. European defendants Bjorlin and Veerboken remain at large, considered fugitives from justice at this writing.

PISZCZEK, Brian: exonerated by DNA evidence
In the early morning hours of July 29, 1990, a female resident of Cleveland, Ohio, was drawn to her apartment door by unexpected knocking. Looking through the security peephole, she saw a stranger standing on her doorstep. When she asked the man to identify himself, he gave the name of a mutual friend, and claimed that friend was parking his car outside. The woman later told police she thought the man's voice was familiar, believing him to be an acquaintance named Tom or Tim, who had visited her home once before. She opened the door to admit him, whereupon the stranger drew a knife, slashing the victim's neck, breast, and stomach before he raped her on the floor.

Two months after the attack, the victim identified suspect Brian Piszczek from a police photo lineup, and later repeated that identification in court. Piszczek acknowledged visiting the woman's home on one prior occasion, with the same mutual friend whose name was mentioned by the rapist in July 1990. Piszczek's alibi, in turn, was corroborated only by his girlfriend, whom jurors found unconvincing. On June 25, 1991, Piszczek was convicted of rape, felonious assault, and burglary, receiving a sentence of 15 to 25 years in prison.

On appeal, with a new attorney from the public defender's office, Piszczek challenged the police photo identification process and complained of ineffective trial counsel, noting that his first attorney had not requested DNA testing of semen recovered from the crime scene. That appeal was rejected, prompting attorneys from the CARDOZO INNOCENCE PROJECT to take Piszczek's case. The new team filed a release-of-evidence motion with the Cuyahoga County Court of Common Pleas, which was granted on March 11, 1994. Test results delivered on July 6, 1994, excluded Piszczek as a donor of the semen found at the crime scene, and one day later the prosecutor's office asked a judge to overturn Piszczek's conviction. Even then, Piszczek remained in custody for another three months, until a judge declared him innocent and ordered his release on October 6, 1994. The case remains officially unsolved today.

PITCHFORK, Colin: first killer convicted by DNA evidence
On November 22, 1983, 15-year-old Lynda Mann was raped and strangled in the English village of Enderby, Leicestershire. Police were still hunting for suspects on July 31, 1986, when 15-year-old Dawn Ashworth was killed in identical fashion, in neighboring Narborough. Convinced that a local man was responsible for both crimes, authorities requested blood samples from all area males between the ages of 16 and 34, for purposes of comparing their DNA "fingerprints" with semen samples recovered from the victims. By July 1987, 3,556 individuals had been cleared of involvement in the crimes, including a 17-year-old Narborough youth already booked on suspicion of committing the Ashworth homicide.

Of 4,196 men in the area, only two refused to submit blood samples when asked. One provided authorities with an undisclosed "legitimate excuse" for refusing, while the other—Colin Pitchfork, a 27-year-old bakery worker from Littlethorpe—seemed curiously evasive. Pitchfork had skipped three appointments with police in January 1987, then finally paid coworker Ian Kelly £200 to donate blood in his name. Kelly complied and Pitchfork was "cleared," until Kelly had a change of heart and informed police of the ruse in August 1987. Pitchfork was thereafter arrested, and detectives got their blood sample, which positively linked Pitchfork to both murders. (The helpful coworker was charged with conspiracy to pervert the course of justice, convicted, and sentenced to 18 months in prison.)

A review of Pitchfork's police record turned up prior convictions for indecent exposure, and Pitchfork confessed to the slayings when confronted with scientific proof of his guilt. At the same time, he was also positively linked to the rapes of two more women who survived his attacks. On January 22, 1988, he pleaded guilty on two counts of murder and two counts of indecent assault, receiving a double life sentence on the murder charges and two concurrent 10-year sentences for the attacks on surviving victims.

PITELIS, Michael: Internet extortionist

Parametric Technology Corporation (PTC), based in Waltham, Massachusetts, is a producer of computer-aided-design software. Its flagship package, dubbed "Pro/Engineer," was created to help manufacturers design and develop new products. It sells for an average $100,000 in CD-ROM format, with the price including key passwords that grant the buyer access to Pro/Engineer's programs and to technical support from PTC. Security of those passwords, as with so much other high-priced software, is critical to the company's survival.

On August 3, 2000, PTC chief executive Richard Harrison received an e-mail signed by one "Bill Myers," asking what would happen if Pro/Engineer's passwords and installation instructions were made public on the Internet. After supplying details of the installation process, Myers wrote that an "unnamed individual" was prepared to pay $250,000 for the information. David Freeman, PTC's senior vice president and counsel, replied on August 10, seeking assurances that payment of the ransom would insure security. "Myers" wrote back the next day, telling Freeman, "We will initially accept a lump sum of $400,000 from PTC to contain this information." He also demanded a "maintenance fee" of $40,000 per month. On August 14 "Myers" reported that an offshore bank account had been established to accept PTC's wire transfers of cash.

PTC's officers contacted the FBI at that point, and agents went to work on tracing "Myers." The extortionist had initially used the e-mail address goldwinO@yahoo.com, until a PTC employee alerted Yahoo to the crime in progress and the account was canceled. Rebounding from that setback, "Myers" had quickly established another account with the address goldwinOO@yahoo.com. This time, instead of shutting down the account, subpoenas were issued for records that enabled agents to trace the elusive writer's telephone numbers. The first two messages from "Myers" were traced to the home telephone of 39-year-old Michael Pitelis, a resident of Tarpon Springs, Florida. Pitelis maintained a website listing him as president and senior associate of Pitelis and Associates, allegedly a firm that "specializes in the application, training and support of (PTC) Pro/Engineer." Subsequent e-mails were tracked to a computer at the Tarpon Springs Public Library.

Agents alerted the library staff that one of their public-access computers had been used to commit a crime, but the librarians were asked not to interfere. Mounting surveillance on Pitelis, the agents trailed him from his condominium to the Tarpon Springs library on August 21, 2000, watching as he typed out his latest threatening message to PTC. This e-mail raised the ante to a flat $1 million. Arrested the following day, Pitelis was indicted for extortion on August 30, with bond set at $25,000 by U.S. Magistrate Judge Mark Pizzo. Conviction on the charge carries a maximum sentence of 20 years in prison and a $250,000 fine, but Pitelis never faced his day in court. He died before the case came to trial.

PLATINUM Technics International: indicted software pirates

A New York-based computer firm, Platinum Technics International (USA) Inc. was indicted by the U.S. Department of Justice on June 22, 2000, charged with trafficking in counterfeit computer software and counterfeit computer central processing units (CPUs or "chips"). Also charged in the same indictment were Platinum's owner, Jinxin ("David") Wu, and sales manager Tai H. ("Danny") Pham. According to the charges, Wu and Pham purchased CPUs from legitimate suppliers, then changed their labels for those of higher-priced, higher-speed Intel CPUs and disabled the chips' speed-lock controls to let them operate at higher speeds than normal (causing them to burn out long before the expiration of their presumed life expectancy). Counterfeit software allegedly sold by Platinum included Windows 95 and Office 97 programs obtained through black market channels.

The federal indictment included three counts for each defendant. The first count charged Platinum, Wu, and Pham with conspiracy to traffic in counterfeit computer chips and software. The second and third counts, respectively, charge the defendants with actually trafficking in counterfeit CPUs and software programs. As a corporate defendant, Platinum faced fines of $5 million on each of the three counts, for a maximum total of $15 million. Individual defendants faced a maximum combined sentence of 25 years in prison for all three counts. A parallel civil action sought forfeiture of any and all proceeds obtained by Platinum, Wu, or Pham through the illicit transactions.

A collaborative effort of the U.S. Secret Service and the New York Electronic Crimes Task Force, these indictments were part of an "Intellectual Property Rights Initiative" announced by the U.S. Justice Department on July 23, 1999. In the wake of the New York arrests, Assistant Attorney General James Robinson told reporters, "This case should serve as a notice that the Justice Department has made prosecution of counterfeiting of computer hardware and software one of its priorities. Those who engage in this activity, whether or not for profit, should take heed that we will bring federal resources to bear to prosecute these cases. This is theft, pure and simple."

PODIATRY, Forensic

Forensic podiatry involves the comparison of footprints or shoeprints from an unknown subject with known suspects in a criminal case, as a means of identification. Depending on the circumstances of a crime scene, feet or shoes may leave visible impressions on any "recording service" with which they make contact. Bare footprints on a receptive surface are left in body oil, the same as fingerprints, and they are equally distinctive, unique to a particular individual. Prints of feet or footwear may also leave traces via transfer of some staining material (blood, paint, grease, ink, etc.) to a hard surface, or by leaving physical impressions in some softer medium (mud, sand, wet cement, loose soil). Where two or more consecutive prints are found, the length of stride may help determine a subject's height. The depth of an impression left in pliable material also permits investigators to calculate the subject's weight.

While bare footprints are as unique as fingerprints, they likewise require a known subject for comparison. Footprints are commonly preserved in ink for many infants born in the United States, but no centralized database or repository exists, and a search of records in all 50 states (not considering foreign countries) would be a near-hopeless endeavor without a name and/or place of birth to launch the exercise. Identification may not be assured even when such records are obtained, however, for as Dr. Anne Wingate notes in her book *Scene of the Crime* (1992), many hospital footprints taken from infants are "cute, fuzzy and illegible." When such comparisons are possible, however, they should prove conclusive. In addition to natural ridge patterns (like those of fingerprints), the sole of every human foot reveals distinct flexion creases that are (at least theoretically) unique to a given individual.

Shoes naturally complicate identification, for while the tread patterns of various athletic shoes may be distinctive as to brand or style, thousands (or millions) of shoes with the same pattern have been sold across the country or worldwide. Smooth-soled shoes, if new, also confound investigators. Fortunately for detectives, though, each shoe begins to show distinctive wear patterns from the day it is purchased. Nicks, cuts, and gouges on the sole are as unique as scars on flesh or imperfections in the barrel of a gun. A worn-down heel or sole also tells much about the subject's style of walking, in some cases enough to spot a distinctive gait on the street.

Footprints may be preserved as evidence by means of photographs or casts, the latter sometimes more useful in terms of demonstrating depth and distinctive physical peculiarities. Such evidence is not immune to fakery, however. In the late 1950s, for example, a sheriff's deputy in Lake County, Florida was found to have "solved" several high-profile cases by confiscating the shoes of different suspects and creating casts from them in his office, then falsely testifying that the casts had been made at crime scenes. The convictions in those cases were ultimately reversed, but not before two innocent suspects were shot to death by police, while three others served long prison terms for crimes they did not commit. The deputy, meanwhile, went unpunished.

POISONED ATM Envelope Warning: Internet hoax

Circulated on the Internet since June 1999, this fear-inducing message is similar to the various NEEDLE

WARNINGS broadcast on the Web, though it transforms the object of dread. Spelling and telephone area code suggest an origin in Toronto, Ontario, but the alleged author and her "crime unit" are figments of the hoaxer's imagination. The original message reads:

Very scary! Please read. . . .

Whenever you go to an automatic teller machine to make deposits, make sure you don't lick the deposit envelopes. (spit on it) A customer died after licking an envelope at a teller machine at Yonge & Eglinton. According to the police, Dr. Elliot at the Women's college hospital found traces of cyanide in the lady's mouth and digestive system and police traced the fatal poison to the glue on the envelope she deposited that day. They then did an inspection of other envelopes from other teller machines in the area and found six more. The glue is described as colourless and odourless. They suspect some sickco is targeting this particular bank and has been putting the envelopes beside machines at different locations. A spokesperson from the bank said their hands are tied unless they take away the deposit function from all machines. So watch out, and please forward this message to the people you care about.

Thanks
Kimberly Clarkson
Crime unit, Department for Public Health
(416) 563-9905

POULSEN, Kevin Lee: hacker "Dark Dante"

The case of California native Kevin Poulsen clearly illustrates the fallacy of arguments contending that "purist" HACKERS are innocent at heart, possessed of no criminal motive, and that they are persecuted by law enforcement for committing simple "crimes of curiosity." So it may have been for Poulsen in the early days of his career in cyberspace, but actions speak louder than words, revealing him in the end as just another mercenary thief.

Born in 1965, Poulsen had developed an unhealthy obsession with the telephone system by age 13. A self-taught "phreaker" who studied the Pacific Bell system in every spare moment, Poulsen obtained his first computer and modem in 1981, logging on to hacker bulletin boards as "Dark Dante." Two years later, he was mesmerized by the apocalyptic scenarios of the movie *War Games* and began to experiment more boldly, accessing restricted computers at the University of California in Berkeley; the Lawrence Livermore Laboratories; the Los Alamos and White Sands, New Mexico nuclear testing facilities; the U.S. Army's Ballistics Research Laboratory; and a military base on Chesapeake Bay, in Maryland. As a joke, in his spare time, Poulsen rerouted calls for directory assistance to his bedroom telephone, directing callers to the appropriate pages of their telephone books in lieu of providing the numbers they sought. Poulsen finally dropped out of high school to pursue hacking full-time, then found himself barred from a technical school by his lack of a high school diploma. He ultimately found work as a programmer for SRI, a Silicon Valley defense contractor, but was fired in 1989 when compulsive phreaking interfered with his work.

Law enforcement officers were on his trail by that time, and Poulsen went underground, living by his modem and his wits as he pursued his hacker fantasy. To support and amuse himself, he invaded Pacific Bell's switching network to rig Los Angeles radio call-in contests, commandeering the phone lines to insure successive wins. In that fashion, Poulsen and two friends collected some $22,000 in cash, several trips to Hawaii, and two $50,000 Porsches. On the side, FBI manhunters maintained, Poulsen also compromised national security wiretaps, invaded the National Crime Information Center and alerted subjects of covert federal surveillance, and jammed the phone lines of TV's *Unsolved Mysteries* after his case was featured on the program. When not playing cat-and-mouse with his pursuers, Poulsen also tapped the phones of various private citizens, including actress Molly Ringwald.

Authorities captured Poulsen on June 21, 1991, charging him with a list of felonies that included espionage, computer fraud, interception of wire communications, money laundering, mail fraud, and obstruction of justice. Once federal prosecutors agreed to drop the dubious espionage counts, which carried a potential life sentence, Poulsen pleaded guilty to the rest and received a 51-month prison term. He was paroled on June 4, 1996, placed on three years' probation that included a ban on use of computers or surfing the Internet. Today, a presumably reformed "Dark Dante" earns his living as a freelance writer, occasional lecturer on topics related to computer security, and as editorial director of the award-winning security news and information website SecurityFocus Online.

POULSEN, Michael: confessed satellite TV pirate

A resident of Mountain View, California, Michael Poulsen was one of 15 defendants indicted by federal authorities in 2000, as a result of an Internet sting campaign dubbed "OPERATION SMARTCARD. NET." In the course of that investigation, U.S. Customs Service agents established a website for the sale of counterfeit access cards granting purchasers the ability to view satellite television transmissions without paying the normal monthly fees. Most of those indicted were themselves "smart card" dealers, purchasing the counterfeit cards for resale to individual customers at higher prices in a scam that reportedly cost one satellite provider more than $6 million in a single year. Poulsen was one of four Smartcard defendants who pleaded guilty as charged in August 2000.

"PREDATOR": computer viruses

From its initial discovery on the Internet, in October 1996, "Predator" has diversified to include a total of seven recognized variants, identified respectively by the numerical suffixes 1063, 1072, 1137, 1148, 1154, 1195 and 1449. All are ranked by analysts as "dangerous," memory-resident, parasitic viruses, with Predator.1072, 1154 and 1449 also being encrypted. The viruses write themselves to the ends of open or executed .com files, sometimes reversing bits in the process. The following text strings are displayed by variants in the family:

Predator.1063, 1137, 1148 and 1195:

> *Predator virus (c) Mar. 93*
> *In memory of all those who were killed . . .*
> *Wookies ain't the only ones that drop! Priest*

Predator.1072:

> *Predator virus (c) Mar. 93 Priest*

Predator.1449:

> *C:\COMMAND.DAT*
> *Predator virus2 (c) Sep. 95 Mc Fly*

"PRIZM": computer viruses

Two different viruses using the "Prizm" name have thus far been reported from the Internet. The first, initially described in February 1999, is an encrypted Word macro virus that replicates in documents as they are opened, saved, and closed. During infection of a new host computer, Prizm employs the host's Dynamic Data Exchange (DDE) instructions, then creates a randomly named .exe file in the Windows temporary directory and writes its program there. When infected documents are printed, Prizm adds the following text at the end: "Battle of life. Capital!!!"

The other, unrelated Prizm virus was discovered on the Internet in January 2001. It is described by analysts as a "very dangerous," memory-resident, parasitic, polymorphic Windows 9x virus that infects .exe files bearing .exe and .dll filename extensions. When infected files are run thereafter, Prizm searches for additional applications and infects them, as well. If an infected program is run on the first, 11th, 13th, and/or 26th day of any month, Prizm erases randomly selected sectors on various drives, overwriting them with its own viral code and displays the following message on a blue screen:

> *Virus Win9x.Chazhma(Chernobil2)*
> *Made by SpAmC0der->[PRiZM]->Vladivostok->Russia*
> *Battle of life. Capital!!!*
> *to be continued . . . Win32.Kursk2000*

"PRO-ALIFE": computer virus

Apparently designed as a spoof of ANTIABORTION propaganda, the "Pro-Alife" computer virus was initially recognized in September 1996. Analysts rate it as a "dangerous," memory-resident, parasitic virus that writes itself to the end of executed .exe files. Whenever an infected program is terminated, Pro-Alife randomly displays one of the following messages on-screen:

> *Kill an evil satanic ANTI-VIRAL product for Jesus today!*
> *Stop Disinfectants NOW!*
> *Ain't aLife A Beautiful Choice?*
> *And God Said, "Let There Be Life!", and there was. . . .*
> *Save the Viruses! They're People Too!!!!*
> *PRO-aLIFE and PROUD! STOP THE VIRUS KILLERS! HALT THE AV!*
> *STORM THE COMPU-CLINICS! DON'T LET THEM KILL THE VIRUSES!!!*
> *Operation Rescue-II, Save the HELPLESS UNBORN Viruses!!!*

Pro-Alife also has a built-in defense against the following antivirus programs: clean.exe, cpav.exe, f-prot.exe, fsp.exe, msav.exe, scan.exe, tbav.exe, tbclean.exe, tbscan.exe, vdefend.exe, virstop.exe and vsafe.exe. When any of those programs is run on an infected host computer, the virus overwrites them with a Trojan program that displays the following message upon execution:

Eddie Lives, Somewhere in time! _____ 1704
*Jerusalem Casino :(;(=(Smeg off! _____ ___ *
Frodo Lives! APRIL FOOLS!
Get a late pass! Datacrime _____ Brain Void-Poem
Your PC is now STONED! ___ OO _____ O __
Copy me, I want to travel!

1,000,000,000 Viruses DIED Today!
And yesterday, and more will die tomorrow!
_/_STOP THE KILLING!_/_
Look What You're Doing To Them!
Below is an aborted virus . . .
Support PRO-aLIFE Activism!
This program has been TERMINATED by the
Virus Survival Underground Movement.
It had long stood as a horrible BABY VIRUS KILLER, and
had to be removed.
Life, What a Beautiful Choice (tm).
—== -----------[OPERATION RESCUE II—SAVING
THE BABY VIRUSES!]-----------==—
Thank you for choosing life over destruction.
Have a Nice Day (tm).

At various other times, Pro-Alife also displays the following messages on-screen:

THE PREDATOR presents the J.TTPOG Virus (c) 1996
SWEDEN!!!!!
THE PREDATOR presents the __ __ __
J.TTPOG VIRUS (c) 1996/03/15 __ __ __
SWEDEN _____ __
And says __ __ __ __ __ __

PROCTER & Gamble Satanism Warning:
Internet defamation

This persistent and malicious hoax predates the advent of the Internet, traceable to the late mid-1960s. Soon after the Church of Satan was first publicized, in 1966, rumors spread that soap manufacturers Procter & Gamble were affiliated with the

Satanic organization, P&G's famous moon-and-stars logo cited as proof of occult influence. Denials notwithstanding, the libelous claim has survived and evolved over time. In the era of TV talk shows, stories initially spread that spokesmen for Procter & Gamble had confessed their Satanic alliance on Phil Donahue's daily program. When Donahue refuted the lie, hoaxers changed their tune to incorporate other sources, flying in the face of repeated exposure to maintain the fraud. Talk show host Sally Jessy Raphael has publicly denied the latest version of the smear campaign, broadcast in July 1999. That version reads (with errors uncorrected):

The President of Procter & gamble appeared on the Sally Jesse Raphael Show on March 1, 1998. He announced that "due to the openness of our society", he was coming out of the closet about his association with the church of Satan. He stated that a large portion of his profits from Procter & Gamble Products goes to support this satanic church. When asked by Sally Jesse if stating this on t.v. would hurt his business, he replied, "THERE ARE NOT ENOUGH CHRISTIANS IN THE UNITED STATES TO MAKE A DIFFERENCE."

Product list includes:

Cleaning supplies: Bold, Cascade, Cheers, Joy, Comet, Dash, Spic & Span, Tide, Top Job, Oxidol, Ivory Dreft, Gain, Mr. Clean, Lest Oil, Bounty Towels
Food: Duncan Hines, Fisher Nuts, Fisher Mints, Dehydrated Fruits
Coffee: Folgers, High Point,
Shortening Oils: Crisco, Puritan, Fluffo
Deodorants: Secret, Sure
Diapers: Luvs, Pampers
Hair Care: Lilt, Head & Shoulders, Prell, Pert, Vidal Sassoon, Ivory
Acne Product: Clearasil
Mouthwash/Toothpaste: Scope, Crest, Gleem
Peanut Butter: JIF
Personal Hygiene: Always, Attend Undergarments
Lotions: Oil of Olay, Wondra
Soap: Camay, Coast, Ivory, Lava, Safeguard, Zest, Oil of Olay
Fabric Softener: Downy, Bounce
Citrus Punch: Sunny Delight
Medication: Aleve, Pepto-Bismol

If you are not sure about the product, look for a Procter & Gamble written on the products, or the symbol of

a ram's horn, which will appear on each product beginning on January 1, 2000. The ram's horn will form the 666, which is known as Satan's number. Christians should remember that if they purchase any of these products, they will be contributing to the church of Satan. Inform other Christians about this and STOP buying Procter & Gamble Products. Let's show Procter & Gamble that there are enough Christians to make a difference. On a previous Jenny Jones Show, the owner of Procter & Gamble said that if Satan would prosper he would give his heart and soul to him. Then he gave Satan credit for his riches. Anyone interested seeing this tape, should send $3.00 to: SALLY TRANSCRIPTS 515 WEST 57TH STREET NEW YORK NY 10019

WE URGE YOU TO MAKE COPIES OF THIS AND PASS IT ON TO AS MANY PEOPLE AS POSSIBLE. THIS NEEDS TO STOP. LIZ CLAIRBORNE ALSO PROFESSES TO WORSHIP SATAN AND RECENTLY OPENLY ADMITTED ON THE OPRAH WINFREY SHOW THAT HALF OF HER PROFITS GO TOWARDS THE CHURCH OF SATAN. >>

PROGESTEREX Warning: Internet hoax

The horrors of "Progesterex," as detailed in this Internet warning message, are mitigated by the fact that no such drug exists. Research conducted by HOAXBUSTERS and the University of Florida College of Pharmacy in March 2002 failed to discover any medication manufactured or sold under that name anywhere on Earth, at any time. The hoax message reads (errors intact):

WAY TOO CLOSE TO HOME!
this was sent by a friend.

Important notice

A woman at Gastown nightclub on Saturday night was taken by 5 men, who according to hospital and police reports, gang raped her before dumping her naked at Neutral Bay. Unable to remember the events of the evening, tests later confirmed the repeat rapes along with traces of rohypnol in her blood. Boyfriends, take heed. Good guys out there, please forward this message to your lady friends. Progesterex, that is essentially a small sterilisiation pill. The drug is now being used by rapists at parties to rape AND sterilize their victims. Progesterex is available to vets to sterilize large animals. Rumour has it that the Progesterex is being used

together with Rohypnol, the date rape drug. As with Rohypnol, all they have to do is drop it into the girl's drink. The girl can't remember a thing the next morning, of all that had taken place the night before. Progesterex, which dissolves in drinks just as easily, is such that the victim doesn't conceive from the rape and the rapist needn't worry about having a paternity test identifying him months later. The drug's effects AREN'T TEMPORARY. Progesterex was designed to sterilize horses. Any female that takes it WILL NEVER BE ABLE TO CONCEIVE. The crooks can get this drug from anyone who is in the vet school of any university. It's that easy, and Progesterex is about to break out big on campuses everywhere. Believe it or not, there is even a site on the internet telling people how to use it. Please forward this to everyone you know, especially girls.

"PROJECT Colt": campaign against telemarketing fraud

An ongoing cooperative effort between Canadian and U.S. authorities, "Project COLT"—for Centre of Operations Linked to Telemarketing Fraud—was launched from Montreal, Quebec, in April 1998. Cooperating agencies in the campaign include the Royal Canadian Mounted Police, the Montreal Urban Community Police, the Sûreté du Québec, the U.S. Customs Service, the FBI, and the U.S. Postal Inspection Service, together with various local law enforcement agencies around the United States. COLT's particular targets are cross-border swindlers who prey chiefly (but not exclusively) on elderly victims, claiming an estimated $70 million in illicit profits per year. (The average U.S. victim loses $3,100 to telemarketers before he stops paying and contacts police.) COLT investigators identify the most common telemarketing frauds as:

1. *Lottery or Sweepstakes Scams.* Con artists telephone victims to tell them they have won a lottery jackpot or other substantial prize. The caller tells the person that in order for the prize money to be released, they must first pay a Customs duty, a tax, or a fee, usually amounting to several thousand dollars. The "winners" are asked to send a check or wire the fee to a bank account or foreign address. Swindlers often pressure their victims by telling them they only have a limited amount of time to send in the fee, before their mythical winnings are returned to a communal "jackpot." Victims are frequently given a phony prize number and telephone number to contact nonexistent lot-

tery officials, but the prize money never arrives. Variations of this fraud include, the Magazines for Life scam, the Mystery Prize scam, and a claim that "You are guaranteed to have won one of five top awards." Some swindlers active in this scheme have misrepresented themselves as U.S. Customs agents, thereby adding yet another felony to their résumés.

2. *Recovery Operations.* In these scams, the swindlers add insult to injury by targeting victims who have been duped previously by telemarketers. The caller claims to be a lawyer, judge, police officer, U.S. or Canadian Customs officer, or a revenue official. Victims are told that a court case has been settled against their long-distance assailants and that as recognized victims, they must first send a fee or pay duties and taxes. The swindlers lend credibility to this audacious fraud by furnishing details of the original crime, including the amount of money lost and the names of companies involved. Some con artists cover their tracks with reference to a "gag order" on the settlement, warning victims not to discuss it with law enforcement officers, friends, or relatives.

3. *Advanced Loan Fees.* Con artists advertise (usually in newspapers or financial publications) that they can lend money to people ranked as poor risks with conventional lenders. Callers who respond are given "loan approval" over the phone, but payment of a fee is required to secure the mythical loan. Once the check is mailed, the "lender" vanishes. In a variation on this theme, swindlers sometimes offer venture capital loans to established entrepreneurs. Victims are required to "deposit" a portion of the loan, sometimes in the tens of thousands of dollars, to secure the loan at a competitive rate. The con artist normally pockets the fee and disappears, but some bold operators return to the victim-investor for more money, claiming that additional funds are needed to convince their board of directors that the loan is a good risk.

4. *Counterfeit Checks.* This fraud is an insidious variation of the lottery or sweepstakes scam. The swindler tells victims that they have won a foreign lottery and solicits an advance fee to secure release of the winnings. With the fee in hand, the telemarketer issues counterfeit checks to the victims in the amount of the bogus lottery prize, doubly victimizing the "marks" when

their own banks seek reimbursement for the worthless checks.

5. *Fraudulent Charitable Donations.* Many dishonest telemarketers claim to represent charitable organizations, often appropriating the names of well-known, legitimate charities with slight variation (e.g., the nonexistent American Kidney Foundation, instead of the legitimate National Kidney Foundation). Police and firefighter organizations are also frequently used in this scam, albeit without their knowledge. Swindlers commonly ask for donations to help police officers buy equipment or to assist families of officers injured or killed in the line of duty. Other variations on the scam seek help for military veterans, sick children, or the homeless—none of whom receive a penny from the proceeds.

6. *Fraudulent Magazine Subscription Sales.* In this scam, swindlers claim to represent a magazine publisher, asking victims to renew a subscription. In most cases, the victimized customer either receives no magazines at all, or else obtains the subscription at an inflated price. Victims may end up with a bill for several hundred dollars and unwanted magazine subscriptions spanning years.

7. *Advance Fee Sweepstakes Fraud.* This scam combines elements from the "advance loan fee" scheme and the lottery/sweepstakes scam. Victims receive a telephone call or a card in the mail, informing them that they have won a prize. In order to collect it, they must first pay a fee, sometime misrepresented as a tax by swindlers who impersonate government revenue agents. As in other variations of this con game, the money is lost forever and victims generally receive no prize at all.

8. *"Reloading" of Fraud Victims.* This scheme, practiced by more aggressive swindlers, again targets prior victims of telemarketing fraud. The "reloader" tries to persuade disillusioned victims that they are eligible for even greater prizes than those offered in the original scam, under the company's "executive" prize promotion—provided that more purchases are made. Senior citizens living on fixed incomes are particularly vulnerable to this swindle, striving in vain to recoup their original losses in the hope that the con artist will "make good" on the original stolen funds. Practitioners of this high-pressure con frequently ask for credit card numbers, and

some have persuaded their victims to take out loans in order to obtain the fees demanded.

9. *Precious Metals and Gems.* Highly popular with swindlers in the mid-1990s, this scheme is practiced chiefly by Canadian telemarketers who purchase cheap gems and sell them to victims at vastly inflated prices. Upon delivery of the "precious" stones, victims are warned not to break the seal on their container. Those who comply with the curious instructions often receive more calls, telling them their stones have increased in value on the world market, urging them to purchase more. When appraised, the actual stones prove to be low-grade gems or entirely worthless.

10. *Investment Scams.* Con artists posing as legitimate investors collect millions of dollars each year from innocent victims, claiming the money will be invested in lucrative banking and real estate ventures. Typically, the swindlers promise huge returns with little or no risk, then pocket the money and move on to their next gullible victim.

11. *Credit card protection scams.* The latest swindle discovered by Project COLT investigators involves swindlers who telephone their victims with a plan to protect their credit cards from devious telemarketers. Callers ask for a fee, typically $300 or $400, and accept payment via credit card. With the card number on file, the swindlers then proceed to charge thousands of dollars in bogus "fees" to the account.

Project COLT was based in Montreal, Quebec, after Canadian law enforcement officers identified that city as the mecca of North American telemarketing fraud. That concentration of swindlers was caused primarily by leniency in handling of nonviolent "white collar" crimes by courts in Quebec and the desire of many swindlers to operate outside U.S. jurisdiction. Hundreds of complaints received by Canadian authorities in the 1990s finally led to creation of the Project COLT initiative, with various American agencies happy to collaborate in cross-border sting operations. An unusual aspect of COLT is the employment of Canadian college students, chiefly police science majors, to return calls from corrupt telemarketers all over North America. Civilian collaborators in Operation COLT include various courier companies who facilitate correspondence for the ongoing sting campaign, including proprietors of some 200 mail drops in greater Montreal alone.

The results to date have been impressive. In its first year of operation, Project COLT recovered $7.6 million for 695 victims, including 63 in Canada and 632 in the U.S., for an average of $10,935 recovered per victim. In its second year, COLT's total of recoveries jumped to $12 million. One sting directed at purveyors of worthless gems bagged 48 suspects from a ring that had swindled several thousand investors out of $52 million. (One victim of that fraud, a Pennsylvania clergyman, had lost $1 million by himself.) In 1999, COLT spokesmen reported they had executed 34 search warrants, including raids on five telemarketing "boiler rooms," plus banks, phone companies and private homes. Nine international extradition cases were pending that year, and December 1998 had already witnessed the first-ever extradition of a Canadian citizen charged with fraud in the United States. On April 30, 2002, Canadian COLT officers staged a series of raids around Montreal, arresting 15 suspects charged with swindling elderly U.S. residents. One of the most notorious defendants—Marvin Redler, director of four fraudulent telemarketing firms in Quebec—pleaded guilty to nine criminal counts on June 4, 2002, closing the case on 3,100 victims who were robbed of $1,040,000.

PSYCHOLOGICAL Profiling

As an investigative tool, psychological "profiling" of unknown subjects at large—UNSUBS in law enforcement jargon—is a relatively new technique, used for the first time in the mid-1950s. It is also one of the most controversial methods used by detectives to track down their prey. In fictional portrayals, such as television's *Millennium* and *Profiler* series, profilers are often depicted as near-psychic, receiving "flashes" from an unknown criminal's mind with every visit to a crime scene, pursuing their quarry with intuitive leaps akin to divine revelation.

Unfortunately, such is not the case.

When hyperbole and hype are stripped away, profiling remains nothing more or less than educated guesswork, based on crime scene evidence and statistical probability. At its best, the guesswork may be highly educated, drawing on experience from previous cases and assisted by computer analysis, refining a fugitive's portrait into fine detail. On the other hand, a bungled profile may be worse than useless, leading investigators down a false trail while the object of their pursuit escapes scot-free. In most cases, the reality of profiling falls somewhere between the two extremes: experts are able to prepare a fair likeness of their UNSUB without providing the essential details of identity required for an arrest.

Ironically, the first application of psychological profiling in modern criminology is also the only case to date wherein a profiler contributed directly to the subject's capture. In 1956, forensic psychiatrist James Brussel prepared an astoundingly accurate profile of New York City's elusive "Mad Bomber," deducing the subject's impotence from the phallic shape of his pipe bombs, generating a sketch that could have passed for the bomber's mug shot, even predicting correctly that the subject would be wearing a double-breasted suit (with the jacket buttoned) on the day of his arrest. More important, however, Dr. Brussel advised police on a means of provoking the bomber to reveal himself by writing to the press, a ploy that led manhunters to his doorstep. No other profiler to date has rivaled Brussel's triumph, and even where specific profiles have proved accurate in the wake of apprehension, the capture is always effected by routine police work.

Two cases often cited as profiling "success stories" demonstrate the gap between hype and reality. In Sacramento, California, sheriff's deputies and FBI agents prepared a profile of an UNSUB blamed for six gruesome murders during January 1978. At his arrest, defendant Richard Trenton Chase was found to match the profile in every respect, yet psychological analysis played no role in his capture. Rather, Chase was seen by a former high-school classmate wandering the streets in bloodstained clothing after the last murder, and was turned in to police, who then found copious evidence in his car and home. Six years later, Florida serial killer Bobby Joe Long was the subject of another FBI profile, which again proved remarkably accurate once police had him in custody. Retired G-men hail their achievement as if they had caught Long themselves, but in fact Long sealed his own fate by leaving his penultimate victim alive, to provide authorities with a description of Long and his car.

When profilers miss their target, meanwhile, the results are sometimes truly bizarre. In 1963, a panel of psychiatrists—including the aforementioned Dr. Brussel—was convened to stalk the "BOSTON STRANGLER." The experts concluded that Boston was plagued by *two* serial killers, one who killed elderly women, and another—thought to be homosexual—who preferred younger females. (In fact, no gay male

in history has ever been identified as a serial slayer of women.) Beyond the divergence in victim selection, many similarities were postulated, including the suggestion that both men were teachers, living alone and killing on seasonal school holidays. Both UNSUBS were diagnosed as sexually inhibited, the products of traumatic childhoods featuring weak, distant fathers and cruel yet seductive mothers. In fact, confessed strangler Albert DeSalvo was a construction worker, living with his wife and two children, an insatiable heterosexual. Examination of his background showed a brutal, domineering father and a mother who was weak and ineffectual. DeSalvo was in his 30s, as projected for the two hypothetical teachers, but there the resemblance ended. Recent DNA testing has cast doubt on DeSalvo's guilt in the Boston murders, his confession notwithstanding, but it should be noted that none of the alternative suspects identified thus far bear any resemblance to the pair of homicidal teachers profiled in 1963.

An even more dramatic failure comes from Los Angeles, where another "expert panel" gathered to profile the brutal "Skid Row Slasher," a serial killer of homeless men. On January 30, 1975 the media broadcast descriptions of the killer as a "sexually impotent coward, venting his own feelings of worthlessness on hapless drifters and down-and-outers." Profilers described the slasher as a friendless loner, probably a homosexual and possibly deformed, "driven to a frenzy to commit these murders as a substitute for normal heterosexual relations." His bloodlust was probably "spurred by an unresolved rage he feels toward his father, who could have been a brutal alcoholic." Sketches drawn to fit the profile showed a white male in his late 20s or early 30s, six feet tall, 190 pounds, with shoulder length stringy blond hair framing a gaunt face. At his arrest, two days later, slayer Vaughn Greenwood was revealed to be a stocky African American with no apparent deformities, whose crimes were the product of ritual occultism, complete with blood-drinking and salt sprinkled around the corpses of his victims.

It is worth noting that profilers themselves disagree on the value of their contribution to crime-fighting. Dr. Norman Barr, one of the Skid Row Slasher panelists in California, belatedly told reporters, "I don't think my statements would make any more sense than those of the average housewife." Across the continent, at Boston University, psychologist Russell Boxley agreed, declaring, "I think the people who do profiles are bastardizing their discipline with a lot of mumbo-jumbo, without really knowing what they're doing. You know, it's a mystical thing, and people are very impressed. It's also a media thing." Boxley concluded that forensic psychiatrists tracking an unknown felon "can't do any better than a college student with the same materials in front of him."

FBI "mindhunters," meanwhile, stand by their record and tactics, with several retired G-men finding new careers as authors of memoirs that relate (and inflate) their achievements. In print, every case appears to hinge upon a brilliant profile, but in fact some of their conclusions are vague, at best. Following extensive interviews with various convicted felons in the 1980s, members of the bureau's Behavioral Science Unit (later Investigative Support Services) divided murderers into two broad categories, "organized" and "disorganized."

Organized killers typically possess good intelligence and are socially competent, tending toward skilled occupations. A review of the subject's childhood, if and when he is arrested, normally reveals a high birth-order status (the oldest or the only child), a father with stable employment, and a home life marked by inconsistent discipline, alternately harsh and lax. In adulthood, the organized killer often lives with a partner, frequently a legal spouse, and is sexually active. Violence is precipitated by "stressors," including marital discord or loss of employment, and is often fueled by alcohol. The killer is mobile, maintaining one or more vehicles in good repair. His mood is controlled on the hunt, and he normally follows the progress of police investigations through the media. Crime scene characteristics of the organized offender betray a crime planned well in advance, reflecting the killer's overall control of his environment. The organized offender typically conceals the bodies of his victims and takes care to leave no evidence behind. If pressed by police, he may flee the area to avoid apprehension.

Disorganized offenders, by contrast, are possessed of average intelligence at best, sometimes mentally retarded, and nearly always socially inept. The subject mirrors his father's unstable work record by quitting or losing one job after another, rarely qualifying for a skilled occupation. The UNSUB's social life is equally barren: the offender typically lives alone and is sexually incompetent, sometimes virginal in adulthood. Disorganized killers rarely drink to bolster their courage, since their crimes are impulsive and unplanned. No serious precipitating stress is seen; rather, the killer strikes at random, almost whimsically, without thinking through his actions. He often lives and/or works near the crime scene, perhaps attacking a neighbor, and displays little interest in media coverage of the case. Crime scenes are sloppy, often rife with forensic evidence. Too distracted or dim-witted to recognize danger, the disorganized offender seldom makes any dramatic lifestyle changes to avoid arrest.

The FBI's profiling categories are deliberately broad, and while fictional slayer Hannibal Lecter may have been unduly harsh in blaming "a real bottom feeder" for the system's conception, federal profilers have admitted its deficiency by creating an intermediate "mixed" category for troublesome cases.

"PUSHER": computer virus

First reported on the Internet in April 1998, "Pusher" is a memory-resident, parasitic, polymorphic virus rated "harmless" by computer analysts. It writes itself to the ends of executed .com files, causing each infected file to grow in size by 740 bytes. When installation of the virus is complete, it copies the following code to the system memory of its new host.

```
MOV AX,Opcode1
PUSH AX
ADD AX,Data1; result is Opcode2
PUSH AX
UB AX,Data2; result is Opcode3
PUSH AX
INC AX; result is Opcode4
PUSH AX
. . .
JMP SP
```

There is no payload for the virus and it seems to have no detrimental effect on the host computer.

QAZA, Abdullah: indicted for CD/DVD piracy

A resident of Brooklyn, New York, born September 23, 1982, Abdullah Qaza was indicted by a federal grand jury on January 11, 2002, charged with copyright and trademark infringement following his arrest in connection with the large-scale manufacture and distribution of counterfeit compact disks (CDs) and digital video disks (DVDs). Prosecutors charge that Qaza and an alleged accomplice, 34-year-old Khalid Ghnaim operated from a Myrtle Avenue storefront in Brooklyn, where they reportedly manufactured bootleg CDs and DVDs in large quantities between March and December 2001. Agents of the U.S. Secret Service raided the establishment and a nearby warehouse on December 13, 2001, confiscating more than 30,000 counterfeit CDs and an equal number of bootleg DVDs, valued at roughly $1 million.

Federal prosecutors maintain that Qaza and Ghnaim specialized in newly released and soon-to-be-released movies on DVD, as well as a wide variety of popular music, earmarked for sale through a nationwide network of outdoor flea markets. Qaza was released on $200,000 bond, while Ghnaim remained in federal custody as a presumed flight risk. If convicted, each defendant faces a maximum of 10 years in prison and/or fines up to $2 million, but the case remains unresolved at press time and authorities stress that indictments are merely accusations of criminal activity and not proof of guilt. All American defendants are presumed innocent until such time as they either plead guilty or else are convicted at trial.

"QPA": computer viruses

Initially reported from the Internet in March 1997, the nonmemory-resident overwriting virus known as "Qpa" now exists in three variants, all rated "very dangerous" by experts in the field. The variants perform in near-identical fashion, seeking out .com files and overwriting them, storing the opening data of each infected file to a new file beginning with the prefix FB. The different versions of Qpa include the following characteristics:

Qpa.256—

Message: Insufficient system memory
Text string: Qpa-XX virus from FBIC:*.COM

Qpa.333—

Message: This program requires Microsoft Windows
Text string: Qpa-XX virus WIN

Qpa.666—

Message: This program requires Microsoft Windows
Text string: Qpa-XXI virus V1.0 from Q6.COM

"QUARK": computer virus

Identified in July 1997, this memory-resident, parasitic virus is rated "not dangerous" by computer analysts. It writes itself to the ends of .com and .exe files as they are executed on the host computer and alters keyboard data. Quark contains a text string reading "smothered to inertness by bendelosangeles Arg~AdeN." If the user alters that text string in any way, Quark deletes its host file and is thereafter inert.

"QUEEN": computer viruses

September 1997 witnessed the Internet discovery of two viruses bearing the "Queen" title, one of which is now recognized in three variant forms—"Queen.a," "Queen.b" and "Queen.c." The triplets are encrypted Word macro viruses that infect a host computer's global macros area when infected documents are opened, afterward saving themselves with new filenames. While each of the three variant forms contains a different number of macros—five, six and two, respectively—all contain the same text string: "(c) 1997 Master of Infection QUEEN FOREVER!!!" All three likewise attach the same message to the end of each document infected. It reads:

> *c) 1997 Master of infection*
> *Queen Hitman Virus inc.*
> *Come and enjoy ;) You can find my url at alt.*.virus.**
> *P.S. QUEEN FOREVER!!!*

Another Queen virus, unrelated to the three discussed above but unleashed on the Internet around the same time, is a macrovirus that infects only Excel worksheets, creating an infected global.xlm file in the Excel startup directory on arrival. Beyond that, however, the virus apparently delivers no payload and does not manifest itself in any visible way.

"QUICK": computer virus

An encrypted Word macro virus, "Quick" was first identified in July 1997. While it does not install itself into a host computer's global macro area, Quick infects documents upon opening, searching each for a list of recently used files and infecting them as well. Finally, Quick disables the infected host's Tools/Macro menu.

"QUOX": computer virus

Rated "harmless" by computer analysts, this memory-resident, stealth boot virus was first identified in June 1996. Upon infecting a new host computer, "Quox" writes itself to the hard drive's Master Boot Record (MBR) and to the floppy disk boot sector, but it has no payload and presents no overt manifestation. It contains the text string "_QUOX_."

"RABBIT": computer viruses

At least seven viruses using the "Rabbit" name have been identified since the first appeared in October 1996. That specimen, a memory-resident boot virus dubbed "harmless" by computer analysts, had two variants—"Rabbit.a" and "Rabbit.b." Both write themselves to boot sectors of an infected computer's floppy disks and to the Master Boot Record (MBR) of the host's hard drive.

The next Rabbit virus appeared on the Internet in February 1998, a "dangerous," nonmemory-resident, parasitic virus that seeks .com files and invades "caves" in their text. A bug inherent to the virus randomly corrupts some files while infecting them, thereby rendering them inoperative. Files without "caves" in their text strings are apparently immune to this Rabbit's attacks.

Eight months later, in October 1998, Web-watchers discovered a new family of Rabbit viruses, including three variant forms, which were the first known viruses written in the Windows Script language. Two of the variants—again dubbed "Rabbit.a" and "Rabbit.b," though unrelated to the earlier viruses tagged with those names—search out and overwrite all files in the current directory that are written in Visual Basic Script (VBS). The third form—"Rabbit.c"—attacks both VBS and Java Script (JS) files. It also contains a bug activated only when Rabbit.c is executed by a browser. In that case, the virus infects every file in the browser's cache and displays their various icons on the monitor screen. These most recent Rabbits display the following comments and text strings:

Rabbit.a—

> *Message: VBSv Version 1.0 by Lord Natas/*
> *CodeBreakers First Windows Scripting Virus*
> *Text: VBSv v1.0 by Lord Natas/CodeBreakers*

Rabbit.b—

> *Message: VBSv Version 1.1 by Lord Natas/*
> *CodeBreakers First Windows Scripting Virus*
> *Text: VBSv v1.1 by Lord Natas/CodeBreakers*

Rabbit.c—

> *Message: VBSv Version 2.0 by Lord Natas/*
> *CodeBreakers First Windows Scripting Virus*
> *Text: VBSv v2.0 by Lord Natas/CodeBreakers*

RADAR/LIDAR Law Enforcement Applications

Radar—from *R*adio *D*irection *a*nd *R*anging—was initially developed as a military tool and later utilized in civilian capacities, primarily for tracking aircraft on their approach to airports. It is used in the same way by U.S. Customs Service agents and members of the Drug Enforcement Administration to track smugglers approaching America's borders with narcotics and other contraband. The police application most familiar to the average citizen, however, is probably the use of radar to monitor ground traffic speeds and apprehend drivers who exceed the maximum posted speed limit.

In essence, radar uses radio waves to detect and monitor various objects. Its original (and simplest) function is to determine distance between two objects by emitting a concentrated radio wave and recording the echoes of any objects that block its passage. Since radio waves move through air at a constant speed, radar devices calculate the distance between the transmitter and its target based on how long it takes the "bounced" signal to return. Radar can also measure an object's speed, by means of a phenomenon called "Doppler shift." When a radar transmitter and its target are both stationary, the echo has the same wave frequency as the original signal. When the target is moving, however, wave patterns are changed. Vehicles moving away from the transmitter "stretch" the waves, while objects approaching the transmitter "compress" the waves,

increasing the frequency. Based on the frequency changes, a radar gun calculates how quickly the target (normally but not necessarily a vehicle) is moving toward or away from the transmitter. Further calculations allow for movement of the radar gun itself, as when mounted inside a police car. If the cruiser is traveling at 50 miles per hour and the target vehicle is moving away from it at 30 miles per hour, then the target must be traveling at 80 miles per hour. (If both vehicles hold a constant speed, there is no deviation in the pattern.)

A newer variation of this tracking system is Lidar—for *Light Detection and Ranging*. As suggested by the name, lidar guns use concentrated infrared light (laser) beams in place of radio waves. Calculations are performed on the same basis as with radar, but using the speed of light, rather than the speed of sound. In place of constant, oscillating radio waves, the lidar gun emits rapid-fire pulses of light to track moving objects over a protracted distance. Many police departments use hand-held or dashboard-mounted lidar guns, but

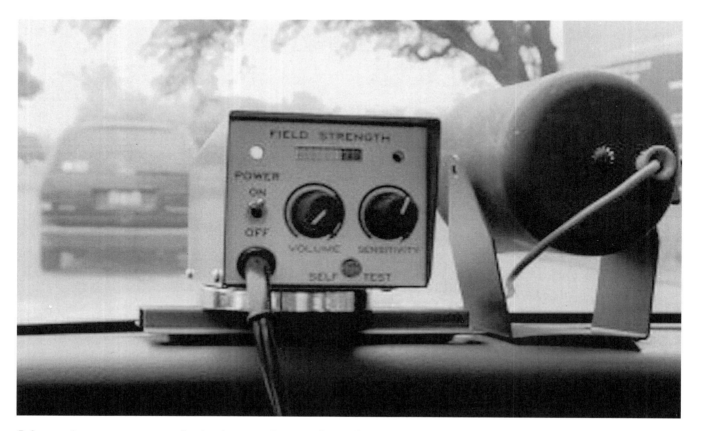

Police and state troopers use "radar detector detectors" to pull over drivers operating illegal radar detectors during travel. (AP/TDPS)

the devices may also be mounted beside highways, continuously operating to monitor the speed of each passing vehicle. Such stationary emplacements frequently include high-speed cameras, employed to snap pictures of the license plates (and sometimes drivers' faces) any time a passing car registers excessive speed. Speeders may thus be traced through computer data banks and receive their citations by mail, without involving officers in time-consuming (and often hazardous) traffic stops.

Lawbreakers normally outdo law enforcement agencies in adopting new technology, and while police initially had the edge in using radar and lidar devices, there is today no shortage of high-tech instruments designed to frustrate their efforts. The simplest evasion devices are radar detectors, basic radio receivers tuned to police frequencies, which (the speeder hopes) will pick up radar signals in time for him to slow down and avoid a citation. Simple detectors are most effective when traffic officers leave their radar guns constantly turned on, without sighting a particular target, thus beaming detectable signals throughout their patrol shift. The detector is useless, though, if an officer turns off his gun until a target is sighted. In that case, the driver's warning comes too late, since his speed has already been recorded.

More sophisticated radar-jamming devices are also available, operating on the same principle used for years by military aircraft to avoid detection by their enemies. Jammers, unlike simple radar detectors, are not passive devices. They register incoming, then transmit their own signal, replicating the original radar gun's signal but mixing it up with additional radio noise, thus preventing an accurate reading. Many U.S. jurisdictions have outlawed radar detectors or jammers, making their possession a separate offense. In those areas, police are often equipped with "VG2" devices—simple high-powered radio receivers tuned to the signal frequency commonly used by radar detectors and jammers. Ironically, a driver with an active radar detector in his car may then be stopped and cited for illegal possession, even if he was not speeding at the time.

Scofflaws have not been lacking in response to lidar technology, either. Many modern radar detectors include a light-sensitive panel to register beams from police lidar guns, but their effectiveness is limited, since lidar guns are best used over short distances and focus strictly on a single target. Thus, again, by the time a detector alerts the speeding driver, he or she has already been "painted" by the lidar beam, with the illicit speed recorded. Some dedicated speeders try to defeat lidar by decreasing the reflectivity of their vehicles. Black paint may be helpful, since it absorbs more light and reflects less than other hues, while certain plastic covers reduce the reflective properties of metal license plates. At best, however, such tricks buy the speeder a few seconds to slow down between the time his car is sighted and his speed is registered by the lidar gun. Lidar jammers are more effective, equipped with their own light-emitting diodes (LEDs) that blind a lidar gun to reflected light.

The prevalence of radar guns in modern traffic enforcement has fostered a number of myths. It is not true, for instance, that inclement weather disables radar guns, although their sensitivity may be somewhat diminished by extremely heavy rain, snow, or dust storms. Radar and lidar do not "prefer" one type or color of vehicle—red sports cars, for instance—over any other (although, as a psychological matter, it may be true that drivers of bright-colored sports cars are more likely to speed and/or draw attention to themselves). Likewise, with the exception of black paint (discussed above), no particular color of vehicle makes detection by lidar less likely (and color has no effect whatsoever on radar). By the same token, radar and lidar guns are *not* infallible. Their readings may be challenged and occasionally proved inaccurate. Various publications detail means of fighting radar/lidar citations in court, and further discussion of the subject may be found at www.CopRadar.com.

"RAGER": computer virus

Logged for the first time in May 1999, "Rager" is a memory-resident, parasitic virus classed as "dangerous" by computer analysts. It writes itself to the end of open .exe files and delivers its payload when the host computer's login utility is executed. On those occasions, Rager displays the following message on-screen before rebooting the computer:

********* Warning ! *********
Novell NetWare report : Hardware A30 error detected.
Registers :
AX :2134 BX :3C23 CX :1841 DX :5421
CS :2451 DS :2023 ES :538A SS :6C8B
SI :46AE DI :94B4 SP :4541 BP :491C
Try restart file-server, if it will not give effect, switch off your network and call trained service-people.

Press any key to restart this computer.
Rager contains the following text strings:
NetWare virus from Avenge (tm) family.
(C)Rager, Simferopol State University

RAINGER, William   See FORD HEIGHTS FOUR

"RAINSONG": computer viruses

Classified as "dangerous" by industry analysts, these memory-resident, parasitic, polymorphic viruses operate on a "per-process" basis, searching out .exe files in the Windows directory and writing itself to the end of each file infected. Rainsong uses the technique of "entry point obscuring" to conceal itself and unlike many other viruses, it does not alter an infected program's entry address. When the host computer runs an infected program, Rainsong searches the opening file for a call command and replaces it with a "JUMP VirusEntry" code, thus seizing control each subsequent time the infected file is opened. A bug in Rainsong frequently corrupts infected files, but it avoids antivirus programs whose names begin with the following prefixes: AN, AV, DR, F-, ID, OD and TB.

The variant forms of Rainsong deliver different payloads once a new host system is infected. On April 6, "Rainsong.3891" produces an error message reading "ASIMOV Jan.2.1920–Apr.6.1992." The second virus form, "Rainsong.3925," freezes the infected host system 11 months after initial infection. These viruses contain the following text strings:

Rainsong.3891:

< The Rain Song Coded By Bumblebee/29a >

Rainsong.3925:

< 99 Ways To Die Coded by Bumblebee/29a >

RANDOLPH, Christopher: satellite TV pirate

A 21-year-old resident of Rantoul, Illinois, Christopher Randolph was among 17 defendants indicted during 2001 as a result of the federal sting operation dubbed "OPERATION SMARTCARD.NET." Those charged were accused of purchasing or selling counterfeit access cards that allowed unauthorized reception and decryption of satellite television services. Prosecutors

estimated that the target company lost $6.2 million in revenue from the fraud between 1998 and 2000, when the sting operation climaxed with multiple arrests. Christopher purchased 35 counterfeit satellite access cards from FBI undercover agents, which he then resold to other individuals. He pleaded guilty as charged on June 14, 2001, facing a maximum sentence of five years' imprisonment and a $500,000 fine.

RAYBURN, Jimmie Earl: indicted for Internet extortion

A 44-year-old resident of Parma, Ohio, Jimmie Rayburn was indicted by a federal grand jury on March 26, 2002, for an alleged campaign of extortion and malicious hacking directed at a national purveyor of telecommunications service and hardware. The 10-count indictment charged Rayburn with the following offenses:

Count 1   That between January 28, 2002, and March 20, 2002, with the intent to extort money or other things of value from the company, he knowingly transmitted one or more interstate threats to damage its protected computer system. The maximum sentence for this offense, on conviction, is five years' imprisonment and/or a $250,000 fine.

Counts 2 through 9   That on various dates between February 6, 2002, and March 7, 2002, Rayburn knowingly and intentionally transmitted programs, codes, information or commands that caused damage to the company's computer system. Conviction of these offenses carries a maximum penalty of 10 years' imprisonment and/or a $250,000 fine on each separate count.

Count 10   That on March 20, 2002, Rayburn knowingly and with the intent to extort from the company, transmitted yet another interstate threat to injure the company's property or reputation. The maximum penalty for this offense, upon conviction, is two years' imprisonment and/or a $250,000 fine.

Rayburn thus faces a potential maximum sentence of 87 years in prison and a $2.5 million fine if convicted on all counts filed against him. Pending trial and final disposition of his case at some future date, unscheduled at this writing, federal prosecutors remind the public that an indictment is only a charge and is not evidence of guilt. A defendant is entitled to a fair trial in which it will be the government's burden to prove guilt beyond a reasonable doubt. All defendants are presumed innocent until such time as they either plead guilty or are convicted at trial.

"README": computer worms

Two separate worm viruses have thus far been identified with the "Readme" title. The first, initially reported in April 1999, spreads through Internet Relay Chat (IRC) channels, appearing on-screen as a DOS program titled readme.exe. When that file is opened, the worm installs itself into the new host computer's DOS memory and proceeds to infect various DOS .com files as they are executed, with the exception of command.com. This version of the Readme worm includes the following text string:

;-)x
whose name means dark matter vir-L

A second Readme worm, discovered in September 2001, is a Windows .exe file written in Visual Basic, spread on the Internet via infected e-mail attachments that appear as shown below.

Subject: As per your request!
Attachment: README.EXE
Message: Please find attached file for your review. I look forward to hear from you again very soon. Thank you.

Once the infected attachment is opened, Readme installs itself in the new host system and copies itself to the Windows directory, while displaying a false error message that reads—

Urgent!
[Open]

WinZip SelfExtractor: Warning
CRC error: 234#21

To spread copies of itself abroad, Readme uses the newly infected computer's Microsoft Outlook program, sending copies of the infected message to all e-mail addresses found in the user's address book. It also writes itself as readme.exe into the root directory of drives found within the new host computer.

REEVES, Jillann: accused software pirate

Jillann Reeves, a 34-year-old resident of Aberdeen, Washington, was arrested by FBI agents on March 23, 2001, charged with criminal copyright violations under terms of the U.S. Code. According to the affidavits filed against her, Reeves operated the web site "koolrcds.com," where pirated copies of computer games and motion pictures were illegally offered for sale. The federal charges specified that Reeves had offered 140 stolen movies, plus more than 2,000 Sony PlayStation, Gameboy, and Nintendo software games, various items of PlayStation and Nintendo hardware, and modification chips for PlayStation hardware.

A variety of private-sector corporations assisted the FBI in its investigation of Reeves and her Internet website. These included Sony Computer Entertainment America; the Interactive Digital Software Association (Washington, D.C.); The Electronic Arts, Inc. (Bellevue, Washington); and the Motion Picture Association of America (representing member companies Buena Vista Pictures, Metro-Goldwyn-Mayer, Paramount Pictures, Sony Picture Entertainment, TriStar Pictures, Twentieth Century Fox Film Corporation, and Universal Studios). Spokesperson Emily Kutner told reporters that the MPAA became aware of Reeves's activities in March 2000, from agents in the FBI's Seattle field office. G-men asked the MPAA for help, including the purchase of various stolen movies and computer games from koolrcds.com. Kutner explained that leaders of the motion picture industry were interested in any efforts to curtail what she called a "cyber-flea market" operating on the Internet, heedless of prevailing copyright laws. "The Department of Justice initiating this case sends the message that the government won't tolerate copyright theft in cyberspace," Kutner declared.

Reeves was charged with two federal violations, one count for copying and selling copyrighted computer game software, and another for bootlegging and selling motion pictures (including some not yet released to the public). Each count carries a maximum sentence of five years in prison and a $250,000 fine, but U.S. prosecutors stress that their charges are only accusations and that Reeves must be considered innocent until convicted at trial. Her case remains unresolved at this writing.

REMINGTON Center Innocence Project

Affiliated with the Frank J. Remington Center at the University of Wisconsin Law School, the Remington

Center Innocence Project (RCIP) is yet another group committed to the legal defense of incarcerated inmates who claim actual innocence of the crimes for which they stand convicted. Founded in 1998, codirected by Professors Keith Findley and John Pray, the RCIP "is interested in cases in which some type of new evidence can be found to prove innocence." As defined on the group's website, "'New' means evidence that was not presented at trial because it did not exist, was inadvertently overlooked by the defense or withheld by the prosecution." The center makes its selection of cases once a year, in August, utilizing a staff of 20 law students to investigate and litigate claims under the supervision of professors. The center takes cases "only after a person has been convicted and all direct appeals have ended or the time for filing a direct appeal has passed." While "nearly all" cases litigated by the RCIP involve Wisconsin inmates, an exception to the rule was CHRISTOPHER OCHOA, liberated from a Texas prison by DNA evidence in 2001. Prisoners seeking assistance on cases within the RCIP's guidelines should address inquiries to:

Innocence Project of Frank J. Remington Center
University of Wisconsin Law School
975 Bascom Mall
Madison, WI 53706

REMOTE Viewing: extrasensory surveillance technique
"Remote viewing" is alleged to be a power or talent possessed by certain gifted individuals who can "see" people, objects, and events at great distances without the aid of mechanical or electronic devices. Described by its proponents and practitioners as something akin to extrasensory perception (ESP), the rumored talent differs from "normal" clairvoyance in that it usually describes events as they happen, rather than predicting the future or delving into the past. Remote viewers are also awake at the time of their "observations," thus separating them from individuals who claim precognitive dreams.

Various popular books—including Elmer Gruber's *The Psychic Wars* (1999), Adam Mandelbaum's *The Psychic Battlefield* (1999), and David Morehouse's *Psychic Warrior* (1997)—detail the alleged exploits of remote viewers in wartime, claiming that various military and intelligence organizations from the U.S. to the Soviet Union have utilized such long-distance spying techniques for

decades. Leaving aside those anecdotal accounts, however, there is little or nothing to document investigation in this field—except for the fact that several remote viewing institutes presently offer lessons in the "psychic" technique to anyone who can afford the going rates. They include:

1. The *Farsight Institute,* a self-described collection of individuals "primarily interested in the process of remote viewing itself, such as how it works and how it can be made more reliable under a wider range of circumstances. According to its website, Farsight is "a non-degree and non-certificate granting nonprofit research and educational institute" devoted to the advancement of "Scientific Remote Viewing®." Farsight research is "totally funded by external donations and grants," but spokesmen for the institute assure potential students that "We exist to serve," being wholly "dedicated to the practical and benevolent use of remote viewing, to solve problems and to answer questions that are otherwise intractable." Farsight researchers "seek to overturn [the] flawed paragigm [*sic*]" that "consciousness is a phenomenon strictly related to brain physiology." Greed and skepticism, they insist, have "inhibited scientific investigation into the nature of the soul." Sounding more religious than scientific, they close their introductory remarks with this proviso: "And let no one doubt that our ultimate goal is no less than to perceive the nature of God."

2. *Remote Viewing Instructional Services, Inc.:* This group defines remote viewing (without registered trademarks) as "a skill by which a person can perceive objects, persons, or events at a location removed from him or her by either space or time." In the RVIS scenario, "neither time nor any known type of shielding can prevent a properly-trained remote viewer from gaining access to the desired target." Far from requiring gifted "psychics," RVIS maintains, "[o]ne of the wonderful things about RV is that virtually anyone can learn to do it"—unless, of course, "there is some sort of physical or mental handicap that prevents it." To prove that point, special training is conducted "in a pleasant classroom setting in the Austin, Texas area by Paul H. Smith, one of the top RV experts in the world." Four-day courses (Wednesday through Saturday) are offered at three different levels, each costing

$2,600 for "approximately 40 hours of training—plus 10 follow-on practice sessions once you return home." In the Basic Course, students "learn to detect and decode the major gestalt of a target, describe sensory impressions from the site, and grasp its fundamental dimensional characteristics." The Intermediate Course (another 40 hours and $2,600) "brings the student the rest of the way through Stage III movement exercises and on to the end of Stage IV (qualitative target evaluation), with an introduction to Stage V (signal line interrogation)." The Advanced Course (40 hours; $2,600) "finishes Stage V and goes through to the completion of Stage VI." While "no one fails" the course, prospective students are reminded that results depend on personal commitment and abilities beyond the control of RVIS instructors. For those remote viewers still lacking focus after 120 hours and $7,800, "RVIS-supplied targets and session support beyond the ten included in the course package are $35.00 each."

3. The *Academy of Remote Viewing through Space and Time,* organized in 1997, promises that "[t]his inborn gifted ability to remote view and influence your reality using the power of your vibratory thought will open your eyes, perhaps for the first time ever, to the One Hidden Force that unlocks your full potential in accomplishments and relationships. When you learn 'this' you will see your whole world differently and your world will automatically change. With no effort on your part." Offering clients an "introduction to the new quantum-leaping freed human of the 21st Century," the Academy spurns costly classroom instruction, instead providing its lessons via a $98 set of audio tapes that purportedly teach listeners "to access and use Delta. Enter the ultimate Portal. The real 'Stargate!'" In addition to the six tapes, billed as "complete, and cover[ing] all aspects of training," Academy students are urged to take advantage of "free lifetime personalized coaching and instruction when requested (given over e-mail or phone) . . . and a lifetime membership to the Academy of Remote Viewing (includes special password entry to restricted Web areas)."

4. The *International Remote Viewing Association,* organized in March 1998 "by selected scientists and practitioners meeting in conjunction with the first professional conference on Remote Viewing

in Alamogordo, New Mexico," has a stated mission to "provide a mechanism for evaluating the discipline called 'remote viewing,' encourage scientifically sound research, propose ethical standards and provide overview educational information to the public." While that educational information is not spelled out on the group's website, the IRVA's vice president is identified as Paul H. Smith, "President and Chief Instructor for Remote Viewing Instructional Services, Inc., of Austin, Texas" (see No. 2 above). It seems fair to assume, in light of that connection, that would-be students may find themselves directed to the RVIS training courses for instruction. An additional twist is added, however, by the IRVA's offer of "standardized on-line testing," though no explanation is offered as to how remote viewing could be tested on-line.

5. When individual instruction proves inadequate, the *Western Institute of Remote Viewing* (founded in March 1997, at Kirkland, Washington) offers contract viewings by "some world class remote viewers" at $600 per session. As summarized by the WIRV's website, "Targets can be past, present, future, important, mundane, well known, unknown, large, small, microscopic, close, far, verifiable, unverifiable, positive, negative, emotional, non-emotional, esoteric, serious, mundane, light, energetic, static, physical, interdimensional, mythological, concrete, intangible, simple, intricate, this timeline, alternative timelines, this universe, other universes. Impose no limits, belief system or paradigm." No guidelines are offered in regard to judging whether WIRV's viewers have, for example, successfully located a microscopic, unverifiable mythological target from the future.

"RENEGADE": computer viruses

The first of two variants in this virus family, dubbed "Renegade.1176," was initially reported in July 1996. Analysts describe it as a memory-resident, encrypted, parasitic virus that is "not dangerous" to the infected host computer. Renegade.1176 writes itself to the middle of executed .exe files, whether they are open or closed at the time of infection, and it displays the following misspelled message on the 17th day of each month: "(c) Renegade 1994. Hello Hacker's!!!"

A second version of the virus, reported in July 2000, is "Renegade.4509." This memory-resident, encrypted, multipartite virus, rated "very dangerous" by experts, infects the Master Boot Record (MBR) of a new host and writes itself to the middle of .com and .exe files as they are opened. (Files known to be immune included adinf, chkdsk, clean, hiew, msav and scan.) As Renegade.4509 infects and corrupts various files, it displays the following message on-screen (errors uncorrected):

Say THANKS to lovely Dr. Web for damage this file . . .

Please wait . . . Hey, LAMER! Are you all right? . . . Not so good ? . . . Oh, don't be afraid my little baby, angry wolf if far away! . . . bUt I aM sTiLL HeRe! AnD i Am HuNGRrry! Aaarrrgghhh! . . . YoU iS _fOxPro or pAsCAL_pROGraMmeR, iSn't It? . . . Oogghh, YeEsss! I WaNt to EaT YoU NoWww! NoW YoU WiLL bEcOme ViCTiM of HACKER's REVENGE!

RH Power/Outback Steakhouse Giveaways:
Internet hoax
Circulated on the Internet since August 2000, this fraudulent chain letter offers gift certificates to Outback Steakhouse restaurants as a reward for participation in a nonexistent e-mail tracking scheme. In fact, there is no such tracking device and neither corporation authorized this phony giveaway. The original message reads:

Well . . . Give it a shot! . . . What the heck! We have rented an e-mail tracker for the next 3 months! We at RH Power Inc. want to see how many people our e-mail can reach in this time! If you forward this mail, you will be PAID MONEY!!! This e-mail must be sent immediately upon receiving this for it to be counted. For every person you send this to, you will receive $413! For every person they send this to, you will receive $139! I, too, Ryan LaGrange, Head Marketing Manager, thought this was a hoax until I did the same thing, and the next month, I got a check for $4,612 in the mail!

*******************BONUS*******************

IF YOU SEND THIS TO AT LEAST 15 PEOPLE RIGHT AWAY, A $25 GIFT CERTIFICATE TO OUT-BACK STEAKHOUSE WILL POP UP ON YOUR

SCREEN. PRINT OUT THIS.—IT IS A GIFT CER-TIFICATE!!!

A variant form of the bogus offer reads:

Subject: Outback Steakhouse

OUTBACK STEAKHOUSE.

We have rented an email tracker for the next 3 months! We at RH Power Inc. want to see how many people our email can reach in this time!
 If you forward this mail, you will be PAID MONEY! ! ! ! This email must be sent immediately upon receiving this for it to be counted.
 For every person you send this to you will receive $413! For every person they send this to you will receive $139! I too (Ryan LaGrange, Head Marketing Manager), thought this was a hoax until I did the same this and the next month got a check for $4612 in the mail!

*******************BONUS*******************

IF YOU SEND THIS TO AT LEAST 15 PEOPLE RIGHT AWAY, A $25 GIFT CERTIFICATE TO OUT-BACK STEAKHOUSE WILL POP UP ON YOUR SCREEN PRINT OUT Gotta try it just for the $25 certificate!

Jo & Bob Wagner
Outback Steakhouse

"RHAPSODY": computer virus
Initially logged in June 2000, "Rhapsody" is a non-memory-resident, parasitic Windows virus that analysts describe as "harmless." Upon invading a new host computer, it searches various Windows directories for .exe files bearing .exe or .scr file names and writes itself to the end of each one discovered. At the same time, it infects DOS batch (.bat) files, writing a "debug" to each which multiplies and saves itself to the hard drive each time the infected file is run.

RIGGS, Sterling: convicted by DNA evidence
On April 15, 1985, 15-year-old Tracey Poindexter was found by Indianapolis police officers, bound, gagged, and drowned in Fall Creek. Semen traces were recovered from her body, but authorities had no

suspect in the case for over 15 years, until the latter part of 2000. At that time, Sgt. Michael Crooke of the Indianapolis Police Department used DNA technology—unknown at the time of the slaying—to compare the crime scene evidence with DNA profiles of 25,000 convicted felons (violent criminals and burglars) maintained in a data bank by the Indiana State Police. In that manner, Sgt. Crooke identified defendant Sterling Riggs, then on parole for his prior conviction in a kidnapping and rape committed nine days after Tracey Poindexter's body was found in 1985. Riggs—who lived in a house adjacent to that of Poindexter's aunt and three blocks from the crime scene—denied any part in the murder, but the scientific evidence was irrefutable. A jury convicted him of first-degree murder on October 31, 2001, and four weeks later he was sentenced to 115 years in prison, assuring that he will never walk the streets again.

RILEY, Brian: software pirate

A resident of Olympia, Washington, born January 13, 1970, Brian Riley was employed by Intel Corporation, a computer firm, in 1998. That December, he joined four coworkers in a criminal conspiracy to defraud Intel by collaborating with an international syndicate of software thieves known as "PIRATES WITH ATTITUDE." The gang maintained an outlaw website based in Quebec, Canada, where stolen software programs were traded and sold. The site's hardware was limited in terms of memory, however, and so the pirates struck a bargain with Riley and his plotters, whereby Intel hardware was illegally diverted to Canada at Intel's expense, without the knowledge of Intel executives. FBI agents were alerted to the theft in July 1999 and launched a full investigation, resulting in the May 2000 federal indictments of Riley and 16 other defendants on copyright infringement charges. Riley and his former coworkers were among those who filed guilty pleas. The rogue Intel employees drew sentences ranging from three to six months community or home confinement, 200 hours of community service, five years' probation, and fines averaging $5,000.

RIVERA, Javier: satellite TV pirate

A 40-year-old resident of Bergenfield, New Jersey, Javier ("Rick") Rivera was among the suspects arrested by federal agents in July 1999, as part of an Internet sting campaign dubbed "OPERATION SMART-CARD.NET." Organized by the U.S. Customs Service with collaboration from commercial providers of satellite television service, the sting snared individuals who trafficked in counterfeit access cards, allowing retail customers full access to satellite TV broadcasts without paying legitimate subscription fees. Before the agents sprang their trap, satellite pirates defrauded the satellite TV industry of an estimated $6.2 million via theft of services.

Defendant Rivera was specifically charged with buying 57 counterfeit "smart" cards from undercover Customs agents, spending $6,250 on cards that ranged in price from $100 to $250. He then sold those cards to friends and relatives for an average of $400 each, turning a handsome profit in the process. On April 3, 2001, Rivera appeared before U.S. District Judge Alfred Lechner Jr., in Newark, and pleaded guilty to a single count of distributing unauthorized satellite TV access devices. The maximum sentence on that charge is five years in federal prison and a $500,000 fine, with financial restitution to the victims and payment of court costs assigned at the judge's discretion.

ROACH Infestation Warnings: Internet hoaxes

Since October 1999 a series of fraudulent warnings have been broadcast on the Internet, alleging danger from cockroach infestation in various settings and products designed to create public alarm. These variations on a classic urban legend falsely claim that ingestion of roach eggs—even under the most improbable circumstances—may cause life threatening infestation of the human body. In fact, digestive fluids would destroy the eggs in the unlikely event they were swallowed at all. Two of the most common hoaxes are reprinted below.

Roach-in-the-taco (October 1999):

Don't eat while you read this.
TRUE STORY:
HEY! HOW ABOUT TACO BELL?

This girl was really in a hurry one day so she just stopped off at a Taco Bell and got a Chicken soft taco and ate it on the way home. That night she noticed her jaw was kind of tight and swollen. The next day it was a little worse so she went to her doctor. He said she just had an allergic reaction to something and gave her some cream to rub on her jaw to help. After a couple of days the swelling had just gotten worse and she could hardly move her jaw. She went back to her doctor to see what was wrong. Her doctor had no idea so he started to run some tests. They scrubbed out the inside of her mouth to get tissue samples and they also took some saliva samples. Well, they found out what was wrong. Apparently her chicken soft taco had a pregnant roach in it, then she ate it-the eggs then some how got into her saliva glands and well, she was incubating them. They had to remove a couple a layers of her inner mouth to get all the eggs out. If they hadn't figured out what was going on, the eggs would have hatched inside the lining of her mouth!!!!!!!!!!

She's suing Taco Bell! Of course.

If you need to find out more about this, it's in the Nov. 19th NY Times. If you still want Taco Bell after this one, you're really brave. PASS THE WORD AND BE VERY CAREFUL!

Roach eggs in envelope glue (March 2001):

A woman was working in a post office in California. One day she licked the envelopes and postage stamps instead of using a sponge. That very day the lady cut her tongue on the envelope. A week later, she noticed an abnormal swelling of her tongue. She went to the doctor, and they found nothing wrong. Her tongue was not sore or anything. A couple of days later, her tongue started to swell more, and it began to get really sore, so sore, that she could not eat. She went back to the hospital, and demanded something be done.

The doctor took an x-ray of her tongue, and noticed a lump. He prepared her for minor surgery. When the doctor cut her tongue open, a live roach crawled out. There were roach eggs on the seal of the envelope. The egg was able to hatch inside of her tongue, because of her saliva. It was warm and moist . . .

This is a true story reported on CNN.

Andy Hume wrote: Hey, I used to work in an envelope factory. You wouldn't believe the . . . things that float around in those gum applicator trays. I haven't licked an envelope for years.

To All: I used to work for a print shop (32 years ago) and we were told NEVER to lick the envelopes. I never understood why until I had to go into storage and pull out 2500 envelops that were already printed for a customer who was doing a mailing and saw several squads of roaches roaming around inside a couple of boxes with eggs everywhere. They eat the glue on the envelopes. I think print shops have a harder time controlling roaches than a restaurant. I always buy the

self sealing type. Or if need be I use a glue stick to seal one that has the type of glue that needs to be wet to stick.

PLEASE PASS THIS ON !!!!

ROBBINS, Justin: confessed software pirate

A resident of Charlotte, North Carolina, born February 10, 1976, Justin Robbins was employed by Microsoft Corporation in 1996, when he joined the international gang of outlaw hackers known as "PIRATES WITH ATTITUDE" (PWA). PWA members operated a website based in Quebec, Canada, which displayed and traded more than 5,000 stolen computer software programs in violation of U.S. and international copyright laws. Robbins, known as "Warlock" to his comrades online, was an important source of software for the group, furnishing Microsoft programs and further granting PWA leader Robin Rothberg use of Robbins's Microsoft password to invade the company's computer system. Federal prosecutors indicted 17 conspirators on May 4, 2000, charging each with multiple felonies, and Robbins was among the first to seek a plea bargain. In return for his cooperation with the government, he was favored with leniency at sentencing. His sentence included an unspecified term of community confinement, following his relocation to Lake Station, Indiana. Without the cooperative attitude, he might have faced five years in federal prison and a $250,000 fine for each count of the indictment.

ROBINSON, John Edward Sr.: first "Internet serial killer"

A native of Cicero, Illinois, born in 1943, John Robinson was well known in his community by age 13, an honor student at Quigley Preparatory Seminary and an Eagle Scout who led a troupe of 120 other scouts in a command performance for Queen Elizabeth II. By 1961 he was enrolled at a local junior college, studying to become an X-ray technician. Three years later, he married Nancy Jo Lynch in Kansas City, Missouri.

Robinson was on the path to a solid middle-class life, but he somehow went astray. In June 1967, while working as a lab technician for a Kansas City doctor, he embezzled $33,000 and was placed on three years' probation. At his next job, as manager of a television rental company, Robinson stole merchandise and was fired, but his boss declined to prosecute. In 1969 he began work as a systems analyst for Mobil Oil. On August 27, 1970, exactly two weeks after his probation officer wrote that Robinson was "responding extremely well to probation supervision," Robinson stole 6,200 postage stamps from the company. This time, he was fired *and* charged with theft.

Moving on to Chicago in September 1970, Robinson embezzled $5,500 from yet another employer. He was fired again, but the victim waived prosecution when Robinson's father repaid the loss. Drifting back to Kansas City, Robinson was jailed for violating his probation and his term of supervised release was extended another five years, until 1976. A probation report from April 1973 records his "good prognosis," unaware that Robinson had recently swindled an elderly neighbor out of $30,000. His probation officer was so impressed with Robinson's improvement, in fact, that Robinson was discharged in 1974, two years ahead of schedule.

It was not the system's first mistake with Robinson, nor would it be the last.

A free man once more, Robinson promptly created the Professional Service Association (PSA), ostensibly formed to provide Kansas City physicians financial counseling. More embezzlement followed, prompting a federal grand jury to indict Robinson on four counts of securities and mail fraud. In June 1976 he was fined $2,500 and placed on three years' probation—another wrist-slap that taught him precisely nothing.

In 1977, with his wife and four children, Robinson moved to Johnson County, Kansas, and took a fling at hydroponic farming behind the corporate front of Hydro-Gro Inc. A community activist who tackled multiple projects, Robinson was voted local "Man of the Year" in 1977 for his work with the handicapped. By 1980 Robinson had taken on a second job as personnel director for a local branch of Borden Foods—where he promptly embezzled $40,000, financing a love nest for kinky liaisons with female bondage enthusiasts. Arrested in that case, he faced a seven-year prison term but spent only two months in jail, with five years' probation added to his tab.

The first of Robinson's suspected murder victims, Paula Godfrey, was employed by Robinson when she vanished in 1984. Police later received a letter, purportedly signed by Godfrey, insisting that she was "O.K." and that she did not wish to see her family. She remains among the missing to this day.

Missouri authorities describe John Robinson as the "first Internet serial killer." (AFP/CORBIS)

In December 1984 Robinson approached a Kansas City hospital and adoption agency, introducing himself as the spokesman for "Kansas City Outreach," allegedly a firm created to provide housing and job training for young unwed mothers. The hospital sent Robinson his first client, 19-year-old Lisa Stasi, in January 1985. Stasi promptly vanished, leaving behind a typed letter explaining her urge to leave Missouri for parts unknown. Robinson's childless brother and sister-in-law took custody of Stasi's newborn daughter, paying Robinson $5,500 for a set of forged adoption papers.

Robinson's next brainstorm was the formation of a sado-masochistic prostitution ring, for fun and profit. FBI agents learned of his venture and sent a female decoy around for a job interview, but the initial conversation was so disturbing that G-men backed out, citing fear for their undercover agent's safety. Robinson's first known S&M employee was

21-year-old Theresa Williams, for whom he rented an apartment and arranged transportation on "dates." In May 1985, after less than one month on the job, Williams woke one morning to find Robinson raging through her apartment with a pistol, furious because she had invited a boyfriend to the flat. FBI agents relocated Williams, while Robinson faced assault charges. His probation was revoked for unauthorized firearms possession, but that decision was reversed on appeal, a higher court finding that the FBI denied Robinson's constitutional right to confront his accuser in court.

The agents found some consolation in January 1986, when Kansas jurors convicted Robinson of another investment scam. Sentenced as a habitual offender, Robinson drew a prison term of six to 19 years, but appeals stalled his incarceration until May 1987. In the meantime, 27-year-old Catherine Clampitt moved from Texas to Kansas, drawn by Robinson's promise of "a great job, a lot of traveling and a new wardrobe." She was never seen again.

In prison, Robinson quickly earned a reputation as a model inmate, using his time to develop a computer program that saved the Kansas penal system $100,000 yearly on administrative tasks. The cooperative attitude and a series of mild strokes earned Robinson the sympathy of prison psychologists. In November 1990 they described him as a "devoted family man" and a "non-violent person [who] does not present a threat to society." Kansas paroled Robinson in January 1991, but he still owed time in Missouri, where he remained incarcerated until spring 1993.

Kansas prison librarian Beverly Bonner admired Robinson so much that she divorced her husband in 1993 and moved to Kansas City as the "president" of Hydro-Gro. She vanished in January 1994, after sending her family a letter explaining that her new job required extensive travel. Six months later, after prolonged correspondence, Sheila Faith left Colorado to join Robinson—her "dream man"—in Kansas City. Faith brought along her teenage daughter Debbie, confined to a wheelchair, and both soon disappeared.

By that time Robinson had discovered the Internet, trolling for fresh victims in cyberspace. One who survived told journalist David McClintock that she lost $17,000 to Robinson on a fraudulent investment scheme, arranged through e-mail correspondence. She was lucky, compared to Izabel Lewicka, a Polish immigrant and freshman at Indiana's Purdue University. Lewicka met Robinson on-line in early 1997, and that June she left home to serve an "internship" with Robinson in Kansas. Communication with her parents ceased abruptly, and they went looking for Izabel in August 1997, leaving Kansas empty-handed, without contacting police. Unknown to Izabel's family, Robinson had coerced her into signing a six-page "slave contract," convincing her the document was legal, while he kept her at an apartment in Olathe, Kansas. Lewicka survived in Robinson's clutches until August 1999, then dropped from sight. He told acquaintances that she had been deported for smoking marijuana.

Robinson's last known victim was 27-year-old Suzette Trouten, a Detroit nurse to whom Robinson offered a job in September 1999. The package was attractive: a $60,000 yearly salary, a company car, and wide-ranging travel. Trouten moved to Kansas City on February 13, 2000, and was last seen alive on March 1.

Kansas authorities, meanwhile, had been building a case against Robinson for sexual assault on yet another victim. They arrested Robinson on June 2, 2000, and searched his Olathe home, seizing five computers and a host of other evidence, including a blank piece of stationery signed by Lisa Stasi 15 years earlier and her last motel receipt, dated January 10, 1985. Searchers visited a storage facility rented by Robinson and found a cache of S&M toys, along with various items related to Izabel Lewicka and Suzette Trouten: more blank stationery with signatures affixed, a birth certificate and Social Security card, Lewicka's slave contract, and sundry photographs (including bondage shots).

On June 3, 2000, police searched Robinson's 16-acre farm near La Cygne, Kansas, recovering two 55-gallon drums with women's corpses packed inside. The victims, both beaten to death with a hammer, were identified as Lewicka and Trouten. Two days later, another raiding party scoured another storage facility rented by Robinson, this one in Cass County, Missouri. They found three more oil drums, sealed with duct tape and planted on mounds of cat litter to mask death's sickly odor. Inside the drums lay Betty Bonner, Sheila Faith, and Sheila's daughter Debbie. Like the rest, they had been hammered lifeless and entombed.

Robinson was charged in Kansas with two counts of capital murder, one count of first-degree murder, and various lesser charges. In Missouri, he faces three additional counts of capital murder. At this writing (in November 2002), a Kansas jury had convicted Robinson of the murders of Trouten, Lewicka and Stasi. He was awaiting trial in Missouri on three additional murder charges. Prosecutors, while outwardly confident in their evidence, stress that indictments are merely accusations and are not proof of guilt. All defendants are presumed innocent until convicted at trial.

ROSS, Johnny: exonerated by blood analysis

For many years, rape was a capital crime in states of the southern U.S., but critics of the death penalty noted that those defendants condemned for nonfatal sexual assaults were nearly always African Americans accused of attacking white victims. Prior to 1960, many of those so accused were lynched without trial, while countless others were convicted and sentenced to prison or death after "confessing" under what amounted to police torture. A modern case in point is that of 16-year-old Johnny Ross, accused of rape and condemned by Louisiana authorities in proceedings that made a mockery of justice.

Ross was 16 years old in 1975, when police in New Orleans accused him of raping a white woman. Ross was beaten by detectives until he admitted the crime, and with that false confession in hand, his capital trial was completed within a few hours. The death sentence was a foregone conclusion, and appeals seemed hopeless until 1981, when Alabama lawyer Morris Dees and his Southern Poverty Law Center took an interest in the case. DNA testing had yet to be discovered, but it hardly mattered, since neither prosecutors nor Ross's original defense counsel had even bothered to check his blood type against semen recovered from the crime scene. When those rudimentary tests were performed, Ross was positively excluded as a suspect, and the New Orleans district attorney's office dismissed all charges, freeing Ross after he had spent six years on death row for a crime he did not commit. The case remains unsolved today.

While Ross was imprisoned, the U.S. Supreme Court addressed the issue of capital punishment for rapists in the case of *Coker v. Georgia* (1977), ruling that execution for rape (or, by extension, any other crime not resulting in death of the victim) constituted grossly disproportional punishment and therefore violated the Eighth Amendment of the U.S. Constitution.

ROTHBERG, Robin: confessed software pirate

A resident of North Chelmsford, Massachusetts, born September 11, 1967, Robin Rothberg was arrested by FBI agents on February 3, 2000, charged with playing a leadership role in the international HACKERS' syndicate known to its members as "PIRATES WITH ATTITUDE" (PWA). According to the charges filed against him, Rothberg (a.k.a. "Marlenus") controlled access to the gang's illegal website based in Quebec, Canada, where more than 5,000 software programs were traded or sold in violation of U.S. and international copyright laws. In furtherance of that conspiracy, Rothberg persuaded PWA member and Microsoft employee Justin Robbins to furnish stolen Microsoft programs and to give Rothberg his company password, permitting Rothberg to penetrate Microsoft's computer system at will. Rothberg also recruited five employees of Intel Corporation to furnish stolen hardware for the PWA website, thereby expanding its capacity to store bootleg programs. Losses to the companies involved were conservatively estimated in excess of $1 million.

By May 2001, Rothberg had joined 12 other PWA defendants in pleading guilty to the charges filed against him, but sentencing was delayed for another year by legal maneuvers and negotiations. On May 15, 2002, U.S. District Judge Matthew Kennelly, in Chicago, sentenced Rothberg to serve 18 months in federal prison. Most of the other conspirators escaped with terms of home or community confinement, varying terms of community service, and fines ranging up to $5,000.

RUNNION, Samantha: murder case solved by DNA evidence

Five-year-old Samantha Runnion was kidnapped outside her Stanton, California, apartment on July 15, 2002, by a man who asked her to help him find a missing dog. Witnesses described the kidnapper as Hispanic, driving a light-green sedan. A massive Orange County search for Samantha and the suspect was in progress, heralded by national publicity, when Runnion's nude corpse was found on July 16, in neighboring Riverside County. Evidence collected at the crime scene proved that she had been sexually assaulted, then asphyxiated.

Relentless broadcasts of a composite sketch and descriptions of the kidnapper's car paid off for police on July 17, when Lake Elsinore neighbors of 27-year-old Alejandro Avila fingered him as a suspect. Authorities placed Avila under surveillance, then arrested him on July 19, 2002. Blood samples were drawn under court order and DNA comparison with the crime scene evidence was completed in near-record time, producing an announcement on July 21 that Avila's genetic profile matched the semen recovered from Runnion's corpse. Avila's sister told police that he had abruptly canceled a family dinner on the night Runnion was kidnapped, and a background check revealed that Avila had faced child-molesting charges two years earlier. He was acquitted by a jury in that case, apparently due to a lack of forensic evidence, but prosecutors in Orange County declared themselves "confident" of his guilt in the Runnion case.

"The evidence is very, very compelling," District Attorney Tony Rackauckas told reporters on July 23. "We are satisfied we have the right person and will be able to bring in a guilty verdict in this case." Avila was charged with murder, kidnapping, and two counts of forcible lewd acts on a child, the latter charges ranked as "special circumstances" that allow prosecutors to seek a death penalty under California's penal code. Prosecutorial confidence notwithstanding, indictments are merely accusations of criminal activity, and all defendants are presumed innocent until they are convicted at trial.

S

"SADMIND": computer worms

Reported in three very similar variants since May 2001, "Sadmind" is a computer worm presumed to have been created by a virus writer with strong sympathy for the People's Republic of China. Designed to replicate between Sun Sparc computers using the Solaris/SunOS operating system, Sadmind's variants specifically target Microsoft IIS v4 and v5 Web servers, replacing their startup page with a message that reads:

fuck USA
Government
fuck PoizonBOx
contact:sysadmen@yahoo.com.cn

Since "PoizonBOx" is the name adopted by a group of hackers known to vandalize Chinese websites, analysts presume Sadmind's author stands opposed to such action—i.e., in favor of the Chinese political system. This deduction remains untested, however, since the creator(s) of Sadmind is still unidentified.

The various forms of this worm—called "Sadmind.a," "Sadmind.b" and "Sadmind.c"—replicate by taking advantage of a weakness in Sun Microsystems software, generating random Internet Protocol (IP) addresses and testing each in turn, by the thousands, until a vulnerable connection is discovered. At that point, Sadmind establishes a connection to its remote host computer and copies itself to the main directory of the new target host. In the process, it modifies the new host's startup files so that Sadmind itself is launched each time the system starts. It then overwrites the latest victim's index page with a new one containing the message quoted above. Minor utility functions differentiate the three Sadmind variants, but their performance is substantially identical.

SALAZAR, Ben: exonerated by DNA evidence

A resident of Travis County, Texas, Ben Salazar was 28 years old in 1991, when police arrested him on suspicion of forcible rape. Although Salazar denied involvement in the crime, prosecutors felt they had enough evidence to proceed with the case. Their suspect smoked the same brand of cigarettes as the rapist, had a tattoo in the same place described by the victim, and possessed a blood profile shared by only one in every 200 Hispanic-American men. Based on that circumstantial evidence and a tentative identification from the victim, jurors convicted Salazar in 1992, and he was sentenced to serve 30 years in prison. Five years later, a new defense attorney submitted semen traces from the crime scene for advanced DNA testing, and the results excluded Salazar as a possible donor. He was pardoned by Governor George Bush and released from prison on November 20, 1997. The state of Texas subsequently paid Salazar $25,000 in compensation for his five years of unjust confinement. The rape case remains unsolved today.

SALGADO, Carlos Felipe, Jr.: Internet thief and swindler
On March 28, 1997, a technician performing routing maintenance duties on an Internet Service Provider (ISP) based in San Diego, California, noted signs of an unauthorized computer intrusion. Searching further, he discovered a "packet sniffer" program used to collect data from various ISP subscribers when they logged onto the system. As a team of technicians continued the search, they discovered that the intruder was still logged onto the ISP, traced back to a computer at the University of California at San Francisco (UCSF). ISP administrators alerted FBI agents to the intrusion and a federal investigation was initiated.

On March 29, an ISP subscriber notified administrators that he had been in contact with a HACKER known on-line as "SMAK," communicating via an Internet Relay Channel (IRC). In the course of their e-mail chat, SMAK had boasted of hacking into the ISP and stealing credit card information. Before the link was severed, SMAK offered to sell the stolen data, along with another collection of 60,000 stolen credit card numbers. Two days later, FBI agents in San Francisco took over the case from their colleagues in San Diego, conducting interviews at UCSF and discovering that SMAK had worked his long-distance mischief after hacking into the computer account of an innocent student. The month of April 1997 was consumed by efforts to identify SMAK and set up a "sting" operation that would lure the hacker into a face-to-face meeting, where he or she could then be arrested.

Once again, the talkative ISP customer in San Diego, now a cooperative witness for the FBI, came to the bureau's rescue. Continuing his chats with SMAK, the informer voiced interest in purchasing the stolen credit card numbers and received an e-mail attachment containing 50 encrypted numbers as a token of "good faith." With the stolen numbers came a message:

There may be a delay in our business together of a day or so. It's not necessarily a bad thing. Let me explain. This morning I was reading a business magazine article about on-line transactions on the Internet and a particular niche in services. A couple companies were mentioned that generated SEVERAL MILLION dollars in credit card transactions a week! I decided to go exploring and got into their sites. The article was right! However, I need to explore the sites for a little while to establish firm control and locate machine extractable data. I think it is worth it. Smak.

On May 5, 1997, the collaborating witness, under FBI direction, asked SMAK, "How many of the credit card numbers are valid?" In response, SMAK sent his "friend" another 710 card numbers at a price of one dollar each, payable after the numbers were confirmed as valid and active. G-men quickly determined that the numbers were indeed active, belonging to cards with credit limits ranging from $5,000 to $12,000. SMAK received his $710 payment via an anonymous Western Union wire transfer, and another transaction was arranged eight days later, this one transferring 580 credit card numbers for five dollars apiece. FBI agents chose 15 of the numbers for random verification, finding that they belonged to active cards with credit limits between $2,000 and $25,000. SMAK received his $2,900 payoff in another Western Union transfer, and agents forged ahead with the last stage of their plan.

A meeting was arranged between SMAK and his presumed customer, for 11:15 A.M. on May 21, 1997, in a smoking room at San Francisco International Airport. The man who kept the date with undercover G-men was Carlos Salgado Jr., a 37-year-old resident of Daly City, California. Arrested on the spot, he was relieved of a CD-ROM containing 100,000 additional credit card numbers, offered for sale at a price of $260,000. Salgado also carried a paperback copy of Mario Puzo's novel *The Last Don.* Agents subsequently determined that the credit card numbers were encrypted, the key to their decryption drawn from the first letter of each sentence in the first paragraph on page 128 of Puzo's book. Authorities told the media that Salgado had hacked into various companies doing business on the Internet and had exploited flaws in their operating systems to download credit card numbers by the tens of thousands. FBI spokesmen estimated that Salgado's arrest had thwarted potential losses of $1 billion to legitimate credit card holders.

Six days after his arrest, Salgado was released on $100,000 bond. A federal grand jury convened on June 6, 1997, and indicted Salgado on five felony charges, including three counts of unauthorized computer penetration, one count of possessing stolen credit card numbers, and one count of trafficking in stolen credit card numbers. The maximum sentence for all five counts, if convicted at trial, was 40 years' imprisonment and/or fines of $1 million, $500 in court costs and three years' supervised probation following release from prison. Intimidated by those prospects, Salgado cut a deal with prosecutors and pleaded guilty to four of the five counts on August 25, 1997. Formal sentencing was set for November 25, 1997, later delayed to January 1998, when Salgado received a 30-month prison term, deferred on condition that he attend a federal "boot camp" program.

SANDUSKY, Christopher Scott: convicted hacker

A South Carolina native, born in 1967, Christopher Sandusky was living in Cedar Park, Texas, in 2001, when he launched a series of long-distance computer invasions targeting Steinberg Diagnostic Medical Imaging (SDMI) in Las Vegas, Nevada. Once employed by a computer consulting firm that assisted in designing SDMI's system, Sandusky sought revenge for termination from his job by invading SDMI's computers on three occasions, maliciously deleting patient billing records, changing employee passwords, and otherwise vandalizing the system so that SDMI's operations were paralyzed. SDMI's system administrator discovered the unauthorized penetration and traced the raids back to Sandusky, whereupon federal authorities were contacted and felony indictments were filed in May 2001.

Eleven months later, on April 17, 2002, Sandusky pleaded guilty in Las Vegas federal court on three counts of unauthorized computer access. Sentencing was deferred until August 2002.

SANFORD, Robert Russell: convicted hacker

On October 12, 2000, 18-year-old Robert Sanford was indicted by a grand jury in Dallas, Texas, on nine counts of theft and illegally obtaining access to computers operated by six state agencies in Texas, the U.S. Postal Service, the Canadian Department of Defense, and Glinn Publishing Company of Milwaukee, Wisconsin. Sanford, a high-school senior residing in the Dallas suburb of Irving, Texas, was identified in press releases as a member of the international HACKER syndicate known as "HV2K." The indictment charged that between November 1999 and January 2000, Sanford illegally penetrated various protected computer systems and defaced various websites in a spree of cybervandalism. (Prior to Sanford's indictment, a Canadian juvenile active in HV2K pleaded guilty to related crimes in Halifax, Nova Scotia, and entered a pretrial diversion program.)

Sanford surrendered to Dallas authorities the day after his indictment was announced, facing a maxi-

mum sentence of 24 years in prison and a $78,000 fine if convicted on all counts at trial. Spokesmen for the U.S. Postal Service in Arlington, Virginia, announced that the indictments resulted from a joint investigation by the Texas Department of Public Safety (whose website was among those vandalized by Sanford), the Royal Canadian Mounted Police, the Canadian Forces National Investigative Service, and the Postal Service Office of the Inspector General. Specific charges included one count of third-degree felony theft (involving losses of $20,000 or more), six felony counts of invading protected computers, and two misdemeanor counts of breaching computer security systems. Bond was set at $11,000 and Sanford was released after being booked into the Dallas County jail. Federal prosecutors declined to pursue the case because Sanford was 17 years old at the time of the offenses, requiring prosecution as a juvenile, while Texas law permitted his trial in state court as an adult.

The hacking indictment was not Sanford's first encounter with the Dallas legal system. In May 1999, he was one of two juveniles charged with dropping LSD into a teacher's coffee cup at Winfree Academy High School. Charges in that case were later dismissed without explanation by Dallas County authorities, but prosecutors in the hacking case asked a judge to consider the drug incident when setting bond for Sanford on the latest charge. As a condition of release on bail, Sanford was barred from using a computer outside the supervision of his parents and was further required to submit urine samples for drug testing.

Eight weeks after his indictment, on December 6, 2000, Sanford pled guilty to six counts of unlawful computer access and one count of theft. He received a 22-year prison sentence, but that term was suspended by the court, with Sanford placed on five years' probation. Further conditions of the plea bargain included payment of $45,856.46 in restitution to various victims of the hacking raids, continued limitations on Sanford's use of computers, random drug testing, an unspecified term of community service, and a court-ordered requirement that Sanford obtain a high school diploma or graduate equivalency degree.

"SANTA": computer worm

Reported from the Internet initially in November 2000, "Santa" replicates in traditional fashion, by sending copies of itself via e-mail attachments to addresses gleaned from the Microsoft Outlook address books of infected computers. Because it is written in Visual Basic Script (VBS), however, the worm functions only on computers which have Windows Scripting Host (WSH) installed. (This includes all systems running Windows 98 or Windows 2000.) Santa is also limited to working with Outlook 98 and Outlook 2000, earlier versions being immune to its corruption. The original message, written in German, reads as follows:

Subject: News vom Weihnachtsmann
Message: Guten Tag, es ist bald Weihnachten. Und wie sieht's aus mit schönen Geschenken? Hierzu ein Tip vom Weihnachtsmann: Unter www.leos-jeans.de gibt es die besten Geschenke im Web! Das bedeutet absolut stressfreies Einkaufen, schnelle und unkomplizierte Lieferung, riesige Auswahl. Also nichts wie hin, und Frohe Weihnachten.
Attached file name: XMAS.VBS

When a recipient double-clicks on the attachment, Santa automatically opens MS Outlook, invades the address book, and sends itself to the first 50 addresses found. Aside from self-replication, the worm has no additional payload and causes no harm to the infected host.

"SANTANA": computer virus

Logged for the first time in April 2000, "Santana" is rated by analysts as a harmless, memory-resident, parasitic, encrypted Win32 virus that writes itself to the ends of .exe files with a text string reading: "Virus 'SANTANA' created by Net'$ Wa$te [RespawneD EviL]." The virus apparently has no payload and does not manifest itself in any visible way, hence the "harmless" rating.

"SATANIC": computer viruses

The first computer virus called "Satanic" was initially reported from the Internet in July 1996, described by analysts as a "very dangerous," memory-resident, parasitic virus that writes itself to the beginning of opened .com files. On Fridays it erases infected disk sectors of the host computer and displays a message reading "Satanic Warrior."

Six months later, in January 1997, a second, unrelated "Satanic" virus was identified, this one described as an encrypted macro virus that infects documents as they are opened or closed. It also infects the host system itself, deleting various menu items when Microsoft Word is opened. On September 30 of any year, Satanic displays the following message on-screen:

Nightmare Joker :-)
You're infected with Satanic

The virus also includes the text string: "Greetings to Dark Night! Thats [sic] good. :-)".

SCHELLER, Suzanne Marie: convicted workplace hacker

A 20-year-old resident of Sacramento, California, Suzanne Scheller was employed by a local bank when she accessed the bank's computers without permission, scanning customer records in search of potential customers for a friend who was launching a real estate business. Unknown to Scheller, some of the information she illegally provided to her friend was later used by two other persons to perpetrate a series of IDENTITY THEFT and bank fraud schemes.

One of the imposters, Katrina Carnes, used a counterfeit California driver's license in the name of a legitimate bank depositor (but bearing Carnes's photograph) to obtain a $14,000 cashier's check from the bank on March 14, 2001. A second swindler, Machelle Christine Groves, used a similar counterfeit driver's license—including a genuine customer's name, address and Department of Motor Vehicles number combined with a photo of Groves—to cash a check for $2,665.23 on June 6, 2000. Both swindlers were subsequently identified and arrested. Groves pleaded guilty to one count of bank fraud on April 20, 2001; on September 28, 2001 she was sentenced to 11 months' imprisonment, five years of supervised release after serving her time, and full restitution of the amount stolen. Carnes likewise pleaded guilty to one count of bank fraud on May 4, 2001; on September 14, 2001, she received a 13-month prison term, five years of supervised parole, and restitution of the amount of $17,000 (including transactions aside from the $14,000 theft).

As for Suzanne Scheller, her duplicity was uncovered, and she pleaded guilty to one count of unauthorized computer access on August 10, 2001. Sixteen weeks later, on November 30, 2001, U.S.

District Judge Garland Burrell Jr. sentenced her to 36 months' probation. Assistant U.S. Attorney Mark Krotoski, in charge of the three prosecutions, told reporters that no legitimate depositors had lost any money to the swindlers, since their deposits were federally insured.

SCHNEIDER, Bjorn See FASTLANE

SCRUGGS, Dwayne: exonerated by DNA evidence

On the night of February 1, 1986, a woman walking home from a bus station in Indianapolis, Indiana, was stopped on the street by a man who approached her from behind, held a knife to her throat, and forced her toward a grassy area beneath a highway overpass. There, while trying to conceal his face, the attacker robbed his victim of six dollars, then raped her and fled the scene on foot. The victim viewed 200 mug shots of convicted sex offenders before identifying suspect Dwayne Scruggs as her assailant "with 98 percent certainty." She later picked Scruggs from a second photograph and repeated her identification in open court. Scruggs denied involvement in the crime, but he acknowledged familiarity with the area and owned a pair of boots resembling those worn by the rapist. Jurors convicted Scruggs of rape and robbery on May 13, 1986, whereupon he received concurrent prison terms of 40 years and 20 years on the respective charges.

Scruggs appealed the conviction on dual grounds, including a lack of sufficient evidence to convict and an "evidentiary harpoon" consisting of a detective's testimony that the victim had selected Scruggs's photo from a group of "individuals who have all been arrested for rape or a sexual assault." The court had warned jurors to ignore that comment, but the defense's motion for a mistrial was denied. The Supreme Court of Indiana rejected Scruggs's appeal in August 1987.

Five years and four months later, on December 18, 1992, Scruggs's public defender petitioned for release of prosecution evidence that included semen traces and a bloodstain from the rapist gathered by Indianapolis police in February 1986. Subsequent motions, filed on February 24 and April 26, 1993, sought DNA testing (unavailable in 1986) on the crime scene evidence and a sample of Scruggs's blood. Permission for the tests was granted on April 27, 1993, and the results excluded Scruggs as a pos-

sible donor of either the semen or blood. Prosecutors verified the test results, then joined Scruggs's defender in a motion to vacate his conviction. That motion was granted on December 17, 1993, and Scruggs was released from prison. His record was expunged by court order on March 29, 1994. The rape remains unsolved today.

SEND-A-REPORT Pyramid Scheme: Internet swindle

Financial pyramid (or "Ponzi") schemes are illegal in all American jurisdictions, but they continue to attract gullible investors and proliferate across the land, more widely since the advent of the Internet than ever before. In this variation on the ancient theme, swindlers try to circumvent the law by pretending to "sell" a worthless product instead of merely soliciting investments. That charade aside, the scheme remains illegal and investors risk their hard-earned cash for naught. The original text of this fraud, circulated since June 2000, reads (with errors intact):

Subject: Invest $25 to get $500,000 in every 4 to 5 months!!

Dear Friend:

AS SEEN ON NATIONAL TV :

"Making over half million dollars every 4 to 5 months from your home for an investment of only $25 U.S. Dollars expense one time"
THANX TO THE COMPUTER AGE AND THE INTERNET !

===

BE A MILLIONAIRE LIKE OTHERS WITHIN A YEAR !!!

Before you say "Bull", please read the following. This is the letter you have been hearing about on the news lately. Due to the popularity of this letter on the internet, a national weekly news program recently devoted an entire show to the investigation of this program described below, to see if it really can make people money.

The show also investigated whether or not the program was legal. Their findings proved once and for all that there are "absolutely NO. Laws prohibiting the participation in the program and if people can follow the simple instructions, they are bound to make some mega bucks with only $25 out of pocket cost".

DUE TO THE RECENT INCREASE OF POPU-LARITY & RESPECT THIS PROGRAM HAS ATTAINED, IT IS CURRENTLY WORKING BET-TER THAN EVER.

This is what one had to say:

"Thanks to this profitable opportunity. I was approached many times before but each time I passed on it. I am so glad I finally joined just to see what one could expect in return for the minimal effort and money required. To my astonishment, I received total $610,470.00 in 21 weeks, with money still coming in".

Pam Hedland, Fort Lee, New Jersey.

Here is another testimonial:

"This program has been around for a long time but I never believed in it. But one day when I received this again in the mail I decided to gamble my $25 on it. I followed the simple instructions and walaa . . . 3 weeks later the money started to come in. First month I only made $240.00 but the next 2 months after that I made a total of $290,000.00. So far, in the past 8 months by re-entering the program, I have made over $710,000.00 and I am playing it again. The key to success in this program is to follow the simple steps and NOT change anything."

More testimonials later but first,

**** PRINT THIS NOW FOR YOUR FUTURE REFERENCE *****

$$$

If you would like to make at least $500,000 every 4 to 5 months easily and comfortably, please read the following . . . THEN READ IT AGAIN and AGAIN !!!

$$$

FOLLOW THE SIMPLE INSTRUCTION BELOW AND YOUR FINANCIAL DREAMS WILL COME TRUE, GUARANTEED!

INSTRUCTIONS:
**** Order all 5 reports shown on the list below.

**** For each report, send $5 CASH, THE NAME & NUMBER OF THE REPORT YOU ARE ORDER-ING and YOUR E-MAIL ADDRESS to the person whose name appears ON THAT LIST next to the report. MAKE SURE YOUR RETURN ADDRESS IS ON YOUR ENVELOPE TOP LEFT CORNER in case of any mail problems.

**** When you place your order, make sure you order each of the 5 reports. You will need all 5 reports so that you can save them on your computer and resell them. YOUR TOTAL COST $5 × 5 = $25.00.

**** Within a few days you will receive, vie e-mail, each of the 5 reports from these 5 different individuals. Save them on your computer so they will be accessible for you to send to the 1,000's of people who will order them from you. Also make a floppy of these reports and keep it on your desk in case something happen to your computer.

**** IMPORTANT—DO NOT alter the names of the people who are listed next to each report, or their sequence on the list, in any way other than what is instructed below in step "1 through 6" or you will loose out on majority of your profits. Once you understand the way this works, you will also see how it does not work if you change it. Remember, this method has been tested, and if you alter, it will NOT work!!! People have tried to put their friends/relatives names on all five thinking they could get all the money. But it does not work this way. Believe us, we all have tried to be greedy and then nothing happened. So Do Not try to change anything other than what is instructed. Because if you do, it will not work for you. Remember, honesty reaps the reward!!!

1. . . . After you have ordered all 5 reports, take this advertisement and REMOVE the name & address of the person in REPORT # 5. This person has made it through the cycle and is no doubt counting their fortune.
2. . . . Move the name & address in REPORT # 4 down TO REPORT # 5.
3. . . . Move the name & address in REPORT # 3 down TO REPORT # 4.
4. . . . Move the name & address in REPORT # 2 down TO REPORT # 3.
5. . . . Move the name & address in REPORT # 1 down TO REPORT # 2
6. . . . Insert YOUR name & address in the REPORT # 1 Position.

PLEASE MAKE SURE you copy every name & address ACCURATELY!

====================================

**** *Take this entire letter, with the modified list of names, and save it on your computer. DO NOT MAKE ANY OTHER CHANGES. Save this on a disk as well just in case if you loose any data.*

**** *To assist you with marketing your business on the internet, the 5 reports you purchase will provide you with invaluable marketing information which includes how to send bulk e-mails legally, where to find thousands of free classified ads and much more.*

There are 2 Primary methods to get this venture going:

METHOD # 1: BY SENDING BULK E-MAIL LEGALLY

====================================

let's say that you decide to start small, just to see how it goes, and we will assume You and those involved send out only 5,000 e-mails each. Let's also assume that the mailing receive only a 0.2% response (the response could be much better but lets just say it is only 0.2%. Also many people will send out hundreds of thousands e-mails instead of only 5,000 each).

Continuing with this example, you send out only 5,000 e-mails. With a 0.2% response, that is only 10 orders for report # 1. Those 10 people responded by sending out 5,000 e-mail each for a total of 50,000. Out of those 50,000 e-mails only 0.2% responded with orders. That's = 100 people responded and ordered Report # 2. Those 100 people mail out 5,000 e-mails each for a total of 500,000 e-mails. The 0.2% response to that is 1000 orders for Report # 3. Those 1000 people send out 5,000 e-mails each for a total of 5 million e-mails sent out. The 0.2% response to that is 10,000 orders for Report # 4. Those 10,000 people send out 5,000 e-mails each for a total of 50,000,000 (50 million) e-mails. The 0.2% response to that is 100,000 orders for Report # 5

THAT'S 100,000 ORDERS TIMES $5 EACH = $500,000.00 (half million).

Your total income in this example is:

1. . . . $50 +
2. . . . $500 +
3. . . . $5,000 +
4. . . . $50,000 +
5. . . . $500,000 . . . . Grand Total = $555,550.00

NUMBERS DO NOT LIE. GET A PENCIL & PAPER AND FIGURE OUT THE WORST POSSIBLE RESPONSES AND NO MATTER HOW YOU CALCULATE IT, YOU WILL STILL MAKE A LOT OF MONEY!

REMEMBER FRIEND, THIS IS ASSUMING ONLY 10 PEOPLE ORDERING OUT OF 5,000 YOU MAILED TO. Dare to think for a moment what would happen if everyone, or half or even one 4th of those people mailed 100,000 e-mails each or more? There are over 150 million people on the internet worldwide and counting. Believe me, many people will do just that, and more!

METHOD # 2: BY PLACING FREE ADS ON THE INTERNET

====================================

Advertising on the net is very very inexpensive and there are hundreds of FREE places to advertise. Placing a lot of free ads on the internet will easily get a larger response. We strongly suggest you start with Method # 1 and add METHOD # 2 as you go along.

For every $5 you receive, all you must do is e-mail them the Report they ordered. That's it. Always provide same day service on all orders. This will guarantee that the e-mail they send out, with your name and address on it, will be prompt because they can not advertise until they receive the report.

_____AVAILABLE REPORTS_____

ORDER EACH REPORT BY ITS NUMBER & NAME ONLY. Notes: Always send $5 cash (U.S. CURRENCY) for each Report. Checks NOT accepted. Make sure the cash is concealed by wrapping it in at least 2 sheets of paper. On one of those sheets of paper, Write the NUMBER & the NAME of the Report you are ordering, YOUR E-MAIL

ADDRESS and your name and postal address.

PLACE YOUR ORDER FOR THESE REPORTS NOW:

===

REPORT # 1: *"The Insider's Guide to Advertising for Free on the Net"*

Order Report # 1 from:
xxx yyyyy
4009-62st.
zzzzz, Alberta
Canada T4V 2W9

REPORT # 2: *"The Insider's Guide to Sending Bulk e-mail on the Net"*

Order Report # 2 from:
aaaaaa bbbbbb
P.O. Box 123456
Sarasota, FL. 34276
U.S.A.

REPORT # 3: *"The Secret to Multilevel marketing on the net"*

Order Report # 3 from:
cccc dddd
9999 Santa Monica Blvd;
Beverly Hills, Ca 90212
U.S.A.

REPORT # 4: *"How to become a millionaire utilizing MLM & the Net"*

Order Report # 4 from:
ccccccc Marketing
88888, 22th Street
Warwick, N.D. 58381
U.S.A

REPORT # 5: *"HOW TO SEND 1 MILLION E-MAILS FOR FREE"*

Order Report # 5 from:
ZZZ Enterprises

PO Box 1111
xxx Lake, ND 58301-0421
U.S.A.

$$$$$ YOUR SUCCESS GUIDELINES $$$$$

Follow these guidelines to guarantee your success:

*** If you do not receive at least 10 orders for Report #1 within 2 weeks, continue sending e-mails until you do.

*** After you have received 10 orders, 2 to 3 weeks after that you should receive 100 orders or more for REPORT # 2. If you did not, continue advertising or sending e-mails until you do.

*** Once you have received 100 or more orders for Report # 2, YOU CAN RELAX, because the system is already working for you, and the cash will continue to roll in!

THIS IS IMPORTANT TO REMEMBER: Every time your name Is moved down on the list, you are placed in front of a Different report. You can KEEP TRACK of your PROGRESS by watching which report people are ordering from you. IF YOU WANT TO GENERATE MORE INCOME SEND ANOTHER BATCH OF E-MAILS AND START THE WHOLE PROCESS AGAIN. There is NO LIMIT to the income you can generate from this business!!!

FOLLOWING IS A NOTE FROM THE ORIGINATOR OF THIS PROGRAM:

"You have just received information that can give you financial freedom for the rest of your life, with NO RISK and JUST A LITTLE BIT OF EFFORT. You can make more money in the next few weeks and months than you have ever imagined.

Follow the program EXACTLY AS INSTRUCTED. Do Not Change it in any way. It works exceedingly well as it is now. Remember to e-mail a copy of this exciting report after you have put your name and address in Report #1 and moved others to #2 ....#5 as instructed above. One of the people you send this to may send out 100,000 or more e-mails and your name will be on everyone of them. Remember though, the more you send out the more potential customers you will reach.

So my friend, I have given you the ideas, information, materials and opportunity to become financially independent. IT IS UP TO YOU NOW!

******* MORE TESTIMONIALS *******

"My name is Mitchell. -*My wife, Jody and I live in Chicago. I am an accountant with a major U.S. Corporation and I make pretty good money. When I received this program I grumbled to Jody about receiving "junk mail". I made fun of the whole thing, spouting my knowledge of the population and percentages involved. I "knew" it wouldn't work. Jody totally ignored my supposed intelligence and few days later she jumped in with both feet. I made merciless fun of her, and was ready to lay the old "I told you so" on her when the thing didn't work. Well, the laugh was on me! Within 3 weeks she had received 50 responses. Within the next 45 days she had received total $147,200.00 . . . all cash! I was shocked. I have joined Jody in her "hobby".

Mitchell Wolf, M.D.,
Chicago, Illinois

"Not being the gambling type, it took me several weeks to make up my mind to participate in this plan. But conservative that I am, I decided that the initial investment was so little that there was just no way that I wouldn't get enough orders to at least get my money back".

"I was surprised when I found my medium size post office box crammed with orders. I made $319,210.00 in the first 12 weeks. The nice thing about this deal is that it does not matter where people live. There simply isn't a better investment with a faster return and so big".

Dan Sondstrom, Alberta, Canada

"I had received this program before. I deleted it, but later I wondered if I should have given it a try. Of course, I had no no idea who to contact to get another copy, so I had to wait until I was e-mailed again by someone else . . . 11 months passed then it luckily came again. . . . I did not delete this one! I made more than $490,000 on my first try and all the money came within 22 weeks".

Susan De Suza,
New York, N.Y.

"It really is a great opportunity to make relatively easy money with little cost to you. I followed the simple instructions carefully and within 10 days the money started to come in. My first month I made $20,560.00 and by the end of third month my total cash count was $ 362,840.00. Life is beautiful, Thanx to internet".

Fred Dellaca, Westport,
New Zealand

ORDER YOUR REPORTS TODAY AND GET STARTED ON YOUR ROAD TO FINANCIAL FREEDOM!

If you have any questions of the legality of this program, contact the Office of Associate Director for Marketing Practices, Federal Trade Commission, Bureau of Consumer Protection, Washington, D.C.

///

ONE TIME MAILING, NO NEED TO REMOVE

///

This message is sent in compliance of the proposed bill SECTION 301. per Section 301, Paragraph (a)(2)(C) of S. 1618. Further transmission to you by the sender of this e-mail may be stopped at no cost to you by sending a reply to: Sophie530@email.com with the word Remove in the subject line. This message is not intended for residents in the State of Washington, screening of addresses has been done to the best of our technical ability.

—— THE END ——

SHAMPOO Cancer Warning: Internet hoax

Circulated on the Web since May 1999, this strange scare message claims that common shampoo causes cancer. The claim has been categorically refuted by the American Cancer Society—cancer is not caused by a "virus" nor by any known shampoo ingredient—yet it continues to surface and presumably terrify various gullible readers. The original message reads (with errors uncorrected):

Subject: FW: Read this about the shampoo you use

Check the ingredients listed on your shampoo bottle, and see if they have substance by the name of Sodium Laureth Sulfate, or simply SLS. This substance is found in most shampoos, and the manufacturers use it because it produces a lot of foam and it is cheap.

BUT the fact is that SLS is used to scrub garage floors, and it is very strong. It is also proven that it can cause cancer in the long run, and this is no joke. I went home and checked my shampoo (Vidal Sasoon); it doesn't contain it; however, others such as Vo5, Palmolive, Paul Mitchell, the new Hemp Shampoo . . . contain this substance. The first ingredient listed (which means it is the single most prevalent ingredient) in Clairol's Herbal Essences is Sodium Laureth Sulfate.

So I called one company, and I told them their product contains a substance that will cause people to have cancer. They said, "Yeah, we knew about it but there is nothing we can do about it because we need that substance to produce foam.

By the way Colgate toothpaste also contains the same substance to produce the "bubbles". They said they are going to send me some information. Research has shown that in the 1980s, the chance of getting cancer is 1 out of 8000 and now, in the 1990s, the chances of getting cancer is 1 out of 3, which is very serious. So I hope that you will take this seriously and pass this on to all the people you know, and hopefully, we can stop "giving" ourselves the cancer virus.

This is serious, after you have read this, pass it on to as many people as possible, this is not a chain letter, but it concerns our health.

SHEPHARD, David: exonerated by DNA evidence

On December 24, 1983, while engaged in some last-minute Christmas shopping, a female resident of Union County, New Jersey, was accosted by two men in the parking lot of a shopping mall. The strangers forced their victim into the backseat of her own car, one man holding her immobile while the other drove them to a nearby residential neighborhood. There, both men raped the woman repeatedly, one calling his companion "Dave" during the prolonged attack. Tiring at last, the rapists shoved the woman from her car

and drove away. The victim's car and handbag were later found near a building at Newark International Airport, where David Shephard was employed.

The victim subsequently identified Shephard by sight and the sound of his voice as one of her attackers. A blood test revealed that Shephard's antigens and secretor type matched those of one rapist. Shephard's alibi was uncorroborated and collapsed under cross-examination at trial, in September 1984. Jurors deliberated for a day before convicting Shephard of rape, robbery, terrorist threats, and weapons violations. Following conviction, he received a 30-year prison term. The second rapist was never identified, as Shephard continued to protest his innocence and refused to name an accomplice.

Shephard's appeals had been exhausted by 1992, when he filed a motion for DNA testing of all semen samples collected by police in 1983 (before such tests were recognized). Prosecutors agreed, and the test results excluded Shephard as the donor of one semen sample recovered from a vaginal swab. Shephard was not exonerated, however, since two rapists were involved and the genetic material found on a second swab produced inconclusive results. Shepard's attorney next sought test results for semen stains on the victim's underpants, where two distinct genetic profiles failed to match Shephard's. Prosecutors theorized that one donor of the underwear stains might be the victim's boyfriend, but further tests excluded him as well. The Union County Superior Court ordered a new trial for Shephard, whereupon prosecutors declined to pursue the case. Shephard was freed on May 18, 1994, after serving nearly 10 years for a crime he did not commit. New Jersey statutes barred financial compensation of defendants wrongfully convicted, but the law was soon changed on the basis of Shephard's case.

"SHOT Spotter" Microphones: audio surveillance technology

Invented by Triton Technology of Los Altos, California, as a means of focusing police response to gunshots fired in urban areas, "Shot Spotter" microphones made their public debut in the high-crime Willowbrook district of Los Angeles in March 2000. Two months later, the devices had produced only one arrest, but law enforcement spokesmen remained hopeful that the system would be useful in the future.

Organized as a privately funded experiment, Shot Spotter microphones were installed atop utility poles and selected rooftops throughout a one-square-mile area of the Willowbrook neighborhood. Each microphone in turn is linked to a computer system that can pinpoint the origin of a gunshot or other similar sounds within a radius of 20 feet, in seven seconds. A parallel system, if activated, places telephone calls to residents in the immediate area of the gunfire, to seek out witnesses and additional information. Willowbrook was selected as a testing ground because its streets had witnessed 120 unsolved homicides in the preceding 30 months. During the first two months of operation, police were startled to note how few gunfire incidents were reported by local residents: of 124 shootings recorded by Shot Spotter, authorities received phone calls on only eight, leaving 94 percent of local shootings unreported.

Reactions to the new technology were mixed. James Pasco, executive director of the Fraternal Order of Police, told *USA Today,* "Any technology that provides police and citizens with more notice of a potentially deadly situation has tremendous public safety implications." Jeff Chester, a spokesman for the privacy-conscious Center for Media Education, took an opposite view, regarding Shot Spotter as the opening wedge of a potential police state. "This is a first visible example that we're creating an infrastructure of surveillance," Chester said. "We want a rapid response to protect public safety, but I think this kind of intrusive technology goes beyond prudent police work. This community eavesdropping is a very dangerous concept." Thus far, local authorities contend, they have received no complaints of privacy invasion from Willowbrook's residents.

"SHOWOFF": computer virus

Reported for the first time in January 1998, this macro virus attacks the Windows operating system, delivering its payload on the 13th day of any month. On that date, "Showoff" creates the file c:\windows\system\nomercy.dll, containing a code for the parasitic virus "NoMercy575." That virus, in turn, proceeds to delete the following files from the infected host computer:

```
c:\*.bat
c:\*.sys
c:\windows\*.grp
c:\windows\*.drv
c:\windows\*.dll
c:\windows\system\*.drv
c:\windows\system\*.dll
```

Showoff then restarts the computer and remains memory-resident, proceeding to infect each .com and .exe file as they are executed. In the process, it displays the following message on-screen (errors intact):

No Mercy II [Hell on WinWord], The Madness Continues . . . wall
NoMercy II ©1997 by CrazybitS
From the land of Smoking Vulcanoes and Gamelan Orchestras
This Macro Virus Was Released for follow his brother No Mercy

On other, unpredictable occasions a different message is displayed, reading (errors uncorrected):

No Mercy II Was Distrub!
Mmmmm . . . you just lost your files!
Don't do it again!

SIMPSON, Orenthal James: acquitted despite DNA evidence

Since the early 1990s, prosecutors and defense attorneys alike have hailed DNA evidence as the "Rosetta stone" of guilt or innocence in criminal cases. Analysis of a suspect's "genetic fingerprint," compared to biological evidence found at a crime scene, may now identify a specific individual to the virtual exclusion of any other person on the planet (except an identical twin). And yet, the strongest evidence is only as good as the prosecutors who present it and the jurors who consider it. The murder case of athlete/actor O. J. Simpson is a perfect case in point.

On the night of June 12, 1994, Simpson's estranged wife, Nicole Brown Simpson, and her male friend Ronald Goldman were attacked outside a private residence in the Los Angeles suburb of Brentwood. Both were slashed to death with a knife, in what appeared to be a frenzied assault. Police responding to the scene found a size-12 shoe print in the victims' blood, and scattered to its left, four drops of blood belonging to neither victim, as if the killer had himself been injured on the left side of his body during the attack. A knitted wool cap lay beside the mutilated bodies. Nearby, a gate revealed more blood, ultimately matched to the four "alien" drops found beside the killer's footprint.

O. J. Simpson was acquitted of murder despite overwhelming DNA evidence. (PACHA/CORBIS)

Mindful of the history surrounding O. J. Simpson and Nicole, including several police reports of wife-beating and death threats, officers proceeded to Simpson's home to question him. There, they found spots of blood inside his Ford Bronco, in the driveway, and inside the house on one of Simpson's socks. A bloody leather glove was also found behind the house, lying in some shrubbery. Simpson sported a fresh, deep cut on the middle finger of his left hand, but told investigators he had no idea how it had happened.

DNA analysis was rapidly performed on the various blood samples found at the crime scene and around Simpson's home. The blood drops found beside the killer's size-12 shoe print (O. J.'s shoe size) and the stain on the gate near the crime scene proved to match Simpson's DNA—in the case of the gate

stain, narrowing the search to one unique person in 57 billion (roughly 10 times the population of planet Earth). Bloodstains from Simpson's car included his own DNA, along with that of Nicole and Ron Goldman. Likewise, the glove found behind Simpson's house bore his own blood, plus blood from both victims. DNA from the blood found on Simpson's sock, inside his house, was a positive match for Nicole.

In addition to DNA evidence, the case also furnished a number of hairs and fibers that helped put the crime in perspective. From the knit cap found in Brentwood, police recovered nine hairs microscopically identical to O.J. Simpson's. A 10th matching hair was recovered from Ron Goldman's shirt. The bloody glove outside Simpson's mansion also carried hair matching O. J.'s and synthetic fibers microscopically identical to the carpet of his Ford Bronco.

Police issued an arrest warrant for Simpson on June 17, 1994, finally taking him into custody after the now-famous "slow-speed chase" that featured Simpson holding a gun to his own head and threatening suicide. In court, Simpson denied any role in the murders, enlisting a so-called "dream team" of high-priced lawyers to defend him. Ironically, the defense team's DNA experts were Barry Scheck and Peter Neufeld, later renowned for their work with the CARDOZO INNOCENCE PROJECT, using DNA evidence to liberate wrongfully convicted inmates. In Simpson's case, their role would be somewhat different.

Former prosecutor Vincent Bugliosi, in his book *Outrage* (1996), noted that there were only three possible explanations for O. J. Simpson's blood being found at the Brentwood crime scene: (1) He somehow cut himself at the scene, while the crime was in progress; (2) he coincidentally spilled blood at the scene on some previous occasion; or (3) samples of his blood were deliberately planted as part of a frame-up. When blood from both victims was found in his car and at his home, the second possibility—sheer coincidence—was effectively eliminated.

Simpson's defenders never offered the court a satisfactory explanation for the fresh cut on his hand. Instead, they devoted their efforts to a two-pronged attack on the prosecution. Simpson had been framed, they said, by racist police who planted the bloody glove at his house, furthermore dribbling blood from the murdered victims on Simpson's sock and the interior of his car. As for his own blood at the crime scene, if it was not planted by authorities to frame Simpson, then the test results were simply wrong, a result of "cross-contamination" in the police crime lab. Barry Scheck branded the L.A. crime lab a "black hole" of contamination, where blood samples were allegedly mixed and mingled indiscriminately. A forensic expert for the defense, Dr. Henry Lee, appeared to testify that "something is wrong" with the state's DNA evidence. (FBI experts refuted that claim, and they also pointed out that marks that Dr. Lee identified as probably footprints of the "real killer" were actually imbedded in the crime scene's concrete pavement, laid years before the murders.)

The "contamination" argument was disingenuous at best. Bugliosi notes, and DNA experts universally agree, that all crime scene evidence samples are contaminated, to some extent, by contact with other physical objects, but such contamination never results in a "false positive" reading. At worst, the results of a test on contaminated blood would be inconclusive, identifying no one. Simply stated, it is physically impossible to take a blood sample from Suspect "A" and mix it with any combination of elements on earth to produce a positive DNA match with Suspect "B." The blood of an unknown killer cannot be altered, transmuted or transformed into the blood of O. J. Simpson by any method known to earthly science.

It simply cannot be done.

Simpson's marathon trial in Los Angeles lasted from January to October 1995, including weeks of scientific testimony, but jurors seemed to have reached their decision far in advance. The panel finally deliberated less than four hours, precluding any real discussion of the evidence, and acquitted Simpson on all charges. One juror, a 72-year-old woman who admitted during pretrial questioning that she never read anything but daily racing forms and "didn't really understand" those, told reporters after the fact, "I didn't understand the DNA stuff at all. To me, it was a waste of time. It was way out there and carried absolutely no weight with me." A second juror found Dr. Lee's discredited testimony the "most impressive" evidence presented—because he had paused to smile at the jury before he testified. Small wonder, then, that journalists described the verdict as a case of "jury nullification," unrelated to logic or evidence. (Lead prosecutor Marcia Clark later described the trial jurors as "moon rocks.")

A second jury listened to the same evidence in 1996, at the trial of a civil lawsuit filed against Simpson by survivors of the two murdered victims, and that panel reached a very different conclusion. In the civil case, Simpson was judged legally responsible for the murders ("wrongful death," outside the venue of a criminal court) and was ordered to pay substantial damages. To date, the winners in that case have reportedly collected nothing.

SKLYAROV, Dmitry: controversial software piracy defendant

A Russian citizen, Dmitry Sklyarov worked in the United States as a programmer for the Moscow-based software firm ElcomSoft during 2001. His troubles with the FBI and federal prosecutors began on June 22 of that year, when his employers posted a press release on the Planet eBook Forum and other Internet pages, announcing the release of a new program called Advanced eBook Processor (AEBPR), designed to remove the encryption from Adobe Acrobat .pdf files and eBooks. Six days later, Adobe Systems released a "fix" to prevent AEBPR from functioning, but ElcomSoft quickly updated its program to defeat the improvement. On July 3, 2001, Adobe formally requested that ElcomSoft stop selling the AEBPR software, and while ElcomSoft agreed, its agents continued to distribute a free "demonstration" version of the program. Frustrated and angry, Adobe technicians purchased a copy of AEBPR for analysis and delivered their results to the U.S. Justice Department in hopes of spurring federal prosecution for copyright violations.

There matters stood on July 16, 2001, when Dmitry Sklyarov—creator of the AEBPR program—prepared to leave Las Vegas, Nevada, on a flight ultimately bound for Moscow. Sklyarov had spent the weekend addressing the DefCon 9 Conference in Las Vegas and was anxious to get home, but FBI agents met him at McCarran International Airport and took Sklyarov into custody on a charge of violating U.S. copyright laws. ElcomSoft managing director Vladimir Katalov denounced the arrest, while members of the Russian consulate and Sklyarov's family alleged that he was being held incommunicado by federal authorities. Spokesmen for the American Association of Publishers praised the FBI's action, while protests poured in from hastily contrived groups like "Free Dmitry!" and "Boycott Adobe Web."

Federal charges against Sklyarov were announced on July 17, 2001. Named as the creator and copyright holder of a copyright circumvention software program, Sklyarov faced a possible five years in prison and a $500,000 fine if convicted for selling his software in the United States. Announcement of the penalties and continuing protests by ad hoc groups on-line convinced Adobe Systems administrators to meet with spokesmen of the Electronic Frontier Foundation on July 23, and they emerged from that conference with a plea for Sklyarov's release from custody. Two weeks later, on August 6, 2001, he was released on $50,000 bond, without his passport, pending formal arraignment on the charges filed against him. That hearing was repeatedly postponed, with defense attorney Joseph Burton advising reporters, "We're talking about whether or not there are any potential ways to dispose of the case." Reports of a plea bargain circulated, but they were premature. On August 28, 2001, a federal grand jury indicted Sklyarov and ElcomSoft on five counts of violating the Digital Millennium Copyright Act of 1998.

While Adobe Systems published position papers detailing its view of the case, Sklyarov's wife and children flew from Moscow to join him in California, where he continued to stay under virtual house arrest. They arrived on September 5, to an outpouring of sympathy from Sklyarov's admirers and "freeware" advocates who profess to believe that copyrights on any computer program (presumably including Sklyarov's AEBPR) are "immoral." Five days later, German police raided the home of a Munich website owner, seizing his computer and peripheral equipment, filing copyright infringement charges after they discovered a "cracked" copy of a newly released book in PDF format, its encryption stripped away by AEBPR.

German sideshows notwithstanding, the main focus of the case remained in California, where preliminary hearings for Sklyarov and ElcomSoft were postponed once more, this time until November 26, 2001. The latest postponement was won by new defense attorney John Keker, selected in a recent survey of California practitioners as the "lawyer other lawyers would hire" to defend them in court. When November finally arrived, the defense won yet another postponement, pushing the preliminary hearing and scheduling of a final trial date to April 15, 2002. In the midst of those legal maneuvers (and the furor caused by the September TERRORISM attacks on Washington, D.C., and New York City), U.S. District Judge Ronald Whyte approved an agreement releasing Dmitry Sklyarov from all criminal charges and permitting his return to Russia on December 13, 2001. Sklyarov was released under terms of the fed-

eral Pretrial Diversion program, which dismissed charges in return for Sklyarov's agreement to testify later as a prosecution witness against ElcomSoft. Company officials declared themselves "thankful" for the plea bargain, although their firm still faced trial as sole defendant in the case. According to CEO Katalov's statement, "ElcomSoft has always made Dmitry's welfare its highest priority. We are very pleased that there has been a solution that minimizes the risk for Dmitry and allows him and his family to return to Russia." Sklyarov, meanwhile, expressed

Russian software programmer Dmitry Sklyarov and his employer ElcomSoft are defendants in a lawsuit involving a controversial new American copyright law.

plans to continue working for ElcomSoft and pursuing his doctorate.

With Sklyarov safe at home, the legal battle continued in California. ElcomSoft's attorneys sought dismissal of all charges on January 28, 2002, while the Electronic Frontier Foundation filed an amicus brief six days later, claiming that the Digital Millennium Copyright Act was itself unconstitutional under the First Amendment's guarantee of free speech. Those motions were rejected, with trial tentatively scheduled for June 2002, but further delays have kept the case in legal limbo up to press time, with no break in sight.

SLATER, Jason: convicted software pirate

A resident of Walnut Creek, California, born April 28, 1970, Jason Slater was a member of the HACKERS' syndicate known to its members as "PIRATES WITH ATTITUDE" (PWA). In May 2000 he was among 17 members or associates of the gang indicted by federal authorities for violation of the 1997 No Electronic Theft (NET) Act. According to the indictments, PWA members conspired to steal thousands of copyrighted software programs, valued at more than $1 million, and to sell or trade them from an outlaw website based in Quebec, Canada. Five employees of Intel Corporation also joined in the conspiracy, providing their PWA colleagues with stolen computer hardware used to keep the website functional. Slater was one of 13 defendants who filed guilty pleas during the 12 months after their indictment. While a few PWA ringleaders were sentenced to prison, Slater and the majority of his codefendants received more lenient sentences, including home or community confinement, community service projects, and financial restitution to their corporate victims.

"SMART" Guns: attempts to improve firearm security

With the exception of religious questions such as legalized abortion and prayer in schools, few public issues raise quite so much heated controversy in America as the issue of "gun control." On one side, proponents of unlimited civilian firepower argue that the U.S. Constitution's Second Amendment guarantee of a "right to keep and bear arms" is sacrosanct, and any legislative effort to abridge that freedom smacks of seditious conspiracy. At the other extreme, proponents of a total firearms ban quote, misquote, and sometimes fabricate statistics to portray guns as a lethal blight on the nation at large. Between those polar opposites lies a body of judicial rulings and some 20,000 federal, state, and local statutes regulating the "right to bear arms" in various U.S. jurisdictions.

One proposed solution to the controversy is development of personalized (or "smart") guns that incorporate technology designed to prevent use of a weapon by anyone other than its rightful owner. Typically employing BIOMETRICS—palm or fingerprints—to identify a firearm's legitimate user, such weapons would theoretically be inoperable in the hands of a stranger, be it a neighbor, a thief, or a curious child. Proponents of "smart" gun technology include Physicians for Social Responsibility (PSR), who deem gun violence "a public health emergency" and view the new technology as critical "in order to reduce the use of firearms in unintentional, homicidal, and suicidal deaths and injuries." Executives of the Colt Manufacturing Company, a leading U.S. handgun producer, announced efforts to produce a "smart" pistol in 1996, declaring that it would save lives in American homes and on city streets, where felons could no longer hope to arm themselves by looting stores or wrestling weapons away from police officers. At the same time, Colt spokesmen declared, the new weapons should make it "less likely that our 2nd Amendment rights will be legislatively reduced or limited." On May 1, 1999, Philadelphia's city council proposed legislation (never enacted) that would penalize buyers, sellers, and shooters alike for any injury inflicted by guns unequipped with "smart" technology.

Critics of the smart-gun concept (and of gun control in general) point out certain built-in problems with the plan that has become a panacea in some quarters. Those problems include:

Unproven technology Today, six years after Colt's announcement of the first smart gun, none are commercially available or found in general use. Critics cite this fact as evidence that the concept is faulty and perhaps unworkable. If smart guns work, where are they?

Combat limitations Police and others required to carry weapons might be placed in jeopardy by smart-gun technology. Since current systems allow programming for only one hand, a right-handed officer wounded in a gunfight could find himself unable to fire his own weapon left-handed in self-defense, with potentially fatal

The "smart gun" uses technology that recognizes the gun's owner and prevents anyone else from firing the weapon. (AP)

results. It is also theoretically possible that while grappling for a weapon, the officer might retain sufficient contact to let his assailant trigger a shot as if he were the authorized shooter.

Feasibility   Americans presently own more than 190 million firearms, including some 65 million pistols. None of them are "personalized," and there is no reason to suppose that gun owners will trade in their weapons, much less spend billions of dollars on new ones to replace the old.

Increased civilian firepower   While a majority of smart-gun advocates are drawn from the ranks of those whose agenda includes the reduction of civilian armament, civilian firepower might actually increase if present gun owners "traded up" to replace their existing weapons with personalized handguns. The reason: a "Guns in America" survey from the 1990s revealed that some three-quarters of all civilian-owned pistols had an ammunition capacity below 10

rounds (reflecting the fact that most were revolvers or older semiautomatics manufactured before the invention of high-capacity magazines). Newer pistols generally accommodate the legal maximum 10-round magazine, thus meaning that legitimate shooters who "go bad" would have increased lethal firepower at their disposal.

Disarming minors   Critics argue that smart-gun technology would have no effect on minors who commit acts of violence with firearms, since persons below age 21 are already barred by law from purchasing pistols, while a 1998 *New York Times* poll revealed that 15 percent of Americans aged 13 to 17 already own other types of firearms. Various arguments that smart guns would thus reduce juvenile violence or suicide are thereby rendered virtually meaningless.

Suicide   Speaking of self-destruction, protestations from the PSR and others notwithstanding, there is no good reason to believe smart guns would prevent suicides. An individual intent on ending his life would simply be required to purchase a weapon and have it programmed to fit his hand.

Accidental shootings Advocates of smart-gun technology assert that it would eliminate "virtually all" accidental firearms injuries and deaths. They refer specifically to deaths of children, who in fact account for barely 15 percent of accidental shooting deaths in any given year. (In 1995, an average year, 181 out of 1,225 accidental firearms deaths involved victims under 15 years of age.) In any case, new technology would do nothing to prevent an accidental shooting by the weapon's "authorized" user, regardless of his or her age.

Black-market sales Smart-gun advocates suggest that the new technology would eliminate many illegal (or "straw") sales, but critics vehemently disagree. Prospective manufacturers such as Colt admit that "smart" firearms could be reprogrammed for new users at will—i.e., no sale is "forever." Nothing would prevent black-market dealers or buyers from adapting the weapons to fit a new user's hand with minimal effort (the equivalent of encoding a new combination on a safe, for example).

Firearms theft While smart-gun proponents claim advancing technology would somehow reduce theft of weapons, critics note that ease of reprogramming would not discourage any thief with access to a cooperative technician. Likewise, circulation of smart guns would do nothing to prevent theft of the 190 million firearms already at large in the country.

At present, in October 2002, the arguments for and against smart-gun technology remain strictly academic. Until such time as personalized weapons are physically available—and then at competitive prices—the theoretical advance in technology will have no real-world impact on crime in the United States.

SMITH, David L.: creator of "Melissa" computer virus

A 31-year-old New Jersey resident, David Smith was arrested on April 1, 1999, charged by state and federal authorities for unleashing a computer virus described by experts as the most prolific created to

David L. Smith, creator of the "Melissa" computer virus. The virus caused millions of dollars in damage by disrupting e-mail systems worldwide in 1999. (AP)

that time. That virus, dubbed "MELISSA," was launched on March 26, 1999, with a posting to the "Alt.Sex" Usenet group. The initial post contained a message luring readers to download and open a document in hopes of finding pass codes to adult-content websites, but in fact it instantly infected computers utilizing Microsoft word-processing software and Microsoft's Outlook e-mail system. Each compromised computer thereupon sent infected e-mails to the first 50 addresses on the user's mailing list, replicating exponentially across the country and around the world. Thousands of personal and corporate computers were thus compromised, resulting in the temporary shutdown of entire networks with significant costs to repair or cleanse computer systems of the virus. Total damages from the Melissa virus were tabulated at $1 billion nationwide.

Arrested at his brother's home in Eatontown, New Jersey, Smith was released on $150,000 bond, pending trial in state and federal court on separate charges. New Jersey state authorities charged Smith with one count of second-degree computer theft, with penalties including a potential 10-year prison term and a maximum fine of $150,000. Federal prosecutors charged Smith with deliberately spreading a computer virus with intent to cause damage, an offense bearing penalties of five years in prison and $250,000 in fines. Investigators initially suggested that the virus was named for an exotic dancer Smith met while living in Florida, but they later backed off that explanation and admitted that the source of Melissa's name remained unknown.

The case was cracked on March 31 by a representative of America Online, who relayed Smith's identity to New Jersey Deputy Attorney General Christopher Bubb, head of the Garden State's Computer Analysis and Technology Unit. Smith was traced to his brother's home on April 1 by a combined force including investigators from the Monmouth County prosecutor's office, the New Jersey State Police High Technology Crime Unit, and the FBI's National Infrastructure Protection Center (INFRAGUARD). Announcing the arrest, New Jersey State Attorney General John Farmer Jr. told reporters, "Computer criminals may think that they operate in a new frontier without boundaries, where they won't be caught. Obviously, that's not true. We've responded by breaking down traditional borders among federal, state, county and local law enforcement. In this case, it helped us to make an arrest in less than a week."

Smith was widely expected to plead not guilty and fight the charges in court, but he surprised and disappointed HACKERS worldwide in December 1999, with his acceptance of a plea bargain. On December 9 Smith pleaded guilty in both state and federal court, confessing his authorship of the Melissa virus in an effort to reduce his legal penalties. In a statement to the press, Smith said, "I did not expect or anticipate the amount of damage that took place," but prosecutors remained unforgiving, New Jersey authorities requesting imposition of the 10-year maximum sentence. U.S. Attorney General Janet Reno warned the architects of future viruses that "this plea is a significant marker in the Justice Department's efforts to stop computer crime. In light of society's increasing dependence on computers, the Department will vigorously investigate and prosecute computer crimes that threaten our computer infrastructure."

Following Smith's guilty plea, New Jersey Superior Court Judge John Riccardi set a sentencing date of February 18, 2000, while U.S. District Judge John Greenaway Sr. postponed federal sentencing until May 15, 2000. Smith remained free on bond pending formal sentencing, waiting to learn his fate. In fact, sentencing was finally delayed until May 1, 2002, when Smith was ordered to serve 20 months in jail.

"SNICKERS": computer viruses

Two unrelated macro viruses, launched on the Internet three years apart, currently bear the name of a popular chocolate bar. The first "Snickers" virus, logged initially in March 1997, infects documents that are loaded into Microsoft Word and scrambles various characters within each document as they are closed. It also inserts its own text within infected Word documents, reading "snickers=mmmhh."

The second version, discovered in February 2000, is a macro virus rated "dangerous" by computer analysts. It also targets Word documents, infecting the host computer's global macro area when corrupted documents are opened. No text is scrambled in this case, however, so users remain unaware of the infection as it progresses. When the affected document is closed, Snickers "encrypts" its text, producing illegible gibberish. Antivirus programs successfully remove Snickers from an infected computer, but since they delete the entire virus code, Word documents scrambled by Snickers on closing remain unreadable. The text can be restored to normal by advanced users, utilizing a Basic routine available for downloading on the Internet from *support@avp.ru*, but it is simpler to restore the damaged documents from backup copies.

SNYDER, Walter: exonerated by DNA evidence

In the early morning hours of October 28, 1985, a female resident of Alexandria, Virginia, was attacked, raped, and sodomized by a stranger who broke through the door of her apartment. The victim, a Caucasian, was initially unable to describe her attacker beyond the fact that he was African-American and wore red shorts. Police prepared a photo array, including a picture of Walter Snyder, a 19-year-old black man who lived across the street from the crime scene. The victim passed over his photo at first, but officers then marched her past a bench in police headquarters where Snyder sat alone. She subsequently selected his photo and picked Snyder from a lineup, declaring herself "100 percent sure" that he was the rapist. A search of Snyder's apartment revealed a pair of red shorts, and his Type A blood matched that of the attacker.

At trial, the victim once again named Snyder as her rapist, while prosecutors introduced the shorts and basic blood evidence. Snyder's alibi—that he was home, asleep, when the attack occurred—was corroborated by his mother, but jurors chose to disregard her testimony. On June 25, 1986, they convicted Snyder of rape, sodomy, and burglary, recommending a 45-year sentence, which the trial judge confirmed and imposed. Snyder's appeal of the conviction was rejected, but he subsequently learned of new advances in the field of DNA testing and "genetic fingerprints." Convinced that such a test would prove him innocent, he sought a lawyer to pursue the case and finally contacted members of the CARDOZO INNOCENCE PROJECT. Staff attorneys agreed to handle Snyder's case on a pro bono basis (free of charge) if his family could raise the money to pay for expensive DNA testing. Virginia prosecutors agreed to release their forensic evidence in May 1992, and a Boston laboratory eliminated Snyder as a suspect seven months later. Prosecutors insisted on repeating the tests, with identical results from the FBI's crime lab.

Snyder should have been released immediately, but Virginia statutes require that any motion for a new trial based on newly discovered evidence must be filed within 21 days of a defendant's conviction. Since more than six years had elapsed from Snyder's trial to the conclusive demonstration of his innocence, state courts rejected any further arguments. The only recourse lay in a request for executive clemency from Governor L. Douglas Wilder. Snyder's prosecutor joined defense attorneys in requesting a pardon for Snyder, but Governor Wilder delayed his decision until public outcry from the press made his position untenable. Wilder finally granted the overdue pardon on April 23, 1993, and Snyder was released after serving nearly seven years for a crime he did not commit. The Alexandria Circuit Court granted Snyder's petition to expunge his criminal record on January 11, 1994. The rape remains unsolved today.

SOPHONOW, Thomas: exonerated by DNA evidence

Shortly before 9:00 P.M. on December 23, 1981, 16-year-old Barbara Gayle Stoppel was found strangled and near death in the women's restroom of a Winnipeg, Manitoba, doughnut shop where she worked after school. Rushed to St. Boniface Hospital, Stoppel was placed on life support, but she was later declared brain-dead, and mechanical support was discontinued later in the week by mutual agreement of her family and physicians. Back at the crime scene, several witnesses described a man seen leaving the ladies' room shortly before Stoppel's body was found. They described the murder suspect as a white male, 21 to 30 years old, with brown hair and mustache, a "scruffy" appearance, and acne-scarred complexion, wearing prescription glasses and a dark-colored cowboy hat. One witness had pursued the suspect and confronted him, but the man escaped after tossing a box, a pair of gloves, and some twine used in the murder off Norwood Bridge. Composite sketches were prepared and circulated to the media.

Police suspected that the killer was a local resident, who may have killed Stoppel in revenge for some previous altercation. That theory was abandoned, though, when detectives mistakenly traced the "unique" nylon twine discarded by their suspect to a manufacturer in Washington state, thereafter focusing their manhunt along the West Coast. (In fact, later analysis proved the twine had been manufactured at Portage la Prairie, 50 miles west of Winnipeg.) While scouring the wrong location, authorities focused their attention on Thomas Sophonow, a 28-year-old Vancouver resident who frequently visited Winnipeg and who vaguely resembled the composite drawing of Stoppel's killer. Sophonow was arrested and charged with the crime on March 12, 1982, but convicting him would be no easy task. The first trial ended with a hung jury, but Sophonow was tried twice more, convicted on both occasions, only to have his convictions reversed by the Manitoba Court of Appeal. He was released in December 1985, after spending three years and nine months in jail, suffering multiple assaults by other inmates. When prosecutors expressed their intent to try him again, that move was blocked by Canada's Supreme Court.

Still, Sophonow remained a prime murder suspect in the public eye, guilty as charged to many casual observers of the case. Another five years passed before Winnipeg police admitted their mistake, with a June 2000 announcement that DNA test results on evidence found at the crime scene had finally exonerated Sophonow of any role in the murder. At the same time, detectives announced their location of an unnamed "new suspect," but that lead proved ephemeral. The slaying remains open today, ranking high among Canada's unsolved mysteries.

As for Thomas Sophonow, falsely accused of murder, robbed of nearly four years' time, his reputation ruined, the road to meager compensation has been long and fraught with frustration. On November 5, 2001, Manitoba Justice Minister Gird Mackintosh released a report by retired Supreme Court justice Peter Cory, recommending payment of $2.6 million to Sophonow, with 50 percent to be paid by the City of Winnipeg, 40 percent by Manitoba's provincial government, and 10 percent from Canada's federal government. Manitoba officials countered with an offer of $1 million for Sophonow and $75,000 to the Stoppel family. At this writing (in July 2002), official intransigence continues to delay payment, despite increasing criticism of government procrastination.

SPATAFORE, Jason Everett: Internet video pirate
A 25-year-old resident of Phoenix, Arizona, known on-line as "Dis-man," Jason Spatafore was charged on September 20, 2000, with four counts of criminal copyright infringement. Federal prosecutors accused Spatafore of illegally copying portions of the Hollywood film *Star Wars Episode I: The Phantom Menace* and distributing those bootleg copies on the Internet for personal financial gain. If convicted on all four counts, Spatafore faced a maximum sentence of four years' imprisonment and fines of $400,000. Spatafore was arraigned before U.S. Magistrate Joseph Spero on October 10, 2000, and he cut a bargain with prosecutors two months later, filing a guilty plea to one count of copyright infringement on December 15, 2000.

SPENCER, Timothy Wilson: serial killer convicted by DNA
A Virginia native, born in 1962, Timothy Spencer was on parole from a burglary conviction, living in a Richmond halfway house and working at a local furniture factory, when he launched a spree of brutal rape-slayings. His first victim, Carol Hamm, was assaulted and strangled at her Arlington home in January 1984. An innocent suspect confessed to that slaying under police pressure and was sentenced to prison, while Spencer managed to restrain himself from committing another attack for three years and eight months. His second victim, in September 1987, was Richmond resident Debby Davis. Two weeks later, again in Richmond, he raped and murdered Dr. Susan Hellams. November 1987 witnessed the identical murder of teenager Diane Cho, in a Richmond suburb. Returning to Arlington for his final murder, Spencer raped and strangled Susan Tucker in December 1987.

Thus far, Virginia's elusive "South Side Strangler" had been careful to leave no fingerprints behind at any of his crime scenes. The only evidence available to the police, therefore, was semen recovered from the bodies and clothing of his victims. Arlington detective Joe Horgas, mindful of recent developments in DNA technology and the British conviction of rape-slayer COLIN PITCHFORK based on such evidence, staked his hopes on snaring the strangler via "genetic fingerprints." He was successful in 1988, linking Spencer to three of the five local murders with DNA evidence. Convicted at trial and sentenced to die for his crimes, Spencer became the first U.S. defendant condemned on the basis of DNA evidence. Virginia's Supreme Court upheld that conviction, and Spencer was executed on April 27, 1994. The innocent suspect who had been coerced into confessing Carol Hamm's murder was belatedly exonerated and released after serving nearly five years in prison for Spencer's crime.

SPIDER-IN-THE-TOILET Warning: Internet hoax
Another false warning with the trappings of an urban legend, this story is not implausible per se. Spiders have been found to inhabit certain unsanitary restrooms and outdoor privies, drawn by a prevalence of flies, and careless humans are occasionally stung in the process of relieving themselves. (Eugene Talmadge, candidate for governor of Georgia in 1946, suffered a near-fatal black widow bite in this manner, at the height of his campaign.) Nonetheless, entomologists report that there is no such arachnid as the "South American Blush Spider," and its alleged scientific name denoted the work of a hoaxer with tongue firmly planted in cheek. The message, first logged on the Internet in September 1999, reads as follows:

Though fairly believable, the spider-in-the toilet warning was just another Internet hoax.

* *

WARNING: From Texas AR&M International University

* *

An article by Dr. Beverly Clark, in the Journal of the United Medical Association (JUMA), the mystery behind a recent spate of deaths has been solved. If you haven't already heard about it in the news, here is what happened.

Three women in Chicago, turned up at hospitals over a 5-day period, all with the same symptoms. Fever, chills, and vomiting, followed by muscular collapse, paralysis, and finally, death. There were no outward signs of trauma. Autopsy results showed toxicity in the blood.

These women did not know each other, and seemed to have nothing in common. It was discovered, however, that they had all visited the same restaurant (Big Chappies, at Blare Airport), within days of their deaths. The health department descended on the restaurant, shutting it down. The food, water, and air conditioning were all inspected and tested, to no avail.

The big break came when a waitress at the restaurant was rushed to the hospital with similar symptoms. She told doctors that she had been on vacation, and had only went to the restaurant to pick up her check. She did not eat or drink while she was there, but had used the restroom.

That is when one toxicologist, remembering an article he had read, drove out to the restaurant, went into the restroom, and lifted the toilet seat. Under the seat, out of normal view, was a small spider. The spider was captured and brought back to the lab, where it was determined to be the South American Blush Spider (arachnius gluteus), so named because of its reddened flesh color. This spider's venom is extremely toxic, but can take several days to take effect. They live in cold, dark, damp, climates, and toilet rims provide just the right atmosphere.

Several days later a lawyer from Los Angeles showed up at a hospital emergency room. Before his death, he told the doctor, that he had been away on business, had taken a flight from New York, changing planes in Chicago, before returning home. He did not visit Big Chappies while there. He did, as did all of the other victims, have what was determined to be a puncture wound, on his right buttock.

Investigators discovered that the flight he was on had originated in South America. The Civilian Aeronautics Board (CAB) ordered an immediate inspection of the toilets of all flights from South America, and discovered the Blush spider's nests on 4 different planes!

It is now believed that these spiders can be anywhere in the country. So please, before you use a public toilet, lift the seat to check for spiders. It can save your life! And please pass this on to everyone you care about.

Officer Sylvia Steele
Texas A&M International University
5201 University Blvd.
Laredo, Tx 78041-1999
956-326-2100

An ironic twist on the "blush spider" myth surfaced in April 2002, when a new rash of e-mails made the rounds—this time within South Africa. The latest message purports to quote an article written by one Dr. Beverly Clark for the *Journal of the Medical Association*, describing fatal spider bites allegedly suffered by nine women in Johannesburg and Pretoria. Once again, the mythical attacks were traced to toilet stalls in various restaurants—and once again, the story was a complete fabrication. There was no such article, no deaths as described—and there is still no such arachnid as the South American blush spider.

"SPUNKBALL" Attack Warning: Internet hoax

Yet another fraudulent warning against nonexistent perils, this scare message surfaced on the Internet in March 2002. The staff of HOAXBUSTERS contacted Allstate Insurance and received assurances that no such warning has been issued by that company (or any other, for that matter). No attacks of this kind have been reported, and the mechanics of the operation as described suggest that it would be impossible for the assailant to commit the act without setting himself on fire. The original message reads as follows (with errors intact):

Subject: Alert from All State Insurance Co
Subject: Very Important

Heard anything about this? Please keep all windows rolled up when stopped at traffic lights, as only cars with windows down are being targeted. Groups of teenagers have been caught, in alarming numbers, playing a new and dangerous game called Spunkball!

Spunkball consists of a group of teens in a car pulling up to a stoplight, and looking around for a car stopped near by with an open window. When one is spotted, the teens shout, "Spunkball", and throw a gasoline soaked rag that has been wrapped in aluminum foil through the open window.

On the outside of the foil attached a small firecracker, with the fuse lit. When the firecracker explodes, it shreds the foil, and the rag is ignited, causing a large flame that may catch the interior of the car on fire.

Spunkball playing has already claimed two lives, caused uncountable injuries due to burns, and caused thousands of dollars in damage to automobiles. The best defense, say authorities, is to keep all windows rolled up when stopped at traffic lights, as only cars with windows down are being targeted.

If you are at a red light and hear a shout of "Spunkball", and notice something come flying in your window, the best thing to do is to have all passengers immediately exit the vehicle. DO NOT try to retrieve the object, as it will ignite once the firecracker explodes.

PLEASE PASS THIS ON TO EVERYONE YOU CARE ABOUT.

Bea xxxxxx, FCLS Allstate Insurance Co

"SQL Slammer": computer virus

Reported for the first time in late January 2002, "SQL Slammer" was named for its primary target, the SQL Server 2000 software produced by Microsoft Corporation. It attacks an unspecified "vulnerability" in SQL, which was initially discovered by Microsoft technicians in June 2003. A patch was offered to correct the problem, but many users of the software either remained unaware of the weakness or chose not to install the patch, thus leaving their systems exposed when SQL Slammer surfaced.

As described by analysts in various media interviews, SQL Slammer "breaks into a server and tries to spread," while generating high volumes of network traffic and thus slowing Internet communication to a crawl. The virus apparently does not affect files stored on computers and had little impact on home PC users. Problems arose when it infected various corporate and government computers, slowing some systems down to the point of virtual inaccessibility. The impact was global, with Reuters news service reporting that networks worldwide were "effectively shut down" for several hours on the first day of SQL Slammer's appearance. Some of the internet victims included

- *U.S. government* While all departments were apparently affected to some degree, the hardest hit were the Departments of Agriculture, Commerce, State, and some units of the Defense Department.
- *Bank of America Corp.* One of the largest banks in the United States reported that SQL Slammer prevented customers from withdrawing cash from its 13,000 ATMs nationwide, although deposits and sensitive personal information were "not at risk."
- *Canadian Imperial Bank of Commerce* The Toronto-based bank suffered ATM problems identical to those faced by Bank of America. All were apparently resolved by day's end without lasting damage.
- *Continental Airlines* Spokesperson reported flight delays of 90 minutes or less caused by computer failures in various cities. Continental's hub in Newark, New Jersey suffered most, but problems were also reported in Cleveland, Ohio and Houston, Texas.
- *Korea Telecom Freetel and SK Telecom* Service failed completely on these systems, leaving millions of South Korean Internet users temporarily without access.

- *Microsoft* Internet congestion prevented consumers from contacting Microsoft via the Internet to unlock anti-piracy features of its newest products, including Windows XP and Office XP software packages.
- *New Media* Associated Press news services were temporarily interrupted, while the Atlanta *Journal-Constitution* reported delays in printing its Sunday edition, and the *Philadelphia Inquirer* suffered "serious computer problems" without missing any deadlines.

STEGANOGRAPHY: data concealment technique

Steganography is a method of hiding computer-encoded data, for whatever reason, within a transmission of unrelated data. It takes advantage of gaps or unused spaces in computer files, filling those gaps with encrypted transmissions meant to be recovered and decrypted by the recipient of the innocent-looking message. The same technique may be used to place a hidden trademark, serial number, or other identifying characteristic within computer images, software, or music— in which case the method is often referred to as "watermarking" or "fingerprinting." While basic steganography is popular with a wide range of users, from small-time HACKERS to outlaw spies and TERRORISTS, watermarking has become a favored technique for protecting copyrighted material in cyberspace.

While software, movie, and music producers increasingly rely on steganographic "watermarking" techniques to protect their merchandise and prosecute bootleggers, U.S. authorities are more concerned with potential abuse of such technology by organized criminals and terrorists. Even before the September 2001 attacks on Washington, D.C., and New York City, journalists and security consultants voiced concern that Middle Eastern terrorist kingpin Osama bin Laden might be using steganography to communicate with his henchmen abroad. On February 6, 2001, *USA Today* reported that bin Laden and others "are hiding maps and photographs of terrorist targets and posting instructions for terrorist activities on sports chat rooms, pornographic bulletin boards and other websites, U.S. and foreign officials say." No specific examples were documented, but the fear remained alive in July 2002, when FBI spokesmen issued warnings that unnamed "known terrorists" were downloading Internet pictures of U.S. sports stadiums, presumably with an eye toward future attacks.

The practice of steganography dates from ancient Greece, when the historian Herodotus described one of his countrymen writing a message on the wood backing of a blank wax tablet. In both World Wars, secret agents of all sides used invisible inks made from such diverse liquids as milk, fruit juice and urine, which dry invisibly but darken when heated. Other techniques employed pinpricks above key letters in a printed text and use of microdots—tiny specks of film concealed as punctuation marks on the page of a book or magazine, their message legible beneath a microscope. Modern cryptographers with access to computer technology are more likely to employ such software programs as "S-Tools," "Steghide," and "White Noise Storm" to conceal their messages in various files.

Debate continues regarding the true extent of steganography in use by global criminals and terrorists. Ex-FBI director Louis Freeh issued numerous warnings of terrorists abroad in cyberspace, a tradition continued under the Bush regime (some critics say to the point of paranoia) by Attorney General John Ashcroft. Author Wayne Madsen, former data analyst for the National Security Agency takes a rather different view. "I think it's all baloney," he told interviewers in 2002. "I think it's all contrived. It's perception management." Indeed, some civil libertarians and critics of the Bush administration (themselves branded "paranoid" by Justice Department spokesmen) regard the incessant barrage of TERRORISM warnings from Washington as a smokescreen for encroachments on privacy and civil liberties of U.S. citizens. To date, no identified terrorist has been apprehended or prosecuted in any global jurisdiction for transmitting illicit data or ordering attacks through concealed Internet messages.

STOCKTON, Jeffrey Alan: convicted software pirate

In December 1999, police officers in Eugene, Oregon, became aware that a local resident was selling bootleg copies of Adobe Systems software on the Internet, using a pseudonym to mask the transactions. FBI agents were alerted to the violation of U.S. copyright laws, and the two agencies collaborated to identify the pirate as Jeffrey Stockton, a 20-year-old student in the University of Oregon's School of Journalism. Officers armed with search warrants raided Stockton's home, post office box, and bank account on January 13, 2000, seizing computer equipment, stolen software programs, and $13,786 in cash obtained from illicit Internet transactions.

Legal maneuvers stalled prosecution of the case long enough for Stockton to graduate in August 2000 and move on to a job as director of corporate communications for Inovaware Corporation, a software development firm in Honolulu, Hawaii, but he could not evade justice forever. Back in Eugene on January 30, 2001, Stockton pleaded guilty to criminal copyright infringement, admitting willful violations of federal law that caused retail losses of some $490,644 to Adobe Systems. According to U.S. prosecutors, he promised full financial restitution and "agreed that his sentence should be enhanced because of the level of planning involved in the copyright infringement." The money seized from Stockton's home and bank account was remitted to Adobe as partial restitution, while Stockton awaited formal sentencing.

A guilty plea on the charge filed against him left Stockton liable to a maximum sentence of five years in prison and a $250,000 fine, but despite the promise of an "enhanced" sentence, he escaped with only a fraction of that jail time. On April 16, 2001, U.S. District Judge Michael Hogan sentenced Stockton to serve 12 months and one day in prison, followed by three years' supervised probation upon his release. In addition to the $13,786 already forfeited, he was ordered to pay Adobe Systems restitution in the amount of $87,391.81—still $389,466 less than Adobe lost through his unauthorized sales of stolen software.

STONE, Mark: convicted software pirate

A 36-year-old resident of Fountain Valley, California, Mark Stone was one of 17 defendants indicted for software piracy by a federal grand jury on May 4, 2000. Known to his on-line friends as "Stoned," defendant Stone was identified as a member of the HACKERS' syndicate known as "PIRATES WITH ATTITUDE" (PWA), an international group with members scattered throughout North America and Europe. As charged in the indictments, PWA members had conspired since 1995 (or earlier) to steal and distribute copyrighted software programs, operating chiefly through an outlaw website based in Quebec, Canada. Employees of Microsoft and Intel Corporation were enlisted by the gang to supply cutting-edge software and computer hardware used to keep the website functional. Mark Stone was one of 13 PWA

defendants who pleaded guilty on reduced charges during the 12 months following release of federal indictments. While a few ringleaders received prison terms, most of the indicted PWA members (including Stone) drew sentences of community or home confinement, community service projects, and financial restitution to their victims.

SULLIVAN, John Michael: computer saboteur

A resident of Indian Trail, North Carolina, born March 24, 1961, John Sullivan was hired by Lance, Inc. (a Charlotte-based snack food manufacturer) in September 1996, to develop a computer program that would track national sales, delivery and inventory data for transmission via telephone modem to corporate headquarters. Sullivan's performance on the job was less than satisfactory, prompting his employers to demote him on May 8, 1998. Two weeks later, on May 22, Sullivan tendered his resignation from Lance, effective on June 2, 1998. Before leaving the firm, Sullivan inserted a date-triggered "code bomb" in Lance's computer system, set to trigger at noon on September 23, 1998. The "bomb" went off on schedule, crashing the computers in various field offices and paralyzing Lance's operations for several days, with financial losses in excess of $190,000.

Sullivan believed himself too clever for authorities, but FBI agents assigned to the sabotage case identified his handiwork and filed charges under the federal Computer Fraud and Abuse Act. That statute makes it a felony for anyone to "knowingly cause the transmission of a program, information, code or command, and as a result of such conduct, intentionally cause damage without authorization to a protected computer." Sullivan denied any involvement in the crime, but jurors convicted him after a four-day trial at Charlotte, in January 2000. On April 3, 2001, U.S. District Judge Richard Voorhees sentenced Sullivan to 24 months in prison, plus financial restitution in the amount of $194,609 and three years' supervised probation following release from custody. In the wake of Sullivan's sentencing, Chris Swecker, special agent in charge of the FBI's Charlotte field office, told reporters, "We commend the Lance Corporation for referring this incident for investigation and prosecution, and hope this sentence provides a significant deterrent. Criminal activity of this nature will be vigorously investigated and prosecuted."

SUNSCREEN Danger Warning: Internet hoax

Since June 1999 a false warning has circulated on the Internet, claiming that certain ingredients of waterproof sunscreen may cause blindness if it comes in contact with the eyes. In fact, no such cases have been reported, and the claim is specifically refuted by the American Academy of Ophthalmology. The original scare message (with errors uncorrected) reads:

Subject: Fwd: WARNING: WATERPROFF SUN-SCREEN LOTION

If you have kids. . . . This is a most read! Sunscreen danger.

To my friends with children or soon to have children. . . . this was passed on to me by my best friend who works for Boeing in Seattle, his own true story . . . FYI

I wanted to tell you a story about a very serious thing. We still use sunscreen on our whole family, but we are more cautious now. I tell you this only to make you more aware and use caution. When Zack was 2 years old, I put on the waterproof sun screen like I always had. I don't know how but he got some in his eyes. Most likely from his hands. It happens so easily at that age or any age really. He started screaming!!! So I tried to flush it out with water. But guess what? Didn't matter . . . Remember *WATERPROOF.* So I just held him and let he cry, thinking the salty tears would flush it all out. But it got worse. I called the poison control center. They told me to RUSH Zack to ER NOW!!! I Was surprised. I got him there and they rushed me back without a second to spare. They started flushing his eyes out with special medications.

Anyway, I found out for the first time that MANY kids each year lose their sight to waterproof sun screen. It burns the eye and they lose complete sight!!! I was appalled. I could not believe the sun screen we use to help keep our kids safe from skin cancer can make them go blind!

Well, I made a big stink about it. I wrote the sun screen company and they admitted to the problem but they said something to the fact that the seriousness of getting skin cancer is much worse then the chance of going blind! I think it's wrong if just one child goes blind!

They should change ingredients or should at least have a huge warning on it. But they claim that if you put a huge warning on it then parents won't use it due

to fear. I kind-of get that but there needs to be a change. We did this huge article in our big city and went on the news warning parents. Education along with the importance of using it. Well, anyway, Zack did go blind for 2 days, it was horrible. So please be careful!!! Don't stop using sun screen, just be very careful your children don't touch there eyes for at least 15-20 minutes after you put it on! And if your child does get it in his/her eyes, then get to the emergency room at once!

PASS THIS WARNING ON!!!

<<WARNING: WATERPROFF SUNSCREEN LOTION>>

SURIS, Yaroslav: convicted software pirate

A resident of Brooklyn, New York, born in 1974, Yaroslav Suris fattened his bank account between February 2000 and April 2001 by bootlegging expensive computer software and selling it over the Internet at drastically discounted rates. The programs that he stole and offered for black-market sale included:

Adobe Acrobat 4.0 (Retail price $369)
Adobe Illustroto 8.0 (Retail $399)
Adobe Page Mill 3.0 (Retail $99)
Adobe Photoshop 6.0 (Retail $609)
Alias-Wavefront Maya Unlimited 2.5 (Retail $16,000)
Corel Draw 9 (Retail $695)
Macromedia Autocad 2000 (Retail $3,750)
Macromedia Flash 9 (Retail $299)
Macromedia Freehand 8.0 (Retail $399)
Side Effects Houdini 4.0 (Retail $17,000)

As an example of the huge discounts offered by Suris to Internet customers, he sold bootleg copies of the $16,000 Alias-Wavefront Maya Unlimited 2.5 for as little as $195, accepting payment from his illicit clients by check, money order, or via the online PayPal network. FBI agents learned of Suris's activities in April 2001 and contacted him in the guise of regular customers, purchasing some $290,000 worth of stolen programs for a total expenditure of $1,310. Suris was subsequently arrested for criminal copyright infringement. He pleaded guilty as charged on February 1, 2002, before U.S. District Judge Thomas Jackson. Federal prosecutors recommended a sentence of 16 months in prison, plus financial restitution to the several corporate victims. On May 31, 2002, Judge Thompson sentenced Suris to two months in jail, followed by 14 months' home detention, with an order for restitution in the amount of $290,556.

SURVEILLANCE Devices

Electronic surveillance—"ELSUR" in FBI parlance—has long been a staple of intelligence agencies throughout the world. In addition to court-ordered surveillance conducted by various law enforcement agencies, the manufacture, sale, and installation of surveillance devices has become a huge covert industry in the United States. A State Department report from the mid-1990s estimated that some $800 million in illegal eavesdropping equipment is imported from foreign sources and installed into U.S. corporate settings each year. Another $6 million per day is spent with domestic suppliers, while any would-be secret agent with a minimal knowledge of electronics can easily construct his own gear from components readily available at stores such as Radio Shack. In New York City alone, more than 85 firms advertise the sale, installation, and monitoring of surveillance devices.

In broad terms, surveillance devices are built to provide audio transmissions, video transmissions, or a combination of both. Audio surveillance is divided into bugs and wiretaps. A "bug" is any listening device installed in a target location to intercept conversation or other sounds and transmit them to a listening post. Depending on the equipment employed, the monitor may be located in an adjacent room or

Surveillance cameras help police identify and track down criminals. (Steve McDonough/CORBIS)

miles away from the scene. The five primary types of bugs are:

Acoustic   The simplest and cheapest method, this technique involves capture of sounds with the naked ear, by means of a stethoscope, water glass, or other primitive listening device inserted into the target area or placed against a common wall, eavesdropping through air vents, and so forth.

Ultrasonic   This method involves conversion of sound into an audio signal beyond the range of human hearing, whereupon the ultrasonic signal is transmitted to a receiver and converted back to audio.

Radio frequency (RF)   The best-known kind of bugging device is a radio transmitter concealed in the target area. Cheap and disposable, such bugs are relatively easy to detect with electronic scanners, but they are near-impossible to trace.

Optical   Optical bugs convert sound or data into a beam of light (optical pulse), which is transmitted to a receiver and there decoded. Expensive and thus uncommon, this variety includes active and passive laser listening devices.

Wiretaps, unlike bugs, specifically involve the interception of communications carried via wires or cables. Taps are most commonly applied to telephones, but in recent years they have also been used to bleed information from PBX cables, local area networks (LANs), closed-circuit television systems, coded alarms systems, and other communications media. The four main categories of wiretaps include:

Hardwired   After gaining physical access to the line of communication, an eavesdropper attaches secondary wires and bridges the signal to a secure location, where it may be overheard and/or recorded. If discovered, this method is the easiest to trace back to a remote listening post, since the wire itself provides a trail.

Record   Similar to a hardwired wiretap, this method simply involves a tape recorder wired into the line of communication. Popular with private investigators and amateur spies, the record wiretap is easily detected by sophisticated scanners and is relatively dangerous to operate because the tapes must be changed frequently. A stakeout on the listening post is vir-

tually guaranteed to catch the wiretapper within a 24-hour period.

Soft   This technique, sometimes called REMOBS (*rem*ote *obs*ervation), involves modification of the software used to run a telephone system, thus permitting interception of messages transmitted. The task may be accomplished at the telephone company (where it would be difficult for surveillance subjects to trace) or through the on-site PBX switchboard (where it can be uncovered more easily). If discovered, the soft wiretap is difficult to trace.

Transmit   This hybrid technique involves attachment of a radio frequency (RF) "bug" to a communications line, which intercepts conversations and transmits them to a remote listening post. The bug's emission of RF energy makes it easy for professional "sweepers" to locate.

Bugs and wiretaps are so well known today that some perennial surveillance targets—members of organized crime, political extremists, intelligence agents, and the like—now routinely avoid any sensitive conversations via telephone or in their homes, offices and automobiles. Open-air conversations may be monitored by a variety of directional (or "shotgun") microphones, designed to pick up sounds from a distance, and lip-readers have been employed (with mixed success) to monitor subjects in various cases.

Video surveillance, unlike certain forms of wiretapping, requires the physical insertion of a camera into the target location. Once unwieldy and obvious, video cameras have been dramatically reduced in size by fiber-optic technology that permits transmission of an image via narrow wires. Such cameras are used not only for stationary surveillance, but also by SWAT officers to "case" a scene before entry to resolve hostage situations. Closed-circuit television and video recorders are widely used for security purposes in banks, schools, airports, hospitals and nursing homes, shopping malls, convenience stores, public transportation centers, parking lots, and in any other location where crimes are likely to occur without an official witness being present. Increasingly, civilians also make use of surveillance cameras (sometimes dubbed "nanny cams") to monitor suspect activity by spouses, children, neighbors, baby-sitters, and employees. Photos or videotape of a crime in progress may be submitted to police and to the courts as evidence, as in the Rodney King and Reginald Hill cases from Los Angeles.

Video technology is so advanced today that cameras mounted on satellites in outer space may be used for surveillance missions, transmitting pictures so detailed that individual persons can often be recognized, while viewers are able to make out addresses, license plate numbers, and other key objects crucial to tracking and identification. Another means of surveillance from beyond the atmosphere involves GPS (global positioning satellite) technology, initially developed for the military but now available for a wide variety of civilian applications. GPS equipment transmits no pictures, but it can determine the location of a targeted person or object precisely, within a matter of inches, at any point on Earth. In one notorious U.S. case, officials of ACME RENT-A-CAR used GPS systems to track their hired cars and illegally fine customers for speeding. Another case, reported in September 2001, saw a judge order Florida defendant Joseph Nichols to be monitored by GPS technology for up to 15 years, following his release from prison on a conviction for squirting young girls with a semen-filled water pistol. Nichols was required to wear a PERSONAL TRACKING UNIT that reports his location via satellite at 10-minute intervals.

Various warning signs may serve as an alert to ongoing covert surveillance. Some of the tip-offs include:

- Revelations that unauthorized persons have knowledge of confidential business, activities, or trade secrets;
- Unusual sounds, interference, or changes in volume on telephone lines;
- Peculiar sounds emanating from a telephone when it is not in use (suggesting the presence of a hidden transmitter);
- Frequent "hang-up" calls when no one speaks or a faint, high-pitched sound is heard on the line;
- Unusual interference on a television or radio (either inside a building or in a vehicle);
- Evidence of break-ins where nothing is stolen;
- Obvious (or subtle) damage or alterations to locks, including sticky tumblers, scratches around keyholes, etc.;
- Small circular discolorations on a wall or ceiling (perhaps indicative of a microphone or camera recently installed;
- Electrical wall plates scratched, smudged, or found slightly askew;
- Crooked or displaced electrical devices (clocks, illuminated signs, smoke detectors, etc.), sprinkler heads, picture frames, posters, furniture, etc.;
- New lumps or ridges under carpets, vinyl floors, or baseboards;
- Traces of dust, sawdust or other debris near the base of walls (suggesting recent drilling);
- The continued, unusual presence of utility trucks, delivery vans, and similar vehicles parked near a potential target location (which may be mobile listening posts).

It is even theoretically possible, with modern technology, to mount surveillance on a subject's silent thoughts. Dr. Lawrence Pinneo, a neurophysiologist and electronic engineer at Stanford University, pioneered this field in 1974, with the development of a computer system that correlated brain waves on an electroencephalograph (EEG) with specific verbal commands. Twenty years later, neurophysiologist Donald York and speech pathologist Thomas Hensen identified 27 words or syllables in brain wave patterns produced by computer software containing a "brain wave vocabulary." Critics of covert surveillance suggest that intelligence agencies are capable of decoding human thoughts "from a considerable distance" by scanning the magnetic field around a subject's head via satellite, then feeding the data to computers, which in turn decode the target's internal "conversation." While that scenario may sound fanciful—and no proof of such surveillance presently exists—concerned civil libertarians dread the day when Big Brother may indeed be watching from the inside of our skulls.

TACY, Gene: convicted software pirate

A resident of Olympia, Washington, born November 13, 1974, Gene Tacy worked for Intel Corporation in 1998, when he and four coworkers joined in a criminal conspiracy with members of the international HACKERS' syndicate known as "PIRATES WITH ATTITUDE" (PWA). The PWA specialized in stealing copyrighted software, then selling or trading it via an outlaw website based on a university campus in Quebec, Canada. The gang forged its alliance with Tacy and company when existing hardware in Quebec proved inadequate to support the storage and traffic in bootleg computer programs. Tacy's coworkers arranged for shipment of stolen Intel hardware to Canada, while Tacy reconfigured Intel's servers to let PWA hackers prowl at will through the company's system, downloading volumes of software. Tacy and his Intel cohorts were among the 17 defendants indicted on federal charges in May 2000, and 13 of the accused (including Tacy) pleaded guilty over the following year. PWA's ringleaders were sentenced to prison, but Tacy and most of the other defendants escaped serving time, slapped with alternative sentences of home or community detention, community service, and financial restitution to their victims.

TAMPON Danger Warning: Internet hoax

Modern physicians agree that some health risks exist, related to the use of tampons, but this March 2001 Internet scare message fabricates a peril where none exists in fact. Spokespersons for various manufacturers, as well as the Food and Drug Administration, agree that tampons pose no threat whatever in terms of asbestos or dioxin poisoning. The original message reads:

Please pass on to as many women as possible . . . If you are a woman and use pads, but especially if you use tampons, read this and pass on to your friends. (For the men receiving this e-mail, please forward it to your friends, significant others, sisters, mothers, daughters, etc.) Thanks!

Check the labels of the sanitary pads or tampons that you are going to buy the next time, and see whether you spot any of the familiar signs stated in this email.

No wonder so many women in the world suffer from cervical cancer and womb tumors. Have you heard that tampon makers include asbestos in tampons? Why would they do this? Because asbestos makes you bleed more, if you bleed more, you're going to need to use more. Why isn't this against the law, since asbestos is so dangerous? Because the powers that be, in all their wisdom (not), did not consider tampons as being ingested, and therefore wasn't illegal or considered dangerous.

This month's Essence magazine has a small article about this and they mention two manufacturers of a cotton tampon alternative. The companies are Organic Essentials @(800)765-6491 and Terra Femme @(800) 755-0212. A woman getting her Ph.D. at University of

Colorado at Boulder sent the following: "I am writing this because women are not being informed about the dangers of something most of us use—tampons. I am taking a class this month and I have been learning a lot about biology and women, including much about feminine hygiene. Recently we have learned that tampons are actually dangerous (for other reasons than TSS). I'll tell you this, after learning about this in our class, most of the females wound up feeling angry and upset with the tampon industry, and I for one, am going to do something about it.

To start, I want to inform everyone I can, and e-mail is the fastest way that I know how.

HERE IS THE SCOOP:

Tampons contain two things that are potentially harmful: Rayon (for absorbency), and dioxin (a chemical used in bleaching the products). The tampon industry is convinced that we, as women, need bleached white products in order to view the product as pure and clean. The problem here is that the dioxin produced in this bleaching process can lead to very harmful problems for a woman. Dioxin is potentially carcinogenic (cancer-associated) and is toxic to the immune and reproductive systems. It has also been linked to endometriosis and lower sperm counts for men-for both, it breaks down the immune system. Last September the Environmental Protection Agency (EPA) reported that there really is no set "acceptable" level of exposure to dioxin given that it is cumulative and slow to disintegrate. The real danger comes from repeated contact (Karen Houppert "Pulling the Plug on the Tampon Industry").

I'd say using about 4-5 tampons a day, five days a month, for 38 menstruating years "repeated contact", wouldn't you? Rayon contributes to the danger of tampons and dioxin because it is a highly absorbent substance. Therefore, when fibers from the tampons are left behind in the vagina (as it usually occurs), it creates a breeding ground for the dioxin.

It also stays in a lot longer than it would with just cotton tampons. This is also the reason why TSS (toxic shock syndrome) occurs.

WHAT ARE THE ALTERNATIVES?

Using feminine hygiene products that aren't bleached and that are all cotton. Other feminine hygiene products pads/napkins) contain dioxin as well, but they are not nearly as dangerous since they are not in direct contact with the vagina. The pads/napkins need to stop being bleached, but obviously tampons are the most dangerous. So, what can you do if you can't give up using tampons? Use tampons, that are made from 100% cotton, and that are UNBLEACHED. Unfortunately, there are very, few companies that make these safe tampons. They are usually only found in health food stores. Countries all over the world (Sweden, Germany, Canada, etc.) have demanded a switch to this safer tampon, while the U.S. has decided to keep us in the dark about it. In 1989, activists in England mounted a campaign against chlorine bleaching. Six weeks and 50,000 letters later, the makers of sanitary products switched to oxygen bleaching (one of the green methods available). (MS magazine, May/June 1995).

WHAT TO DO NOW:

Tell people. EVERYONE. Inform them. We are being manipulated by this industry and the government, let's do something about it!

Please write to the companies: Tampax (Tambrands), Playtex, O.B., Kotex. Call the 800 numbers listed on the boxes. Let them know that we demand a safe product—ALL COTTON UNBLEACHED TAMPONS.

TANG, Wilson See OSOWSKI, GEOFFREY

"TEDDY Bear": computer virus

Discovered on the Internet in April 2000, "Teddy-Bear" is a parasitic Windows virus with "backdoor" capabilities. When the user opens an infected file, TeddyBear's installation routine creates a file named dllmgr.exe in the host computer's Windows directory, containing the virus code. That file, in turn, is registered in the auto-run section of the host computer's system registry, thereby causing Windows to open and run the file automatically on each startup. Thereafter, TeddyBear remains memory-resident in Windows and its "backdoor" routine is executed, opening a connection to its remote host computer and awaiting the command to transmit files. So far, the identified TeddyBear virus functions only with Windows 9x systems and cannot infect Windows NT, although analysts predict refinement by Teddy-Bear's unknown author at some future date. Internal bugs prevent the virus from spreading in some cases, but the interruption is erratic and unpredictable, occurring in a minority of cases.

TELECOMMUNICATIONS Fraud

This criminal activity is broadly defined as including any theft or fraud involving the use of telecommunications service or equipment. Such activities are subdivided into two main categories: (1) the theft of service from commercial providers and (2) use of telecommunications services to defraud third parties.

Theft of telephone service is the province of "phreaks"—the designation self-applied to individuals who swindle telephone companies for fun and profit. Prior to the advent of computer modems, dedicated phreaks constructed homemade devices like the "BLUE BOX" to mimic the 2600-hertz tone sounded by telephone switching systems, thereby granting access to long-distance lines free of charge. Enterprising phreaks thus saved money on telephone calls and also earned income by selling their illicit devices to others. (Author Steve Ditli reports that the founders of Apple Computers, Steve Wozniak and Steven Jobs, manufactured blue boxes during their undergraduate days in college, selling them off to classmates for $80 each with an unconditional guarantee of satisfactory performance.) By the mid-1970s, AT&T spokesmen reported yearly losses of $30 million due to telephone fraud. In February 1998, estimated yearly loss to long-distance fraud ranged from $4 billion to $8 billion.

The advent of wireless telephones opened a whole new world of telecommunications fraud to zealous phreaks. In the 1990s, CELL PHONE CLONING was all the rage, with transmitter codes snatched from thin air and transferred to computer chips inside one or more "clones" of the original phone, off-loading astronomical bills to the accounts of legitimate service subscribers. Cities hardest hit were those with large concentrations of narcotics dealers, since the pushers found a double benefit in cloned cell phones: aside from saving money on their calls, any discussions of their outlaw business intercepted by police would lead investigators not to the dealer himself, but to the innocent user of the telephone whose code had been hijacked. In 1994, the mayor and police commissioner of New York City both fell prey to cell phone pirates, proving that the crime wave recognized no barriers of rank or privilege.

Other forms of telecommunications fraud include:

Modem fraud In the simplest method, hackers penetrate a computer system and gain access to its local area network (LAN), thereafter routing free long-distance calls through that circuit instead of using their home telephones.

Toll-free fraud In a variation on the previous scenario, computer-savvy phreaks penetrate a legitimate company's toll-free system, find an outside line monitored by another computer, and proceed to make long-distance calls at the corporate victim's expense.

Subscriber fraud This technique involves registration for telephone service under a false name, either an alias plucked from thin air or (more commonly today) the name of an actual person acquired by means of IDENTITY THEFT. Use of real identities is preferable, since many customers pay their phone bills without checking specific calls, and thieves can spread the cost around by using multiple stolen identities, thus often forestalling detection.

PBX fraud Some hackers take advantage of a private branch-exchange (PBX) system that permits employees of a given firm to place calls through the company's home office (typically on a toll-free line) from locations outside the workplace. By using a personal identification number (PIN), the employees may then bill calls to the company as if they were dialing from work. Hackers who penetrate a company's system sometimes obtain employee PBX passwords and make their own calls, untraceable since the corporate office is billed as the source of the calls.

Credit card fraud Hackers steal credit card numbers on-line, or individuals purchase the stolen numbers (sometimes in bulk, by the hundreds or thousands), then use them to purchase goods and services by telephone or through e-commerce. Estimates of yearly losses to such swindlers vary widely, but Visa reported a $490 million loss to credit card fraud in 1997, and all sources admit that the problem grows worse every year.

Telemarketing fraud Long-distance swindlers use various fraudulent games, giveaways, and investment scams to milk cash from their victims, often calling internationally. Montreal, Canada, is recognized as a hotbed of telemarketing fraud, targeted since the late 1990s by a collaborative team of Canadian and U.S. authorities in a sting operation dubbed "PROJECT COLT." Elderly persons living on fixed incomes are the favored prey of fraudulent telemarketers, but no one with a telephone is entirely safe.

Consumer advocates and law enforcement agencies advise consumers to use common sense and exercise normal caution to avoid being victimized by some form of telecommunications fraud. The obvious safeguards include:

1. Maintaining strict security over telephone calling cards, PIN numbers, credit card numbers, computer or voicemail passwords, and other personal data that enable unauthorized users to launch an illicit spending spree in an innocent party's name.
2. Exercise caution in any purchase made on-line or on the telephone. Recognize that some avenues of e-commerce are safer than others, and insist on certain minimal security precautions.
3. Verify a telemarketer's credentials before agreeing to any transaction. Again, be extremely cautious when giving out credit card numbers and other important personal information.
4. Dismiss out of hand (and report to the proper authorities) any approach by practitioners of the various telemarketing scams detailed in the entry on Project Colt, above.
5. Immediately report any loss or theft of cell phones, calling cards, credit cards, or similar items that thieves may use to run up bills on your account.
6. Use caution when discussing any personal matters or financial transactions on a cellular telephone. The calls are *not* secure and may be intercepted in various ways.
7. If long-distance or overseas calls are not anticipated, ask your cellular phone provider to remove or disable those functions, thereby barring another party who steals or finds your telephone from running up long-distance bills.
8. Report frequent hang-ups or "wrong number" calls received on a cellular phone, which may indicate unauthorized use of a cloned version by some unknown party.
9. Thoroughly check all telephone bills for unauthorized calls and report any suspicion of fraud to the service provider.

TENNEBAUM, Ehud: Israeli hacker

On February 3, 1998, in the midst of ongoing tension between the U.S. government and Saddam Hussein's

Israeli hacker Ehud Tennebaum, who called himself "The Analyzer," leaves a police station near Tel Aviv. (AP)

Baghdad regime, concerning the presence of United Nations weapons inspectors in Iraq, a U.S. Air Force computer security system known as ASIM—Automated Security Incident Monitors—detected root-level penetration of an Air National Guard computer at Maryland's Andrews Air Force Base. One day later, members of the Air Force Computer Emergency Response Team (AFCERT) at Kelly Air Force Base in Texas detected additional penetration of air force computers in Texas, New Mexico, and Mississippi. While none of the compromised systems were classified per se, all were involved in buildups for a possible military strike against Iraq, thus sparking fears that foreign spies or terrorists might be involved in the incident.

In response to those computer intrusions, federal investigators from the FBI and CIA joined agents of the Army, Navy, Air Force, National Security Agency, the National Aeronautics and Space Administration, and other government bodies in a sweeping investigation code-named "Solar Sunrise." Computer experts traced two of the HACKERS to their homes in northern California, identifying them as a pair of 16-year-olds known on-line as "Mak" and "Stimpy." (Actual names were withheld because the offenders were juveniles.) Following their arrest by FBI agents, the teenagers identified a third accomplice in the Solar Sunrise penetrations as "Analyzer," a hacker based in Israel who launched his U.S. probes from Maroon.com, a website located in College Station, Texas.

Investigators soon obtained court orders permitting them to monitor traffic at Maroon.com, tracing "Analyzer" to Jerusalem, where he was identified as 19-year-old Ehud Tennebaum, and arrested by Israeli police on March 18, 1998. Once Tennebaum was in custody, authorities recognized him as the same hacker who had recently granted an interview to the website AntiOnline, freely admitting penetration of 400 different computers maintained by the U.S. Department of Defense. An Israeli police spokesperson told reporters that Tennebaum was arrested with two unnamed 18-year-olds, alleged to be accomplices in his global hacking spree. Authorities in Jerusalem grilled the trio, then confiscated their passports and forbade them from contacting one another until further notice.

Reviewing Tennebaum's interview with AntiOnline, U.S. authorities determined that his motive was apparently personal amusement, sparked by a feeling that worldwide chaos was a "nice idea." One of his unnamed cronies, known online as "Makaveli," explained the adventure in terms that belied his highly touted IQ: "It's power, dude. You know, power." The Israeli trio, fond of calling themselves "The Enforcers," pleaded not guilty on criminal charges of penetrating protected computer systems in the United States, including those maintained by the Pentagon and NASA. Tennebaum's attorney maintained that his client had broken no laws when he hacked into various official computers, including that of the Israeli Knesset, because there was no official notice declaring them restricted. In the final event, none of the Israeli youths were extradited for trial. "Mak" and "Stimpy" were processed through the California juvenile justice system.

"TENTACLE": computer viruses

Three computer viruses named "Tentacle" are presently known to Internet analysts. The first, logged in April 1996, is dubbed "Tentacle.1958," a nonmemory-resident, parasitic virus rated "not dangerous" by expert technicians. Upon invading a computer, it searches the NewEXE header in the current and c:\windows directories, writing itself to the end of all such files discovered. During infection of the new host, Tentacle.1958 also creates a temporary file named c:\tentacle.$$$, selecting blocks of text from that file and inserting them into various infected documents before the temporary file is finally deleted. If the host computer is active during the first 15 minutes of any given day, from 12:00 A.M. to 12:15 A.M., Tentacle.1958 searches for an icon resource in the system and, if one is found, overwrites it with a different icon contained in the virus code. Tentacle.1958 contains the internal text strings—

C:\TENTACLE.$$$
C:\WINDOWS*.EXE

A second Tentacle virus, this one named "Tentacle_II," was initially reported in September 1996. Like Tentacle.1958, it is a nonmemory-resident, parasitic virus targeting NewEXE files, and analysts rate it "not dangerous." Tentacle_II writes itself to the end of the NewEXE header located in the host's current directory and then proceeds to search for more in the following directories:

c:\win\
c:\windows\
c:\win31\
c:\win311\
c:\win95\

One target file is infected in each directory, with the exception of c:\windows\, where two may be infected. After running its course with NewEXE files, Tentacle_II searches the current directory for *.scr files and may infect them, as well. Analysts note that Tentacle_II pays "special attention" to the file winhelp.exe and "patches it in some way," but the method and purpose of that infection remain unexplained in available texts. If the infected host computer is active between 1:00 A.M. and 2:00 A.M., the virus creates a file named c:\tentacle.gif and there writes a .gif image depicting an octopus tentacle. That done, Tentacle_II proceeds to alter the Extensions text string used in viewing .gif files and inserts its own code, so that the tentacle graphic appears each time the user attempts to view *any* .gif file. Tentacle_II contains the following internal text strings:

```
c:\win\
c:\windows\
c:\win31\
*.exe *.scr
c:\win311\
c:\win95\
\shell\open\command
```

The third (and thus far final) Tentacle virus was discovered in December 1997 and named "Tentacle_III.10496." It is a memory-resident, parasitic, polymorphic virus rated "dangerous" by computer analysts, which writes itself to the end of open or executed .exe files. As with Tentacle_II, this virus also attacks .gif files and overwrites them with the image of a writhing cephalopod tentacle. It contains the following internal text strings (errors uncorrected):

IFSHLP
TBDRVXXXSCANX
TBCHKXXXTBMEMXXXTBFILXXXTBD-
SKXXXTBLOGXXX
WARNING! Your system is contaminated with the Tentacle Virus.
IMPORTANT: Don't open any GIF file!
.GIF.gif.EXE.exe\TENTACLE.

TERRORISM

The terrorist attacks that claimed more than 3,000 American lives on September 11, 2001, were the culmination of a relatively low-tech conspiracy. While several of the airline hijackers were graduates of private U.S. flight schools (available before 9/11 to any literate applicant with sufficient funds to cover the tuition), they commandeered the aircraft using only simple box cutters and made the planes themselves their weapons, avoiding even the need to construct a crude bomb. Even the wave of anthrax mailings that followed the September 11 assaults seemed poorly conceived, disorganized, their chaotic nature perhaps

contributing to the fact that those involved remain at large nearly a year after the crimes.

Those facts notwithstanding, U.S. authorities were naturally fearful of further attacks, perhaps involving high-tech weapons or techniques designed to damage the nation's critical communications infrastructure. Likewise, law enforcement spokesmen have stated repeatedly (without supporting evidence thus far) that global terrorists, including 9/11 mastermind Osama bin Laden and others, communicate regularly on the Internet, holding the equivalent of conference calls in cyberspace via e-mail, chat rooms, and encrypted messages posted to various websites. Ten days after the September 2001 attacks, a *Washington Post* report claimed that "for at least three years, federal agents had found evidence that bin Laden's group embedded secret missives in mundane e-mails and on Web sites. But efforts to track down and decipher the messages have floundered."

Skeptics are inclined to ask how FBI agents and others know such communications are ongoing, if they have been unable to "track down" a single coded message, but simple logic dictates that some terrorists, somewhere on earth, must by now have exploited the Internet's broad range of possibilities. Encrypted messages are only part of the package, in a realm where even teenage HACKERS have penetrated corporate and government computer systems, defacing websites and deleting vital data, looting bank accounts around the world, paralyzing businesses, and forcing the White House website itself to go off-line for repairs. What else might terrorists accomplish if they truly set their minds to it? Diverting troops or weapons? Raiding classified files to unmask confidential informants and double-agents? Retrieving the launch codes for nuclear missiles?

The ultimate worst-case scenario for high-tech terrorism involved use of nuclear weapons to spread mass destruction. Prior to 1991 and the collapse of Soviet communism, such incidents were confined to best-selling novels, action films, and sporadic anonymous threats proved groundless by agents of the U.S. NUCLEAR EMERGENCY SEARCH TEAM. Over the past decade, however, persistent reports have suggested that the bankrupt governments of former Soviet states and satellites, confronted with hardship and virtual anarchy in some cases, may be selling off their nuclear warheads at random to the highest bidders. Members of the global "Russian Mafia," likewise, are said to traffic in weapons of mass destruction, though once again, no such cases have been publicly documented so far.

Two months after the 9/11 attacks, in November 2001, reports circulated that Osama bin Laden's al-Qaeda terrorists in Afghanistan had attempted to build a nuclear weapon from scratch, but the "plans" recovered from an abandoned house in Kabul suggested that bin Laden had been duped by an Internet prankster. Cyber-journalist Jason Scott, writing for the Internet newsletter rotten.com, reportedly traced the blueprint to a spoof originally published in 1979, titled "How to Build an Atomic Bomb in 10 Easy Steps." The original article, run in the short-lived *Journal of Irreproducible Results*, suggested that a warhead constructed in the price range of $5,000 to $30,000 "is a great ice-breaker at parties, and in a pinch, can be used for national defence." Bin Laden and his Taliban associates were presumably confounded by "decadent" Western humor, or else received the "plans" without their accompanying satirical text.

The pursuit of terrorists in cyberspace is serious business, however, and thus far the results for American hunters has been disappointing. If terrorists are, in fact, using the World Wide Web to communicate among themselves, they have so far been able to cover their tracks absolutely. Encryption techniques such as STEGANOGRAPHY make a "cold hit" on any particular message or sequence of code a virtual impossibility, while evasion of physical traces may be as simple as shifting from one Internet café to another between transmissions. David Lang, director of the computer forensics department at the Virginia-based Veridian Corporation, explained the problem to a *New York Times* reporter in March 2002. "The Internet presents two main challenges," Lang said. "One is it's ubiquitous—you can access it from just about anywhere in the world. The other thing is you can be easily hidden."

One of the few known instances wherein terrorists have been tracked down via e-mail was the kidnap-murder of Daniel Pearl, a reporter for the *Wall Street Journal* in Pakistan. The kidnappers used Hotmail, a Microsoft e-mail service, to announce Pearl's kidnapping on January 30, 2002, and their transmission was traced to New Skies, a company based in the Netherlands that provides Internet access to many nations via satellite. From there, investigators were able to identify and locate the computer used in the transmission, resulting in the arrest of Pearl's kidnappers. Four defendants in that case were convicted on

Hundreds of volunteers participated in rescue efforts at the site of the collapsed World Trade towers. Terrorist hijackers conspired to launch a relatively low-tech attack, commandeering planes with knives and using the planes themselves as weapons. (FEMA)

July 15, 2002, with one condemned to hang and the other three sentenced to life imprisonment.

Tracing the perpetrators of real-world crimes via computer is one thing, but protecting computers themselves from a cyberattack is even more challenging. Since the 1980s, various government, corporate, and university computers have been penetrated repeatedly by hackers ranging from curious adolescents and disgruntled employees to industrial spies and transnational bank robbers. No system is truly secure, as demonstrated by penetration of every major telephone company, the White House, FBI headquarters, the Justice Department's National

According to law enforcement officials, global terrorists like Osama bin Laden and his network communicate regularly via the Internet. (AFP/CORBIS)

Crime Information Center, various Pentagon computers, systems operated by the National Aeronautics and Space Administration, and computers housed at various military bases throughout the U.S. Whether the hackers responsible are engaged in childish cybervandalism or downloading of classified information, deleting priceless files or uploading the latest computer VIRUSES, each penetration confirms the inherent weakness of a society dependent on computers and the Internet. As Rep. Jane Harman (D-Calif.) told USA Today reporter Tom Squitieri in May 2002, "Cyber terrorism presents a real and growing threat to American security. What I fear is the combination of a cyber attack coordinated with more traditional terrorism, undermining our ability to respond to an attack when lives are in danger."

Various domestic cyberattacks caused a reported $12 billion in damages across the United States during 2001, and while some are clearly pranks—like the

July 2002 assault on USA Today's website, inserting spurious news items amidst the legitimate reports—other attacks are clearly carried out with the desire to harm (if not destroy) specific corporate targets. President George W. Bush sought $4.5 billion for new computer protection systems in his budget for 2003, but skeptics wonder if any amount of new technology can hold the line for long against determined hackers.

The nearest thing to all-out cyberwar began 11 months before the 9/11 attacks on America, and it came—perhaps predictably—in the strife-torn Middle East. Hackers sympathetic to Palestinian militants fired the first broadside on October 6, 2000, defacing 40-odd Israeli websites in a matter of hours. Pro-Israeli hackers swiftly retaliated, bombarding Palestinian websites with floods of e-mail from computers based in Israel and the United States. The terrorist group Hezbollah's website, featuring appeals for Palestinians to kill as many Israelis as possible, was overwhelmed and crippled by millions of rapid-fire "hits" from abroad, coordinated from a pro-Israeli site called "Attack and Destroy Hizballah" (www.wizel.com). Arab hackers disabled the Israeli government's official website and the website of its foreign ministry on October 25, 2000, using identical techniques. When Hezbollah established "mirror" sites of its original web page, enemies tracked them, adorning each in turn with Stars of David and messages in Hebrew. Palestinian hackers, meanwhile, disabled still more Israeli websites, including those maintained by the ministries of defense, immigrant absorption, religious affairs, industry, and trade, along with that of the Tel Aviv Stock Exchange and private organizations including a number of Hebrew schools. Aftahat Ma'Khevim, the military unit charged with maintaining Israeli computer security, reported that most of the attacks were traced to Lebanon and the Persian Gulf states, but also that many originated from Muslim students enrolled at American universities.

Israeli retaliation in the ongoing Mideast cyberwar has thus far been an unofficial project, at least from outward appearances. A group calling itself Israeli Hackers (www.israelhackers.cjb.net) led the charge, ably assisted by members of another group dubbed "m0sad" (presumably unconnected to Israel's Mossad intelligence network) and various independent operators. Public calls for an "army of Israeli soldiers on the net" to perform "search and destroy" missions against a list of Arab websites have led to further escalation in the so-far bloodless conflict. Pro-

Israeli sites in the United States have also come under fire, as when a hacker known as "Dr. Nuker," based in Pakistan, penetrated the American Israel Public Affairs Committee (AIPAC) website on November 1, 2000, posting a list of "Israeli massacres" and other derogatory comments. According to investigators, "Dr. Nuker" also accessed credit card numbers and other personal information of recent contributors to AIPAC, and sent the group's 3,500 e-mail subscribers a message proclaiming that "it's a shame Hitler didn't finish what he set out to do" in slaughtering Jews during World War II.

With 70-plus Middle Eastern websites vandalized or temporarily disabled in the first month of conflict, James Adams, chairman of the iDefense computer security firm told reporter Carmen Gentile and *Wired News,* "We expect to see more wars like this one being waged out there. Their weapon of choice, the laptop, is easily available, and the ammunition, viruses and hacking programs, is free on the Internet." Arab hacker gangs like Unity, a group with ties to Hezbollah, vow to continue their "e-jihad" against Israel, threatening to expand attacks from government targets into "phase four of the cyber war," attacking Israeli e-commerce to cause "millions of dollars of losses in transactions." An independent hacker known on-line as "dodi," meanwhile, has threatened to shut down NetVision, the Israeli internet service provider (ISP) that hosts nearly 70 percent of Israel's Internet traffic. Groups including m0sad and the Israeli Internet Underground, meanwhile, vow to defend their nation's computer infrastructure and retaliate in kind for any new attacks. One faction ready to face that challenge is Gforce Pakistan, an activist group that recently claimed credit for penetrating the website at Jerusalembooks.com, inserting the name "Palestine" in flaming letters, with messages asking Israelis if the Torah teaches them to rape women and murder innocent children. In mid-July 2001, hackers from m0sad struck a stunning 480 Arab websites in what Internet reporter James Middleton called "a political hack that probably took less than a minute."

Not unexpectedly, the Arab-Israeli conflict in cyberspace has drawn attention—and unwelcome participation—from hackers around the globe. Ben Venzke, director of intelligence production at iDefense, told reporter Brian Krebs in late November 2000, "We're starting to see groups that have no connection or relationship to anything going on in the region jumping into the fray because they think it's a neat thing, [and they] want to be part of it." That reaction intensified after September 11, 2001, with reports that American hackers planned retaliation against computer systems in Pakistan, Iraq, and other alleged "terrorist states." No actual incursions were reported, but they may well have been lost in the confusion of cyberwar already raging throughout the region. Attacks on Iran's Ministry of Agriculture and Ministry of Foreign Affairs, for example, were reported even before 9/11, presumably conducted by hackers sympathetic to Israel.

No such concerted political attacks have thus far been directed against the U.S. government or e-commerce outlets, though "recreational" hackers have briefly disabled such on-line giants as Yahoo and Amazon.com. Given the state of world affairs and America's continuing involvement in regions fraught with turmoil, it would be naïve to assume that the United States can maintain long-term immunity against attacks in cyberspace. No death or physical destruction may result from such incursions, but victims will experience disruption in their daily lives as cyber-terrorism spreads around the globe.

THORNTON, Eric John: convicted software pirate

A resident of Virginia Beach, Virginia, born in 1975, Eric Thornton formerly operated an Internet website called "No Patience," at www.nopatience.com, where he illegally offered bootleg copies of copyrighted software without permission from the legitimate vendors. FBI agents learned of Thornton's operation in January 1999 and arranged for a civilian collaborator to download various software applications valued at $9,638 over the next two months. Thornton was subsequently arrested and charged with criminal copyright infringement under the No Electronic Theft (NET) Act of 1997. Three days before Christmas 1999, defendant Thornton pleaded guilty as charged before U.S. Magistrate Judge John Facciola. Thornton faced a maximum sentence of one year in prison and/or fines up to $100,000, but the court settled for an act of public shaming instead. Thornton was ordered to maintain his "No Patience" website for a minimum of 18 months, posting a notice of his federal conviction with a statement that his computer had been seized by authorities. U.S. Attorney Wilma Lewis told reporters that Thornton's prosecution "represents the latest step in a major initiative of federal and state law enforcement representatives working together to prosecute electronic crimes."

"TINY": computer viruses

More than a dozen computer viruses presently wear some variation of the "Tiny" name, divided into three virus "families." The first group, initially reported from the Internet in August 1996, includes three viruses named "Tiny.330," "Tiny.340" and "Tiny.Fred." All are memory-resident parasitic viruses that install themselves in the DOS data area of an infected host computer. Thereafter, the viruses write themselves to the ends of .com files as those files are executed or loaded into the system as overlays. Tiny.330 also infects av.exe or scan.* files, deleting them when they are executed, while the monitor screen displays—

This scan program can't find me
I'm a GHOST in your machine!!

Tiny.Fred also corrupts .exe files, causing them to freeze the host computer whenever one of the infected files is opened or executed.

A second group of Tiny viruses, the "Dutch_Tiny" family, was first recognized in January 1998. The family includes at least seven variants, all parasitic encrypted viruses described by computer analysts as "primitive" and "harmless." They infect only files launched from the Jump (jmp) command, attaching themselves to the end of each file infected. Different variants of the Dutch_Tiny family sometimes display the following messages:

D_Tiny.251—

Tiny-D version 1.1 by

D_Tiny.284—

*** NIGHTCRAWLER V 2.0 ***
Written by the Weasel! (C) Sector Infector Inc

D_Tiny.286—

*** NIGHTCRAWLER V 1.0 ***
Written by the Weasel! (C) Sector Infector Inc

D_Tiny.Brenda—

(C) '92, Stingray/VIPER Luv, Brenda

D_Tiny.Kennedy (on June 6, November 18 and 22)—

Kennedy er d¢d—l'nge leve "The Dead Kennedys"

D_Tiny.Stigmata—

Greetings to Ps!ko, The Dark Avenger, Zodiac, Data Disruptor, John McAfee (Who would probably be living in a cardboard box if it weren't for people like us . . .), ProTurbo, Jennifer (FUCK YOU BITCH!), Flash Force, Heidi (The Homosexual Greek Warrior), Lazarus, Phoney Phreak, Banadon, Traci (you slut you), The Maggie, Duckee, Daniel (The Homosexual French Pimp with a Purple Hat), The Dead Milkmen, Circle Jerks, Ministry, Nirvana, Nine Inch Nails, Pixies, and all the other virus authors out there, wherever they may be.
Remember: Drugs don't use Winners!
And . . . I'm not as think as you stoned I am.
(c) 1991 -SiTT-

D_Tiny.Wild—

This is a Wild Thing
Programmed By Admiral Bailey [YAM]
(C) 1992 YAM Inc.

Finally, we have the Tiny family of Word macro viruses, initially reported in February 1999. All are extremely short viruses, containing only one macro each (AutoOpen, which causes the viruses to replicate when infected documents are opened). All use a "hot-keys" trick to replicate, programming Word to copy the virus each time specific keyboard keys are pressed.

"TITANIC": computer virus

Initially catalogued in July 1999, "Titanic" is a non-memory-resident, parasitic, Windows 95 virus, rated as "harmless" by computer analysts. In action, it searches out .exe files in the host computer's current drive directory and infects those located. During infection, Titanic creates a new section at the end of each file, bearing its own name, and there writes its code. Beyond that infection process, however, the virus has no payload and does not otherwise manifest itself.

TORRICELLI, Raymond: convicted hacker

A resident of New Rochelle, New York, known online as "rolex," Raymond Torricelli was identified in 1998 as the leader of a loosely knit HACKERS' syndicate called "#conflict." Members of the group enjoyed penetrating government computer systems, including two maintained by the National Aeronautics and Space Administration's Jet Propulsion Laboratory in Pasadena, California, and using one of those computers to host an Internet chat room for hackers. Working from his home, Torricelli used his personal computer to penetrate various systems and upload a software program known as "rootkit," which permits unauthorized users to access various functions without permission from the system's owners. Mixing business with pleasure in his penetration of a pornographic website, Torricelli invited friends to view the site's offerings, while he collected 18 cents per minute for each visit, for an average income of $300 to $400 per week.

On December 1, 2000, Torricelli pleaded guilty in federal court to penetrating the NASA computers and turning them to personal profit, as well as intercepting user names and passwords on a computer system maintained by San Jose (California) State University, using a password-cracking program called "John-the-Ripper" to break any encoded passwords he encountered, thereby gaining access to still more computers. A third charge confessed by Torricelli involved possession of stolen credit card numbers, found stored on his home computer when FBI agents raided his apartment, and use of those numbers to fraudulently purchase long-distance telephone service. On September 5, 2001, Torricelli was sentenced to four months in prison, followed by four months of home confinement. He was also ordered to pay NASA $4,400 in restitution for unlawful use of its computer systems.

TOWNSEND, Jerry Frank: exonerated by DNA evidence

In retrospect, the worst anyone could really say about Jerry Townsend was that he seemed eager to please others—including the Florida detectives who falsely accused him of multiple murders and rapes. Diagnosed with an IQ somewhere between 50 and 60, equivalent to the mental capacity of an eight-year-old child, Townsend proved malleable in the hands of police interrogators who fed him information on a series of sex crimes around Miami and Fort Lauderdale, then took down his "confessions" as a way to close outstanding cases with a minimum of effort.

Townsend, age 27 at the time of his arrest for raping a pregnant Miami woman on a public street in 1979, did not initially confess any wrongdoing, but

the victim and several bystanders pointed him out to police. Persistent grilling eventually produced statements that led to his indictment for two unsolved Fort Lauderdale murders. Investigators knew there were serious problems with Townsend's confessions, even then. In the case of Terry Cummings, a 20-year-old McDonald's restaurant employee found dead in a burned-out building, still wearing her uniform, Townsend "remembered" killing a woman dressed in shorts, in her own apartment. (Tape recordings of Townsend's confessions reveal police correcting him and "refreshing his memory" when he offered inaccurate statements.) Nonetheless, prosecutors proceeded to trial and jurors convicted Townsend on both counts of first-degree murder. Once incarcerated, he confessed in 1980 to four more slayings and a nonfatal rape, piling one life sentence upon another. (One published report claims Townsend may have confessed to as many as 23 serial slayings, but the rest were never formally charged against him.)

Townsend sat in prison for 21 years after that spate of false confessions, before DNA evidence finally cleared him on all charges. Broward County prosecutors asked the court to vacate Townsend's convictions in May 2001, after DNA analysis of bodily fluids retrieved from three local crime scenes identified another suspect, one Eddie Lee Mosley, as the actual offender. (Mosley, in fact, had been a suspect at the time of Townsend's confession, but those statements caused police to abandon their search for further evidence.) Broward County Sheriff Ken Jenne visited Townsend's cell to deliver a personal apology on June 8, 2001, and Miami judge Scott Silverman ordered Townsend's release a week later, calling his imprisonment "an enormous tragedy."

Miami Assistant Police Chief James Chambliss explained to the press how such a miscarriage of justice could happen. "He liked the cops," Chambliss said. "He wanted to be with the cops. They were his buddies, and frankly that's a great tool if you get suspects to like you. That's a good thing." Collusion in the imprisonment of an innocent man, however, is itself a criminal offense in every U.S. jurisdiction, though it seems unlikely anyone involved with Townsend's case will ever see the inside of a cell. Still, there are some who feel regret for the way his case was handled. While defense attorneys branded Townsend "a human parrot," willing to confess any crime to please his interrogators, Miami detective Confesor Gonzalez told reporters, "The confessions do not fit the physical evidence. This case was bad."

"TRIPLICATE": computer virus

Noted for the first time in February 1999, this highly specialized, multi-platform macro virus infects only Office97 components, including Word documents, Excel sheets, and PowerPoint presentations. It disables antivirus software in all three target programs, but once infection is accomplished the several forms of Triplicate—variously labeled Triplicate.a, b, c and d—present no manifestations whatsoever.

Computer analysts report that Triplicate.b and Triplicate.c are merely "bug-fix" variants of Triplicate.a, suggesting the virus writer's attempt to perfect his brainchild, but Triplicate.d contains some independent features, using a breach in Word97 to invade new host computers from the Internet. Initially launched from a remote website, Triplicate.d penetrates new hosts with an already-infected Word document, which disables any Word antivirus systems presently in place and proceeds to search out other documents for successive infection.

Triplicate infection of Word documents is accomplished simply, by writing the virus code into the normal template (normal.dot) of various documents. Excel infection requires Triplicate to use the CreateObject application in Excel, first disabling antivirus protection, then creating a new WorkBook in the system registry and saving this infected item as book1 to the Excel startup folder. After a computer restart, any spreadsheet opened from Excel thereafter carries the Triplicate infection. PowerPoint infection is achieved in a manner similar to the Excel infection, Triplicate first searching for a presentation titled "Blank Presentation.pot" and infecting it if present, otherwise creating a presentation of that name to receive its viral code.

"TUNGUSKA": computer virus

Initially reported from the Internet in December 1997, "Tunguska" takes its name from the Siberian region devastated by a massive explosion of still-disputed origin on June 30, 1908. Written in Italian, Tunguska is an encrypted macro virus that infects the global macros area of host computers when an infected document is opened, thereafter writing itself into other documents when they are saved and saving them with new names unintended by the user. It

creates the following text strings in Microsoft Word (the winword6.ini file section):

DictionaryHelp=1
DOC-PATH=<NORMAL.DOT directory>

Additionally, Tunguska contains the following text:

Virus: TUNGUSKA

Variabile in Winword6.ini:

CheckCRC$: se = 1, il virus NON infetta il MIO computer
Debug$: se = 1, visualizzo i messaggi di Debug
DictionaryHelp$: se = 1, scattata una certa data

MACRO Italiane	MACRO Inglesi	COMMENTO
AutoClose	*AutoClose doppio-click*	*intercetta*
AutoExec	*AutoExec avvio Word*	*intercetta*
AutoOpen	*AutoOpen apertura file*	*intercetta*
FileApri	*FileOpen Dialogo Apri*	*intercetta*
* FileChiudiO ChiudiT.	*FileClose chiusura file*	*intercetta*
FileSalva	*FileSave salva file*	*intercetta*
FileSalva ConNome	*FileSaveAs Dialogo Salva ConNome*	*intercetta*
* FileModelli	*Templates Dialogo Modelli*	*intercetta*
GuidaInformazioni	*GuidaInformazioni*	*virus*
GuidaSupporto	*GuidaSupporto*	*per controllo presenza virus*

TURNER, Makeebrah and Williams, Patrice: bank swindlers

On August 7, 2001, a federal grand jury in Cleveland, Ohio, indicted 32-year-old Makeebrah A. Turner and 26-year-old Patrice M. Williams with two counts of consumer fraud. Both defendants were former employees of Chase Financial Corporation in Cleveland, a subsidiary of Chase Manhattan Bank. Count 1 of the indictment charged that between November 1999 and December 2000, Turner and Williams penetrated their employer's computer system without authorization, to obtain credit card numbers and other account information about 68 of Chase Financial's customers, whose aggregate credit limits totaled some $580,700. The stolen information was then faxed to cohorts in Georgia, who used the credit card numbers to fraudulently obtain goods and services valued at $99,636.08. Count 2 of the indictment charged Turner and Williams with penetrating protected computer systems "for purposes of commercial advantage and private financial gain, and in furtherance of criminal violations of U.S. and Ohio law." The maximum penalty on each count, if convicted, is five years' imprisonment and/or fines of up to $250,000.

Makeebrah Turner bargained with federal prosecutors for a reduced charge, resulting in a guilty plea to the indictment's first count on October 9, 2001, while the second count was dismissed. On January 8, 2002, U.S. District Judge Solomon Oliver Jr. sentenced Turner to serve 12 months and one day in federal prison. Patrice Williams pleaded not guilty and took her chances at trial in January 2002, but she was convicted and received an identical sentence from Judge Oliver on February 19, 2002.

TWEETY Bird Chain Letter: Internet hoax

Proving once more that cyberspace harbors as many gullible and superstitious denizens as any other realm of human activity, this May 1999 chain letter actually promises to make a wish come true for anyone who follows the instructions. Needless to say, there is no record to date of any such wish being fulfilled. The original message reads (errors uncorrected):

Subject: DO NOT DELETE!! THIS REALLY WORKS!!!!]

I'm SO sorry about this, but I had to keep it going.

The last time sent this exact e-mail out, I got a new job and now I'm superstitious. Start thinking of something you really really want, cause this is astounding . . . the person that sent this to me said their wish came true 10 mins after they read the mail so I thought what the heck.

```
               ,,:cc,,,;.
           cc$$$$$$$$$$$$$cc
          cc$$$$$$$$$$$$$$$$$cc
         $$$$$$$$$$$$$$$$$$$$$$$c
       c$$$$$$$$$$$$$$$$$$$$$$$$$$$
      ,c$$$$$$$$$$$$$$$$$$$$$$$$$$$$$
     ,d$$$$$$$$$$$$$$$$$$$$$$$$$$$$$$$$,
    ,$$$$$$$$$$$$$$$$$$$$$$$$$$$$$$h$$$'
   ,$$$$$u$$$$$$$$$$$$$$$$$$$$$$$$$$$$$$$
   J$$$$$$$$$$$$$$$$$$$$$$$$$$$$$$$$$$$b$
   $$$$$$$$$$$$$$$$$$$$$$$$$$$$$$$$$$$$$$$
   $$$$$$$$$$$$$$$$$$$$$$$$$$$$$$$$$$$$$$$
   '$$$$$$$$$$$$$$$$$$$$$$$$$$$$$$$$$$$$$'
     '$$$$$$MMMMM'$$$$$$$MMMMM'$$$$$$'
     '$$$$$$MMMM.$$$$$$$$,MMMM $$$$$$$'
    $$$$$,M";;;'$$$$$$$$$'M",,'",$$$$$$$'
    ?$$$$,<(    ') $$$$$$$$$$(' ) $$$$$'
    ?$$$,<(     ) $$$$$$$$$$(   ) $$$$?
    '$$$$$.'-' $$$$$$$$$$$,'-',$$$'
     $$$$$$$$$$$$????$$$$$$$$$$'
   d$$$$$$$$$$         $$$$$$$$$$b
   $$$$$$$$$$$$c,,,,,c$$$$$$$$$$$$$
    "?$$$$P""" "$$$$$???$$$$??"
            $$$$$
            $$$$$$c
           ,$$$$$$$"c
          z$$<$$$$$$$'$,
          z$$<$$$$$$$$$'$c
          <$$$$$$$$$$$$;?$
          '$$<$$$$$$$$$$$:$
          ?L$$$$$$$$$$$$:$
          ?$$$$$$$$$$$$$d'
          '$$$$$$$$$$$$F
           '?$c'??3$F
           ccc    ccc
          ·,,,,,·
          ··,,,,,·
```

You have been seen by the tweety bird. He will grant you one wish. Make your wish when the count down is over.

10..
9..
8..
7..
6..
5..
4..
3..
2..
1..

**** MAKE A WISH******

Send this to 10 people within the hour you read this. If you do, your wish will come true. If you don't it will become the opposite.

2400 Baud Modem Virus Warning: Internet hoax

One of the first computer virus hoaxes, originally circulated in October 1988, this "warning" cautioned readers against a nonexistent peril. The original message read:

SUBJ: Really Nasty Virus
AREA: GENERAL (1)

I've just discovered probably the world's worst computer virus yet. I had just finished a late night session of BBS'ing and file treading when I exited Telix 3 and attempted to run pkxarc to unarc the software I had downloaded. Next thing I knew my hard disk was seeking all over and it was apparently writing random sectors. Thank god for strong coffee and a recent backup. Everything was back to normal, so I called the BBS again and downloaded a file. When I went to use ddir to list the directory, my hard disk was getting trashed again. I tried Procomm Plus TD and also PC Talk 3. Same results every time. Something was up so I hooked up to my test equipment and different modems (I do research and development for a local computer telecommunications company and have an in-house lab at my disposal). After another hour of corrupted hard drives I found what I think is the world's worst computer virus yet. The virus distributes itself on the modem sub-carrier present in all 2400 baud and up modems. The sub-carrier is used for ROM and register debugging purposes only, and otherwise serves no other purpose. The virus sets a bit pattern in one of the internal modem registers, but it seemed to screw up the other registers on my USR. A modem that has been "infected" with this virus will then transmit the virus to other modems that use a subcarrier (I suppose those who use 300 and 1200 baud modems should be immune). The virus then attaches itself to all binary incoming data and infects the host computer's hard disk. The only way to get rid of this virus is to completely reset all the modem registers by hand, but I haven't found a way to vaccinate a modem against the virus, but there is the possibility of building a subcarrier filter. I am calling on a 1200 baud modem to enter this message, and have advised the sysops of the two other boards (names withheld). I don't know how this virus originated, but I'm sure it is the work of someone in the computer telecommunications field such as myself. Probably the best thing to do now is to stick to 1200 baud until we figure this thing out.

Mike RoChenle

The modem virus hoax inspired a spoof, which began to circulate in November 1988. That tongue-in-cheek reply read:

Date: 11-31-88 (24:60) Number: 32769

To: ALL Refer#: NONE
From: ROBERT MORRIS III Read: (N/A)
Subj: VIRUS ALERT Status: PUBLIC MESSAGE

Warning: There's a new virus on the loose that's worse than anything I've seen before! It gets in through the power line, riding on the powerline 60 Hz subcarrier. It works by changing the serial port pinouts, and by reversing the direction one's disks spin. Over 300,000 systems have been hit by it here in Murphy, West Dakota alone! And that's just in the last 12 minutes.

It attacks DOS, Unix, TOPS-20, Apple-II, VMS, MVS, Multics, Mac, RSX-11, ITS, TRS-80, and VHS systems.

To prevent the spread of the worm:

1. *Don't use the powerline.*
2. *Don't use batteries either, since there are rumors that this virus has invaded most major battery plants and is infecting the positive poles of the batteries. (You might try hooking up just the negative pole.)*
3. *Don't upload or download files.*
4. *Don't store files on floppy disks or hard disks.*
5. *Don't read messages. Not even this one!*
6. *Don't use serial ports, modems, or phone lines.*
7. *Don't use keyboards, screens, or printers.*
8. *Don't use switches, CPUs, memories, microprocessors, or mainframes.*
9. *Don't use electric lights, electric or gas heat or air-conditioning, running water, writing, fire, clothing or the wheel.*

I'm sure if we are all careful to follow these 9 easy steps, this virus can be eradicated, and the precious electronic fluids of our computers can be kept pure.
—RTM III

TYREE, Scott W.: indicted for cyberstalking and abduction

A 38-year-old resident of Herndon, Virginia, employed as a computer programmer with the local office of Computer Associates International, Scott Tyree was arrested at work by FBI agents on January 4, 2002, charged with kidnapping a 13-year-old girl from Pittsburgh, Pennsylvania. Before arresting Tyree, the agents raided his home and found victim Alicia Kozakiewicz tied to a bed. The raiders also seized a number of bondage and sadomasochistic items from Tyree's dwelling, many of them pictured on the Web page where Tyree advertised himself as a "master for teen slavegirls." The page described Tyree's hobby as "training young female slaves to serve me in all ways," while the section on "latest news" announced that he was "looking for your slavegirls to train in real life."

Kozakiewicz disappeared from her Pittsburgh home around 6:00 P.M. on New Year's Day, allegedly after corresponding with Tyree on the Internet and agreeing to meet him in person. Authorities claim that Tyree, a divorced father of one, drove to Kozakiewicz's home and picked her up after dropping his own 12-year-old daughter at the local airport. (Pittsburgh lies roughly 150 miles northwest of Fairfax County, Virginia.) Investigators refused to describe what they thought had transpired between Tyree and Kozakiewicz, and affidavits filed in support of their warrants were sealed due to Kozakiewicz's age, but Tyree was held without bond on a federal charge of transporting a minor across state lines for sexual purposes, while Virginia prosecutors announced their intent to file additional sex-related charges. Kozakiewicz was reunited with her family on Saturday, January 5, her parents informing reporters that the girl had not been seriously injured. The case highlighted fears of CYBERSTALKING, fueled in some cases by the widespread availability of Internet CHILD PORNOGRAPHY, but state and federal prosecutors stressed the fact that indictments are only accusations of criminal behavior, and Tyree must be considered innocent until convicted by a jury of his peers. No trial date had been scheduled for his case at press time.

TZENG, Anna: convicted software pirate

A 44-year-old resident of Rowland Heights, California, a Los Angeles suburb, Anna Tzeng was arrested by U.S. Customs Service agents on June 8, 2001, for trafficking in counterfeit Microsoft products, including the first bootleg copies of the new Windows Millennium Edition operating system seized anywhere by U.S. authorities. Tzeng made her first court appearance on January 14, with bond set at $150,000 by U.S. Magistrate Carolyn Turchin. A 29-page affidavit filed in support of the charges accused Tzeng of procuring "cutting-edge pirated software" and shipping it to confederates in Georgia for retail distribution. Five search warrants were executed in conjunction with Tzeng's arrest, resulting in seizures of counterfeit Microsoft products valued between $4.5 million and $7 million. Aside from the Windows Millennium Edition, Tzeng was also found in possession of software for the Microsoft Office 97 Professional Edition, Microsoft Windows 98 Special Edition, and Microsoft Office 2000 Professional Edition.

If convicted on all counts filed against her, Anna Tzeng faced a maximum sentence of 10 years in federal prison, but she ultimately bargained with her prosecutors to plead guilty on reduced charges. On May 20, 2002, U.S. District Judge Nora Manella sentenced Tzeng to 21 months' imprisonment, plus an order to compensate Microsoft in the amount of $356,024.

U

"UFO": computer viruses

The first of two viruses bearing the "UFO" title (so far) was discovered on the Internet in May 1996. It is a memory-resident, multipartite virus, rated "not dangerous" by analysts, which writes itself to the ends of .com and .exe files as they are accessed on an infected host computer. While leaving the host and its files undamaged, UFO displays the following message on-screen:

> *The U F O Club*
> *UFO-4 By Faisal-Andre-Akhmad Klp Gading Jakarta*
> *Utara*

A second UFO virus, discovered in July 1996, is dubbed "UFO.1468" to differentiate it from the original. Analysts describe it as a "dangerous," memory-resident, encrypted parasitic virus that writes itself to the ends of .exe files as they are accessed. Every 3,000th keystroke following infection produces the following message on-screen:

> *THEY . . . are here!*
> *We will see who is gonna survive, motherfuckers!*
> *You are all some fuckin Unknown Flying Objects!*
> *UFO has come to destroy the fucking thresh around*
> *here!*

After the 10th display of that message—i.e., on the 30,000th keystroke following infection, UFO.1468 erases the host computer's complementary metal-oxide semiconductor (CMOS) and displays one final message, reading: "I am sick of a bullshit like e-Ön-Öf<¢F<ô."

"UGLY": computer viruses

Initially reported from the Internet in May 1997, the "Ugly" viruses—identified specifically as "Ugly.6047" and "Ugly.6048"—are memory-resident, polymorphic and stealth multipartite viruses, ranked by analysts as "very dangerous." Both infect .com and .exe files, in addition to the Master Boot Record (MBR) of the host computer's hard drive and the boot sectors of floppy disks. Infection of the host computer's MBR is achieved when infected files are executed or loaded from an infected floppy disk. From that point, the Ugly viruses infect all files and floppy disks thereafter accessed, while searching the current directory for more .com and .exe filed to corrupt. The Uglies may also erase a host computer's complementary metal-oxide semiconductor (CMOS) and various hard-drive sectors chosen at random. The following files are presently immune from Ugly infection:

> chkdsk.exe
> command.com
> dosx.exe
> gdi.exewin386.exe
> krnl286.exe
> krnl386.exe

user.exe
wswap.exe

"UKRAINE": computer viruses

The Soviet Union's collapse in 1991 produced (or exposed) a rash of criminal behavior in the states of the former USSR and abroad, including numerous incidents of computer theft and cyber-vandalism. Contributions to the realm of computer viruses include several bearing the "Ukraine" title, initially reported from the Internet in June and July 1996.

The first reported is properly known as WestUkrain.274, ranked by analysts as a "dangerous," nonmemory-resident, parasitic virus that searches out .com files on an infected host computer and writes itself to the ends of all such files discovered. In its 25th generation, the virus begins to corrupt files instead of merely infecting them and replicating, thereby rendering them useless. It contains the following text string:

*.com
Western Ukraine

July 1996 witnessed the exposure of a new virus family on the Internet, also dubbed "Ukraine." These memory-resident, polymorphic, stealth viruses, classified as "very dangerous" by experts, write themselves to the ends of .com, .exe, and .ovl files as they are accessed on an infected computer. On the 24th day of any month, the viruses display a Ukrainian flag on the monitor screen, playing that country's national anthem, and proceed to erase various sectors of the infected host computer's hard drive.

"UNASHAMED": computer viruses

Three variants of this virus—called "Unashamed.a," "Unashamed.b," and "Unashamed.c"—have been discovered on the Internet since March 1998. All are memory-resident boot viruses, rated "harmless" by computer analysts, that write themselves to the boot sectors of floppy disks and to the Master Boot Record (MBR) of an infected host computer's hard drive. Unashamed.a and b are apparently designed to freeze infected computers while displaying a message that reads "the Unashamed Naked!" but bugs in the viruses prevent them from delivering their payload. Unashamed.c is somewhat more effective, displaying the following message on-screen:

I'm the great UN, say, the Unashamed Naked! Yeah! of course, I'm the pride of yo nud(ll)ity! I'm here to nakedly spread my HELPS, say, my AIDS along with my UNashamed & AmeriKindily famous dinocracy, yo girl & pearl$ in my heart! Uh! I this game! Pray fo peace guys, while I seize, strip, kis & $queeze! You'd enjoy the scene & hold yo hate, I've no shame, once I'm spreading AIDS, for (the) sake (of) yo peace! Sure! In Songola, Moznia, Amalia, Bozambique, . . . my strip-squeeze's going on, UNashamed & NAKEDly!

UN, watch yoself! . . . Black Synapse advises!

"UNBIDDEN": computer virus

Initially described from the Internet in July 1997, "Unbidden" is a nonmemory-resident parasitic virus classified as "dangerous" by computer analysts. It searches out .com files and writes itself to the end of each one discovered, but an internal bug causes the virus to erratically and unpredictably corrupt some of the files infected, thereby rendering them inoperative. Otherwise, Unbidden delivers no payload and does not manifest itself in any visible way. It contains the following text strings:

*.com *.exe *.*
<1996Nov3\Fryazino\Mikhail G.\Unbidden v1.00>

"UNIS": computer worm

Prowling the Internet since January 2001, the "Unis" worm spreads via infected e-mail attachments and through Internet Relay Chat (IRC) channels. It may also attach itself to files found in the infected host computer's Reverse Address Resolution (RAR) archive. The basic worm—a Win32 .exe file—is in fact merely a "loader" that connects the newly infected host to a remote Web page found at http://hyperlink.cz/benny/viruses/ (based at an unknown location in the Czech Republic) and downloads five components ("plugins") to make itself functional. Internal bugs usually freeze the host system before Unis has a chance to replicate and spread itself abroad on the Internet, indicating that it is deliberately mailed on most occasions when it is encountered.

When an infected e-mail attachment is opened, Unis copies itself to the Windows system directory as a file named msvbm60.exe and remains in the system as a hidden "service" application. Next, it establishes a connection to the remote Czech website and downloads its five plugins, installing them in the Windows directory under the following filenames:

msvbvm6a.dll
msvbvm6b.dll
msvbvm6c.dll
msvbvm6d.dll
msvbvm6e.dll

Unis then "sleeps" for a randomly selected length of time (no longer than five minutes) and repeats the downloading routine.

The worm delivers its payload in stages that include altering the default settings for Microsoft Explorer, changing the host computer's wallpaper design, randomly moving blocks of the host's desktop, and sending reports on its progress with the newly infected host to its remote website. At the same time, Unis scans all HTML files in the infected computer's Internet cache directory for addresses and sends the following message (errors uncorrected below) to all those found:

From: "Microsoft Support" <support@microsoft.com>
Reply-To: "Peter Szor" <pszor@symantec.com>
To: "Mikko Hypponen" <mikko.hypponen@f-secure.com>
Subject: Virus Alert
Attached file name: uniclean.zip

Text: Dear user F-Secure, Symantec and Microsoft, top leaders in IT technologies have discovered one very dangerous Internet worm called I-Worm.Universe in the wild. Author of this viral program is well known hacker from Europe under "Benny" nickname from 29A virus writting group. Universe is fast-spreading worm that already destroyed computer systems in FBI and Microsoft. It is heavilly encrypted and very complex. It consists from many independed parts called "modules", which are very variable—every second hour is produced one new module, that completelly changes behaviour of worm, including anti-detection tricks. You should check your system by our anti-virus attached to this mail. All reports please send to our mail address: universe@microsoft.com and/or universe@f-secure.com Have a nice day, F-Secure, Symantec and Microsoft, top leaders in IT technologies.

The attached file contains Unis's loader component, and any recipient opening that file infects his or her computer, starting the process all over again.

URBAN Legend Warning: Internet hoax

In the age of mass communication, when urban legends are often reported as fact (and Hollywood chimes in with a series of slasher films about serial killers using urban legend motifs to slay their victims), it is sometimes difficult to separate truth from fiction. The Internet hoax, circulated for the first time in April 2002, spoofs the rash of scare reports broadcast in cyberspace—and doubtless snared a few believers of its own. The original text reads (with errors uncorrected):

Subject: Fw: Important Hoax Information!

The following was forwarded to me and it is absolutely true. Everyone knows that I don't send out erroneous emails. This completely clears up all the misunderstandings concerning internet hoaxes, conspiracy theories, pranks, schemes etc. Of course, the following information has been confirmed by CNN and/or the United States government. So next time you are unsure if an email that you have received is true or not, please check with the following to confirm its accuracy. If you feel that any particular hoax or theory has been left out, please email it to me with the details and I will include it in future mailings. Once again, the following is 100% true and well worth the read.

P&G Flash Report

The KKK is endorsed by Procter and Gamble, who also supports the satanists, and who sold Mrs. Field's cookie recipe to Neiman Marcus for $2,000 after the kiddie tatoos laced with LSD that were supposed to be used for satanic ritual abuse at that day care center in Beaufort were mistakenly eaten by the choking doberman who was bitten by the snake that came out of the fur coat that was worn by the escaped homicidal maniac whose hook prosthesis was found hanging from the door of the car of the teenagers who high-tailed it out of a lover's lane when they heard that he had escaped and then went to the pot party where the kids who were supposed to be babysitting got high on marijuana and were so stoned they accidentally put the baby in the oven instead of the turkey that makes you sleepy because it contains tryptophan because the microwave was ruined by the exploding poodle that the girl with the beehive hairdo that turned out to contain roaches who had gotten an automatic "A" at college because her roommate had committed suicide had put in to dry after it had gotten wet chasing the vanishing hitchhiker *who had tried to warn the girl that her insides were cooked because she had stayed too long under the sun lamp at the local tanning salon while her dad poured a load of concrete into a new convertible parked outside of the house because he thought it belonged to a guy who was having sex with his wife but was really a prize he had won in a contest at that radio station that played rock records that contained hidden commands and subliminal messages planted by the Jews, international bankers, the Trilateral Commission, the Council on Foreign Relations, the Illuminati, the New World Order, multinational corporations, right wing militias, Jerry Falwell, the Christian Coalition, Planned Parenthood, and the spooks at Hanger 18 of Area 51 in Dreamland who performed the autopsies on the aliens who crashed at Roswell, New Mexico while on a mission to abduct people and conduct weird sexual and reproductive experiments on them because they knew we use only ten percent of our brains and that engineers had "proven" that bumblebees can't fly and that sugar wakes you up even if you're a CIA agent who has recovered memories about conspiring with organized crime and anti-Castro extremists to kill JFK with a magic bullet, and then killed dozens of other people whose odds of all dying within the period in which they did are infinitesimal even if you don't count their near-death experiences in which an angel guided them to the light before they were called back because it wasn't time for them to die like Mikey from the Life cereal commercials did after eating Pop Rocks(R) candy when his friend Alice Cooper who was Eddie Haskell on Leave it to Beaver woke up after a one night stand in a hotel only to find that the girl he was with was gone and had written "Welcome to the world of AIDS" in lipstick on the bathroom mirror which terrified him because he knew that it is just as easy to get AIDS from heterosexual intercourse as it is from homosexual sodomy with an IV drug user because when the US government created AIDS to commit genocide against blacks who aren't adversely affected by the minimum wage with the aid of Korean grocers who don't give anything back to the community they knew that Anne Klein had said on the Donahue show that she didn't want blacks buying her clothes because when the poison they put in that fried chicken at Church's so The Rich could keep the poor down because they can't be rich if nobody is poor there would be a massive coverup like the Philadelphia*

Experiment or the carburetor that can allow a car to get 100 mpg in perpetual motion just like Nikola Tesla had done a hundred years ago using the same principal that Uri Geller uses to bend spoons and psychic friends use to give you valuable insights that improve your life for amusement purposes only while smoking a cigarette that has no more been proven to give you cancer than evolution has been proven to occur because it's only a theory and there are no transitional fossils and it violates the second law of thermodynamics unlike creation science which is not religious and fear of irradiated food which is rational because we know it's bad just like the assault weapons that are more dangerous than other semi-automatic weapons because they look scary and ugly and they're ok to ban because the second amendment wasn't meant to preserve the rights of individuals against the state like the other nine amendments in the Bill of Rights but instead is the only amendment designed to protect the state against individuals because if there is no effective way to keep guns out of the hands of criminals the next best thing is to keep them out of the hands of law abiding citizens and make sure only the state has them because countries where the state doesn't permit its citizens to own guns are never oppressive and the government doesn't become arrogant and intractable and corrupt because the government can improve our lives by suspending the laws of supply and demand to make prices fair and deciding how many people of each race and sex should be in colleges and jobs which is good because when control of everyday life is centralized in the state the people who get to make the decisions are never capricious or highhanded or make decisions favoring their friends and family and people who pay them money because if only we can get the right people into positions of control it will be safe to let them run things because smart people can figure out how to allocate resources and what fair prices are for goods and services and labor and who should be allowed to do what much more efficiently and constructively than just letting millions of people make their own decisions about what they should eat or drink or smoke or for whom they should work for under what conditions for how much money on what schedule based on their own perceptions concerns and plans in accordance with their best interests.

But I digress . . .

"VAMPIRO": computer viruses

At least three computer viruses are presently known under the "Vampiro" title, two of them variants within a single family, first reported in September 1996. Those variants are encrypted parasitic viruses, rated "dangerous" by experts in the field. The first variant, dubbed "Vampiro.1000," is a nonmemory-resident virus that searches infected host computers for .com files and writes itself to the end of each one found (except command.com), while also deleting the file named chklist.ms. On various unpredictable dates Vampiro.1000 displays the following on-screen message:

> *Zarathustra & Drako les comunican que llego la*
> *hora de ir a dormir.*
> *Shh! Vampiro Virus.*

The second variant of this family, also written in Spanish, is a memory-resident virus called "Vampiro.1623." It writes itself to the ends of executed .com and .exe files, also deleting anti-vir.dat and chklist.ms files. Occasionally it displays the following message:

> *NO NO NO!! Que hace todavia despierto?!?!*
> *Drako & Zarathustra le OBLIGAN a dormir.*
> *Que sea la última vez, ok?!?! En caso contrario,*
> *morira.. JAJAJAJAJAJA*
> *Vampiro 2.4 Versión de Batalla—(C) Digital Anarchy*
> *Viral Development*

Yet another "Vampiro" virus was discovered on the Internet in September 2000. This one is a nonmemory-resident, polymorphic, parasitic virus that searches for .exe files in a host computer's current directory and writes itself to the end of each one located. Because it does not manifest itself in any known way, analysts deem this version of Vampiro "harmless."

VAUGHN, Kevin See FASTLANE

"VCELL": computer virus

Initially reported from the Internet in April 2001, "Vcell" is a nonmemory-resident, parasitic Windows virus, rated "not dangerous" by computer analysts. It searches a host computer's current and parent directories for .exe files, and writes itself to the end of any such files discovered. On the 30th day of any month, Vcell delivers its harmless payload by displaying the following message on-screen (errors intact):

> *W32/Cell Virus*
> *My evolution is complete*
> *Cell is born anew into the Win OS*
> *take a hex editor and open some PE Exes*
> *and look at the end of the file*
> *why? because youll laugh*
> *why? because Cell is in them*

under your nose i have made more akin to me!
Cell Virus

When the user has had time to read that message, Vcell causes the Internet Explorer program to seek out and open an "adult" website featuring pornographic photos, and the gag is complete.

"VD": computer viruses

The first known virus with the "VD" label, now known as "VD.1664," was discovered on the Internet in June 1996. It is ranked by analysts as a "dangerous," memory-resident, parasitic virus, which writes itself to the end of .exe files as they are opened or executed. A bug in VD.1664 corrupts some of the files it infects, causing them to malfunction and freeze the host computer.

A second VD virus—"VD.568"—was reported for the first time three months after its predecessor, in September 1996. A nonmemory-resident, encrypted, parasitic virus that writes itself to the ends of .com files, VD.568 is considered "not dangerous." After infecting some files, dependent on their length, it displays the following on-screen message:

[2J[10;25H[5;33m—- Be careful VIRUS !! —-

VEERBOKEN, Mark: fugitive software pirate

A citizen of Belgium, Mark Veerboken (a.k.a. "Shiffie") was one of 17 defendants indicted by U.S. authorities in May 2000, when federal prosecutors cracked down on the international HACKERS' syndicate known as "PIRATES WITH ATTITUDE." Following a series of arrests spanning North America, Veerboken and Swedish national KAJ BJORLIN (a.k.a. "Darklord") were the only defendants remaining at large.

As detailed in the federal indictments and in the subsequent guilty pleas of 13 defendants, members of "Pirates with Attitude" (PWA) conspired with employees of Microsoft and Intel Corporation to steal valuable copyrighted software programs, making them available for sale or trade through a website based in Quebec, Canada. A group of renegade Intel employees also supplied computer hardware to keep the Canadian website functional. By May 2001, most of the PWA pirates and their accomplices had either filed guilty pleas or else had been convicted at trial. Ringleaders of the gang received prison sentences, but the majority were treated more leniently,

sentenced to home or community detention, periods of community service, and financial restitution to their victims.

Belgian authorities so far profess themselves unable to locate Mark Veerboken, and U.S. prosecutors question whether they could win an extradition fight in any case. That said, spokesmen for the Department of Justice are careful to point out that indictments are merely accusations of criminal activity, not proof of guilt. Indicted defendants are presumed innocent until such time as they are convicted at trial.

VEILLETTE, Todd: convicted software pirate

A resident of Oakdale, Connecticut, born November 21, 1959, Todd Veillette was one of 17 defendants indicted by the U.S. Department of Justice in May 2000, for involvement with the international HACKERS' syndicate known as "PIRATES WITH ATTITUDE" (PWA). The group, including members throughout North America and parts of western Europe, maintained an outlaw website in Quebec, Canada, where thousands of computer software programs were offered for sale or trade without permission from their copyright holders. In addition to stealing, copying, and trafficking in stolen software, PWA members also conspired with employees of Intel Corporation to transport stolen computer hardware into Quebec, where it was used to maintain and expand the illicit website.

By May 2001, a year after indictments were returned, Veillette and 12 other PWA defendants had filed guilty pleas in federal court. Ringleaders of the gang received short prison terms, but Veillette and most of the others were treated more leniently, receiving sentences of house arrest or community confinement, various terms of community service, and financial restitution to their corporate victims.

"VENGEANCE": computer viruses

Eight variant forms of this virus are presently recognized, the first reported in November 1997. All are nonmemory-resident parasitic viruses that seek out and infect *.c* files; half of the eight are rated "very dangerous" by computer analysts, while the remainder apparently pose no threat at all to infected host computers. The first three dangerous variants—known as "Vengeance.252," "Vengeance.390" and "Vengeance.435"—overwrite the files they infect and contain the following text strings (errors uncorrected):

Vengeance.252—

.C *Vengence-B virus. Lastest release from Swedish Virus Association. Released 8:th of May 1992. Satan will come and rule his world and his people!*

Vengeance.390—

.C *Vengence-C virus. Lastest release from Swedish Virus Association. Released 8:th of May 1992. Satan will come and rule his world and his people!*

Vengeance.435—

Vengence-D virus. Lastest release from Swedish Virus Association. Released 12:th of May 1992. Satan will come and rule his world and his people!

The four nondangerous Vengeance viruses—known as "Vengeance.613," "Vengeance.639," "Vengeance.656" and "Vengeance.657"—write themselves to the beginning of infected *.c* but do not corrupt or disable those files. They present near-identical on-screen displays to identify themselves, as follows (errors intact):

Vengeance.613 and 639—

Vengence-E virus. Debugging session unlimited.

Vengeance.656 and 657—

Vengence-F virus. Debugging session unlimited.

The final variant, dubbed "Vengeance.723," seeks out .com files and writes itself to the end of each one found, afterward erasing disk sectors of the host computer and thereby earning its "very dangerous" rating. It also displays the following on-screen message:

*** *Vengeance is ours!* ***
SKISM/Phalcon '92

VICTORIA'S Secret Giveaway: Internet hoax
This Internet hoax, circulated for the first time in November 1999, bears a strong resemblance to the BATH & BODY WORKS giveaway fraud. Whether broadcast by the same author or not, it is likewise entirely spurious. The original message reads (errors uncorrected):

Subject: Fw: Victoria Secret Gift Certificate

My name is Victoria Johnson, founder of Victoria's Secret. In an attempt to get our name out to more people in the rural communities where we are not currently located we are offering a $50 gift certificate to anyone who forwards this email to 9 of their friends. Just send this email to them and you will recieve a an email back with a confirmation number to claim your gift certificate.

Sincerely
Victoria Johnson
Founder of Victoria's Secret

Hey guys, DONT DELETE THIS EMAIL It really works, I tried it and got my Gift certificate confirmation number in 3 minutes.

"VIRTUAL Card" Virus Warning: Internet hoax
Circulated for the first time in March 2001, this bogus warning—like so many others before it—describes a virus that does not exist. The scare message reads:

URGENT ALERT

Please read the following carefully and send it to EVERYONE you know. Send it to all contacts you have, for I agree with the message, I'd rather receive this 25 times as to not at all. . . .

A new virus has just been discovered that has been classified by Microsoft www.microsoft.com) and by McAfee (www.mcafee.com) as the most destructive ever! This virus was discovered yesterday afternoon by McAfee and no vaccine has yet been developed. This virus simply destroys Sector Zero from the hard disk, where vital information for its functioning are stored. This virus acts in the following manner: It sends itself automatically to all contacts on your list with the title "A Virtual Card for You". As soon as the supposed virtual card is opened, the computer freezes so that the user has to reboot. When the ctrl+alt+del keys or the reset button are pressed, the virus destroys Sector Zero, thus permanently destroying the hard disk. Yesterday in just a few hours this virus caused panic in New York, according to news broadcast by CNN (www.cnn.com). This alert was received by an employee of Microsoft itself. So don't open any mails with subject "A Virtual Card for You". As soon as you get the mail, delete it. Please pass on this mail to all your friends. Forward this to everyone in your address book. I would rather receive this 25 times than not at all. Also: Intel announced that a new and very destructive virus was discovered recently. If you receive an email called "An Internet Flower For You", do not open it. Delete it right away! This virus removes all dynamic link libraries(.dll files) from your computer. Your computer will not be able to boot up.

SEND THIS TO EVERYONE ON YOUR CONTACT LIST!!

VIRUSES, Computer: definitions and history

Experts have thus far been unable to agree on a universally accepted definition of the term "computer virus." Some bridle at discussion of "worms" and "Trojan horses" in the same breath, insisting that each is a distinct and separate entity, while other analysts casually lump all three together as variations of the same phenomenon. Broad definitions will suffice for the purposes of our discussion, leaving micromanagement of details to the denizens of antivirus think tanks and university classrooms.

In general, then, a *computer virus* is an executable code that attaches itself to ("infects") some other code within a host computer system in a bid to replicate itself. *Malicious* viruses are those specifically designed to alter or delete data, crash the host system, and so forth; other viruses, while not intended to cause lasting damage, may still impair the host system by devouring memory or delivering unwanted "prank" payloads. Computer *worms* are self-replicating codes that need not attach themselves to a separate "healthy" code to reproduce. *Trojan horses* do not replicate, but are designed to perform some hidden, undesired action in addition to their ostensible function (e.g., collecting passwords or other data for transmission to an unauthorized recipient outside the host system).

Within these broad definitions lie different classes and categories of computer viruses. The most common varieties include:

1. *Cluster infectors*, designed to modify a host computer's file system, thereby superseding programs called by the user.
2. *File infectors* that attach themselves to various programs within the host system, thereby being executed each time an infected program is run.
3. *Macro viruses* featuring instructions in Word Basic, Visual Basic for Applications, or other macro programming languages. These viruses take advantage of an infected program's auto-execution capabilities to spread whenever the program is opened.
4. *System infectors* that store themselves in the boot sectors of a host computer's operating system, thus being executed any time the infected disk (hard or floppy) is used to boot the system.

Expert analysts note that while some viruses are rated "harmless" or "benign," delivering no destructive payload, there is still no such thing as a "good" computer virus. None are helpful to the infected host computer, and even those designed to cause no harm may impede performance over time through the simple act of replicating endlessly (and thus devouring the computer's memory).

California resident Jim Hauser claimed to have written the first computer virus in 1982, collaborating with an unnamed college student to create a harmless program designed to provide "guided tours" of the early Apple II computer. Hauser termed his program an "electronic hitchhiker," and publicly acknowledged the potential for abuse of such codes. Others were still disputing his role as the first virus writer in March 1989, when Hauser died of a brain aneurysm at his home in San Luis Obispo.

November 1988 witnessed the first great panic caused by a computer virus, when a worm created by 23-year-old graduate student ROBERT MORRIS infected some 6,000 networked military computers across the United States in two days. An investigating commission at Cornell University, where Morris was enrolled, decided that the outbreak "may simply have been the unfocused intellectual meanderings of a HACKER completely absorbed with his creation and unharnessed by considerations of explicit purpose or potential effect," but federal prosecutors disagreed. In the wake of that incident, 1989 witnessed numerous reports of computer viruses running amok "in the wild." Those outbreaks and the actions undertaken in response included the following:

January 11 Administrators for the University of Oklahoma at Norman blamed a computer virus for crashing terminals and printers at the campus library, ruining several students' papers in the process.

January 13 Hundreds of IBM computer owners in Britain reported near-simultaneous malfunctions blamed on a "Friday the 13th" computer virus. Investigators announced that the virus was similar, if not identical, to one that crashed computers at Jerusalem's Hebrew University on May 13, 1988.

January 27 Spokesmen for the Library of Congress belatedly announce that the library was struck by a computer virus three months earlier, apparently delivered via infected software obtained from the University of Maryland. According to reports, no data was damaged or lost to the infection.

February 3 The U.S. Department of Defense announced formation of a new Computer Emergency Response Team (CERT), seeking volunteer civilian experts to assist federal agencies in combating computer viruses.

February 27 A Computer Protection Act was proposed in the U.S. House of Representatives, imposing a maximum sentence of 15 years in prison and a $250,000 fine for any defendant convicted of tampering with computer hardware or software. Though specifically aimed at hackers who penetrate computer systems, the law also included virus writers.

March 22 Administrators at William Beaumont Hospital in Royal Oak, Michigan, announced that a computer virus had recently altered data on two hospital computers. A day later, three more Michigan hospitals announced damage to their computer files by a similar (if not identical) virus between August and October 1988.

March 24 The periodical *Government Computer News* announced the impending formation of federal antivirus response centers to "provide authentic solutions to virus attacks as they occur." The centers were to be developed and managed by the National Institute of Standards and Technology, with start-up funds from the U.S. Department of Energy.

May 16 FBI Director William Sessions (later fired for corruption by President Bill Clinton) testified before a Senate Judiciary subcommittee on computer crimes, calling such violations "the most elusive to investigate," since they are often "invisible." Sessions reported that the FBI had trained more than 500 agents to investigate computer intrusions and virus attacks.

May 23 According to statistics cited in *Network World* and the *Dallas Morning News,* American business lost $555.5 million, 930 years of human labor and 15 years of accumulated computer time due to hacker and virus attacks in the past 12 months. As a result, the number of computer "vaccine" programs offered for sale to the public had increased from 1,000 in January 1988 to almost 20,000 by November.

June 27 The *Bangkok Post* reported that a new computer virus, described as "the most destructive yet discovered," had damaged computer systems at two Thai banks and on the campus of Chulalongkorn University. Investigators called it "the Israeli virus," since its first appearance was recorded there, in early May 1988.

July 31 British researchers reported discovery of a new virus called "Datacrime," apparently primed to attack MS-DOS systems on October 12, 1989 (Columbus Day in the United States). According to reports, the virus had been at large but lying dormant since early March. On September 10, U.S. military bases were officially alerted to prepare for a Columbus Day virus attack.

September 12 An Australian newspaper, *The Dominion,* reported that sensitive data in Defense Department computers was destroyed by "the Marijuana virus," recently making the rounds of computer installations in the South Pacific region. The virus, thought to have originated in New Zealand, is named for its payload, which presents a pro-drug message on monitor screens.

September 20 An infected hospital bookkeeping program crashed computer systems in 100 hospitals across the United States, forcing accountants to abandon their terminals in favor of pencils and paper until the problem could be corrected.

September 22 The so-called Datacrime virus surfaced again, this time infesting Denmark's Postgiro network, a system including 260 personal computers, described as the largest such network in Scandinavia. A team of 20 specialists was deployed to check some 200,000 floppy disks for possible corruption. Two weeks later, on October 4, IBM released a program designed to check personal computers for the "Datacrime" virus.

Computer viruses and worms have only proliferated in number since 1989, multiplying into the thousands through the 1990s and the early years of the new millennium. A few of the recent examples not covered elsewhere in this work include—

"TROJ_SEPTER.A" An information-stealing Trojan horse program disguised as an application from the American Red Cross, reported from the Internet in late October 2001, which asks the infected user to furnish personal information including credit card numbers. Instead of forwarding that data to the Red Cross, it sends the information off to the Trojan author's remote website.

"PE_NIMDA.E" A fast-spreading Internet worm and file infector, reported for the first time in early November 2001, which arrives as an e-mail attachment titled sample.exe. The prolific virus propagates itself by four methods: through file infection; via unprotected servers; through shared network drives; and by hijacking an infected host computer's e-mail address book.

"JS_SEEKER.W" An encrypted JavaScript Trojan program, initially reported in November 2001, this virus alters the host computer's Internet Explorer startup page, directing the user to a pornographic website. Injured sensibilities aside, it has no destructive payload.

"TROJ_KLEZ.C" A destructive worm reported for the first time in November 2001, this virus propagates itself via infected e-mail attachments or through local area networks (LANs). On the 13th day of any odd-numbered month (i.e., January, March, May, July, September and November) it attempts to execute a destructive payload, overwriting all files on the hard disk with zeroes.

"WORM_PETTICK.A" Yet another virus reported for the first time in November 2001, this virus spreads via infected e-mail attachments titled anthrax_info.exe. The subject line of the attachment reads "What is Anthrax?" The message body reads: "I will send you some information about Anthrax. Click on the attached file."

"WORM_BADTRANS.B" A memory-resident Internet worm that infected more than 20,000 computers (including the author's) in November 2001, badtrans traveled worldwide by year's end, using vulnerabilities in e-mail systems linked to Internet Explorer with infected e-mail attachments that open automatically, independent of any action taken by the recipient.

"WORM_GONE.A" Described by analysts as a destructive memory-resident worm written in Visual Basic, propagated via e-mail using Microsoft Outlook, this virus surfaced in December 2001. It seeks out selected files in a host computer's memory and terminates their functions, afterward deleting the files entirely. Delivery is made via an e-mail reading as follows:

Subject: Hi
Message: How are you? When I saw this screensaver, I immediately thought about you. I am in a harry [sic], I promise you will love it!
Attachment: GONE.SCR

"WORM_UPDATR.A" Reported for the first time in December 2001, this virus arrives as an infected e-mail attachment with various subject lines and titles. Once installed, it seeks and copies files with the extensions .doc, .exe and .txt, adding the file extension .vbs to each. It also propagates itself by e-mail, sending two copies of the infected message to each address found in the host computer's address book.

"WORM_GOKAR.A" Another discovery from December 2001, this worm is written in Visual Basic and propagates via Microsoft Outlook. It arrives as a randomly titled e-mail attachment, and while it delivers no destructive payload, it has the capacity to install a "backdoor" in the host computer system, potentially granting access to intruders.

"WORM_SHOHO.A" Reported from the Internet in late December 2001, this virus replicates via infected e-mail attachments and damages its host computer by randomly deleting files in the current directory.

"WORM_ZOHER.A" Discovered around Christmas 2001, this worm establishes a connection between its host and a remote website, from which it downloads various e-mails and attachments used to replicate itself. Those messages are then dispatched to addressed gleaned from the host computer's e-mail address book.

"JS_GIGGER.A" A mass-mailing worm written in JavaScript, discovered on the Internet in

January 2002, this virus propagates by e-mail and arrives via messages appearing as one of the following.

Email Sample 1:
Subject: Outlook Express Update
Message Body: MSNSofware Co.
Attachment: MMSN_OFFLINE.HTM

Email Sample 2:
Subject: (email address of recipient)
Message Body: Microsoft Outlook 98
Attachment: MMSN_OFFLINE.HTM

On dates including the numerals 1, 5, 10, 15, or 20, the worm deletes the contents of various files found on the host computer's hard drive.

"WORM_MALDAL.I" Another mass-mailing worm written in Visual Basic, this one discovered in February 2002, the virus arrives and propagates itself via infected e-mail attachments. Moments after infection, the worm displays an onscreen message reading "ZaCker Is N YoUr MaChiNe." Rapid replication slows the functions of an infected host computer with each rebooting.

"WORM_MYLIFE.A" At large on the Internet since March 2002, this memory-resident worm propagates via infected e-mail messages that appear as follows:

SUBJECT: my life ohhhhhhhhhhhhh
MESSAGE BODY: Hiiiii
How are youuuuuuuu?
look to the digital picture it's my love
vvvery verrrry ffffunny :-)
my life = my car
my car = my house
ATTACHMENT: My Life.scr

"WORM_KELINO.A" Another Internet worm spread via e-mail attachments, this one reported for the first time in April 2002, KELINO hijacks a host computer's address book to spread itself abroad. It arrives in a message that appears as follows [with errors uncorrected]:

FROM: "Microsoft Support" <support@microsoft.com>
SUBJECT: Support Message

MESSAGE: During the last time, many bugs were found in our software. Because of our product philosophie, we want to give our custumers as much security as possible. So we decided to send out to all known Microsoft custumers the NetBios patch Version 1.0. This patch will fix all the known and possibly unknown bugs and securityholes on port 137 and 139 . The patch is completly free and easy to install. Our patch will install itself after starting and run as background process. After a successfull installation you should get an OK message box. Thanx for using Microsoft products.
Your Microsoft Support Team
ATTACHMENT: "netbiospatch10.exe"

"WORM_KLEZ.G" A mass-mailing, memory-resident version of the WORM_KLEZ virus (see above), this virus arrives in an e-mail attachment with a randomly selected subject line and is capable of spreading via shared drivers or folders. It disables an infected host computer's running processes and sometimes deletes executable files of popular anti-virus programs.

"VBS_VBSWG.AQ" This destructive Internet worm, written in Visual Basic Script, arrives in an infected e-mail attachment bearing the name of popular musician Shakira. Once installed, it copies itself to all .vbs and .vbe files found in the system, overwriting and thereby disabling them. Its original e-mail appears as follows:

Subject: Shakira's Pictures
Message: Hi : i have sent the photos via attachment have funn . . .
Attachment: ShakiraPics.jpg.vbs

"W32/PERRUN" Identified by McAfee Security in June 2002, this is the first known virus capable of infecting JPEG (Joint Photographic Experts Group) image files. As such, it may be spread through Internet websites containing infected image files. McAfee experts reported on June 18, 2002, that the virus was not yet found "in the wild," but fears of rapid propagation have prompted manufacturers of antivirus programs to work overtime on an antidote.

"WORM_LILAC.A" Another Internet worm spread via infected e-mail attachments, this virus also commandeers a host's address book to broadcast itself across the Web. It arrives with an e-mail appearing as follows:

Subject: LILAC project video attach
Message: Things that the govt. dont want you to know
Attachment: LILAC_WHAT_A_WONDERFUL-NAME.avi.exe

"WORM_FRETHEM.K" Circulating on the Internet in July 2002, this nondestructive, memory-resident worm virus replicates via e-mail attachments, with a message that appears as follows (errors uncorrected):

Subject: Re: Your password!
Message: You can access very important information
By this password DO NOT SAVE password to disk use
your mind now presscancel
Attachment: decrypt-password.exe and password.txt

New viruses, worms and Trojan horses will undoubtedly continue to proliferate in ever greater numbers, challenging analysts and security specialists to keep pace with the efforts of "malware" aficionados. At the time of this writing, in July 2002, the 10 most prolific viruses found on the Internet are:

1. WORM_KLEZ.H
2. JS_NOCLOSE.E
3. TROJ_SUA.A
4. WORM_DANDI.A
5. PE_NIMBDA.E
6. BKDR_LITMUS.203
7. WORM_KLEZ.E
8. WORM_APLORE.A
9. PE_NIMDA.A-0
10. PE_ELKERN.D

"VOODOO": computer viruses

Two different computer viruses presently carry the "Voodoo" name, the first a nonmemory-resident boot virus initially reported in May 1997, rated "dangerous" by analysts. It overwrites the boot sectors of drives C and A (if a disk is inserted in the latter), and also contains several bugs that may result in stalling the infected host system, with occasional corruption of non-DOS boot sectors. Voodoo contains the following text but is generally unable to display it on-screen, due to additional bugs:

[VooDoo]
Yar harddisk's gone now..

Eighteen months passed before the second Voodoo virus—dubbed "Voodoo.1537"—was reported from the Internet in November 1998. This is a memory-resident, encrypted, parasitic Windows virus, rated "harmless" by experts, that infects files in the Windows "C:\Program Files" directory and others. A bug in the virus allows it to operate only in Windows 95, and it has no payload manifestations in any case. Voodoo.1537 contains a text string reading: "Star0—Magic Voodoo."

VRANESEVICH, John: founder of "AntiOnline"

A self-declared enemy of HACKERS everywhere, John Vranesevich calls his AntiOnline website "a valuable tool in the fight against 'CyberCrime,'" providing tips on computer security, advice on the legality of downloading software, instructions for "profiling" hackers and learning their real-world identities, a directory of schools that offer courses in on-line security, and so forth. While widely praised by law enforcement officers and spokesmen for major industries, Vranesevich has also predictably come under fire from hackers and "free data" advocates who brand him (among other things) a "self-anointed junior G-man wannabe" devoted to "misguided cyber-vigilantism." His critics liken Vranesevich to Red-hunting Senator Joseph McCarthy in the 1950s, trampling the alleged "rights" of Internet surfers to go where they will in cyberspace, including penetration of protected government and corporate computers.

Vranesevich has a simple answer for his critics. "I know some of you are playing what you feel is a game," he writes on-line. "A game that you think you are winning. Some of you sit back and laugh at organizations like the FBI. You make sure that you provide enough information to make it obvious who you are, yet are careful not to provide enough information to actually have it proven. I have been watching you these past 5 years. I know how you do the things you do, why you do the things you do, and I know who you are."

Hacker antipathy to Vranesevich and AntiOnline is not limited to snide comments. Vranesevich reports that his website is under constant attack by those who regard him as an enemy of unfettered "freedom" in cyberspace. "We average between 200–500 intrusion attempts against one of our systems AN HOUR," he writes on-line, "and every time I piss another segment of the cyber-population off, that number skyrockets." As to the outpourings of vitriol and name-calling,

Vranesevich told *Slashdot* in a November 2001 interview: "To be honest, at this point in my life, my goal is not to become loved in the hearts of the masses. I'm not running for political office, so popularity doesn't count. I have goals in my life that I want to achieve . . . Sure, I have to put up with a lot more flack and B.S. than the average 21 year old. But I'll tell you this, every minute is worth it."

"VULCAN": computer viruses
Reported initially in December 1997, the "Vulcan" family of computer viruses presently includes four variants, all described by analysts as "harmless," memory-resident, parasitic viruses. Known variously as "Vulcan.307," "Vulcan.480," "Vulcan.484," and "Vulcan.496," they write themselves to the beginning of .com files and to the end of .exe files as they are opened or executed. None of the variants deliver any payload or present any manifestations of themselves, hence the harmless rating for the entire virus family.

"WADIM": computer viruses

Spawned in Russia and initially logged on the Internet in December 1996, the "Wadim" virus family included two known variants, identified as "Wadim.481" and "Wadim.531." Both are memory-resident, parasitic viruses, described by expert analysts as "harmless." Wadim.481 installs itself into a host computer's Interrupt Vectors Table, then writes itself to the end of any .exe files it discovers. It includes a text string reading: "Wadimka v2.1 (c)Copyright 1996 Wadim in Moscow." Wadim.531, by contrast, writes itself to the beginning of .com files as they are opened. It contains the text string "Wadimka v1.1 (c)Copyright 1996 Wadim&Gurre in Moscow." Their "harmless" rating derives from the fact that neither variant appears to manifest itself in any way.

WALID, Mohammad: convicted satellite TV pirate

A resident of Yorktown Heights, New York, Mohammad Walid was one of the defendants arrested by U.S. Customs Service agents in the sting operation known as "OPERATION SMARTCARD.NET." The operation targeted individuals trafficking in counterfeit access cards, which permit their users to watch satellite television broadcasts without paying normal subscription fees to the service providers. Customs agents and industry spokesmen estimated that such fraud was costing legitimate providers like DirecTV an average of $6.2 million per year at the turn of the century. Walid pleaded guilty in August 2000 to charges of dealing in counterfeit "smart" cards, but he still had not been sentenced at press time. The U.S. Department of Justice's website lists the sentence for Walid and his several codefendants as "TBD"—To Be Determined at some unknown future date.

WALKER, Tony See FASTLANE

WAL-MART Flag Alert: Internet hoax

Another cyberspace message spawned in the wake of terrorist attacks committed on September 11, 2001, this anonymous broadside attacks the Wal-Mart chain of discount stores for failing to consistently display American flags. Since the majority of shops and stores in the United States do not fly flags, the reason for singling out Wal-Mart remains unclear. The original call to arms reads (with errors uncorrected):

Quite honestly, I had not noticed that Wal-mart does not fly our flag. What a surprise. I have run across a situation that I think should be changed; it upset me and so I decided to put it out on the Internet. If you decide to forward this note to your friends, that's fine-if not, that's okay, too.

Maybe I'm wrong in feeling this way, but this is what I found on Friday, October 12, 2001.

I ran to our local Wal-Mart store before I went to work. I needed a couple of items before we left at noon for a short vacation. While I was being checked out at the counter, I realized that I had not noticed an American Flag flying outside and asked the clerk why there wasn't one.

I was told that the policy is that Wal-Mart does not provide flags to their stores—rather, each store must provide their own—at this store, the employees would have to take up a collection among themselves to make the purchase of the flag, pole & flood light.

I was sure there was a misunderstanding in that policy somewhere, but needed to hurry off to work, so I didn't pursue the problem. As I drove to work I became more and more upset to think that the Company "seems" to encourage patriotism and "Buy American" won't even, in these days of horror and heroism and war on terrorism, provide their stores with flags to show their support!! When I got to work I told my co-employees what I had found that morning and they agreed that I must be mistaken—Wal-Mart would not have a policy that made individual stores/employees purchase their own flag, "for heavens sake"!!

My co-employees suggested I just call Wal-Marts corporate offices and there I would discover the truth to this misunderstanding. So, I did. I called the Corporate office and spoke to their representative.

By the way, their number is 1-800-Wal-Mart.

Do you know what I was told? I wasn't misunderstanding their policy! Each store must provide their own flag—if the store can't fit the expense into their budget, then the employees have to take up a collection.

Now, I find this a disgrace. I have always noticed the large flags flying at every Perkins Pancake House—they always fly the flag, even when there isn't a National Emergency. But here's Wal-Mart, the company who has become wealthy beyond measure in this great Country of ours; who claims to be "one big happy family," who recommends we "Buy American," but who cannot/will not provide a flag pole/flag and light to each of their stores wherever they are.

Would this be expensive? Oh, somewhat, I agree, but I hear that Wal-Mart is planning to build many new stores in the near future and that, possibly, they will make every existing store into a "super-store." Now, I realize that expanding like that will bring in more money and make them wealthier still—where providing flags to all their stores would only COST money and not add money to their fortune. Maybe, just maybe, not providing flags to their stores and not flying the flag in

support of our Country will start costing them more money—maybe I will start looking more closely for the flag before I shop and begin supporting the smaller stores who don't worry so much about the "bottom line," but rather are happy to spend some money to show they really love America.

Do you think I am really way off base on this, or do you feel the same. Thanks for taking the time to think about this with me—if you feel the same, forward this on to your address list—if not, that's what your "Delete" is for.

WANG, Tae Yuan   See FASTLANE

"WASP": computer viruses

The summer of 1996 witnessed discovery of two computer viruses bearing the "Wasp" title. The first, logged initially in June 1996, is known as "Wasp.1655," a memory-resident, parasitic virus rated "dangerous" by expert analysts. Wasp.1655 writes itself to the end of open or executed .com files, its code containing a text string that reads: "Wasp" ver 1.0—Underground Laboratory "FLY"—Moscow 1993. On the third day of any given month, the virus reformats the first track of a host computer's hard drive and displays the following message at 10:00 P.M. in the upper left-hand corner of the monitor's screen:

Hello—Im Your New Virus
- WASP -
A.J.Poshukaev Call Neighbour

A second Wasp virus, dubbed "Wasp_II.1312," was reported a month later, in July 1996. It is identified as a "very dangerous," nonmemory-resident parasitic virus that seeks out .com files in a host computer's various directories and writes itself to the beginning of each one located. It also overwrites the A drive's boot sector with text reading:

I'm W.A.S.P.
Fuckyourself!

At the same time, Wasp_II.1312 displays these messages on the monitor's screen:

Insufficient memory
Incorrect DOS version

When that message has been delivered, a small memory-resident program "shakes" the screen, causing the images to blur.

WATERS, Kenneth: exonerated by DNA evidence

In 1980, Ayers, Massachusetts, resident Katharina Brow was stabbed and beaten to death in a brutal robbery. Suspect Kenneth Waters was indicted after two ex-girlfriends told police that he had boasted to them of committing the crime. At trial, in 1983, Waters argued that he was in court at the time of the slaying, on an unrelated charge of assaulting a police officer, and thus could not be guilty. Court records confirmed his presence on the day of the murder, but could not pin down specific times. His ex-girlfriends testified for the state, and prosecutors claimed that Waters sold some of the victim's jewelry six weeks after the murder. Jurors convicted Waters of first-degree murder and robbery on May 12, 1983. He subsequently received a sentence of life imprisonment.

Kenneth's younger sister, Betty Ann Waters, devoted her life to proving his innocence. Although a high school dropout and divorced mother of two at the time of his trial, Betty Ann went on to earn her GED, then her bachelor's and master's degrees, finally graduating from law school at Roger Williams University, in Rhode Island. While still at Roger Williams, she began to correspond with attorneys from the CARDOZO INNOCENCE PROJECT concerning her brother's case. Attorney Barry Scheck agreed to take the case, after a court clerk directed Betty Ann to a box of old case evidence stored in the courthouse basement. The stash included blood samples from the presumed killer, found at the crime scene, and DNA testing excluded Kenneth Waters as a donor of the evidence. He was released on March 15, 2001, after 18 years in prison, while prosecutors announced their intention to hold a new trial.

Despite the threat of another trial, Waters seemed confident, telling reporters that the true story of his wrongful conviction was "going to come out and it is going to be a shocker." That trial would not take place, however. On September 6, 2001, in Middletown, Rhode Island, Waters fell from a 15-foot wall while taking a short cut to his brother's home for a family dinner. He fractured his skull in the fall and died on September 19, in a local hospital.

"WEIRD": computer viruses

Initially reported from the Internet in September 1997, the first "Weird" computer virus is formally known as "Weird.1800," a nonmemory-resident, encrypted parasitic virus that writes itself to the end of any .com files located on an infected host computer. It also deletes certain antivirus files—specifically anti-vir.dat, chklist.cps and chklist.ms—while overwriting the c:\dos/msd.ini file with the following text:

You are now looking at the name/passwords of your network! Greetings, ThE wEiRd GeNiUs. Check your MSD.INI once in a while!

It also prints the C:\DOS.MSD.INI file on the first of every month, but despite such pranks, Weird.1800 is rated "not dangerous" by analysts.

The same rating is applied to "Win32.Weird," a memory-resident parasitic virus logged initially in June 1999. This Weird variant writes itself to the end of .exe files and also affects the explorer.exe file if found, renaming it explorer.e on the next Windows startup. Win32.Weird also has a "backdoor" function that opens an Internet connection to a remote website and awaits orders to download, upload or delete files on command. This function would appear to challenge the virus's "not dangerous" rating, since it allows invasion and vandalism of the infected host computer.

"WEREWOLF": computer viruses

Initially reported in October 1997, the "WereWolf" virus presently exists in at least 16 variant forms, all rated as "dangerous" parasitic viruses that corrupt sectors of an infected host computer's hard drive. The many variants perform in different ways, and are therefore best considered in sub-families.

Five of the variants—WereWolf.658, 678, 684.a, 684.b and 685—are nonmemory-resident encrypted viruses that seek out .exe files and write themselves to the end of each one discovered. They also seek and delete files labeled ant*.dat, *.cps and *.ms. They contain the following text strings:

*WereWolf.658,678: Home Sweap Home
(C)1994-95 WereWolf*

WereWolf.684.a: CLAWS (C)1994–95 WereWolf

WereWolf.684.b,685: FANGS
(C)1994–95 WereWolf

WereWolf.1152m 1168, 1192, 1193, 1208, 1367, 1450, 1500.a and 1500.b are memory-resident viruses that infect .com and .exe files as they are opened or executed. Variants 1192, 1193, and 1208 write themselves to the beginning of .com files and to the end of .exe files; the other forms all write themselves to the ends of both .com and .exe files. Were-Wolf.1500a and 1500b also corrupt randomly selected bytes in the data buffer of any disk they infect. These viruses contain the following text strings:

WereWolf.1152: SCREAM (C)1996 WereWolf
WereWolf.1168: SCREAM! (C)1995–96 WereWolf
WereWolf.1192,1193,1208: BEAST (C)1995 WereWolf
WereWolf.1367: FULL MOON (C)1995–96 WereWolf
WereWolf.1450: [WULF] 1996 WereWolf
WereWolf.1500.a: WULF 1996 WereWolf
WereWolf.1500.b: [WULF] (c) 1995–1996 WereWolf

Two final variants, WereWolf.Wave 2662 and 2845, are polymorphic viruses, with WereWolf.Wave.2845 containing a bug that corrupts .com files as they are infected. Both variants of the WereWolf include the following text strings:

WAVE v0.9 WereWolf Advanced Viral Encryption
[HOWL] (c)1996 WereWolf

"WILDLICKER": computer virus

Initially reported in November 1996, "WildLicker" is a memory-resident, parasitic polymorphic virus, rated "harmless" by computer analysts. It writes itself to the ends of open or executed .com files. WildLicker may also infect write-protected floppy disks, using a special function to prevent display of the standard DOS error message during infection. If the user decompresses an infected file, that action simultaneously corrupts the file and erases WildLicker's virus code. WildLicker contains the following text strings:

3 . . . 2 . . 1 . . . WILD LICKER !!! a PKWARE+NUKE+TRIDENT virus for your fucked pentium (bug inside)
thanks to [NuKE] N.R.L.G. AZRAEL
thanks to PKWARE

PKLITE Copr. 1992 PKWARE Inc.
All Rights ReservedNot enough memory and thanks to [MK / TridenT]
[TPE 1.4]

WILHOIT, Gregory R.: exonerated by forensic odontology

In the early morning hours of May 31, 1985, Kathy Wilhoit was found dead in her home at Pawhuska, Oklahoma, the victim of a brutal rape and murder. Investigators determined that she had been strangled with a telephone cord. They found a fingerprint on the telephone receiver and retrieved a lone pubic hair from a pool of blood near the corpse. A bite mark on the victim's breast was photographed and measured by technicians.

Kathy Wilhoit's estranged husband, Gregory, was an immediate suspect. The couple had separated barely two weeks earlier, and Gregory lived in Tulsa, 40 miles southeast of Pawhuska. Gregory kept odd hours and had no alibi for the time of the murder, but he was initially encouraged when his fingerprints failed to match the one on Kathy's phone and microscopic study of the suspect pubic hair revealed no match with his. Still, the prosecution forged ahead, claiming that Wilhoit's teeth matched the bite mark found on his wife.

A competent defense attorney would have challenged that assertion with expert testimony, but Wilhoit had the grave misfortune to be represented by George Briggs, a 78-year-old brain-damaged alcoholic who had been censured by the American Bar Association weeks before he took Wilhoit's case. Constantly intoxicated, Briggs had been known to soil his own trousers in court, and he vomited several times in the judge's chambers during Wilhoit's 1987 trial. Worse yet, from his client's perspective, Briggs was so confused throughout the proceedings that he failed to challenge the bite-mark testimony offered by the prosecution. Wilhoit was convicted of the slaying, so despondent at the outcome of his trial that he requested execution in lieu of a life sentence. The judge obliged him, and Wilhoit was packed off to death row. (George Briggs was disbarred soon after the trial and died a short time later.)

When Wilhoit recovered from the shock of his conviction, he appealed the verdict and death sentence. Attorney Mark Barrett handled the appeal, swiftly recognizing that forensic ODONTOLOGY was the key to Wilhoit's guilt or innocence. Copies of the bite-mark photos and Wilhoit's dental records were sent to 11 recognized experts in the field, including technicians employed by the FBI and the Royal Canadian Mounted Police, as well as dentists who had reviewed evidence in the Ted Bundy and "Hillside Strangler" serial murder cases. The verdict was unanimous: Greg Wilhoit's teeth had not inflicted the bite mark on Kathy's breast.

The appellate court granted Wilhoit a new trial in 1993, on grounds that his original defense counsel had been "ineffective" (to say the least). With the new forensic evidence in hand, he was acquitted by a second jury. The murder of Kathy Wilhoit remains unsolved today.

WILLIAMS, Dennis See FORD HEIGHTS FOUR

WILLIAMSON, Ronald See FRITZ, DENNIS

"WIN a Holiday" Virus Warning:
Internet hoax
Sometimes it seems there are as many false virus warnings at large in cyberspace as there are actual computer viruses. The following message, strongly reminiscent of the "JOIN THE CREW" hoax, warns readers of a malicious e-mail that does not exist in fact. The original text reads:

VIRUS WARNING !!!!!!

If you receive an email titled "WIN A HOLIDAY" DO NOT open it. It will erase everything on your hard drive. Forward this letter out as many people as you can. This is a new, very malicious virus and not many people know about it. This information was announced yesterday morning from Microsoft; please share it with everyone that might access the Internet. Once again, pass this along to EVERYONE in our address book so that this may be stopped. Also, do not open or even look at any mail that says "RETURNED OR UNABLE TO DELIVER" This virus will attach itself to your computer components and render them useless. Immediately delete any mail items that say this. AOL has said that this is a very dangerous virus and that there is NO remedy for it at this time. Please practice cautionary measures and forward this to all your on-line friends ASAP.

WINGEART, Jerald Leroy: convicted by DNA evidence
A resident of Chesaning, Michigan, 20-year-old Dawn Lee Magyar vanished on a shopping trip to Owosso on January 27, 1973. Her father-in-law found Dawn's car the next morning in a supermarket parking lot, the driver's door open, bags of groceries on the front seat, with Dawn's keys lying on the ground nearby. A two-day search by law enforcement officers and some 4,000 volunteers failed to discover any further traces of the missing young woman. On March 4, 1973, two boys found Magyar's body discarded in a neighboring county. She had been raped and shot three times at close range with a .22-caliber weapon. In 1974 police found a pistol they believed to be the murder weapon, discarded in the Shiawassee River near the scene of Magyar's abduction, and Magyar's wallet was found on a riverbank in the same area two years later, but the clues brought detectives no closer to Dawn's killer.

The advent of DNA testing raised hopes among Michigan State Police investigators, but those hopes were dashed in 1995, when testing cleared an Owosso resident, their only real suspect to date, of any involvement in the crime. Another four years passed before investigators traced the .22 pistol's original owner, and he in turn directed them to 59-year-old Jerald Wingeart, residing in Center Line, Michigan. Wingeart, police discovered, had been convicted of robbing and raping a blind college student in 1961, receiving concurrent sentences of 9–30 years for robbery and 10-30 years for sexual assault. He was paroled in 1968, five years before the Magyar slaying.

Unable to present sufficient evidence to secure a court order for Wingeart's blood, detectives lifted cigarette butts from his household trash (considered public property once garbage is placed outside the home for pickup) and matched DNA from Wingeart's saliva to the semen samples recovered from Magyar's corpse 26 years earlier. Wingeart was arrested on murder charges in March 2001 and tried nine months later. Convicted on November 28, 2001, he received a mandatory life prison term on January 19, 2002. Circuit Judge Gerald Lostracco noted that "a life sentence for someone who's 61 years old has less of an impact," regretting that Wingeart had not been captured in 1973, when life imprisonment might have had "some meaning." Still, Lostracco observed, "I'm convinced if you were still out in the streets that you would strike again, so it's not too late for the protection of society."

"WOBBLER" Virus Warning: Internet hoax

This spurious warning, circulated on the Internet since May 1999, claims that a virus called "Wobbler" is in circulation, carried by a file named "California." In fact, research by IBM and HOAXBUSTERS has demonstrated that neither the virus nor its alleged host file exist. The alert is simply another Internet hoax. Broadcast in both English and French, the original text (English version) reads:

Subject: FW: New Virus Warning

Dear ALL

Thought you might be interested in this message. If you receive an email with a file called "California" do not open the file. The file contains the "WOBBLER" virus.

This information was announced yesterday morning by IBM. The report says . . . "this is a very dangerous virus, much worse than 'Melissa' and there is NO remedy for it at this time. Some very sick individual has succeeded in using the reformat function from Norton Utilities causing it to completely erase all documents on the hard drive. It has been designed to work with Netscape Navigator and Microsoft Internet Explorer. destroys Macintosh and IBM compatible computers. This is a new, very malicious virus and not many people know about it at this time. Please pass this warning to everyone in your address book and share it all your online friends asap so that the destruction it can cause may be minimized"

All the best
Dan

WOODALL, Glen Dale: exonerated by DNA evidence

In 1986, two female residents of Huntington, West Virginia, were kidnapped in separate incidents from the parking lot of a local shopping mall. In each case, the male offender wore a ski mask and brandished a knife, ordering his victims to keep their eyes shut. In the first attack, he drove around aimlessly in the victim's car, then stopped and raped her repeatedly, stealing a gold watch and $5 in cash before he fled. The victim opened her eyes long enough to see that the rapist wore brown pants and was uncircumcised. The second victim, also raped repeatedly and robbed of a gold watch, glimpsed the attacker's hair and

boots, further confirming that he was uncircumcised. Both victims told police that their attacker exuded "a distinctive smell."

Detectives eventually settled on suspect Glen Woodall, a gravedigger from Charleston, West Virginia. Prosecutors based their case on a variety of evidence, including a "partial visual identification" by one victim, another victim's identification of brown pants found in Woodall's home, confirmation from both victims of an odor pervading Woodall's workplace, and the fact that Woodall was uncircumcised. In terms of scientific evidence, hairs recovered from one victim's car were found to be microscopically "consistent" with samples from Woodall's scalp and beard. Finally, state police chemist FRED ZAIN opined that Woodall's blood secretions matched semen evidence recovered from the victims.

In a pretrial hearing, Woodall's attorney asked the court to perform "experimental new" DNA tests on the crime scene evidence, but the motion was denied in favor of chemist Zain's "more conventional" evidence. On July 8, 1987, jurors convicted Woodall on two counts of kidnapping, two counts of aggravated robbery, one count of first-degree sexual assault, and one count of first-degree sexual abuse. At sentencing he received two life prison terms plus separate terms of 203 and 335 years, the four terms to be served consecutively. The trial court belatedly ordered a DNA test after Woodall was convicted, but ruled the results "inconclusive."

West Virginia's Supreme Court affirmed Woodall's conviction on July 6, 1989, but he continued filing appeals for new DNA testing on the crime scene evidence. Permission for testing was finally granted and the results excluded Woodall as a donor of the semen found at either crime scene. The trial court vacated his conviction on July 15, 1991, and released him on $150,000 bond, monitored by an electronic PERSONAL TRACKING UNIT while further investigation continued. Research on the case revealed a romantic liaison between one rape victim and a primary investigator, along with the fact that both victims had been secretly hypnotized to "enhance" their memories of the crimes. A second round of DNA tests once again excluded Woodall as the rapist, in April 1992, and all charges were dismissed the following month. Subsequent investigations of chemist Fred Zain in West Virginia and Texas have reopened scores of cases wherein Zain apparently perjured himself to convict various defendants. Glen Woodall was awarded $1 million for his wrongful conviction and false imprisonment in West Virginia.

WOODSIDE Literary Agency: Internet fraud and harassment

The Woodside Literary Agency, based in New York City, apparently began soliciting clients on-line in January 1996. Its advertisements were posted to the Usenet newsgroup misc.writing, where they drew attention from freelance author Jayne Hitchcock. Hitchcock telephoned the agency and spoke to an agent who identified himself as James Leonard, afterward sending Woodside a book proposal. The response combined lavish praise with Woodside's demand for a $75 reading fee, a practice barred by ethical guidelines of the Association of Authors' Representatives. Hitchcock advised Woodside that their advertisements made no mention of a reading fee, and her proposal was returned.

In April 1996, several posts to misc.writing criticized Woodside's unusual fee schedule, noting that the charges were not limited to reading fees, but also included additional charges for a variety of services. Several newsgroup subscribers inaugurated a "contest," mailing Woodside the worst prose they could manage, whereupon all but one were welcomed among the agency's "exclusive 5 percent" of chosen clients. Each acceptance notice was accompanied by bills for reading fees in various amounts. Hitchcock and author Jack Mingo (*Juicy Parts, Couch Potato Guide to Life,* etc.) posted warnings about Woodside's practices on the newsgroup, whereupon Woodside retaliated with a blizzard of "spam" messages from multiple Internet service providers (ISPs). James Leonard, writing as "Doctor-Day," followed that campaign with an August 1996 message warning would-be writers to "stay clear" of Jack Mingo, falsely claiming that "his manuscript has been rejected by all literary agencies" and that Mingo therefore sought to frustrate competitors by defaming honest agents.

In response to Woodside's attacks, Jayne Hitchcock sent the firm another book proposal, using the pen name "Anne Doyle." Woodside sent another enthusiastic response, this time doubling the price of their reading fee to $150. By December 1996, as complaints against Woodside multiplied on Usenet, the company launched another spam offensive against misc.writing and several similar newsgroups. One of the messages traced to Woodside was forged in Jayne Hitchcock's name, including her home address and telephone number with an invitation for sado-masochistic sexual fantasies. At the same time, Woodside initiated a campaign of E-MAIL BOMBING against Hitchcock, her husband, her new literary agent, and the Maryland college where she was employed.

Hitchcock filed a civil lawsuit against Woodside for aggravated harassment in January 1997, naming the agency and two of its officers—James Leonard and Ursula Sprachman—as defendants. By early February 1997, the war of attrition against Hitchcock had expanded into "snail mail," with various magazine subscriptions, CD club memberships, and similar mail-order purchases forged in her name. The campaign was costly for Woodside, however, as the agency was dropped from one ISP after another, including AOL, CompuServe, IDT, IBM and Prodigy. Trying another tack, Ursula Sprachman complained to the FBI that Jack Mingo had threatened her life. (Two agents interviewed Mingo at his California home and the complaint was later dismissed.) Sprachman filed similar complaints about Jayne Hitchcock with the FBI, the Maryland attorney general's office and the Maryland State Police, but each in turn was dismissed.

On the legal front, U.S. District Judge Nina Gershon rejected Woodside's motion to dismiss Jayne Hitchcock's lawsuit in April 1997. Hitchcock, meanwhile, found sympathetic ears in Maryland's state legislature and helped promote a law to punish e-mail harassment with three years' imprisonment and/or a $500 fine. (The bill was passed in April 1998 and took effect six months later.) Woodside resurfaced on Usenet in May 1997, using a Florida address and the name Photo Phoenix International to solicit new clients, but the ruse was soon exposed and "Photo Phoenix" joined its parent company as an Internet pariah. On November 27, 1997 the New York attorney general's office filed its own civil suit against Woodside for false advertising, deceptive business practices, fraud and harassment. Woodside briefly rallied with a countersuit against Jayne Hitchcock, in June 1998, but the end was near. By the time New York County Supreme Court Justice Abdus-Salaam pronounced Woodside guilty of misleading clients and misrepresenting its services, in February 1999, the agency had closed up shop. Jayne Hitchcock, victorious, had meanwhile gone on to create the volunteer watchdog organization known as WORKING TO HALT ONLINE ABUSE (WHOA).

WORKING to Halt Online Abuse:
Internet watchdog group

A volunteer organization created in 1997, WHOA (or WHO@) describes its mission as an ongoing effort "to educate the Internet community about on-line harassment, empower victims of harassment, and formulate voluntary policies that systems administrators can adopt in order to create harassment-free environments." To that end, its members work with victims of on-line harassment in ways similar to the techniques of CYBERANGELS. Founder and president Jayne Hitchcock, a freelance journalist, was inspired to create WHOA after her own experience with harassment by the WOODSIDE LITERARY AGENCY. Today, she speaks frequently at training seminars convened by law enforcement agencies and other interested groups. Hitchcock and her volunteers also lobby state and federal legislators in support of new and stricter laws against CYBERSTALKING and similar crimes. WHOA's website lists the groups long-term goals as follows:

1. To educate the Internet community about harassment and means of prevention.
2. To empower targets of harassment in their own defense.
3. To provide model policies for a better Internet community, including bans on threats of any kind or posting of any potentially libelous material.

WORLD Record E-mail Contest: Internet hoax

Staffers for the *Guinness Book of World Records* confirm that this Internet chain letter, launched in May 1999, is a hoax with no validity whatever. Simple logic dictates that tracking and counting of e-mails such as that described would be impossible, meaning that no world record could be verified. The original text reads:

If we keep this going until September 9th, 1999 (9-9-99), I PROMISE YOU that everyone's name who this was sent to will be in the Guinness Book of Records. AND I HAVE PROOF! I e-mailed them and told them I would start one and they said they'd save a spot for all of us in the 2000 Special addition! So, if we keep this going. . . . We'll all be a part of the book. . . . So please, have some heart and send this to a few people. It would really be nice. You get something out of it too! So, send this right now to everyone you know on-line!

Thanks very much!

"WORM.INFO": computer viruses

Three variants of the "Worm.Info" virus had been documented since December 1996, all memory-resident, encrypted stealth worm viruses, rated "not dangerous" by software analysts. Each variant announces its arrival by displaying a message on the new host computer's monitor screen, as follows:

Worm.Info.2141—

-*- INFOSYSTEM -*-
version 1.04
(C) 1995 by Ziff Co.
Reading System Information . . .
Computer type: IBM PC

Worm.Info.2191—

InfoSystem version1.01
Reading System Information . . .
Computer type: IBM PC

Worm.Info.2259—

Reading System Information . . .
Computer type: IBM PC

After thus declaring itself, each virus then checks the type of computer and displays one of the following strings:

AT
Convertible
Junior
Original
PS/2
Unknown
XT

Next, this message is displayed on the host computer's monitor:

Checking HDD controller . . .
SCSI controller type: Unknown (Error14)

The Worm.Info variants then proceed with infection, searching the host's directories and writing its code to newly created info.com files. It next begins to search for .bat (batch) files in the various directories and writes the following commands to the beginning of each one found:

```
@if not exist info.com goto noinfo
@info>nul
:noinfo
```

On Friday the 13th, Worm.Info plays a prank on its host by changing the video ports on the infected host computer's Video Graphics Array (VGA).

"XALNAGA": computer virus

Initially reported from the Internet in December 2000, "Xalnaga" is a Windows "Trojan horse" virus that modifies certain registry keys on the infected host computer, thereby removing icons from the desktop and making it impossible to restart the computer by normal methods. Xalnaga modifies registry keys with the following codes and results:

Key 1 Removes all standard desktop icons—

HKEY_CURRENT_USER\Software\Microsoft\Windows\CurrentVersion\Policies\Explorer
NoDesktop = 1

Key 2 Removes the "Start" menu items "Run," "Find," and "Shut Down"—

HKEY_CURRENT_USER\Software\Microsoft\Windows\CurrentVersion\Winlogon
NoRun = 1
NoFind = 1
NoClose = 1

Key 3 Disables the standard WinNT registry editors:

HKEY_CURRENT_USER\Software\Microsoft\Windows\CurrentVersion\Policies\System
DisableRegistryTools = 1

Key 4 Displays a message (see below) on startup—

HKEY_LOCAL_MACHINE\Software\Microsoft\Windows\CurrentVersion\Winlogon
LegalNoticeCaption = <<< Xal Naga was here >>>
LegalNoticeText = The human era has come to an end, the new breed of humans will evolve right now!!! Behold and despair!!!

A bug in Xalnaga prevents its alteration of Key 3 from taking effect as intended by the virus writer, and it is possible to repair the altered keys by following these steps:

1. Run "Regedit.exe"
2. Select "Start\Programs\Windows Explorer"
3. Find and run "Regedit.exe"
4. Set the affected keys for "0" or delete them.

"XANAX": computer worm

Named for a popular prescription tranquilizer, "Xanax" is an Internet worm discovered in March 2001. Like so many other Internet viruses, it spreads via e-mail by sending infected messages from host computers or by mailing a copy of itself to Internet Relay Chat (IRC) channels. In addition to mass replication, Xanax also infects .exe files in a host computer's Windows directory.

Xanax is essentially an .exe file written in Microsoft Visual C++ language, which copies itself into a new host's Windows system registry with two names: xanax.exe and xanstart.exe. The latter file is next registered into the host registry's auto-run key, so that Xanax is automatically run each time Windows is booted. As soon as infection is achieved, the worm initiates its e-mail replication routine, gaining access to Microsoft Outlook's address book and sending infected messages to the first 1,000 addresses found there. The message appears as follows:

Message Subject: Stressed? Try Xanax!

Text: Hi there! Are you so stressed that it makes you ill? You're not alone! Many people suffer from stress, these days. Maybe you find Prozac too strong? Then you NEED to try Xanax, it's milder. Still not convinced? Check out the medical details in the attached file. Xanax might change your life!

File Attachments: xanax.exe

At the same time, Xanax searches its new host computer for any connections to an IRC system and, if found, thereafter sends a copy of itself to everyone who logs on. Meanwhile, it scours the host's Windows directory for .exe files and infects some of those found by writing itself to the beginning of each. Files whose names begin with the letters E, P, R, S, T and W are apparently immune to Xanax infection. When Xanax is run from a file with "R" as the penultimate letter in its name, the following message is displayed on-screen:

Xanax
8-Chloro-1-methyl-6-phenyl-4H-s-triazolo (4,3-alpha)(1,4) benzodiazepine

As a "bonus" of sorts, Xanax also creates three new files within the host computer's system: hostfile.exe appears in the Windows system directory, while winstart.bat and xanax.sys are found in the Windows directory. hostfile.exe contains an uninfected version of the last file run, while xanax.sys includes this text string: "Win32.HLLP.Xanax (c) 2001 Gigabyte." The winstart.bat file orders its host to display the following message on-screen:

Do not take this medication with ethanol, Buspar (buspirone), TCA antidepressants, narcotics, or other CNS

depressants. This combination can increase CNS depression. Be sure not to take other sedative, benzodiazepines, or sleeping pills with this drug. The combinations could be fatal. Do not smoke or drink alcohol when taking Xanax. Alcohol can lower blood pressure and decrease your breathing rate to the point of unconsciousness. Tobacco and marijuana smoking can add to the sedative effects of Xanax.

XIE, Jing Ping: convicted software pirate

Jing Ping Xie was a resident of Maryland, employed as a research scientist with the National Institutes of Health (NIH) in November 1997, when he began to moonlight with a second career in software piracy. Xie's wife, Shenglan Liu, assisted him in the illicit scheme to reproduce copyrighted computer software on compact disks and sell them on three different Internet websites, accessed via Xie's computer at the NIH. The operation continued until June 1999, with the couple advertising their illicit products on the Internet. Buyers were required to send Xie an e-mail reading "I swear I am not a law enforcement officer, [and] I can not use the coming CD(s), by any means, against the CD maker." Personal checks were refused as payment, in Xie's words, "for both our protection." Software programs offered for sale at rates far below their legitimate retail price included Adobe Acrobat and Pagemaker, Microsoft Office 97 Pro and Visual Basic5, and Symantec Norton Utilities, among others.

Xie and his wife typically sold programs valued at $4,000 for as little as $40, but the bargain-basement sales still produced a tidy sum. Between December 1997 and May 1999, income from bootleg software sales exceeded Xie's legitimate NIH salary by some $47,000, according to the couple's banking records. On June 2, 1999, federal agents and county sheriff's deputies raided Xie's apartment, confiscating more than 300 CDs containing 2,903 software programs (labeled "Xie's Collection"), 165 blank CDs, plus more than $7,000 in cash and money orders. Xie, who possessed four college degrees, including a Ph.D. in molecular biology, was proficient in three computer languages and had a working knowledge of four others, thus facilitating his bootleg scheme. Shenglan Liu, though a physician in her native China, had worked only menial jobs in the U.S. prior to helping Xie launch their excursion into software piracy.

Both defendants pleaded guilty to federal copyright violations on March 16, 2001, facing a maximum penalty of five years in prison and a $250,000 fine. Sentencing was scheduled for July 20, 2001, but a full year later, in July 2002, the Department of Justice's website lists the sentences of Xie and Lie as "TBD"— To Be Determined at some unknown future date.

"XM": computer viruses

This memory-resident, encrypted parasitic virus was written in Russia and found "in the wild" during June 1998. It writes itself to the end of .com and .exe files (except command.com) as they are opened, executed, or renamed. In roughly one-eighth of all cases, the virus—rated "not dangerous" by computer analysts—also displays the following message on-screen: "[XyeBo_MHe], (c) Midnigh+Pr0wler."

A separate and distinct XM virus, dubbed "XM.2379," is rated as a "dangerous," memory-resident, polymorphic parasitic virus with built-in anti-debugging routines. XM.2379 also writes itself to the end of .com and .exe files as they are executed, passing over command.com, dos4gw.exe and ibmio.com. At the same time, it scans the host computer's c:\autoexec.bat file and infects various files listed therein.

"X-RAY": computer virus

Discovered on the Internet in August 1996, "X-Ray" is a memory-resident, encrypted, parasitic virus that writes itself to the ends of .com and .exe files as they are accessed, simultaneously deleting the antivirus programs anti-vir.dat and chklist.ms if they are installed on the host computer. The virus encrypts its Terminate and Stay Resident (TSR) code to avoid detection and may appear under any of the following names:

AVP.
AVPV
BAIT
CHEC
CLEA
CPAV
-D.C
DEBU
F-PR
GOAT
ITAV
MSAV
NAV.

ORGA
PCSC
PROS
PV.E
SCAN
TBAV
TBCL
TBDI
TBDR
TBFI
TBGE
TBKE
TBLO
TBME
TBSC
TBSE
TBUT
TD.E
TEST
THDP
-U.C
VDS.
VIRS
VPRO
VPRU
XRAY

X-Ray also displays the following message on-screen, the timing of its appearance determined by the host system's date and time:

The X-Ray virus sends greetings to everyone who is reading this text . . . No panic, I'm harmless!

"XUXA": computer viruses

Initially reported in September 1996, at least eight variants of the "Xuxa" virus are currently recognized, identified as Xuxa.1037, 1045, 1088, 1096, 1405, 1413, 1984, and 2058. All are memory-resident viruses that infect various files on host computers, but they are rated "not dangerous" by expert analysts.

Xuxa.1037, 1088, and 1096 are encrypted viruses which write themselves to the ends of executed .com files (excluding command.com). They also delete the antivirus files anti-vir.dat and chklist.ms if found, while infecting the host computer's c:\dos\format.com file and may freeze the computer, depending on the time of day when infection occurs. Xuxa.1037 contains the following Spanish text strings:

Si no viste el Show de Xuxa por T.V, ni en vivo . . . ahora podes verlo en tu PC!.—XOU DA XUXA 1.0 By Leviathan.

Xuxa.1088 and 1096 display the following message, also in Spanish:

Si no viste el Show de Xuxa por T.V, ni en vivo . . . ahora podes verlo en tu PC!.—XOU DA XUXA 1.2 By Leviathan.

Xuxa.1405 and 1413 write themselves to the beginnings of .com files as they are executed and also play a musical tune over the host computer's speakers. Xuxa.1045 displays the following message in Spanish:

Si no viste el Show de Xuxa por T.V, ni en vivo . . . ahora podes verlo en tu PC!.—XOU DA XUXA 1.3 By Leviathan.

Xuxa.1656 writes itself to the ends of both .com and .exe files as they are executed. It displays the following message on various occasions, determined by the host computer's time and date:

Xuxa Park 1.0 _ By Hades "Y luchemos para que todos los niños delmundo tengan derecho a soñar, a soñar por igual"

Xuxa.1984 and 2058 are encrypted stealth viruses that write themselves to the ends of .com and .exe files that have been executed or closed, also deleting the antivirus programs anti-vir.dat and chklist.ms if

they are found. Data compression utilities are not infected, but both variants contain internal bugs that sometimes freeze the host computer. On the 27th day of every month, these viruses display the following messages:

Xuxa.1984—

_ XUXA PARK 2.0 _ By Hades _ Todo el mundo esta feliz?

Xuxa.2058—

XUXA PARK 2.1 _ BY HADES "Y LUCHEMOS PARA QUE TODOS LOS NIÑOS DEL MUNDO TENGAN DERECHO A SOÑAR, A SOÑAR POR IGUAL"

"XXX": computer virus

Reported for the first time on October 1996, this memory-resident parasitic virus is rated "very dangerous" by computer analysts. It writes itself to the beginnings of .com files accessed by the DOS functions FindNext FCB and ASCII, corrupting those it infects to render them useless. On the 19th day of any month, XXX also reformats various disk sectors of the infected host computer and displays the following message on-screen:

My dear xxx:
Happy birthday and happy a new year!
Yours xxx.

YANG, David Tzu Wvi See HSU, EUGENE

"YANKEE/VACSINA": computer viruses
Initially reported in January 1998, this family of non-memory-resident parasitic viruses now includes more than 40 recognized variants, treated collectively by expert analysts and deemed "not dangerous." Variants numbered 1 through 25 infect executed .com and .exe files; numbers 26 and above infect .com and .exe files that are loaded into the host computer's memory. Variants numbered 1 through 23 infect .exe files in an unusual fashion, by transforming them into the format of .com files, revising the file's address and adding 132 bytes of virus code to each infected file. The alteration leaves .exe files vulnerable to later infection by other viruses that normally attack .com files.

The viruses in this family produce sound effects on their host computers. Yankee erratically plays the melody to "Yankee Doodle Dandy," either at 5:00 P.M. on selected days or when the user presses the Alt-Ctrl-Del keys simultaneously. Vacsina, meanwhile, is satisfied with the sound of a chiming bell. On some occasions, "Vacsina.06" also displays an on-screen message reading "Az sum vasta lelja." A curious side effect of these viruses is their built-in inclination to attack certain other viruses if found within the host. Versions 2 and 3 take various measures against the "Cascade" virus and also deactivate the memory-resident portions of the "PingPong" virus.

From the sheer proliferation of viruses in this family, experts report that many—perhaps most—were created by copycat authors, primarily in Russia. Some of the more peculiar variants include:

Yankee.1905 First seen in Irkutsk, Russia, it presents a message challenging "Yankee.53" with a claim to the latter variant's numerical designation. (No reason for the dispute is known, but it may suggest a personal feud between independent virus writers.)
Yankee.2189 At unpredictable times, it "rolls" (inverts) the various symbols—, / , \ , and |.
Yankee.3045 Contains text strings reading "LOGIN.EXE SUPERVISOR. HESLO."
Yankee.Estonia.1716 At 2:00 P.M. on any Monday, it displays an on-screen message reading "Independent Estonia presents," then plays a short tune and restarts the infected host computer.
Yankee.Flip.2167 On various programmed dates it "flips" the monitor screen, inverting images and text displayed there.

YARIMAKA, Igor See ZEZOV, OLEG

"YB": computer viruses
First logged in November 1996, the "YB" family of nonmemory-resident parasitic viruses today includes

at least 13 recognized variants, all rated "harmless" by expert analysts. All versions search for .com files and write themselves to the ends of any that are found. Variant YV.402 displays random data on the monitor screen and freezes the infected host computer, while YB.405 creates empty directories. These viruses contain the following text strings:

YB.299 and 300: INSERT YOUR NAME HERE
*.?OM
YB.316: Silent Runner by Nostradamus [NuKE'94]
YB.402 and 405: \DOS Abraxas 13
00000001. OUCH!
YB.425, 426 and 466: YB-1 & Handsome Dick
Manitoba/Köhntark*.com
YB.647 and 2277: YB-2/Köhntark*.com
YB.2328 and 2330: YB-1/Köhntark*.com
YB.Funkware.235: AV Funkware Evaluation League of
[NuKE'94]*.c?m

"YEKE": computer viruses

A family of memory-resident, parasitic encrypted viruses, initially reported in December 1996, all "Yeke" variants are rated "dangerous" by computer analysts. They uniformly write themselves to the ends of executed .exe files, but deliver various payloads following infection. Some variants play a tune, then freeze the infected host computer after displaying a message that reads: "Be Careful. YEKE Controls Your Computer." One version, dubbed "Yeke.2425," erases the computer's Complementary Metal-Oxide Semiconductor (CMOS) and various disk sectors, while playing a tune and displaying this message on-screen:

TERMINATOR 2 lives . . .
The Judgement Day has come!
Your system has been terminated.

"YOSHA": computer viruses

There are presently two separate virus families that share the "Yosha" label, including a total of 11 known variants between them. The first family, recognized since April 1998, includes eight DOS viruses with different impacts and danger ratings from computer analysts. Those variants include:

Yosha.745 A memory-resident, parasitic virus that writes itself to the ends of executed .exe

files, rated "not dangerous" by experts. It deletes the antivirus files anti-vir.dat and chk-lis5t.ms if they are found on the infected host computer. Finally, it creates a file named c:\win.com and there writes a program that displays an on-screen message reading: "Windoze crashes your system." It contains the following German text strings:

Kein Mehrheit für die Mitleid
KMFDM by Yosha/DC

Yosha.975 and 980 Ranked "dangerous" by analysts, these memory-resident, encrypted parasitic stealth viruses both write themselves to the ends of closed or executed .com files, also deleting the protective anti-vir.dat file if it exists on the infected host computer. These viruses also search for the Microsoft CD file in the computer's current directory and eject any disk in the machine, while displaying an on-screen message that reads: "Give Yosha cold Mountain Dew!" Both contain the text string "[Dew-Bug] (C) 1996 Yosha/DC."

Yosha.LT Described as a "dangerous," memory-resident, parasitic virus, this Yosha variant writes itself to the host computer's Interrupt Vectors Table, as well as to the ends of various .com files. Some of the infected files are corrupted and thus rendered useless. Yosha.LT contains a text string reading: "Malaria by Yosha/LT."

Yosha.MDK An encrypted, memory-resident overwriting virus, classified as "very dangerous" by analysts, this variant copies itself to the host computer's DOS data area and overwrites various files as they are executed. Disk sectors are also randomly erased, based on the host system's timer. Yosha.MDK contains the text string "Murder-Death-Kill by Yosha/tCS/DC."

Yosha.Smegma Depending on the reader's point of view, this virus derives its name either from the Greek term for "cleansing medicine" or the common name for a greasy discharge found on unwashed human genitals. In either case, it is a memory-resident, parasitic polymorphic virus, rated "harmless" by computer experts. The variant writes itself to the ends of .com and .exe files as they are executed, opened or accessed via the host computers Get/Set File Attribute DOS function. It contains the text string "[Smegma] by Yosha," but presents no manifestations of itself.

Yosha.Stercor Continuing the trend begun by its predecessor, this variant derives its name from the Latin term for dung. It is a memory-resident, companion stealth virus, deemed "not dangerous" by analysts, that creates "companion" .com files when .exe files are accessed on the host computer. Various video effects may be displayed, depending on the system's timer. Yosha.Stercor contains a text string reading: "Stercor by Yosha[LT/RSA]."

Yosha.Zadig A "harmless," memory-resident, polymorphic virus, this version writes itself to the ends of executed .com files. It contains the text string "Zadig by Yosha[LT]."

The second family of Yosha viruses, recognized since August 2000, includes three variant forms. Once again, their actions and danger ratings vary widely from one version to the next. They include:

Yosha.440 A memory-resident, multipartite virus, rated "harmless," it writes itself to the Master Boot Record (MBR) of the host computer when an infected file is executed. Thereafter, the virus loads from the infected MBR, writing itself to the ends of .com files as they are opened or executed. It contains the text string "ELDOB1X by Yosha/DC."

Yosha.512 A stealth virus that infects .exe files and the MBR of the host computer's hard drive, this version is ranked by experts as "very dangerous." Infected disk sectors are also corrupted, ultimately rendering them useless. The virus also decreases system memory by altering the size of infected .exe files.

Yosha.Novacane Like its predecessor, this variant also infects .exe files and the host computer's Master Boot Record, but it earns a "harmless" rating from computer analysts. It contains the text string "NovaCane by Yosha/DC."

"YUKOM": computer viruses

Initially reported from the Internet in June 1996, this family of viruses included three variants, all ranked as "dangerous," nonmemory-resident, parasitic viruses. They seek out .com and .exe files, writing themselves to the end of each file located, with numerous bugs in the different versions frequently crashing infected host computers. Erratic sound effects also occur, depending on the host system's date. Yukom's variants include the following similar text strings (suggesting that the virus's name may be a clumsy misspelling of "Yukon"):

> *Yukom.389: My Name is Yukom Pete and I am a Virus*
> *Yukom.392: My Name is Yukom Pete and I am your Virus*
> *Yukom.402: My Name is Yukom Pete and I am your unfriendly Virus*

"YZ": computer viruses

These memory-resident, parasitic viruses, initially described in November 1996, include three variants, all rated "very dangerous" by expert analysts. They write themselves to the ends of executed .com and .exe files, erasing infected disk sectors on March 8 and displaying a message that reads: "It is my birthday!!!" Version YZ.1230 presents that message at 3:00 P.M., while times may vary for the other versions. YZ.1339 and YZ.1434 accompany the on-screen announcement with beeping sounds from the host computer's speakers.

Z

ZAIN, Fred Salem: police chemist accused of fraud

A troubling case of apparent official malfeasance, reminiscent of the JOYCE GILCHRIST scandal in Oklahoma, involves serologist Fred Zain, employed for 13 years at the West Virginia State Police crime laboratory, and afterward in Texas. Like Gilchrist, Zain stands accused of faking test results and testifying falsely under oath in numerous felony cases, sending numerous innocent defendants to prison. Once revered as "a god" by West Virginia prosecutors, Zain was totally discredited in 1993, when West Virginia's Supreme Court ordered a review of every case on which he worked, ruling that "as a matter of law, any testimonial or documentary evidence offered by Zain at any time should be deemed invalid, unreliable and inadmissible."

Zain began his tenure at the West Virginia crime lab in 1977, at age 26, quickly building a reputation as an expert who could nail down even the most difficult cases, assuring prosecutors of convictions with a scientific basis. District attorneys who adored Zain were presumably unaware of his curious tactics, but the same cannot be said about his supervisors at the laboratory. In some cases he testified to positive results for tests the crime lab could not even perform, since it lacked the necessary equipment, but none of his superiors came forward to correct him. In 1985, FBI lab director James Greer informed Zain's boss that Zain had lied about his credentials to obtain the West Virginia post—he had, in fact, failed basic courses in forensic serology and bio-

chemical methods of testing bloodstains—but Zain remained on the job. At least two other crime lab employees also complained to their superiors about Zain's methods, and they likewise were ignored. Zain's public reputation began to unravel in 1991, after alleged rapist GLEN WOODALL—convicted chiefly on Zain's testimony in 1987—was exonerated by DNA evidence.

Fred Zain, meanwhile, had left West Virginia for Bexar County, Texas—coincidentally the scene of numerous false autopsy reports filed by pathologist RALPH ERDMANN—in 1989, where he served as chief of physical evidence for the county's medical examiner. Alerted by the West Virginia controversy, Texas prosecutors charged Zain with perjury and jury tampering in one of his cases, but the charge was thrown out on grounds that the statute of limitations had expired. Around the same time, in 1994, Zain was indicted for perjury in Marion County, West Virginia, a grand jury concluding that he lied during the 1991 rape and robbery trial of defendant Paul Walker. (West Virginia prosecutors continued to use Zain's testimony even after he left the state for Texas.) One count of the perjury indictment was dismissed prior to trial, jurors acquitted Zain of a second charge, and deadlocked on the third (an accusation that he lied under oath regarding fees he received for a double-murder trial). Another West Virginia grand jury, in Kanawha County, indicted Zain again in March 1998, but Judge Andrew Mac-Queen dismissed the charges nine months later, on grounds that the state government could not be a legal victim of fraud. The state supreme court reversed that ruling in 1999, and Zain also faces a new trial in Texas, though legal delays have postponed both events beyond press time.

Zain, for his part, denies any wrongdoing in even a single case, much less the hundreds in which he stands accused of falsifying evidence. In a rare 1997 interview with reporter Sandy Wells, Zain claimed that he "would never want anybody put in jail—having been through trial myself—who was innocent of what he is being charged with." Rather than taking personal responsibility for years of false testimony, Zain advanced the novel defense of blaming various prosecutors who put him on the witness stand, as well as his supervisors at the West Virginia crime lab. He was, Zain claimed, an innocent "scapegoat" for the sins of others. Defense attorney Sam Bayless, meanwhile, seemed ready to admit that his client had testified falsely in various cases, but told reporters in September 2001, "I think there's no criminal intent."

Whether he finally avoids prison or not, however, more court battles loom in Zain's future. Jack W. Davis, a Texas defendant falsely convicted of murder on Zain's testimony, has filed a civil lawsuit against Zain, seeking $10 million in damages for the time he wrongfully spent in prison.

"ZAMOL": computer viruses

Initially reported from the Internet in December 1997, the "Zamol" virus now exists in at least five variant forms. All are memory-resident, partly encrypted, parasitic viruses that write themselves to the beginnings of .com files and to the ends of .exe files as they are opened or executed. Files are temporarily renamed during infection by these viruses. Three of the variants—Zamol.2024, Zamol.3390, and Zamol.4358—rename files as "acula.trs"; the other variants, Zamol.2153 and Zamol.2743, rename their infected files as "++++++.!!!"

While Zamol.2024 presents no manifestations of itself on the infected host computer, the other four variants make themselves known in various ways—playing tunes, disabling the "Enter" and "Delete" keys, blocking access to the computer's floppy disk drive, and overwriting hard disk sectors with programs that display various messages on-screen. Some of those messages include the following (errors uncorrected):

Zamol.2153—

> Greetings from Timishoara !
> Call 040-96-113821

Zamol.2743—

> ZAMOLXIS VIRUS
> Se dedică mortilor din DEC. 89!
> Nu se dedică lui Ion Iliescu!
> Romania Timisoara 1994/am!
> Liceul de Informatica Grigore Moisil

Zamol.3390—

> ROMANIAN 13 VIRUS
> Dedicate to Bosnia-Hertegovina
> and special for romanian youngs
> dead in "The War For Liberty."
> Romania Timisoara 1994/am !
>
> Timisoara phone: 040/096/
>
> "DRACULA's spirit"
> original scotch by Transilvania . . .
> . . . call "Transilvania General Import/Export"
>
> "RIO" soft drink! Quality guaranted!
> Romania Timisoara cod 1900 Ghirlandei nr. 4
>
> To everytime Whores! Call 166894. (Taxi Bimbo)
>
> "Eco Tours"! More a man dead! (123450)

"ZAPPER": computer virus

Reported for the first time in May 1996, "Zapper" is a nonmemory-resident, encrypted parasitic virus that searches for .com and .exe files, writing itself to the beginnings of any it finds on an infected host computer. In the process, Zapper creates a temporary file named c:cX1849.com. It earns a "dangerous" rating from computer analysts by erasing various disk sectors and deleting the following files:

> *.D??
> f:\public\chklist.*
> c:\dos\chklist.ms

Zapper contains the following text strings that may assist in its identification:

*.com
*.exe
c:\dos\format.com
f:\public\map.exe
ZAPPER

ZEZOV, Oleg and Yarimaka, Igor: international hackers
On August 10, 2000, two citizens of Kazakhstan were arrested in London, on charges of penetrating Bloomberg L.P.'s computer system in New York City, attempting to extort money from the Bloomberg financial empire. The HACKERS were identified as 27-year-old Oleg Zezov (a.k.a. "Oleg Dzezev") and 37-year-old Igor Yarimaka, both residents of Almaty, Kazakhstan.

According to the charges filed against them, Zezov sent various e-mails to Michael Bloomberg, founder and owner of Bloomberg L.P., demanding $200,000 in exchange for information concerning the penetration of Bloomberg's computer network. Bloomberg replied with a suggestion that they meet in London, whereupon Zezov—writing as "Alex"—demanded the establishment of an offshore bank account with a deposit of $200,000 prior to the meeting. Bloomberg complied, establishing an account with the Deutsche Bank in London, after which Zezov and Yarimaka flew from Kazakhstan to London on August 6, 2000. Four days later, they met with Bloomberg and two London police officers posing as Bloomberg board members. In that meeting, Yarimaka claimed to be a former Kazakhstan prosecutor, now in private practice, who represented "Alex" in the pending transaction. Both would-be extortionists were arrested and held without bail, while U.S. authorities processed a formal extradition request.

Prosecutors determined that Zezov had gained access to the international Bloomberg computer network in the spring of 1999, while employed by Kazkommerts Securities, in Almaty. Bloomberg L.P. had provided Kazkommerts with database services called "Open Bloomberg," which granted access to the firm's system at large. From there, Zezov used his computer skills to ferret out classified data which, if released, might have seriously damaged Bloomberg's business.

Zezov and Yarimaka were extradited from London to New York on May 21, 2002, each facing charges of unauthorized computer intrusion, conspiracy, extortion, and interfering with commerce by using extortion. If convicted on all counts, each defendant faces a maximum penalty of 28 years in prison and a $250,000 fine (or double the gross pecuniary loss resulting from the crimes committed in each count). Trial is pending on the charges, and federal prosecutors stress that indictments are merely accusations of criminal activity, not proof of guilt. All defendants are presumed innocent until convicted at trial.

"ZHENGXI": computer virus
A polymorphic, stealth, parasitic virus, reported initially in November 1997, "Zhengxi" is rated "very dangerous" by expert analysts, described in some publications as the most complex DOS virus thus far discovered. Zhengxi infects .exe, Library (lib), and Object (obj) files, also attaching .com-droppers to certain compressed files located on the host computer (.arj, .rar, and .zip archives). It contains the following text strings:

*Abnormal program termination
The Virus/DOS 0.54 Copyright (c) 1995 Zhengxi Ltd
Warning! This program for internal use only!*

Zhengxi's installation routine is apparently foiled if the intended host computer has Microsoft Windows installed, if its boot drive is either A: or B:, or if the host's date and time stamp represents the current date of attempted installation.

When successfully installed, Zhengxi infects .exe files by three distinct methods, variously appending its code to some, inserting the code into others, or infecting archives of self-extracting files (.arj, .rar, or .zip files). Files shorter than 1,024 bytes are ignored, while Zhengxi attaches itself to the ends of files between that length and 32K; in the case of files longer than 32K the virus inserts itself at some point following the first 6K of data. Archives are attacked by the insertion of infected .com-droppers, randomly titled with such names as doo.com, haif.com, vlg.com, and so forth. When attacking .zip files, the virus targets only those created since 1996, deleting both the files and their entire subdirectory tree.

"ZHENGZHOU": computer viruses
This family of Chinese viruses, initially reported in October 1996, presently contains three variant forms. All are memory-resident, multipartite viruses, rated "very dangerous" by computer analysts. They write themselves to the ends of executed .com and

.exe files, then proceed to infect the host computer's Master Boot Record (MBR) while the affected files are working. The variant ZhengZhou.3576 also infects the boot sectors of floppy disks, while ZhengZhou.3584.b deletes the wmset.com file (but ignores the files clean.exe and scan.exe). Various hard-drive sectors of infected host computers are erased at random intervals by these viruses. The variant ZhengZhou.3584.a attempts to reformat the hard drive but fails due to internal bugs, displaying an on-screen message that reads:

> *Do not turn OFF the computer when WOLF is working!*
> *Insert DOS diskette in drive A:*
> *Strike any key when ready . . .*

ZhengZhou.3584.a also contains the following text strings:

> *Zheng Zhou, China. 1993*
> *Thank for your helping, Good-bye!*

"ZOMBIE": computer viruses

Four different computer viruses are presently identified by variations of the "Zombie" label. The first, reported in November 1997, is "Zombie.4584," a nonmemory-resident, encrypted Windows 95 virus rated "not dangerous" by expert analysts. Upon invading a new host computer, it searches the Windows directory for New.exe Portable Executable files in the C:. D:, E:, and F: drives, infecting each one found. The infection routine includes creation of a new file section labeled with the .zombie suffix. Various zsetup.exe files are also created in the host system, containing Zombie's virus code. It includes the following text strings:

> *ExitProcess FindFirstFileA FindNextFileA CreateFileA-*
> *   SetFilePointer*
> *ReadFile WriteFile CloseHandle GetCurrentDirectoryA-*
> *   SetCurrentDirectoryA*
> *GetWindowsDirectoryA GetCommandLineA WinExec*
> *GetFileInformationByHandle*

> *.Z0MBiE*
> *Z0MBiE 1.01 (c) 1997*
> *My 2nd virii for mustdie*
> *Tnx to S.S.R.*
> *\ZSetUp.EXE*

A new family of Zombie viruses, including three variant forms, was reported from the Internet in June 1999. The first version identified, "Zombie.3592," is described by experts as a "dangerous," nonmemory-resident, polymorphic parasitic virus that writes itself to the ends of .com files (ignoring those with the names adinf*.*, aids*.*, avp*.*, .command*.*, drweb*.*, emm386*.* and web*.*). It also contains a program to erase the host computer's Complementary Metal-Oxide Semiconductor (CMOS), but internal bugs prevent that function from working.

Another variant, dubbed "Zombie.PM.4592," is a nonmemory-resident, polymorphic parasitic virus that writes itself to the ends of .com files. Internal text strings include the lyrics from a 1990 rock song by The Scorpions, "Wind of Change," in addition to the following text:

> *z0mbie$$.$$$*
> *Z0MBiE.PGPMorph Version 1.00 (c) 1997, 1998*
> *   Z0MBiE International*
> *Now we can infect Dr.WEB addons . . .*
> *homepage: http://www.chat.ru/~z0mbie*
> *e-mail: z0mbie@chat.ru*
> *Scorpions is BEST!*
> *@SONG: WIND OF CHANGE*

The final recognized variant, "Zombie.ZCME .16384," is a nonmemory-resident, parasitic polymorphic virus rated "harmless" by analysts. It searches the host computer's current directory for .com files and writes itself to the beginning of each one located. It contains a text string reading "ZCME 0.01 Z0MBiE's Code Mutation Engine (c) 1997."

ZUCCARINI, John: Internet "mousetrapper"

A resident of Andalusia, Pennsylvania, John Zuccarini was one of the Internet's most prolific "mousetrappers"—a reference to websites that are rigged to snare unsuspecting browsers with a blizzard of pop-up advertisements for various products or services. Zuccarini refined the process by creating dozens of websites with names similar to those of popular products, companies, or celebrities, thus snaring Net "surfers" who misspell the name of their intended destination. Escape from one of Zuccarini's websites was virtually impossible for hapless victims, since the buttons normally used to close the windows were either disabled or rigged to trigger still more rapid-fire advertisements.

Zuccarini was nothing if not industrious. At one time in 2001, according to the Federal Trade Commission (FTC), his 5,500 mousetrap websites included 15 with names similar to that of the Cartoon Network and 41 with variant spellings of pop singer Britney Spears's name. Another of his websites, named after tennis star and fashion model Anna Kournikova, led visitors inexorably to 29 different Internet browser windows. By the FTC's estimate, Zuccarini earned an average of $800,000 to $1 million per year from advertisers seeking a captive audience in cyberspace.

Any thriving business has its risks, and Zuccarini's was no exception. Operating behind 22 different corporate names, many including the word "Cupcake"—Cupcake Incident, Cupcake Messenger, etc.—Zuccarini lost 53 state and federal lawsuits prior to 2001, with some 200 Web addresses transferred by court order to legitimate copyright holders. Finally, in October 2001, the FTC filed what it hoped would be one last lawsuit against Zuccarini, chairman Timothy Muris telling reporters, "Scams that capture consumers and hold them at sites against their will while exposing Internet users, including children, to solicitations for gambling, psychics, lotteries and pornography must be stopped." A federal court agreed on May 29, 2002, filing an order that barred Zuccarini from diverting Net surfers with any sort of unwelcome advertising or promotion and forbade him from launching any further look-alike websites. At the same time, Zuccarini was ordered to refund a substantial portion of his advertising income, which the court termed "ill-gotten gains."

"ZYX": computer virus

Initially reported in July 1996, this is a nonmemory-resident, encrypted parasitic virus, rated "very dangerous" by analysts for its ability to detect and evade antivirus software. Zyx writes itself to the end of any .com and .exe files located on the infected host computer. In the process, it corrupts and/or deletes antivirus files from the system and writes the following message to the beginning of files whose names end in the extensions .asm, .bak, .c, .doc, .me, .pas, or .txt (errors intact):

> To Karen
> In the realm of a greek deity, I dreamt of you.
> A weird reverie,
> Typewriters were like clouds, high in the sky,
> The floor was made of paper,

> Pencils stood for trees,
> A light bulb, low on the horizon, made a perfect sunset.
> And it rained words . . .
> Then you came, more beautiful than ever,
> The only one real in my cyberspace.
> I felt like holding you im my arms, touching your hair,
> Telling you how much I loved you,
> How much I wanted to lose myself in your
>   pretty brown eyes.
> I was almost in heaven.
> Suddenly it was pitch dark,
> The greek god had turned off the PC. It said:
> 'Buddy you're just a damned cyberpunk
>   whose only friends are NPCs.'
> I opened my eyes, it was dawning outside.
> You weren't there.
> I miss you. I really miss you.

> Zyx
> From the slums of
> Beverly Hills.

Zyx contains the following internal text strings:

I'M Wack Oki Dt Heb Rain Child Of Zyx
Stopsnoopingintomywork
Itoldyoutostop
Ifyuwanagoontakesomeflowerstoyourgirltoday&make-
herhappyok
.
Ihateturksazerbaijanisand KARABAGH belongstous
ME M
*.COM *.EXE
SCANVAL.VAL FSIZES.QCV
SCAN.EXE NAV.EXE TBSCAN.EXE
STACKER.COM
COMMAND
CONFIG.SYS
NAV_.NAV&.EM
CHKVIRUS.CFG
NAV_*.*
CHKLIST.MS
VSAFE.
*._XE *._OM
SIGNTURE.DAT
.. OMSPEC=
PAS DOC \ CHKLIST.CPS
BAK ASM
C TXT
Sowhatdidyougainwiseass
wishIhaddonesomethingelse

Glossary

@m Suffix often attached to a computer virus's name, indicating that the virus is a SLOW MAILER.

@mm Suffix frequently attached to the name of a computer virus, identifying it as a MASS MAILER.

alias Describes any of the several names applied to a single computer virus, since there is no standard, universally accepted rule for naming viruses.

anti-antivirus virus Alternative name for a computer RETRO-VIRUS.

anti-emulation A trick employed by some POLYMORPHIC viruses to defeat scanners that employ code EMULATORS to identify and isolate known viruses.

anti-heuristic Techniques employed by virus writers to avoid detection of new viruses by HEURISTIC DETECTION.

antivirus virus Hypothetical technique for making a computer antivirus program viral in itself, to replicate wherever and whenever needed. Reputable antivirus researchers shun the idea as dangerous.

appender/appending virus Any computer virus that inserts a copy of its code at the end of an infected file.

armored virus A computer virus utilizing special tricks to frustrate detection and/or disassembly.

AVED Antivirus Emergency Discussion list: an on-line mailing list for professional computer antivirus researchers, designed for rapid notification of a new virus "crisis" or emergency. A separate list facilitates secure distribution of virus samples for breakdown and analysis.

backdoor A method of accessing a computer system or software application commonly unknown to its legitimate users. Backdoors are typically inserted by a program's developer, but may also be created by HACKERS.

bait file A dummy file written to the drives of a computer to facilitate virus detection. The files are routinely monitored for any changes caused by a computer virus infestation. Also known as "decoy files" and "goat files."

bimorphic virus An encrypted computer virus that has two forms of decryption code, randomly selecting one or the other when writing its decryptor to a newly infected file.

binary code Complex series of 1s and 0s used to write computer programs.

boot infector/boot sector infector Any computer virus that infects the "boot"—startup—sector of any logical drive, whether hard disk or floppy, thereafter preventing the drives from operating properly.

boot sector virus A computer virus that travels on the "boot sector" of computer disks, read on startup from a floppy disk. Infection occurs when a floppy disk is inadvertently left in the computer at startup.

bootlegging Making unauthorized copies of commercial software, prerecorded videocassettes, etc., for illegal resale.

bulletin board A means of on-line communication in which messages are posted by modem to a host computer for later viewing by others.

byte One byte equals eight bits (binary digits) of data, the basic unit of measurement for computer memory.

carders Hackers who specialize in stealing credit card numbers for personal use or resale to others.

CARO Computer Antivirus Research Organization: an informal group of professional antivirus researchers.

cavity infector A computer virus that seeks out "holes" in programs and inserts its code in the gaps. It thus avoids telltale increase in size of files that might otherwise signal a virus at work.

central processing unit (CPU) A computer's "brain," which dictates various functions.

class infector A computer virus whose code resides in one or more of a program's class modules, developed shortly after the release of Word 97.

cluster virus A DOS computer virus that saves its code to a computer's hard drive, rather than attaching it directly to the beginning or end of infected files. Also called "link viruses," since the infection interferes with linkage of cluster chains assigned to a file.

collection virus Alternative name for a ZOO VIRUS.

companion virus A virus that copies itself to a system as a complete program, triggered whenever the program is run. *Program execution order companion* viruses operate from the command-line of DOS and its Windows relatives, activated by command prompts. *Path order companion* viruses rely on a copy of the virus being made in a directory path ahead of the directory housing the target file. A third variety renames target programs to a nonexecutable extension, then copies the virus to the original location, filename, and extension of the target, effectively replacing it.

computer languages Short combinations of letters used by programmers to feed computers their instructions.

constructor kit A program designed to guide nonprogrammers through the steps required to create and unleash their own computer viruses.

cracker Hacker jargon for someone who gains unauthorized access to protected systems; often a pejorative term, contrasting those with criminal motives to "pure hackers."

cybercrime Criminal activity relying for the most part on computers.

cyberethics The ethics of computer use, often honored more in the breach than in observance.

cyberspace A term coined by science-fiction author William Gibson to describe the internal realm of computer networks.

data diddling Unauthorized alteration of computer data, usually for profit or as a form of vandalism.

DDoS "Distributed Denial of Service": a coordinated hack attack by multiple computers on a single system, pooling resources to exhaust bandwidth and memory.

decoy file An alternative name for a BAIT FILE.

DoS "Denial of Service": an attack on a computer system designed to reduce or block service by legitimate users, through techniques of wasting bandwith or memory. Not to be confused with DOS.

DOS Disk operating system: a computer's primary system of operation, whether MS DOS, IBM DOS, or some less common system.

dropper Any program that installs a virus but is not itself infected.

Dumpster diving Raiding trash cans to obtain data, including credit card numbers, computer passwords, financial records, etc.

e-mail virus Described on several Internet websites as a "hoax" or "urban myth," this term refers to any virus transmitted by the simple act of receiving and opening an e-mail, in the absence of infected attachments. Denials notwithstanding, the first straight e-mail virus—BubbleBoy—was identified in 1999.

e-mail worm Misnomer for a MASS MAILER virus.

emulator A common method for detecting POLYMORPHIC viruses. Emulators run a harmless portion of a program's code to see if viruses are thereby triggered and exposed.

encrypted virus An early attempt to evade virus detectors via self-encryption with a variable key.

encryption Coding computer transmissions by means of scrambled data.

entry point obscuring virus Parasitic viruses that bypass headers of an infected file and conceal their point of entry to retard detection. The first viruses to use the technique were "Lucretia" and "Omud."

false positive/false negative Inaccurate readings from a virus scanner, indicating the presence of a virus where none exists or failing to detect one hidden in a system.

fast infector As opposed to "slow infectors," any virus that infects programs not only as they are executed, but also if merely opened or accessed.

fast mailer alternative term for a MASS MAILER.

FAT File Allocation Table: a crucial part of the standard file systems used in all versions of DOS and Windows 9x, which records the chaining of disk clusters and the final cluster in a file.

field sample/field virus   See IN THE FIELD.

file infector   Usually, a virus that attaches itself to (or entirely replaces) .com and/or .exe files, though some have also been identified that infect files with extensions including .bin, .cpl, .dll, .ovl, .sce, and .sys.

file system virus   Synonym for a CLUSTER VIRUS.

generator kit   Synonym for a CONSTRUCTOR KIT.

germ   The first-generation sample of a virus.

ghost positive   A form of FALSE POSITIVE in which erroneous readings by a virus scanner are caused by remnants of a virus detected and falsely reported as an active infection.

gigabyte   A measure of computer memory equal to 1 million bytes.

goat file   A standard synonym for a BAIT FILE or DECOY FILE; some antivirus researchers use the term to describe the "standard" files employed to replicate viruses for study.

"Good Times"   Alleged to be the first e-mail virus capable of infecting target computers without using an attachment, Good Times never existed. The same function is performed, however, by "BubbleBoy" and a few other real-life e-mail viruses presently found on the Internet.

hardware   The physical equipment of a computer system.

hardware damage   A persistent urban myth of cyberspace, contending that software viruses are capable of physically damaging computer hardware.

heuristic detection   The use of "relaxed" scanners that detect suspect codes typically used by virus writers, without making specific identification of a known virus.

hoax   In cyberspace (as elsewhere), any false message, alert, or warning. Internet hoaxes typically warn of a nonexistent virus, solicit funds for some mythical charity, or announce spurious giveaway programs from major companies.

immediate acting   Describes a virus payload that strikes the newly infected host computer as soon as the virus completes self-installation or is initially run (as opposed to waiting for a pre-programmed date or event to trigger the action).

in the field   An intermediate virus dispersal stage found only in a particular, restricted setting (as within the computers of a specific system), as opposed to those IN THE WILD.

in the wild   A reference to viruses widely dispersed on the Internet, sometimes (as with "MELISSA" and others) appearing throughout the world.

in-the-wild lists   Rosters of viruses commonly found "in the wild," prepared and published by antivirus researchers.

joiner   A program that attaches one file to another.

joke program   "Harmless" programs written and transmitted by cyber-pranksters to aggravate their recipients without causing real damage to the affected systems, often by display of a rude or humorous image on-screen.

key logger   Any program that records computer keystrokes, generally used by hackers to steal passwords and other data from unsuspecting victims.

kilobyte (K)   A measure of computer memory equal to 1,024 bytes.

kiting   Use of normal delays in processing financial transactions to make assets appear where none yet exist, employing the bogus assets to secure loans, cover cash withdrawals, etc.

lapping   Employee diversion of incoming cash to a bogus account, while thefts are covered with funds from other incoming accounts. This scam works primarily when one employee (or a group of conspirators) are responsible for both handling cash and recording transactions.

link virus   A synonym for CLUSTER VIRUS.

logic bomb/time bomb   A code that delays execution of a virus payload, typically calling for action on a certain date, at a specific time, or after a predetermined period of time.

macro virus   Any virus featuring instructions in Word Basic, Visual Basic for Applications, or other macro programming languages.

malware   Malicious software, generally including all viruses, worms and Trojans.

mass mailer   A virus that distributes itself via e-mail to multiple addresses captured from the host computer's address book. These are frequently identifiable by the "@mm" suffix attached to a file's name.

master boot record (MBR)   The boot sector at the beginning of a computer's hard drive.

master boot record infector   Any virus that infects a host computer's master boot record.

megabyte (Mb)   A measure of computer memory equal to 1,048,576 bytes.

microchip/microprocessor   Small silicon wafers containing a series of electrical circuits that relay impulses to drive a computer. Expensive brands are frequent targets of counterfeiting.

middle infector   An uncommon synonym for an ENTRY POINT OBSCURING virus.

money laundering   The "cleansing" of illicit income (as from drug sales) through legitimate business accounts, thus enabling criminals to show "normal" sources of income and pay taxes without revealing their true occupations.

multipartite virus   Any virus capable of infecting two or more different types of computer systems (e.g., DOS and Macintosh); also refers to viruses that infect both boot sectors and files on the same computer.

multiple cavity infector   An expansion of the CAVITY INFECTOR technique, wherein a virus breaks its code into multiple pieces, lodging each in a different niche of the target.

network creeper   Viruses that find new hosts by seeking out and infecting writable network drives ("shares").

oligomorphic virus   An encrypted virus whose decryption code has several alternative forms, randomly selected when installing itself to a new host computer or writing replicants.

overwriter   The simplest form of computer virus, one that copies itself on top of existing programs in the host computer.

parasitic virus   Any computer virus that modifies an existing code within the host computer to achieve replication, as opposed to companion viruses and overwriters [see above].

payload   The ultimate, presumably negative effect of a computer virus (as distinct from any collateral damage caused by bugs or defects). While many viruses deliver a payload no worse than a humorous or annoying video display, others may destroy files or crash the host system.

phreaks/phreaking   Slang terms for hackers who concentrate primarily on penetrating telephone systems, either for the sake of pranks or to illegally obtain free services.

piggybacking   A synonym for SHOULDER-SURFING.

polymorphic virus   An improvement on encrypted viruses, designed to frustrate detection by employing multiple encryption/decryption.

prepender   A virus that writes itself to the beginning of a file.

RAM   Random Access Memory: computer memory used for revisable data storage (as opposed to ROM), also required for viruses to remain active within a system.

remnant   Any portion of a virus that remains within a system after it is disinfected, sometimes producing GHOST POSITIVES.

remote access Trojan (RAT)   A program that secretly grants access to a computer system by outsiders via a concealed, unauthorized network connection.

resident virus   Any virus that remains running and active within an infected system, as opposed to one that delivers its payload and then becomes inactive.

retro-virus   A computer virus that specifically attacks antivirus products or programs, drawing its name from biological viruses that attack a victim's immune system.

REVS list   Rapid Exchange of Virus Samples: a mailing list for antivirus companies and researchers, enabling them to transmit samples on short notice during emergency situations.

ROM   Read-Only Memory: a program whose contents may only be "read" by a computer, but which cannot be altered or modified.

salami slicing   Small thefts (of data, cash, etc.) by a computer operator from numerous larger sources, achieved by altering data to conceal the losses.

shoulder-surfing   Low-tech theft of personal identification numbers and other data by peering over a subject's shoulder during transactions.

slack space   "Wasted" space on any disk, unused by the programs it contains; slack space is sometimes used by viruses to hide themselves, since it is rarely scanned by antivirus programs.

slow infector   A virus seeking to avoid or postpone detection by infecting only files that are newly created or modified, as opposed to FAST INFECTORS.

slow mailer   A virus that distributes itself from infected host computers via e-mail, but without the blitz attack of a MASS MAILER. Slow mailers are frequently identifiable by the @m suffix to their titles.

slow polymorphism   Describes polymorphic viruses that change their codes sporadically, rather than each time they replicate.

social engineering   Various personal methods of duping another person into revealing passwords or other sensitive data via conversation; an alternative to CRACKING, DUMPSTER DIVING, and SHOULDER-SURFING.

software   Any and all instructions that make computer hardware perform its various functions.

software piracy   Theft of copyrighted software, either for personal use or illicit resale.

sparse infector A virus that avoids early detection by replicating only occasionally—e.g., after 50 or 100 programs run on the infected host computer.

stealth virus Any virus that takes active steps to conceal itself from detection, in some cases intercepting efforts to read or scan disk sectors where it resides.

system infector A computer virus that gains control after a host system is booted up.

time bomb A synonym for certain LOGIC BOMBS.

TOM Top of Memory: the limit of a computer's conventional memory. Any reduction in a computer's known TOM may indicate the presence of a virus.

trapdoor A synonym for a BACKDOOR.

trashing A synonym for DUMPSTER DIVING.

trigger The specific condition or circumstance that causes a virus to deliver its payload, often a specific time or date in the case of LOGIC BOMBS, the execution of a specific program or number of programs, etc.

Trojan/Trojan horse A harmful program that does not replicate after delivering its payload (erasing files, etc.). Failure to replicate makes Trojans much less common than other viruses and worms.

virus Any program that replicates itself from one computer to another by attaching itself to disks, files, or programs, usually but not always altering or destroying data in the process.

warez A slang term for bootleg copies of computer software sold or traded on the Internet.

warhead A synonym for PAYLOAD.

WildList Created by antivirus researcher Joe Wells in an effort to catalog viruses found IN THE WILD. The "top half" of the list includes those viruses confirmed in the wild, while the "bottom half" lists viruses reported IN THE FIELD.

wild virus Any virus found IN THE WILD.

wire fraud Criminal use of any telephone system to steal or extort money, information, etc.

worm Variously defined as a program that reproduces itself "like a virus," but without destroying data, or one that spreads among computers on a network without attaching itself to other programs in the process. Some sources treat worms as a variant form of virus, with definitions subject to ongoing debate.

zoo virus Any virus known to exist without having caused any real-world infection, and/or those made obsolete and rendered harmless by computer evolution, despite having once been widespread.

Bibliography

Alexander, Michael. "Operation Sundevil Nabs First Suspect." *Computerworld* (17 February 1992).

"Alibris Pays $25,000 To End Charges It Kept Amazon.com E-mail." *Bloomberg News* (25 November 1999).

American Civil Liberties Union. "18 Years Later, DNA Evidence Acquits Death Row Inmate." *ACLU News* (4 July 1996).

Anderson, Barrie and Dawn Anderson. *Manufacturing Guilt: Wrongful Convictions in Canada.* Halifax, Nova Scotia: Fernwood Publishing, 1998.

Baker, Al. "Couple Charged in Sex Abuse Waive Right to Speedy Trial." *New York Times* (16 August 2001).

———. "Girl Describes Ordeal of Rape and Captivity." *New York Times* (14 August 2001).

Balmer, Crispian. "French Army Veteran Faces Trial for 1980s Killings." Reuters (14 August 2001).

Banks, Michael. *How to Protect Yourself in Cyberspace: Web Psychos, Stalkers and Pranksters.* Albany, N.Y.: Coriolis Group Books, 1997.

Bardwell, S. K. "Search Team Members Indicted on Child Porn Charges." *Houston Chronicle* (30 August 2001).

Batty, David. "The Internet Twins: Timeline." *Guardian Unlimited* (9 April 2001).

"B.C. Child Pornography Trial Begins Monday." *Canadian Press* (20 January 2002).

Becker, Robert. "Ford Heights 4 Offered Huge Settlement." *Chicago Tribune* (5 March 1999).

Begley, Sharon, and Melinda Liu. "Foiling the Clipper Chip." *Newsweek* (13 June 1994).

Bequai, August. *Techno-Crimes: The Computeriza-tion of Crime and Terrorism.* Lexington, Mass.: Lexington Books, 1987.

Berger, Leslie. "Computer Hacker Who Jumped Bail Gets 41 Months." *Los Angeles Times* (28 November 1995).

Bieglow, Bruce. "To Some Hackers, Right and Wrong Don't Compute." *San Diego Union-Tribune* (11 May 1992).

Burtman, Bob. "Innocent At Last." *Houston Press* (3 August 2000).

Cabrera, Luis. "Can DNA Solve Green River?" Associated Press (27 August 2001).

———. "DNA Testing Breakthroughs May Help Identify Who Killed 49 Women in Northwest in the 1980s." Associated Press (12 September 2001).

"Calif. Judge Arrested for Child Porn." Associated Press (10 November 2001).

"Child Porn Law Challenger in Court." *Vancouver (British Columbia) Sun* (20 January 2002).

"City of London Surrenders to Cyber Gangs." *Times* (London) (2 June 1996).

Clark, Kim. "The Cruelest Con." *U.S. News & World Report* (28 August 2000).

"Computer Hacker Accused of Unfairly Winning Prizes." *Los Angeles Times* (23 April 1993).

"Convicted Murderer Getting Closer to Freedom." *Click10.com* (7 June 2001).

Coyne, Tom. "Man Cleared by DNA Test After Being Sentenced to 70 Years." Associated Press (12 December 2001).

Craig, Andrew. "Telecom Fraud Software Looks and Learns." *Internet Week* (29 April 1998).

"Crown Witness Admits to Lying." *Regina (Saskatchewan) Leader Post* (4 March 1992).

De Angelis, Gina. *Cyber Crimes*. New York: Chelsea House, 1999.

DeHaven, Judy. "High-tech World Faces Low-Life Realities." *Detroit News* (10 January 1996).

Delio, Michelle. "Rent-a-Car Motto: Speed Bills." *Wired News* (12 July 2001).

———. "Wireless networks in big trouble." *Wired News* (20 August 2001).

Dibbell, Julian. "The Prisoner: Phiber Optik Goes Directly to Jail." *Village Voice* (New York) (12 January 1994).

"DNA Evidence Frees Retarded Man After 22 Years in Jail." Associated Press (16 June 2001).

"DNA Links Convicted Rapist to Women's Slayings in 1987." Associated Press (11 December 2001).

Duffy, Shannon. "Convicted Rapist Wins Right to Seek DNA for Testing in Federal Court." *Legal Intelligencer* (27 March 2001).

Dugas, Christine. "FBI Cybercops Hunt Hackers: Agents Armed with Laptops Nab Robbers." *USA Today* (3 March 1998).

———. "Visa: Card Fraud at All-time Low." *USA Today* (16 February 1998).

Elmer-Dewitt, Philip. "Terror on the Internet." *Time* (12 December 1994).

Fegelman, Andrew. "DNA May Clear 4 in Grisly '78 Murders." *Chicago Tribune* (8 June 1996).

Fields, Gary. "'Spotter' Pinpoints a Shot in the Dark." *USA Today* (16 June 2000).

Forester, Tom, and Penny Morrison. *Computer Ethics: Cautionary Tales Ethical Dilemmas in Computing*. Upland, Pa.: DIANE Publishing, 1998.

Freeze, Colin. "One Arrested, 200 Sought in Porn Crackdown." *Globe and Mail* (Toronto) (21 January 2002).

Gambill, Gary. "Who's Winning the Arab-Israeli Cyber War?" *Middle East Intelligence Bulletin* (November 2000).

Gegax, T. Trent. "Stick 'Em Up? Not Anymore. Now It's Crime by Keyboard." *Newsweek* (21 July 1997).

———. "Israeli Hackers Vow to Defend." *Wired News* (15 November 2000).

Gohring, Nancy. "Big Brother at the Wheel?" *Interactive Week* (3 September 2001).

Goodyear, Charlie, and Erin Hallisy. "The Other Side of DNA Evidence: An Innocent Man is Freed." *San Francisco Chronicle* (18 October 1999).

Gralla, Preston. *Complete Idiot's Guide to Protecting Yourself Online*. Indianapolis: Que Education and Training, 1999.

Guisnel, Jean. *Cyberwars: Espionage on the Internet*. New York: Plenum, 1997.

Hafner, Katie, and John Markoff. *Cyberpunk—Outlaws and Hackers on the Computer Frontier*. New York: Simon & Schuster, 1991.

Haring, Bruce. "Cybermusic Pirates Agree to Stop Pilfering." *USA Today* (22 January 1998).

Harmon, Amy. "Cyberspace: Caltech Harassment Case Illustrates Growing Problem." *Los Angeles Times* (15 November 1995).

"He Has Nowhere To Turn." *Regina (Saskatchewan) Leader Post* (13 April 1992).

Heckman, Candace. "One DNA Link Is Firm; Other Two Are Less So." *Seattle Post-Intelligencer* (4 December 2001).

Hodel, Martha. "Questionable Testimony Sends Crime Lab Chemist Back to Court." Associated Press (6 September 2001).

Hucks, Karen. "Making the DNA Case." *Seattle News Tribune* (10 December 2001).

Jackman, Tom. "Fairfax to Pursue Charges in Sex Case." *Washington Post* (8 January 2002).

Johnson, John. "Fugitive Hacker Leaves Trail of Strange Claims." *Los Angeles Times* (4 August 1994).

Johnson, Kevin. "FBI Takes Page From Mormons' Data Book." *USA Today* (22 March 2002).

Judson, Karen. *Computer Crime: Phreaks, Spies, and Salami Slicers*. Berkeley Heights, N.J.: Enslow Publishers, 2000.

Kataoka, Mike. "DNA Testing Casts Doubt on 1988 Rape Conviction." *Riverside (CA) Press-Enterprise* (10 February 2000).

Keegan, Paul. "High-tech Pirates Collecting Phone Calls." *USA Today* (23 September 1994).

Kelley, Jack. "Agents Pursue Terrorists Online." *USA Today* (21 June 2002).

"Kids Tricked into Giving Perverts Their Pictures." *The Province* (Manitoba) (20 January 2002).

Kofman, Jeffrey. "Oklahoma Death Sentence Overturned." *ABCNEWS.com* (15 August 2001).

Koren, William. *Hackers No More*. New York: Random House, 1994.

Kornblum, Janet. "Rental Car Firm Spied on Drivers, Conn. Says." *USATODAY.com* (5 July 2001).

Krane, Jim. "Hackers Hit USA Today Web Site." Associated Press (12 July 2002).

Krebs, Brian. "Hackers Worldwide Fan Flames in Middle East Conflict." *Computer User.com* (25 November 2000).

Kurtz, Michele. "DeSalvo DNA Can't Be Tied to Murder Victim." *Boston Globe* (7 December 2001).

Landreth, Bill. *Out of the Inner Circle—A Hacker's Guide to Computer Security.* Bellevue, Wash.: Microsoft Press, 1985).

Larrabee, John. "Cyberspace a New Beat for Police." *USA Today* (26 April 1994).

Lawrence, J. M. "AG's Office Questions Motive Behind Strangler Guilt Probe." *Boston Herald* (6 December 2001).

———. "Kin Say DNA Absolves DeSalvo in Strangler Case." *Boston Herald* (7 December 2001).

Lemos, Robert. "Car Spy Pushes Privacy Limit." *ZDNet News* (20 June 2001).

Littman, Jonathan. "The FBI Takes On Hackers." *CNET, Inc.* (20 November 1997).

———. *The Watchman: The Twisted Life and Times of Serial Hacker Kevin Poulsen.* New York: Little, Brown and Company, 1997.

"Man Cleared of Charges after 15 Years in Jail." Associated Press (8 December 2001).

Markoff, John. "How a Computer Sleuth Traced a Digital Trail." *New York Times* (15 February 1995).

Masters, Brooke. "Death Row to Freedom: A Journey Ends." *Washington Post* (13 February 2001).

———. "Va. Killer Executed in Landmark DNA Case." *Washington Post* (15 March 2002).

———. "Bond Denied in Teen Girl's Abduction." *Washington Post* (9 January 2002).

McAfee, John, and Colin Haynes. *Computer Viruses, Worms, Data Diddlers, Killer Programs, and Other Threats to Your System.* New York: St. Martin's Press, 1989.

McAndless, David. "Warez Wars." *Wired* (April 1997).

McClintick, David. "Fatal Bondage." *Vanity Fair* (June 2001).

"MCI Worker in Phone-Card Ripoff." *Chicago Tribune* (4 October 1994).

McIntyre, Mike, and Bruce Owen. "Child-Porn Horror: Nudists' Volunteer Photographer Charged; Victims May Be As Young as 2." *Winnipeg (Manitoba) Free Press* (15 December 2001).

"Milgaard Was Suspicious Character to Police." *Regina (Saskatchewan) Leader Post* (13 April 1992).

Morin, Monte. "O.C. Judge Faces New Charges." *Los Angeles Times* (29 November 2001).

O'Neill-Hill, Lisa. "Man Jailed 12 Years Files Damages Claim." *Riverside (Calif.) Press-Enterprise* (8 September 2000).

"Online Methods Elude Federal Agencies." *Washington Post* (20 September 2001).

Orman, Neil. "Fighting Check Fraud." *Austin (Texas) Business Journal* (16 September 1996).

Orr, Patrick. "Exonerated Man Tells of Surviving Prison." *Idaho Statesman* (12 December 2000).

Oxley, Chuck. "Freed Death Row Inmate Not Bitter." *New York Times* (24 August 2001).

Parker, Donn. *Crime by Computer.* New York: Charles Scribner's Sons, 1976.

———. *Fighting Computer Crime: A New Framework for Protecting Information.* New York: John Wiley & Sons, 1998.

Paulson, Tom. "New DNA Match Technology Broke Case." *Seattle Post-Intelligencer* (1 December 2001).

"Preying on Hope." *cbsnews.com* (25 January 2001).

"Profile of a Virus Writer." *PC World* (March 1997).

Protess, David, Rob Warden, and Robert Warden. *A Promise of Justice.* New York: Hyperion, 1998.

Quinn, Andrew. "Teen Hackers Plead Guilty to Pentagon Attacks." *Time* (30 July 1998).

Quittner, Joshua. "Invasion of Privacy." *Time* (25 August 1997).

Reynolds, Dave. "Confessed Murderer Cleared by DNA Tests." *Inclusion Daily Express* (10 May 2001).

———. "Townsend Freed After 22 Years." *Inclusion (Fla.) Daily Express* (18 June 2001).

———. "Townsend Should Be Released, Prosecutors Say." *Inclusion Daily Express* (15 June 2001).

———. "Townsend's Case Not Isolated." *Inclusion Daily Express* (18 June 2001).

Richtel, Matt. "Virus Hunters: Stalking 'Disease' on the Net." *New York Times* (15 September 1998).

Riley, Mark. "DNA Testing Gives Freedom to 64th Inmate." *Sydney Morning Herald* (1 April 2000).

Robison, Melissa. "DNA Evidence Casts Doubt on DeSalvo as Boston Strangler." Associated Press (6 December 2001).

———. "Scientists Have New Evidence in Boston Strangler Case." Associated Press (6 December 2001).

Ryckaert, Vic. "Man Sentenced in 1985 Slaying." *Indianapolis Star* (29 November 2001).

Sanchez, Rene. "Police Want Site More than Web Address for Escaped Calif. Hacker." *Washington Post* (10 December 1998).

Sanminiatelli, Maria. "Killer Found Through Search of DNA Database Executed." *Hampton Roads (Virginia) Daily Press* (15 March 2002).

Schwartz, John. "Inside the Head of a Hacker." *Newsweek* (29 July 1991).

———. "One High-End PC Cracks Data-Scrambling System." *Washington Post* (18 July 1998).

Scheeres, Julia. "Looking to Adopt? Beware the Web." *Los Angeles Times* (21 May 2001).

"Sheriff Apologizes to Inmate." *Click10.com* (6 June 2001).

Slatalla, Michelle, and Joshua Quittner. *Masters of Deception: The Gang That Ruled Cyberspace.* New York: HarperCollins, 1995.

Smith, Graham (ed). *High-Tech Warfare.* New York: Crescent Books, 1991.

Southern Poverty Law Center. "Active 'Patriot' Groups on the Internet in 1999." *Intelligence Report* 98 (Spring 2000): 22–24.

———. "Active 'Patriot' Groups on the Internet in 2000." *Intelligence Report* 102 (Summer 2001): 36–38.

———. "Hate groups on the Internet." *Intelligence Report* 89 (Winter 1998): 26–28.

———. "Hate groups on the Internet." *Intelligence Report* 93 (Winter 1999): 43–45.

———. "Hate on the Net: As New Sites Arise, So Do Legal Issues." *Intelligence Report* 93 (Spring 1999): 46–47.

———. "The Neo-Confederates." *Intelligence Report* 99 (Summer 2000): 28–31.

———. "The patriot movement on the Internet." *Intelligence Report* 90 (Spring 1998): 36–39.

———. "The patriot movement on the Internet." *Intelligence Report* 94 (Spring 1999): 32–35.

Squitieri, Tom. "Cyberspace Full of Terror Targets." *USA Today* (5 May 2002).

Sterling, Bruce. *The Hacker Crackdown—Law and Disorder on the Electronic Frontier.* New York: Bantam Books, 1992.

Stockman, Farah. "Man Held in Hooker Scheme." *Boston Globe* (23 August 2001).

Stoll, Clifford. *Silicon Snake Oil: Second Thoughts on the Information Highway.* New York: Doubleday, 1995.

Stone, Keith. "Computer Criminal Pleads Guilty to Fraud Charges." *Daily News of Los Angeles* (28 March 1995).

———. "Computer Hacker Caught After 10 Months on the Run." *Daily News of Los Angeles* (30 August 1994).

———. "Former FBI Informant a Fugitive After Helping Track Hackers." *Daily News of Los Angeles* (31 July 1994).

Strauss, Gary. "Employees, Ex-Workers Get Even." *USA Today* (20 August 1998).

Sullivan, Christopher. "Taking a Byte Out of Crime." *Minneapolis Star Tribune* (18 February 1995).

Suro, Roberto. "The Hackers Who Won't Quit." *Washington Post* (1 September 1999).

Taft, Darryl. "No Electronic Theft." *Computer Reseller News* (29 September 1977).

"Task Force Forming to Find Green River Killer." Associated Press (29 June 2001).

Taylor, Chris. "Hackers Plunder NASA, Pentagon." *Time* (23 April 1998).

———. "Justice a la Modem." *Time* (30 July 1998).

Thornburgh, Nathan. "2 Russian Hackers Nabbed in FBI Sting." *Moscow Times* (28 April 2001).

"Tracing Terror's Digital Footprints." *New York Times* (30 March 2002).

Underwood, Graham. "Ex-Medical Examiner to Remain in Beaumont Prison." *Avalanche-Journal* (Lubbock, Texas) (4 March 1997).

Van Dine, Lynn. "Crooks Lurk Behind Phony Web Sites." *Detroit News* (25 February 1997).

Vistica, Gregory, and Evan Thomas. "The Secret Hacker Wars." *Newsweek* (1 June 1998).

Weinstein, Henry. "States Resist DNA Tests That Could Free the Wrongly Convicted." *Los Angeles Times* (21 February 2000).

Weise, Elizabeth. "Feared Hacker Fined $4,125, Could Be Freed in January." *USA Today* (11 August 1999).

Whitaker, Barbara. "Judge Facing Pornography Charges Is Unopposed on Ballot." *New York Times* (2 March 2002).

Wickert, David, and Sarah Duran. "Advances in DNA Tests Help Police Solidify Case." *Seattle News Tribune* (3 December 2001).

Zorn, Eric. "To Set Case Right, Find Out Why It Went Wrong." *Chicago Tribune* (9 June 1996).

Index

Kaiser, Tom 195
Kaney, Ken 131
Kashpureff, Eugene **171–172**
Keating, Frank 125
Keeper virus **172**
Keker, John 288
Keller, Bob 166
Keller, Sharon 69
Kelly, Ian 249
Kelsey Brook Jones hoax
  172–173
Kenadek, Richard **173**
Kendall, Joe 199
Kennedy, Thomas **173**, 235
Kennelly, Matthew 273
Kerplunk virus **173–174**
Keypress virus **174**
KGB 74
Khizhnjak virus **174**
Khokhlov, Nikolai 55
kidney harvest hoax **174–175**
Kilshaw, Alan and Judith 3–4
King, Rodney 302
Kirk, Paul 39
Kislyansky, Leonid **175**
Kislyansky, Michael **175**
kiting 72
Kline, Ronald 60–61
Klingerman virus hoax **175–176**
Koball, Bruce 204
Kotler, Kerry **176–177**
Koval, Edward 70
Kozakiewicz, Alicia 317
Krebs, Brian 311
Krieg, Jason 60
Krogman, William 13
Krotoski, Mark 279
Ku Klux Klan 16, 143*f*, 144,
  321
Kusumah virus **177**
Kurner, Emily 265
Kwon, Il **177–178**

L

Ladopolous, Eli 195
LaMacchia, David **179**
Lance, Al 111
Lapchuk, George 201

lapping 72
Larsen, Bryan 61
Lashmanov, Alexei 182
"Launch Nuclear Strike Now"
  virus hoax **179–180**
Lechner, Alfred, Jr. 269
Lecter, Hannibal 258
Ledbetter, Ron 177
Lee, Henry 287
Lee, John 195
Lee, Kent **180**
Lee, Samuel 177
Legion of Doom 72, **180–181**,
  194–195, 236
Legion virus **180**
Leonard, James 339
lethal rodent offal hoax **181–182**
Levin, Vladimir 72, 130,
  182–183
Levy, Jeffrey **183**
Lewicka, Izabel 272, 273
Lewis, Adrienne 3
Lewis, Guy 164
Lewis, Wilma 311
Library of Congress 327
lidar **262–263**
Lindsly, Corey 245
Linscott, Steven **183–184**
Lionberg, Larry 119
Lirola, Maria 168, 169
Lisi, Mary 12, 173
List, Robert 15
Lithium virus **184**
"A Little Girl Is Dying Hoax"
  10–11, 81
Little Girl song hoax **184**
Lizard virus **184–185**
Llerta-Plaza, Carlos 116
Lloyd, Timothy **185**
Long, Bobby 257
Long, Wei 125
Loschin, Beth 62
Lostracco, Gerald **337–338**
Louarn, Max **185**
Loveletter worm 129, **185–188**
LSD 55, 57, 277
Lucy virus **188**
Ludlam, Evelyn 93
Lunchtime virus **188–189**
Luster, Dale **189**

Lyell, Jerry 96
Lynch, Nancy 270

M

Mackintosh, Gird 294
MacQueen, Andrew 351–352
Macy, Bob 125, 126, 246
Madsen, Wayne 297
Magyar, Dawn 337
"Make a Loan" pyramid scheme
  191
"Make Money Fast" pyramid
  scheme **192–194**
"Make Money Fast" virus hoax
  194
Ma'Khevim, Aftahat 310
malicious programming 73–74
Malmberg, Kaj 146
Malvsi, Dennis 16
Mandelbaum, Adam 266
M & M giveaway hoax **194**
Manella, Nora 317
Manley, Martin 10
Marino, Achim 228
Markham, John 168
Martin, Glendon 112, 113
Massachusetts Institute of
  Technology 137, 151, 179
Masters of Deception 1, 72, 181,
  194–195
Masters of Downloading 74
Matthews, Dave 81–82, 82*f*
Mayer, J. A. C. 115
Mayes, Larry **195–196**
Mayes, Michael 69
McBarron, Thomas 60
McCarty, Curtis 125
McCarty, Richard **196**
McChesney, Kathleen 231
McClintock, David 272
McCloskey, James 53*f*
McClurg, John 113
McDougal, Mike 69
McIntyre, Shane 112, 113
McKenna, Patrick **196**
McMillan, Clark **196–197**
Meagher, Stephen 116–117
Meek, Michael 58